Investigation and Prosecution of Child Abuse

THIRD EDITION

Investigation and Prosecution of Child Abuse

THIRD EDITION

National Center for Prosecution of Child Abuse

SAGE Publications
International Educational and Professional Publisher
Thousand Oaks ■ London ■ New Delhi

For information:

Sage Publications, Inc.
2455 Teller Road
Thousand Oaks, California 91320
E-mail: order@sagepub.com

Sage Publications Ltd.
6 Bonhill Street
London EC2A 4PU
United Kingdom

Sage Publications India Pvt. Ltd.
B-42 Panchsheel Enclave
Post Box 4109
New Delhi 110 017   India

Printed in the United States of America

Library of Congress Cataloging-in-Publication Data

Investigation and prosecution of child abuse/American Prosecutors Research Institute—3rd ed.
    p. cm.
Includes bibliographical references and index.
ISBN 0–7619–3090–6 (cloth)
    1. Child abuse-Law and legislation—United States.
2. Child abuse—Investigation—United States. 3.   Prosecution—United States.
I. American Prosecutors Research Institute.
KF9323.I58 2004
345.73′025554—dc22

                                   2003018363

03   04   05   06   10   9   8   7   6   5   4   3   2   1

Acquisitions Editor:	Arthur T. Pomponio
Editorial Assistant:	Veronica K. Novak
Production Editor:	Melanie Birdsall
Copy Editor:	Ruth Saavedra
Typesetter:	C&M Digitals (P) Ltd.
Proofreader:	Kristin Bergstad
Indexer:	Kathy Paparchontis
Cover Designer:	Edgar Abarca

Contents

List of Figures and Tables

CHAPTER V

CHAPTER VI

Foreword

Having served as both a juvenile prosecutor and an elected District Attorney, I am aware of the many critical issues and challenges facing today's child abuse prosecutors. As a District Attorney, I had the privilege in the early 1980s of starting the first Children's Advocacy Center. This effort led to better investigations and prosecutions of child abuse in a multidisciplinary setting. Later, as a United States Representative, I championed the cause of children by marshalling congressional support for both my National Children's Advocacy Center in Huntsville, Alabama, and the National Children's Alliance, a coalition of Children's Advocacy Centers from across the nation that is headquartered in Washington, D.C.

In 1985, the United States Congress approved an authorization for the American Prosecutors Research Institute (APRI) to establish a National Center for Prosecution of Child Abuse (NCPCA). NCPCA provides front line investigators and prosecutors with quality training at the national, state, and local levels as well as technical assistance in individual cases. Equally important, NCPCA produces quality publications that provide practical guidance to those called on to handle these complex cases. Perhaps its most important publication is this manual, *Investigation and Prosecution of Child Abuse*. Now in its third edition, the manual will be of invaluable assistance to prosecutors and allied professionals in the field.

I want to commend the attorneys and staff of the National Center for Prosecution of Child Abuse for their tireless efforts in producing this important work, as well as the many authors who contributed to this project. It is my hope that it provides valuable guidance to all those who selflessly serve children in need.

Congressman Robert E. "Bud" Cramer, Jr.
United States House of Representatives

Preface

Since its inception 18 years ago, the American Prosecutors Research Institute's National Center for Prosecution of Child Abuse (NCPCA) has become a beacon for prosecutors seeking training, research, and one-to-one advice on these complicated and gut-wrenching cases. Aimed at providing a central resource for improving responses to child physical, sexual, and fatal abuse as well as criminal neglect, NCPCA serves child abuse professionals nationwide and internationally.

When *Investigation and Prosecution of Child Abuse* was first published in 1987, prosecutors had for the first time a current and comprehensive guide to handling some of the toughest cases many had ever faced. Praised for its thoroughness, practicality, and readability, the manual was widely known as the child abuse prosecutor's "bible." In 1993, the manual was revised and expanded.

Since that time, child abuse cases have generated a great deal of case law, along with an outpouring of medical, psychological, and other important research. This third edition of *Investigation and Prosecution of Child Abuse* has been updated and expanded to address many of these changes. I have no doubt that the third edition will be invaluable to prosecutors striving to keep abreast of these developments.

I am deeply grateful to the dedicated staff of the National Center for Prosecution of Child Abuse for the many hours spent putting this publication together. In addition, NCPCA attorneys travel to 30 or more states each year, training as many as 14,000 child abuse prosecutors and investigators. NCPCA also responds to several thousand requests for technical assistance, publishes a monthly newsletter, and produces law review articles, book chapters, and other scholarly works.

No organization means as much to front-line child abuse prosecutors as does NCPCA. NCPCA has demonstrated that accountability for offenders goes hand-in-hand with interdisciplinary cooperation and child abuse prevention efforts. Through the leadership of APRI's National Center for Prosecution of Child Abuse and the dedication of America's child abuse prosecutors and investigators, the world will be a safer place for children.

Newman Flanagan
President, American Prosecutors Research Institute
Executive Director, National District Attorneys Association

Acknowledgments

As I travel around the country, I'm amazed at the number of child abuse prosecutors and investigators who tell me they still have on their shelves and still frequently refer to the second edition of *Investigation and Prosecution of Child Abuse*. To many in the field, the manual continues to be referred to as the "bible" of our professions.

In the 10 years that have passed since the publication of the second edition, much has happened in the field of child protection. Advanced technologies enable perpetrators to commit old crimes in new ways. Defenses abandoned over the past decade have given way to new tactics to discredit victims and those who seek to protect them.

Although new defense tactics and new methods of committing the crime of child abuse will be a constant, negative pattern in this field, there have been many positive developments as well. Prosecutors are getting involved earlier in these cases and, in many jurisdictions, are present when child victims are being interviewed in the local child advocacy center. As a whole, the profession is better trained, and many parts of the country report marked improvement in the ability to handle these cases.

In recognition of the changing landscape and in response to the demand from those of you on the front lines, we offer this third edition of the manual. It is my fervent hope that these pages will assist you in the high calling of protecting children in need.

I am grateful to the contributors to this manual who built on the work of contributors to earlier editions. In alphabetical order, these contributors are Jeff Brickman, Mary-Ann Burkhart, Cindy Christian, Dan Davis, Paul DerOhnessian, Carl B. Hammond, Mindy Mitnick, John E. B. Myers, Rob Parrish, Robert Reece, Domenic Trunfio, Bill Walsh, and Robin Wilkinson. I am also appreciative of my colleagues at the National Center for Prosecution of Child Abuse both past and present for their hard work on this project. In particular I wish to thank Dawn Wilsey for assisting with myriad administrative details in the publication of this book. I am also grateful to Brian Holmgren and Laura Rogers for the many hours spent in selecting and editing the appendixes. I am indebted to Mary-Ann Burkhart for her careful reading of each chapter to ensure all information was substantively correct.

Finally, a special thanks to Minnesota prosecutor Michelle Zehnder-Fischer for her diligent reading of the manuscript and her efforts to turn it into polished prose.

I have been blessed to work with and to otherwise know many of the best and brightest child protection professionals in the world. This magnificent manual is a testament to the selfless labors of so many of them. If there are any errors or weaknesses in this manual, the blame rests squarely with me.

Victor I. Vieth
Director, APRI's National Center for Prosecution of Child Abuse

About the Contributors

Jeffrey H. Brickman, Assistant United States Attorney, Atlanta, GA

Mary-Ann R. Burkhart, Assistant State's Attorney for Baltimore City, Homicide Unit, Baltimore, MD

Cindy W. Christian, MD, Associate Professor of Pediatrics; Chair, Child Abuse and Neglect Prevention, The Children's Hospital of Philadelphia, Philadelphia, PA

Daniel W. Davis, MD, Assistant Medical Examiner, Hennepin County, Minneapolis, MN

Paul DerOhannesian, Esq., Trial Consultant, Albany, NY

Michelle Zehnder Fischer, Assistant Nicollet County Attorney, St. Peter, MN

Carl B. Hammond, Director of Casework, Vanished Children's Alliance, Los Gatos, CA

Brian Holmgren, Assistant District Attorney General, Nashville, TN

Mindy Mitnick, EdM, MA, Licensed Psychologist, Edina, MN

John E. B. Myers, Professor of Law, University of the Pacific, Sacramento, CA

Robert Parrish, Managing Attorney, Second District Office of the Guardian Ad Litem, Bountiful, UT

Robert M. Reece, MD, Director, Clinical Professor of Pediatrics, Tufts University School of Medicine; MSPCC Institute for Professional Education; Executive Editor, the Quarterly Child Abuse Medical Update, Boston, MA

Rick Trunfio, Chief Assistant District Attorney, Onondaga County, Syracuse, NY

Victor Vieth, Director, APRI's National Center for Prosecution of Child Abuse, Alexandria, VA; Director, APRI's National Child Protection Training Center, Winona, MN

Lieutenant Bill Walsh, Dallas Police Department, Dallas, TX

Debra Whitcomb, Director of Grant Programs and Development, American Prosecutors Research Institute, Alexandria, VA

Dawn Doran Wilsey, Senior Attorney, ARPI's National Center for Prosecution of Child Abuse, Alexandria, VA

Introduction to the Third Edition

The Benefits of Working as a Multidisciplinary Team

A premise of this manual is that successful prosecution of child abuse requires different practices than those used to respond to other types of crime. One of the major differences is the critical role that information from a variety of individuals and agencies—law enforcement, child protective services (CPS), medical personnel and mental health professionals—plays in building strong child abuse cases. Experts who deal with children, abuse issues, courts, and trials on a daily basis agree that the optimal response to child abuse involves a coordinated multidisciplinary approach to share information and establish agency responsibilities.

The process of developing a shared investigative approach can itself be beneficial. It can reduce the number of interviews a child undergoes, minimize the number of people involved in the case, enhance the quality of evidence discovered in the investigation, make more efficient use of limited resources, educate each agency concerning the needs and interests of the other agencies involved, and minimize the likelihood of conflicts among those agencies. At the same time, it can diminish the defense's ability to play one agency against another. Not only does a multidisciplinary approach directly assist the victim and family, but it provides the impetus for improving the overall approach to child abuse. Independent investigations, in contrast, often overwhelm the child; result in evidence being ignored, lost, or tainted; disrupt the lives of those who might otherwise cooperate; and produce other problems detrimental to the search for truth. If independent investigations must be made, the police and CPS should at least coordinate activities and attempt to share their interview session or sessions with the child.

Of particular interest to prosecutors is information about the child relating to the filing of criminal charges, taking the case to trial, and making sentencing recommendations. Since all these actions will concern professionals from other disciplines, they will certainly be discussed in the team review setting. At a minimum, the prosecutor participating on this team can learn how the child is doing at home and school and how the child is reacting to all that is happening. The prosecutor can also share information with team members on next steps and difficulties anticipated in the criminal justice system. While the team should not assume responsibility for charging decisions, it can make recommendations for the prosecutor's consideration.

Current approaches range from casual arrangements for concerned professionals to discuss common problems and new developments to formal teams of designated agency representatives responsible for investigating and recommending action in alleged child abuse cases in their communities. Currently, at least 30 states have recognized the value of coordinating public agency responses by mandating or authorizing implementation of joint investigation teams including law enforcement and CPS officials.

ESTABLISHING A COORDINATED SYSTEM

Creating teams to address problems in the workplace is not a new concept. Organizational units are used in areas as diverse as designing automobiles and providing mental health treatment to seriously disturbed patients. Such teams frequently bring together individuals from independent public and quasi-public agencies that may have conflicting interests. The process is not easy and does not generally produce dramatic results overnight. The results in improved case handling, however, are well worth the effort.

Team development generally involves a series of activities including reviewing current practice in the jurisdiction and planning, implementing, and evaluating the team approach. This process involves considerable "up front" work by the prosecutor, who recognizes the problems associated with fragmented child abuse investigations and undertakes to change the process.

The Prosecutor as Coordinator

Communities in which the prosecutor has taken a leadership role in designing the investigation process tend to be the same communities that have demonstrated the greatest success prosecuting child abusers. When agencies conduct independent investigations, the opportunity to prosecute the offender successfully may be lost. Multiple interviews by multiple agencies often lead to situations in which the child recants or is no longer willing to talk about the incident by the time the case is reviewed for criminal charging. In addition, damage to a child's mental health can result from repetitious interviews with different people.

The prosecutor must develop policies requiring prompt, thorough, objective, sensitive, and coordinated investigations despite the initial drain of such planning on time and personnel, especially in offices without investigators or victim advocates. It may be necessary to overcome resistance from law enforcement, CPS, and medical and mental health personnel. However, once the prosecutor takes a leadership role and begins to work with the agencies involved in child abuse investigations, the task becomes easier. Because of prosecutors' prominence in the charging process, they are in the best position to ensure the success of a coordinated approach.

The liability implications of active involvement in investigations mean that prosecutors must structure their involvement accordingly. Prosecutors have traditionally been afforded absolute immunity from civil liability for any actions "intimately associated with the judicial phase of the criminal process" (*Imbler v. Pachtman*, 424 U.S. 409, 430 [1976]). Legal advice concerning admissibility of evidence should fall within this category. Should the prosecutor lose absolute immunity, qualified immunity generally protects the prosecutor from liability unless the conduct was plainly incompetent or constituted knowing violation of the law. (See generally *Id.* at 430; *Burns v. Reed,* 111 S. Ct. 1934 [1991]; *Buckley v. Fitzsimmons,* 113 S. Ct. 2606 [1993].). Prosecutorial involvement in developing interagency protocols or providing consultation on child abuse cases should not subject prosecutors to civil liability. Know the law and custom in your jurisdiction, and if liability is a concern, discuss the issue with risk management personnel or agency counsel.

Reviewing Current Practices in Your Jurisdiction

The first step is to assess the effectiveness of the current system. The axiom, "If it isn't broken, don't fix it" applies. If your system has been successful in securing reporting from all mandated reporters, reducing the hardship children can experience in the investigative and litigation process, and prosecuting a range of cases effectively, the best approach may be to leave the system alone. Past successes, however, do not always predict future ones, and your perception of the system may not be shared by victims or other professionals. The need for change may also arise because of a greater volume of cases, changes in the quality of case handling, or the need for more communication and sensitivity. Quality control requires ongoing evaluation to identify problems.

Surveying victims, witnesses, and key professionals through questionnaires or interviews is a good place to start and can be adapted to provide regular feedback regarding strengths and weaknesses in the existing system. Communities that conduct regular evaluation of their services' effectiveness are in the best position to respond quickly to challenges. (See Appendix III.14 for an evaluation form used by a prosecutor's office for victims and their families.)

At least once a year, each multidisciplinary team should evaluate the effectiveness of the team and its protocol and make any necessary adjustments.

Prosecutor's Office

The starting point for a review and possible system modification should be your own office. Gather as much information as possible about how child abuse cases are currently prosecuted. If you are not directly involved in trying these cases, talk to the lawyers who are. You may wish to consider the following factors:

- How well do other agencies, particularly police and CPS, cooperate in sharing information?
- What is the quality of information provided?
- Are cases referred to your office promptly and in compliance with state reporting requirements?
- After the cases are referred, what happens to them?
- How long does it take to make charging decisions?
- How many referred cases are accepted for prosecution?
- How many referred cases are declined and for what reason? (If a significant number are declined owing to insufficient evidence, a problem may exist in the investigation practices of police or CPS or in the screening practices of the prosecutor.)
- Does your office designate particular prosecutors to handle all child abuse cases?
- What kind of caseload do the child abuse prosecutors carry?
- What is the rate of turnover of the office?
- How does that compare with the specialized unit?
- How does it compare with the caseloads of other prosecutors in the office?
- Do the child abuse prosecutors receive specialized training regarding child abuse?
- How much prosecution experience do these prosecutors have?
- Do you have vertical prosecution of child abuse cases?
- What percentage of cases results in guilty pleas (to original charges and reduced charges), and how many go to trial and end in conviction or acquittal?
- How much time passes between the filing of charges and verdict or guilty plea? Between conviction and sentencing?
- What agencies have input at the sentencing phase?
- How do actual sentences compare with prosecution recommendations and with those imposed for other crimes?
- Are other agencies notified of decisions to charge or decline prosecution and of outcomes (verdict, sentencing)?

After you are thoroughly familiar with your office's response to child abuse cases and have taken any necessary corrective action, look at how other agencies are approaching these cases. Your initial decision to review practices and policies should be pursued informally. Public disclosure of your intentions may make other agencies reluctant to cooperate unless you have enlisted their support beforehand.

Identify key agencies and personnel involved in child abuse intervention: agency administrators, policymakers, supervisors, and those who work in the field as well. A rough understanding of each agency involved in child abuse is necessary before contacting it. Staff members who deal with child abuse cases can provide an initial description of the agencies and individuals with whom they work. Your review should focus on:

- Disclosure and reporting procedures
- Investigation and court processes
- Quality and level of interagency communication and information sharing
- Amount of time involved in case processing
- Counseling and support services
- Training needs and opportunities

Law Enforcement

Following evaluation of your own office, continue the analysis with law enforcement agencies. Many jurisdictions have numerous law enforcement agencies with investigative responsibilities, and all of them should be reviewed despite an apparent lack of responsibility for child abuse cases. For example, while the sheriff's department may have no investigative role regarding child abuse reports, it may be heavily involved in locating and arresting fugitives charged with child abuse crimes.

One of the major problems in child abuse cases arises in jurisdictions with multiple police agencies. Often one jurisdiction will have a county or borough-wide police department, many municipal police departments, a sheriff's department, state police, military police, or federal law enforcement agencies serving federal enclaves—each having differences in resources, experience, training level, and capabilities. A small, ill-equipped, inexperienced municipal police department should not be expected to investigate child abuse allegations within its jurisdictional boundaries if there is a fully equipped child abuse unit at the county level. This problem has generally been resolved by interagency agreements assigning responsibility for child abuse investigations to the police agency best equipped to handle them.

Jurisdictions without a child abuse unit in the police agency may still have some personnel with expertise in the investigation of child abuse. Most medium-to-large law enforcement agencies not only divide investigative responsibilities but provide personnel with a variety of training as well. In agencies with homicide, sexual assault, burglary, juvenile, or violent crime sections, the sexual assault investigator is likely to be responsible for adult or child-related sex offenses, and the juvenile investigator may handle physical abuse.

Child Protective Services

The agency with statutory responsibility for protecting children and investigating complaints of child abuse and neglect is an essential participant in a coordinated approach. Since the CPS worker usually has the first contact with a child and family following a report of suspected abuse, the information gathered by CPS can have major implications for the success of any subsequent prosecution. Learning the procedures that govern the initial CPS investigation can alert you to areas in which changes may be needed to improve the quality of information. Problems often arise owing to a lack of coordination between CPS, law enforcement, and the prosecution. Determine how and when CPS notifies law enforcement and/or the prosecutor's office regarding reports. Prompt notification of appropriate law enforcement agencies by CPS of all child sexual abuse and, at a minimum, "serious" physical abuse should be delineated. Identify the level of coordination among CPS, law enforcement, and the prosecutor regarding the investigative process and protection of the child victim (i.e., removal of the defendant, court-issued protective orders and their enforcement, law enforcement protection for CPS workers if needed, and information sharing regarding the status of civil and criminal court hearings).

Health Care and Treatment Communities

Key participants in a coordinated approach include representatives of the health care community, especially physicians likely to be involved in examining potential victims of abuse and mental health workers specializing in treating abused children and their families. Other important treatment providers include the probation department, private mental health clinics, crisis centers, and private therapists who provide services to the court or court-related agencies on a contract basis.

Support for a child and family through the trauma associated with abuse and sometimes difficult justice system procedures should start at the time of disclosure and continue for as long as necessary. Counselors or mental health practitioners to whom the child and family have been referred must be able to work with medical professionals, police, and prosecutors and must be sufficiently knowledgeable about the criminal justice system to respond to the child's anxieties.

Victim Advocates and Guardians *Ad Litem*

Many jurisdictions have sexual assault or rape crisis centers that provide medical treatment and counseling to victims, family members, and sometimes offenders. These centers can be valuable resources, and their support for a coordinated response should be sought early in the process. They are usually natural allies of the prosecutor because of their orientation toward victims and tend to be in more frequent contact with police investigators and prosecutors than other agencies. Because funding for these centers sometimes depends on their services to the criminal justice system, they often welcome opportunities to work with the jurisdiction's chief law enforcement official.

Hundreds of prosecutors employ full-time victim-witness advocates. Such personnel often take the lead in assisting prosecutorial efforts to create strong working relationships with other agencies serving victims and families. In addition, they play an important role in guiding the child through the criminal justice process. Since the presence of resourceful and sensitive victim advocates can go far to minimize the hardship of the criminal justice process, they are a significant part of any coordinated approach.

Guardians *ad litem* or court-appointed special advocates (CASAs) are increasingly involved in civil dependency proceedings in child abuse cases. Prosecutors may find it beneficial to solicit their assistance in the related criminal case and may wish to request court appointment of a guardian or CASA to assist the victim in the criminal case.

The Courts

Frequently, the child abuse victim and family are involved in related actions in the civil court system including divorce proceedings, dependency hearings, or removal actions. Coordination of these actions with cases in the criminal court is crucial. Make sure you are aware of the steps taken in civil actions that affect the stability of the child's placement, since this could significantly influence the child's ability to testify and participate in the criminal trial. In addition, consider how multiple proceedings involving the same victim in criminal, dependency/removal, and domestic relations cases can be synchronized. Find out which court will assume responsibility for common aspects of the cases, such as decisions related to the defendant's contact with the child and his removal from the home, and pursue agreements regarding the timing of hearings.

In jurisdictions in which the prosecutor's office is responsible for representing the state in dependency, neglect, or removal actions, coordination is simplified, but in many others, responsibility falls on agency attorneys such as those representing CPS or guardians *ad litem* who are *not* directly linked to prosecutors handling criminal cases. Although both the prosecutor and agency attorney may be faced with proving the same facts in court—e.g., that a child was sexually abused by a parent—they are often unaware of the other's parallel processes. It is important to become familiar with the operation of the juvenile and family court in your community and include an agency attorney and administrator or judge in your team review meetings.

Information must be shared when court rulings in one system affect other agencies. For example, school authorities and agency attorneys should be notified when a "no contact" order has been issued barring an offender from access to the child. Failure to establish a process of routine notification can result in conflicting court orders or a tragic confrontation. Moreover, if a no contact order has been issued, group or family counseling that involves the offender cannot be recommended as part of a parole or probation agreement. Alerting school officials to possible defense attempts to obtain the school records or to speak with school personnel can also result in closer cooperation with the prosecutor's office on these sensitive matters.

Other Agencies

Secondary groups of agencies and resources to consider for information sharing and cooperation on special projects are:

Administrative and Funding Agencies. Consider how key officials in your local government, particularly those concerned with resource allocation, can be helpful to maintaining cooperative procedures. Plan for early involvement of a staff member from the mayor's or county executive's office, county council or county board of supervisors to encourage a community-wide and agency commitment for better services for abused children and troubled families.

Citizen and Special Interest Groups. Consider the role of special interest groups concerned with children or citizen advocacy groups. Your decision to broaden the base of your review depends on your stage of system reform and assessment of the value of their participation for the overall success of the effort. Many of the same individuals involved in community child abuse prevention programs and victim support groups will also have roles in the litigation process or treatment services.

Schools. Review school policies and procedures regarding child abuse. Research indicates that children often disclose abuse to a trusted teacher or counselor, so school reporting practices to investigative agencies are of paramount importance. Like information from CPS, information gained early by school personnel may be essential to your case. Teachers and counselors also have a great deal of contact with the child after the disclosure. Accordingly, school personnel support and sensitivity toward the child is critical.

Outside Experts. Finally, consider resources outside your community. National organizations concerned with child abuse litigation such as the National Center for Prosecution of Child Abuse, the National Child Protection Training Center, and the American Bar Association Center on Children and the Law are available to assist with technical expertise in addressing administrative and legal issues. There is no need to reinvent the wheel. State prosecutor associations can often help organize and interpret the information you collect. Explore the experiences of other jurisdictions in developing a multidisciplinary system and talk to the prosecutors. While approaches differ, the problems most communities face are remarkably similar.

BEGINNING THE PROCESS OF CHANGE

To guarantee the success of a coordinated approach to child abuse cases, the prosecutor must build commitment to coordination among staff members of the agencies mandated to respond to child abuse reports—specifically CPS and law enforcement. Using information from your initial review of current practices, discuss problems with administrative heads of these agencies and seek their cooperation in implementing changes in policies and procedures that enhance each agency's response.

At this point, you may consider enlisting the assistance of an outside consultant to act as facilitator in managing the development of improved policies and protocols. Participation of a neutral third party has several advantages:

- An outside person can push participants to examine and resolve controversial issues without being perceived as having a vested interest in the outcome.
- A person not involved in the day-to-day response to child abuse can see problems that are not apparent to participants.
- Participation of a third party frees the participants to focus on issues of importance to their agencies and the community.
- Regular meetings with a consultant can provide incentive to pursue the process that might otherwise be abandoned because of the pressure of job responsibilities.
- A trained consultant can help team members become more skillful in identifying and resolving problems.

Qualified consultants can be found in almost any community, particularly on the faculty of local universities, in civic organizations, or among private practitioners in the area. Look for individuals who have experience working with groups and knowledge of organizational development and group dynamics. Professional consultants may cost more than a local group is able to pay. Because skills vary widely, interview potential consultants carefully about their approaches and the services to be provided. Speaking with former clients is essential.

Even though coordinated systems exist in many jurisdictions, much of the information about implementing and maintaining an effective team is still anecdotal. For many communities, *The New Child Protection Team Handbook* (Bross et al., [Eds.] [1988]. New York: Garland) is an indispensable tool for assembling the multidisciplinary team. Another respected reference work is *Handbook of Clinical Intervention in Child Sexual Abuse* (Sgroi, S. M. (Ed.). [1982]. New York: Lexington Books). All efforts, however, share at least four goals:

- Educating all disciplines involved in responding to child abuse reports about the dynamics of victimization, child development, and the criminal justice process as it relates to children

- Establishing and maintaining consistent reporting practices
- Providing better-quality investigations and eliminating duplication of effort
- Ensuring sensitive treatment of the child victim and family throughout the investigative and trial process

Types of Multidisciplinary Teams

Generally teams can be divided into three types: investigative, service planning, and systems coordination. These functions are not mutually exclusive and may be combined in one team or carried out by many of the same people (particularly in small communities) on several teams. *The primary team for prosecutors is the investigative team.*

Investigative Teams

Investigative teams include individuals mandated to respond to child abuse cases on a day-to-day basis: the prosecutor, the CPS investigator, and the law enforcement investigator. These people often receive joint specialized training in handling child abuse cases and already work together to conduct the investigation and manage the criminal court process. Depending upon community organization and the volume of cases, health and mental health care professionals, victim-witness advocates, and school officials may also be part of the team.

The purpose of this team is to review cases currently under investigation or pending court action to ensure that all members are aware of case status and unresolved issues. In large jurisdictions with several investigators and prosecutors, this team may meet regularly, have a designated coordinator, and have a formal procedure for discussing cases. In jurisdictions with single investigators from each agency, meetings may be less formal or occur over the telephone. In jurisdictions with few child abuse reports, the team may assemble only when a case is under investigation or pending court action.

Service Planning Teams

Service planning teams consist of professionals providing therapeutic and other support services to abuse victims and families during the investigative and adjudicatory stages and following court disposition. These teams must include CPS workers, mental health practitioners, victim-witness advocates, and school guidance counselors or social workers. The purpose of this team is to coordinate the services provided to individual victims and families, to ensure that needed services are available, and to maintain consistency among agencies in dealing with abuse victims and families.

While the participation of the prosecutor and other law enforcement personnel is not as crucial in this team as it is in the investigative team, it can be mutually beneficial. Knowledge of services provided to a victim and family and their responses can affect the prosecutor's decisions concerning presentation of the victim in court, alternatives to in-court testimony, and additional avenues of investigation. A multidisciplinary team made up of skilled social service professionals is an excellent mechanism for increasing the prosecutor's understanding of the dynamics of child abuse. This understanding will enhance the prosecutor's credibility in pretrial negotiations and in the courtroom.

Systems Coordination Teams

These teams can consist of the same individuals who participate in the service planning team but can also include county or city administrators, citizen advocacy groups, and others. This team provides feedback to the people in the "system" concerning public perceptions about child abuse and how it is being addressed. This group can identify gaps in services and advocate for increased resources. It can assume responsibility for organizing public awareness events and generate support for prevention efforts.

Organizing the Investigative Team

The first step in organizing a team is defining the problem the team will address and the purpose for which it is being created. In many communities, the impetus for creating a multidisciplinary investigative team is a particularly complex, sensational, or poorly handled case that has generated public demand for increased information sharing among agencies handling child abuse cases. In other communities agencies work well together, but scarce resources limit their effectiveness in responding to child abuse. In other cases, an increased awareness of child abuse is needed among all community residents.

Agency representation need not be confined to a single person. The police may wish to have a supervisory-level detective and uniformed officer on the team because of their different responsibilities in child abuse cases. CPS may be represented by both an intake worker and a person responsible for providing ongoing services to abused children and their families. If the social services agency employs a therapist to provide counseling to child abuse victims, this person may be invited to join the team.

As the convening agency and leader of the multidisciplinary team, the prosecutor's office should be represented by the elected or appointed prosecutor or an assistant who has the authority to speak and act on behalf of the chief prosecutor. If the prosecutor's office has an active victim-witness program, the program's coordinator or child advocate should join the team.

Since change in traditional agency interaction can be threatening and provoke strong resistance, team membership should be initially limited to agencies and individuals who play major roles in the investigation and prosecution of child abuse—usually prosecution, law enforcement, and CPS. If change is being implemented in an environment of institutional antagonism, assembling a group of agency representatives to develop a system to improve coordination will be time-consuming for the prosecutor.

Clarity of Roles

It is essential that individual roles and responsibilities of team participants be clearly delineated from the outset. Multidisciplinary teams have recently come under defense attack as promoting a bias toward concluding that children have been abused and reinforcing inaccurate conclusions about abuse. To guard against this possibility and perception, it should be made clear that each team member retains responsibility and accountability to independently evaluate the case; authority should not be abdicated to the team. For example, the prosecutor is solely responsible for deciding what crimes to charge, if any. Team consultation should be used to share information, enabling the prosecutor to make an informed decision. Decisions should never be made by group vote.

Documentation and Confidentiality

Most teams have opted to keep paperwork and administrative responsibilities to a minimum. The aim of the team approach is to promote discussion and problem solving, not create additional burdens. Usually, the investigative team will be composed of very busy professionals who cannot assume additional administrative responsibilities. Yet, each may be able to volunteer limited clerical support and meeting space on a rotating basis.

Some organizational duties may be necessary, such as agenda preparation and meeting notifications. These responsibilities can be divided equally. However, the team should have a chairperson who selects cases for review, leads discussions, manages time, and summarizes group discussion. While the chairperson can be chosen by appointment or vote, many teams prefer rotating chair responsibilities.

Teams should consider what kind of records they wish to maintain. Meeting attendance, a log of cases reviewed, recommendations of participants on issues raised, case outcomes, and task assignments can be documented. This information is necessary for evaluating the impact of the multidisciplinary approach on case handling if the team wishes to analyze its progress.

However, important considerations are confidentiality and the free exchange of information. Privilege statutes, professional standards regarding confidentiality, and statutes regarding privacy normally allow for such information sharing. The work sessions themselves should be confidential, and privacy rights of the victims and their families should be a priority (also addressed in some state statutes). The team may wish to disguise the victims' names during the review process, especially when outside observers such as representatives from potential funding organizations, interested professionals who wish to organize a multidisciplinary team in their own jurisdictions, or others attend. The team could also decide not to discuss specific cases if a nonteam member attends and instead devote the meeting to communication or prevention efforts.

Be aware that, should cases reviewed by the investigative team enter the criminal court system, defense attorneys may request team records as part of discovery. In light of that probability, the team should discuss what type of records are appropriate. Try to avoid duplicative paperwork and refrain from placing privileged materials (e.g., psychiatrist's reports) in the records. Some teams maintain very brief meeting records or opt for none at all.

Reporting statutes, laws authorizing formation of multidisciplinary teams, and court-ordered cooperation form a basis for implicit agreements to share information and preserve confidentiality of agency records. Some teams sign explicit agreements allowing them to share information and maintain confidentiality within the context of the team. Team members may want to establish a policy that prohibits the team records from being disclosed unless the team agrees to do so for a particular purpose.

Team Activities

The frequency of team meetings will be decided by the team. Whether the team meets daily, weekly, monthly, or less frequently will depend upon the tasks and goals identified by the team. Team functions should be identified early. Some teams review every reported case of suspected sexual or physical child abuse; other teams address broad policy issues. A jurisdiction with relatively few cases and inexperienced members may make multidisciplinary training its first priority. Immediate tasks will differ from jurisdiction to jurisdiction.

Protocol Development

The first goal of many teams is to develop a protocol. A child abuse team's protocol is simply an agreement among agencies to follow certain procedures when faced with a report of child abuse. Clarification of roles, duties, and expectations is a prerequisite to drafting the protocol. Discussion should be open, honest, and constructive, with the paramount goal of improving services to children.

Protocols can be short, long, complex, or simple, but they must be clear and should be in writing. The National Center maintains a collection of protocols from across the country. They range from 1 page to more than 250 pages and address topics ranging from case investigation to offender treatment.

Each protocol should begin with a statement of purpose—a useful exercise for clarifying team expectations. The statement should explain why the team was formed, set forth general challenges, and indicate how the team expects to meet them. It should state the signatories' commitment to a coordinated approach to the investigation and prosecution of crimes against children. A statement of purpose helps ensure that the vision of the team remains constant and serves as a public statement from leaders in the community that crimes against children will be taken seriously. The types of cases (e.g., neglect, serious physical abuse, sexual abuse, child homicide) covered by the protocol should also be identified and defined.

A general but concise statement of the mission of each agency signing the protocol should be included. This has several benefits. First, it requires agencies to define their missions, perhaps for the first time. Second, it helps others understand the reasons for an agency's policies. Third, it serves as a foundation for procedures set forth in the protocol. Team members may want to define the statutorily imposed duties of participating agencies. For instance, if law enforcement is required to remove children from their homes under certain circumstances, those criteria should be cited in the protocol. CPS responsibilities to investigate child abuse reports, including mandated time limits for interviewing children suspected of being abused and criteria for referral to the prosecutor, should also be delineated and supporting statutes cited.

Recognizing that each agency has unique skills and information, some communities have made provisions in their protocols for interagency assistance. Such assistance is typically sought when the assisting agency has no statutory duty to investigate but has expertise useful to the requesting agency.

The protocol must identify the agency with primary responsibility for particular aspects of the investigation. If joint interviews are envisioned because of agreement or statute, specify methods to be followed. The description of the investigative procedure must be specific enough to be used as a guide, yet general enough to allow flexibility under varying conditions. As in any process, one agency has the ultimate responsibility for coordinating the investigation, but the coordinating agency need not be the same under all circumstances. For instance, if it is clear that the purpose of a particular investigation is not to determine whether a crime was committed, it may be reasonable to identify CPS as the coordinating agency. The determining criteria must be clearly stated. The protocol may also include procedures for resolving disagreements. While friction is inevitable, the existence of a conflict resolution method allows the investigation to proceed without undue disruption.

Remember, the purpose of a protocol is not to burden investigative agencies with more bureaucracy but to enhance the community's response to the challenges of crimes against children. If regular team meetings are unnecessary, some provision should be made to convene the team when unusually demanding cases arise. Consultation with experts can also produce helpful insights into seemingly insoluble problems.

Limit those who investigate cases of abuse. Most jurisdictions accomplish this by selecting a handful of officers and social workers and pouring all training into these individuals. The protocol provides that only investigators receiving this specific training will be allowed to handle a case of child abuse.

Limit those who prosecute a case of child abuse. If only a handful of prosecutors are assigned to handle a case of child abuse, these professionals will develop greater expertise by doing it more often.

Involve the prosecutor early in the case. Ideally, a prosecutor should be contacted shortly after the report is received and be allowed to give input into the case. If a child-friendly interview room with a two-way mirror is constructed, the prosecutor can and should be present for the interview.

Develop one or more child-friendly interview rooms. If video equipment is to be used, care must be given to select high-quality taping and recording equipment that can capture the low voices and whispers of children. Though toys and artwork interesting to children would be appropriate for a waiting area, the interviewing room itself should be free of toys or wall decorations that may be distracting to a child. Chairs comfortable and sized to fit children should be selected. Beanbag chairs often fit this description. A sketch board, visible to the camera, that can be used by the interviewer to draw pictures and take notes the child can see should be placed between the interviewer and the child's chair. Anatomical dolls should not be immediately visible to the child but should be stored in a box or cabinet near the interviewer where they can be readily accessed if necessary. If the taping equipment does not have a clock or other mechanism that discloses to a viewer the time of the interview, you may wish to place a clock above the sketch board so that it is visible to the camera. When selecting the room, make sure it is easily accessible. If you have a designated room in the police station, for instance, make sure the room is not used for other meetings that cannot be canceled on a moment's notice. Also, can the child be ushered in and out of the building with as little fanfare as possible? If the child has to go past a number of other rooms and officers before getting to the interview room, the child may be intimidated by the whole process. In small jurisdictions, investigators must do the best they can with the facilities available. In selecting a color for the room, you may wish to consult with a local child counselor. Some colors are believed to make children more comfortable than others.

Train your interviewers in the art and science of interviewing child abuse victims. There is no substitute for comprehensive, intensive training of child interviewers. Many jurisdictions have expended time and resources on videotape cameras, child-friendly interview rooms, and even child advocacy centers without having ever taken the prerequisite step of adequately training forensic interviewers. A child-friendly environment may enhance a child's ability to communicate, but atmosphere alone cannot make a bad interview good. Experience is also not a substitute for training. As one commentator noted, "Some of the poorest interviews that we have observed were done by workers who had been interviewing children for years." (Wood, J., McClure, K. A., & Birch, R. A. [1996]. Suggestions for improving interviews in child protection agencies. *Child Maltreatment, 1*, 223.) At a minimum, investigative interviewers must be well-versed in linguistics, child development, memory and suggestibility issues, the dynamics of abuse, and commonly accepted interview guidelines. (Wood, et al. Suggestions for improving interviews in child protection agencies. *Child Maltreatment, 1*, 223.) To address the need for training, APRI offers basic and advanced education in investigative interviewing of children.

Develop an interview protocol. It is important to develop a protocol for the interview of child abuse victims. Many investigators have an understanding of child development and linguistics but are unsure how to begin an interview and transition to different topics. An interview protocol can overcome this obstacle. An interview protocol "provides structure and guidelines for what often can be an unwieldy process . . . the protocol provides checkpoints that interviewers learn and use to orient themselves throughout the interview process." (Davies, D., et al. [1996]. A model for conducting forensic interviews with child victims of abuse. *Child Maltreatment, 1*, 189.) An interview protocol "facilitates internal consistency among interviewers and uniformity between interviews" (*Id*). There are many interview protocols in use around the country. There are strengths and weaknesses to each protocol, and no one protocol represents a panacea to the problems inherent in the interviewing of children. In selecting a protocol, investigators must choose a model that is supported by the research on interviewing children and that can be defended in court. The protocol should be flexible to allow for variations between interviews, depending on the developmental level of the child. One protocol is RATAC. Each letter stands for a different component of the interview. The "R" stands for rapport. The "A" stands for anatomy identification. The "T" stands for touch inquiry. The second "A" stands for abuse scenario. The "C" stands for closure. For more information about RATAC, contact CornerHouse Interagency Evaluation Center, 2502 Tenth Avenue South, Minneapolis, MN 55405, (612) 813–8300.

Train investigators to obtain corroborating evidence, including incriminating statements from the suspect. For example, Cottonwood County, Minnesota's protocol requires each officer to receive specific training in obtaining incriminating statements.

Review your protocol yearly. Note any attacks in court and make any needed alterations.

Joint Training

Team members often designate multidisciplinary training as a top priority, since joint training in investigative skills and team development gives members access to state-of-the-art techniques and information about investigation and prosecution as well as the opportunity to learn and appreciate the functions of others. Provisions for joint and cross-training are often incorporated into team protocols.

Joint training serves a variety of additional purposes. It allows members to work together in the relatively relaxed setting of training sessions. It provides a break from work, thus reducing stress. It often pools financial resources, permitting access to resources perhaps not otherwise available. Shared training also ensures that all participants have essentially equivalent tools, thereby lessening situations in which one agency does not perform at the level of other agencies or does not understand why a strategy is needed. Simply, joint training enhances teamwork. It need not be elaborate or expensive, and there are often experts within local agencies who can offer special training. At a minimum, the protocol should explicitly endorse the concept of joint training.

Team Flexibility

The roles of team participants should be flexible, recognizing that problem solving in child physical and sexual abuse cases is difficult in a rigidly structured environment and that professionals should have the opportunity to explore ideas freely. The issues in child abuse demand a flexible, pragmatic approach that respects the views of others in addressing problem areas such as reporting, investigation, case assessment, child protection, risk assessment, treatment plans, and progress monitoring. Priorities also change over time. Flexibility allows the team to address new problems as they arise.

Child Death Review Teams

Interagency child death review teams are an increasingly important investigative tool for prosecutors. Missouri was the first state to have local teams in all 115 counties as well as a state team. Colleen Kivlahan authored a landmark study on the lack of agency coordination in investigating or recording abuse-related deaths and was pivotal in the passage of Missouri H. Bill 185, Gen. Assembly, 1st Sess. (1991), requiring changes in the investigation of suspicious deaths. Among its provisions is a requirement that prosecutors convene a child death review team for their county or city to investigate suspicious deaths of children under 15. (For further information on child death review teams, see Chapter II, Section IX.R.)

CLOSING THOUGHTS

Coordinating a community's response to child abuse is one of the most challenging and rewarding activities a prosecutor can undertake. A coordinated approach not only benefits professionals responsible for responding to uniquely painful and frustrating situations, but it lessens the trauma of victims and families suffering simultaneously from the revelation of abuse and the intrusion of social service and criminal justice procedures in their lives. An effective system can protect the rights of victims and meet the needs of families. It can also engender community support, improve investigative procedures and case outcomes, and build professionalism in public service.

Interagency communication is critical to the effectiveness of child abuse investigations and prosecutions. Whether a community creates a multidisciplinary team to review all child abuse reports, establishes protocols to govern agency responses, or adopts another approach to coordination is a matter for each jurisdiction to decide. But decide it must. The crime of child abuse is too complex to investigate and too far-reaching in its effects to be dealt with by any one agency. Working together multiplies your chances of success in protecting child victims and holding offenders accountable—truly an area in which the whole is greater than the sum of its parts.

Dynamics of Victimization

Child abuse is uniquely difficult to prosecute. No other type of case consistently presents such complex psychological and social dynamics. No other type of case so often requires the prosecutor to go to trial with a child as its crucial witness. The pressure on victims is also uniquely painful. In addition to the devastating effects of the abuse itself, the discovery of the crime frequently results in the child or offender being removed from the home, leaving families sometimes permanently disrupted and often chaotic throughout the adjudicative process. In the vast majority of cases, the offenders are trusted authority figures such as family members, neighbors, babysitters, members of the clergy, scoutmasters, or teachers who physically or sexually abuse or neglect the children in their care. Unlike victims of most other crimes, child victims of abuse are sometimes castigated as villains by family members and friends who hold them responsible for the breakup of the family.

The controversy surrounding children as witnesses in the criminal justice system runs the gamut from arguments that children live in a fantasy world and cannot be believed to assertions that children never lie. Obviously, neither of these assumptions is correct. Experience and research show that children are no more or less reliable as witnesses than adults. They are witnesses whose testimony must be evaluated in light of their specific developmental capacity. Their ages, ability to communicate, and limited life experiences will affect their testimony. Like adults, they can be confused and deceived. However, it is rare for children to deliberately lie about abuse except to minimize its frequency or deny its actual occurrence.

To be effective, prosecutors must learn as much as they can about children and their capabilities and about the dynamics of child abuse. Specialized training is now more widely available and recommended. At a minimum, prosecutors should consult books and articles on child development and child abuse. Experiences with children from both professional and personal lives can be a helpful reference. Knowing how to talk to children and what to expect from those who have been abused will immeasurably improve the ability to evaluate and prosecute cases. Moreover, a sensitive and caring approach will gain the trust of children and their families and elicit the most accurate accounts of criminal activity. The following material provides a basic framework for understanding the dynamics of child abuse and dealing with child victims.

I. OVERVIEW OF VICTIMS AND VICTIMIZATION

A. The Victims

Victims of child abuse include boys and girls of all ages, from infancy through adolescence. They come from all ethnic and cultural groups, social and economic classes, and rural and urban areas, and they have varying levels of intellectual and physical abilities. They are abused and neglected in a variety of ways, from single incidents of brutal discipline to multiple physical assaults, from a single act of sexual fondling to years of forced intercourse, and from a single instance of dangerously inadequate supervision to prolonged ignoring of serious medical problems.

Although most children dislike the experience of being abused or neglected, they also have a strong need to be part of a family. Young children have no frame of reference for what is appropriate caregiving except what they experience. Older children may come to realize that what is or has happened to them is wrong or illegal, but they may also recognize that disclosure can harm people they care about or are dependent on. Abusers can easily trick or manipulate children into silence by telling them, for instance, the child will not be believed, the child will be punished after disclosure, or the family will be permanently separated. Equally effective deterrents to revealing abuse are threats to kill the victim, family members, or pets. Bribes such as money, special attention, or alcohol for adolescents, encourage victims to protect offenders, leading many children to feel like active participants in their own victimization.

B. The Vulnerability of Children

By their very nature, children make perfect victims. Authorities recognize children's vulnerability and they point to widely recognized factors that make children ideal targets of abusive behavior.

1. Children Are Dependent on Adults

Children are raised to respect and obey adults. This is ingrained in them through parental child-rearing techniques and the child's total dependence upon adults. To a child, adults hold positions of power and authority and generally exercise some control over the child. Moreover, mere physical size differences play an important part in the child's world and certainly enhance the dominating presence of the adult in that world.

The most significant and influential people in a child's world are those with whom they have the most frequent contact and whom they are taught to obey—parents, teachers, religious leaders, relatives, youth leaders, and babysitters. Parents may warn their children not to talk to strangers, but the abuser is usually someone well known to the child. The combination of authority and trust enhances the victimizer's likelihood of success. With greater access to the child and more control over the child, the victimizer can limit the child's self-protective actions and prevent disclosure. The child experiences additional confusion because the child loves and needs the offender.

2. Children Are Naturally Trusting and Curious

The trust that children place in the adults who care for them and are familiar to them also puts them at risk of physical and sexual abuse. This is especially true for very young children who have no choice but to rely on their caregivers. Young children also have a natural curiosity about everything, including sex, and that natural curiosity can be manipulated to engage the child in abuse scenarios. They generally have little to no understanding of sex despite the prominence it plays in television programming, movies, magazines, advertisements, and overheard conversations. Even so, their curiosity can be exploited by child molesters who establish rapport over time and gradually undertake the process of victimization.

Children's developmentally appropriate and healthy curiosity can frustrate parents who respond with excessive punishment and physical abuse. Young children's intellectual curiosity, typified by "Why" questions, can result in verbal aggression by parents unable to tolerate these challenges. Verbal aggression by parents may include statements such as "Shut up" and "You're so stupid."

3. The Need for Attention and Affection

The need for attention and affection from parents, siblings, and peers is a child's single most exploitable characteristic. Children seek to be included in the activities of friends and people close to them. This is particularly true when those activities involve attention from an adult. Attention helps children feel important and worthwhile. When a child's need for affection is not met, the child may seek to fulfill this need at all costs, thus increasing the risk of physical abuse and especially the risk of sexual exploitation. Often the offender is the only person in a child's life who offers affection, binding the child to the offender. This vulnerability is well known to offenders, who often admit they select victims who appear lonely and sad.

4. Adolescent Defiance and Peer Pressure

Adolescent defiance of parental controls increases tensions in the home, often exacerbating the level of physical punishment and abuse. In addition, incest offenders often become jealous when the child starts socializing with peers or dating, resulting in threatened and actual physical violence or an escalation of the sexual abuse.

Nonfamilial offenders use adolescent defiance of parental controls to their advantage by influencing a victim to disobey parents more often and associate more with the offender. An adolescent who is told to stay away from the offender is less likely to disclose the abuse for fear of blame or punishment. The offender may enhance the attractiveness of his company with alcohol or drugs, prohibited video games, and sexually explicit materials. The offender may initiate the teen into a group of other adolescents who also spend time with the offender, thus providing a circle of peers for lonely and isolated teens.

Sex offenders will sometimes take pictures of the adolescent engaged in sexual activity and then use these to coerce the teen's silence. Once adolescents are lured or tricked into participating in these activities, the threat of public disclosure helps to ensure continued participation or submission.

5. Children With Disabilities

The natural vulnerability of children is magnified when the child has a physical, emotional, or developmental disability. The disability may impair major areas of life activities such as self-care, receptive and expressive language, learning, self-direction, and independent living. Disabled children are even more dependent on adults to assist them with daily needs and may have a greater desire to please caregivers. The severely disabled, often in institutional settings, are usually totally dependent on their caregivers and they are even more vulnerable to physical and sexual abuse. The disabled child's greater dependence increases the offender's ability to trick, manipulate, or simply overpower the child.

A child's developmental disabilities can add stress to the already difficult job of raising a child. Children with multiple disabilities may display significant behavior problems that pose special challenges to parents. These behavior problems may include head banging, screaming, violent tantrums, and swearing. These disabilities are generally permanent and the chronicity of the special care required is highly taxing on parents' coping abilities.

Children with cognitive and communication disabilities are easy targets for abuse since they have significant difficulty reporting their experiences. Disabled children may be more socially isolated because they lack the social skills to maintain supportive peer relationships. Children with physical handicaps experience obstacles in interacting with peers, leaving them even more dependent on caregivers for attention, affection, and social interaction. (Ammerman, R. [1997]. Physical abuse and childhood disability: Risk and treatment factors. In R. Geffner, S. Sorenson, & P. Lundberg-Love [Eds.], *Violence and sexual abuse at home.* New York: Haworth Press.)

Some children have intellectual deficits that restrict their ability to recognize their experiences as abusive. These deficits can also limit their ability to report, seek help, and identify the offender. If communication deficits accompany the intellectual deficit, children can experience difficulty in describing the events, context, and location of the abuse. This creates challenges for investigation and interviewing. Some of these children may also have a speech impairment, necessitating the involvement in the interview process of someone familiar with the child's speech patterns. These deficits alone should not be a bar to prosecution. These children simply need greater assistance through the use of appropriate interviewing techniques and additional preparation for court.

Children with visual and auditory challenges may nevertheless be able to describe in detail what they experienced if they are assisted by the use of an interpreter or reporting aid. Facilitated communication involves an adult assisting the child with communication, such as the adult helping the child type answers. Such facilitation is highly controversial, and there is no current information that this method produces reliable reports of abuse. Care should be exercised when evaluating allegations of abuse involving the use of facilitated communication. Some disabled children are credible and competent witnesses, although they may require the assistance of interpreters and technological aids to allow them to participate in the legal process. They require special advocacy in the criminal justice system. It is the prosecutor's job to find a method of presenting the child's information so the child feels competent in the court process and appears credible to the jury.

C. Types of Abuse and Neglect

In the past, professionals have tended to think categorically about abuse, investigating and prosecuting it as a single form of maltreatment. Information from large-scale national studies suggests more than one type of maltreatment often occurs at once—for instance, physical and sexual abuse, physical abuse and medical neglect. Although a child may be referred for investigation of only a single incident of abuse or for only one type of maltreatment, professionals need to be willing to look for signs of other co-occurring forms of maltreatment, looking holistically at the full scope of family violence. (Davidson, H. A. [1995]. Child abuse and domestic violence: Legal connections and controversies. *Family Law Quarterly, 29,* 357.) When investigating suspected abuse of one child in the family, the possibility that other children have also been victimized must be explored.

1. Physical Abuse

Severe physical abuse often leads to permanent injuries and even death. From 1986 to 1993, there was a 299% increase in the number of reports of serious injury from all forms of maltreatment, abuse, and neglect. (Sedlak, A., [1997]. Risk factors for the occurrence of child abuse and neglect. In R. Gefner, S. Sorenson, & P. Lundberg-Love [Eds.], *Violence and sexual abuse at home.* New York: Haworth Press.) However, there is good reason to believe that statistics based on reports to child welfare and law enforcement agencies seriously underestimate the scope of the problem. A series of studies conducted by phone with parents have consistently indicated much higher rates of abusive behavior than were previously estimated. A recent survey conducted by the Gallup Poll in 1995 found the number of physical abuse victims to be six times higher than the estimate from the National Center for Child Abuse and Neglect. One in five parents also reported they received severe physical punishment when they were children. For parents who themselves had been abused in childhood, severe abuse of their own children was ten times higher than parents who were not abused. (Straus, M. et al., [1998]. Identification of child maltreatment with the parent-child conflict tactics scales: Development and psychometric data for a national sample of American parents. *Child Abuse and Neglect, 22,* 249.)

"Battered child syndrome" (BCS) involves repeated or serious injuries to a child that are nonaccidental. It is also common for BCS children to have poor health, poor hygiene, soft tissue injuries, malnutrition. (See Kempe, C. H., et al. [1962]. The battered child syndrome. *Journal of the American Medical Association, 181,* 105.) It is not uncommon to discover multiple injuries in various stages of healing when a child dies from abuse-related injuries. Physical abuse must, of course, be distinguished from medical conditions, such as osteogenesis imperfecta that may result in fragile bones or easy bruising.

Physically abused children frequently suffer repeated abusive behavior, often in the name of discipline. Abused children are often told they are bad or incorrigible and deserving of punishment. They are made to feel responsible for the abuse ("If you got dressed when I told you the first time, I wouldn't have to hit you.") and begin to believe they are indeed at fault. While most states do not criminalize mild corporal punishment, severe corporal punishment is clearly abusive and illegal. (See Vieth, V. [1994]. Corporal punishment in the United States: A call for a new approach to the prosecution of disciplinarians, *Journal of Juvenile Law, 15, 22.*) Excessive corporal punishment and other forms of physical abuse have been linked to a rise in delinquent acts, aggression, and a host of other behavioral and mental health problems. Factitious disorder by proxy, also known as Munchausen syndrome by proxy, involves a serious and potentially fatal form of abuse committed most frequently by mothers. The abuse consists of repeated steps of (1) inducing symptoms of illness in a child by acts such as suffocating a child until she stops breathing and then resuscitating her, (2) presenting the child for medical care expressing great concern for her welfare, and (3) claiming ignorance of the source of the illness. Parents may also alter laboratory specimens and may fabricate symptoms that never existed. These fabrications are often medically complex, and medical care providers have difficulty pinning down the nature of the illness. These parents seek the excitement of the hospital setting, the positive attention given to them by medical staff when they are so knowledgeable about their child's condition, and the praise from family members and others for being heroic in saving the child over and over again. When the child has medical crises, the abusing parent is the only one present and is able to "save" the child, call for assistance, and describe to care providers the symptoms supposedly observed. (See Ayoub, C., & Alexander, R. [1998]. Definitional issues in Munchausen by proxy. *APSAC Advisor, 11, 7.*)

Drug and alcohol abuse by pregnant women has generated debate about the prosecution of the mothers because of the large number of infants born with potentially long-term problems attributable to such abuse. Some criminal cases also involve parents giving children illegal drugs to calm them or leaving drugs where children can find and ingest them. Forced intervention for drug-exposed infants has not been demonstrated to prevent the problem or decrease the incidence of illicit substance use during pregnancy. Initial research suggested long-term cognitive, affective, and developmental problems in drug-exposed infants and toddlers. More recent research suggests some of those effects may be due to other intervening factors such as poverty and poor prenatal care and that some problems will resolve by the time children enter school. The American Academy of Pediatrics' position paper supports preventing intrauterine drug exposure by educating women about the hazards of drugs to the fetus and providing readily available drug treatment programs. Although criminal prosecution is not supported, the American Academy of Pediatrics does see benefits to civil litigation, such as in juvenile courts, to ensure the mother's participation in treatment. (Committee on Substance Abuse. [1995]. Drug-exposed infants. *Pediatrics, 96, 364.*)

2. Exposure to Domestic Violence

Awareness of the effects of domestic violence to children is growing. Three to ten million children per year experience the psychological trauma of seeing a parent beaten or otherwise assaulted. (Jaffe, P., Wolfe, D., & Wilson, S. [1990]. *Children of battered women.* Newbury Park, CA: Sage.) A child may directly witness violence, hear it, or infer it after seeing a parent's injuries or destroyed furnishings. A child's exposure to domestic violence is the single best predictor for transmitting violence across generations. (1996. *Violence and the family.* Washington, DC: American Psychological Association.)

When domestic violence occurs, the risk of physical and sexual abuse to children also increases dramatically. Estimates vary from 30% to 60% regarding the frequency of the co-occurrence of physical abuse of children and domestic violence. Daughters of women who are assaulted by their partners are much more likely to be sexually abused in the home or by someone else. Mothers beaten by their partners are twice as likely to abuse their children, and fathers who frequently beat their wives are more likely to beat their children. (Straus, M., & Gelles, R. [1990]. *Physical violence in American families*. New Brunswick, NJ: Transaction.)

Violence against an intimate also puts children at risk if the parent—usually the mother—is unable to protect her children from abuse and the effects of witnessing violence. The co-occurrence of domestic violence and child abuse represents a unique form of trauma in which not only is the child harmed, but the person to whom the child would otherwise turn for comfort, support, and safety is also being assaulted.

3. Neglect

Neglect, defined as the failure to provide the essential care for a child's physical, emotional, or intellectual well-being, ranges from failure to provide sufficient food, adequate clothing, or safe shelter to neglect of medical care, supervision, or schooling. It also includes exposing children to threatening or dangerous conditions, including criminal activity. Forty percent of child fatalities owing to maltreatment are the result of neglect. (Daro, D., & McCurdy, K. [1994]. Preventing child abuse and neglect: Programmatic interventions. *Child Welfare, 73*, 405.)

Neglect is often associated with poverty and can result from extraordinary inattentiveness or deliberate acts. Neglect may be the result of poor mental health, chemical dependency, or developmental disabilities in the parent. Situational neglect may develop when divorce, hospitalization, or job loss overwhelms a parent's resources.

Medical neglect includes the caretaker's failure to obtain needed immunizations and physical examinations, provide adequate care for disabled children, or obtain treatment that is medically required for the child's welfare. Some parents reject medical care for their children based on religious beliefs, relying solely on prayer to restore their children to health. Children may suffer needlessly and sustain permanent injuries or die when denied the benefits of medical procedures that could control or cure disease.

Failure to thrive is a poorly defined condition that refers to a child's subnormal growth pattern. Pediatricians make the diagnosis by conducting a physical examination and by evaluating the child's history. Most victims are under two years of age and generally weigh less than the third percentile, when corrected for height, on standard growth charts. Some failure-to-thrive children fail to gain weight, while others seem to be developing normally and then show a steady weight loss. The condition may be due to an inadequate caloric intake or too many calories being excreted and/or lost internally. Growth failure may be associated with poor overall health, decreased responsiveness to stimuli, and apathy. The causes can also include environmental deprivation and feeding problems. (Monteleone, J. [1998]. *Child maltreatment* [2nd ed., pp. 357–369]. St. Louis: G.W. Medical.)

Supervision neglect involves failure to provide guidance or protection suitable to the child's age and developmental abilities. This type of neglect includes expecting slightly older siblings to care for infants or choosing inappropriate babysitters. Leaving young children at home alone places them at risk of serious injury. Leaving older children alone places them at risk of sexual exploitation, substance abuse, or delinquency.

4. Psychological Maltreatment

Psychological maltreatment, or emotional abuse and neglect, involves a pattern of caregiver behavior that attacks a child's development of self and social competence. Acts of omission and commission convey to children that they are worthless, unloved, unwanted, endangered, or only of value in meeting another's needs. (American Professional Society on the Abuse of Children. [1995]. *Practice guidelines: Psychosocial evaluation of suspected psychological maltreatment in children and adolescents.* APSAC.) Psychological maltreatment is widespread: The 1995 Gallup Survey found that 22 million children were subjected to severe verbal aggression in the previous year. Reported cases of emotional neglect nearly tripled between 1986 and 1993.

Since parents and other caregivers are not perfect, everyone may send occasional harmful messages to children. However, psychological maltreatment does not involve a few isolated incidents over a child's lifetime, but rather a consistent parenting style that is part of the child's daily life. Six types of psychological maltreatment have been identified: (1) rejecting/spurning, (2) isolation, (3) terrorizing, (4) ignoring, (5) exploiting/corrupting, and (6) mental health, medical and emotional neglect.

Rejecting/Spurning involves a combination of rejection and hostile degradation such as singling out one child for punishment and criticism. *Isolation* includes confining a child physically or preventing social interactions by locking a child in his room all day. Acts involved in *terrorizing* include threats to hurt, kill, or abandon the child; exposing the child to domestic violence; and leaving the child unattended in dangerous circumstances. The modeling of antisocial acts or the encouraging and condoning of deviant behaviors, such as using a child to shoplift items or selling the child for sexual purposes, constitutes *exploiting and/or corrupting* the child. *Ignoring,* or denying the child emotional responsiveness, may involve failing to express affection and caring for the child, refusing to interact with the child, or being psychologically unavailable. Psychological unavailability can occur, for instance, when a parent suffers from depression. Parents may also deny the need for or refuse to allow the child to receive needed mental health treatment, medical care, or special education services. (See Hart, S., & Brassard, M. [1990]. Psychological maltreatment of children. In R. Ammerman & M. Hersen [Eds.], *Treatment of family violence: A sourcebook* [pp. 77–112]. New York: John Wiley.)

Child victims of psychological maltreatment may show evidence of severe emotional or behavioral disturbance, failure to attain normal developmental milestones, or impaired relationship skills or lack a positive, secure attachment to a parent or parent figure in the home. Because psychological maltreatment may be difficult to assess, it is generally not the focus of criminal prosecution. However, these forms of maltreatment often co-occur with and exacerbate the effects of other types of abuse and neglect. Psychological maltreatment that is at the heart of other abuse helps explain why so many children delay reporting or make seemingly unconvincing reports.

5. Sexual Abuse

Awareness of the problem of child sexual abuse has dramatically increased in the past 15 years. Most adults now report knowing someone who has been sexually abused and understand the widespread nature of this problem. Research with sexual offenders and telephone surveys of the public demonstrate that statistics based on reported cases seriously underestimate the true number of sexual abuse crimes. Reported cases of sexual abuse increased 125% between 1986 and 1993. The Gallup Survey estimated 10 times the number of sexually abused children than are reflected in the actual reports: 1.3 million children per year compared to 130,000 reports. Prior victimization of any type—earlier sexual abuse, physical assault, witnessing abuse of a family member—places children at greater risk for later sexual abuse. (Boney-McCoy, S., & Finkelhor, D. [1995]. Prior victimization: A risk factor for child sexual abuse and for PTSD-related symptomatology among sexually abused youth. *Child Abuse and Neglect, 19,* 1402.)

Knowledge about the process of sexual victimization has also grown, helping professionals understand the varied mechanisms by which children are manipulated, coerced, and forced into unwanted or developmentally inappropriate sexual activity. Both intrafamilial and extrafamilial sex offenders known to the victim use a variety of strategies to involve the child in a sexual relationship, including tricking the child into believing the contact is appropriate, manipulating the child through the use of bribes, and threatening severe consequences for disclosure. Strangers who sexually assault children also rely on trickery and threats to obtain compliance and maintain secrecy.

Child sexual abuse victims may be involved in highly deviant behavior or bizarre scenarios. They may be drugged to diminish their resistance and undermine their credibility when they report these unusual acts. Discrediting the victim's account because it involves acts that are shocking and offensive to ordinary sensibilities or to a mistaken stereotyping of offender behavior can mean that serious crimes go undetected. While many would rather ignore these accounts or believe children fantasize and invent these bizarre stories, the possibility that they may be based on actual events should be carefully explored. A skillful investigation should always attempt to determine why such things are being described. (See Everson, M. [1997]. Understanding bizarre, improbable, and fantastic elements in children's accounts of abuse. *Child Maltreatment, 2,* 134.)

Intrafamilial sexual abuse places children in the unique situation of disclosing events that may be embarrassing, painful, and shameful, but disclosure also implicates loved ones and trusted family members. Similarly, nonoffending parents may be criticized for failing to know the abuse was occurring. These parents often must choose between believing and protecting the vulnerable victim and believing and supporting a loved spouse, older child, or extended family member.

While many cases of sexual abuse involve female victims, boys are often victims of sexual abuse. However, males are much less likely than females to disclose the abuse. Boys experience the same feelings of guilt, shame, and confusion. However, depending on the case characteristics, boys may suffer from the added dynamic of homophobia. The fear of being labeled homosexual suppresses reports of male child sexual abuse.

Victims of both genders tend to blame themselves for abuse, with thoughts such as "I didn't stop him" or "I knew what he would want if I went over there." The perpetrator often encourages these thoughts by telling the child "You're so sexy" or "You like it. I know you do." If children do not report sexual abuse after the first incident, they become the guilty bearers of this awful secret. (Summit, R. [1993]. The child sexual abuse accommodation syndrome. *Child Abuse and Neglect, 7,* 177.)

Victims may try to cope with abuse in both active and passive ways. Their very coping mechanisms—running away, acting out sexually, or defiant behavior at home—may be used to discredit them when they do report. The victims' passive coping mechanisms, including minimizing the impact on themselves and dissociating the pain from conscious awareness, may also be used to undermine the reliability of a disclosure. Skepticism about delays in reporting and identifying abused children as "disturbed" are also common techniques to block investigation and prosecution efforts.

A number of factors can increase the impact of sexual abuse on children:

- Lack of a relationship with a supportive adult or sibling
- A poorly functioning family
- Multiple types of sexual abuse
- Physical restraint of the victim
- Victim's fear of negative consequences for disclosure
- Victim's perception of the relationship with the perpetrator as positive
- Closeness of relationship between victim and offender

SOURCE: Conte, J., & Schuerman, J. [1987]. Factors associated with an increased impact of child sexual abuse. *Child Abuse and Neglect, 11*, 201.

D. The Need for Sensitivity

1. General Principles

Child abuse and child abuse prosecution typically invoke intense emotions in the families impacted by the offense and the professionals who seek to investigate and prosecute these crimes. Prosecutors and investigators dealing with these cases are often faced with individuals who are extremely upset and for whom the effects of victimization fade slowly. The effects may become worse before becoming better. The goal of prosecution should be the protection of children without retraumatizing the children or their family members. As victims, children are least likely to understand the complexities of the legal system and they are least able to effectively express their interests. The fears of separation, loss, and blame that result from the disclosure can overwhelm children. The need for sensitivity on the part of prosecutors dealing with child abuse cases is thus especially critical. Extra time must be set aside for victims and their families to overcome their natural apprehension about the criminal justice system, often magnified in sexual abuse cases, and to instill confidence in the system.

It is important to communicate respect for children and their families' feelings and circumstances and to listen without reacting negatively or judgmentally. A victim and family will not appreciate being treated as though their case is only one of many or less serious than another case. Clear, honest answers and explanations about the prosecutor's role and what to expect from the process will help establish trust.

Victim-witness advocates within a prosecutor's office and other victim support and advocacy services in the community can provide valuable support for victims throughout the criminal process. Prosecutors should take advantage of such programs and work with them to respond more effectively to the needs of child abuse victims and their families. Even a successful outcome will make little difference to the victim and her family if the process itself was not positive and responsive.

2. Ethnic and Cultural Diversity

An effective prosecution response must be sensitive to ethnic and cultural differences. Cultural values, parenting approaches, views of law enforcement and public agencies, family constellations, beliefs about sexuality, to say nothing of language differences, can all affect the investigation and prosecution process.

First, sensitivity demands that prosecutors and investigators support efforts to see that residents of every ethnic and racial background in their community are encouraged to come forward to report abuse and cooperate with investigations. Frequently, non–English speaking victims fail to report crimes because they are not aware of the available resources, they are unable to communicate, or they fear exposure and retribution. Prosecutors need to reach out to minority communities to ensure awareness of child abuse laws and resources for help.

Second, communication with a child of a different background can be significantly enhanced if you consult with other professionals familiar with the child's community. Children and their families' prior experiences with the legal system, either their own or others in the community, may have been negative, leading minority families to expect prejudice, discrimination, or at best, misunderstanding from public employees. An individual who can serve as an intermediary or translator between the prosecutor, the child, and the family can help reduce discomfort with a system that is often confusing and intimidating. The use of the same interpreter throughout the process will help establish rapport and trust between the victim, the victim's family, and the interpreter.

Even when the victim speaks English, there may be language barriers resulting from the family's use of unfamiliar terms to discuss certain matters. Legal and medical terms that may be familiar to most members of the dominant culture may be unfamiliar to members of a minority culture. Cultural beliefs that are different from state laws about child abuse may lead individuals to emphasize certain aspects of the abuse while ignoring others. The concern for privacy may be extremely high. It may be bolstered by family networks that exert strong resistance to openly discussing what is perceived as shameful or to overly intrusive intervention into family matters. This may be especially problematic in a culture where the extended family also serves as a vital support network for the child victim.

Children from differing backgrounds may have had prior experiences with discrimination, taunting about their physical differences, language difficulties, or generalized insensitivity to their values. They may be highly reluctant to participate in a process they can only expect to produce these same dynamics. Recognize and be sensitive to the special impact the litigation process may have on individuals of different ethnic backgrounds and respect their values. The prosecutor should avoid the temptation to generalize based simply on membership in a particular minority group. Each case is unique and will demand special attention. Policies and programs regarding cultural competence for staff members will also help in making victims and their families feel comfortable with the criminal justice system.

E. The Offenders

Understanding the victimization process requires recognition of the dynamics of deviance that propel the offender. However, there is no single profile of a physical or sexual abuse perpetrator, just as there is no typical victim. Offenders come from every age, gender, socioeconomic, and geographic category. Youthful offenders (adolescents and younger children) are increasingly coming to the attention of authorities.

The sole responsibility for the exploitation and victimization of children lies with perpetrators who take advantage of children's vulnerability and inability to defend themselves. Plainly and simply, children do not cause abuse. Rationalizations offered by abusers do not excuse the crime or guarantee it will not be repeated. A perpetrator who blames the victim, denies the behavior, or minimizes the seriousness of the crime makes the repetition of abuse a virtual certainty.

1. Physical Abuse

A number of models have been proposed to explain the development of physically abusive behavior toward children. These models emphasize parental psychopathology, the importance of social factors, or the interaction of individual and situational contributors. [In the latter model, abuse occurs at the nexus of individual characteristics, such as difficult infant temperament and the parents' own histories of abuse, family factors such as marital problems and domestic violence, and community factors such as a lack of access to services and cultural tolerance of violence.] (Kolko, D. [1996]. Child physical abuse. In J. Briere et al., [Eds.], *APSAC handbook on child maltreatment* [pp. 21–50]. Thousand Oaks, CA: Sage.)

Persons who physically abuse children may have greater environmental stressors than nonabusive parents, but regardless of the intensity or types of stress, their responses differ. Adults at risk to commit physical abuse tend to be more responsive to stress stimuli and to experience more distress. They exhibit greater autonomic reactivity with heightened levels of arousal that interfere with their coping skills. They also report more anxiety, depression, and low self-esteem related to their inability to cope. (See Milner, J., & Dopke, C. [1997]. Child physical abuse: Review of offender characteristics. In D. Wolfe, R. McMahon, & R. deV. Peters [Eds.], *Child abuse: New directions in prevention and treatment across the life span* [pp. 25–52]. Thousand Oaks, CA: Sage.) These characteristics directly relate to how a parent might respond to precipitating stimuli such as a child's crying or normal setbacks in toilet training.

The social factors that appear to make adults more likely to commit physical abuse include [poverty, lower educational achievement, unemployment, and crowding.] The presence of domestic violence is often found in failure-to-protect cases. Most abused individuals do not go on to commit physically abusive acts as adults, although a victimization history is associated with abuse of one's own children. Finally, the adults' physical health problems, chemical abuse, and disabilities are linked with an increased risk of abusive behavior.

Parents or adults in parenting roles, such as a mother's live-in partner, who are at risk for committing physical abuse often perceive children as disruptive and disobedient. Their expectations of the child's behavior exceed the child's developmental capability. These can include expectations of extreme compliance, excessive ability for self-care or care of younger siblings, and no need for parental attention. They hold the children responsible for misdeeds and misbehavior while not acknowledging the children's successes and good behavior. These parents tend to interact less, use more punitive discipline strategies, and use more physical punishment. They communicate and relate poorly and are less expressive and more aggressive, rather than assertive. A higher rate of alcohol abuse has also been linked to more frequent and severe aggression and physical abuse. However, alcohol abuse is only moderately related to "general" child abuse. It may be that alcohol interacts with other factors, such as depression or stress, to increase the level of dysfunction.

2. Neglect

Parents who neglect their children tend to be apathetic and uninvolved, with a history of abuse or neglect in their own childhood. These parents may come from unloving, unreliable, and indifferent parents who simply ignored them or from unstable drug- or alcohol-plagued environments. Neglect appears more likely to pass from generation to generation than either physical or sexual abuse. Basic parenting skills and empathy appear to be very difficult skills to learn in adulthood. As adults, such parents appear unable to perceive their child's problems and needs. In other cases, a battering relationship prevents the parent from protecting the child from the abuser and limits the attention and energy devoted to parenting. Some neglectful parents demonstrate limited intelligence or mental illness, but others enjoy high incomes and job status.

3. Psychological Maltreatment

Parents and parent figures in the home may engage in psychological maltreatment owing to inadequate and emotionally abusive parenting in their own childhood. Some parents engage in this behavior because of acute stresses such as divorce or unemployment. For others, emotional abuse and neglect are chronic patterns of interaction. One group of parents may become verbally aggressive toward and denigrate their children only under the influence of alcohol or drugs but not when they are sober. Undetected or untreated parental mental illness can also be associated with patterns of emotional neglect and abuse that do not remain when the mental illness is treated.

4. Sexual Abuse

While sex offenders do not neatly fit into a profile, general observations can be made. Abusers are usually in a position of authority, power, trust, or control over the victim. Many perpetrators appear to be normal, intelligent, successfully employed, and active in community affairs and they do not have prior criminal records. A number of typologies have been proposed for categorizing types of child molesters, but no typology is universally accepted owing to the lack of research data strongly supporting any one typology.

No single theory explains why offenders are attracted to children. Common developmental characteristics of offenders include a history of childhood abuse, feelings of inadequacy, depression, isolation, poor impulse control, and rigid sexual and religious values. A number of other factors are also associated with child molesting. These include an empathy deficit, inadequate social skills, cognitive distortions, deviant arousal patterns, and a sense of entitlement. The overriding commonality among child molesters is access to children through career choices, living arrangements, offers to "help" single parents, and volunteer work.

Offenders may target specific children based on appealing physical characteristics or perceived vulnerability. Others may be opportunistic and take advantage of an unsupervised child. A variety of techniques may be used to engage children, including spending time in pleasant activities with them, engaging in nonsexual touch, or showing them sexual materials to pique their curiosity or desensitize them. Children may be manipulated into sexual contact by convincing them they are special to the offender, giving them gifts or special privileges, or telling them the offender knows they are sexual with their girlfriend or boyfriend. When forced into sexual contact, the threat may be overt or implicit. These techniques include telling the child that if she allows the contact she will not get hurt, reminding her what happened when her mother disagreed with the offender, or threats to abuse younger siblings if she does not comply. Other sexual crimes against children are rapes with violent force, use of weapons, and physical assault in addition to the sexual acts.

Sex offenders also utilize a variety of strategies to break down children's emotional and psychological boundaries to allow the abuse to occur. It is not unusual for a sexual abuser to devote a great deal of time and attention to a needy child for the purpose of eventual exploitation. Some sex offenders choose their victims, pursue them, and "groom" them until they can successfully victimize them. Some offenders begin the process by talking inappropriately to children, while others begin with inappropriate touch they convince the child is accidental. Younger children may not reject inappropriate touch because of their lack of knowledge. Older children may become confused and assume the touch was accidental or that they misunderstood. Offenders try to convince children the contact is acceptable or minimize the seriousness of the acts. The offender may play on the child's feelings for the offender or develop a caretaking role with the child by making comments about things such as how lonely the child is. Later, children may be made to feel responsible when offenders begin to shift the blame to the child through statements such as, "You didn't tell me to stop" and "You must be enjoying it if you didn't tell." Others will use emotional coercion to maintain compliance by telling the child, "People will think you're a slut if they find out" and "Your mom will never believe you over me." (See Conte, J., Wolf, S., & Smith, T. [1989]. What sexual offenders tell us about prevention strategies. *Child Abuse & Neglect, 13,* 293.)

The grooming process may move very slowly, as some offenders enjoy the excitement and intrigue of this phase of the abuse. Other offenders move from nontouch to very invasive touch in short periods of time. This is particularly true if the offender knows he will only have access to a victim briefly, such as during a family reunion.

Offenders engage in their own cognitive distortions that allow the behavior to proceed. These thinking errors allow the offender to rationalize that some good will come from the contact by thinking, "She learned about sex from someone who loves her," minimize the impact on the victim with thoughts that "most 15-year-olds have done it," deny the sexual intent by believing, "My penis just fell out of my pants," and project the blame by thinking, "She shouldn't have been running around in her underwear." Offenders distort events and portray themselves as victims by stating, "My wife put her in bed with me," while at the same time professing remorse and the intention of never letting the abuse occur again. Such statements of remorse usually result only after the perpetrator is caught and not from any genuine concern for the victim. These promises are rarely reliable, and if no consequences follow disclosure, offenders may feel emboldened to proceed against that victim or others with impunity. (Abel, G., et al. [1987]. Self-reported sex crimes of non-incarcerated paraphiliacs. *Journal of Interpersonal Violence, 2,* 3.)

While courts generally prohibit the use of offender profile evidence at trial, understanding typical offender behavior and specific patterns of individual defendants might assist investigators during interrogation and prosecutors at sentencing.

5. Female Offenders

The true incidence of molestation by females is unknown, but it appears to be in excess of 10% of all sexual victimizations. Since women typically provide most of the physical care for children, acts committed against young children may go unreported. Further, the cultural norm that it is acceptable for a young male to be initiated into sexual behavior by an older female lowers the rates of reporting. There is also a deeply ingrained societal belief that women do not harm children.

Adult and adolescent females may molest children alone or in concert with a male offender. They may molest their own or relatives' children, children for whom they provide care, or those with whom they have a guidance role such as a coach. Some women may be reenacting their own victimization. Others may be living out their fantasy that they are attractive to adolescents. As with male offenders, these women are likely to have deviant fantasies and cognitive distortions, such as, "We love each other." Women who act in concert with male offenders may be victims of domestic violence trying to attract and keep a boyfriend or spouse. These women tend to be more violent and typically follow the male's lead rather than initiating the sexual contact.

Some female sexual offenders exhibit psychiatric disturbances including personality disorders. They may appear to lack a sense of competence, be isolated and dependent, and have distorted views of the role of sexuality in relationships. (Matthews, J. [1993]. Working with female sexual offenders. In M. Elliott [Ed.], *Female sexual abuse of children: The ultimate taboo* [pp. 61–78]. United Kingdom: Longman.)

6. Adolescent Offenders

Adolescents are increasingly being identified as being responsible for large numbers of sex crimes against children, with numbers as high as 30%–50% of all child molestation. (Becker, J., et al. [1986]. Characteristics of adolescent incest sexual perpetrators: Preliminary findings. *Journal of Family Violence, 1,* 85.) Over one-half of all sex offenders committed their first offense as an adolescent. Child molesters who are attracted to young boys had the earliest offense onset: 53% reported deviant arousal patterns by age 15 and 74% by age 19. Those who began offending as teens committed an average of 380 crimes by the time they were interviewed as adult offenders. (Abel, G., et al. [1987]. Self-reported sex crimes of non-incarcerated paraphiliacs. *Journal of Interpersonal Violence, 2,* 3.)

In the past, adolescent sexual offending has often been dismissed as naïve and harmless experimentation. However, we now know that true "experimentation" involves peers of the same age and does not require the use of coercion, force, or bribes. Although the percentages range from 25% to 70% on whether adolescent offenders are likely to have a history of being sexually abused, there is greater consensus that about 75% of adolescent offenders have been physically and/or emotionally abused or neglected.

Adolescent offenders and their parents are not accurate reporters of the teens' behavior. Adolescents significantly underreport their use of force and number of victims. Parents of adolescent offenders may lack information about their child's secretive sexual behavior and they are highly likely to minimize and deny the importance of the behavior they do know about, such as stealing underwear from family members. Adolescents who molest show similar patterns of deviant arousal and cognitive distortion to adult offenders. Those who have been sexually victimized may tell themselves, "It's no big deal. It didn't bother me when it happened."

Types of adolescent offending range from appropriate behavior with an inappropriate partner, to inappropriate behavior with an appropriate partner, to inappropriate behavior with an inappropriate partner. Some will have no prior history of acting out; for others, sexual offending will be one among many types of antisocial acts. (Pithers, W., et al. [1995]. Children with sexual behavior problems, adolescent sexual abusers, and adult sex offenders: Assessment and treatment. *Review of Psychiatry, 14,* 779.)

Adolescents in treatment programs report the following motivations to molest:

- Exploration and experimentation with newly developing sexual feelings
- Achieving acceptance, closeness, or a sense of importance or autonomy
- Gaining sexual pleasure
- Power, expressing anger, or humiliation of the victim
- Alleviation of anxiety or tension coupled with sexual gratification

Some of the adolescents appear to be isolated, under-socialized, and have poor self-confidence, while others are successful, have good social skills, and appear to have friends. Another group is seen as quite impulsive and disturbed, with reality testing problems, chemical abuse, and learning difficulties. (See Hastings, T., Anderson, S., & Hemphill, T. [1997]. Comparisons of daily stress, coping, problem behavior, and cognitive distortions in adolescent sexual offenders and conduct-disordered youth. *Sexual Abuse: A Journal of Research and Treatment, 9,* 29; Mathews, R., Hunter, J., & Vuz, J. [1997]. Juvenile female sexual offenders: Clinical characteristics and treatment issues. *Sexual Abuse: A Journal of Research and Treatment, 9,* 187.)

II. INDICATORS OF ABUSE

Abused children usually demonstrate behavioral, cognitive, and emotional reactions to the abuse. Children's responses may be affected by such factors as gender, age at onset of abuse, duration and severity of abuse, number of different types of abuse, relationship with the perpetrator, physical effects of the abuse, and quality of the relationship with the nonoffending parent(s). The problems that develop as a consequence of the abuse may be short term or long term or show some continuity throughout childhood; others appear to be transient or age-specific.

Indicators, standing alone, cannot be used to diagnose or conclude that the child was abused. As with any unusual change in a child's behavior, efforts should be made to explore alternative explanations and to determine the cause of the change. The opposite is also true: The absence of these indicators cannot be used as proof that abuse has not occurred since some abused children may be extremely resilient and effective at coping with their experiences.

While the following indicators are clearly not conclusive, when they accompany other evidence of abuse, especially medical evidence and the child's verbal report, they can provide crucial corroboration of an allegation. (See Beitchman, J., et al. [1991]. A review of the short-term effects of child sexual abuse. *Child Abuse & Neglect, 15,* 537; Beitchman, J., et al. [1992]. A review of the long-term effects of child sexual abuse. *Child Abuse & Neglect, 16,* 101; Kendall-Tackett, K., Williams, L., & Finkelhor, D. [1993]. Impact of sexual abuse on children: A review and synthesis of recent empirical studies. *Psychological Bulletin, 113,* 164.)

A. Behavioral Indicators of Abuse

1. Aggression and Acting Out

Running away from home, committing criminal acts, or turning to prostitution are behaviors common to abused children. Research reveals that the majority of runaways are escaping neglectful, abusive, and violent families. Children who become involved in prostitution are overwhelmingly characterized as having a history of sexual abuse. Their low self-image, combined with a belief that sex is their only valuable asset, makes them natural prey for exploitation through prostitution. A child's entry into delinquency is often a product of a dysfunctional family life and subsequent susceptibility to negative peer pressure. The violence or severity of criminal acts by young offenders seems to be correlated with the level of violence and neglect they experienced at home.

Children who have been physically abused are prone to acts of aggression against younger children and animals, defiance against authority figures, and exaggerated temper outbursts.

2. Regression or Pseudomaturity

The stress from physical or sexual abuse, together with demands that exceed the child's developmental capacity, can result in regression. Regression is characterized by children acting younger than their chronological age. Children may revert to earlier levels of development with symptoms of wetting and soiling, separation anxiety, difficulty with previously mastered skills, and a return to baby talk.

Under pressure to act older than their age, some victims develop a precocious adult-like facade. They may become the main caregiver for younger siblings, assume responsibility for many household tasks, and present as decision makers in the family. Sexually abused girls may dress in adult clothing with excessive makeup. They may also respond in sexualized ways to nonsexual situations.

3. Grooming Habits and Hygiene

Changes in the child's grooming habits and hygiene may signal body shame or fear of detection of the abuse. These changes may include dressing in clothing that hides the body, especially when it is out of season; refusal to bathe or bathing excessively; or an abrupt increase in modesty. Sexually abused children may have the mistaken belief that their bodies are somehow marked by their sexual experiences, while physically abused children may seek to hide obvious bruises and welts. Some sexual abuse victims become obsessive about their hygiene, for instance, brushing their teeth or showering repeatedly, in an effort to cleanse themselves after their repugnant experiences. Neglected children's hygiene may deteriorate owing to the lack of supervision or even the inability to take a bath or shower because of the lack of soap or shampoo.

4. Eating Problems

Some sexual abuse victims may develop eating disorders, such as anorexia (starving oneself) and bulimia (bingeing and purging). A child's wish to change his or her appearance to avoid being attractive to the perpetrator may result in the child gorging or refusing to eat. Neglected children may gorge or hoard food when it is available because they are uncertain when they will be fed next. Some psychologically maltreated youngsters are told they are fat or ugly and develop eating problems in response to these negative messages. Other abused children find food intake is the only aspect of their lives that they can control.

5. Sexual Behavior

Perhaps the strongest behavioral indicator of sexual abuse is developmentally inappropriate sexual behavior and sexual knowledge. These children may be sexually preoccupied, make drawings and tell stories with sexual content, or tell sexual jokes. Their conversations may contain frequent or unusual sexual references and their activity may be focused around their sexualized interests. It is common for children to be curious about body parts, have a desire to look at another's body, and to ask questions about procreation. However, research shows that there are a number of sexual behaviors that occur with such low frequency that they can be considered red flags for sexual abuse. These include:

- A child putting his or her mouth on another's sex parts
- A child asking to engage in sexual acts
- A child masturbating with an object
- A child inserting an object into his or her own anus or vagina
- A child imitating intercourse
- A child making sexual sounds
- French kissing by a child
- A child talking about explicit sexual acts
- A child undressing others
- A child asking to watch explicit sexual television or movies
- A child using sexual words
- A child imitating sexual acts with dolls

SOURCE: Friedrich, W., et al. (1992). Child sexual behavior inventory: Normative and clinical comparisons. *Psychological Assessment, 4*, 303.

Some sexually abused children reenact their experiences with siblings, pets, and peers. If a child persists in sexual behavior after being told that behavior is inappropriate, a careful assessment of how the child learned the behavior is essential to protect the child.

The list of behaviors by themselves should not be considered diagnostic of abuse. Some children model these behaviors after interactions with peers who have over-stimulated their sexual interest or after repeatedly witnessing adults engage in sexual acts. A careful evaluation and investigation is needed to distinguish inappropriate peer interaction from criminal sexual conduct by someone older than the child.

6. Post-Traumatic Responses

When physical or sexual abuse overwhelms the child's coping ability, leaving the child feeling helpless, terrified, and over-stimulated, traumatic responses may follow. A child's response to events that appear traumatic is based upon the child's resilience and ability to cope during the trauma. The three most common post-traumatic reactions involve reexperiencing, avoidance, and increased physiological arousal. *Re-experiencing* involves repetition of the trauma in dreams, thoughts, play, or actions. Flashbacks and reenactments of the abuse are also forms of reexperiencing. An *avoidance* reaction includes efforts not to be reminded of the abuse by avoiding thoughts, places, people, and things associated with the trauma; suppressing one's emotional responses; and denying that the abuse occurred. (See Mitnick, M. [1997]. *Trauma in the lives of children.* Minneapolis: University of Minnesota Department of Continuing Education.) *Increased physiological arousal* may take the form of rapid heart rate and sweating when reminded of the abuse, inability to fall or stay asleep, and an exaggerated startle reaction.

7. Self-Injurious Behavior

Some abused children demonstrate self-inflicted harm such as burning, cutting, disfiguring, or hair pulling. These behaviors may reflect a desire to punish themselves for not stopping the abuse or an attempt to gain some control over their own bodies or to feel alive through the infliction of pain when they feel dead inside.

B. Cognitive Indicators of Abuse

1. School-Related Problems

Since abused children have no security and are torn by the conflicting emotions of love, hate, anger, fear, and despair, they often have a great deal of trouble concentrating at school. A sudden drop in academic performance or generalized under-achievement may accompany this. Children may be described as "not learning" even though they have no learning disabilities. In other children, problems with attention span can mimic an attention disorder.

A child's listless behavior in school may reflect fatigue from being up all night, being afraid to sleep, or having to take care of younger siblings. The child's lack of participation in school events and extracurricular activities may also reflect excessive responsibilities at home, being isolated from peers by parents, or the parent's wish to have the child available for sex at all times. A child's refusal to go to school may signal a desire to stay away from an abuser. A fear of discovery, shame, and embarrassment may be reflected by abrupt changes in personal relationships and aloofness from long-time friends.

Children may develop attitude problems toward authority figures who remind them of an abuser. Teachers may notice unexplained hostility, aggressive anger, and bouts of destructiveness. Since abused children often carry a great deal of rage and frustration, they may act out the angry thoughts that they cannot express in words. If school officials are unaware of the presence or dynamics of abuse, they may be antagonized by such "problem" students. The school official's common reaction to punish or separate these children further increases the child's alienation and isolation.

2. Distorted Self-Image

Abused children often internalize their parent's negative view of them. The parent's negative view may be expressed by word or action. The parent's distorted view of the child can result in the child seeing him- or herself as ugly, stupid, lazy, boy-crazy, or out of control, thus reflecting the parents' distorted views of the child.

Some abused children put on a facade of physical and emotional toughness to hide their fragile self-esteem that has resulted from thinking they are never good enough to be treated as other, nonabused children are.

3. Problem-Solving Skills

Abused children show deficits in nonviolent problem-solving skills. Victims often utilize the learned modeled behavior of impulsive, violent, or verbally aggressive methods to deal with conflict with children or adults. They appear to lack strong internal controls, demonstrating instead a weak conscience development that prevents them from understanding the impact of their actions on others.

C. Emotional Indicators of Abuse

1. Depression

Depression develops out of the sense of loss of control and hopelessness that comes with prolonged and repeated acts of abuse and neglect. In children, depression may be manifested in two ways. A child who internalizes problems may have seemingly unprovoked crying spells, be withdrawn, have decreased energy, psychosomatic complaints, little appetite, and an increased need for sleep. A child externalizing problems may show heightened aggressiveness, "hyper" behavior, temper tantrums, irritability, and mood swings. Even young children may express suicidal thoughts such as wanting to kill themselves or wanting to sleep forever. Older children may be preoccupied with death or killing, and may make overt suicide attempts. Reckless behavior such as running into the street, seeking access to weapons, or dangerous driving may mask the suicidal feelings these children have not expressed verbally. Psychological maltreatment is often recreated in the self-denigrating comments made by depressed abuse victims.

2. Dissociation

Dissociation is a powerful coping mechanism to manage the psychic and physical pain of abuse. It involves splitting off from the consciousness of experiences. Dissociation occurs along a continuum from normal dissociation such as "tuning out" and not remembering what you just read, to pathological dissociation involving significant problems with memory and identity. (See Putnam, F. [1993].

Dissociative disorders in children: Behavioral profiles and problems. *Child Abuse & Neglect, 17*, 39.) Dissociative disorders include amnesia or incomplete memory of a distressing event, detachment from one's experiences, or the splitting of one's identity into multiple personalities. Examples of dissociative coping mechanisms include victims' describing themselves as feeling detached from their bodies and watching the abuse or anesthetizing themselves by pretending to be somewhere else.

Dissociation appears to facilitate transmission of abuse across generations. Abuse victims who deny, minimize, and poorly recall their abuse are more likely to abuse their own children. (Egeland, B., & Susman-Stillman, A. [1996]. Dissociation as a mediator of child abuse across generations. *Child Abuse & Neglect, 20*, 1123.)

3. Post-Traumatic Responses

Children cannot manage the overwhelming anxiety produced by traumatic abuse. In addition to the behavioral responses described above, traumatized children may show a dramatic increase in sensitivity to noise, to being touched unexpectedly, or to being approached by someone quickly. Physically abused children may flinch reflexively if someone moves quickly. Hypervigilance, an extreme sensitivity to what is going on around oneself, may develop as a means of protection. For example, the child may constantly scan the environment for cues of danger.

4. Unusual or Excessive Fears

A child who suddenly refuses to visit a noncustodial parent, relative, or friend's home may be responding to abuse. Abrupt changes in behavior reflecting intense fear, such as refusal to sleep in her bedroom, a refusal to be left with a caregiver, or hysterical crying when unable to find a parent in the house, may signal that the child has had extremely frightening experiences. Traumatized children often develop incident-specific fears of certain clothing, sounds, smells, or touches to particular parts of their bodies. Unlike with typical childhood fears of the dark, monsters, or bugs, abused children generally cannot be reassured that they have nothing to fear. They appear to have intense, catastrophic reactions to whatever frightens them. Some abused children shift from being relatively easy-going to highly anxious and easily overwhelmed emotionally. There are personality changes that parents and others notice.

A Summary of the Indicators of Abuse

Behavioral Indicators

- Aggression and acting out
- Regression or pseudomaturity
- Grooming habits and hygiene
- Eating problems or disorders
- Sexual acting out
- Post-traumatic responses
- Self-injurious behavior

(Continued)

(Continued)

Cognitive Indicators
- School-related problems
- Distorted self-image
- Impaired problem-solving skills

Emotional Indicators
- Depression
- Dissociation
- Post-traumatic responses
- Unusual and excessive fears

III. CHILD DEVELOPMENT FACTORS

Children think, feel, and act differently from adults. Cognitive, emotional, and social growth begins at birth and gradually develops through childhood. There are developmental limits at each stage defining the child's ability to recall and relate events. The child's perceptions of, feelings about, and responses to abuse are also determined by individual factors. These individual factors include the child's rate of growth, temperament, physical development, health, and personality style. The child's family characteristics, other life experiences, and the social and cultural environment also shape the child's reaction to the abuse. Preexisting physical or psychological problems or disabilities play a significant role in the impact of the abuse. Characteristics of the abuse itself, including duration, the victim's relationship to the offender, use of force or threat of force, and the possible consequences of disclosure, influence whether the child will report and what she will say when that happens. Investigators and prosecutors must consider the impact of these factors along with the child's developmental stage when evaluating and dealing with a child who reports and describes abuse.

A. Infants and Toddlers/Preverbal Stage

Newborn infants and toddlers are completely dependent and vulnerable. Children under the age of 2 are developing attachments to caregivers. Their primary needs are security and consistently responsive caregiving. Children's later views of the world develop from their earliest interactions with caregivers. The significant milestones at this stage include walking, weaning, and being able to separate comfortably from parents.

More than half of all child deaths occur before the age of 1, and over two thirds occur before the age of 5. Children who are unable to give verbal accounts of abuse may use their rudimentary verbal skills together with gestures and behaviors that suggest an abusive incident. For instance, the child may point to a bruised arm or her genital area and say, "Owee, Dadda, owee." Some preverbal children reenact abuse in play or other activities. Examples of this include the child lying back in the crib and spreading her legs wide or the child pounding over and over on a stuffed animal. In addition to these clues, there must be additional evidence to form a basis for concluding abuse, such as medical evidence, eyewitnesses, or evidence of the child's unusual or changed reactions to the offender. The change in reaction may include fear, crying, or a refusal to be touched by the perpetrator. With this group of children, an investigation may need to involve ongoing recording of the child's behavior and emotional reactions by the nonoffending parent along with an assessment by a professional skilled in working with very young children. (See Hewitt, S. [1998]. *Assessing allegations of sexual abuse in preschool children: Understanding small voices.* Thousand Oaks, CA: Sage.)

B. Preschoolers (2–5 Years Old)

Children at this age are still completely dependent on adults to meet all their physical and emotional needs. Their thinking is egocentric, meaning that they see themselves as the center of the world with everything revolving around them. If their security needs have been met in the previous stage, their new concern is with autonomy, power, and control. Significant milestones include talking, toilet training, increased independence, gender identification, and the roots of conscience.

Preconceptual, concrete, and intuitive thinking are characteristic of this developmental stage. Preschool children do not understand causality, abstractions, metaphors, analogies, or irony. Early autobiographical accounts are likely to be loosely organized, circumstantial, brief, and confusing to the listener. Although preschoolers can recall events, they cannot give accurate information regarding antecedents, sequences, or context. Time and space are personalized and not necessarily logical. Their statements will frequently be tied to behavioral routines such as naptime, bedtime, or bathing. Their concepts of "before" and "after" are likely to be inconsistent, and they are unable to give accurate information about time, dates, and the frequency or duration of events. A young child's verbal and cognitive abilities may not be consistent. For example, a 5-year-old is likely to be able to count to 5 or 10 but may be unable to count the rooms in a house from memory.

A preschooler's verbal account may be brief because of a short attention span rather than an inability to recall events. Young children are unable to monitor verbal interactions. They may assume they understood a question when they did not and be unaware of the listener's confusion about their reports. Preschoolers may appear to be inconsistent because they often describe different details of the experiences each time the event is discussed. These very young children are especially dependent on adults to ask the right questions. They do not know what information is important to report and are literal in their interpretations of verbal communication. An example of the child's literalness is as follows: Q: "Who lives with you at your house?" A: (silence, then child shrugs—she lives in an apartment.) Their accounts may contain what appear to be bizarre or imagined elements owing to their lack of familiarity with words to describe the abuse scenario. An example of this is Q: "Tell me what happened at Uncle Jerome's house." A: "He touched me with a pink snake." Q: "Did anything else happen?" A: "It hissed." In this example, the child was penetrated with a flesh-colored dildo, but she had no experience to draw upon to describe it other than knowing what a snake looked and sounded like.

The offender is almost always a relative or caretaker since this age group does not usually have independent relationships. If abused by an authority figure, children will be fearful of telling since they see adults as omnipotent. Preschool children assume adults know everything about them. They may, therefore, not report abuse, as they may feel adults already know. Preschool children may also report the abuse in subtle ways that are not recognized by adults, such as by saying they do not like the offender. When sexual abuse is involved, they do not know the behavior is sexual or wrong. They may only be aware that it hurts, feels good, or is unusual because it is concealed. The need to conceal the abuse is conveyed with statements such as, "Don't tell Mommy about our special game." Even when they might try to disclose abuse, these reports are often dismissed initially because preschool children lack the words and concepts to describe their experiences. When abuse is suspected in this age group, the clues may come from the child's behavior.

There is sometimes a bias among professionals to dismiss allegations of abuse against young children. They may believe that children are prone to fantasy and vulnerable to the influence of television. However, children at this age are unable to independently make up sexually explicit stories and they are extremely unlikely to have learned about adult sexual behavior except through direct experience. In addition, children's fantasies are wishful, and the child tends to emerge as the hero or victor, not the victim. Professionals also may not pursue these cases vigorously because of the care required to interview children reliably. The professional also must spend more time preparing the child to testify. There is a fear of being unable to convince a jury with the child's report. It is essential to remember that the child's report is but one leg on which the case stands and that there is often other evidence to present that bolsters the child's credibility.

C. First Through Fifth Graders (6–10 Years Old)

Once in school, children begin to have a life of their own with activities and relationships outside the family. Their world expands to include friends and other adults such as teachers and neighbors. Their sources of information also increase. Although this group of children continues to rely on the family for taking care of most of their physical and emotional needs, there is a gradual shift to increasing reliance on this expanding network. Peers become important as playmates, but not as a basic source of emotional support. Same sex relationships are common, often accompanied by negative attitudes toward the opposite sex. The mastery of social, academic, athletic, and artistic skills is a primary focus in this age group. Other significant developmental milestones include understanding rules, learning right from wrong, sex-role identification such as, "Boys like to play with race cars," the development of cooperation and competitiveness, and identification with the same-sex parent such as, "When I get bigger, I'm going to hunt with my dad."

At this stage, children still think in fairly concrete terms, but they begin to understand concepts and symbolism at the later end of the age range. They generally feel responsible for external events, like their parents' divorce. This feeling of responsibility leads them to believe they will be punished or suffer consequences for disclosing abuse. As their cognitive ability increases, they begin to develop a time sense but still have difficulty using the units of time correctly. Children in elementary school develop the ability to think logically and to understand cause-and-effect relationships. By the end of this stage, children are likely to connect events as related and, therefore, to report more information without prompting. An example of this is the following: Q: "Then what happened?" A: "My sister fell down the stairs and then she didn't get up." Elementary school–age children may be able to report some details of events while being able to provide only sketchy descriptions of other aspects of the experience because of difficulty paying attention to multiple aspects of an event at one time.

Because children are still concrete in this stage, they remain dependent on the questions asked to frame their narrative report. A question asking a child about a touch she received will likely not elicit any description of her being forced to touch the offender. Questions that ask the child to tell what happened to her would not produce reports of what happened to other children who were present. Similarly, questions that focus on one perpetrator will not provide the child the opportunity to report that there were multiple perpetrators. These questions also will not allow the child to tell that her mother watched the abuse and gave her instructions about the act.

At this developmental stage, children are better able to describe the location and the context of the abuse. They may be able to describe a time frame through the use of identifying markers such as grade in school or the house they lived in at the time. They often are able to describe the offender's method for establishing and maintaining secrecy and control over the child.

Abused children in this age group generally know that certain behavior is unacceptable since it occurs under forced or deceptive circumstances. Because of their expanding world, children also begin to learn that not everyone is locked in their room after school, spanked so hard they get bruised, or used as their stepfather's sexual partner. Their lack of control over their lives still prevents them from challenging or resisting abuse. They may also have learned that attempts to prevent or elude abuse result in an escalation of harm to them. Since abused children have a variety of reactions to abuse, there can be no "expected" response. Some children are fearful and confused, others appear resigned to the abuse, and still others appear to tolerate the abuse because they receive something in exchange. Once they have become part of an ongoing situation, children may feel as much to blame and as worthy of punishment as the offender.

D. Middle School Children (11–13 Years Old)

The physical changes of puberty affect girls about 1–2 years earlier than boys. For both, their developing bodies produce feelings of self-consciousness and awkwardness. Sexual thoughts and feelings begin at this time and almost everything is embarrassing. The changes in hormones and the accompanying major physical developments cause moodiness, extreme swings in feelings, and emotional outbursts.

The major issue of this age group is peer acceptance, with anyone who is seen as different being ostracized. Friendships start to be significant sources of emotional intimacy, while family relationships become conflict ridden, although still the primary source of support. The child often begins a tentative challenge of familial and societal rules. Drug and sexual experimentation may be attempted.

Children are now often able to think hypothetically, that is, to reason from past experience and draw conclusions about events that have not yet occurred. The child is now able to think through what will happen "if I tell." The child now clearly understands possible consequences for the perpetrator, the child, and the child's family.

In this stage, children are often good at telling a story in sequence, though they may not start at the beginning. Instead, the child may start at a point in the abuse narrative that is individually significant. Children this age are able to think logically, but the emotion or the confusion of multiple similar events may appear to overwhelm their cognitive processing ability.

Prepubescent abused children usually know the behavior is wrong. Their feelings of self-consciousness, fear of blame, and feeling responsible for the abuse, perhaps because of their own physical changes, all inhibit them from disclosing the abuse. They may tell a friend or indirectly indicate something is happening, then feel guilty about their participation and previous silence. They may even deny to themselves that anything has happened to them and act as if everything is fine. If directly asked, the child may deny that abuse is occurring.

When children in this age group are being victimized, their behavioral changes may be interpreted simply as part of normal early adolescent development. Precocious sexuality, aggressiveness, problems with authority, or use of drugs and alcohol can easily be mistaken for adolescent experimentation instead of efforts to cope with maltreatment.

E. Adolescents (13–17 Years Old)

The shift toward greater independence is heightened at this stage and is often accompanied by a high level of testing behavior. Conflict with authority, represented by parents and societal expectations, is normal. Adolescents may be intense, have extreme reactions to situations, and take themselves very seriously. They want to appear competent and find it hard to admit when they need help. Abused adolescents may have a long history of abuse by a parent whose behavior they are no longer willing to tolerate. The adolescent is now aware of the difference between what is normal and what their own experiences as victims have been. They may begin to consider alternatives to living in an abusive situation. Adolescents may threaten the offender with physical violence or with exposure of the abuse. The adolescent may also threaten to or actually run away.

This age group is almost fully physically developed. Many adolescents are sexually active with peers to some degree, with most adolescents being aware of and interested in sexual matters. Romantic relationships grow in importance as a source of intimacy and emotional support.

An adolescent's cognitive abilities may be similar to an adult's or, after years of maltreatment, the adolescent's abilities may resemble those of a younger child. Professionals must balance the adolescent's need to be treated as mature while still targeting the interview to the developmental capacity of the teen.

Adolescents, like younger children, demonstrate a spectrum of behaviors that include both internalizing and externalizing modes of accommodating abuse. The teen's efforts to deal with the abuse, such as truancy, chemical abuse, promiscuous sexual behavior, lying to conceal activities, or other overt behaviors, are often cited as reasons not to trust or believe adolescents instead of being seen as the teen's coping mechanism.

Summary of Developmental Tasks in Childhood

Infants and Toddlers

- Attachment and bonding
- Establishing a sense of security
- Regulating bodily states such as hunger and sleep
- Separating from parents
- Using first communication skills
- Learning about limits

Preschoolers

- Using fantasy and imagination
- Expressing curiosity
- Learning right from wrong
- Developing a gender identity
- Using language to express needs and feelings
- Using language to establish and maintain relationships
- Storing information
- Developing a conscience

School Age Children

- Focusing on learning
- Mastering skills
- Learning about rules
- Developing logical reasoning
- Developing social relationships beyond the immediate family
- Learning about cooperation and competition
- Shifting to primary dependence on peers
- Beginning to deal with the changes of puberty

Adolescents

- Emancipating from the family
- Testing rules and societal expectations
- Revisiting old issues such as power struggles
- Developing an identity, including morality, religious beliefs, future goals
- Expressing sexuality

IV. REPORTING ABUSE

The abuse report can come from many sources: children disclosing either intentionally or accidentally; family members suspecting maltreatment based on witnessed events or observed changes in the child's behavior and emotional state; professionals suspecting abuse based on the child's behavior or verbal reports; and neighbors or other community members who see, hear, or infer maltreatment based upon the child's condition. Children disclose the abuse for a variety of reasons and motivations. It is the younger child who is likely to make an accidental disclosure by blurting out reports, including sexual touches, "owies," or of being left alone. Children make intentional reports for many reasons, including seeing a program about abuse on television after being asked directly what is troubling them, and when they fear that younger siblings are also being harmed. Sometimes a school presentation or public service announcement alerting victims to available community resources and encouraging them to seek help triggers disclosure. Other children report abuse after a friend discloses a history of physical or sexual maltreatment. For the first time, this child may have a feeling of support and a sense of hope. Numerous psychological and developmental factors affect how and when children report and describe abuse.

While there have been claims that child abuse is over reported, that reports are increasingly unsubstantiated, and that parental rights are infringed upon by investigations, the research indicates otherwise. Research actually reflects that many abuse cases go unreported, that many reports are not being investigated, and that the true incidence of abuse appears to be increasing. (Sedlak, A., & Broadhurst, D. [1996]. *Third national incidence study of child abuse and neglect.* Washington, DC: Department of Health and Human Services.; Finkelhor, D., Moore, D., Hamby, S., & Straus, M. [1997]. Sexually abused children in a national survey of parents: Methodological issues. *Child Abuse & Neglect, 21,* 1.) Further, the percentage of children whose maltreatment was officially investigated dropped significantly between 1986 and 1993. Child protective services investigated only 26% of the seriously and moderately injured children in 1993. (See Sedlak, A.J., & Broadhurst, D. D. [1996]. *Executive Summary of the Third National Incidence Study of Child Abuse and Neglect.* National Center on Child Abuse and Neglect.)

A. Reliability of Abuse Reports

While many reports are classified as "unfounded" or "unsubstantiated," these terms do not mean a child or reporter has made a deliberately false accusation of abuse. These terms are used by social service agencies when they conclude there is no basis for further involvement. "Unfounded" reports can result from vague complaints or legitimate suspicions that cannot be investigated because a perpetrator cannot be identified, the victim has moved and cannot be located, or the abuse does not involve a caretaker or child protection issue. A number of studies have found that substantiation rates are misleading because factors other than the presence of abuse heavily influence maltreatment findings by child protection agencies. For instance, reports by mandated reporters are more likely to be substantiated than reports by nonmandated reporters. Other factors such as the victim's age, the characteristics of the incident(s), and the sex of the perpetrator also influence the levels of substantiation.

Definitions of "unfounded" and "unsubstantiated" reports vary from state to state, and these labels may be used because of inadequate resources or an unwillingness to do complete investigations. For instance, the report may be labeled "unsubstantiated" if a young child is unable to provide a detailed statement even though no attempt was made to interview the alleged perpetrator or obtain any forensic evidence to corroborate the report. When investigative agencies such as police and child protective services lack resources, experience frequent staff turnover, offer little training, and maintain poor record-keeping practices, the thoroughness of child abuse investigations suffers.

Both experience and research establish that children are much more likely to minimize or deny abuse than to fabricate incidents of abuse because of pressure or fear. In many cases, physically abused children offer alternative explanations for their injuries, and sexual abuse victims recant or refuse to repeat the allegation. This emphasizes that when most children lie, it is to avoid punishment or unpleasant consequences. Children are less sophisticated than adults in their ability to lie, and their lies are easier to detect. In research studies, many children acknowledge uncertainty or retract an erroneous part of a statement when gently challenged about whether they are sure about reports of nonabuse events. It is rare that unfounded abuse reports are attributable to deliberate deceit by children. There have been no studies demonstrating that children can be influenced to fabricate detailed abuse reports despite accusations of "brainwashing" by parents or professionals.

There is also no scientific evidence that children are capable of fantasizing abuse experiences. Most imagined events have some basis in actual experience, especially for young children. In rare instances, an older child with a prior history of abuse may be confusing a past experience with current events, but these cases generally involve known diagnoses of serious psychiatric disorders. Nevertheless, the emotionally disturbed child's reports of abuse cannot be dismissed without a careful assessment, because symptoms may represent a response to severe abuse.

The belief that divorce and custody disputes routinely provoke false allegations of child sexual abuse, particularly by the mother, is a popular misperception. Two large studies have found the rate of reports of abuse during custody and parental access disputes to be only 2%–5%, and the rate of substantiation of these reports is the same as for reports that do not occur during custody disputes. (See Thoennes, N., & Tjaden, P. [1990]. The extent, nature and validity of sexual abuse allegations in custody/visitation disputes. *Child Abuse & Neglect, 14,* 151; Brown, T., et al. [1998]. Problems and solutions in the management of child abuse allegations in custody and access disputes in the family court. *Family and Conciliation Courts Review, 36,* 431.) There may be higher rates of reporting abuse after a separation or divorce for a number of reasons not associated with the validity of the report: the abuse caused the relationship breakdown; separation creates opportunities for abuse; dating and remarriage bring children into contact with people who abuse them; children may be more likely to disclose abuse once they are no longer under the control of the abuser; and the nonabusing parent is more likely to support the child's report after the separation.

The emergence of various "validation" methods such as legitimacy scales and checklists, mainly in the context of divorce or custody proceedings, has made shortcuts to a thorough investigation appealing. Researchers have not validated these tests as reliable tools, and a single instrument should not replace a full investigation.

B. Children's Memory and Suggestibility

No area of child abuse research has generated as much interest or controversy as the area of children's memory and suggestibility. Interest in these topics is relatively recent. Since 1992, there has been an explosion of studies designed to assess children's reliability as witnesses. A new wave of research developed after a few highly publicized multivictim, multiperpetrator cases in the 1980s led researchers to attempt to understand more about children's ability to recall and report abuse experiences. The research shifted from studying children's ability to recall word lists and recognize previously seen pictures to "ecologically valid" studies of children's ability to describe actual events in which they were participants or observers.

Two different types of research have emerged that tend to focus primarily on either the child's strengths or the child's weaknesses as a participant in the judicial process. The latter body of research received a great deal of attention after the publication of the 1995 book, *Jeopardy in the Courtroom: A Scientific Analysis of Children's Testimony* by Stephen Ceci and Maggie Bruck. One area focuses on false reports of abuse and the other on the failure to substantiate actual abuse. Because of this difference in emphasis, similar findings in different studies may be summarized and reported in very different ways. For instance, a research finding that 9% of 4-year-old children presented with anatomical dolls demonstrate suggestive positioning in free play might be interpreted in two ways, by one group to show how few children engage in this behavior or by another group to show how many children engage in this behavior.

The issues about children's memory and suggestibility occur almost exclusively in sexual abuse cases, where medical evidence is much less common and young children have difficulty explaining details of sexual behavior. Although defense experts frequently cite the Ceci group's research as proving the unreliability of children's reports of abuse, the researchers themselves describe children as capable of providing "accurate, detailed and useful information." (Bruck, M., Ceci, S., & Hembrooke, H. [1998]. Reliability and credibility of young children's reports: From research to policy and practice. *American Psychologist, 53,* 136.)

In attempting to understand and utilize the new wave of research in investigating and prosecuting cases, it is essential to remember that no study can replicate the actual circumstances of child abuse or the disclosure process. Studies of children's ability to describe a genital medical exam, a touch by a stranger during a game, or whether someone who came into the classroom broke a toy are certainly useful approximations of real childhood negative experiences. However, such research cannot replicate the high levels of arousal, confusion of responsibility, methods to maintain secrecy, or the lack of support from the nonoffending parent associated with abuse. Similarly, these studies cannot fully explore the impact on the child and the disclosure process of factors such as disclosing abuse by a loved one, the embarrassment that accompanies the disclosure of repeated sexual contact, or the threats of harm if the child reports the abuse.

Many factors inherent in the nature of social science research affect the results reported. It is often very difficult to compare studies because of differences in the research paradigm. Many aspects vary between studies: what the child must remember, the way the child is questioned about the task, how responses are scored as correct or incorrect, the length of delay since the event, and the ages of the children studied. In general, the research results are reported in terms of groups. For example, inaccurate reports by 3- to 4-year-old children of a witnessed event were cut in half with gentle challenges. However, this statistic does not allow for a conclusion about whether a particular 3- to 4-year-old will change an inaccurate answer after a challenge. Because of the methodological differences noted, research on children's memory and suggestibility often seems contradictory across and even within studies. The information that follows has been tested across multiple studies and is considered to be reliable. Nevertheless, there is significant disagreement among experts as to the appropriateness of using this information to bolster or undermine a child's testimony. See Chapter V for a discussion on the use of expert witnesses in child abuse cases.

1. Memory

Memory involves three different processes: encoding, storage, and retrieval. There are developmental differences in the degree to which children accurately encode, store, and retrieve memories from preschool to adolescence. Children find it more difficult than adults to understand complex events, relationships, feelings, and intentions. When children do not understand events, it is difficult for them to encode the memory accurately. For instance, a child who has never seen a penis will have to compare this novelty to what is already stored in memory to encode it. The penis may then be described as a stick, a snake, or the word the child was given by the perpetrator. Children and adults are unable to attend to all aspects of an experience, resulting in some information not being encoded and, therefore, unavailable for retrieval later. Children are likely to pay attention to aspects of an event that are salient to them as opposed to aspects of the event the investigator needs to know about. Stress and the number of similar events the child has experienced can also affect the child's encoding ability. Young children's ability to remember familiar people, objects, and events is very good.

Information is first stored in short-term memory and then in long-term memory if it is to be retained. The ability to store information is not significantly affected by age. Memories can be weakened or strengthened while in storage by the time elapsed since the memory was stored and the number of times the original information has been recalled. Experts do not agree on the way stored memories may be affected by subsequent similar experiences.

Retrieval is the process whereby information is accessed although not necessarily reported. The complexity of the event to be remembered, children's limited ability to use memory strategies, whether the event is personally meaningful, and motivation and emotional state affect children's event memory at the time of remembering. Older children and adults rely on more complex mnemonic strategies. They are able to use categories to store information, have a greater knowledge base, and have more practice in recalling events. By third grade, the use of retrieval strategies has increased and improved. However, adult techniques are not mastered until adolescence. Research indicates that children's memories fade more quickly than do adults' memories, especially for peripheral details, but this is not absolute. Children may have an easier time recalling events that are personally meaningful to them and those in which they participated.

Memory also involves three tasks: recognition, reconstruction, and free recall. *Recognition,* the simplest task, involves skills such as the ability to identify people and recall where familiar objects were in a room. *Reconstruction* involves reinstating the context in which the original event occurred. This is the memory task necessary to provide a narrative account. Memories for events are reconstructed through complicated cognitive processes that mature as children develop. (Myers, J., Saywitz, K., & Goodman, G. [1996]. Psychological research on children as witnesses: Practical implications for forensic interviews and courtroom testimony. *Pacific Law Journal, 28,* 1.) *Free recall* is the most difficult task for younger children and it is strongly age related. There are clear developmental trends in the amount of information children are able to provide about experiences through the use of free recall. Kindergartners and first graders recall one or two facts without prompting, while seventh and eighth graders can recall six facts. In children, free recall is highly accurate but also highly incomplete. Because younger children have more difficulty with free recall, more direct questions are needed that tap into the child's recognition memory. A comparison of these questions is as follows: "Tell me what happened at your dad's house" (free recall) versus "Did someone hurt you?" (recognition). Children are more likely to make errors of omission than commission with free recall tasks.

A child's ability to report an event is determined by the child's cognitive development and language acquisition, the length of delay between event and interview, and inducements to keep secrets. Stress and intimidation can affect both memory and reporting. Conflicting research suggests both positive and negative effects of stress on memory. Stress alone may improve memory, especially if it is not overwhelming. Stress coupled with intimidation may harm memory.

Narration of life events by children is also a skill with clear developmental trends in both the amount and type of information reported. Preschool children are still learning the "rules" involved in telling about an event. Young children generally report the usual aspects of an event. As the child matures, she reports the more unique and distinctive aspects of an event. Both children and adults have difficulty distinguishing any one of a set of similar events from the others. Young children are more likely to report a "script" based on the general aspects of the similar events. (Fivush, R. [1993]. Developmental perspectives on autobiographical recall. In G. Goodman & B. Bottoms [Eds.], *Child victims, child witnesses: Understanding and improving children's testimony* [pp. 1–24]. New York: Guilford.)

Young children's narratives, consistent with their egocentric perspective, are sketchy, lack detail, and are loosely organized. They have not mastered the convention of telling a story from beginning to middle to end. Thus, they can appear confused, disorganized, and inconsistent in their recounting of events. Their expectation is that the adult already knows what they are going to report. Children will try to answer questions they do not fully understand, utilizing information from the beginning or end of the question, as a cue to the question's meaning. The child's apparent inconsistency should not be confused with inaccuracy or insincerity, but it should be understood as a function of developmental differences between children and adults. In some cases, the explanation for the child's apparent inconsistency does not rest with the child's memory or communicative competence, but with the interviewer's inability to ask reliable questions that are geared to the child's developmental level. Researchers have identified a number of factors that explain children's seemingly inconsistent reports.

Explanations for Children's Inconsistent Statements

- Children lack skills for monitoring their statements for errors, omissions, inconsistencies, or contradictions.
- The interviewer lacks skills to ask developmentally appropriate questions.
- Children lack skills to monitor how well they understand what the adult said.
- Children assume adults know what they are talking about.
- Children provide different information about experiences at different points in time.
- Children rely on adults' questions to guide their recall.
- Children's ability to retrieve information at any given moment in time is affected by fatigue and fear.
- Children's level of comfort with the interviewer affects their willingness to disclose the information they do recall.

2. Suggestibility

"Suggestibility concerns the degree to which children's encoding, storage, retrieval and/or reporting of events can be influenced by a range of internal and external factors." (Ceci, S., & Bruck, M. [1993]. The suggestibility of the child witness: A historical review and synthesis. *Psychological Bulletin, 113*, 403.) Suggestibility is not a single trait, but it is related to situational factors. Overall, 3- to 4-year-old children are the most suggestible, with a significant developmental shift in suggestibility occurring at 6–7 years of age. By 10–11 years of age, the child's suggestibility approaches that of an adult. No sweeping generalizations can be made that children are more suggestible than adults. A child who is suggestible in one set of circumstances may be resistant to suggestion in another circumstance. If a child incorrectly remembers one aspect of an event, there can be no assumption that she will incorrectly remember other aspects of the same event. There is no evidence that gender or intelligence is related to suggestibility.

The following factors are known to be associated with children's suggestibility:

The interviewer's mind-set. Interviewers who begin with assumptions about what the child knows may elicit that information from a child even if it is erroneous. Children may be swayed by adults' interpretations of events that children do not understand well.

Stereotypes. When children are repeatedly presented with negative stereotypes, such as "the bad man," they are more likely to report negative information that conforms to the stereotype.

Delay. Children's memory for details fades more quickly than adults' memory, especially for peripheral details. This leaves the child more vulnerable to suggestion about those details.

Intimidating environment or interviewer. Children are more likely to agree with the suggestions of an intimidating interviewer. There are conflicting research results as to whether children actually adopt the suggestions of an intimidating interviewer or simply conform to the demands of the situation by agreeing.

Form of the question. Children provide more erroneous information in response to yes or no questions than to open-ended questions.

Inducements to keep a secret or lie. By age 5, children frequently lie or omit information to protect the adults who have asked them to do so.

Source monitoring. Young children have more difficulty than do older children or adults with remembering the source of their knowledge. The child has difficulty determining, "Did it happen to me or did someone tell me it happened to me?"

Leading or misleading questions. Not all leading questions have an equal impact on the child's account. An example of a leading question is, "Did something happen to your vagina?" A misleading question is, "When your dad touched inside your vagina, how did it feel?" if the child said he touched her *on* her vagina. A coercive question is, "Your dad touched your vagina, didn't he?" Children will have a hard time correcting the interviewer when coercive questions are asked. Researchers currently disagree about whether suggestive questions permanently affect the original memory or whether the memory remains intact.

Misleading questions can be a source of postevent contamination that can affect the recall of preschoolers. A child's compliance with misleading questions decreases through age 8 or 9. By this time, there is no difference in a child's compliance with misleading questions when compared with adults.

Young children are more influenced by leading and misleading questions when they are

- Asked for information about unfamiliar people rather than events
- Pressed for additional details
- Asked about an event when their memory is uncertain or incomplete
- Questioned under intimidating circumstances
- Questioned by someone in an authority position
- Presented with a negative stereotype about someone
- Questioned with misleading suggestions over many weeks

SOURCE: Batterman-Faunce, J., & Goodman, G. (1993). Effects of context on the accuracy and suggestibility of child witnesses. In G. Goodman & B. Bottoms (Eds.), *Child victims, child witnesses* (pp. 310–330). New York: Guilford.

Repeated Questioning. The use during an interview of repeated questions that are open-ended and nonsuggestive does not diminish the accuracy of reports. The child's repeated exposure to misleading information or suggestive questioning, either within or across interviews, can be responsible for erroneous reports. Single suggestive questions are unlikely to alter memories and do not negate the validity of other statements.

Practice Recommendations to Improve the Reliability of Young Children's Reports

- Ask questions that are simple and contain familiar words.
- Ask questions about salient aspects of events rather than peripheral details.
- Match the questions to the child's developmental capacity.
- Do not pressure hesitant children to provide answers.
- Present an attitude of friendliness and neutrality rather than an authoritarian or accusatory style.
- Avoid stereotyping labels, e.g., "the bad touch."
- Pair specific questions with open-ended questions: "Did he put his peter in you one time or more than one time? Tell me about that."

SOURCE: Adopted from Saywitz, K., & Goodman, G. (1996). Interviewing children in and out of court: Current research and practice implications. In J. Briere et al. (Eds.), *APSAC handbook on child maltreatment* (pp. 297–318). Thousand Oaks, CA: Sage.

The key to accurate reports is skillful, prompt, and sensitive interviewing that focuses on the child's developmental capacities and the impact of abuse on his or her ability to disclose experiences.

Concerns about possible "therapist contamination" of children's reports have been raised in regard to therapy undertaken concurrently with prosecution. While there may be instances of therapists' influencing children's statements, this is not a widespread problem. Prosecutors should make a careful attempt to document the child's statements prior to and outside therapy. This practice minimizes claims of therapist contamination.

C. Delayed Disclosure

The child who delays disclosing may confuse professionals and jurors who do not understand the dynamics of abuse. Delayed disclosure is the norm rather than the exception with abused children. (Finkelhor, D. [1979]. *Sexually victimized children.* New York: Free Press; Russell, D. [1986]. *The secret trauma: Incest in the lives of girls and women.* New York: Basic Books.) Abuse by family members is less likely to be reported and to be concealed for long periods of time than is abuse by someone outside the family unit. The child's silence is maintained because of fear, shame, and concern about being believed. In addition, the child may not fully comprehend that the abusive behavior is wrong, and the offender's insistence on secrecy is also a powerful influence.

Children may report at seemingly inopportune times, such as when parents are going through a divorce, and for what appear to be suspect motives, such as anger at a mother for requiring the adolescent to babysit on weekends. Children may report when they find themselves in trouble for misbehaving at school, after a suicide attempt, while in chemical dependency treatment, or in therapy for depression. When the child reports abuse in such situations, adults and peers may display unsympathetic and disbelieving reactions. The very problems that have developed in an effort to cope with abuse are then seen as reasons to discount the reports.

It is not surprising that more and more adults are coming forward to report their childhood abuse experiences, given the powerful reasons victims have for concealing abuse during childhood and the increasing public awareness of the extent of child sexual abuse. Numerous retrospective studies and anecdotal reports have demonstrated that abuse memories may be forgotten for long periods of time only to be recalled at a later time. (See Epstein, M., & Bottoms, B. [1998]. Memories of childhood sexual abuse: A survey of young adults. *Child Abuse & Neglect, 22,* 1217; Williams, L. [1995]. Recovered memories of abuse in women with documented child sexual victimization histories. *Journal of Traumatic Stress, 8,* 649.) While there remains controversy over whether traumatic memories can be truly repressed, research suggests that at least 30% of adults with known histories of abuse have had partial or total amnesia for the event(s) at some point in their lives. (Elliot, D. M., & Fox, B. [1994]. *Child abuse and amnesia: Prevalence and triggers to memory recovery.* Paper presented at the annual meeting of the International Society of Traumatic Stress, Chicago.) The focus on the "false memory" debate detracts from the reality of abuse recollections by children.

D. Recanting

The victim's propensity to recant allegations of abuse is a common problem in child abuse cases. Recantation, however, is understandable in view of the dynamics of child abuse, especially in intrafamilial abuse cases. The professional should consider the victim's dilemma when everything the abuser warned her would happen should she disclose does in fact happen. The perpetrator may have threatened that no one would believe her, and in fact, the child's mother, the most important support person in her life, does not believe her. The perpetrator may have predicted that her relatives and friends would blame her, and they do. The perpetrator may be arrested, her parents may separate, and everyone who is important to her may be labeling her a "slut" or a "freak." The child's fears, if not the abuser's threats, may all come true. For the child, life after disclosure may appear worse than the abuse. The child may come under intense family pressure to withdraw the complaint. The decision, therefore, to retract her earlier allegations may seem the only logical course to stop the pain and turmoil.

The investigator must be aware that an individual's statement to a child that brings about a recantation from the child may not be intended for that purpose. For example, a member of the clergy meeting with the child may say that the perpetrator is truly sorry and has been forgiven by God, and that the appropriate thing for the child to do is to forgive the perpetrator as well. The child may see that the only way to forgive is to stop the process by recanting the original statement.

If a child does recant, the investigator must look for the reason. A child's recanting legitimate abuse allegations can and does occur. (See Summit, R. [1983]. The child sexual abuse accommodation syndrome. *Child Abuse & Neglect, 7,* 177 [reprinted as Appendix SA.4].)

V. EXPECTATIONS OF THE PROCESS

Children do not ordinarily report abuse in order to have the offender prosecuted. Many do not even know it is a crime or that they are protected by laws. They definitely do not understand the requirements, procedures, or laws governing criminal investigation and prosecution. Other children may want offenders punished for the wrong they have done, although they may not wish for a lengthy prison sentence.

While going to court may be stressful for children, it can also help the victim regain a sense of empowerment and a sense of being believed, especially when a guilty verdict is obtained. Prosecutors can take a number of steps to reduce a child's anxiety. A prosecutor should oppose defense efforts to postpone the trial date. In some jurisdictions, the prosecutor can demand a speedy trial on behalf of victims. A prosecutor must keep the victim, victim's family, and other professionals working with the child apprised of the status of the case. The delays and other pitfalls of the criminal justice system are easier to handle when a prosecutor makes an effort to explain the process both during and before the events happen. If a trial is necessary, the prosecutor must take the time to properly prepare the child for court. These steps not only help protect the child, but they facilitate her competence and thus boost her credibility with the jury.

Prosecutors must make it clear that they, not the victim, are responsible for the outcome of the criminal justice process. This must be communicated to the child at the outset and reinforced frequently to offset her sense of responsibility for harming the offender and causing trouble in the family. Finally, the child should have the help of professionals and supportive family members to guide her through the process as comfortably as possible.

II

Investigation

The purpose of this section is to assist investigators and prosecutors in interviewing children reliably and credibly about their abuse experiences. The principles presented also apply to later interviews for court preparation. The primary goal of the investigative or forensic interview is to obtain and preserve information that the victim is uniquely able to provide. If the child is able to talk, a thorough interview is the first and probably the single most important part of the investigation. It will serve in almost all cases as the basis for evaluating the child's credibility.

Techniques used in interviewing adult crime victims will not work with children. Preschool, grade school, and adolescent children must each be handled differently. It is essential that the interviewer is both able to communicate effectively with children and knowledgeable about the legal system. An understanding of the dynamics of child abuse and the developmental abilities of children of different ages will help the interviewer succeed in obtaining information from child victims. The prosecutor must be able to judge the quality of the prior interview(s) and must be competent in talking with children to prepare the child for court and to obtain the child's account on direct examination.

There is no single right way to interview children. The American Prosecutor's Research Institute's (APRI) National Center for Prosecution of Child Abuse urges investigators and prosecutors to receive thorough training in the art and science of interviewing children. For information and quality forensic interview training in your region, contact the National Center for Prosecution of Child Abuse at (703) 549–4253. It is also important to develop a protocol for conducting interviews. Although experts in the field have advanced many protocols, the various models are more similar than dissimilar. Investigators and prosecutors should select a protocol that is appropriate for their jurisdiction and that can be defended in court. A protocol facilitates uniformity between cases and reduces defense attacks on the reliability of the investigation and the credibility of the child victims. Essential to the interview process is a comfort level in talking with children that comes only through practice. An interviewer's experience in talking with children facilitates the smooth flow of the interview process, communicates confidence in the interviewer for the child, and reduces the likelihood of serious errors.

The interviewer elicits the greatest amount of, and most reliable, information by adopting a neutral and supportive approach during the interview. This means starting the interview with no assumptions about whether abuse occurred, the identity of the perpetrator(s), or how the child feels toward the perpetrator(s). The interviewer allows information to flow from the child and never tells the child what happened or how she "must" feel about her experiences. The process should never revictimize children through coercive approaches ("You can go as soon as you tell me what happened"), threats ("Your mom's going to be mad if you don't talk"), or manipulation ("Dad said you're going shopping as soon as you tell me what happened"). Interviewers must be careful not to make promises to children about whether a perpetrator will or will not go to jail, whether any part of the interview will "just be between us," or not having to talk about the abuse with anyone after the initial interview. These promises usually cannot be kept and only undermine the child's already damaged sense of trust in adults.

A. Preparing for the Interview

Prior to the interview, the investigator or prosecutor should thoroughly review all known information, including previous police or child protection reports, medical findings, and other available materials. If possible, the interviewer should speak to others involved in the case such as the teacher who made the report, the physician who examined the child, the child's parent or guardian, or the therapist who has been treating the child. This allows the interviewer to gain better insight into the case, the child's developmental status, and any special issues that would affect the interview process. Biographical information such as the child's age, grade in school, family members, residence, relationship to the alleged perpetrator, and whether the child suffers from any physical, mental, or learning difficulties is essential to know before the interview takes place. When caregivers cooperate with the investigation, it is important to caution them not to question or rehearse the child prior to the interview, but it is appropriate to prepare the child to talk with someone who will want to know about what has been happening in the child's life.

Determine what the child has revealed about the abuse thus far: what took place, where, when, by whom, and to whom it was reported. What was the child's reaction to the abuse and the process of disclosure? Determine whether there were any behavioral or physical signs of distress and who noted them. It is also important to learn the reaction of those close to the child and whether the child is in a safe, stable, and supportive environment. Finally, the interviewer must use the gathered information to assess the potential problems and defenses faced if criminal proceedings are instituted against the perpetrator.

Some defense attorneys and defense experts advocate "allegation-blind" interviews on the theory that having the interviewer know nothing of the background of the alleged abuse will eliminate any chance the child will be influenced during the interview. Without a blind interview, it is argued that the child may provide false information as a result of the interviewer's expectations that are communicated through suggestive questions.

Recent research utilizing an allegation-blind interview format did not result in a decrease in disclosures from children interviewed. This process involves a three-stage interview in which the interviewer obtains as much information from the child as possible, then meets with the referring agent if possible, and then asks additional questions if necessary. (Cantlin, J., Payne, G., & Erbaugh, C. [1996]. Outcome-based practice: Disclosure rates of child sexual abuse comparing allegation blind and allegation informed structured interviews. *Child Abuse & Neglect, 20*, 1113.) While this approach may have promise in the future, few allegation-blind interviews are currently conducted. Measures other than allegation-blind interviews can be taken to assure reliable interview results.

When a child has a disability, the interviewer may need a therapist, a personal care attendant, or a special education teacher present both to assist the child in communicating information and to help the interviewer understand the answers. When a child is deaf, the interviewer will need the assistance of someone trained in sign language to provide exact duplications of questions and answers.

Special planning is needed when the child speaks a different language. An interpreter proficient in the child's language will need to be present during the initial interview, subsequent meetings, and court appearances. Some communities have skilled, sensitive bilingual personnel available through child and family welfare services or community organizations. In others, more effort will be required to locate an appropriate interpreter. If possible, the same interpreter should be used throughout the entire process. In all cases, the prosecutor will need to provide orientation and training to prepare the interpreter for the unique role of participating in an abuse case. This should include an instruction not to show signs of being upset when the child describes the abuse experience.

B. Interview Location and Circumstances

The number of investigative interviews should be limited to one whenever possible. Multiple sessions are stressful for the child, are often unnecessary, and can lead to seemingly inconsistent statements. Single interviews prevent defense attacks on the use of repetitive questioning with children.

Research confirms professional experience that children provide more accurate detail in informal, private settings. (Saywitz, K., & Nathanson, R. [1993]. Children's testimony and their perceptions of stress in and out of the courtroom. *Child Abuse & Neglect, 17*, 613.). The interview room's surroundings should encourage the child's sense of well-being and be free from distracting commotion. Traditional police department facilities are generally not conducive to child interviews. Children can feel intimidated by the large number of busy adults, some wearing guns and uniforms, as they are being led to the normally stark detective's office or interview room. In recognition of this feeling, many police agencies and prosecutors' offices have set up special interview rooms to accommodate the needs of child witnesses.

The appearance of the interview room should make children feel welcome. An attractive wall with cheerful posters or familiar storybook figures can be helpful. Some prosecutors and investigators put up artwork made by other child witnesses to demonstrate that other children have had similar experiences and the interviewer has talked with those children. Some interviewers allow children to photocopy their hands after the interview and then hang these on the wall, while other interviewers display photos of their own family, which conveys a sense that the interviewer likes children. On the other hand, some investigators make the interview room too child friendly. This can happen when the room is so full of toys, games, and artwork that the child gets distracted and cannot keep on task during the interview. It may be wise to have games, toys, and artwork in a waiting area and avoid having these items in the interview room itself.

Some interview rooms have child-sized furniture to help the youngest victims be physically comfortable. Other settings have stuffed chairs or a love seat rather than traditional office furniture. A few toys, such as stuffed animals, can be available for a child to hold during the interview, but these can be distracting or children may hide behind them making it difficult to hear their answers. Many interviewers prefer a relatively small space so children maintain proximity to the interviewer, reducing the need to repeat questions and answers because the child was too far away. If the interview is being videotaped, the furniture will need to be set up so the child's gestures and facial expressions can be seen.

Anatomical drawings and dolls that will be used should be in the room but put away at the start of an interview. In this way, the anatomical dolls and drawings are easily accessible, but the interviewer can maintain control over when and if to use them. A flip chart may be useful to the process if the interviewer needs to draw the layout of the house or for an older child to demonstrate where others were positioned during the abuse. Drawing can be an effective way to keep a child engaged during the interview.

Defense experts have criticized the use of anatomical dolls. It is said that the dolls are inherently too suggestive, they elicit false reports of sexual abuse, and the child confuses the dolls for play objects rather than a forensic tool. Most research findings conclude that these critiques are unfounded or exaggerated. Nevertheless, as with any interview procedure, the interviewer should be familiar with the appropriate uses of anatomical dolls and document the use accordingly. (See Boat, B., & Everson, M. [1996]. Concerning practices of interviewers when using anatomical dolls in child protective services investigations. *Child Maltreatment, 1*, 96.) In most cases, the dolls should be produced only after a child has made a verbal disclosure. A substantiation of abuse should not be based solely on a child's interaction or demonstration with the dolls. Anatomical dolls should be used only by interviewers trained in their use. The dolls can be used with any child who can make the representational shift. That is, the child must be able to understand the doll represents him/her or another person and is being used as a demonstration aid. Most children can make this shift by the age of 5.

The location of the interview should provide the child with a feeling of privacy. Victims often feel an enormous amount of shame and guilt and are less likely to speak openly if there are interruptions. It is also much more difficult for the child to follow the interview flow if the phone rings or the interviewer is called out of the room. The interviewer should turn off beepers and cell phones so they do not distract or alarm the child.

The interviewer or prosecutor should avoid giving the child food, such as juice and crackers, during the interview. The interviewer should also avoid promising a snack when the interview is over. These behaviors facilitate defense attacks focusing on "bribing" the child with food.

The interviewer should work with parents, whenever possible, to choose a time for the interview when the child is not likely to be sleepy, hungry, or otherwise distracted. A decision to take the child out of school should be discussed with caregivers, as some children resent the disruption to their routine, while others prefer not to miss after-school activities. If possible, the time of the interview should be flexible enough so that the child and others involved will not be too inconvenienced.

It is also important to allow enough time so that the interview is not rushed. While some children will complete an interview in less than 30 minutes, others will need more time. Some children's energy and attention span are exhausted much sooner than others. Many preschoolers cannot stay focused for more than 15 minutes. The length of the interview should be dictated by an assessment of the child's capacity. An interviewer demonstrates trustworthiness to the child by keeping appointments without numerous changes, being on time, and by beginning the interview promptly. Delays heighten children's anxiety and decrease their confidence in the process.

C. Who Should Be Present During the Interview

A parent or other caregiver may walk the child to the interview room and show the child where he or she will be waiting. In rare circumstances, the parent of a very young child may need to be present for the introduction of the interviewer and an explanation of the interview process. Children should be interviewed alone even when parents ask to be present. The presence of a caregiver opens the interview to attacks of pressure, nonverbal prompting, or other contamination of the process. The caregiver should encourage the child to talk to the interviewer and tell the truth, without telling the child what to say.

When setting up the interview, the prosecutor or investigator should let the caregiver know he or she will not be in the interview room. The caregiver's questions should be answered ahead of time so the child is not exposed to any conflict between the interviewer and caregiver or anxiety on the caregiver's part about separating from the child.

The interviewer's comfort with children and interviewing skills are more significant factors in the success of the process than is the gender of the interviewer. Sensitivity to child abuse dynamics and good communication skills are far more important qualifications. In rare situations, the child may demonstrate significant discomfort with an interviewer of one gender. In this circumstance, accommodation should be made to allow the child to be interviewed by someone else even if it means rescheduling the interview.

Multidisciplinary cooperation from the start of the investigation is likely to reduce the number of interviews and improve the quality of evidence obtained. Joint interviews require that one person assumes the lead in asking questions but may ask the other professionals if there are any other questions before ending the interview. Law enforcement personnel should interview children in plainclothes without any weapons, handcuffs, or other implements on their person. Uniforms may have a chilling effect on children who associate police officers with being arrested and being in trouble.

Many agencies have a one-way mirror set up for children's interviews. As with taping, this procedure should be explained to the child. At an agreed-upon signal, the interviewer may call the others to see if there are additional questions, or the other members may call or send in additional questions for the interviewer to pursue.

In some cases, more than one interview will be necessary to obtain a complete account of the child's experiences. It is important for the same interviewer to conduct all investigative interviews, just as it is essential that one prosecutor be assigned to the case from start through trial. In the subsequent interview, the child should not be re-interviewed about information previously disclosed unless there is a substantial reason to do so, such as contradictory answers. The purpose of an additional interview is to provide the child the opportunity to completely disclose all of the abuse experiences.

D. How to Record Information From the Interview

Some jurisdictions have enacted laws requiring audiotaping or videotaping of forensic interviews with children. Most investigators prefer to preserve the first interview to reduce the number of interviews, to maintain an exact record of the child's information as close in time to the actual events as possible, and to provide a clear picture of the child's affective responses. There are persuasive arguments for and against videotaping. Some investigators see the videotape as a tool for the defense to misuse. It allows defense counsel to show a flawed interview process by showing the jury a single leading question. If children make additional disclosures after the forensic interview, defense counsel use these statements incorrectly to argue inconsistency when the child may be talking about different instances of abuse. Some defense attorneys may use the child's videotaped statement not for court preparation but for illegitimate purposes, such as showing the tape to the media or displaying the videotape at defense bar training courses. Any misuse of this evidence may revictimize the child. Investigators who do videotape the interviews find the tapes to be a powerful tool when interrogating suspects and eliciting confessions. The tape can be showed to nonoffending parents to help them learn the details of the abuse and see the child's emotional reactions to her experiences. In some jurisdictions, the videotape can be used at trial as substantive evidence if the child is unable or unavailable to testify or as a prior consistent statement if the child testifies. In some states, videotaped statements may be admissible in civil child protection proceedings even if the child does not testify.

If taping is done, high-quality equipment must be used, and the taping process must be explained to the child. A simple explanation might include a statement that the interviewer wants to be sure not to forget anything the child tells him. Since the vast majority of children are familiar with watching videos, they are likely to be much more comfortable being on tape than they might have been even a decade ago. If the child is a victim of pornography or was in any way photographed or videotaped by the perpetrator, the interviewer should assure the child the videotape will not be sold at video stores or be shown on television but will only be used for legitimate law enforcement purposes.

When taping is not used, it is essential to record the details of the interview accurately. Generally, it is best to have one person interview the child and the other take careful notes. Skilled interviewers are able to fulfill both functions. The interviewer should explain to the child the need to take notes and that it may be necessary for the interviewer to check with her to be sure that her words were recorded correctly. The documentation should include the child's exact words and as many of the questions as possible since the wording of questions is often the focus of defense attacks. The interviewer should document gestures, facial expressions, and affect such as crying. The recording of these nonverbal responses provides a fuller representation of the interview. The interviewer may want to limit the documentation to what is seen and heard as opposed to personal impressions. The interviewer must keep in mind the discovery rules as they relate to these notes.

A few methods have been developed that purport to assess the credibility of sexual abuse allegations, including the Sex Abuse Legitimacy Scale, Statement Validity

Analysis, and Content-Based Criteria Analysis. These methods generally involve reviewing video or audio recorded interviews and then rating the content of the interviews. Although the methodologies differ, each claims to differentiate true and false allegations. While these techniques contain a variety of thought-provoking ideas to ensure a thorough investigation, they have not demonstrated scientific reliability in separating valid from invalid allegations. However, their proponents, some with impressive credentials, are often effective in persuading juries of their acceptability as a means of critiquing interviews with children. (See Faller, K., & Corwin, D. [1995]. Children's interview statements and behaviors: Role in identifying sexually abused children. *Child Abuse & Neglect, 19,* 71; Lamb, M., et al. [1997]. Criterion-based content analysis: A field validation study. *Child Abuse & Neglect, 21,* 250.)

E. Conducting the Interview

1. Introduction and Rapport Building

Interview protocols are increasingly being used to make the interview process easier and more productive for the investigator, the prosecutor, and most important, the child victim. Two examples of interview protocols include those used by the National Children's Advocacy Center, Huntsville, Alabama, and the CornerHouse Interagency Abuse Evaluation Center, Minneapolis, Minnesota. The various protocols share a model of conducting the interview in stages to assist the child in becoming comfortable with the unfamiliar process of a forensic interview before eliciting information about the suspected abuse. The introduction and rapport-building stages of the interview also allow the interviewer to become familiar with the child's communication style and adjust the questions' complexity in response to the child's developmental capacity. The information that follows is a guide to interviewing children; it is not intended as a specific interviewing protocol.

Greet the child in a friendly way, preferably at eye level for the child. Since some children are reluctant to tell their names to a stranger, the interviewer may want to begin by telling his own name and asking the child to confirm her name: "Hi. My name is Jim and this is Helen. She'll be with us today. And you're Nicky?" The child should be told where the interview will take place and where the caregiver will be waiting. The interviewer should avoid touching children being interviewed, as this may intimidate or otherwise remind the children of unwanted touches in the past. However, if a young child reaches for your hand, it will be comforting to the child if you take the hand offered.

Once in the interview room, give the child a choice of where to sit, if possible. If the child must sit in a particular spot because you are taping the interview, then simply direct the child to that location: "I need you to sit in this chair."

Begin by explaining your job: "I talk to kids about things that have happened so that I can try to help." Asking, "Do you know why you're here?" will often elicit a "No" because children are reluctant to immediately begin talking about the abuse. It is very important never to argue with a child by responding: "Yes you do. Your mom told me you know why we're talking today." Questions such as, "What do you think my job is?" may provide an opportunity to correct the child's misperceptions that the interviewer is the judge or that the interviewer will be putting the alleged perpetrator in jail. Children are more familiar than ever before with court proceedings, but they usually obtain their information from television shows that do not resemble your actual role with the child. If the child is misinformed about what will be happening during the interview, let the child know she made a good guess and then correct the misunderstanding. Also be sure to tell the child what her job is during the interview: answering questions. The child should be told that she is not expected to have all the answers: "It's OK if you don't know an answer."

Research has indicated that teaching and practicing a few rules at the start of the interview with grade school children and adolescents improves the accuracy of information provided. (See Reed, D. [1996]. Findings from research on children's suggestibility and implications for conducting child interviews. *Child Maltreatment, 1*, 105.) These rules include

- Encourage the child to tell what she knows but not to guess. To test the child's understanding of this rule, some interviewers use questions such as, "Where do I live?" and others use nonsense questions like, "How many pazingas do you have at your house?" If the child responds, "I don't know," praise the child for following the instruction. If the child guesses an answer, praise the child for making a "good guess" but remind her that for the purposes of this interview, guessing is not allowed. Then, the interviewer should try another question to make sure the child understands.
- Allow the child the opportunity to correct the interviewer if a mistake is made. When the child's name is Taneesha, "If I called you Tawana, what would you say?"
- Let the child know that if a question is repeated the interviewer is not trying to get a different answer: "Sometimes I ask a question more than once. If I do, that doesn't mean you gave me the wrong answer. It means I forgot I already asked."
- If the interviewer has a concern that the child is saying "I don't know" when she actually does know, the interviewer may offer an instruction about the need to provide information: "If you don't know the answer I want you to tell me, but if you do know the answer I want you to tell me what you know."

NOTE: See Saywitz, K., & Geiselman, R. [1998]. Interviewing the child witness: Maximizing completeness and minimizing error. In S. Lynn & K. McConkey [Eds.], *Truth in memory* [pp. 190–226]. New York: Guilford.

Instructions That May Clarify Interview Task Demands for School-Age Children

1. Your job is to tell the best you can what you saw and what you heard. Tell the truth. Just tell what you really remember. Do not guess and do not make anything up.
2. Do your best. Try your hardest.
3. Tell me what happened from the beginning to the middle to the end. Tell as much as you can about each part.
4. You may not understand all the questions I ask. Some may be easy and some may be hard to understand. When you don't understand a question, tell me that you don't understand. You can say "I don't get it" or "I don't know what you mean."
5. I may ask some questions more than once. Sometimes I forget that I already asked you that question. You don't have to change your answer. Just tell me what you remember the best that you can.

(Continued)

(*Continued*)

6. If you do not want to answer a question, you can say, "I don't want to answer that question."
7. Sometimes you may not know the answer to a question. That's okay. Nobody can remember everything. If you don't know the answer, then say, "I don't know," but do not guess or make anything up. It is very important you tell me only what you really remember and only what really happened.
8. If you don't know the answer, you can say, "I don't know." But if you do know the answer, tell me the answer.
9. Sometimes I may put my guess into a question. You should tell me if I'm wrong. I was not there and I do not know what happened.
10. I want to write down what we say because what you're telling me is important. Later, if I forget what we said, I can look it up.
11. Tell me as much as you can about what happened. Tell me everything, even the little things that you might not think are important.

SOURCE: Saywitz, K, & Geiselman, R. [1998]. Interviewing the child witness: Maximizing completeness and

This list is not intended to be read as a script to the child. The interviewer should choose instructions that are appropriate for the interview circumstances. Keep in mind that the younger the child, the shorter the attention span. If an interviewer spends too much time on instructions, the opportunity to fully discuss the alleged abuse may be lost. Also, if all the instructions are given at the beginning of an interview, children may not remember them when needed. As any parent can attest, if you give preschoolers three or more instructions (e.g., go upstairs, brush your teeth, comb your hair) they may not remember them all. For this reason, some interviewers incorporate instructions throughout the interview. If, for example, a child corrects the interviewer, the interviewer will stop and provide an instruction. The interviewer might say, "Thank you for correcting me. If I make any other mistakes, please let me know."

Some interviewers then move to a fixed set of rapport building questions, while others tailor these questions to information known about a particular child. The rapport building portion of the interview should contain questions that are easy for the child, such as, "Tell me who lives with you" and "What's your favorite part of school?" The goal of rapport building is to assist the child in getting comfortable with the question-and-answer format of the forensic interview; it is not to have a conversation with the child or to disclose personal information about the interviewer.

Since the most reliable information comes in response to open-ended questions, this part of the interview can "teach" the child to provide narrative descriptions rather than one- or two-word answers. A sample interaction would be, Q: "What's your favorite part of school?" A: "Gym." Q: "What do you like about gym?" This is a much more effective strategy than repeated questions requiring limited production from the child: Q: "What's your favorite part of school?" A: "Gym." Q: "What else do you like about school?"

Rapport building should be as brief as possible to avoid wasting the child's precious attention span on irrelevant information. If a child asks a personal question of the interviewer, such as, "Did anything like this ever happen to you?" the interviewer should be prepared with a brief honest answer, such as "No, but I talk to a lot of kids who tell me what happened to them."

If the interviewer chooses to determine whether the child knows the difference between telling the truth and telling a lie during the initial interview, it is extremely important that this be done in a developmentally appropriate form. (See Lyon, T. [1996]. Assessing children's competence to take the oath: Research and recommendations. *APSAC Advisor, 9,* 1.) Traditionally, interviewers ask children to distinguish between the abstract concepts of "truth" and "lie," and children are notably poor at this task. For example, Q: "What's the difference between the truth and a lie?" A: "A lie is something that isn't true." Other interviewers ask more specific questions that do not represent the concepts of telling the truth and lying. For example, Q: "If I said your sweater is red, would that be the truth?" A: "It's pink." Older children can be asked hypothetical questions to elicit their understanding of these concepts. For example, Q: "If your brother ate some cookies and said you did, would that be the truth?" The interviewer should avoid using himself as the individual in an example about lying, as the child may be very reluctant to indicate the interviewer, an authority figure, is a liar.

A new technique has been developed using simple concrete examples to facilitate even a young child's ability to demonstrate she can distinguish accurately between the truth and a lie. For example, a child is shown a picture with a boy and a girl and an object, like a banana, between them. The child is then asked: "The boy says that's an apple on the table. Is that the truth?" and, "The girl says that's a banana on the table. Is that the truth?" Children can also be asked to describe what happens if they do not tell the truth: "Tell me what happens when someone tells a lie."

The interviewer must be flexible. Children may say and do unexpected things that require the interviewer to remain calm, not convey frustration, and maintain an orderly flow to the interview. The goal is to establish trust, reaffirm that the interviewer is there to help the child, and elicit an accurate account of what happened. The interviewer may have to remind a child to speak louder, if necessary, or that this is a time to answer questions and not to play. If a child is whispering or is otherwise soft-spoken, the interviewer may want to raise his voice a little in the hope the child will follow, or mirror, the interviewer. The interviewer will likely have to redirect the child's attention back to the abuse inquiry when her attention wanders.

2. Approach to the Abuse Inquiry

Moving from rapport building questions to the abuse inquiry requires a specific shift of focus. Some interviewers make the transition directly through their questions: "Now I need to ask about what happened at school. Tell me about what happened." Another approach involves the introduction of anatomical drawings.

In the latter approach, drawings of a boy's and a girl's body are shown to the child. The child is asked which drawing looks most like her. The interviewer then asks the child to name body parts from head to toe. While many children may be reluctant to provide words for genitals, breasts, and buttocks, the use of gentle encouragement usually elicits the names they use for those parts: "It's OK to say what you call this part." Some interviewers wait to introduce body drawings for identification purposes after a disclosure has been made: "I'm going to show you a picture of a boy/girl and I want you to show me where the (child's word for genitals) is."

Use of body drawings early in the interview teaches children that it is all right to talk about their bodies. On the other hand, the defense may try to attack the use of such pictures as a suggestive form of questioning in and of itself. The prosecutor must be prepared to show through questioning of the interviewer that not all children shown these pictures disclose abuse.

Without a tool like anatomical drawings, children may identify body parts by touching their own bodies or the investigator's body. The use of anatomical drawings eliminates the need to remind children of unwanted touch on their own bodies and spares them from the discomfort of having to demonstrate on a stranger's body. (See Holmes, L. S., et al. [2002]. The use of anatomical diagrams in child sexual abuse forensic interviews. *Update, 15*[5].) Drawings and dolls can also be presented in court as a demonstration tool during the child's direct examination.

It is important to avoid asking children to simply repeat their prior report with questions such as: "I want to know what you told your mom about the babysitter." This may limit the child's disclosure to the contents of that conversation rather than to tell everything she can recall about her experience(s). A better opening would be: "Did you tell your mom about something that happened with the babysitter?" If the child responds affirmatively, follow up with: "I wasn't there, so I need you to tell me everything you remember about what happened even if you don't think it's very important."

3. The Use of Appropriate Language

Remember to ask simple questions using easy language. As professionals, we become accustomed to asking compound questions using professional jargon with adult witnesses: "I want to talk to you about the defendant's behavior on the night that he entered your premises." Ask one question at a time: "What were you wearing? What was he wearing?" rather than "What were you and he wearing?" The investigator should allow some time to pass before concluding a child does not want to answer a question or does not understand the question. If the child does not understand, offer to rephrase the question and never communicate that the child has done something wrong by not answering: "That was a hard question. Let me try an easier one."

Children have no familiarity with legal and technical concepts. Words such as *offender, penetrate,* or *erection* are often beyond the comprehension of children even into their teens. Even seemingly easy words like *describe* can be phrased in simpler form: "Tell me . . ." The interviewer should replace legalistic phrases: "What, if anything . . ." with "What did you do next?"; "Did there come a time that . . ." with "Did you go to his house?"; "Let me direct your attention to . . ." with "Let's talk about . . ."; and "Can you describe for the court . . ." with "Tell me about . . ."

Forensic linguists and developmental psychologists who have studied children's linguistic and cognitive development along with actual transcripts of court proceedings have suggested a number of other guidelines for interviewing children. (See Saywitz, K., & Elliott, D. [1994]. *Interviewing children in the forensic context: A developmental approach.* Washington, DC: American Psychological Association; Walker, A. [1994]. *Handbook on questioning children: A linguistic perspective.* Washington, DC: American Bar Association.) These guidelines include

- Use names of people instead of pronouns: "Uncle Rodney" instead of "him."
- Use names of places instead of vague referents: "your uncle's house" instead of "over there."
- Use concrete words instead of abstract terms: "gun" instead of "weapon."
- Avoid abstract concepts like "abuse" and "threaten."
- Avoid using vague quantifiers like "some" and "most of the time."
- Avoid asking younger children to use units of measurement such as height, speed, weight, and distance.
- Avoid asking children to make estimates of elapsed time: "How long did he lie on top of you?"
- Avoid asking children how many times they were abused. Instead ask, "Did it happen one time or more than one time?"
- Utilize anchors to determine the duration of the abuse: "What grade were you in the first time Jenny babysat? What grade were you in the last time Jenny babysat?"
- Utilize familiar concrete indicators of location: "What color was the house you were living in when your dad touched your bottom?"
- Help the child present a narrative in sequence: "What happened next?" "Just before he put his peter in your butt, what happened?"
- Avoid moving forward and backward in time without telling the child: "Now I need to go back and ask you a few more questions about the first time Jenny babysat."
- Remember that children can be very literal in their understanding of language: Q: "Where were you when you were in bed with your dad?" A: "In bed."
- Be sure to ask both about touching done to the child and touching the child had to do.
- Avoid using relationship words instead of names: "Julio" rather than "your step-dad."
- Avoid asking about "good touch" and "bad touch" as young children may have no concept that what happened was "bad" and older children who were not hurt may not identify the abuse in those terms.
- Use the child's words without correcting the use of those words. If the child describes the abuse as "tickling," but says, "it hurt," continue to use her words rather than replacing them with your own words such as "hurting you."
- Do not ask the child to tell you her "story" so there can be no question at the end of the interview whether the account was factual or a product of fantasy. For the same reason, avoid the word *pretend*.
- Never ask the child to "guess."
- Avoid tag end questions: "Your mom wasn't home, was she?"

4. *How to Ask Questions*

The most reliable information elicited from children comes in response to open-ended questions such as, "Tell me about that" or "Tell me more about that." Less reliable information comes in response to multiple-choice questions, especially when the accurate choice is not part of the question: "Did he touch your bootie when you were in the bedroom or living room?" when the abuse happened in the bathroom. Multiple-choice questions can create a need to ask multiple questions instead of just one. For example, the question, "Did he touch your bootie with his finger or something else?" can result in the child responding, "Something else," leading to the next question, "What did he touch your bootie with?" The latter question should have been used initially. The least reliable information comes in response to "yes or no" questions: "Did he tell you not to tell?" The following chart represents the continuum of questions used to interview children about alleged abuse.

Table II.1	A Continuum of Types of Questions Used in Interviewing Children Alleged to Have Been Sexually Abused and Confidence in Responses			
	Question type	*Example*	*Child's response*	
Open-ended	A. General	How are you?	Sad, 'cause my dad poked me in the pee-pee.	More confidence
	B. Focused	How do you get along with your dad?	OK, except when he pokes me in the pee-pee.	
	C. Multiple choice	Did he poke you with his finger, his ding-dong, or something else?	He used his ding-dong.	
	D. Yes-no	Did he tell you not to tell?	No, he didn't say anything like that.	
	E. Leading	He took off your clothes, didn't he?	Yes.	
		Didn't he make you suck his penis?	Yes.	
Closed-ended				Less confidence

SOURCE: Faller, K. C. [1990]. Types of questions for children alleged to have been sexually abused. *APSAC Advisor*, 3(2).

Do not ask questions that sound accusatory, such as, "Why didn't you try to stop him?" "Why did you let him touch you?" or "Why did you wait so long to tell anyone?" Questions like these will only make the child feel guilty and reluctant to be open with you.

When asking a child open-ended questions, the interviewer must allow her to complete her answer before following up for additional details. Interrupting children to clarify may serve the interviewer's needs, but it will likely disrupt the child's flow of thought and may lead her to believe the information first asked about is not wanted.

The flow of questions in the abuse inquiry should be from open-ended questions to focused questions with as few yes-or-no questions as possible. Nevertheless, some yes-or-no questions may be needed in every interview to secure information children are unable to provide with more open-ended inquiry. It is essential to follow up multiple-choice and yes-or-no questions with an open-ended question such as: "Did someone tell you not to tell? Tell me about that."

Whenever possible, the interviewer should try to obtain information using who, what, when, or where questions. For example, "What were you wearing?" elicits more information from the child's own recollection than, "Were you wearing your pajamas?" which clearly provides information to the child she has not previously offered. Similarly, "Where were you in your bedroom when Uncle Jim humped you?" is preferable to "Were you on the bed or the floor or someplace else?" Yes-or-no questions and multiple-choice questions should not be used as the first attempt to secure information from the child.

Focused questions, such as clothing worn and persons present, may be needed to introduce topics that were not provided by the child in her initial narrative. Other focused questions will help the interviewer learn more details about topics introduced by the child. These details could include a description of the clothing worn and what the others present were doing when the abuse took place.

Leading questions are discouraged but sometimes unavoidable if the interviewer is going to learn the full scope of what happened to the child. In some cases, for instance, a medical evaluation will produce clear physical findings of penetration, but the child does not spontaneously report penetration. Questions that introduce this concept are then necessary: "Where was (suspect's name)'s (child's word for penis)?" Some questions are so leading and coercive that they indicate to the child there is only one correct answer: "You're not mad at your dad, are you?" This form of leading question must never be used with children.

Some direct questions are much more suggestive than other questions. Even when leading questions must be asked, the interviewer can reduce the extent of suggestion. For example, "Did something happen to your (child's word for vagina)?" is better than, "Did your dad do something to your (child's word for vagina)?" or "Did he put something in your (child's word for vagina)?" (Lamb, M., Sternberg, K., & Esplin, P. [1998]. Conducting investigative interviews of alleged sexual abuse victims. *Child Abuse & Neglect, 22,* 813.)

Erroneous questions introduce information that children must respond to. If the child has said that the offender's clothes were off, the question, "When he took off his shirt, what did you see?" assumes the offender took off his shirt. The offender may have been wearing a sweater or he may have been wearing only pants before he took his "clothes" off. Children are unlikely to correct the interviewer's error and may become confused and unable to respond to a question that may seem to require a lie for an answer.

Children do not understand the need to tell a story from beginning to end. They often begin their narrative accounts at points that are of particular interest or meaning to them. Young children, in particular, tell narratives that are loosely organized and sketchy in detail. (See Fivush, R. [1993]. Developmental perspectives on autobiographical recall. In G. Goodman & B. Bottoms [Eds.], *Child victims, child witnesses: Understanding and improving testimony.* New York: Guilford.) Children need the interviewer's help to sequence their account with questions that prompt an orderly flow of information: "Right after he laid on top of you, what happened?" "Just before he walked out of your room, what happened?" and "And just before that, what happened?"

Avoid asking questions that sound accusatory, such as "Why didn't you run away?" Questions like those will only make the child feel guilty and reluctant to be open with you. You may want to ask instead, "Were you able to try to stop him?" "How were you feeling?" "What did you do when he touched you?" and "Did you say anything to him? What did you say?" A question such as, "Did you tell someone about what happened?" will help the interviewer determine what the child has really told. The child may believe that someone knew about the abuse when no one did. The child may also believe that she told someone about the abuse, but she did so in such a way that the other person did not know the child was being harmed. The child's statement may have been: "I don't want to stay home with Roger when you go to the store." A question asking what the offender said to the child may elicit threats, bribes, and intimidation.

Children often make cryptic statements. Rather than guessing about or ignoring these statements, clarify what the child means: "I'm not sure what you mean when you say 'He looked like in the movies.'" This is important because the defense can use unusual or unclear statements to discredit the child's statement or impeach her testimony. The interviewer is also vulnerable to the accusation that he selectively attended to information that confirmed abuse when these clarifying questions are not asked of the child.

Never threaten or try to force a child to continue an interview. The use of pressure during the interview can cause a self-conscious and anxious child to withdraw and be further traumatized. For an overly compliant child, pressure can cause the child to embellish the account to please the interviewer or to get the interview over with. If the child becomes distressed, the interviewer should try a supportive statement like, "Talking about this can be real hard" and wait a minute or two. Some children will allow you to return to a particularly upsetting topic at the end of the interview: "Let's talk about something else now and we'll come back to this at the end." If the child still indicates she does not want to talk about it or is obviously denying all knowledge about the event, stop the interview. The interview can be conducted again.

If a child appears too fearful to disclose what happened, ask directly whether she is scared to tell you and, if so, what frightens her. Try to address her fears honestly. If she has been threatened, let her know how you can protect her. If she is afraid the suspect will go to jail, explain that it will be up to the judge to decide whether jail is needed, but that it will not be her fault if that happens. The child's extreme anxiety in divulging the abuse is understandable. Many children may love the abuser, but they want the abuse to end. Other children have kept their silence for years in the face of threats or the wish to keep the family together. The benefits to the child of telling this "special secret" are uncertain. This is especially true when family members have denounced the child and pressured her to recant. The interviewer must respect and acknowledge the great risk the child may be taking by telling about the abuse.

F. Possible Questions for the Sexual Abuse Inquiry

The following questions are intended to elicit information about suspected abuse. Not all will be appropriate in every situation, and additional questions may be necessary depending on the facts of the case. Always use the child's descriptive names for body parts.

1. General Inquiry Questions

"Tell me what happened when. . . ."

"Have you had any touches you didn't like or made you feel uncomfortable?"

"How did the touching start? What happened next?"

"What did (suspect's name) touch you with?"

"You said (suspect's name) touched you with his (child's name for body part). Did (suspect's name) touch you with anything else?"

"What did (suspect's name)'s hand/finger/(child's word for penis) do?"

"What part of your body did (suspect's name) touch?"

"How did the touching feel?"

"How did it feel when (suspect's name) put his (child's word for penis) in your private spot?"

"Did (suspect's name) touch you somewhere else on your body?"

"Did you ever see (suspect's name) touch anyone else's private spot?"

"Did anyone see (suspect's name) touch your private spot?"

"Where were you when (suspect's name) touched your private spot?"

"Did (suspect's name) touch your private spot when you were at any other places?"

"Did (suspect's name) touch your private spot once or more than once?"

"Did (suspect's name) have you touch any parts of his body?"

"How did your clothes come off?"

"What did you see when you were in that room?"

"What did you hear when (suspect's name) was touching your private spot?"

2. Penetration Questions

"Where was (suspect's name)'s (child's term for penis)?"

"Did (suspect's name)'s (child's word for penis) touch you anywhere?"

"What part of your body did (suspect's name)'s (child's word for penis) touch?"

"Did your (child's word for own genitals) hurt? What made it hurt?"

"Did (suspect's name)'s (child's name for penis) touch inside or outside your (child's word for own genitals)? How did you know? How did that feel?"

"Did (suspect's name) ever put anything else inside that part of your body? Did (suspect's name) ever put anything on that part of your body?"

"Did (suspect's name)'s (child's word for penis) touch you on your clothing or on your skin?"

"Did (suspect's name) put anything on his (child's word for penis)? What did it look like?"

3. Erection/Masturbation Questions

"What did (suspect's name)'s (child's word for penis) look like?"

"Were there any marks on (suspect's name)'s (child's word for penis)?"

"Tell me more about what (suspect name)'s (child's word for penis) looked like."

"Did (suspect's name) want you to touch him anywhere? How did he want you to touch him?"

"Did (suspect's name) want you to touch his (child's word for penis) in a certain way?"

"What did (suspect's name) do while he made you do that?"

"What did (suspect's name) say when he made you do that?"

"How did (suspect's name)'s (child's word for penis) feel when you touched it?"

"What did you hear when you were touching (child's word for penis)?"

4. Ejaculation Questions

"What happened to (suspect's name)'s (child's word for penis) after he made you touch it?"

"What did he call the (child's word for semen)?"

"What do you call that stuff?"

"Where did (child's word for semen) come from?"

"After (child's word for semen) came out of (child's word for penis) where was the (child's word for semen)?"

"What did (child's word for semen) look like?"

"What did (child's word for semen) feel like?"

"What did (child's word for semen) taste like?"

"Did (suspect's name) say anything when (child's name for semen) came out?"

"Did (suspect's name) ask you to do anything after (child's word for semen) came out?"

"What did (suspect's name) do after (child's word for semen) came out?"

5. Nudity Questions

"What were you wearing when . . . ?"

"What was (suspect's name) wearing when . . . ?"

"Was there anything special about (suspect's name)'s clothes?"

"How did your clothes come off?"

"How did (suspect's name)'s clothes come off?"

"Were all of your clothes off?"

To clarify confusion about conflicting reports that her clothes were on but penetration occurred ask: "You said your clothes were on. You said he put his peter in your private spot. I don't understand that part. Tell me more about that."

6. Oral Contact/French Kissing Questions

"Did (suspect's name)'s mouth touch you anywhere?"

"What did (suspect's name) do with his mouth?"

"Did (suspect's name)'s mouth touch any other parts of your body?"

"Did (suspect's name) want you to kiss him anywhere? Did (suspect's name) want you to suck him anywhere else? Did (suspect's name) want you to lick him anywhere else?"

"What did (suspect's name)'s mouth do? What did (suspect's name)'s lips do? What did (suspect's name)'s tongue do?"

"How did (suspect's name)'s mouth feel? How did (suspect's name)'s lips feel? How did (suspect's name)'s tongue feel?"

"How did (suspect's name)'s kisses feel?"

7. Pornography Questions

"Did (suspect's name) show you any pictures/books/magazines/movies/videos?"

"What were the pictures/books/magazines/movies/videos about?"

"What did you see in the pictures/books/magazines/movies/videos?"

"Did (suspect's name) show you anything when he (child's word for abuse) you?"

"Did (suspect's name) take any pictures/videos? What did he take pictures of?"

"Where does (suspect's name) keep the pictures/videos?"

"Did (suspect's name) show the pictures/books/magazines/movies/videos to anyone else?"

"What were the movies/videos about?"

"Where was the camera when (suspect's name) took pictures/videos?"

G. Possible Questions About Physical Abuse

Physical abuse allegations will most often involve the child's parent or another caregiver. If the abuse was discovered by means other than the child's own report, the child may be difficult to interview. The child may have been led to believe she deserved to be punished and may not recognize that what she experienced was abuse. For good reason, the child may fear worse punishment if she tells. Further, she may be ashamed of the abuse and the bruises or scars it has left on her body.

It can be helpful in such cases to begin the abuse inquiry with a discussion of the kinds of punishment used in the child's home. Be careful to broach this subject in a nonjudgmental way so the child does not misinterpret your line of questioning and think she is in trouble with you.

The following questions may be appropriate in some, but not all, physical abuse cases.

"What happens if you do something you're not supposed to?"

"What else happens when you do something you're not supposed to?"

"Who punishes you?"

"What does (the person named) do?"

"When was the last time (suspect's name) (child's word for abuse) you?"

"What does (suspect's name) use to (child's word for abuse) you with?"

"Where on your body does (suspect's name) (child's word for abuse) you? Any other places?"

"How does that feel?"

"What did you think about that?"

"What does (suspect's name) do when your brother/sister does something he/she is not supposed to?"

"What was the worst punishment you ever got? What had you done to get that punishment?"

"Does (suspect's name) ever say anything when he does that? What does he say?"

"Did anyone see (suspect's name) do that to you? How do you know?"

"What happened after (suspect's name) did that to you? Did you go to the doctor?"

"Has anyone else done (child's word for abuse) to you?"

"Who spanks you? What does he/she spank you with? Where on your body does he/she spank you? How does it feel?"

(If the child has used the word *hurt*) "Have you been hurt in any other way?"

If the child has injuries such as bruises or scars, you may ask directly, "How did that happen?" If the child gives an unlikely explanation, and especially if she is reluctant to talk, reassure her that she is not in any trouble with you and then ask her for help in understanding what happened: "I don't understand. Tell me everything you remember about how you got that bruise."

Because physical abuse covers such a range of circumstances, questions will vary and you will need to be flexible. The interviewer must try to be matter-of-fact during the interview no matter how brutal the child's description. Abused children are extremely sensitive to the reactions of others and may seek to protect your feelings by not disclosing more or react to your upset with heightened distress that may interfere with their ability to report.

H. Possible Questions About Witnessed Abuse

Children may produce highly valuable testimony about witnessing the assault or murder of a sibling or parent. The questions discussed in other sections can also be used to obtain a complete account of the event. The following questions may also be appropriate.

"Tell me what you saw when . . ."

"Tell me what you heard when . . ."

"Tell me about the other times you saw . . ."

"Where were you when . . ."

"When (suspect's name) did that, how did he look? What did he say?"

"Right after (suspect's name) did that, what happened?"

"Did anyone else see (suspect's name) do that?"

"Has (suspect's name) ever done that to anyone else? Tell me all about that."

"Have the police ever come to your house? Why did they come?"

I. Possible Questions About the Child's Fears or Reasons for Secrecy

The interviewer may wish to determine if threats, promises, requests, or rewards were used to prevent the child from disclosing the abuse. This type of information may be difficult to discover because of the coercion applied or because of the child's positive feelings for the offender. The interviewer should also inquire whether other family members, especially a nonoffending parent, applied similar pressure on the child.

"Did someone tell you not to tell? Who? What did he/she say would happen if you told?"

"Did you ever tell anyone besides (name of person child most recently disclosed to)? What happened after you told him/her?"

"What made you decide to tell what happened?"

"Has someone asked you to keep a secret? What was the secret?"

"Did (suspect's name) tell you he would do something for you if you didn't tell? What did he say?"

If it appears that the child has been threatened and is particularly frightened, address her fears directly: "Sometimes kids are really scared to tell what happened to them. You seem scared to talk to me. Tell me about that." Be aware that it could be an accomplice or someone close to the abuser who made the threat rather than the abuser. It is helpful to inquire about whether the child witnessed any violence in the home. Domestic violence often has a chilling effect on a child's willingness to divulge her own abuse. Once domestic violence is disclosed, it may be easier to break the intimidator's hold on the child by discrediting unrealistic threats and reassuring her that the investigator will do everything in his power to protect her.

Sometimes an indirect approach is needed. The interviewer can ask the child about the people in her life, with whom she likes to spend time, and with whom she does not like to spend time. The interviewer can then ask questions about what the various people do whom she does not like.

J. Discovering the Offender and Determining Who Was Involved

Most children know their offenders and will be able to name them, although in some cases children may not fully understand their relationship to the offenders. The interviewer should be able to learn from other sources about the nature and extent of the relationship. The interviewer should not be surprised if the child has mixed or conflicting feelings about the offender. Children commonly report they like the offender, but they do not like what he did. A sensitive investigation will document both the good and bad parts of the relationship, as a previously or currently close relationship between the offender and child will help undermine assertions of a motive for revenge on the part of the victim.

The interviewer needs to ask questions to establish if anyone else was present when the abuse occurred, if the child knew where that person was when the abuse occurred, and if that person participated in the abuse act. Questions should also be asked to determine whether anyone should have reason to suspect that abuse had occurred. Find out whom the child first told and whether she told more than once.

The following questions may be appropriate in some cases.

"Did (suspect's name) ever do anything else you didn't like?"

"Does anyone else know about (child's word for abuse)? Who? How does he/she know?"

"Who was the first person you told? Who was the first person you tried to tell? What happened after you told him/her?"

"What did that person say/do?"

"Was anyone else there when (child's word for abuse) happened? What was/were he/she/they doing while (suspect's name) (child's word for abuse) you?"

"Do you know if (suspect's name) has done this to anyone else? Who? How do you know?"

"Has anyone else ever (child's word for abuse) to you?"

"Has anything like (child's word for abuse) ever happened to you before?"

K. Finding Out When and How Often the Child Was Abused

Learning from the child precisely when the abuse took place is difficult, if not impossible, depending on the child's age and developmental capacity. Children have poorly developed concepts of time and do not use names for units of time accurately until they are older. Children may not be able to describe the first incident if they have been abused many times, since the events may all blur together in their memory. The best description will likely be of the most recent incident since it will be the freshest in the child's mind.

The interviewer should avoid asking the child to state the exact number of times abuse occurred. If a child has had a number of abuse experiences, the types of abuse committed may not be identical. For example, she performed oral sex six times, but the offender only attempted penetration five times. A broad question such as, "How many times did he do that?" may elicit a confused account, as children do not keep track of the number of the different types of incidents. Allow the child to provide her view of the number or frequency of events without pushing her to be more specific: Q: "Did this happen once or more than once?" A: "Lots."

To determine when the abuse occurred, the interviewer should use anchors that are familiar to the child. These anchors may include age; grade in school; the house lived in; people who lived there; season of the year; daytime or nighttime; before or after school; during the summer or during the school year; holidays, birthdays or other special days; before or after a favorite television show; or when Mom was at a specific location. Sometimes a cooperative parent or guardian can provide information about these markers to help facilitate the questioning. The interviewer may also ask the child how old she was the first time she was abused and how old she was the last time she was abused.

An older abuse victim occasionally will keep a diary or journal. The child may have written letters to someone referring to abuse incidents, the abuser, or other events coinciding with the abuse. These areas must be asked about. Similarly, compulsive offenders often keep records of the details of their crimes in computers, diaries, calendars, or special hiding places. The child needs to be asked if she is aware of such records.

L. Finding Out Where the Abuse Took Place

Abuse frequently occurs in the child's or offender's home. However, it can occur anywhere: in public restrooms, in vehicles, outdoors, at camp, in church, and in the classroom. If a child has moved, the location is important to determine the appropriate jurisdiction. The interviewer should not end the interview if it is discovered that the abuse occurred somewhere outside the interviewer's jurisdiction. The interview should continue to determine if any acts happened in the interviewer's jurisdiction as well. The interview also needs to be completed so that the child's confidence is not suddenly cut off, preventing a full disclosure and to avoid the need for multiple interviews. The child should be told that the interviewer needs to let someone else know about what the child said because the abuse happened somewhere else.

Besides determining the general location of the abuse, the interviewer should ask for as many details about the location as possible. This prevents the account from being attacked as vague. It also assists in gathering physical evidence, such as the blanket where the offender ejaculated, or evidence to corroborate the child's statement, such as the red comforter on the bed or the picture of the horse on the bedroom wall. The interviewer should always ask if there was more than one location where the child was abused.

M. Alternative Hypothesis Testing

Every interview must include the opportunity to test the possibility that someone else has abused the child or that there is some other explanation for an intimate touch, e.g., a bath. The following questions may be appropriate depending on the specific circumstances of your case.

"Has anyone else ever (child's word for abuse) you?"

"Has anyone else ever touched you in a way you did not like? Has anyone else ever made you feel uncomfortable?"

N. Sensitivity to the Child's Emotions

Sometimes it is difficult to maintain poise when a child reveals something shocking. The interviewer should be prepared for anything, remain neutral, and respond in a nonjudgmental manner. Extraneous comments like, "Oh, no!" or "I'd hate that, too" should be avoided. If taken by surprise, saying something like, "And what happened next?" can allow the interviewer to collect his or her thoughts. If the interviewer feels pressured to get information from the child, or exhibits anxiety, revulsion, or enthusiasm in response to what the child has described, the child is less likely to be open during the interview. The interviewer must always consider how the questions, tone of voice, and body language may be interpreted by the child and adjust them to set the child at ease. A child may also feel pressured to provide information and hurry to answer questions or move restlessly. The use of techniques such as slowing down the pace of the questions and maintaining a calm demeanor can help the child calm down. Avoid reprimanding a child for moving around. As long as she is able to answer questions, it doesn't matter if she is standing on her head. If, however, a child needs to be refocused, one simple technique is to ask the child if you can trace her hand. If the child places her hand on the flip chart in the interview room, trace the hand slowly as you resume questioning.

It is often helpful to acknowledge and normalize the difficulty a child has talking to you. These statements can help in such situations: "Sometimes it can be kind of scary/embarrassing/sad/confusing to talk about these things." "Lots of kids feel sad/embarrassed/scared/confused talking about stuff like this. How are you feeling?" "I would like to understand what might be bothering you so I can help." Never tell a child how she is feeling by saying, "You must be sad about seeing your dad" or "You seem angry about being in the foster home." Since none of us can know how a particular child feels, it is important to let each child express herself in her own way. Guessing the wrong feeling communicates to a child that you are not listening sensitively and reduces the child's trust in the interviewer. Children may also conclude there is a right feeling and experience added shame that they are not feeling like they are supposed to feel.

O. Special Strategies

1. Anatomical Dolls

Anatomical dolls should be used only with children who can make the representational shift. That is, the child must understand that a doll or dolls represent the child or another person. By the age of 5, most children acquire this ability. If anatomical dolls are to be used, an appropriate introduction tells the child these dolls are not for play: "I have some special dolls. We don't play with these dolls. We use them to show what has happened." Whenever possible, the interviewer should have dolls of the appropriate age, gender, and race to facilitate accurate demonstration. The interviewer should choose which dolls to use, making sure that the dolls chosen for the child and the perpetrator are both developmentally and racially correct. "Show me . . ." allows the child to then demonstrate what happened. Sometimes children will have described nudity but begin their demonstration with the dolls clothed. The interviewer should not interrupt the demonstration. When the child is done demonstrating, the interviewer should ask whether her clothes were like those on the doll. The demonstration should be provided by the child. The interviewer can use requests to facilitate additional demonstration, such as, "You said (suspect's name) (child's word for the abuse). Show me how that happened." If you are still unclear after a demonstration you may ask the child to do it again or ask follow-up questions: "Tell me again where he had his (child's word for penis)."

Dolls should always be introduced fully clothed, and the interviewer should never position them in any way or assist the child in demonstrating the abuse.

Examples of inappropriate uses of dolls by interviewers would be

- Presenting the dolls to the child unclothed
- Encouraging play with the dolls
- Naming the sexual parts of the doll for the child
- Probing the dolls' genitals or breasts
- Using the dolls to demonstrate sexual behavior to the child
- Failing to elicit a verbal description of the abuse before presenting the dolls to the child
- Clarifying incorrectly what the child demonstrated

Only forensic interviewers trained in the use of these tools should use anatomical dolls. For information on available training, contact the National Center for Prosecution of Child Abuse at (703) 549–4253. (Adapted from Boat, B., & Everson, M. [1996]. Concerning practices of interviewers when using anatomical dolls in child protective services investigation. *Child Maltreatment, 1,* 96; see also Holmes, L. S. [2000]. Using anatomical dolls in child sexual abuse forensic interviews. *Update, 13*(8).)

2. Reluctant or Recanting Children

Prosecutors and investigators handling child abuse cases should not be surprised or discouraged by a child's reluctance to disclose abuse. The complex nature of an abusive relationship or incident creates a natural unwillingness to tell. Reluctance or recantation might also be a sign that abuse did not occur. Never assume the child was abused and set out to prove that theory. It is essential to maintain an open mind and demand a thorough investigation to uncover the reasons for the child's reticence before reaching a conclusion. Some children may not be able to disclose abuse in the forensic interview context and will need to be referred to a mental health professional skilled in working with children. The American Professional Society on the

Abuse of Children has developed guidelines for accepted practice in the psychosocial evaluation of a suspected abused child. A perpetrator can still be prosecuted after a disclosure in the more therapeutic setting.

Children recant for a variety of reasons including loyalty to family members, fear of rejection by family members, threats by the offender or others, feeling responsible for the offender's arrest or removal from the home, and a genuine caring for the offender and not wanting to get him into trouble. If the interviewer believes the child was abused but has recanted, it is appropriate to let her know that other children sometimes decide to say it did not happen because it is so difficult to handle what happens after disclosure. You may want to tell the child: "I wasn't there and so I don't know what happened, but (name of person child reported to) believed you when you told him/her." A question to the child about why she said one thing before and another thing now may elicit an explanation such as a statement that the abuse really did occur, her motivation for recanting, or an explanation that does not make sense.

Still another approach is to ask the child what she would do if something like this did happen to her or what should happen to a person who does this to a child. A recanting child commonly says she would not tell and nothing should happen to the offender. The interviewer may then ask the child to explain her reasoning for these answers. Ask the child about her current circumstances and recent developments in her life. In one case, for example, a recanting child informed the investigator that her mother was diagnosed with cancer and had told the child she would like her husband, the alleged perpetrator, to be released from jail so that he could care for her. Information such as this can help the prosecutor explain the recantation to the jury.

Sometimes cooperative caregivers or others familiar with the child will be able to offer explanations for the recantation that can then be incorporated into the discussion with the child. It may be necessary to find out who has had access to the child and her reactions to those contacts. Contacts, such as phone calls from Mom to the child in foster care or letters from the perpetrator to the mother that are read to the child, can greatly influence a child.

The child who recants is almost certainly a child in turmoil, and aggressive confrontation rarely, if ever, helps to resolve the turmoil. The interviewer's best chance of gaining or regaining trust lies in showing the child genuine empathy to the pressures she faces. Only when she believes that revealing the truth will result in more positive than negative repercussions will the child be comfortable enough to do so.

3. Adolescents

A plan to interview an adolescent should include an approach and questions targeted to the developmental capacity, and not the chronological age, of the child. Chronically abused adolescents may function cognitively like much younger children or they may be age-appropriate in their ability to participate in the interview process.

Adolescents generally prefer to be dealt with directly and may be extremely sensitive to any technique that seems manipulative to them, such as the interviewer being overly friendly. Adolescents may present with an attitude that reflects their negative experiences with adults in general and authority figures in particular. The interviewer should not be put off by this attitude or try to joke with the adolescent. The interviewer will facilitate the interview by maintaining a calm demeanor, being frank with the youth about the process, and ignoring a hostile tone. Be aware that an adolescent's associations with police and prosecutors may be negative ones. An interviewer who is personable but professional will go a long way toward undermining the adolescent's negative stereotypes.

Adolescents should not be asked to name body parts at the beginning of an interview, and anatomical dolls should be used only if they can be introduced in a way that does not appear to the adolescent to be insulting. Anatomical drawings or dolls might be introduced to reduce confusion about the abuse report after the verbal disclosure has been made, but explain to the adolescent the drawings and dolls are only used to clarify important points.

Adolescents often respond to requests for additional information as if the interviewer were stupid. The interviewer must ignore the attitude and explain that it is necessary to be sure that what she is telling you is being understood. If an adolescent uses a phrase requiring further explanation, a statement such as, "I talk to lots of kids. I need to know what you mean when you say 'He Frenched me,'" can allow the interviewer to obtain clarification.

Embarrassment can be the biggest hurdle with this age group. Adolescents may feel particularly responsible for the abuse, confused about why they did not report right away, and as if they "should have known better." The interviewer must take care not to proceed upon assumptions that may not be true, such as that the adolescent knew how to prevent pregnancy.

If the suspect's knowledge of the child's age is an issue or potential defense, the interviewer should cover this with the adolescent. Find out what she told the suspect about her age, whether he knew her birthday or grade in school, whether he knew she has a driver's license, or any other information that would have demonstrated her age.

If the adolescent describes abuse that involved intercourse, the interviewer should always ask if the adolescent was concerned about becoming pregnant. If she indicates she was not, the interviewer should find out what the suspect did or said to remove that concern. The adolescent may then describe the condoms used or the offender's explanation of a vasectomy. Each description is a potential source of evidence and corroboration. Adolescents may also be able to describe their fear of contracting a sexually transmitted disease (STD) or their attempts to determine if they had an STD by setting up a doctor's appointment or a visit to the school health clinic.

The interviewer should alert the adolescent of the need for her not to disclose the details of the abuse to others, including friends. Care should be taken not to alarm the adolescent, but apprise her of the possibility that the defense will use investigators. Along with this warning, the interviewer should explain that the defense can subpoena anyone to whom she has spoken about the abuse. Let the teen know that her false denials to others that are intended to avoid the embarrassment or stigma associated with abuse can be damaging should a trial become necessary. Depending on the laws of the jurisdiction, the adolescent should be assured that attempts will be made to protect her identity. An adolescent may also be relieved to know that she can have a support person present if she has to testify.

P. Ending the Interview

Interviews generally end at a point at which the child is no longer able to provide additional information. It is important to allow the child to leave feeling good about her participation rather than a failure for not being able to answer questions. Statements such as, "You can go now" can leave children feeling uncertain about whether they did what they could. Interviewers can finish the interview by asking the child, "Is there anything else you want to tell me today? Is there anything you want to ask me?" Thank the child for her hard work, sitting still for so long, or for helping you understand what happened. If appropriate, tell the child what will be happening next with statements like, "I'll walk you out and spend a little while talking with your mom before you go home today." Many interviewers give children their name and phone number on a card in case they want to contact the interviewer in the future. Other interviewers tell the child they will give that information to the parent or guardian.

Avoid asking the child to promise to tell what she told again in court. Children cannot project themselves into an unknown situation or predict how they will behave in the future. Aside from this, an immediate statement to the child that she will have to disclose the abuse again may have a chilling effect on her willingness to cooperate in the future.

Q. After the Interview: Meeting With Parents or Caregivers

After the interview, the interviewer or another team member should meet privately with the parents or other caregiver to address the parent's or caregiver's concerns. This should be done without the child being present. The parent or caregiver will normally want to know what happened to the child. If the interview has been videotaped, parents may wish to view the tape with a team member. If it was not videotaped, tell them what the child disclosed while adjusting the level of detail to the questions they ask. An exit interview will allow the adult time away from the child to manage emotions. It also provides the team member with an opportunity to offer suggestions about how to respond to the child and how the adults might want to express their own feelings to the child. Some children want to participate in telling their parents about the abuse. The interviewer can repeat what has already been shared to the parents in front of the child and allow the child to tell the parents how she feels. It is important to prepare parents to control their emotions in front of the child and to focus their efforts on offering support to the child. Parents may also need assistance in understanding the child's reaction to the abuse and the offender. This may be especially true when the child's reaction is different from the parent's reaction. For instance, the child may not be angry with the person who abused her but want the perpetrator to get help. In contrast, the parents may prefer serious consequences for the perpetrator.

Even with young children, the interviewer might want to discuss with the child the acceptability of talking to her parents or caregiver, rather than other persons, when she wants to talk about the abuse. While the child should be allowed to talk to her parents about the abuse, parents should be told that they are not to act as an investigator with the child. The parent should be warned to not question the child about the abuse but simply allow the child to talk about the abuse. A team member should encourage the parent to document and disclose to authorities additional information the child discloses.

A team member should provide the parents or caregiver with simple, straightforward information about the criminal justice system. This should include the expected time frame and the possibility of a trial. As with children, team members should avoid making promises to parents or caregivers that cannot be kept, such as being able to clear the courtroom when the child testifies. The parents or caregiver should be told that the child's name and address will be protected as much as possible. They should also be warned of the possibility that defense investigators may contact them. Be careful not to give parents or caregivers the impression that they will decide whether the child will testify or if a trial will be held. Enlist the parent's or caregiver's cooperation and let them know whom they can call for status reports on the progress of the case. The interviewer should express appreciation and understanding of the effort involved in making the report, in bringing the child in for the interview, and following through with the process.

General practical suggestions for interviews include

1. Develop a child-friendly interview location.

2. Adopt a neutral, friendly attitude.

3. Make no assumptions about the abuse or how the child feels about it or the perpetrator.

4. Develop or use a protocol that has the stages of

   - Introduction
   - Rapport building
   - Instructions
   - A method for beginning the abuse inquiry
   - An abuse inquiry
   - Closure

5. Elicit a free recall narrative account before asking follow-up questions.

6. Explain taping procedures when they are utilized.

7. If using anatomical dolls, introduce them when they are needed and only after a verbal disclosure has been completed.

8. Keep appointments and be prompt.

9. Schedule interviews that are consistent with the child's routine; avoid naptime or important school events.

10. Avoid making promises.

11. Never pressure a child to respond to questions.

12. Make sure your forensic interviewers have been trained in a quality forensic interviewing training program, such as APRI's Finding Words. For information about forensic interviewer training, contact the National Center for Prosecution of Child Abuse at (703) 549–4253.

II. ASSESSING VALIDITY IN SEXUAL ABUSE CASES

Determining whether a report of sexual abuse is valid is a process of evaluating available information and evidence. Evidence such as eyewitness statements, confessions, or pictures or videos depicting the abuse should leave virtually no doubt about the authenticity of an allegation. Likewise, the existence of conclusive medical and forensic evidence will make the determination easy. Realistically, however, this kind of definitive corroborative evidence is rare in child sexual abuse cases. In the majority of cases, the evidence consists only of the child's statements, together with evidence that may be consistent with abuse but does not prove the abuse occurred. This other evidence may include emotional and behavioral characteristics of the child and suspect seen by others, indirect medical findings, objects similar to the descriptions given by the child, and known contact with the offender. The absence of other evidence results in an examination of the child's statements for information that can be used to assess the validity of an abuse report. Although there are no factors that conclusively demonstrate a report's validity, a working knowledge of reliability indicators may assist the prosecutor in preparing the case and presenting it to the jury. (See Myers, J. [1996]. Taint hearings for child witnesses? A step in the wrong direction. *Baylor Law Review, 46*, 873.)

A. Elimination of Other Explanations

Throughout the investigation, the investigator must consider alternative explanations for the child's statements that would indicate there was no abuse. As the child is interviewed, the investigator should look for sufficient confirmation of the people involved and the circumstances described so that the possibility of deliberate falsehood, misinterpretation of innocent contacts, or coaching by someone else can be ruled out. The investigator must always keep in mind the potential defenses the suspect can use and determine whether the other possibilities that might account for the child's statements can be eliminated.

B. Spontaneity

Spontaneous statements from children are reliable statements. These statements are unlikely to be the result of prompting or manipulation by an adult or suggestive questioning by an interviewer. The initial report may have been spontaneous. There also may be elements of the investigative interview that are clearly spontaneous. For instance, if an interviewer asks, "What were you wearing when Andre asked you to sex him?" and the child replies, "My clothes. It was my jeans and my Steelers shirt," the spontaneous details lend credibility to the account.

C. Consistency

The consistency of the child's statements, both internally and externally, is very important. Internal consistency is the consistency of the child's statements within a single interview. External consistency is the consistency of the child's statements throughout time, such as during the initial report, the forensic interview, the medical exam, and the child's testimony in court. This is not to say that the child's account must be exactly the same each time. In fact, a statement that sounds like a rote recital when repeated should be scrutinized carefully for the possibility of coaching. A child who has been coached to fabricate or is lying on her own may tell an entire story from the beginning to the end without hesitation. On the other hand, a child who has been interviewed a number of times or a traumatized child may exhibit a self-protective numbness that makes her style of relating sound like a rote recital. A review of the circumstances of her initial disclosure should allow for a more confident evaluation of the statements.

A valid report will be consistent for core events and the individuals involved. There may be variation about more peripheral aspects, particularly when multiple incidents of abuse have occurred. If multiple incidents are involved, statements may also appear inconsistent because the child is actually revealing an additional incident or new details about a previously reported experience. Progressive disclosure is a well-documented process in child abuse literature. (See, e.g., Sorensen, T., & Snow, B. [1991]. How children tell: The process of disclosure in child sexual abuse. *Child Welfare, 50, 3.*)

The inability of a victim who has been repeatedly abused over a long period to identify dates should not in itself detract from the victim's credibility. For example, in *State v. Brown*, 780 P.2d 880 (Wash. Ct. App. 1989), an 11-year-old victim could identify the date of only one of hundreds of times her stepfather molested her. The appellate court upheld convictions on six separate counts, noting that it would be impractical to require victims to pinpoint dates when the accused has had virtually unchecked access to the victim. The victim was able to provide detailed descriptions for each count, leading the court to hold that "rendering such testimony inadequate [would mean] the most egregious child molesters effectively would be insulated from prosecution. We cannot countenance such a result." (*Id.* at 886.)

D. Sexual Knowledge or Behavior That Is Developmentally Unusual

When young children verbalize or act out adult forms of sexuality, ask others to perform sexual acts, or use sexual talk, they are demonstrating developmentally unexpected sexual behavior and knowledge. On the other hand, when children are using "poop" and "pee" talk, asking about others' bodies, or even trying to touch others out of curiosity, they are likely demonstrating age-appropriate sexual behavior. For instance, a child who is bathing with a parent and reaches for her breasts or his genitals is more likely showing natural curiosity than deviant sexual knowledge. See Chapter I for further discussion of children's sexual behavior as an indicator of abuse. An investigator should explore what knowledge or behavior is developmentally appropriate and what is not appropriate.

E. Developmentally Appropriate Language

Children's disclosures should be expressed using language that is consistent with their age and developmental capacity. The interviewer must let the child establish the terminology and then adopt the child's terminology during the interview. For example, a 3-year-old child's description of sexual abuse as, "My dad peed on my tummy . . . he was pressing his butt against my butt and we were stuck together" is graphic and appropriate to that age. It is unlikely an adult would have coached a child using such a description. Children coached to make a disclosure are likely to use language unexpected for children their age. They often use abstract terminology, such as, "He abused me," or descriptions that are unlike those typically heard from young children, such as, "He exposed himself to me" rather than, "He showed me his wiener." Statements with poor grammar such as, "He be's naughty to me" are likely the child's own words.

This being said, an investigator should still closely examine a child's account that uses unusual language, as she may simply be precocious in her ability to use adult terminology. The words and phrases taught by the parents or caregiver should also be explored to determine if exact terminology is used with the child, such as vagina versus "pee pee." The investigator should identify a witness who can testify concerning the terminology used by the family and the education the child received about names for body parts. If a child uses an unexpected word or phrase, the investigator should be alert for these same terms in the suspect's statement. If the words are the same as the offender's words, the prosecutor can effectively use these similarities during his or her argument.

Later statements of a child may include language used by others and may sound less credible. In such cases, the investigator should look at the child's earlier statements and descriptions and then ask who taught the child those more adult-like words.

F. Play and Gestures Indicative of Abuse

The abuse of the child may have been detected because the child engaged in sexualized play with toys or pets. Again, the interviewer must consider whether the play is normal sexual play or exploration. After the child discloses the abuse, the parent or caregiver may connect the report of abuse to previously observed sexual play. If the parent punished the child for the play, the child may be unwilling to describe the "play."

Many children make spontaneous gestures during their interviews that vividly demonstrate their sexual knowledge and how the abuse was perpetrated. One example might be a child putting her hand on the back of her head to show how the perpetrator kept her mouth on his penis.

G. Idiosyncratic Detail

While it is possible for children to fabricate detailed accounts, details consistent with the account can be persuasive. These details may include perceptual information such as how the suspect's genitals smelled or how his beard felt. A young child who has been sexually abused will often demonstrate an accurate knowledge of sexual anatomy and functioning that is inconsistent with the child's developmental age. For example, a 4- or 5-year old child may describe the suspect's penis becoming erect and then the suspect ejaculating, perhaps after masturbation, with such description and detail that there can be little doubt that the child witnessed the sexual act by the male suspect.

The details disclosed by the child may include information the child could know only if he or she was abused by the perpetrator. For example, the child may know about a tattoo on the perpetrator's body or where the perpetrator keeps his condoms. A child's description of details such as taste or the texture of semen will help eliminate other potential sources of knowledge for this information such as cable television, pornographic magazines or movies, or witnessing others engaged in sexual activity.

Often a child will recount idiosyncratic or highly personalized details that lend credibility to her statement, such as stating what she was thinking, how the abuse act felt, or details significant to the child. A child's total inability to furnish details that demonstrate familiarity with the sex act forced upon the child may indicate the absence of abuse. Still, the child's lack of richness of detail may be due to the child's cognitive or linguistic abilities or to the difficulty the child has in disclosing the abuse.

H. Content of the Statement

In addition to assessing the child's vocabulary, the details provided, the consistency of the statement, and the general emotional response of the child, the investigator must also consider whether the actions that the child describes make sense. Is the child describing something that is physically impossible? Could the child or someone else have misinterpreted an innocent touch as sexual? Does the child's description seem to fit common patterns of abusive situations? The investigator must elicit all the details and use common sense when evaluating the child's account of an abuse act. Suzanne Sgroi, in *Handbook of Clinical Intervention in Child Sexual Abuse* (Free Press, 1982), considers the presence of the following factors indicative of credibility:

- Descriptions of multiple incidents over time, particularly when the suspected offender is known to and has a relationship with the child.
- A description of a progression of sexual activity over a period of time, rather than in a single incident, especially if the abuse is occurring within the family. For example, the child may describe the abuse as beginning with fondling, followed by the offender introducing oral sex prior to vaginal or anal intercourse.
- Elements of secrecy indicating an express or implied understanding between the suspect and the child that the child is not to tell.
- Elements of coercion indicating the offender's misuse of power and authority including
  - The engagement phase: a misrepresentation of moral standards and/or the use of bribes or coercion to force or trick a child into submitting to sexual activity
  - The secrecy phase: tactics similar to those in the engagement phase to prevent disclosure
  - The suppression phase: pressure to undermine the child's credibility and force the child to withdraw the complaint following disclosure.

Even when the child describes something that sounds fantastic, it does not necessarily mean everything he or she is saying is false. The child may be repeating something she is convinced of because of the abuser's explanations. Some commentators suggest that it is helpful to view the statements of very young children along a continuum from activity that is impossible to acts that are possible but improbable, to those that are probable, and those that are confirmed. A child's description should, moreover, be interpreted from the child's point of view. The investigator must avoid jumping to conclusions. Is there a logical explanation for a child's story of dismantling and reconstructing the day-care building before her parents arrived to take her home? Could the child be talking about a replica of the day-care building made of blocks? Similarly, if a child said the suspect kept lions in the basement, could an adult have said that to ensure that the child stays out of the basement? If the child's statements are viewed in the context of a continuum, it is possible to see that because a child says one thing that does not seem literally true, it does not follow that his or her entire account is untrue. Finally, the investigator can sometimes corroborate the child's statements by physical evidence, photographs, and confessions.

At some point during the course of a career, the investigator will likely encounter descriptions of abuse that sound very strange and even unbelievable. These could involve pornography or sadistic or ritualistic behavior, perhaps with satanic or other cult-type overtones. This behavior can occur in both physical and sexual abuse situations. The more outrageous the abuse described, the more skepticism it creates, since most people prefer not to believe such acts could actually be perpetrated against children. Practices involving urination (urolagnia) and defecation (coprophilia) in connection with abuse may be outside the knowledge of some professionals, who either discount the child's statement or prematurely conclude such activity inevitably signals cult activity. In fact, such ordinary sexual deviance is often unrelated to Satanism or cults. A child's detailed description of bizarre behavior, assuming the things described are not physically impossible and the child is otherwise in touch with reality, can add to, rather than detract from, the child's credibility. When children report what appear to be bizarre or improbable details in their accounts, the investigator must not dismiss these reports without first trying to understand what the child is trying to describe and the possibility the child is correct. (See Everson, M. D. [1997]. Understanding bizarre, improbable, and fantastic elements in children's accounts of abuse. *Child Maltreatment, 2,* 134; Lanning, K. [1992]. *Investigator's guide to allegations of "ritual" child abuse.* Quantico, VA: National Center for the Analysis of Violent Crime; Lanning, K. [1992]. *Child sex rings: A behavioral analysis* [2nd ed.]. Alexandria, VA: National Center for Missing & Exploited Children.)

I. The Child's Manner and Emotional Response

A child's reactions and general demeanor during the interview may give the investigator a sense of whether an account is genuine. The investigator must note all of the child's verbal and nonverbal emotions during the interview and include those emotions in the written report of the interview. The ability to capture the child's emotions is one of the greatest advantages of videotaping the child's interview.

When a child is hesitant to discuss questions related to anatomy or abuse, take note whether she appears to feel shameful or afraid, especially if she tells how she is feeling. A child who feels guilty about the abuse, fearful of her revelation's negative consequences, or truly concerned for the welfare of the suspect, is showing characteristics compatible with honesty. Children who become fearful and evasive are probably afraid. Listen to the child's tone and watch for nonverbal cues. For instance, a child describing oral sex may make a face when she says, "It was yucky!" While an emotional response increases the reliability of the report, the absence of emotionality is not automatically an indicator the child was not abused. The absence more likely reflects the child's resignation to the abuse, the use of dissociation as a coping mechanism, or the child's resilience in his or her ability to manage the abuse without emotional problems.

It is dangerous to place too much weight on the interpretation of any particular emotional response since behavior is more subjective than objective. While the literature on child sexual abuse suggests that certain reactions from victims can be expected, there is no single "normal" reaction of a "real victim" during an interview. Children, like adults, are individuals and their reactions vary greatly based on their individuality.

J. The Existence of a Motive to Fabricate

The assessment should consider what motives the child may have to fabricate the abuse or the motives others may have to coach a child to allege abuse. The investigator should remember that when children lie it is normally to avoid trouble rather than create it, and the disclosure of abuse typically has many negative consequences. The younger the child the less able she is to invent or maintain a cohesive story about abuse, particularly sexual abuse. Further, the mere existence of motives to fabricate should not lead the investigator to conclude that an allegation is invalid. For instance, an adolescent being sexually abused by her stepfather may finally report the abuse after he imposes severe restrictions on her freedom. Offenders are adept at trying to confuse motive and reliability. It is essential not to confuse the motive for reporting with the truthfulness of the report.

If the child is old enough to tell an investigator, ask her what she would like to see happen as a result of having disclosed the abuse. This response should be compared for consistency with the feelings expressed about the abuse and the perpetrator. Some children simply wish for the abuse to stop but wish no negative consequences for the perpetrator. Other children are angry and want to see the perpetrator punished. They may express their anger in extreme ways with statements, such as, "He should go to prison for life so he can't do this to anyone else."

The investigator must consider the possibility that the child may be seeking a result that occurred before, or in the situation of a recantation, the child may be trying to avoid a result that happened before. Consider the following factors:

- How did the police, social workers, teachers, and others treat the child?
- Was the child removed from the home? If so, where was the child placed?
- How did the child get along in the out-of-home placement?
- Did the child have to change schools? How did the child feel about the change?
- What happened to the family financially?
- How did people (family and nonfamily) react to the child?
- Did the child get special attention, or did other family members ostracize the child?

It must also be remembered that an abused child is often victimized by more than one abuser. This is true with both physical abuse and intrafamilial and nonfamilial sexual abuse. The child who has been sexually abused may equate affection with sex and may behave provocatively (consciously or subconsciously) to attract attention or exhibit behavior that can make the child vulnerable to further abuse. Similarly, a child exposed to physical abus in a violent family may continue to be abused after the initial offender has left the home if the nonabusing parent continues to have relationships with abusive people.

A common defense is to present the disclosure not as a purposeful manipulation, but as confusion on the child's part. Be sure to provide an opportunity in the interview for the child to demonstrate that she can distinguish between previous and current abuse experiences. An example of such an opportunity is to use statements such as, "Did your dad do the same thing the babysitter did when you were little? Tell me what's different."

K. The Child Corrects the Interviewer

Look for instances where the child corrected or failed to agree with the interviewer. When the child corrects the interviewer, it is clear she is listening attentively and is not overly suggestive. When yes-or-no questions are asked and the child replies, "No," she is demonstrating that she is not merely agreeing with the interviewer as the defense may contend, but she is relating what did and did not occur.

Summary of Indicators of Report Validity in Sexual Abuse Cases

- Medical evidence
- Forensic evidence
- The child's statement
- Statement spontaneity
- Consistency—both internally in the statement and across the statements
- Developmentally unusual sexual knowledge/behavior
- Idiosyncratic detail
- Developmentally appropriate language
- Play and gestures indicative of abuse
- The child's manner and emotional responses
- Lack of motive to fabricate
- The child corrects interviewer
- The offender's statement

L. Allegations of Abuse in Divorce and Custody Cases

In no other circumstance is the concern about false allegations greater than when the accusation against a parent surfaces during a divorce or a custody dispute. These situations are among the most difficult to assess, but they still deserve serious attention. All the factors previously discussed must still be considered and evaluated. (See MacFarlane, K., et al. [1986]. *Sexual abuse of young children* [p. 121]. New York: Guilford Press.)

The primary worry about disclosures during a divorce and custody dispute is that one parent coached the child in order to hurt the other parent or to gain custody. Many professionals who deal regularly with abuse cases recognize that, while false allegations are not impossible, they are most likely rare. (See Thoennes, N., & Tjaden, P. [1990]. The extent, nature and validity of sexual abuse allegations in custody visitation disputes. *Child Abuse & Neglect, 14,* 151.) Parents who genuinely care for their children are unlikely to put them through the distress that accompanies abuse allegations unless they really believe something happened.

The investigator should pay attention to the origin of the initial report. Did the report originate from the child or from the parent? If the child confided in someone other than her parent, there may be less reason to suspect coaching. Carefully investigate whether the child made a prior complaint, such as to a friend, that has been kept secret. Factors that indicate coaching include the child's eagerness to talk about "abuse," the use of adult words, the lack of variation in the descriptions, and a lack of convincing detail in the statements.

Legitimate reasons may exist for a delay in disclosure or a disclosure after the initiation of a divorce or custody battle. The investigator should try to determine the child's reasons for disclosing abuse at the time of the divorce or custody proceedings. However, the investigator must be careful with the use of "why" questions. The use of "why" questions in an inappropriate manner may cause the child to feel guilty or shameful and result in an untrue recantation. The following factors should be considered as alternative reasons for the disclosure during a custody battle:

- The abuse may have started after the couple separated, and it was precipitated by the stress of the separation.
- The offender's motivation may have less to do with sexual propensities and more to do with a desire to punish the other parent.
- The offender may be a parent's new partner or the child of a parent's new partner, and so the abuse did not begin until after the separation.
- The period following the separation may be the first safe opportunity for the child to reveal abuse by a perpetrator who is now gone from the home or about to leave.
- The child may also fear the prospect of having to visit or live alone with the abuser.
- The nonoffending parent may, for the first time, feel safe enough to make a report.
- The nonoffending parent may, for the first time, be receptive to the child's allegation and willing to offer support.

When interviewing the child, simply ask the child if she has spoken with the nonoffending parent about the abuse and what the nonoffending parent said to the child. In addition, ask the child for sensory detail. If a child describes performing fellatio on her father, ask the child about the taste, smells, and sounds. It is possible that a nonoffending parent may have coached a child into describing an act of fellatio, but it is unlikely the child was coached about sensory details of the act. A child who provides sensory details is, more probably than not, a victim of abuse.

The investigator can also learn a lot by meeting with and evaluating the reactions of the nonoffending parent. It is often possible to tell if this parent has coached the child to lie. For instance, the parent may refuse to let the investigator speak with the child alone or respond with a pleased reaction in learning of the child's "disclosure." In other circumstances, a parent who is fabricating abuse may refuse to accept that the child did not disclose abuse during the interview and may begin the process of "expert shopping" until "abuse" is substantiated. Talking with a parent also allows the opportunity to consider whether there is a possibility of misinterpretation or overreaction to what someone saw or something the child said or did. It can also help uncover whether the child could have a reason for making an untrue allegation. It is always important to remember that children and parents infrequently make deliberate false allegations.

III. COMMON PROBLEMS ENCOUNTERED IN INTRAFAMILIAL SEXUAL ABUSE CASES

The following discussion includes a list of the most commonly encountered problems that prosecutors and investigators deal with when handling intrafamilial sexual abuse cases. Many people are unwilling to accept that a biological parent or stepparent would engage in sexual activity with his or her child. It is much easier for community members to believe that the child is confused and misinterpreted an innocent touch or an act, or that the child is lying out of vindictiveness toward the suspect.

The best method to battle against disbelief of this type of abuse is *ongoing* education of the public. The public needs to be made aware of and understand that intrafamilial sexual abuse happens in all socioeconomic classes and in all communities. This information can be disseminated through effective use of the media by way of public service announcements and press releases after a conviction. Information about intrafamilial sexual abuse can also be incorporated into existing public talks about domestic violence, child abuse, and other forms of victimization.

A. Disclosure Reasons

It is common to mistakenly believe that the disclosure that initiated the case is the first and only disclosure the child has made. This is not typically the case. In fact, thorough interviews with people associated with the case will likely reveal that the child made a series of gradual disclosures over a period of time before making the disclosure that started the investigation. For example, an interviewer might discover the child made statements about having problems with the offender or about not wanting to be alone with the offender. The child might have told someone that she did not like the way the offender hugged her. All of these statements may have occurred before the child finally disclosed the perpetrator's abuse. This "full" disclosure should not be viewed as the only outcry, but rather as the culmination of a series of small disclosures. The investigator must look for these types of statements when interviewing potential witnesses.

While there are any number of situations or circumstances that may bring about the child's disclosure of sexual abuse, many of these situations are twisted by defense attorneys to suggest that the allegation is false and motivated by reasons other than sexual abuse. The following reasons may prompt a child to disclose the abuse.

1. Restricting the Child's Growth Away From the Family Unit

As children grow older and develop their social skills, they desire to be with their peers and develop relationships outside the family. While this type of growth may be very normal, it can be somewhat disturbing for parents to see their children become independent and grow away from them. It is natural for many parents to struggle with this new independence and, at some level, restrict or supervise this growth. A defense attorney may be able to convince a jury that the parent's appropriate restrictions and supervision prompted a false report by an angry child.

For the intrafamilial offender, control over the victim is paramount. Control ensures the perpetrator's ownership of the victim and reduces the likelihood of a disclosure. Often, this control becomes a strong point of contention between the victim and the perpetrator, and the victim may disclose the abuse as a means of breaking the control. The investigator must identify the controls and restrictions used by the offender. Many times the prosecutor may be able to demonstrate that the perpetrator went to the extreme and that these excessive controls and restrictions were really a reflection of the offender's desire to maintain an abusive relationship.

2. Outside Intervention and Influences

A common defense argument is that outside interventions and influences "planted ideas in the child's head" and thus brought about a false allegation. This defense can be very effective because it offers an explanation for the allegation without attacking the victim directly. The most common of these outside interventions and influences are school sex education programs, boyfriends and girlfriends, therapists, movies, publications, and various other outside sources. Many incest victims do disclose when exposed to information and supportive persons. However, it must be understood that the disclosure is not the result of a fantasy or implanted idea, but rather the result of the child discovering that this type of activity is not normal behavior and is against the law.

3. The Perpetrator Accuses the Child of Being Promiscuous

Unfortunately, many sexual abuse victims adopt sexually active and/or risky behaviors. This type of behavior, especially in smaller communities, may be known to the jury and can easily be used by the defense to explain the reactions of the perpetrator. The key point for the investigator and prosecutor to remember is that much of the literature indicates that these behaviors are "learned." The victim has learned these behaviors from the perpetrator. If this type of behavior exists, the investigation must work toward identifying where the child learned the sexual behavior. To the extent the behaviors come into evidence at all, the prosecutor can argue the behaviors do not detract from, but rather enhance, the reliability of the allegations.

4. Molestation of Younger Siblings

It is not uncommon in intrafamilial cases for the perpetrator to turn his or her attention away from an older sibling toward younger siblings in the family. This may be the result of the current victim's resisting a certain activity or even leaving the family. Many people assume that a victim discloses abuse to protect younger siblings when the perpetrator begins to "groom" them for molestation or to actually molest them. While this is the reason for disclosure in some cases, it is not the most common reason. The most common reason for the disclosure under this circumstance is that the current victim resents being replaced, pushed aside, and losing status within the family unit. Disclosing the abuse is a way to fight back. Regardless of why the victim discloses, it is unlikely that the other siblings will back up the disclosure.

Unless they have observed the abuse or have been abused themselves, the siblings who are not abused can be jealous of the attention that is given to the victim by the perpetrator. During the grooming process, the sibling recognizes that she is now getting some of the attention that she has longed for and will very quickly align herself with the perpetrator against the victim. The cooperation of these siblings with the investigator and prosecutor is normally very limited, and they are protective of the perpetrator. The approach in this situation is for a skilled interviewer to gather information from the siblings that demonstrates a distinct change in attention toward them by the perpetrator. This may enable the prosecutor to argue that these children are being groomed for future molestation.

5. Jealousy Between Mother and Child

The dynamic of jealousy between mother and child is sometimes noted in long-term molestation cases. Some incestuous relationships develop to the point that the child is given the status within the family unit normally reserved for the nonabusive spouse. When this level of substitution takes place, it can create a power struggle within the family and may result in the nonabusive spouse making the disclosure to the authorities. When this happens, the perpetrator and the victim may join forces to discount the allegation of the nonabusive spouse. Be aware that conducting the forensic interview of the child too quickly could result in the child's denying the allegations. The most effective approach in this circumstance is to separate the victim from the influence of the perpetrator before conducting the interview.

6. Parental Discovery or Confrontation

Parental discovery occurs when the nonabusive spouse catches the perpetrator and the victim engaged in some form of sexual activity. This direct and undeniable confrontation will generally bring about a disclosure by the confronting spouse. The investigator should move quickly to isolate the victim from the influence of the suspect. Given the opportunity, perpetrators can be very effective in convincing the victim that the situation may be blamed on her and convince the child to deny that anything was going on. It may be appropriate to obtain a protective order or no contact order to prevent the suspect from having contact with the child. At the same time, the investigator and prosecutor should carefully evaluate whether it is appropriate to leave the victim in the care of the nonabusive parent. If the nonabusive parent is not supportive of the victim, it may be wise to place the child elsewhere. Unless it is stressed and constantly reinforced to the victim that she has done nothing wrong and that she has no blame or fault in the situation, the prosecutor may very quickly have a recanting victim.

7. The Child Becomes a Habitual Runaway

It is not uncommon for a victim to run away to escape the abuse. For a number of reasons, the perpetrator will act like most parents and work very hard to locate the child and have the child returned home. However, the victim will continue to run and eventually will become known or classified as a habitual runaway. The victims often do not trust the system and are therefore unlikely to make a disclosure. Because of the activities that many runaways engage in during the running episodes, their credibility is seriously questioned when they finally disclose. In this situation, the investigative process should concentrate on identifying early disclosures before the child began to run away. While there are exceptions to the rule, it is critical to understand that most children do not run away simply for the sake of running.

B. The Victim

Victims of intrafamilial sexual abuse may display a wide range of defenses and coping mechanisms. At one extreme, the child may be withdrawn, quiet, and choose not to interact with anyone. The child may intentionally make herself unattractive in order to discourage the perpetrator and others from having contact with her. At the other extreme, the child may engage in risky behaviors, become very sexually active, develop a threatening or provocative appearance, or exhibit seductive behavior toward adults.

Investigators must understand that all of these behaviors are learned behaviors. The investigator should try to identify and document when these changes in the child began to take place. If the investigation establishes a correlation between when the child began to exhibit these behaviors and the onset of the sexual abuse, this evidence can be used very effectively to corroborate the child's statement.

C. The Family

In a large percentage of cases, the victim's family is supportive of the offender by the time the case comes to trial. For this reason, it is critical that the family's early statements, made while they are still cooperating, be well documented. The safest assumption for the investigator and prosecutor to make is that the family members will come to the support of the perpetrator.

D. Delayed Reporting

There are commonly two types of reporting delays in intrafamilial sexual abuse cases, and each poses a unique problem during prosecution. One delay occurs between the time when the abuse begins and the time when there is a disclosure that results in the investigation. On average, it takes 3 to 5 years before the incestuous relationship comes to the attention of the authorities. Many individuals, especially jurors, react to the length of the relationship with the belief that if it were as bad as it seems, why did the victim wait so long to disclose the abuse? Again, this is when the investigator should work to identify other disclosures the victim made during the time of the abuse.

The second reporting delay occurs between the time of the last assault and the time of the actual report. The problem posed by this delay is the loss of any physical evidence. This delay results from the emotional struggle that the victim faces when deciding whether to disclose and the consequences that may result from that disclosure.

E. Evidence

A major problem when prosecuting most intrafamilial sexual abuse cases is the perceived lack of evidence. It is true that many of these cases lack hard, conclusive physical and medical evidence. This lack of hard evidence results from a variety of reasons, including victim behavior such as delayed reporting, the secrecy of the crime, victim grooming, and the proximity of the perpetrator to the victim. However, it is imperative that investigators still employ *all* of the standard evidence-gathering techniques that would be used for any type of sexual assault crime. Far too often, the crime scene, most often the residence, is not processed by law enforcement because the delay in reporting causes evidence to be lost or destroyed. It is also believed that if trace evidence is found, it would be expected because the victim and perpetrator both live in the residence. However, this is not always the situation. For instance, it may not be uncommon to find the perpetrator's pubic hairs in the bed of the victim because they live together. However, the prosecutor may be able to argue that the quantity of pubic hair far exceeded that which would be found from normal cohabitation. Generally, there are plausible explanations for the lack of hard physical and medical evidence in these cases.

The most common form of evidence in these cases is the circumstantial and corroborative evidence that can demonstrate that the child is a credible witness and an accurate historian of the facts. For this reason, the investigator and prosecutor should identify the various segments of the child's statement that can be corroborated by other individuals. For instance, the child states her father was wearing a pair of underwear that had a specific pattern or tear in them. The investigator should obtain a search warrant to locate that article of clothing. The child may have stated that right after the abuse incident, she watched a particular episode of a television program. The investigator should check with the programming division of the television station to corroborate the child's statement. This type of information may also help to establish the date and time of the assault.

F. Information Sharing

In child abuse cases, a number of agencies can have information that is valuable to the investigation and to the prosecutor when making decisions about the case. These groups or agencies could include social services, schools, mental health professionals, medical professionals, public health, clergy, and many others. The failure to obtain this information in a timely manner directly impacts the prosecutor's ability to make an informed case decision. This issue can be avoided by creating a multidisciplinary team that is built on policies, procedures, and protocols that ensure a free flow of case-relevant and case-appropriate information. If a multidisciplinary team does not exist or is ineffective, the prosecutor should give serious consideration to subpoenaing the records from each of these agencies that pertain to the child and the family.

IV. INTERVIEWING WITNESSES IN SEXUAL AND PHYSICAL ABUSE CASES

A. Purpose

Law enforcement investigators should always be involved in an interview if a violation of criminal law is suspected. During the interview, the interviewer should be alert for direct and circumstantial evidence as well as for potential defense claims. The prosecutor should encourage investigating officers to begin identifying and interviewing potential witnesses as soon as possible. Some witnesses will be obvious, such as the person who reported the allegation to authorities, the suspect's spouse, and other members of the child's family. Other witnesses can be identified from the interview with the child victim. The primary objectives for interviewing witnesses are discussed below.

Determine the person's knowledge of the offense(s). Child sexual abuse, especially the act of incest, is normally a very private crime. It is unusual to have nonparticipating witnesses who can say they saw the act take place. Most witnesses are unaware that they have any information that is helpful to prove or disprove the allegation. For these reasons, the interviews of these witnesses focus more on events and incidents that occurred before and after the abuse.

Identify potential defense claims. Witnesses who support the suspect may state that the child has had problems in the family, school behavior problems, emotional problems, or problems in the community.

Establish corroboration for the child's statement. It is critical that the forensic interview of the child be structured to obtain information concerning events leading up to and after the assault being described. Following the interview, collateral witnesses can be interviewed to corroborate the child's statements about events that occurred before and after the abuse. These witnesses can also help determine when the suspect had access to the child, in order to establish a time frame for the abuse.

Gain an understanding of the family dynamics in intrafamilial cases. In intrafamilial cases, witnesses can provide the investigator with an understanding of the family dynamics by relating their observations of how the family functions. This information is helpful to the prosecutor to document behaviors that may be unusual.

B. Witness Stages

Potential witnesses in child abuse cases can go through several reaction stages depending on their individual ties to the family unit, the victim, and the suspect and their response to the heinous nature of the assault. However, these stages are most noticeable in cases of intrafamilial sexual abuse as opposed to extrafamilial. There is no formula for determining how long an individual will be in a particular stage. The depth of the individual's connection to the interested parties will determine how many of these stages the investigator and prosecutor will see. Witnesses's reactions primarily depend on their closeness to the situation and their feeling about the nature of the offense.

1. Shock and Self-Defense

This stage occurs when the investigator or prosecutor first approaches the individual and that individual realizes that he may become involved in the case. The witness generally expresses shock and disbelief that the suspect could or would commit such an act. It is generally not wise to push the individual for information at this stage, as that will not generally yield a positive result.

It is normally better to give the witness an opportunity to deal with his emotions and simply let that person know that at some point in the investigation he will be asked to provide a statement. It is a good idea for the investigator to provide the witness with contact information so he can get in touch with the investigator.

2. Cooperation

Most potential witnesses eventually react with some degree of cooperation. It is at this stage that the investigator has the opportunity to gather information relevant to the investigation. It is imperative that all information gathered during this stage be well documented. Depending on accepted practices in individual jurisdictions, a very useful tool is a tape recorder. This enables the investigator to document exactly what was said and how it was said. This type of documentation can prove invaluable to the investigator during interrogation of the suspect and to the prosecutor to impeach or challenge the credibility of the individual at trial.

3. Offender Support

Unfortunately, the majority of witnesses will enter the final stage of supporting the offender because of the dynamics and denial surrounding child abuse. At this point, these individuals will become very uncooperative and any information obtained is questionable. It is not uncommon for an individual to contact the investigator and want to change or recant statements that were made during the cooperation stage. This is why it is critical that the information obtained is well documented and preferably tape recorded. The investigator should not assume that witnesses who support the offender cannot be helpful to the prosecutor. Ask each of these witnesses if he or she has spoken to the defendant about the allegations and, if so, what the defendant has said. In many cases, the defendant will have denied the event to his relatives and friends, but the denial will vary in significant ways. For example, the defendant may have given an alibi to one friend and, to another, said he was with the victim but claim that others were present who could verify his innocence. Variations in the defendant's denials can be powerful evidence that it is not the child, but the defendant, who is inconsistent when speaking about the allegations.

C. The Benefits of Early Interviews

Early interviews by specially trained police investigators are crucial. Early interviews will help avoid unpleasant surprises later. The investigator can pin down the witnesses' statements before they forget relevant details or before their accounts are tainted by information from outside sources or by bias toward the child or suspect. Early interviews help police uncover additional evidence before it is lost, hidden, or destroyed. The interviews can also help educate and enlist cooperation of additional witnesses. While a prosecutor will undoubtedly want to talk with some of these witnesses prior to a charging decision and trial, the prosecutor should not be the first or only person to contact the witness. Besides being too late to obtain the maximum benefit from any information the interview might produce, a one-on-one interview leaves the prosecutor without a witness to testify at trial for impeachment or on rebuttal. For this reason, prosecutors who interview potential witnesses should make a practice of having a third party present.

D. Conducting the Interviews and the Content of Reports

All witnesses should be interviewed separately, and investigators should refrain from telling one witness what others have said. The facts related by these witnesses should be set forth in the officer's report in as much detail as possible and in the witnesses' own words. The investigator should use quotation marks only to indicate the witness's *exact* words. The investigator should try to obtain a tape-recorded or signed statement from all witnesses. The safest approach for investigators is to work with an assumption that all witnesses might change their statements before trial. Some investigators ask witnesses to read and sign their notes. Other investigators obtain notarized statements. Although witnesses can be asked to write their own statements, this type of statement will not always cover everything the investigator would ask about and want to know. Prosecutors can sometimes use grand jury proceedings to obtain sworn testimony from uncooperative witnesses.

Investigators should consider using a tape recorder for documenting interviews with all witnesses. Tape recorders are easy to use, nonthreatening, and portable. The investigator must ensure that this is in compliance with departmental policy and procedures and that the tapes are handled like any other piece of evidence. There should be no more than one interview per tape. Each interview should begin by stating on tape the date, place, time, and persons present. Given the option to have the interview recorded or to provide a handwritten statement, most witnesses will agree to the tape recorder. A recorded interview can prove invaluable to the investigator during the interrogation process. It is also helpful to the prosecutor during trial when faced with witnesses who have decided to support the defendant.

Investigators should not insert personal opinions or conclusions in their reports. This is especially important in child abuse cases because defense attorneys will seize on any opinions appearing in the reports to discredit the child or to argue that the officer's bias tainted the entire investigation. Claims that investigators "program" children to make unfounded allegations or engage in witch hunts can be defeated if a thorough and objective approach is reflected in investigative reports.

The investigator should talk with witnesses in person rather than over the phone so that observations about the appearance and demeanor of the witness can be recorded. Besides providing information with which to assess the credibility of the witness, a face-to-face meeting allows the witness to assess the competence of the investigator and, one would hope, for the investigator to instill trust and a desire to cooperate. The interviewer must be professional and must not mislead the witness or make false promises.

Witnesses likely to be in contact with the child or each other should be instructed not to question or rehearse the child, not to investigate the case on their own, and not to compare notes. Explain that these requests are aimed at assuring that information provided by the child and others is accepted as reliable and free from outside influence. For the same reason, the investigator should carefully consider the implications of relaying explicit details of the child's statement to the parents. There cannot be strict rules that apply to all situations. If the decision is made to withhold details, the investigator should reassure parents or concerned witnesses that such information will be shared after the case is resolved.

Witnesses should be asked to contact the investigating officer or the prosecutor immediately if they remember further information or observe anything new regarding the child or suspect. Encourage witnesses to document questions, observations, and statements made by the child or others. The investigator should make referrals to support groups or therapy when appropriate. To avoid a claim of contaminated testimony, the investigator should discourage the parents from involving the child in group therapy, especially with victims of the same offender(s), prior to trial. If the child's therapist feels strongly that the child needs to join a group therapy program, the investigator should make sure the child has given a detailed statement prior to the first group session. This statement will be useful at trial to rebut any implication of contamination of the child's testimony owing to therapy.

E. Reporters and Others to Whom the Child Made Statements

The person who first reported the allegation to authorities should be promptly interviewed to determine what precipitated the report. If the child's revelation caused the complainant to suspect abuse, the investigator needs to ascertain the circumstances of the disclosure. The same information should be sought from anyone else to whom the child made statements about the abuse. Pay careful attention to whether these witnesses have anything to gain or lose as a result of the allegation. Pertinent factors include their relationship to the suspect and child, attitudes toward each person, and the person's attitudes toward the allegation. Explore the following areas during questioning:

- What were the circumstances of the disclosure?
- Did the child deliberately and voluntarily disclose the abuse or did the child accidentally say something that caused the witness to suspect abuse?
- Was anyone else present during the disclosure?
- What were the exact words the child used?
- What was the child's emotional state during the disclosure?
- How does the child typically react when upset or under stress?
- What concerns did the child express about disclosing the abuse?
- Did he or she provide details? If so, what were they and how were the details elicited?
- What was the child's attitude toward the suspect?
- How did the witness react to the child's disclosure?
- What did the witness say to the child?
- Is the witness aware of any reason the child might lie about what happened?
- Does the witness know of any other source from which the child could have learned sexually explicit information that would enable her to make a credible sounding, but false, complaint?
- If the child has physical injuries or if there is medical evidence, does the witness know of a reason for the injuries or evidence that is inconsistent with the child's account?
- Does the witness know anything else about the child or suspect that might be relevant?

In addition to providing the investigator with useful information, the witness's responses to all of the foregoing questions will affect whether the child's statements can be introduced as evidence at trial under special or traditional hearsay exceptions.

If the person reporting the abuse allegation has not spoken with the child, the interviewer must ascertain precisely what the reporter saw or heard. Even if the reporter did not speak to the child, the reporter's attitudes, relationship to the child and suspect, and motives are equally important. Such information will form the basis for further investigation aimed at verifying or refuting the allegation.

F. Nonoffending Parents or Caregivers

The child's parent(s) or caregiver(s) are an extremely important source of knowledge about the child. The caregiver's support or lack of support for the child is a crucial factor in the success of the prosecution, since this involvement can be either a tremendous help or hindrance to the process.

Interviews with the child's parent(s) or caregiver(s) should first focus on their concerns. Investigators can then attempt to enlist their cooperation, instill confidence, and obtain information about the child and the suspect. These witnesses should be asked questions about the child's well-being and behavior before and after disclosure. Their general observations as well as the details the child may have shared with them can corroborate the allegation and thus should be solicited immediately. If more than one child is involved, parents will often want to know what the other child is disclosing. The investigator must explain why this information cannot be shared with them. The investigator must also explain why the parents need to refrain from seeking that information themselves. Caution them against investigating the case on their own. The investigator or prosecutor should maintain contact with the parents throughout the criminal justice process and provide updates on the progress of the case.

Suggested questions for the parent(s) or caregiver(s) include:

- What, if anything, did the child say about the abuse?
- Does the child talk about the abuse?
- Did the child exhibit any unusual behavior before or after disclosure such as changes in sleep patterns, bad dreams, bedwetting, changes in conduct or school performance, clinging, fear of the suspect, complaints of pain, or any other possible reactions to abuse?
- What is the child's medical history? The investigator should secure written permission to obtain hospital and medical records.
- Has the child been abused before or made previous allegations of abuse? Who was the perpetrator and what was the nature of the allegations?
- Can the witness verify any fact related by the child? This verification could include the suspect's access to the child including time spent alone with him or her; the timing of activities such as vacations, outings, and celebrations; moving to a new house or starting or ending school; unusual features of the suspect or his home, car, and belongings; and any other corroborating details.
- What was the quality of the relationship between child and suspect?
- What else is going on in the child's life? This area should cover the child's relationships with friends; involvement in hobbies or outside activities; any physical, mental, or learning disabilities; juvenile court involvement including dependency proceedings; and any other events that might be affecting the child.
- What was the witness's response to the child and the allegation? Was the witness supportive?
- Can the witness think of any reason that the defense would say the child is fabricating?
- In sexual abuse cases, what was the child's exposure to or awareness of sexual matters through contact with others, television, videos or movies, magazines, observation of adults, sex education, or other sources of sexual knowledge?

G. The Suspect's Spouse or Partner in Intrafamilial Abuse Cases

The suspect's spouse, former spouse, or significant other should always be interviewed as soon as possible. As with all potentially hostile witnesses, it is wise to either tape-record the interview or have another witness present during the interview. In many cases, the suspect's spouse or other partner is the child's nonoffending parent or caregiver. Elicit as much information about the suspect as possible from this witness.

The approach to the interview will probably depend on the witness's attitude toward the suspect. The spouse who supports the suspect will often be called as a witness by the defense if the case goes to trial, so determining her story early in the investigation has obvious advantages. She will often be the best source of information about what defense will be raised at trial. Further, the spousal privilege and spousal incompetency provisions do not apply in most states in child abuse cases. The prosecution may wish to call the spouse or significant other as a witness.

In both physical and sexual abuse cases, the following areas might be explored. The investigator should use care not to give a hostile witness information that may cause her to destroy or hide evidence or contrive a statement tailored to contradict the case.

- What has the suspect said about the allegation or the child?
- How did the suspect learn about, react to, or explain the allegation?
- Looking back, can the witness recall anything unusual, even if she did nothing about it at the time? The witness may need some encouragement if she feels guilty about not reacting and is concerned about her reputation or culpability.
- Does the suspect own, or has he ever owned, items, clothes, weapons, or other articles described by the child? If he no longer has the item, when, where, and why did he discard it?
- Was the suspect ever alone with the child? When, for how long, and who else can verify this?
- Was the suspect ever responsible for the child's care?
- What was the suspect's relationship with the child, and were there any problems between them?
- Does the witness know of a motive for the child to lie about the suspect?
- Does the suspect have contact with other children? This may assist in identifying other victims.
- Has the suspect previously been arrested for or convicted of any crime?
- Where has the suspect lived and worked?
- Have prior accusations ever been made against the suspect even if not reported to the authorities?
- Does the witness or the suspect keep a diary, calendar, address book, computer records, or other records?
- If the case involves sexual abuse alone, explore the following areas:
  - Has the suspect ever bathed the child?
  - What were the sleeping arrangements?
  - Does the suspect have any scars, tattoos, or birthmarks? Is the suspect circumcised or does he have any unusual features on or near his genitals? This information should be compared to the information provided by the child, and the suspect should be examined and photographed if appropriate.

- Does the suspect have or use pornography, such as photographs, magazines, movies, or videos; sexual aids or implements; or birth control devices?
- Has the suspect had an STD and sought treatment?
- Has the witness ever contracted an STD?
- Does the suspect engage in any distinctive sexual practices? This should be compared to the child's descriptions of the sexual abuse.
- Has the suspect had a vasectomy? This is useful if the child has indicated she was told by the suspect not to worry about pregnancy because he was "fixed."

Another area of questioning is that of the sexual relationship between the witness and the suspect. Much to the surprise of many investigators and prosecutors, nonoffending spouses or partners will provide very detailed information about this topic if they are not questioned in an accusatory or threatening manner. The reason for obtaining this information is to detect parallels and similarities in the sexual activities that the suspect engaged in with the spouse or partner and the child. It is not unusual for the incestuous relationship to be a substitute for the offender's sexual relationship with the spouse. The investigator should gather information that details not only specific sex acts but also the terminology that is used by the suspect and his patterns of behavior before and after the act.

If the case involves physical abuse alone, the questioning should explore the following areas:

- Was the suspect responsible for the discipline of the child?
- If so, what methods, implements, and/or amount of force were used?
- Was the suspect violent with the witness or anyone else?
- Did anyone else ever hit the child?
- Where was the child taken for medical care?
- Who examined and/or spoke to the child? The investigator should obtain releases for the medical records.

H. Other Family or Household Members

Other people in the child's family and household, including other children, should be interviewed. Determine whether the child told these witnesses about the abuse. Sometimes these witnesses can provide direct or indirect corroboration. Did they see or hear some aspect of the abuse, or were they asked to conceal information by either the child or the suspect? Were they asked to leave, locked out of the house or room, or otherwise distracted to prevent their witnessing the abuse? Did they observe behavioral, emotional, or physical signs of abuse? How did the child and suspect interact? Can others in the family or household verify details given by the child?

1. Grandparents

The information from grandparents should be examined closely. It is not uncommon for incest to be passed from one generation to the next. Therefore, the investigator may be talking to a perpetrator of abuse against the victim's parent or even to a perpetrator who the current victim has not yet disclosed. Even if the grandparents of the child are not potential suspects, the investigator needs to determine the relationship between them and the suspect prior to the disclosure and balance that with the information provided by the witnesses.

2. Siblings and Other Children in the Home

The victim's siblings and other children in the home can be an important source of information. If the suspect is a family member or someone known to the family, try to determine whether other children in the home were victimized. The same sensitivity called for in interviewing the reported victim should extend to other children. If they also were abused, their fear, guilt, and embarrassment can be more intense than that of the current victim since they have not yet disclosed.

a. Children still in the home. Children still living in the home may not rush to the defense and support of the disclosing victim. They may, in fact, be the first to move to the offender-support stage and do all they can to discredit the victim. These children may resent the victim because of their perception that the victim is the perpetrator's favorite child. The victim may have been given special privileges that the other children were not allowed, such as staying up late at night to watch television, not having to share a room, or taking special trips with the perpetrator.

These children may also view the victim as being responsible for

- Breaking up the family
- Putting Daddy in jail
- Causing the loss of the family home
- Preventing an older brother or sister from going to college
- Preventing the perpetrator from spending time with the family
- Upsetting the other family members

Whatever the reason for these feelings, the investigator must explore the basis for them. If the suspect is telling the other children this information to manipulate or intimidate the victim, the prosecutor can use this information at trial. This information may also explain why the child might later recant statements because the pressure at home is too much to bear.

b. Siblings or children out of the home. Contact children who have left the home to ascertain their reasons for leaving. It is not unusual to find that these children are former victims. Individuals suspected of being former victims may be very distrustful of the system, especially if they previously reported sexual abuse and the report was not handled to their satisfaction. Survivors may take pride in having survived without the help of the system and simply take the attitude that their sibling should do the same. One approach that may work with these reluctant witnesses is to offer them the opportunity to be for the current victim what no one else was for them—an advocate. The identification and cooperation of survivors can provide some of the most powerful corroboration of the child's statement.

If these individuals decide to cooperate, it is critical that their statements be taken before they have any unsupervised contact with the victim. This avoids claims that the survivor coached the current victim and contaminated the victim's statement. The investigator should look for parallels between the survivor's victimization and that of the current victim.

Investigators should also approach with caution individuals who are suspected of being a perpetrator who was pushed out of the home to avoid competition with the parent perpetrator. These individuals will protect the parent perpetrator in order to protect themselves. These individuals may also have been victims of the suspect, so they may feel the need to hide not only their own perpetration, but also their own victimization. If this situation is suspected, the first contact with the individual should be a joint interview by the investigator and prosecutor. In this situation, the prosecutor may decide to offer the individual immunity from prosecution in exchange for cooperation in the prosecution of the adult perpetrator.

If the suspect has been married before, former spouses, extended family members, and children may also be potential sources of information.

I. Additional Witnesses

1. Other Children Accessible to the Suspect

In nonfamilial abuse cases, it is extremely rare for a person to commit a single act of abuse against a single child. However, this does not mean that the perpetrator will molest or abuse every child he has contact with. The case may involve a perpetrator who has very specific characteristics for the children he abuses. These characteristics may or may not be obvious. The investigator should identify the characteristics of the current victim such as age, sex, gender, physical development, and vulnerability, and then look for other children with similar characteristics. If the suspect has access to other children through family, work, or recreational or volunteer activities, the investigator should find out who these children are and whether they have been approached or abused by the suspect. Physical evidence such as pictures in the suspect's possession or address books may provide leads regarding other possible victims. The investigator should also be aware that just because the current victim is in the family unit, this does not mean that the perpetrator did not go outside of the family unit to molest. These additional victims will most likely be other children in the neighborhood and/or friends of the current victim.

2. Other Persons in Regular Contact With the Child or Suspect

The investigator must make sure that those who may have had contact with the child or suspect during the investigation and prosecution know how to reach the investigator or prosecutor with more information or questions. This can prevent behavior that could be detrimental to the child or case, such as questioning of the victim about the abuse, spreading rumors, or changing accounts based on outside influences. When the suspect is prominent in the community and character is likely to become an issue, it is especially important to question witnesses about their knowledge of the reputations of the suspect and the child. Lock in these witnesses as early as possible in the investigation to prevent later influence by others. If the defendant is in custody prior to trial, the investigator should consider interviewing cell mates since the defendant may have revealed important information to them, including details of the crime or explanations that will be asserted as defenses at trial.

a. School personnel. It is important to remember that sexual abuse does not happen in a vacuum. When a child is abused, chances are there will be some outward reaction to the violation. The reaction will depend on the individual child's ability to cope. Therefore, it follows that the investigation must identify individuals who can attest to these reactions. No one group of professionals has more contact with school-aged children than school personnel—teachers, counselors, bus drivers, nurses, coaches, and parent volunteers. These individuals should all be interviewed to determine if they have noted behavioral changes in the child or if they have noted anything that may be a behavioral indicator of abuse. When interviewing these individuals, it may be necessary to inform them that they are mandated reporters and they cannot honor an agreement of confidentiality that they may have made with a student.

An important evidence source may be the teacher's documentation. By either state law or by school district policy and procedure, teachers and counselors are required to maintain their classroom records, such as their planning books and grade books, for a period of time usually ranging from 2 to 4 years. These records may corroborate some of the child's statements. For example, a child in one case talked about the first time, several years earlier, that her father had penetrated her. She could not provide any specifics on the date and time. However, she did remember that this was so upsetting to her that she could not think in school the next day, and as a result, had failed a history test. Her former history teacher still had her grade book and was able to document the exact date that the child failed the test. In addition, she had made a note that the child was upset about something and she had sent her to the counselor. The counselor also had notes that the child had been sent to her and was obviously upset, but would not say why. The counselor sent her to the school nurse to rest for a while before going back to class. The school nurse also had this in her records. This information provided the prosecutor with

- The exact date of the assault
- Three credible independent witnesses that the child was distraught
- Written documentation of the child's behavior following the assault
- A demonstration that the child was an accurate historian of facts

The investigator should interview the school's attendance officer to obtain the child's school attendance records, records for early dismissal, and in-school suspensions. The investigator should also interview the school nurse to identify visits to the health room and complaints of ailments. Bus drivers should be interviewed to determine the child's behavior on the bus and whether the child expressed or demonstrated any reluctance to go home.

b. Employers. An employer may not want to believe or have clientele believe the company has hired a child molester. For this reason, the employer may be defensive and supportive of the suspect. Normally, the employer can only address what kind of employee the suspect is or was. Since child abuse is unrelated to job performance, the investigator should not be surprised if the suspect is a good employee.

The employer should have the suspect's work schedule, sick leave, and vacation leave history. This may provide valuable information. For instance, a child indicated that one of the times she was molested by her father occurred on a day that she had stayed home from school sick and her father had also come home sick in the middle of the day. The employer's records showed a day of leave for the father that matched with a day the child was sick and out of school.

If there is reason to believe the suspect may collect erotica or have keepsakes from his victims, the investigator should consider obtaining a search warrant for the suspect's office, locker, or other potential hiding places at work.

3. Friends of the Victim

The investigator should identify the current and past close friends of the victim. It is likely that the victim may have made some type of statement or disclosure to one or more of these individuals. Children do not have the forethought or patience to develop a false allegation over a long period of time. If the investigator can show that the victim made some reference to the abuse at some time in the past, the prosecutor will have facts to defeat the common defense that the child is lying. The investigator should not rely just on the child and cooperative family members for friend identification. School officials and friends of the child should be asked for additional names as well.

V. ADDITIONAL INVESTIGATIVE TECHNIQUES

A. Forensic Analysis

Traditional forensic experts available through public or private crime laboratories may play a role in the investigation of child abuse cases. The investigator should take advantage of these resources whenever an investigation produces evidence that requires analysis, such as biological specimens for DNA analysis. Prosecutors handling child abuse cases should visit local facilities to gain a firsthand understanding of their capabilities. Criminologists are usually happy to explain what they can do to help the prosecution. A prosecutor who makes an effort to establish personal contact with these experts will usually be rewarded later.

B. Polygraph and Psychological Stress Evaluations (PSE)

Polygraphs (lie detectors) and psychological stress evaluations (PSEs or voice-stress analysis) are used by a number of police agencies in criminal investigations. Opinions about their reliability differ greatly. The prosecutor must be aware of whether these tools are used in the jurisdiction, and if so, how. Their primary usefulness in child abuse investigations will be with suspects. Suspects cannot be forced to undergo these examinations. The results of these tests are generally inadmissible at trial owing to their lack of scientific reliability. These investigative tools should never be the controlling factor in a decision about whether to proceed with a case. The results should represent only one more factor to consider when evaluating a case. Moreover, the results should not be a substitute for a thorough and complete investigation.

Some jurisdictions have used polygraph and PSE to validate a victim's allegation. This is strongly discouraged because of its impact on the child victim. These tools were designed with adults in mind and thus are not appropriate for use with children under 12. More often than not, this technique does not produce useful information when used with victims, and it leaves the victim feeling not believed by the investigator and prosecutor. It also sends a message to the community that child abuse victims are not as reliable as other crime victims, who are not required to undergo polygraph examinations or PSE tests before their allegations are taken seriously. In California, Colorado, and Illinois, investigators and prosecutors are prohibited from requiring or requesting an alleged victim of a sexual offense to submit to a polygraph examination as a prerequisite to filing charges. (Cal. Code § 637.4, Colo. Rev. Stat. § 18–3–407.5(2), 725 Ill. Comp. Stat. 200/1, 735 Ill. Comp. Stat. 5/2–1104.)

C. Hypnosis

A decade ago, hypnosis was widely used by police to facilitate a witness's recall of details. Today, it is used less frequently after a number of unfavorable appellate court decisions. However, the U.S. Supreme Court, in *Rock v. Arkansas,* ruled that a per se rule of exclusion for hypnotically refreshed testimony infringes on a criminal defendant's right to testify on his or her own behalf under the Sixth Amendment. (483 U.S. 44 [1987]). Some states' case law generally admits hypnotically refreshed testimony, and California, Nevada, and Oregon have statutes that explicitly outline requirements for admitting such testimony. (Cal. Evid. Code § 795, Nev. Rev Stat. Ann. § 48.039, Or. Rev. Stat. § 136.675, .685, .695.)

Witnesses to a crime who have been hypnotized are generally allowed to testify only about facts recalled before hypnosis and in some cases, may not testify at all. Hypnosis of witnesses in child abuse cases, especially the child, is therefore not recommended. The investigator must be sure to tell parents and caregivers in any case with the potential for prosecution not to have the child undergo hypnosis. If hypnosis has occurred or it is being contemplated in a case, the applicable jurisdictional law must be reviewed very carefully.

D. Single-Party Consent Taping

"Single-party consent taping" and the "pretext phone call" are the audio recording of a telephone conversation between two or more individuals with the knowledge and consent of only one of the parties involved in the conversation. Most commonly, the technique involves having the victim call the suspect, engage him in a conversation, and obtain some type of disclosure or admission to the assault. This technique can also be used effectively by having other cooperative individuals such as a spouse, coperpetrator, or other relatives call the suspect.

Table II.2	States Permitting Single-Party Consent Taping
Alabama	ALA. CODE § 13A-11-30
Alaska	ALASKA STAT. § 42.20.310
Arizona	ARIZ. REV. STAT. §§ 13–3005, -3012
Arkansas	ARK. CODE ANN. § 5-60-120
Colorado	COLO. REV. STAT. § 18–9–303
Georgia	GA. CODE ANN. §§ 16-11-62, -66
Hawaii	HAW. REV. STAT. ANN. § 803–42
Idaho	IDAHO CODE §§ 18–6701, -6702
Indiana	IND. CODE § 35–33.5–1–5
Iowa	IOWA CODE § 727.8
Kansas	KAN. STAT. ANN. §§ 21-4001, -4002
Kentucky	KY. REV. STAT. ANN. § 526.010
Louisiana	LA. REV. STAT. § 15:1303
Maine	ME. REV. STAT. ANN. TIT. 15, § 710
Minnesota	MINN. STAT. ANN. § 626A.02(3)(B)(2)
Mississippi	MISS. CODE ANN. § 41–29–531(E)
Missouri	MO. REV. STAT. § 542.402(A)(3)
Nebraska	NEB. REV. STAT. §§ 86–701, -.702(2)(C)
Nevada	NEV. REV. STAT. § 200.620(1)(A)
New Jersey	N.J. REV. STAT. §§ 2A:156A-3, -4(D)
New Mexico	N.M. STAT. ANN. § 30–12–1(3)
New York	N.Y. CRIM. PROC. LAW § 700.05(3)
North Carolina	N.C. GEN. STAT. § 15A-287
North Dakota	N.D. CENT. CODE § 12.1–15–02(3)(B)
Ohio	OHIO REV. CODE § 2933.52(B)(4)
Oklahoma	OKLA. STAT. ANN. TIT. 13, § 176.4(5)
Oregon	OR. REV. STAT. §§ 165.540(1)(A), -543
Rhode Island	R.I. GEN. LAWS § 11–35–21(C)(3)
South Dakota	S.D. CODIFIED LAWS ANN. §§ 23A-35A-1, -20
Tennessee	TENN. CODE ANN. § 39–13–601
Texas	TEX. PENAL CODE ANN. § 16.02
Utah	UTAH CODE ANN. § 76–9–403
Virginia	VA. CODE ANN. § 19.2–62(B)(2)
West Virginia	W. VA. CODE §§ 62–1D-3, -6
Wisconsin	WIS. STAT. § 968.31(2)(C)
Wyoming	WYO. STAT. ANN. § 7–3–702(B)(IV)
U.S. Code	18 U.S.C. §§ 2510 TO 2522

NOTE: This compilation lists and summarizes all the statutes that permit the audio recording of telephone calls when one party to the call voluntarily consents to the recording. This table includes all legislation passed through January 2002, as verified through Lexis Nexis.

1. Legality

Some states allow single-party consent taping without the requirement of a wiretap or overhear warrant. Other states require that the call be treated as a wiretap. Before this technique is used, the investigator and prosecutor must determine its legality. If the call is being made across jurisdictional boundaries, the investigator and prosecutor should check the requirements in both jurisdictions. The prosecutor needs to determine the receptiveness of the courts to this technique as well.

2. Cautions

While this is a very effective technique, it is simply another investigative tool. It is not a substitute for a thorough investigation, and it should never be used as a shortcut. This technique is not appropriate for every suspected case of child abuse, and it should be used only after careful consideration and discussion between the investigator and prosecutor. It is also wise to consult with the child's therapist or other professional to be sure the victim is emotionally able to confront the offender.

The caller has to call the suspect under some type of false pretense in order for this technique to work. In essence, the investigator and prosecutor not only give the caller permission to tell a lie, but they are also encouraging her to lie. This can and will be used by the defense not only to attack the credibility of the investigation, but more important, to attack the credibility and trustworthiness of the caller. Not all suspects will confess to the caller, and in some situations, they can come off looking like they are the victim of a vicious and unfounded allegation. The investigator must also consider how the suspect may react to the victim. The suspect may very well make an admission but may also be verbally abusive to the victim, causing the victim to recant or refuse to testify.

Along with the negative aspects of this technique, there are also some positive ones. Having the suspect make an admission of what he did to the child and knowing that others have heard this admission will validate the child. It can be a major step toward the victim's regaining her self-esteem and a feeling of control over her life. The investigator's possession of a recorded single-party consent tape during interrogation will greatly increase the likelihood of a confession. This type of evidence can be so damaging that there is a very good likelihood of a guilty plea, thus sparing the child the need to testify.

The key to having this technique work in an effective manner is preplanning and being prepared to deal with the unexpected. This is generally a one-shot opportunity and it must be well orchestrated.

3. When to Use This Technique

A common misconception is that if the suspect becomes aware that the investigation is underway, this technique is ineffective. Therefore, some individuals rush to use the technique as soon as possible after the disclosure. This technique can be used effectively at all stages of the investigation. The decision on the timing of the call should be based on

- The ability and emotional state of the caller, the primary consideration
- The perpetrator
- The amount of information available concerning the incident

4. Preparation for the Call

Once the decision has been made to employ the technique, the first step should be to obtain the appropriate consents and releases for the caller. Normally, this is not an issue unless the caller is a child. The investigator must be aware of the releases needed in his jurisdiction. The person able to give consent for the call will be determined by who or what agency has legal custody of the child. If the child is in the custody of the Department of Social Services, it may be necessary to obtain state-level approval or a court order for the call.

Next, the investigator must determine what approach the caller will use with the suspect. This is a critical step in the process since it will often determine what information, if any, will be obtained during the phone call. The approach will depend on the caller's relationship to the suspect, the caller's ability to be convincing, the caller's emotional state, the type of activity that took place between the caller and the suspect, the amount of contact between the caller and suspect, the suspect's emotional state, and the suspect's knowledge of the investigation and/or allegation. Whatever the approach, it must be comfortable for the caller and seem logical and believable to the suspect. Once the suspect is aware that the caller is calling to discuss the allegation, he will quite often want to know where the call is being placed and whether anyone else is there. The caller must be prepared to provide information that will make the suspect feel at ease.

The investigator must also determine who should be present during the telephone call. As a general rule, the fewer people present, the better. At a minimum, those present should include the investigator and a support person for the child, preferably a mental health counselor.

5. Equipment

The equipment needed for the call is a telephone interface device that is a hard wire or direct connect. The instrument must provide a high-quality recording of both the caller's and suspect's voices. The device should be tested each time it is used to ensure that it is working properly and that the suspect cannot hear any audio feedback or echoing. Interface devices are not expensive and can be obtained at any electronics store. The suction cup–type devices should not be used because of their poor sound quality and the likelihood of their falling off during the conversation. As with the interface device, the tape recorder itself should be of a quality that will clearly record the conversation. Most cassette tape recorders will provide the quality needed. An AC power source can be used, but there should also be a battery backup in case of a power outage. The cassette tape should be new, not recorded over, and it should be tested before the call.

6. Determining the Call Location

The investigator should consider the following factors when determining where the call should be placed:

- The location should provide privacy with no chance of interruption or distractions.
- The location should be quiet with no background noise that will distract the caller, alert the suspect, or interfere with the quality of the recording.
- The caller should not feel threatened or uncomfortable with the location.
- The recording device must be compatible with the telephone equipment. Some locations that have multiple line phone jacks may not work with the interface device.
- Does the suspect have caller ID? Even if the suspect does not have caller ID, or if the phone being used is blocked, the suspect may still be able to use a

callback feature. What will the caller do if the suspect becomes suspicious and asks the caller to give him a number so he can call the caller back?

7. Preparation of the Caller

First, the investigator and the caller should prepare a list of questions that the caller will ask the suspect, along with a list of statements the caller may make in response to things the suspect might say or ask. The list that is generated should be maintained, along with the investigator's notes, for disclosure by the prosecution. The caller can assist the investigator in determining the reason that will be used for the call to the suspect. The caller's opening statement will often determine how the call will proceed. The investigator should have the caller become familiar enough with the statements and questions so that the caller will not have to read them during the call. Be sure to let the caller know that it is all right to feel scared or nervous about making the call. It is vital that the caller knows that she is not responsible for anything that is said by the suspect or happens during the phone call. Let the caller know that it is okay to lie to the suspect during the call. A critical failsafe is to provide the caller with a way to end the call if she gets too nervous or scared of the suspect's reaction, or if the suspect does not want to let her off the phone. This might be as simple as the caller stating to the suspect, "Someone is walking in, I will have to call you back later."

If the caller is a child, one effective technique for preparing the child is to let her make a practice call to the investigator. The investigator should take on the role of the suspect and attempt to respond as one might expect the suspect to respond. This will also provide one last test of the equipment to ensure that all is working properly. If a practice call is to be used, the prosecutor should approve it in advance to avoid a complication during the court process.

8. Making the Call

When all of the appropriate preparation has been done and the caller is ready to make the call, all unneeded individuals should leave the calling area. The caller must be able to concentrate totally on dealing with the suspect. If the investigator is going to listen in on another phone, he must ensure that neither the caller nor the suspect will be able to hear him on the line. Once the call has started, there can be no mid-course change. Regardless of how well or how poorly the call goes, no one should interrupt the caller or display any emotions. The call should just be allowed to happen. In some situations, it may be acceptable or possible to make a second call if it is deemed necessary.

9. After the Call

Once the call is completed, the caller's well-being should be the primary concern. Regardless of the outcome of the call, the caller should be praised for what she has done. This is when the counselor/therapist is most important, to debrief the caller, take care of the caller's needs, and help her understand the feelings she may be experiencing.

VI. ALLEGATIONS INVOLVING MULTIPLE VICTIMS AND SUSPECTS

It is impossible to conduct a thorough investigation of a case involving multiple alleged victims or suspects without understanding the dynamics of "child sex rings." A child sex ring is defined as one or more offenders involved sexually with several children. A ring does not necessarily mean group sex, although that may take place. Offenders are more likely to be sexually interacting with one child at a time. Further, recent sex ring cases illustrate the evolving nature of offenders' sexual involvement with their victims. For example, the proliferation of the Internet has spawned chat rooms in which members exchange stories about their sexual contact with minors and digital files containing homemade pornographic photos and videos of the offenders' sexual acts with children. (See *U.S. v. Tank*, 200 F.3d 627 [9th Cir. 2000]; see also *U.S. v. Laney*, 189 F.3d 954 [9th Cir. 1999]).

Sex ring cases typically involve children in day-care, school, and institutional settings. They can also include a single father who uses his children to recruit others into a club with sexual intent or a youth leader who is drawn to children as his primary sexual outlet. (For a detailed understanding of the dynamics of child sex rings, consult Burgess, A. [1984]. *Child pornography and sex rings*. Lexington, MA: Lexington Books; Lanning, K. [1992]. *Child sex rings: A behavioral analysis* [2nd ed.]. Alexandria, VA: National Center for Missing & Exploited Children.) Kenneth Lanning, an FBI expert in child exploitation cases, describes four important differences between a sex ring and typical cases of child sexual abuse. The first is the interaction between multiple victims. In intrafamilial cases, the sexual activity is usually a secret the child has discussed with no one, except perhaps a trusted friend sworn to secrecy. In child sex rings, there are multiple children who are often aware of one another. Some children may have participated in recruiting other children at the suspect's request. Most have witnessed other children engage in sexual activity with the suspect. Sometimes the children have engaged in sexual activity with each other at the behest of the suspect. Offenders exploit the fact that most children, especially adolescents, want to be part of a peer group and maintain control over them through a combination of bonding, competition, and peer pressure. Offenders operating sex rings have used scout troops, sports teams, or school clubs or created their own group of victims.

Second, in certain types of sex rings, offenders trade information, material, and sometimes children with other offenders. The interaction is an important element of the investigation. Some police agencies have capitalized on this characteristic by engaging in proactive investigations by having officers pose as pedophiles to gather enough information to make an arrest even though no child has disclosed the abuse. While multiple offenders can pose an investigative difficulty, they can be an advantage, since the more offenders involved, the greater the odds of a weak link to corroborate the abuse.

The role of the child's parents is a third major difference between child sex rings and intrafamilial child sexual abuse. Intrafamilial cases usually involve an abusing and a nonabusing parent. A nonabusing mother may protect the child, pressure the child not to talk about the abuse, or persuade the child to recant the disclosure so the perpetrator does not face the criminal justice system. In child sex ring cases, parents are rarely the abusers, but their interaction with the child can be crucial to the case. If parents interrogate their children or conduct their own investigation, the results can damage law enforcement's pursuit of the facts and decrease the chances of a conviction. It is also possible, of course, that a child being sexually exploited in a sex ring is also sexually, physically, or psychologically abused at home.

The gender of the victim is the fourth major difference between intrafamilial abuse and child sex ring cases. Unlike intrafamilial sexual abuse cases, where the most common reported victim is a young female, the victims in child sex rings are often adolescent males. (See Lanning, K. [1991]. *Child sex rings: A behavioral analysis* [2nd ed.]. Alexandria, VA: National Center for Missing & Exploited Children.)

The keys to the successful handling of an investigation of this magnitude include the effective management of *all* components of the investigation, the establishment of protocols to guide the investigation and ensure information sharing in a timely manner, and being prepared for and anticipating the unexpected.

A. Definition of Agency Roles

Sex ring investigations place extra demands on an investigator's time, energy, and resources. If police staff, or the agencies with which the police work, have no experience in the investigation of sex rings, immediately arrange for a knowledgeable outside prosecutor, therapist, caseworker, detective, or other expert to meet with those working on the case and suggest how to approach the investigation. Consult with a specialist in handling sex ring cases *before* problems arise, and when asking for help, be sure the individual has experience with multiple victim, multiple suspect cases.

Early decisions can make or break the case, so the prosecutor should be involved at the onset. Arrange for the police and child protective service agencies to notify the prosecutor immediately about any allegations of multiple victim, multiple offender cases. The prosecutor should then make sure that the rights of alleged victims and suspects are preserved and that the investigation is conducted expeditiously.

Many of the following suggestions are based on a protocol developed by the Los Angeles County Inter-Agency Council on Child Abuse and Neglect after several controversial cases of suspected mass victimization disrupted that community. (See Los Angeles County Inter-Agency Council on Child Abuse and Neglect, Multi-Victim Multi-Suspect Child Sexual Abuse Subcommittee Protocols [1988]). The most common problems in these investigations include insufficient resources to investigate the allegations in an expedient manner, inadequate training, confusion about leadership during the investigation, contamination of evidence, failure to assure confidentiality of the investigation, and simply the overwhelming magnitude of the investigation. Many of these cases become even more complicated when allegations arise in a preschool setting involving very young children. To develop a plan before disaster strikes, local prosecutors should bring together policy-level representatives of all agencies that may become involved in multiple victim, multiple suspect cases to agree on the guidelines for the investigation. It is much easier to implement a pre-existing plan than to try to form one during a crisis. With responsibilities defined, agency coordination will be improved and the duplication of effort reduced. The Los Angeles protocol, a good model to follow, documents the following interagency agreements.

- *Law Enforcement.* The primary responsibility for criminal investigations of serious abuse rests with law enforcement. Law enforcement is in charge of the investigation until the allegations are determined to be unsubstantiated or have been investigated and presented to the prosecutor's office for filing.

- *The Prosecutor's Office.* The prosecutor's office should be an active member of the investigative team throughout the investigation. The prosecutor's role is to provide ongoing legal advice, help draft search warrants, observe interviews of potential witnesses, and provide any other assistance deemed appropriate.

- *Child Protective Services Agency.* The department administering children's services is part of the investigative team when the circumstances of the case mandate involvement, such as when the suspects are parents, caregivers, educators, or other licensed care providers. It is the child protective services agency's responsibility to ensure the safety of children who require protective custody, make placement recommendations, and coordinate the assessment and interviews of children and adults with appropriate law enforcement and licensing agencies. They may be part of the investigative team for only a portion of the investigation or throughout the duration of the investigation.

- *Licensing Agency.* The primary responsibility of the licensing agency is to investigate allegations of child abuse and neglect in a licensed out-of-home care facility and to coordinate its efforts with those of the law enforcement investigative team and child protective agency. The licensing agency provides back-up assistance when requested by the investigating law enforcement agency and may be part of the investigative team during all or part of the investigation. It is responsible for administrative action involving any licensed facility, including revocation or suspension of the license and the investigation and prosecution of unlicensed activity, regardless of the outcome of the criminal investigation.

- *Victim-Witness Agency.* The victim-witness agency is part of the investigative team when children are identified as victims. Victim advocates work with law enforcement; make referrals for medical examinations, therapeutic evaluations, and treatment; assist the family with processing applications for the Victim-Witness Assistance Fund; and provide support for the child and family throughout the investigation and subsequent court process.

- *Medical Practitioner.* Medical practitioners conduct medical examinations of suspected victims in accordance with state guidelines and protocols. Medical personnel provide additional assistance to the investigative team by giving expert opinions regarding the existence and nature of abuse, coordinating examinations with the investigative team, and providing medical expertise to the team as needed.

- *Licensed Therapists.* Licensed therapists include evaluators and treatment therapists previously identified by the investigative agency. Evaluators selected for their experience and training in evaluating suspected victims of child abuse provide evaluations of children as requested by the investigative team. They also provide written findings and fill out mandated forms upon receiving any disclosures from children when abuse is suspected. Evaluators may be part of the investigative team for a portion of or throughout the investigation. They prepare children for investigative interviews and conduct evaluations in conjunction with investigators, depending on what procedure serves the best interests of the children and the investigation. Licensed therapists with experience and training may receive referrals from the investigative team to provide treatment to children who have disclosed abuse or are suspected victims because of behavioral symptoms. Their treatment is considered confidential and need be revealed to the investigative team only when and if children disclose additional suspects or additional crimes. Therapists who provide such evaluations and treatment must do so in a manner that does not compromise the integrity of the investigation.

• *Schools.* Schools are not involved in the investigative process; however, the victim will normally continue to attend school. Schools play an important role in protecting the children from the media, suspects, and agencies working on the suspect's behalf. They may also be a valuable source of information to the investigation team for identifying potential problems with victims.

• *Multidisciplinary Investigation Team.* A multidisciplinary investigation team is a voluntary association of law enforcement agencies, the prosecutor's office, county welfare and/or probation departments, child protection agencies, and state or county licensing agencies established to share information and coordinate investigations and reports of multiple victim, multiple suspect child abuse cases. The team can include specialized medical practitioners and licensed therapists and might call on additional consultants.

B. Interviewing Large Numbers of Children

1. The Initial Assessment

If a child discloses abuse and it appears that there is the potential for multiple children as either victims or witnesses, many children must be interviewed. The lead investigative agency must make a timely assessment regarding what resources are going to be assigned to the investigation and it must activate the interagency investigative team or a law enforcement investigative team. It is far more effective to allocate sufficient resources in the beginning of the investigation than to attempt to assess the situation with only one or two investigators. If allegations prove to be baseless or involve only a small number of children, the extra personnel can be returned to normal duties. If the reverse is true, the team will be in place to continue the investigation without the interruption of new members or the loss of valuable time.

The first phase and highest priority of the investigation involves assessing the risk to any children currently in the care of the alleged offender(s) so they can be protected. A determination must be made regarding the existence of abuse, how many alleged victims and witnesses exist, what evidence has been collected, and what additional evidence is needed. The interviews of alleged victims and medical examinations should be conducted without delay. If the alleged victims are very young, determine whether there are older children who can corroborate their statements.

2. Team Interviewing

The primary defense focus in multiple-victim sexual abuse cases is often on the investigative process, especially the interviewer(s) and interview methodology. A common defense argument in mass victimization cases is referred to as the "biasing effect" of interviewers on alleged victims. The defense frequently claims that the children were led to fabricate the allegations by the manner of questioning employed, coupled with the interviewers' expectations and relationship with the children.

Dividing children among different teams of investigators can defeat this argument. The information generated by each team is passed vertically up to a supervisor but is not shared horizontally with other investigators or interviewers. If a child names other children as victims or witnesses, the responsibility for interviewing them is delegated to another interviewer with no information about the allegations. The supervisor controls the information shared among interviewers, notes whether patterns of behavior or other aspects of abuse emerge, and documents when any information is released. The process minimizes contamination of information and maximizes the spontaneity of any disclosures. If distinctive patterns emerge, it is clear that the information originated with the children and not the investigators or interviewers. It is a good safeguard to continue this practice throughout the investigation until trial.

3. Additional Interviews

Based upon the findings from the initial assessment, proceed to phase two of the investigation—interviewing children who were previously exposed to the suspect to determine whether they were victimized. The investigators should obtain the names and addresses of all children who could have been the subjects of the abuse as well as an employee list if the allegations arose in an institutional setting. Investigators should conduct home interviews of the children exposed to the suspect(s) as quickly as possible. If the alleged victims have not attended the institution for an extended period of time, it may be wise to bring the victims to the school or facility to help them remember events.

Prosecutors usually cannot interview large numbers of children and should rely on the investigative team to conduct initial interviews. The prosecutor who tries the case may need to limit interviews to children who recount being abused. If there are numerous alleged victims, it may be necessary to have several prosecutors conduct interviews. If so, the prosecutor who interviewed a particular child should handle the examination of that individual at trial.

Interview the children separately and without parents present. Efforts should be made to schedule interviews so that several children do not wait in the same area. Try to determine through separate interviews whether there seems to be a common pattern of offender behavior. Look for patterns that suggest motive or opportunity to commit the alleged crimes. Did the suspect take the children individually to one area or a few children to different areas at different times? Did any child witness acts involving other children? Did anyone photograph the child or others in the child's presence? Was sexual paraphernalia used, and can the child describe or draw the items? What were other teachers and children doing before, after, and during the time the child was being victimized? How did the suspect(s) ensure the children's silence?

C. Parents of Suspected Victims

1. Assignment of a Liaison or Victim-Witness Advocate

Parents who are outraged by revelations, concerned for their children, and frustrated by the response of the social service and criminal justice agencies can undermine the best investigative team with the most exemplary protocol. Frustrated with the delays associated with a complicated criminal justice system, parents may take their feelings out on investigators or the prosecutor. Assigning a liaison officer or victim-witness advocate to work directly with parents can save countless hours of prosecutor and investigator time. While the liaison should represent the "system," he or she should not perform an investigative function. The liaison plays several important roles. One is to keep parents informed regarding the general status of the investigation. The liaison should also explain why details of the investigation, such as the allegations of other children, cannot be shared because of potential defense complaints of cross-germination of information. Parents who feel "left in the dark" about the case are much less likely to cooperate. The liaison should attempt to maintain regular contact with all of the alleged victims' parents, even when there are no new developments. Further, the liaison should not pressure anyone to participate in an investigation.

The liaison is also responsible for referring parents and children to counseling and therapy. Information concerning community resources and qualified therapists should be close at hand. With regard to emotional health, the liaison should emphasize the importance of keeping the family's life as stable and routine as possible and not to let the abuse become the focal point. Parents should be encouraged to deal with their anger and grief outside their children's presence.

Parent support groups, a natural outgrowth of parent meetings held by a victim-witness advocate, have sometimes proved crucial to the success of a case. One of the ground rules of such groups has been a prohibition against discussing the facts in the case to avoid defense claims of contamination of children's disclosures. The opportunity to meet other parents who are undergoing similar family crises as a result of the allegations, however, clearly provides some comfort in an often long ordeal.

2. Group Therapy

Children and/or parents may be involved in group therapy with other children and their parents. This raises separate problems. It is natural to compare notes with others in a therapeutic setting. Whether these discussions actually influence recollection or later testimony, the opportunity for cross-germination creates an issue to be exploited by defense attorneys. Defense attorneys will suggest that children learned additional facts about sexual abuse in group therapy and subconsciously incorporated them into their experience, confusing fact with fantasy and rendering everything they say suspect. Everyone involved with the case should strongly recommend against group therapy prior to trial. Individual therapy is much less likely to lead to criticism by defense attorneys. Whatever the situation, the children's accounts of abuse should be carefully documented prior to participation in any therapy.

3. Civil Actions

The investigator and prosecutor must determine whether civil actions related to the case have been filed or are being contemplated. While parents obviously have the right to bring such actions, the parents should be advised of the ramifications of filing civil actions prior to the conclusion of the criminal case. If a civil case has already been initiated, the prosecutor should work with the lawyer representing the child and, if possible, take appropriate action to preclude civil defense interviews or depositions while the criminal case is pending.

D. Electronic and Other Surveillance

Various forms of surveillance can be useful in investigating multiple victim, multiple suspect cases. The investigator should consider using consensual monitoring or undercover police officers. Wiretaps and disguised video cameras in areas where abuse is expected to have occurred can help monitor activities of the suspects, particularly regarding interactions with children. Obviously, the police should not wait to record the victimization of a child, but must intervene quickly if the child appears to be in danger. Attempts at surveillance should take place early in the investigation, before the suspect has been alerted and behavior patterns changed. In many jurisdictions, a search warrant is necessary to enter the building, and timing of execution is always important.

E. Search Warrants

Obtain and execute search warrants within 48 hours after the disclosure whenever possible or as soon as probable cause emerges on new suspects. When a case involves multiple suspects, some offenders are often unknown when the investigation is in its early stages. The decision to move quickly regarding known suspects will obviously alert unknown suspects, but it may be necessary given the prosecutor's assessment of how to "make the case" and the need to protect children from further abuse. Be alert for evidence of conspiracy among multiple suspects.

F. Whether to Arrest

If the suspect is known, the evidence is clear, and arrest will not interfere with the continuing investigation, make an arrest. If this cannot be accomplished, try to prevent the suspect's continued contact with children. In institutional settings, realize that the supervisor may be a participant and will likely be protective of the suspect. Depending upon the information surrounding the allegation and implications of even the confidential release of this information the authorities, the suspect's suspension or transfer away from children under the watchful eye of others may be possible.

G. Developing the Case When Suspect Identity Is Uncertain

If suspect identities are unknown, pursue the case as a criminal conspiracy. Until the scope of investigation narrows, assume all children may be victims and all adults are suspects. Consider the consequences of all actions carefully. For example, letters sent prematurely to parents of suspected victims may have the unintended result of alerting suspects and causing the loss of important evidence.

Obtain employee photographs for display to alleged victims for identification purposes. Placing alleged victims in concealed locations to identify the suspect is also a possibility, depending on the case and the legal requirements of each jurisdiction.

Since statements of identification are not hearsay and are admissible so long as the declarant testifies and is subject to cross-examination in some states, assign someone to record the child's verbal and behavioral reactions.

H. Interviewing Collateral Witnesses

In sex ring cases, interview all employees, volunteers, or others who frequent the location of the abuse, if the alleged sexual abuse occurred in an institution. Investigators should determine the collateral witness's relationship with the suspect and child(ren), work habits, personal idiosyncrasies, activities, likes, and dislikes. Some witnesses may know about the abuse but have been shamed or threatened into silence. Tracking the daily schedule of all persons with access to the children can provide clues to those who had an opportunity to commit the abuse.

I. Investigative Support

The investigative team should consider using computer databases to record pertinent data. This is a valuable method not only at the investigation stage, but also as demonstrative evidence at trial. Assign sufficient clerical staff so reports can be prepared on schedule and investigators can spend their time investigating and not typing.

J. The Use of an Investigative Grand Jury

The grand jury's proven benefit as a tool for uncovering complex, organized criminal activity can be extended to large-scale child sex rings, particularly when some offenders are unknown and individuals with knowledge of the abuse refuse to cooperate with investigating authorities. Grand jury investigations can generate a myriad of leads for corroborative evidence and a wealth of volunteered information from outside witnesses in highly publicized cases. The strength of the grand jury lies in its ability to compel testimony. Its contempt powers generally ensure answers from even the most uncooperative witness, while the threat of perjury may keep the witness closer to the truth than he might otherwise have been. Grand jury sessions not only lock in witness testimony, but the secrecy of the proceedings protects the investigation as well. Moreover, grand jury subpoenas are an effective way to obtain needed documents.

Since an individual whose testimony has been compelled is immune from prosecution (with "use immunity" automatic in most jurisdictions), exercise care in choosing whose testimony to compel if a waiver of immunity cannot be obtained. Compelling testimony from a witness believed only to have peripheral information who then confesses to molesting scores of children is obviously undesirable. However, this is rare. Investigating authorities should be able to steer the prosecutor to witnesses who are not principally involved but who have helpful information. Starting with known victims and uninvolved employees and moving toward those who may be peripherally involved should lead the prosecutor to other victims and the principal offenders. Then, if necessary, the prosecutor can consider granting immunity to the least culpable offender if the case cannot be successfully prosecuted without turning one offender against the others.

Not all children who have been victimized need to testify before the grand jury. The grand jury will generally rely on the prosecutor to decide whom to call as witnesses, although it can call anyone it wishes. The grand jury investigation should not disrupt the manner in which a prosecutor interviews children, although one or more of the children may be required to testify. In most jurisdictions, grand jury proceedings are less formal than regular court hearings. Having the child testify before trial permits the prosecutor to evaluate each child's strengths and weaknesses in a setting similar to but not as stressful as the actual trial.

The possibility of a "runaway" grand jury concerns some prosecutors, especially with investigations likely to catch the public's eye. Sweeping indictments by a grand jury despite a disparity of evidence concerning the suspects can destroy the credibility of the investigation and jeopardize the outcome of future efforts. Although runaway grand juries are extremely rare, they are generally caused by the prosecutor's inability to control the direction and momentum of the investigation. A prosecutor is responsible for educating members of the grand jury. It is not in everyone's best interests for the prosecutor to serve only as a person who presents evidence and as a legal advisor without taking a position on the case.

K. Dealing With the Media

Any case involving multiple victims and suspects is certain to get the attention of the state and local media, and perhaps the national media as well. This type of coverage can be beneficial or it can be disastrous. All agencies involved in the case should agree early in the investigation that all press releases or conferences will be managed and handled through one source. A professional with extensive experience in dealing with the media should be selected for this assignment. A resource for this person may be the larger metropolitan or state law enforcement agencies that may have a public information officer (PIO) who is familiar with managing the media in sensitive situations. Investigators, prosecutors, social workers, and other front-line personnel should never deal with the media directly.

L. Agency Supervisor Updates

The case supervisor should schedule regular joint meetings of the chief agency supervisors of the involved agencies to update them on the status of the investigation. This will go a long way in preventing agencies from breaking rank and not supporting the multidisciplinary investigation team.

M. Contingency Plans

The investigation team, in cooperation with the agency supervisors, should develop contingency plans for dealing with problems normally associated with these types of cases. The most common problem areas are

- Uncooperative parents and/or family members
- Resource depletion
- Media problems

- Personnel problems
- Involved and uninvolved agencies

VII. MEDICAL EXAMINATIONS IN SEXUAL ABUSE CASES

A. Reasons for Medical Examination

The presence of an STD, pregnancy, forensic evidence of sperm or semen, or residua of certain types of tissue damage represent pathognomonic findings of sexual abuse. The history given by the child is the most important part of the diagnosis. The presence of sexualized behaviors is additional evidence favoring the diagnosis of sexual abuse. The majority of sexual abuse cases, however, do not involve conclusive medical findings. A number of factors account for this lack of medical evidence. First, any evidence that may exist immediately following an assault, such as bleeding, bruises, and the presence of seminal fluid, will not remain long. Second, it is possible that whatever injuries originally existed have healed because of the manner in which victims are groomed and the progression of sexual activity. The sexual activity may progress from oral-genital contact to anal penetration, and then to vulvar intercourse which consists of the penis, finger, or other object being placed inside the labia but not completely through the hymen. Third, a physician usually cannot tell just by looking whether a child experienced sexual abuse.

The absence of medical evidence does not doom a case to failure. In fact, in one jurisdiction, child sexual abuse cases without medical evidence have been found to have a somewhat higher rate of conviction. (See DeJong, A., & Rose, M. [1991]. Legal proof of child sexual abuse in the absence of physical evidence. *Pediatrics, 88,* 506.) A physician with expertise in this area can explain that the absence of definitive medical evidence can still be consistent with abuse.

Medical evidence can, however, provide powerful and convincing corroboration. Since children who have been victims of sexual abuse often initially minimize its extent, a medical examination may reveal more about what really happened. The medical examination also makes it possible to screen for STDs, provide needed treatment, and reassure the child about her well-being. Finally, the examination prevents the defense from attacking the sufficiency of the evidence based on the absence of a medical examination.

B. Who Should Do the Medical Examination

Not all doctors, including pediatricians and emergency room physicians, have sufficient training, experience, or interest to perform the kind of sensitive and thorough medical evaluation needed in cases of alleged child sexual abuse. Although awareness of the issues involved in these examinations is increasing within the medical community, many physicians have not had training to conduct these exams and they are not familiar with the current research. Since the untrained individual may miss positive evidence of abuse or misinterpret equivocal evidence, it is imperative to learn which doctors are conducting the medical exams. In many communities, the process is haphazard. At times, child protective services, caseworkers, or the police have not requested medical examinations, or they have requested them without specifying that a qualified doctor perform the evaluation.

For reliable results from the medical examination, it is necessary to coordinate the community's prosecutors, police, child protective services workers, hospitals, and doctors. The police and the prosecutor should make efforts to standardize the process so that all of these agencies refer children to the most qualified doctors. In many communities, children's advocacy centers have been established. These centers use a multidisciplinary team to perform child abuse evaluations in a child-friendly environment. This allows a complete evaluation to be performed only once and obviates the need to subject the child to multiple encounters in numerous sites. The national network of children's advocacy centers (National Children's Alliance) has produced standards of care, and the centers must conform to these standards in order to be part of the national network. The investigator should check with professionals in the community to determine available resources. Many medical teaching hospitals sponsor child abuse intervention programs. For help in identifying specialized training for doctors, contact the National Center for Prosecution of Child Abuse.

Local experts should engage in regular continuing medical education programs relating to sexual abuse. Membership in professional organizations including the interdisciplinary American Professional Society on the Abuse of Children, the American Academy of Pediatrics, and the American Academy of Family Physicians and participation in ongoing peer reviews are excellent ways for physicians to stay current with recent developments. In addition, the investigator and prosecutor should consider participating in joint training programs with medical professionals to develop a mutual understanding of the issues and levels of expertise. Prosecutors and physicians can do much to educate each other about their respective needs and capabilities.

C. The Development of Protocols

As a way of standardizing the medical examination, many communities have developed protocols indicating when and where a suspected victim is to be examined. Some protocols specify certain procedures such as using a colposcope, photographing injuries, and specifying how evidence should be marked, preserved, analyzed, and documented. These protocols should be individually designed to fit the personnel, methods, facilities, and legal requirements of the community.

At a minimum, prosecutors need to review existing protocols to understand the current practices and to identify areas that need improvement. If protocols do not exist in the community or if changes are called for, the prosecutor should meet with hospital administrators, doctors, nurses, lab technicians, criminologists, police officers, child protective services representatives, and local rape/abuse crisis center personnel to design new guidelines. Even if cases are currently handled effectively within the community, a formal multiagency agreement is valuable for training new staff. While it may be difficult to persuade everyone who should be involved to participate, the results are usually well worth the effort.

D. The Procedures and Components of the Examination

The following considerations for conducting a medical examination are not intended as a how-to for doctors, but as an overview for prosecutors. Readers wanting more detailed information on any aspect of the medical examination should start by consulting the medical bibliography in the appendixes or contacting the National Center for Prosecution of Child Abuse.

1. Obtaining Consent

When a child is examined in response to an allegation of abuse, especially in the hospital or emergency room, it is necessary to obtain appropriate consent before the exam, treatment, and evidence collection. Hospitals generally have consent forms developed specifically for this purpose, and the staff can inform the child's caregiver, or the child if she is old enough, about the procedures involved with the examination. The explanations that are given depend on both state law and hospital policy and they can reflect agreements with other professionals involved in the investigation.

Mandatory reporting requirements should be explained to patients and caregivers so that they understand that medical personnel are required to report suspected child abuse to law enforcement and/or the local social services agency. If the patient or caregiver refuses to allow the collection of samples or other evidence, staff should explain the consequences. These consequences might include the inability to analyze potential evidence, and the lack of evidence may undermine the civil or criminal case.

While parents must generally authorize an examination, treatment, and evidence collection related to their own child, parental consent is generally not required in suspected child abuse cases. In the case of parental refusal, children may be taken into protective custody by the local law enforcement or child protective services agency. A representative of the child protective services agency can then sign an appropriate consent form as the temporary guardian of the child to authorize the procedures. Many states have laws permitting children between 12 and 17 years of age to give consent for hospital, medical, and surgical care related to the diagnosis or treatment of alleged sexual abuse or assault and the collection of medical evidence. These laws often relate to the prevention, diagnosis, or treatment of pregnancy and STDs. Laws requiring medical professionals to attempt to contact parents or legal guardians about treatment generally do not apply when medical personnel have reason to believe that the parent(s) or guardian(s) committed the abuse. Furthermore, at least eight states have enacted laws that specifically permit minors to consent to medical treatment when there has been suspected sexual abuse or generally permit examination without parental consent by the physician's discretion that the treatment would maintain the child's well-being. (See Ariz. Rev. Stat § 13–1413, Cal. Fam. Code § 6928, Kan. Stat. Ann. § 65–448, 41 Ill. Comp. Stat 210/3, Md. Code Ann. Health-Gen. I § 20–102(c)(7), 32 Me. Rev. Stat. tit. 32, § 2595, S.C. Code Ann. § 20–7–290, Tenn. Code Ann. § 63–6–222, Tex. Fam. Code § 32.005.)

The medical professional and the investigator should seek permission for any photographs taken during the medical exam, and the photographs must be taken with the understanding they may be used as evidence. Most states permit photographs to be taken of known or suspected child abuse victims without parental consent and further allow the photos to accompany reports to child protective services or law enforcement agencies. The medical professional and the investigator should be sensitive to the child's possible embarrassment about the need for photographs, and they should make sure the photograph is taken in the least intrusive manner necessary to document findings.

2. The Examiner's Approach and the Medical Interview

It is critical that medical personnel exercise great sensitivity when dealing with children who are alleged to have been sexually abused. The child should be approached in a relaxed and nonjudgmental manner. Privacy, reassurance, and support are of critical importance.

The medical interview provides data that can assist the physician in diagnosing and treating the child and to help the investigator understand what happened. The child's statements during the medical evaluation can be especially helpful to prosecutors in jurisdictions that admit hearsay statements made for purposes of medical diagnosis or treatment. Prosecutors should therefore ensure that the doctors examining children are familiar with hearsay requirements and recommended interviewing techniques. When interviewing young children, it is essential to explain the physician's role to the child and explain that the child's answers will be used in diagnoses and treatment. This can be as simple as, "My name is Dr. Jane. I am a doctor. My job today is to make sure your body is all right. To do that, I have to ask you some questions. I need you to tell the truth so I can make sure your body is all right. Do you understand?" The physician must document this part of the conversation in the child's medical records. If not, a defense attorney may claim the child was not aware of the purpose of the examination and thus lacked the selfish motive to be truthful to the doctor that is necessary for the statement to be admissible under the medical diagnoses exception to the hearsay rule.

Hospital or other medical forms can be designed with sections for recording not only the child's statements and observations, but also the caregiver's statements. Before the exam, the investigator should inform the doctor of the information gathered to date and encourage the doctor to record what the child says in her own words. The medical record should include observations of the child's general appearance, emotional state, and reaction to the exam. The physician should not ask leading or suggestive questions. Routine information about the child's age, gender, and situation should also be included in the medical interview. The following list suggests areas pertinent to the medical diagnosis and treatment as well as to the prosecutor's evaluation of the criminal case.

- Details of the assault, including
  - The number of assailants
  - The assailant's relationship to the child
  - Time elapsed since most recent assault
  - The type of sexual contact involved, including whether there was attempted or actual vaginal, anal, or oral penetration, and if so, with what object
  - Whether ejaculation occurred
  - Whether a condom or other birth control device was used
- The use of coercion, including the use of weapons, threats, or injuries inflicted as part of the coercion
- The child's symptoms following the assault, including pain, bleeding, bruises or cuts, loss of consciousness, nausea, vomiting, diarrhea, and discharge
- If the assault was recent, the child's activity after the assault, including whether the child bathed or took a shower, douched, urinated, defecated, ate, drank, used toothpaste or mouthwash, changed clothing, or used drugs or alcohol
- If the assault occurred within three days of the examination, the child's prior sexual contact with others. This information is necessary to eliminate other

possible sources of physical evidence recovered from the child during the exam, such as seminal fluid or pubic hairs.

- The child's medical history, including any allergies, chronic illnesses, current acute illnesses and medication, especially antibiotics, constipation, and urinary tract infections
- The child's physiological development and gynecologic history, including menstruation, pregnancy, the use of contraceptives, and STDs

The assailant's identity should always be a focus of the physician's inquiry because it relates directly to the child's current physical and emotional condition as well as prevention of future injury. If an STD is detected, the perpetrator must be tested and treated. If the child is still at risk because of the assailant's access to her, the doctor may choose to admit the child to a hospital or call child protective services to arrange for a safe placement.

E. Examination Techniques and Evidence Collection

The type of medical examination performed will depend to some extent on how much time has passed since the most recent abuse incident. If it occurred within the preceding 72 hours, the exam should be performed immediately. The physician should be alert for evidence indicative of a recent assault and use a sexual assault kit to take all appropriate samples. If more than 72 hours has passed since the most recent assault, an immediate exam is necessary only if the child reports bleeding, genital pain, or discharge. An examination should be conducted, however, without too much delay because of the speed of healing in these areas. The collection of samples is generally not warranted.

It is often helpful to allow a support person for the child to be present during the examination. This person could be a supportive parent who is not emotionally distraught, a hospital social worker, or a victim advocate. The medical professional should begin the examination with general procedures, such as an overall assessment of the child's physical appearance, blood pressure, pulse, and temperature to put the child at ease. The examination can then progress from the least intrusive parts of the exam to the most sensitive and intrusive procedure. For example, if a recent assault is suspected, the examination should begin with the collection of clothing or fingernail scrapings before moving to the inspection of the genital area and the taking of oral, vaginal, or anal samples.

1. Evidence of Injury

If the child was restrained during the assault, there may be injuries reflecting the force used, such as bleeding, abrasions, bruises, bite marks, broken bones, and tenderness of the scalp where the hair was pulled. Physicians should be alert for signs of severe lacerations of the vagina, urethra, rectum, or abdominal cavity that can occur in young children or with a brutal assault on a child of any age. It is unusual to find serious intra-abdominal penetration and injury even when objects other than a penis or finger have been inserted into the vagina or anus. It is also rare for such penetrations to cause internal damage without additional evidence of external injury. Immediate injuries such as bruising, erythema (redness), focal edema (localized swelling), and tenderness of the vaginal or anal area can occur as a result of vulvar intercourse and attempted or actual penetration by a finger, penis, or other object and can last from a few hours to a few days. In forcible assaults, doctors may find round, blunt trauma caused by a penis or curved thin lacerations from a fingernail.

Injuries should be photographed during the medical exam and include a centimeter measure to verify size and a color chart to compare to the color of any bruises. A good 35-mm or digital camera should be used. The physician should also describe the photographed (or unphotographed) injuries in her report and sketch them so that the extent and location of the injury is clear. Many hospitals use "traumagrams" or standard diagrams for this purpose.

2. Vaginal Findings

The hymenal ring is a fine membrane separating the external genitalia from the vagina. Hymens are present at birth in all girls. (See Berenson, A. B., et al. [1991]. Appearance of the hymen in newborns. *Pediatrics, 87,* 458; Jenny, C., et al. [1987]. Hymens in newborn female infants. *Pediatrics, 80,* 399.) The absence of the hymen as an isolated birth defect is a myth. The surface and edge of the membrane may have irregularities including bumps, tags, cysts, and clefts. It varies considerably in thickness and elasticity from person to person, and these characteristics also vary depending upon the child's age. The term *intact hymen* is meaningless and unlikely to be used by properly trained physicians experienced in conducting vaginal examinations of young girls. Contrary to popular opinion, sexual abuse often occurs without leaving obvious and lasting hymenal or vaginal findings.

Injuries to the genital area are usually described by reference to a clock face depending upon the position of the patient during examination. When the child is on her back, the clitoris is in the twelve o'clock position, the anus and median raphe[1] in the six o'clock position and a line between nine and three o'clock across the hymenal orifice. In the knee-to-chest position, the references to the clock face are reversed. Consequently, it is important that the physician enter a notation in the medical chart as to the child's position during the examination. Ideally, the child should be examined in both supine and knee-to-chest positions. Penile penetration may cause lesions in the posterior fourchette[2] without any lesions of the hymenal ring itself. These lesions usually occur between the five o'clock and seven o'clock positions, are most common at the six o'clock position, and may even involve the perineum. Some physicians believe that trauma parallel to the hymenal opening may occur with both penile and digital or instrument penetration.

Scarring, although unusual, is possible when there is trauma such as lacerations to this area and this trauma may be evident during a later examination. The physician may observe healed transections (cross sections), synechiae (anterior or posterior adhesions), hymenal deformity, hymenal thickening with scarring and changes in vascularity, and rounded and attenuated hymenal remnants. In children who have been chronically abused, the only evidence may be an absent or thinned hymenal

---

[1]The median raphe is the ridge or furrow of skin that marks the line of union of the two halves of the perineum, lying between the vulva and the anus in the female.

[2]The posterior fourchette, or frenulum of the labia majora, is the external tissue extending from the hymen toward the anus, contained within the labia majora.

ring or a markedly enlarged vaginal opening as a result of gradual stretching and the loss of the normal hymenal tissue. Normal diameters of vaginal openings in children prior to puberty have been described as ranging from one to ten millimeters. This measurement is affected by a number of factors including the examination position, the amount of traction used, the child's degree of relaxation, and cycles of respiration. Concluding that a certain measurement is proof of abuse is hazardous in the absence of other more specific findings. Similarly, small or normal vaginal openings are possible in sexually abused children as a result of healed or contracted scars.

Martin Finkel assessed changes in vaginal and anal injuries in children, concluding that without further sexual abuse, superficial wounds can heal completely within 48 to 72 hours. (Finkel, M. A. [1989]. Anogenital trauma in sexually abused children. *Pediatrics, 84,* 317, 320.) His findings are helpful when the defense is arguing for a second examination of the child months after the initial evaluation. These finding may also be valuable in determining that sexual abuse has ceased or in confirming that it has reoccurred (*Id.* pp. 321–22).

3. The Colposcope and Other Enhancing Instruments

The colposcope is a binocular optical instrument providing magnification of the genital area. Equipped with a high-quality light, many colposcopes include cameras for photographs, slides, or videotapes. The colposcope is not intrusive and does not touch the child.

Gynecologists traditionally have used colposcopes for early detection of cervical cancer. With abuse victims, the colposcope can help physicians detect traumatic lesions of the anogenital region or anal areas. It also gives the physician a better view of obvious injuries. In addition, the colposcope allows for second opinions regarding the examination because of the ability to take photographs, slides, or videotapes, thereby protecting the child from repeated examinations.

If colposcopy is available in your community, it can be extremely helpful in detecting and documenting injuries caused by sexual abuse. It will not produce miracles, and physicians must be trained and experienced in diagnosing sexual abuse to use it effectively. When a photo or video colposcope or other magnifying instrument with photograph or video capabilities is not available, evidence-grade comparable photographs of genital or anal trauma can be obtained using a 35-mm camera and a 1:1 macro lens. This relatively common instrument is also much less expensive.

4. Anal Findings

The anus appears perfectly normal in many cases of anal penetration. Just as an anus can accommodate a large, hard stool, it can accommodate an object such as an adult male penis. The use of lubricants, the amount of force, and the number of penetrations are factors that can affect the appearance of the anus. The examining physician may occasionally note reflex relaxation of the child's anal sphincter, complete or partial loss of sphincter control, the loss of normal skin folds around the anus, thickening of the skin and mucous membranes, and skin tags or fan-shaped scars in the anal area of a child who has been sodomized. A gaping anus, meaning over 15 mm, surrounded by an enlargement of the perianal skin is thought by some physicians to be indicative of chronic sodomy. Other physicians suggest dilation that is irregular or over 20 mm is indicative of prior anal penetration. These injuries are most likely when the child has described painful penetration accompanied by bleeding, and these findings are strong evidence to support a child's account of abuse. McCann, however, noted a relatively high level of perianal soft tissue changes in children who were not believed to be sexually abused. (See McCann, J. J., et al. [1989]. Perianal findings in prepubertal children selected for non-abuse: A descriptive study. *Child Abuse & Neglect, 13,* 179; Muram, D. [1989]. Anal and perianal abnormalities in prepubertal victims of sexual abuse. *American Journal of Obstetrics and Gynecology, 161,* 278.) The physician should exercise caution when evaluating the reasons for soft tissue changes in the anal region of a child.

5. Sexually Transmitted Diseases

The child may acquire an STD as a result of the sexual abuse. Transmission occurs in the genitalia, in the mouth and throat, or in the anus. Doctors should have specimens from the child cultured to identify bacterial or other agents that could cause disease if the suspect is infected or at high risk for an STD, if the child has a discharge or other signs and symptoms suggestive of infection, or if the history or circumstances suggest that an STD is present. Samples should be taken regardless of when the assault occurred, since sexually transmitted diseases may persist and not manifest themselves until well after the infection has begun. Physicians should also keep in mind that children might not initially reveal the full extent of sexual abuse. Thus, a child might disclose only sexual touching when in fact sexual intercourse occurred, and the lack of culturing might result in the child going undiagnosed.

Testing for STDs usually requires taking specimens from the mouth, throat, and rectum. In boys, the urethra is included. In girls, the vaginal area is included, specifically the endocervix, or mucous membrane of the cervical canal, in the adolescent girl and the vaginal pool in the prepubertal girl. If a child has a discharge, samples should be taken for smearing and staining for microscopic examination and for culture. A speculum exam of the vagina is necessary for a prepubertal girl only if the patient has active bleeding, signs of significant genital trauma, or the suspicion of a foreign body in the vagina. Examination under anesthesia is recommended in these cases since intracavity exams can be extremely traumatic.

If there is evidence of a sexually transmitted disease, immediate steps should be taken to have the alleged perpetrator tested. The investigator should act quickly to obtain appropriate warrants or court orders. Others who may have contracted the disease from the suspect should be contacted, including household members.

The following conditions in the child could indicate sexual abuse:

• *Urethritis* is the infection of the urethra secondary to gonorrhea. Subtyping of the gonococcus is possible in some research labs; this allows a comparison to be made of the bacterial strains infecting the child and the suspect. Gonorrhea in children who are not newborns or young infants makes the diagnosis of sexual abuse a medical certainty, even in the absence of a positive history, when the congenital form of gonorrhea is excluded. (American Academy of Pediatrics. [1999]. Guidelines for the evaluation of sexual abuse of children: Subject review. *Pediatrics, 103* 186, 189.)

• *Cervicitis* is the infection or inflammation of the cervix. It is seen usually in adolescent children.

- *Pelvic inflammatory disease* is the infection of the fallopian tubes and/or ovaries. It is also seen in adolescent children.

- *Pharyngitis* is the inflammation of the pharynx, which is the cavity at the back of the nose and throat. Pharyngitis can be caused by having oral sex with a person infected with gonorrhea.

- *Proctitis* is a rectal infection. Proctitis is a clinical manifestation of gonorrhea, marked by an inflammation of the rectal mucosa.

- *Perihepatitis* is an inflammation of the serous, or watery, covering of the liver, which is a clinical syndrome caused by gonorrhea or chlamydia.

- *Syphilis* in its primary stage causes chancres (ulcerating lesions) in the genital area or mouth. Dark field examination of secretions from these lesions can identify spirochetes. Secondary syphilis causes such things as fever; rashes; enlarged liver, spleen, or lymph nodes; and other complications. Blood tests can identify a syphilitic infection, but only after the patient has had several weeks to develop antibodies. Syphilis in children who are not infants is certainly caused by sexual contact.

- *Chlamydia trachomatis* can cause urethritis, cervicitis, conjunctivitis, trachoma (disease of the eye causing inflammation of the inner surface of the eyelid), and additional vaginal, rectal, or other infections. Discharge may or may not be evident. Chlamydia is commonly transmitted from an infected mother to a newborn at the time of delivery, and has been documented to persist for as long as three years in some children. This infection presents diagnostic difficulties for many laboratories since the organism is difficult to culture and there is a significant false-positive rate among rapid tests identifying chlamydia with fluorescent antibodies, the ELISA test, or gene probe techniques. In prepubescent children, physicians must use a culture in order to identify chlamydia since a rapid screen is not reliable.

- *Human immunodeficiency virus (HIV)* usually results in the acquired immune deficiency syndrome (AIDS). The infection may be undetectable for years after exposure, and it requires a blood test to diagnose. Sexual contact is one of the principal methods of virus transmission. If a child is diagnosed with HIV or AIDS, sexual abuse is the most likely cause unless the child contracted the disease through fetal acquisition or tainted blood transfusions.

- *Herpes simplex viruses* are commonly referred to as Type 1 or Type 2. Either can be sexually transmitted, but Type 2 is more commonly transmitted through sexual contact. The Type 2 virus causes genital lesions and is strongly suggestive of sexual abuse. The Type 1 virus commonly causes mouth sores and is of little concern unless it appears in the vagina. Type 1 can be transmitted to the vagina by sexual or nonsexual means. Culture studies are necessary to determine if the virus is Type 1 or Type 2.

- *Trichomoniasis (Trichomonas vaginalis)* can cause urethritis and vaginitis, with purulent or watery vaginal discharge common in infected females. Males often have no symptoms. It is so rare in prepubescent girls beyond the first six months of life that sexual abuse is the likely cause. It is also only rarely found in sexually abused children and must be distinguished from *Trichomonis hominis,* a nonsexually transmitted species.

- *Venereal warts (Condyloma acuminata)* are common in sexually active adults and adolescents. These warts are caused by the human papilloma virus, which has several subtypes according to DNA typing. While such subtyping is currently performed only in selected labs, it may prove of significant forensic value in the future. At this time, the literature describes numerous modes of acquisition of genital warts in young children, including genital warts in close contacts, particularly genital warts in mothers of infected children. Nonsexual transmission does occur, and incidence rates for sexual acquisition vary from study to study. (Fraser, L. [1998]. Genital warts in children. *APSAC Advisor, 11,* 9.)

- *Nonspecific or bacterial vaginitis* is characterized by mucosal inflammation and purulent discharge. It is usually seen in preadolescent children. Bacterial vaginosis is diagnosed by characteristic "clue cells" seen on microscopic examination of vaginal secretions and the distinctive odor in these secretions. The condition is thought to result from the overproduction of organisms normally found in the vagina, including *Gardnerella vaginalis* and other anaerobic bacteria. The condition in children may result from nonsexual causes and is only rarely encountered in sexual abuse cases.

- *Pubic lice* may be transmitted to a child by sexual contact with an infected adult.

- *Granuloma inguinale,* which is thought to be spread most frequently through anal intercourse and causes painless ulcers that enlarge and easily bleed, is a strong indication of abuse.

The foregoing list does not include every potential sexually transmitted disease. Others such as hepatitis, *Ureaplasma urealyticum, Mycoplasma hominis,* and *Molluscum contagiosum* are more commonly nonsexually transmitted. Sometimes a child tests positive for one of these viruses, bacteria, or agents without having had any observable symptoms. If one of these conditions is present in a child who describes being sexually abused, consult with an expert to determine the likelihood of sexual transmission of the disease, especially if the suspect has the condition as well.

Acording to the 1989 Sexually Transmitted Diseases Treatment Guidelines issued by the Centers for Disease Control, "some diseases (e.g., gonorrhea, syphilis, and chlamydia), if acquired after the neonatal period, are almost 100% indicative of sexual contact." (Centers for Disease Control and Prevention. [1998]. 1998 guidelines for treatment of sexually transmitted diseases. *Morbidity and Mortality Weekly Report, 47*[RR-1], 119.) Whenever this type of evidence is present, the investigator should consult with a medical expert. Testimony addressing the characteristics of the disease, methods of transmission, likelihood of transmission by other than sexual contact, and any other issues should be elicited from an expert at trial.

6. Additional Steps When the Assault Was Recent

Whenever information suggests that an incident of sexual abuse occurred within the past 72 hours, the medical exam should include additional steps. The physician will base the decision about what evidence to collect on the nature of the suspected abuse and how much time has passed.

Wood's Lamp. A Wood's Lamp is an ultraviolet light that can scan clothing or the body for evidence of dried or moist secretions, stains, or subtle injury. Most hospitals and many doctors use this lamp when a child is being examined within 72 hours of a suspected abusive incident. Semen usually reflects a green or blue fluorescence under this light but may not fluoresce when fresh. Furthermore, seminal stains may appear as areas of absent or diminished fluorescence on clothing made of fluorescent synthetic material or washed in light optical density detergent. Subtle bodily injury, such as rope marks and recent contusions, can often be seen. However, various skin infections, pigmentary changes, and chemicals including systemic and topical medications, cosmetics, soaps, and industrial chemicals may also fluoresce under ultraviolet light. Physicians should use diagrams to record the location and extent of stains and injury.

Clothing. The child should not be required to undress until the exam is ready to begin. If the child's clothing has possible evidentiary value, it should be collected by medical staff and appropriately packaged and labeled before being turned over to the investigating officer. If the child does not have a change of clothing, the investigating officer should accompany the child home after the exam to collect the clothing for later submission to the appropriate crime laboratory.

The examining physician should describe the condition of the clothing if it was worn during or immediately after the abuse. The presence of rips, blood or semen stains, dirt, hairs, or other foreign material should be noted. Many physicians place clean paper on the floor, then another piece of clean paper or a sheet on top of that, and have the child disrobe while standing on the paper or sheet. The physician then folds the top layer to collect loose material that falls from the clothing.

Wet clothing should be allowed to dry before packaging, then each piece should be placed in a separate paper bag. Do not use plastic storage methods since plastic retains moisture and can cause the clothing to deteriorate. Clothing should not be folded across any stains and care should be taken to avoid transfer of stains to the bag, other garments, or different areas of the same garment. Medical personnel often place tissue paper against stains and fold the clothing inward. Investigating officers should arrange for analysis of the stains by a crime laboratory.

Fingernail scrapings and foreign material collection. Fingernail scrapings are generally taken from a child who may have scratched the suspect during a recent assault. Similar scrapings would be taken from the suspect if he scratched the child. Recovered evidence can include blood, tissue, fibers, or possibly even feces if digital anal penetration is suspected. A clean knife, toothpick, or manicure stick can be used to collect these scrapings into paper bindles, usually one for each hand. Other foreign materials, such as grass and dirt found on the child's body, can also be placed in paper bindles with careful notation of their location. This kind of evidence should be submitted to a crime laboratory for analysis.

Bite marks. Although assailants sometimes bite children they abuse and vice versa, physicians often fail to recognize bite marks. If the child has been bitten, the physician or forensic odontologist should swab the immediate area of the mark to collect saliva for later crime lab analysis. Photographs should also be taken. They should be of good quality with as little distortion as possible. Position the camera directly above and perpendicular to the mark and take close-ups. Place a centimeter ruler next to the bite mark when photographing to clarify the size of the mark. Marks may be only faintly visible if the child is seen immediately after an assault. Additional photos can be taken in 24 to 36 hours when bruising may be more fully developed. Consult with a forensic odontologist and consider making impressions of the suspect's mouth for comparison with the photographed bite marks if identity of the suspect is an issue.

Hair samples. A doctor will usually inspect the child for hairs from the suspect if the examination occurs soon after the alleged sexual assault. The hairs collected should be placed in a bindle and sealed. The postpubescent child is seated on a paper towel while a clean comb or brush is used to remove loose hairs or foreign material from the pubic area. The paper can then be folded and placed in an envelope.

If the investigator needs to match these specimens to the suspect's hair, reference head and/or pubic hair samples from the child must be pulled and turned over to the criminologist for analysis. Some jurisdictions collect reference samples at the time of the medical exam unless it is clearly unnecessary, while others wait until a case is going to trial and hair analysis is needed. Crime labs, doctors, and hospitals should determine how many hairs should be cut or plucked. Recently, some crime laboratories have begun using mass spectrometry to test hair for past drug use. This may be useful in child abuse cases to verify or refute allegations that the suspect used or provided illegal substances to the child.

Foreign debris. The presence of lubricating agents, such as petroleum jelly or baby oil, used by offenders to facilitate penetration often provides strong circumstantial corroboration of a child's allegation. Investigators should encourage the examining physician to check for such residues when the child is examined after a recent victimization. A laboratory, such as the FBI, can often provide verification of such a discovery, as they can often distinguish one manufacturer from another through analysis, and even isolate one batch of lubricant from another produced by the same company. A range of foreign objects, including chewing tobacco, coins, and pubic hairs, recovered from the vaginas of young girls have also corroborated claims about abuse.

The collection of samples to detect sexual contact. At the same time specimens are taken for determining the presence of STDs, the examining physician should take specimens from the child's mouth and genital areas to test for sperm and seminal fluid whenever there appears to have been recent ejaculation. Positive findings constitute convincing evidence of sexual contact by a male offender.

Because sperm and seminal fluid indicators deteriorate rapidly, the likelihood of positive results will depend on how recent the assault was; whether the child washed, urinated, or defecated; and what area of the body was involved. Because salivary enzymes cause deterioration, evidence of semen in the mouth can rarely be detected more than 6 hours after an assault. The longest such evidence can survive in the vagina and rectum is estimated to be 48 hours, although sperm may survive in the cervix and be detectable in samples from the endocervix for several days. While studies of sperm survivability have been done only on adult women, they can be used to estimate the rate of sperm deterioration in child victims.

Mouth specimens are collected by swabbing the gums, fold of the cheek, under the tongue, and the pharynx. On occasion, the physician may deem it helpful to have the child blow her nose on a gauze square. Vaginal and rectal specimens can be collected with swabs during speculum or bimanual exams or by using a saline wash and saline-moistened swabs. Because of the discomfort involved in a speculum exam, endocervical samples are not usually obtained from young girls unless it appears necessary.

Heavily crusted blood or semen stains can be scraped with the edge of a clean glass slide or the back of a clean scalpel blade into a paper bindle. Hairs matted with secretions can be cut and placed in a paper bindle. Thinner stains are collected with swabs moistened in distilled water, then air-dried and packaged in an envelope or tube. Secretions that are still moist can be collected with dry swabs to avoid dilution, air-dried, and similarly packaged. Normally, these specimens would then be submitted by law enforcement to a crime laboratory for analysis. The following items most commonly indicate semen.

The presence of sperm: Wet mount and permanent smears. Wet mount slides are generally made immediately after specimens are collected by combining a drop of the secretion from a swab or pipette with a drop of nutrient medium or saline on the slide. The examining physician or lab technician then examines the slide under a high-power microscope to determine the presence of motile or nonmotile sperm. Motile sperm indicate a recent ejaculation within 8 hours. Factors affecting motility or presence of sperm include body temperature, amount of ejaculate, vaginal acidity, the use of contraceptives, the existence of vaginitis or other infection, postassault hygiene, whether the child was lying down or upright at the time of the assault, and whether the offender has had a vasectomy.

Permanent smears (dry mount slides) are usually also made from the samples. They can be stained to help visualize sperm, examined by medical or crime lab personnel, and kept indefinitely. Sometimes nonmotile sperm can be seen on dry mount slides when no sperm were seen on the wet mount, owing to the increased visibility of the stained smear. Both wet mount and permanent smears need to be appropriately labeled and retained as evidence. Hospital personnel and professionals from the crime laboratory should establish protocols for obtaining sperm specimens and preparing them for analysis.

Acid phosphatase. Human acid phosphatase is an enzyme found in significantly higher concentrations in seminal fluid than in other bodily fluids, including vaginal secretions. The acid phosphatase found in seminal fluid can be differentiated from other sources of acid phosphatase. It is present in semen even when the male has had a vasectomy and there are no sperm in his semen.

Elevated levels of acid phosphatase in samples taken from the child's vagina, rectum, or mouth are consistent with recent ejaculation. Acid phosphatase levels in the vagina may return to normal within as few as 3 hours of ejaculation and usually within 72 hours. Normal levels return more rapidly to the mouth and rectum. High levels may be detectable on clothing or other surfaces for months or years. Tests can be conducted in hospitals or crime labs using aspirated secretions or cool air–dried swabs. Refrigeration is necessary for wet samples and helpful for preserving dried samples.

P 30 (semen glycoprotein of prostatic origin). Some jurisdictions test for the presence of P 30, which is especially important when acid phosphatase is found in high concentrations but no sperm are found. Specimens are collected in the same manner as those for acid phosphatase testing. The test for P 30 is particularly valuable when the suspect has had a vasectomy or is sterile for some other reason. P 30 is present in high levels in seminal fluid, in low levels in male urine, and absent in vaginal fluid, female urine, or saliva. Both normal and vasectomized males have P 30 present in their semen. A positive P 30 test indicates that sexual contact occurred within 48 hours of the specimen being taken. Like properly preserved nonmotile sperm and acid phosphatase on other surfaces, P 30 may be detectable for much longer in its dried state. The prosecutor must determine, through a discovery motion or search warrant, whether the suspect has had a vasectomy or is otherwise sterile whenever P 30 is detected (proving the sample is semen) but sperm is not (indicating sterility). Failure to do so creates an argument regarding reasonable doubt for the defense.

Genetic markers in bodily fluids: Blood group substances and DNA. Additional tests of blood and saliva may help identify the offender. All comprehensive crime labs are equipped to perform traditional tests for genetic markers found in the bodily fluids of people who are secretors. A secretor is an individual whose bodily fluids, including saliva, semen and vaginal secretions, contain a water-soluble form of the antigens of the ABO blood group, which makes up 80% of the population. Genetic markers include blood group antigens such as ABO blood type, PGM-phosphoglucomutasetype, EsD-esterase D-type, Pep-A type, and others. A growing number of labs can conduct tests that identify distinctive patterns in the DNA (deoxyribonucleic acid) found in biological specimens. DNA is found inside the cells of all living organisms. In humans, DNA is found in practically every cell of the body and determines all inherited characteristics. No two people have identical DNA molecules unless they are identical twins.

DNA typing offers a number of advantages over traditional serological tests. Its distinguishing feature is that it makes positive identification possible. If a crime suspect's DNA matches biological samples taken from a child, that suspect can be linked with the crime. Traditional tests serve only to exclude persons from the matter under investigation and allow scientists only to express the odds of whether the suspect was the source of the specimen. If DNA samples match, the expert can testify conclusively about the match between the suspect and child. The suspect is exonerated if the samples do not match.

DNA typing is also useful for establishing parentage in incest and rape cases. Tests can produce a DNA "print" composed of components inherited from the child's mother and putative father. By comparing DNA prints, scientists can establish family blood lines with unprecedented precision. This technique uses tissue from an aborted fetus or samples taken from the newborn and should be considered the scientific test of choice when a sexual assault victim is impregnated.

Specimens of the child's blood and saliva needed for comparison to the suspect's blood and saliva samples should be collected during the medical exam. The chain of custody of both the child's and suspect's evidence sample is of paramount importance, and procedures to ensure its integrity must be strictly followed and documented. Any error in this process will jeopardize the test's ability to identify the guilty suspect, and the court may refuse to allow test results to be admitted at trial. Laboratory testing procedures should be clearly delineated and followed. (See Stolorow, M., & Clarke, G. [1992]. Forensic DNA testing: A new dimension in criminal evidence gains broad acceptance. *The Prosecutor, 25*(4), 13.) Local or state police laboratories or the FBI laboratory in Washington, DC can be contacted for possible DNA testing. Ask for a referral to one of the private laboratories throughout the country that does DNA testing if government laboratories are unable to conduct the tests. It is important to keep in mind that DNA testing can be time-consuming and expensive and may not be necessary in every case.

The prosecutor should not rely solely on one piece of evidence to make the case. If the results of tests are deemed inadmissible, the prosecutor must then use more traditional types of proof to persuade the jury of the defendant's guilt. Do not forgo thorough interviewing and preparation of the witnesses simply because of a positive test result. For additional information, see the Resource List at the end of Chapter III. (National Research Council, Committee on DNA Technology. [1992]. In *Forensic science, DNA technology in forensic science.* Washington, DC: National Academy; *People v. Wesley,* 533 N.Y.S.2d 643 [N.Y. County Ct. 1988], *aff'd,* 589 N.Y.S.2d 197 [App. Div. 1992], *aff'd,* 83 N.Y.2d 417 [1993]).

Additional tests as needed. Additional tests may be appropriate depending on the case and timing of the medical exam. For instance, a pregnancy test should be done with a postpubertal girl whenever pregnancy is possible. Blood alcohol testing and toxicology screens can be done when an assault has occurred recently and there is reason to believe the child ingested drugs or alcohol prior to or during the abuse. If too much time has passed for toxicology screens to be of assistance, consider having samples of the child's hair examined by mass spectrometry for drug ingestion.

Evidence collection procedures and use of "rape kits." Evidence must always be labeled, preserved, and stored properly. It is especially important to properly handle evidence collected during the medical exam. Protocols should delineate

- Where samples are collected, including from what parts of the body
- When samples should be taken and who should take samples
- How samples are collected so contamination and improper processing are avoided
- How samples are packaged, sealed, and labeled, including specification of the date, the doctor's and child's identity, the area of the body from which the sample was taken, and other identification information
- Who handles samples and how the chain of custody is recorded
- How samples are stored, e.g., in a locked space such as freezer, refrigerator, or evidence room to which others have limited or no access
- How and when samples are transferred between medical personnel and law enforcement

Proper packing and storage of samples are two of the most important aspects of evidence collection procedures. Swabs and slides must often be air dried, preferably in a stream of cool air, to promote rapid drying and maximum preservation of genetic marker enzymes. Once dried, they are ordinarily refrigerated or frozen. Blood samples need to be stored in the appropriate type of tube and usually need to be refrigerated. Both medical and law enforcement staff must be able to package and store such samples properly.

It is advisable to keep the number of people who handle evidence to a minimum so it will later be easier to determine and present evidence about chain of custody. The names of those involved in the medical examination and the handling of evidence must be legible and enough information must be provided to locate them if their testimony is needed.

Many hospitals use commercially available sexual assault or rape kits designed to facilitate the collection of forensic evidence in recent sexual assaults, including those in which the victim is a child. These kits can be very useful in smaller jurisdictions since they promote uniformity in sample collection. Larger hospitals often develop their own kits. The rape kit commonly includes checklists of specimens to be collected, paper bags for collecting clothing, tubes with swabs to collect secretions, glass slides, special tubes for blood-typing syphilis serology, combs for pubic and scalp hair collection, orange sticks for fingernail scrapings, envelopes for hair samples and other evidence, items needed to collect saliva samples such as gauze squares or swabs and tubes, and forms for recording chain of custody information.

Both the prosecutor and the investigator must be familiar with these kits and determine whether they adequately cover needed evidence. They should take steps to incorporate additional procedures into the current evidence collection protocol if appropriate, or find another kit including everything needed or wanted. Medical personnel must follow recommended procedures for any rape kit that is used.

F. Medical Evidence in Sexual Abuse Cases

1. Evidence Characteristic or Symptomatic of Sexual Abuse

a. Acid phosphatase, sperm, and semen. The presence of acid phosphatase, other biomedical markers found in semen, or sperm in or near the child's vagina, rectum, or mouth is considered conclusive evidence of sexual abuse. This evidence generally indicates that the sexual abuse took place within the past 12 hours, although some markers can be found in body orifices up to 72 hours later. The presence of acid phosphatase or sperm usually results in reliance on an "identification" defense.

Finding such definitive evidence of sexual abuse is rare since cases are seldom reported quickly, children are frequently bathed in the interim, and the sexual abuse of children may not include ejaculating in or on the child's body. Acid phosphatase, an enzyme produced in the prostate, and other markers of semen are rapidly lost on or in the body after intercourse, but are better preserved on items such as clothing, bedding, or carpeting. Acid phosphatase may persist for months in dried stains. If ejaculation is suspected, the case investigator should submit items such as clothing and bedding for forensic examination even if there has been a long delay. The biological evidence from these items can be tested and used to identify the perpetrator.

b. Sexually transmitted diseases. Theoretically, STDs can be transmitted by one of three mechanisms: sexual activity, nonsexual contact, and vertical transmission from mother to fetus or newborn. The identification of certain STDs outside of the newborn period is conclusive proof of sexual abuse. The American Academy of Pediatrics has published guidelines for the evaluation of sexual abuse of children, which show the probability of sexual abuse when various STDs are found in the child.

When a child is diagnosed with an STD, it is essential to know the method used to make the diagnosis, as there are standards for diagnosing STDs in children that do not apply to adults. In addition, the incubation period (time from transmission of the infection to symptoms of the disease), rate of transmission, and time to cure should be ascertained for purposes of determining when the abuse occurred and whether the suspect will show symptoms of the disease. If the victim tests positive for an STD, obtain a search warrant or court order for samples from the suspect immediately. Consider subpoenaing the suspect's medical records to determine if there is any evidence of treatment for an STD. If the defendant and the child are infected with the same STD, the prosecution will likely need to call the examining

Sexually Transmitted Disease (STD) confirmed	Sexual abuse
Gonorrhea*	Diagnostic[1]
Syphilis*	Diagnostic
HIV**	Diagnostic
Chlamydia*	Diagnostic***
Trichomonas vaginalis	Highly suspicious
*Condylomata acuminatum**	Suspicious
Herpes (genital location)	Suspicious ****
Bacterial vaginosis	Inconclusive
Candida albicans	Unlikely

SOURCE: American Academy of Pediatrics. [1999]. Guidelines for the evaluation of sexual abuse of children. *Pediatrics, 103,* 186, 189.

NOTES: 1. "Diagnostic" means the presence of the particular STD makes the diagnosis of sexual abuse a medical certainty when its congenital forms have been excluded or ruled out.

* If not acquired during childbirth

** If not acquired during childbirth or transfusion

*** Culture only reliable diagnostic method

**** There must be an investigation to determine whether there is a clear history of autoinoculation (inoculation with a vaccine made from microorganisms obtained from the recipient's own body).

physician, the technician who took the sample from the victim and suspect, the laboratory examiner, an expert in STDs, and the clinician who compared the samples in order to tie these facts together.

If the suspect does not have the STD by the time he is tested and there is convincing evidence that the suspect is in fact the perpetrator, the prosecution will need expert testimony to explain this circumstance. The expert will need to explain the rate of spontaneous remission of the STD, that a person can be cured and within days have no trace of most STDs, and that antibiotics for a non-STD infection such as an upper respiratory infection may also cure the STD. The expert can further address the type of testing available for STDs, limitations on testing, e.g., some infections can be reliably diagnosed only when active lesions are present, the sensitivity and specificity of the testing method used, and the fact that improper laboratory techniques and testing procedures may fail to reveal an existing organism.

The investigator should seek out another person such as a spouse or significant other who was sexually involved with the suspect at the time it is believed that the abuse occurred. Determine if that person is or was infected. A third party match, such as the suspect's spouse and the victim having the same strain of gonorrhea even though the defendant does not, can be quite persuasive. Such a finding may also allow the prosecution to argue that the suspect must have destroyed evidence by getting treated.

If the defendant has an STD but the child does not, the prosecution will also need an expert witness to talk about the rates of transmission and how the disease is transmitted. Using the expert testimony, the prosecution may then be able to argue that the contact between the suspect and the child would not be expected to transmit secretions or the infection. It would also be important to point out that the transmission rates of STDs are based upon adult subject studies, not transmission rates with children owing to understandable ethical constraints. The expert should discuss the applicability of adult studies to the rates of transmission from an adult to a child. (See Ingram, D. L. [1991]. Controversies about the sexual and nonsexual transmission of adult STDs to children. In R. D. Krugman & J. M. Leventhal [Eds.], *Child Sexual Abuse: Report of the Twenty-Second Ross Roundtable on Critical Approaches to Common Pediatric Problems* [p. 14]; Hammerschlag, M. R., et al. [1998]. False positive results with the use of chlamydial antigen detection tests in the evaluation of suspected sexual abuse of children. *Pediatric Infectious Diseases, 7,* 11; Whittington, W. L., et al. [1988]. Incorrect identification of Neisseria gonorrhoea from infants and children. *Pediatric Infectious Diseases, 7,* 3.)

c. **Genital injuries**. Although few findings on the genital examination are proof of sexual abuse, a child will occasionally sustain a severe genital or anal injury that is conclusive evidence of sexual abuse. When such injuries occur, the injury may be extensive and involve the external and/or internal genital tissues. Its extent will not be expected from accidental trauma. In addition, a verbal child may be able to provide a history of sexual assault that explains the injury. The expert physician, however, will not testify that sexual abuse is the cause of the injury. The prosecutor cannot ask the physician whether sexual abuse caused the injury. Rather, the questions and answer might be as follows:

Q: Doctor, what might cause this injury besides an object being forced into the child's vagina?

A: Nothing I'm aware of. This injury is diagnostic of a penetrating genital injury.

Q: Did you find any indication of a disease or condition present in this child that may account for these injuries?

A: No.

Physicians can generally rule out self-infliction of serious injuries by excessive masturbation. If the examining physician can rule out excessive masturbation, have him do so. If the physician will not do so, do not raise it or it might become a suggestion to the defense and give the theory some legitimacy. If it is a possibility, it might be better to let the defense raise it. The state's redirect would then consist of questions that elicit answers that it is "possible" but not likely that the injury occurred in this manner and that the physician received no history of excessive masturbation from any source.

In the event that the physician finds hymenal tears, the physician should be able to testify that tears are painful and children will not masturbate to the point of causing themselves pain. The doctor should further be able to relate that when young children masturbate, they generally manipulate the clitoris, not the hymen. The physician should be able to conclude that the injuries, such as those in the present case, are not expected from masturbation.

2. Medical Evidence That Is Nonspecific to Sexual Abuse

Children frequently have complaints related to their genital area, most of which have nothing to do with sexual abuse. Kellogg reviewed the medical records of 157 children with anogenital signs or symptoms who were referred for a medical examination for possible sexual abuse but did not have a history of abuse or behavior symptoms. Only 15% of the children had medical findings suggestive or definitive for sexual abuse. The majority of these children had medical problems unrelated to sexual abuse or had normal examinations. (Kellogg, N. D., et al. [1998]. Children with anogenital symptoms and signs referred for sexual abuse evaluations. *Archives of Pediatric and Adolescent Medicine, 152*, 634, 636.)

Because physicians do not always perform routine genital examinations in young girls, many are unfamiliar with variations of normal anatomy or with common and uncommon vulvovaginal problems. Although many of the findings discussed below may be the result of sexual abuse, they are nonspecific and should be treated as such.

a. Redness (erythema). General redness (erythema) of the vulva, vagina, penis, or anus is a common problem in young children. It is very often the product of poor hygiene rather than a specific indication of sexual abuse. Erythema caused by sexual abuse can represent a superficial injury caused by a *recent* sexual contact. The healing of superficial injuries in these areas is rapid, and the redness is unlikely to persist for more than a few days following the injury. On occasion, the redness may be a secondary problem related to an infection. When calling a physician to testify about redness in the genital area, the prosecutor should elicit testimony about the redness and its other possible causes. The prosecutor should use care to not let the physician overstate the case. The more evenhanded the physician's testimony, acknowledging the possible alternative causes, the more likely the jury will give the physician's testimony greater weight. If the redness appears coincidentally with a report of molestation, and especially if it is a problem only when the child has had contact with the suspect, it is certainly relevant.

b. Hymenal opening. Hymenal opening size should not be used as evidence of sexual abuse. Although much attention has been paid to this issue in the past, the size of the opening varies from child to child and may depend upon the position of the child, the amount of traction used to separate the labia, and the degree of her cooperation during the doctor's genital examination. Be aware that physicians who are skilled in examining children for sexual abuse often differ in their assessment of girls' genital findings. (Paradise, J. E., et al. [1997]. Assessments of girls' genital findings and the likelihood of sexual abuse. *Archives of Pediatric Adolescent Medicine, 151*, 883.)

More important than the size of the hymenal opening is the condition of the hymenal tissue around the opening. Is the surrounding tissue attenuated, absent, or irregular? Significant irregularities, usually in the posterior rim of the hymenal tissue, may be indicative of penetrating trauma into the vagina. The difficulty with such evidence is that the defense might claim that excessive masturbation accounts for the finding. If this defense is asserted, the prosecution will need to call a qualified physician to testify that irregular tissue surrounding the hymenal opening is a result of the insertion of some object and is not found in children absent some manipulation. Depending on the medical findings, the physician may be able to minimize the likelihood of self-infliction. The prosecution should also corroborate the medical evidence through other witnesses that the child does not masturbate excessively. The prosecutor is then left with a significant medical finding that corroborates the child's testimony.

c. Enuresis. Enuresis, the involuntary passage of urine, occurs commonly in young children and is generally of no concern to medical professionals. Occasional nighttime bed-wetting in children up to ages 7 or 8 is normal. Children with urinary tract infections often experience enuresis. However, a physician should examine a child over 4 who experiences regular pant-wetting during the day. Similarly, it is a cause for investigation if a child who has stopped nighttime bed-wetting for a number of years suddenly starts wetting the bed again. Such cases of enuresis may be caused by a medical problem, the maturation process, or psychological problems that may or may not be related to sexual abuse. Talk to a physician who is an expert in the area of child abuse about the child's symptoms.

The prosecution may decide that expert testimony is necessary to explain the connection between the child's enuresis and the sexual abuse. The prosecution must be careful not to overstate this issue, however, because it is likely that a jurist may have been a bed-wetter or has a child or relative with enuresis that is unrelated to abuse. This is a common, nonspecific pediatric problem, and care must be used when it is introduced to support an argument of sexual abuse.

d. Encopresis. Encopresis is the passage of formed or semiformed stools in inappropriate locations that occurs after age 4 and has no medical cause. The anal sphincter is a ring-like muscle that normally maintains constriction of the anal opening. Encopresis can result from sexual abuse because the anal sphincter becomes dilated from multiple penetrations. The child might also have learned to relax this muscle to reduce the pain of the penetration. However, not all encopretic children are abused. Encopresis may be associated with neurologic or muscle disorders and psychological problems. Some abused children with normal sphincters develop encopresis because of the emotional problems created by the abuse.

If encopresis is present in the child, consider testimony from a physician about this condition. There is a very logical connection between sexual abuse and the repeated relaxation of the anal muscles as an act of self-protection by a child. If a physician can explain this in a manner that makes sense, the prosecution should elicit this testimony.

e. Anal fissures. Anal fissures are common causes of anal pain and mild bleeding, but their cause is not well understood. Trauma from fecal mass and increased tone of the internal anal sphincter seem to be important factors in the development of anal fissures. The significance of anal fissures depends on their size, location, and number. They may be related to constipation, but they are also associated with anal trauma caused by excessive stretching of the anal mucosa. A physician may feel comfortable testifying that multiple anal fissures are inconsistent with constipation but may be unable to state that they were the result of sexual abuse because they are also not specific for sexual abuse. With nonspecific evidence, the defense will suggest numerous potential causes of the condition. The prosecution must always be prepared on redirect to ask questions that generate answers that acknowledge other causes of the condition to give the physician credibility but also demonstrate that anal fissures are consistent with injuries caused by abuse. (See McCann, J. J., et al.

[1992]. Genital injuries resulting from sexual abuse: A longitudinal study. *Pediatrics, 89,* 307.)

3. Lack of Medical Findings in Sexual Abuse Cases

Most sexual abuse cases lack significant medical evidence. There are three simple reasons for the lack of medical evidence. First, the abusive acts may not have caused any injury. Second, the genital area heals quickly, so minor injuries may have healed by the time of the examination. Finally, there is generally not a timely examination because of a delay in reporting or because of a delay in scheduling the examination. Joyce A. Adams et al. have reported that two factors correlate with an abnormal examination: (1) the time since the last assault being generally within 72 hours and (2) a history of blood being reported at the time of the assault. (Adams, J. A., et al. [1994]. Examination findings in legally confirmed child sexual abuse: It's normal to be normal. *Pediatrics, 94*(3), 310.)

The decision whether to call a doctor who may have found nothing has no simple answer. Some prosecutors believe it wise to always have a physician testify, if for no other reason than to explain why the lack of medical findings is not inconsistent with the abuse account. Cases involving oral copulation, fondling, or digital penetration some time in the past are unlikely to have medical findings. Other prosecutors prefer not to call the physician with the hope the defense will, so that prosecutors can elicit testimony during cross-examination that medical findings would not be expected in such circumstances and that to suggest otherwise is foolish. However, some physicians may not know that medical findings are unlikely, so the prosecutor must be cautious. If a young child testifies that painful penetration and bleeding occurred, the jury will expect medical findings or an explanation of their absence. Have an expert explain to the jury why it is common to find no medical trauma and why the examination is not inconsistent with the child's statement of events. The failure to do so may result in an acquittal.

Children may experience pain as a result of some manipulation that does not actually cause injury, since pain is a protective reflex that causes the child to draw away from the source of pain before injury actually occurs. The use of lubricants such as Vaseline and lotion also decreases the possibility of injury. The physician should point out that the hymen is recessed in the introitus[3] and protected by the labia. A perpetrator putting his penis, a finger, or other object between the labia (referred to as vulvar coitus) is usually interpreted by the child as "in the vagina" and may meet the statutory definition of penetration, but the hymen may not actually be damaged. The rapidity and nature of the healing process may also account for the lack of injuries or scars. Healing may progress so rapidly that examinations 3 to 7 days later may show no indication of prior injury. (See McCann, J. J., et al. [1992]. Genital injuries resulting from sexual abuse: A longitudinal study. *Pediatrics, 89,* 307; Dejong, A., & Rose, M. [1991]. Legal proof of child sexual abuse in the absence of physical evidence. *Pediatrics, 88,* 506; Finkel, M. S. [1989]. Anogenital trauma in sexually abused children. *Pediatrics, 84,* 317; see also *People v. Rowland,* 841 P.2d 897 [Cal. 1992] (finding the *Frye* test not applicable to expert medical opinion that absence of genital trauma was consistent with nonconsensual sexual intercourse because testimony implicated no new scientific technique, and was based fundamentally on physical examination of victim.)

---

[3]The introitus is the entrance into a canal or hollow organ, as the vagina.

4. Sample Questions

The following list of questions was adapted from the 1983 manual of Shirley C. Anderson and Lucy Berliner titled *Evaluation of the Child Sexual Assault Patient in the Health Care Setting: A Medical Training Manual.* All the questions will not be appropriate or allowed in every case or jurisdiction. The prosecutor must add questions tailored to the facts of the specific case and the law in that jurisdiction. A prosecutor should always review the questions with the witness before testimony to avoid surprises during the testimony. In addition, some physicians will not answer questions that are phrased in a certain manner, but they may be willing to provide the answer the prosecutor is looking for if the question is phrased differently.

General qualifying questions:
- State your name, address, and current occupation.
- Please list your educational background including degrees, board certification, licensing, postgraduate training, and work experience.

Qualifying as an expert witness:
- Describe your training, education, and clinical experience in the field of sexual assault examinations.
- Have you written or presented papers in the area of sexual assault examinations?
- At approximately how many conferences have you presented lectures, speeches, or workshops on the subject?
- Have you qualified as an expert in this or other courts in the areas of sexual assault?
- Estimate the number of times you have done so.

Questions regarding the medical examination:
- Did you examine (victim's name) on (the date)?
- For what purpose was the examination performed?
- Where did you perform the examination?
- Did you obtain a history from the child? (Note that in some circumstances, a forensic interview will have been completed before the physician sees the child, and the physician will not have obtained the history of assault from the child. The physician should have obtained a routine medical history, however.)
- For what purpose did you obtain the history?
- Was the history critical to your diagnosis and treatment of the child?
- Did you tell the child what you were going to do?
- What did you tell the child?
- Describe the general appearance and behavior of (victim's name) during that examination.
- Did you perform a physical examination?
- Could you briefly describe the nature of that examination?
- What were your findings?
- Did you perform any medical tests? Describe them and the reasons why they were done.
- Does your hospital/clinic have written standard procedures for the evaluation of a victim of sexual assault?
- Are you familiar with these procedures?
- Were those procedures followed in this case?

(Continued)

(Continued)

Questions regarding injuries:

- In your report, you state that injuries were found. Please list the type and location of those injuries.
- Did you photograph the injuries? Is this the photograph taken of the injuries?
- Did you take or witness the taking of this photograph?
- Is this a true and accurate representation of the injuries you have described?
- Can you give an estimate of the age of the injury you described, that is, when it occurred?
- Are the injuries noted consistent with the history given regarding the type of sexual abuse experienced by the child? If so, how? If not, why not?
- What else might account for the kind of injuries you observed? Do you have any reason to believe that such a cause accounts for the injuries to this child? Why not?
- You state no injuries were found. Would this be consistent with the history given as to the type of sexual abuse described by (victim's name)?
- Would you always expect to find injuries if a child was sexually abused? Why not?
- You note there were no genital injuries, and specifically, no injury to the hymen. Is this inconsistent with a history of attempted or actual digital/penile penetration? Please explain why or why not.

Questions regarding infection:

- What laboratory tests were performed?
- What were the results of these tests?
- What is a sexually transmitted disease?
- List the more commonly occurring sexually transmitted diseases.
- Could a person contract a sexually transmitted disease as the result of sexual abuse?
- In your opinion, could the sexually transmitted disease seen in this child have been a consequence of the sexual abuse reported?
- Are any of these diseases transmitted in nonsexual ways? How often does this occur? (Note that nonsexual transmission of STDs occurs with varying frequency for different diseases, and for children, controversy may exist regarding nonsexual transmission rates.)

Questions regarding forensic evidence of sexual contact: (Note that these questions may be asked of the physician or criminologist who analyzed the forensic evidence.)

- Did you collect any samples, specimens, or other evidence from the child?
- If so, what were they? What was your purpose for doing so?
- What is a wet mount? What is the purpose for taking such a sample?
- How long would you expect to find motile/nonmotile sperm in the mouth? In the vagina? In the rectum? (Note that no data or studies exist for these occurrences in children.)
- Are you sure what you saw was sperm? How many times have you performed this test?
- What is the purpose of the permanent smear? Why are the sperm seen more easily on the stained slide?

(Continued)

(Continued)

- What is acid phosphatase?
- What is the test for acid phosphatase? Why is it performed?
- What were the results of the test? (If the sample was sent to a forensic laboratory, the health care provider may not have the results.)
- What do the results mean?
- Can other body fluids or other fluids contain acid phosphatase?
- Can a female have acid phosphatase in her vagina/urethra?
- The analysis for acid phosphatase was negative. Is it possible for a sexual assault to have occurred even if it is not present?
- The tests were negative for spermatozoa, yet positive for acid phosphatase. Explain how this can occur.

Questions regarding tests to identify the offender:

- What tests were done to aid in the identification of the perpetrator?
- What is the purpose of:
  - A pubic hair combing
  - Collecting secretions for antigen testing
  - Collecting secretions for genetic marker testing
    Fingerprints/bite marks
- Usually at this point, the doctor, unless an expert in this area, will defer to an appropriate expert in the field.
- What were the results of these tests?
- What are the limitations of such tests?

VIII.   INTERROGATION OF THE SUSPECT

Child abuse cases are among the most challenging investigations conducted by law enforcement officers. In many investigations, there are no witnesses or physical evidence that can be used to corroborate the victim's allegation. Even in those cases in which medical evidence is present, it only proves that the child was sexually or physically abused, but it does not prove by *whom* unless DNA is involved. Except for the occasional case where a photograph or videotape is recovered that shows the offender committing the abuse, or where there is an eyewitness to the crime, there is probably no evidence more powerful than the offender's own admission of guilt. In the eyes of many jurors, physical and medical evidence cannot compete with the suspect who readily confesses guilt. For this reason, the proper interrogation of a suspect is an important investigative tool in child abuse cases.

The successful child abuse investigator understands that the interrogation is an integral part of the criminal investigation, not an independent activity. The interrogation is no more important than any other part of the investigative process, including the forensic interview of the victim, witness interviews, the medical examination, background checks, and search warrants. During an interrogation, the interrogator's goal is to obtain a truthful confession from the suspect that corroborates the victim's allegations and the other evidence in the case. In many states, a suspect cannot be convicted solely on the basis of an uncorroborated confession.

An investigator has two important goals in every interrogation. The first is to influence the suspect to cooperate with the interrogator by telling the truth. The second goal is to accomplish this in a manner that satisfies both the applicable legal and departmental requirements. Achieving the first goal is no small task. This requires that the suspect do something that is against his best interests and will most likely result in punishment. The second goal is often a difficult task, as confession admissibility is regulated by the Fourth, Fifth, Sixth, and Fourteenth Amendments of the United States Constitution as well as applicable state laws and departmental policies. An interrogator's job is to convince the suspect to tell the truth, not force or compel him to do so. The successful interrogator must be able to accomplish both goals. Investigators must understand that an interrogation that results in a confession might eliminate the need for a trial or for the child to testify.

A. Interviews

Even though the terms are often inappropriately interchanged, *interviews* and *interrogations* are not the same activity. An interview of an individual, including a suspect, is an exchange of information accomplished through a two-way conversation. The interview setting is usually cordial and nonaccusatory. During an interview, it is common and acceptable for the investigator to take notes. Miranda warnings are generally not required since interviews are usually noncustodial situations and the person being interviewed can leave at any time. On average, interviews usually last between 30 and 60 minutes. In addition to gaining information from people, interviews are useful for "locking them into a story." Locking a person into a story is important so that the person cannot later change that version of events as new evidence comes to light or as the case develops. In order to successfully lock a witness into a story, the statement must be reduced to writing and signed or electronically recorded. Occasionally, when a suspect is interviewed, he may give the investigator a preview of a future alibi or defense. The suspect may also give the investigator information for possible themes and strategies that can be used later, during the interrogation.

B. Interrogation

An interrogation is a systematic method of obtaining information from a suspect through a combination of questioning, confronting, suggesting, and influencing. By its very nature, the interrogation setting is one that is accusatory, as there is reason to believe that the person being interrogated is guilty of committing a crime. The reason for this belief may be that the victim named this person as the offender or that the investigation has identified this person as responsible. Without a strong basis for believing in an individual's guilt, a suspect should not be subjected to an interrogation in the hopes that a confession will result. The circumstances in which the interrogation is conducted may differ from one case to another. In one instance, the suspect being interrogated may be under arrest, while in the next the suspect may just be the focus of the investigation. Unlike the interview, the interrogation is very often a custodial situation because the suspect is either under arrest or not free to leave.

Law enforcement investigators, not child protection services (CPS) workers, should be responsible for conducting interrogations. Police investigators are trained in the requisite legal issues and they are experienced in dealing with criminal suspects. In addition, only law enforcement personnel can arrest the suspect or execute a search warrant if such actions are deemed necessary as a result of the suspect's statements. Law enforcement officers enjoy the advantage, both tactically and legally, of being able to deceive the suspect during the interrogation. They may also be able to attempt a single-party consent phone call to the suspect prior to the interrogation. For further information regarding single-party consent phone calls, see Section V.D in this chapter. CPS investigators may be prohibited from using these practices because of their professional ethics. While CPS workers may need to interview the suspect for purposes of their investigation, they should wait until the law enforcement interrogation is completed. If CPS interviews a suspect before an interrogation is conducted, the element of surprise is lost and the opportunity for a successful interrogation is diminished. However, if a suspect is first interrogated and confesses, a CPS worker's subsequent interview will probably be more productive. Moreover, CPS will most likely be able to use the information given by the suspect during the interrogation without having to interview the suspect again. Another question that arises if CPS conducts an interrogation of a suspect is whether the CPS worker must advise the suspect of his constitutional rights. All of these problems can be eliminated if the CPS investigator is allowed to observe the interrogation while it is being conducted and/or interviews the suspect after the law enforcement interrogation.

The interrogator should approach the interrogation without a guiding idea as to how long the interrogation will take to complete. There is no universal legal ruling or policy that dictates how long an interrogation can last. Interrogators must never convey to the suspect, through word or deed, that they are impatient or have to be somewhere else. This will usually cause the suspect to stall and/or just wait the interrogator out. Though the interrogator's training and experience will have some impact on the length of the interrogation, it is the suspect who ultimately decides how long the interrogation will last. The suspect will confess when and only when he is psychologically ready and motivated to do so.

Once the interrogation begins, there should be no unplanned interruptions. Unplanned interruptions may cause the interrogator to lose his train of thought, continuity, and momentum. Interruptions may also allow the suspect time to regain confidence, composure, and become more resolute in his denials.

While some investigators have an innate talent for interrogation, others may have to work harder to acquire the requisite skills. Regardless of natural abilities, investigators can always improve their interrogation skills by obtaining proper training, by observing more experienced interrogators, and by practicing what they have learned. There are many characteristics of a successful interrogator. Interrogators must both possess and demonstrate the following to the suspect during the interrogation:

- Confidence in the investigation
- Patience
- Knowledge of human behavior, the suspect, and the case
- The ability to be a good bluffer
- Experience with child abuse investigations
- The desire to obtain the truth

- Thoroughness in the investigation
- A nonjudgmental attitude toward the suspect
- Self-control
- Empathy for the suspect and his or her situation
- Professionalism
- Understanding

During the interrogation, it is recommended that the investigator refrain from taking notes until the suspect has confessed. If the suspect observes the investigator writing down everything that is said, it may cause him either to stop talking or to become more careful or circumspect in what is said.

Interrogations should always be conducted in a one-on-one setting. Joint interrogations by law enforcement are not recommended. It is psychologically easier to admit a mistake to one person at a time. Private settings ensure that the suspect does not receive verbal or nonverbal cues that the interrogator does not want him to have. A third person in the room may ask the wrong question or make a wrong statement that the interrogator may not want the suspect to hear at that moment. The third person's body language may also convey a message that is contradictory to that of the interrogator. An interrogator cannot control the comments or body language of a third person. There must be only two variables in the interrogation room: the interrogator and the suspect. It is the interrogator's job to influence the suspect's behavior and not allow the reverse to happen. Interrogators must remain in control of their speech, body language, and emotions during the interrogation.

1. Using Interpreters

While it is always preferable for the investigator to communicate directly with the suspect, there are times when this is not possible and an interpreter may be necessary. Interpreters are needed when the suspect speaks a different language than the investigator or when the suspect is deaf. Investigators should be familiar with any applicable state laws or departmental policies governing the use of interpreters. When the suspect is legally deaf, some states require that the interpreter be certified in sign language and present for the entire interrogation. If interpreters are used, they should be cautioned against reacting to what they hear the suspect or investigator say, no matter how shocking or explicit it may be. Interpreters should be made aware that they will have to testify in court at a later date regarding their participation in the interrogation.

2. Observation

In addition to the interrogator, it is strongly recommended that another investigator observe all interrogations. This can be accomplished through the use of visual (a one-way mirror), audio (a microphone), or video (a hidden camera) mechanisms. If the investigator's facilities do not allow for any of these methods, an inexpensive audio monitoring system can be set up using a baby-monitor. There are several reasons for having the interrogation observed by a third party. First, it protects the interrogator from physical assaults by the suspect. Second, it protects the interrogator from false allegations made by the suspect of verbal abuse, physical abuse, sexual harassment, or the use of racial slurs. Third, and most important, it provides the interrogator with someone who can act as a coach and give advice during breaks as to possible themes, strategies, and questions that should be pursued. The observer can also suggest what does and what does not appear to be working. The observer may provide an additional opportunity for obtaining a confession from the suspect if the first interrogator is unsuccessful. The observer, having seen and heard what has already transpired, can pick up where the first interrogator left off without repeating an unproductive line of questioning. If the suspect does not confess to the first interrogator, he should not be asked to give a written or recorded statement. If the second interrogator is able to obtain the suspect's admission and a statement, the jury will view the two conflicting statements with suspicion. Lastly, the observer can act as a witness to the interrogation and take notes on what is observed and heard.

3. Legal Issues

There are many legal issues involved in suspect interrogation. In addition to the constitutional protection against self-incrimination set out by *Miranda v. Arizona*, 384 U.S. 436, 468–69 (1966), the investigator has to comply with departmental or state policy. There are some states that *allow* for either the video or audio recording of the suspect's statement, while other states *require* it. If state law does not require electronic recording and an interrogator is asked why he did not make a video or audio recording of the interrogation, a suggested answer is, "It is not required by law." Policy decisions regarding whether an agency will audiotape or videotape a suspect's statement should be made after consulting with either the agency's legal adviser and/or the prosecuting attorney. Just like the debate surrounding the videotaping of forensic interviews of children, there are pros and cons to recording interrogations and statements.

One universal legal principle that investigators must follow is that when the suspect invokes his right to remain silent or have an attorney present, the investigator cannot attempt to talk the suspect into changing his mind. If the suspect makes an ambiguous or equivocal statement about his desire to remain silent, the investigator should attempt to clarify the suspect's desires. For example, if the suspect says, "Maybe I shouldn't say anything without talking to an attorney first," it would be appropriate for the investigator to ask, "Do you want to talk to an attorney before you answer any more questions?"

Addressing the many state laws and departmental policies governing interrogations is beyond the scope of this manual. Accordingly, investigators should confer with their local prosecutor and/or departmental legal adviser regarding applicable laws and policies in their jurisdiction.

4. The Timing of the Interrogation

The timing of the interrogation will vary from case to case. As a general rule, the investigator should try to balance the need for maintaining the element of surprise with sufficient preparation. The challenge is to know when the interrogator is sufficiently prepared so that a thorough interrogation can be conducted. A mistake is made when so much time is spent in preparation that the suspect becomes aware of the investigation. When this happens, the interrogator loses the element of surprise. If the suspect learns about the investigation prematurely, he may do one or more of the following:

- Apply pressure on the victim to recant the allegation
- Attempt to harm or threaten the victim
- Conceal, remove, or destroy evidence
- Construct and rehearse an alibi or a defense
- Obtain the services of a defense lawyer
- Flee from the jurisdiction
- Commit suicide

When CPS or other investigative agencies are involved, it is critical that the investigator coordinate and communicate with all interested parties prior to the interrogation and throughout the investigation. This will prevent the suspect from becoming prematurely alerted to the investigation. Investigators must understand that the CPS worker may have a departmental policy that dictates a time frame in which the suspect must be contacted and informed of the investigation. Problems are certain to arise in cases where two agencies are conducting separate investigations on the same case. A team approach to the investigation will reduce these problems. Both law enforcement and CPS must understand and respect each other's practices and policies in order to work together successfully. Both agencies and the child victim will benefit if the suspect is interrogated properly and confesses to the abuse.

In most cases of physical and sexual abuse, the victim either is related to or knows the suspect. In these situations, the investigator may have to act to prevent the victim from contacting the suspect prior to the interrogation. The victim may want to threaten the suspect or get back at him by telling the suspect that the police are aware of what he has been doing. In some cases, the victim might have a change of heart and feel the need to warn the suspect that the police are involved. In either event, the result will be the same—the loss of the element of surprise.

In some cases, preparation will be less important than the element of surprise. For example, consider a situation in which a patrol officer observes and arrests a local businessman in the act of committing a sex act with a runaway. An investigator called to the office to handle this case will probably need little preparation before beginning the interrogation. The investigator may want to interview the victim and the patrol officer first but could then begin the interrogation without doing much more preparation. In this case, the interrogator has the patrol officer's reliable eyewitness account to use in confronting the suspect with his guilt. In another situation, such as an anonymous letter detailing allegations about a new band teacher involved in sexually abusing students, an investigator may have to do a great deal of preparation before even considering an interrogation of the band teacher. The investigator will first need to identify a victim, conduct an interview to establish if a crime occurred, and complete other tasks before interrogating the suspect. In every case, the investigator must decide when the timing is right to conduct the interrogation.

5. Preparation for the Interrogation

The investigator's preparation prior to walking into the interrogation room is almost as important as what transpires in the room itself. To be successful, the investigator must demonstrate to the suspect that a thorough investigation has been conducted and that the investigator knows the details of the case. The investigator must know the evidence in the case and know how it relates to the statements of the victim, the witnesses, and the suspect. The more information the investigator has, the easier it will be to detect the suspect's deception and overcome denials.

The interrogator should know the following information before beginning the interrogation:

- The victim's account of the abuse
- Statements made by the child to an outcry witness
- The medical, physical, and testimonial evidence in the case
- The suspect's account, if it has been given
- The facts of the case, including the who, what, where, when, how, and why

The properly conducted forensic interview of the victim will provide the investigator with the foundation on which to build the investigation. In sexual abuse cases, the investigator must know the extent of the abuse. Is fondling or penetration alleged? Were pictures or videos made of the victim? How long was the abuse going on? When did it start? What has the suspect done to ensure the victim's compliance and silence? Did the suspect give the victim gifts? Drugs? Money? Special privileges? Did the suspect threaten to harm the victim or members of the victim's family?

In physical abuse cases, the investigator must know the extent of the child's injuries. What is the child's prognosis? What explanation(s) have the caregivers already given? Do medical professionals believe the injuries were inflicted or accidental? By knowing the answers to these and other questions relevant to the abuse, the investigator not only demonstrates the thoroughness of the investigation but will have information on which to base questions and themes.

Before beginning any interrogation, the investigator should always consider the evidence already available in the case. If there is physical evidence or witnesses who corroborate the child's allegations, this evidence can be very important in overcoming the suspect's denials and detecting any attempts at deception. The investigator may want to consider if there is additional evidence or information that *should* be obtained before the suspect is contacted or the interrogation is started. For example, should a search warrant be executed on the suspect's residence to obtain corroborative evidence? Does this case lend itself to the use of a single-party consent telephone call? Once the suspect has been contacted and/or interrogated, the value of both of these investigative techniques is greatly diminished.

6. The Location of the Interrogation

There are obvious advantages to conducting the interrogation in the investigator's office. As this location is under the investigator's control, it will ensure there are no unplanned interruptions, and distractions can be minimized. The investigator gains a psychological advantage by conducting the interrogation on home turf. If a suspect is interrogated at his home or office, the interrogator cannot control interruptions from family and friends or ensure that weapons are not accessible. Conducting interrogations at the investigator's office also allows for third-party observation and the resulting advantages that this affords. In addition, this location affords the interrogator easy access to required forms like affidavits, voluntary statements, and consents to search.

7. *The Suspect*

In addition to knowing what the victim has alleged and what evidence there is, the more the investigator knows about the suspect, the better prepared the investigator will be to conduct a successful interrogation. Each interrogation must be tailored to the specific dynamics of the case and the personalities of the individuals involved. Different suspects must be approached differently. A line of questioning or a specific theme that will be productive for a preferential child molester, who relates a love for the victim, would probably not work on a situational offender who did not even know the victim. The experienced interrogator will treat people differently, knowing that one approach will not work with everyone.

Just as there is no profile that fits all offenders, there is no single approach to interrogation that will fit all offenders. Though it may not be necessary or practical in every case, the following information about the suspect may be useful to the interrogator:

- The suspect's prior criminal history
- The suspect's employment and volunteer history
- The suspect's prior contacts with law enforcement
- The suspect's financial status
- The suspect's prior involvement with CPS
- The suspect's reputation in the community
- The suspect's history of alcohol or substance abuse
- The suspect's history or reputation for violence
- The suspect's medical condition, disabilities, and use of medications
- Any statements the suspect has made about the alleged abuse

C. The Interrogation Process

While each interrogation will be different, there is a progression of events that applies generally in most interrogations:

The introduction

The constitutional rights advisory

The preconfrontation interview of the suspect

Confronting the suspect with his guilt, the evidence, and the results of the investigation

Overcoming the suspect's denials, objections, and claims of innocence

The use of questions, themes, and strategies to obtain the first admission of guilt from the suspect

Building on the first admission to obtain additional admissions and a complete narrative account of the conduct

Clearing up any inconsistencies and misunderstandings

Obtaining a formal statement, written or otherwise

Conducting the postinterrogation interview

Conducting the follow-up investigation

1. Introduction

The first thing the investigator should do in the interrogation room is introduce herself to the suspect if they have not already met. During the introduction, the investigator has two goals. The first is to establish both the investigator's identity and her control over the situation. For example, the investigator may say, "I'm Detective Susan Jones and I'm in charge of this investigation. I will decide what is going to happen in this case after I talk to you today." This type of statement highlights the investigator's role and importance to the suspect. The second goal is to plant the idea in the suspect's mind that there is an advantage to him in talking to the investigator. For example, the investigator may say, "I am very thorough and I want to be certain I have all the facts before I decide what I am going to do in this case. I know there are always two sides to every story. Up until now, I have only heard one side of this and I want to give you an opportunity to tell me your side before I decide what I should do next." The suspect may feel that by talking to the investigator, he can talk his way out of the situation or at least minimize his actions. The goal is to encourage the suspect to talk and not invoke his right to remain silent or request an attorney.

2. The Constitutional Rights Advisory

The investigator must follow applicable federal laws, state laws, and departmental policies when it comes to the issue of whether constitutional (*Miranda*) warnings are necessary before interrogating a suspect. Many prosecutors prefer that all suspects who are interrogated be advised of their rights, even if they are not under arrest and are not the subjects of custodial interrogations. Though this is more than the *Miranda* decision requires, state laws and local policies are often more restrictive. If a suspect needs to be warned of his constitutional rights, the investigator should read the constitutional rights from a printed card or form and not rely on doing it from memory. It is also advantageous for both the investigator and the suspect to sign and date the form from which the rights were read. This will make it more difficult for the suspect to claim later that the investigator did not advise him of his constitutional rights. The signed card or form should be saved as evidence, as it may later be needed in court.

After the rights are administered, the investigator should ask the suspect if he understood everything that has been read and if he has any questions about what he has heard. The suspect must knowingly and voluntarily waive his rights. The investigator should then ask the suspect if he "would like to tell his side of things." This again encourages the suspect to talk to the interrogator, if for no other reason but to try and deny the allegation.

3. Preconfrontation Interview

The preconfrontation interview may not be applicable in all interrogations. In the previously stated example of the local businessman arrested in the act for sexual abuse, the interrogation could probably begin without the preconfrontation interview. In other cases, it may be helpful to use the preconfrontation interview to establish a baseline for the suspect's verbal and nonverbal (body) language. By asking the suspect questions not related to the case, such as the suspect's name, address, and date of birth, the investigator will be able to determine how the suspect answers questions and how he acts when being truthful.

The preconfrontation interview may also be useful to establish possible strategies and themes for use later during the interrogation. For example, the suspect may claim he would never commit sexual abuse because he loves the child involved. Later during the interrogation, the interrogator can explain how these two behaviors are not always incompatible. The investigator may also use this nonconfrontational interview with the suspect to ask questions like, "What do you think should happen to someone who sexually abuses a child?" If the suspect answers, "Well, it depends on the situation. If it was the first time and the child went along and wasn't hurt, maybe the person should have to get counseling." This answer suggests the investigator should pursue the "first time" issue and highlight that this was not a "chronic situation." The investigator may also raise the issue that no force or injury was involved. It is often helpful if the interrogator can contrast the current incident with a previous "really bad case," real or fictitious. The investigator can say that it was a situation involving chronic abuse and the child was severely hurt. Then the investigator can point out that while the suspect made a mistake, it was a "one-time thing" and not as serious as the other case.

4. Confronting the Suspect

After the preconfrontation interview is conducted, the interrogator should make a very direct statement to the suspect about his guilt. It may be something like, "Bob, our investigation proves you are responsible for sexually abusing the girl who lives next door to you." This statement has to be made in a very convincing and unequivocal manner. The investigator will most likely be interrupted at this point by the suspect saying that there is a mistake and he is innocent. The investigator should disregard the suspect's objection and continue talking, asking the suspect to hear her out. The investigator may then follow up that statement with, "Bob, the reason I am taking the time to talk to you today is to find out why this happened, as I already know what happened."

5. Overcoming the Suspect's Denials, Objections, and Claims of Innocence

Rarely will the suspect who has been accused of committing any type of crime, especially child abuse, sit quietly after he has been accused. The investigator can expect that the suspect will deny his involvement, object to the results of the investigation, and claim that he is innocent. The investigator must remain firm that the suspect is responsible for the crime of which he is accused. At this point, the investigator must overcome the denials and objections offered by the suspect. The investigator must dominate the conversation at this point and not engage the suspect in a debate. The investigator should confidently explain that the suspect's guilt is not in question, only the reason for why the abuse happened. Regardless of what the suspect claims, the investigator must convince him that it does not change the fact that he is guilty of the crime. For example, the suspect may ask, "Why would I sexually abuse that girl? I have a beautiful wife at home." In response, the interrogator may say, "Bob, it doesn't have anything to do with having a beautiful wife. There are other reasons people make mistakes like this."

If the proper themes are used during the interrogation, the suspect will begin to become less vocal and make fewer denials. It is often the case that as the interrogation progresses, the guilty suspect will become less resistant to the interrogator's allegations. The suspect will become quiet and carefully listen to what the interrogator says. At this point, the suspect is weighing his options and listening for a possible out or explanation that he can offer for his conduct. It is the interrogator's job to suggest the correct explanation that the suspect is willing to accept.

[handwritten margin note: even when remaining neutral?]

6. Questions, Themes, and Strategies

Depending on the dynamics of the case and the suspect involved, the interrogator has to select the appropriate questions, themes, and strategies for the interrogation. In a case involving intrafamilial sexual abuse, the investigator could suggest that the suspect is not a predator or the kind of person hanging around schools trying to lure a vulnerable child. The investigator should highlight the fact that the suspect loves the child. The theme the interrogator must use is that even though the suspect made a mistake, he does not want to compound that mistake and deny what the investigator can and will prove. To do so will cause additional pain to the victim he claims to love. The investigator should remain flexible throughout the interrogation. If one theme or strategy does not appear to be working, the investigator must be able to switch to another.

It is an important turning point when the interrogator observes that the suspect is no longer arguing but is listening carefully. At this point the investigator should use alternative or forced-choice questions. These questions are ones in which a suspect must answer a question using one of two answers the interrogator has offered. By forcing the suspect to choose one answer, he is forced to admit wrongdoing. The only option for the suspect is to choose the answer he feels minimizes his culpability. Examples of alternative or forced-choice questions include

> Pete, there is no doubt that you had sexual intercourse with your daughter, I can prove that. I just need to know, did you plan this thing out in advance or is it something that just kind of happened?

Before the suspect can answer, the interrogator may add while nodding affirmatively,

> It just kind of happened didn't it, Pete? Didn't it?

In the same case, the interrogator could also say,

> Pete, there is no doubt that you had sexual intercourse with your daughter, I can prove that. I just need to know, is this the first time you have done this, or have you done it many times before?

Before the suspect can answer, the interrogator may add while nodding affirmatively,

It was the first time wasn't it, Pete? Wasn't it?

The easiest thing for the suspect to do in each of these situations is to simply nod affirmatively in agreement with the interrogator. At this point, the interrogator is only attempting to obtain the first admission of wrongdoing, not a complete account of the abuse. If the suspect does admit to having sexual intercourse on one occasion, the interrogator can build on this admission to get a full confession. The use of alternative and forced-choice questions can now be used to solicit further details from the suspect. The questions may be phrased to address the many issues involved in child abuse cases including, but not limited to, the number of incidents, the type of abuse involved, the use of force, the number of victims, and the premeditation involved.

a. Deception. It is very important that investigators and prosecutors understand that deception is both legally permissible and an important strategy that may be useful during an interrogation. The United States Supreme Court has upheld the conviction of a murder suspect who confessed after police falsely advised that his accomplice had confessed. *Frazier v. Cupp,* 394 U.S. 731 (1969).[4] Investigators again are reminded to check with local legal advisers for the legal parameters of deception in their jurisdiction. The use of deception must be understood and carefully used. The investigator must adhere to two qualifications when using deception. First, the deception must not be conducted in such a fashion as to shock the conscience of either the court or the community. Second, the deception cannot be used in a manner that would tend to make an innocent person confess to a crime he did not commit. As a practical matter, the investigator must not use any deception the suspect does not believe. If the suspect does not believe that he can trust the interrogator, the latter will have a very difficult, if not impossible obstacle to overcome.

The investigator may use deception as it relates to the following issues in a child abuse case:

- The existence of witnesses
- The existence of medical and/or physical evidence
- The statements of other victims and/or offenders
- The existence of diaries, photographs, videos, or recorded telephone calls
- The existence of laboratory and scientific tests involving DNA, trace evidence, and fingerprints

---

[4]Frazier has been criticized by the Second Circuit in *Ortiz v. Kelly,* 687 F.Supp. 64 (E.D.N.Y. 1988) and distinguished by the First, Third, Fourth, Fifth, Sixth and Ninth Circuits. *Ortiz* held that *Frazier's* significance is diminished because it was decided without considering the effect of *Miranda v. State of Arizona,* 384 U.S. 436, 448-56, 476 (1966), an opinion highly critical of the use of deceptiveness and trickery by law enforcement officials to obtain confessions. Further, *Santiago* found that voluntariness requires an inquiry into whether the confession was "freely given" (*Id.* at 66). Nevertheless, the *Santiago* court upheld the petitioner's conviction based on "the ambiguity of the law dealing with voluntariness and police trickery" (*Id.* at 66-67).

b. Minimization of Criminal Culpability. Allowing the suspect to minimize his level of criminal culpability is another important strategy that is useful in child abuse interrogations. With this theme, the interrogator allows the suspect an opportunity to confess in a manner that is psychologically acceptable to the suspect. It may also allow the suspect to view his conduct as less reprehensible than that of other individuals described by the investigator. The suspect may minimize the gravity of the conduct in his own mind. It may also allow him to transfer all or some of the blame onto the victim or other people. Lastly, this theme allows the suspect to view himself as the victim. Although this theme is useful to investigators conducting interrogations, other professionals criticize its use. Some therapists claim that by allowing the suspect to minimize culpability, the investigator makes it harder for the suspect to accept responsibility for the acts and to be treated. This argument ignores the fact that the perpetrator was completely in denial and wholly untreatable prior to the confession. Moreover, it is doubtful that any suspect truly believes the investigator's themes. The suspect merely embraces them in an attempt to escape full responsibility for his crimes.

In any case of abuse, there is probably a more severe case, real or imagined, that the investigator can offer to the suspect for comparison with his actions. The following is an illustration of the themes the investigator can use with the suspect:

Less Severe Forms of Abuse	More Severe Forms of Abuse
One time	Many times
One victim	Multiple victims
One offender	Many offenders
Spontaneous act	Premeditated act
Fondling	Oral sex
Oral sex	Sexual intercourse
Sexual intercourse	Deviate sexual intercourse with an object
No force	Force involved
No injury	Victim injured
Temporary injury	Permanent injury
Victim not made pregnant	Victim made pregnant
Victim not infected with a STD or HIV	Victim infected with a STD or HIV
No weapon	Weapon used
No child pornography involved	Child pornography involved

c. Themes and Strategies. In addition to themes that allow the suspect to minimize culpability, there are themes that allow the suspect to transfer some or all of the blame for the sexual abuse onto another person. While the suspect and only the suspect is responsible for the abuse, the following themes are useful in getting the suspect to admit to the crime while mentally placing responsibility on someone else.

Blaming the Victim. Regardless of the child's age, the type of sexual activity involved, or the force used, many suspects will try to blame the child for the sexual abuse. The following themes capitalize on the suspect's attempt to transfer the blame to the victim. The interrogator may suggest to the suspect that the victim may be to blame for

- Initiating the sexual contact and/or seducing the suspect
- Exaggerating the extent of the abuse, the number of times it happened, the force involved, or the use of a weapon
- Being sexually promiscuous and sexually active
- Provoking the suspect into committing the sexual abuse by teasing or daring him
- Blackmailing the suspect
- Misinterpreting the suspect's actions
- Failing to say "No" and in fact cooperating with the suspect

Blaming Others. In addition to trying to transfer the blame for his actions to the victim, the suspect may be inclined to blame the child's parents for their child's sexual abuse. This theme may also be used by the suspect in the case of intrafamilial sexual abuse, in which the offender blames the spouse for the abuse. Examples of this theme include

- The parent/spouse allowed the child to be alone with the suspect, thereby providing the suspect with the opportunity to commit the abuse.
- The parent/spouse ignored the child's need for love and attention, so the child turned to the offender to fill these needs.
- The parent/spouse was negligent in supervising the child, otherwise she would have noticed something was wrong and stopped it.
- The parent/spouse has failed as a parent and did not raise the child properly.
- In the intrafamilial sexual abuse case, the interrogator may suggest to the suspect that the wife (or girlfriend) is to blame, as she was unwilling and/or unable to satisfy the suspect's emotional and sexual needs, forcing him to turn to the child.

Blaming Outside Factors. The following themes are useful with a suspect who wants to blame things beyond his control for the behavior. If not for these circumstances, the suspect claims he would have never committed the abuse. It was as if "the stars were just aligned right."

- The suspect was under unusual stress due to work, health issues, financial issues, etc.
- At the time of the abuse, a combination of factors existed in the suspect's life that caused him to act irrationally.
- Society is to blame for mistreating the suspect.
- The victim was physically mature for her age.
- In cases in which the suspect was previously incarcerated or treated for sexual abuse, the interrogator may suggest to the suspect that the prison, the therapist, CPS, the probation officer, or the parole department is to blame for not rehabilitating him.

Blaming Alcohol and Drugs. Some suspects will blame the sexual abuse on an addiction, disease, or intoxication. As intoxication is not a defense to child abuse, the suspect may be told the following about alcohol and drugs and their effect on an individual:

- They depress inhibitions
- They make people aggressive
- They stimulate sexual interest
- They impair judgement

The interrogator could also ask the suspect, "You wouldn't have done that if you were sober, would you?"

Suspect Themes. The following themes are specific to the suspect, and the interrogator must decide which are most likely to work with each suspect.

- The suspect is not a bad person, but the behavior was wrong.
- The suspect was showing affection for the child and went too far.
- The suspect was educating the child about sexual matters and not doing it for sexual gratification.
- The suspect was sexually abused as a child and committed the abuse because of that.
- The suspect did not intend for the sexual abuse to happen. It was unplanned. It was an accident.
- This is the suspect's first mistake and it will never happen again.
- The suspect's actions were not as bad as other cases the investigator has handled.

With the intrafamilial offender, the interrogator should say that the stranger who molests a child he does not even know or care for is the really terrible person. With the nonfamilial offender, the interrogator should say that the person who molests his own child is the really terrible person.

Other Themes. There are other themes and strategies that are either combinations or variations of those listed above. The interrogator can ask the suspect, "Is this all you did or are you also responsible for . . . ?" This can be used on the suspect who is trying to minimize the severity of the sexual abuse or the number of victims. For example, in a fondling case, the interrogator could ask the suspect, "Did you just touch the girl or did you have sex with her?"

The interrogator could also tell the suspect, "You cannot change what you did before you entered this room today. What's done is done. All you can do now is be a man and take responsibility for what you have done and I can prove. You will only cause the child more suffering by denying what both you and I know you did."

7. Building on the First Admission

Once the suspect has made the first admission of guilt, the interrogator's job is to build on that admission to obtain a full account of the suspect's actions. After making this first admission, many suspects will attempt to convince the interrogator that they have made full disclosure of their conduct. This is almost never the case. Most suspects will attempt to give the interrogator as little information as possible, hoping that if they admit to the least serious act, or to doing it only once, the interrogator will be satisfied. The interrogator should not accept too little, too soon. After the suspect has made the admission, the interrogator should acknowledge that the suspect has told the truth, but qualify these statements and let the suspect know that the interrogator knows there is more to tell. The interrogator could try the following approaches with the suspect:

> Bob, I'm glad that you have finally admitted that you fondled your daughter. I know that was not an easy thing to admit. But Bob, if you are going to be honest with me, you have to be completely honest. You know and I know that you did it more than once, right? It was more than once, wasn't it, Bob?

> You know that I have already interviewed your daughter and I know it happened more than once. Listen, if you lie to me now and say it was only once, when I know it was more, I'm going to have to think you are lying when you said that all you did was touch her. It was more than once, right? Was it 5 or 6 times, or 10 or 20 times? It was 5 or 6, right?

There are many variations of these themes that the interrogator can use to influence the suspect to be more forthcoming. The interrogator must remember what information she has from the victim and witnesses and the evidence in the case and compare this with the suspect's statements. The interrogator must also consider that the victim's account may not be totally accurate for various reasons.

After the suspect has fully disclosed his involvement in the case, the interrogator should give the suspect a chance to start over and give a full narrative account of his actions. The interrogator should listen carefully to the suspect's account and ask the suspect to clarify any statements that appear to be inconsistent with the interrogator's understanding of the facts of the case. Before the suspect is asked to give a formal statement, the interrogator should make sure the relevant issues in the case are addressed. In addition to the standard who, what, where, when, how, and why questions, the interrogator may ask the suspect to address the issues of motivation, intent, attempts to conceal the conduct, and any other facts important to explaining his actions.

8. Clearing Up Any Inconsistencies

The investigator must be prepared for inconsistencies between the suspect's verbal admission, the victim's account, and the evidence available. There may be several reasons for these inconsistencies. The suspect may be trying to minimize his culpability and the extent of the abuse. The victim may not have made a full disclosure of what happened. The child may have been too embarrassed to discuss acts to which the suspect has confessed. As it is the investigator's goal to obtain the most accurate statement from the suspect, the investigator should challenge the suspect on statements that do not match the victim's account or the evidence. If the suspect's statement is going to be given proper consideration by a judge or jury, it must be accurate and corroborated by the other evidence in the case.

9. Obtaining a Formal Statement

The method by which the suspect's formal statement is obtained will vary from one jurisdiction to another, even within the same state. In some agencies, the suspect is asked to write a voluntary statement in his own handwriting. There are some agencies that prefer to have the suspect dictate the statement to either a stenographer or the interrogator. The statement is then written or typed for the suspect's signature. Other agencies audiotape or videotape the formal statement or the entire interrogation from start to finish. Regardless of which method is used, the interrogator must ensure that the formal statement contains all of the relevant issues that have been previously discussed. If state law or agency policy directs that a witness be present when the suspect gives a formal statement, the witness should be instructed to show no reaction to what the suspect says.

10. Postinterrogation Interview

Now is also the opportune time to ask the suspect about other victims, other crimes, and other evidence. While this ploy is not always successful in gaining additional information, it may occasionally lead to other victims or other crimes. The interrogator can say something like the following to the suspect:

Other victims. "Bob, I'm glad you told me about what happened with your daughter. It was the right thing to do. But now, I need to know about those other children that you have been involved with. See, I know about them also."

Other crimes. "Bob, I'm glad you told me about what happened with your daughter. It was the right thing to do. But now, I need to know about those other incidents you have been involved in. See, I know about them also."

Other evidence. "Bob, I'm glad you told me about what happened with your daughter. It was the right thing to do. But now, I need to talk to you about those pictures you took of her. I know you said you destroyed them all, but would you be willing to sign a consent to search your apartment, so I can tell my supervisor that I made sure there are no more pictures left?"

After the interrogator has obtained the suspect's formal statement, there are still several issues the interrogator must consider. First, the interrogator must refrain from speaking harshly to a suspect who has just confessed to committing a crime of sexual abuse, no matter how horrible the abuse. Not only would such comments be unprofessional and inappropriate, but they would be counterproductive. At trial, the investigator's conduct during the interrogation is going to be scrutinized. An investigator should not give the defense any ammunition with which to attack her professionalism. Second, additional victims or unforeseen consequences may require further interrogations. Accordingly, the investigator must not close off communication by humiliating the suspect.

After securing the suspect's admission, the interrogator may want to ask the suspect *why* he confessed. While there are no assurances that the suspect will tell the real reason(s), it is a way for the interrogator to obtain some feedback on interrogation style. For example, the suspect may offer that the reason was because the interrogator treated him with respect or because the interrogator had obviously thoroughly investigated the case. Regardless of what the suspect says, the interrogator can decide if the information may prove to be useful in future interrogations.

Take the suspect's picture after he has given a formal statement. This will document that he has not been mistreated. If the suspect has injuries, photographs of the injuries should be taken and the file documented prior to the interrogation.

No confession. In situations where the suspect does not confess, the interrogator must realize that time was not wasted. Even if the suspect denies his guilt, he may have provided information that can be useful during the subsequent investigation and during trial. The suspect may have said something that can be used at trial for impeachment. The suspect's denial may include alibi witnesses that can be contacted by the investigator to lock them into their story so they cannot change it at trial. Occasionally, the suspect may give a statement that locks him into a version of events. Finally, the suspect may give a preview of what his defense to the allegation is going to be. For example, the suspect may claim that he could not have committed the crime because he was out of town at the time. A subsequent investigation may be able to prove otherwise.

11. Conducting the Follow-Up Investigation

Finally, the suspect has confessed and given a formal statement. The postinterrogation interview has been completed and the investigator is finished with this case, except perhaps for testifying in court, right? Wrong. The interrogator is back to being an investigator and cannot stop working yet. Suspect confessions are ruled inadmissible every day in courtrooms across this country for reasons too numerous to list here. As such, the investigator must continue working to build a case that can win in court in the event the confession is suppressed. Finding additional victims will usually result in a stronger case against the suspect. The investigator should work to corroborate the details of both the victim's allegations and the suspect's confession.

IX. CHILD PHYSICAL ABUSE AND CHILD HOMICIDE

A. Introduction

Despite the fact that physical assaults and neglect are by far the most common forms of child abuse, some prosecutors have concentrated their attention primarily on sexual abuse cases. The reasons are obvious. State laws and social values clearly prohibit sexual contact between adults and children. Definitions of illegal physical treatment of children, however, tend to be murky, with the circumstances and motivation of the offender playing significant roles in culpability. Brutality is often defended as an individual style of discipline. Even when punishment ends in the death of the child, defendants successfully argue that it was unintentional or accidental. Although more and more states are banning corporal punishment of children at school, the issue remains controversial. Even more controversial are proposals adopted in some European countries, and supported in this country by such organizations as Parents Anonymous, to ban corporal punishment in the home. The result of a double standard in attitudes toward sexual and physical assaults is that far fewer cases of physical abuse are reported to prosecutors' offices and far fewer prosecutors have comparable experience in child physical abuse and homicide.

A number of forces are at work to change this situation. One is the rising number of child fatalities caused by abuse and experts' belief that known maltreatment deaths are dwarfed by the actual number of child homicides. Supporting this belief are studies indicating wide divergence in data collection on child deaths and little communication among the agencies charged with responding to fatal child injuries. Establishment of child death review teams to share information, improve case handling, and protect surviving siblings is an important outgrowth of professional awareness that many child deaths signed off as "accidental" may not be. (See this chapter, Section IX.R.)

Another force propelling change in criminal investigations is the medical profession's strides in the past 25 years in identifying child physical abuse. The justice system has only recently begun to catch up with the dramatic advances in medical diagnostic capability. Prosecutors and investigators must develop a working knowledge not only of state-of-the-art pediatric medicine but also of forensic methods now available to medical examiners and coroners. Cause of death can now be determined with much greater reliability, even though the perpetrator may be unknown. Explanations inconsistent with injuries, evidence of old injuries, and a history of similar past behavior with the alleged victim or siblings may reveal the perpetrator's identity. These are all areas in which close collaboration with medical professionals can be crucial to the case.

Familiarity with the "battered child syndrome", a term coined by the late C. Henry Kempe in his landmark article, is essential. (See Appendix 5A.2.) There are two general categories of serious child physical abuse and homicide cases. One is the classic battered child syndrome in which the child has multiple types of injuries at various stages of healing. The other kind of case involves a single explosive incident leading to serious injury or death—often a massive head or abdominal injury. These often horrifying cases present convincing evidence to convict a defendant, assuming there is solid evidence to place the child in the defendant's control at the time the injuries occurred. Investigators must explore not only the current injury but also the child's medical history and the conclusions of medical personnel who examined the child on previous occasions. The prosecutor will have to determine whether prior medical conditions will be admissible at trial. They can represent corroborative evidence critical in proving an intentional act of abuse.

Virtually every appellate court in the country, including the United States Supreme Court, has ruled that expert testimony on the existence of the battered child syndrome is admissible. (See *Estelle v. McGuire*, 112 S. Ct. 475 [1991].) Most courts have gone farther to hold that evidence of prior acts of abuse by the perpetrator against the alleged victim are admissible as prior uncharged misconduct evidence to show a pattern of conduct or to refute an implication or claim that the injury was caused by accident. (See Myers, J. E. B. [1988]. Uncharged misconduct evidence in child abuse litigation. *Utah Law Review*, p. 479.)

B. Indicators of Neglect

Neglect is traditionally defined as the parent's or guardian's failure to provide a child with one or more essential elements for the child's physical, intellectual, or emotional capacities. It also includes the parent's or guardian's abandonment of the child. Neglect can be further divided into categories of physical, medical, emotional, and educational neglect. The caregiver's omissions cause the neglected child to suffer physical or mental injury that harms or threatens to harm the child's health or welfare.

Physical neglect may be manifested by

- Signs of malnutrition or growth failure, also called failure to thrive
- Inappropriate clothing for weather conditions
- The child not receiving the minimal standards of personal hygiene
- The child being left with an inappropriate caregiver
- The caregiver's failure to protect the child from environmental harm such as
  - Failure to provide supervision for prolonged periods of time
  - Inadequate or inappropriate shelter
  - Exposure to violence, including exposing the child to domestic violence
  - Exposure to controlled substances
  - Exposure to extreme hot or cold conditions
  - Exposure to safety hazards such as unsupervised baths, flammable materials, toxic materials, fall hazards, or staircases
  - Failure to provide safety equipment such as smoke detectors and car seats
  - Exposing the child to danger because of irresponsible behavior such as speeding or driving under the influence of alcohol or other substances

Medical neglect occurs when an infant or child

- Is repeatedly denied routine immunizations
- Is not taken for routine medical and dental care
- Is not taken to a doctor for a timely diagnosis of illness or disease
- Is not given the prescribed therapy for a diagnosed medical, dental, or mental health disorder
- Repeatedly misses medical, mental health, or dental appointments

Emotional neglect occurs when an infant or child

- Is not given the nurturing required for sound personality development
- Is disparaged, bullied, shouted at, or humiliated

Educational neglect is present when a child is denied appropriate education as prescribed by local law.

C. Indicators of Physical Abuse

Suspicion of physical abuse should arise if the caregivers are evasive, contradictory, or belligerent when asked about the child's injury or state a history of minor trauma that is not a plausible explanation for the child's injury. This is often referred to as a "discrepant history." Investigators should also be concerned when parents have behaviors suggestive of alcohol or other substance abuse, interpersonal difficulties, antisocial attitudes, or mood disturbances. A parent's history of previous encounters with law enforcement, especially when those encounters involved assaults or violent behaviors, should also be an alert to possible physical abuse. Investigators should also be concerned about parents who express or demonstrate little concern for the child and who are disinterested in the child's prognosis. Some perpetrators are noticeably eager to get away from the hospital without making sure the child is safe and secure.

Behavioral signs of physical abuse in the child may include the appearance of having been neglected and/or showing emotional extremes of depression, irritability, hypervigilance, fright, or extreme anxiety. Some children may be withdrawn, with blunted affect, lying motionless, devoid of all facial expression, and attempting to hide under the sheets of the examination table. Some children may cling to the nonperpetrating caregiver and be quite fearful of the perpetrator, while other children may exhibit role reversal and try to protect the nonperpetrating parent. Some children may take on the role of the perpetrator and be quite aggressive. Other children are pleased to be admitted to the hospital and do not exhibit the normal response of fear in this unfamiliar and threatening environment. Richard Galdston ([1965]. Observations on children who have been physically abused and their parents. *American Journal Psychiatry, 122*(4), 440) describes some abused children as appearing as if their "inner psychic life . . . has been completely suspended."

An investigator should have suspicions when the child has physical signs of old injuries, especially those in different stages of healing. There may be evidence of numerous traumatic episodes while the child is in the home. During hospitalization, however, no new injuries will appear. Radiographic findings often do not correlate with the alleged time interval between injury and examination, or the severity of the injury is not consistent with the description of how the injury occurred.

In fatal cases, the parent or caregiver inadequately describes the circumstances surrounding the child's death. The parent or caregiver may not be able to offer an explanation for the child's injuries, stating, "I just found him this way." Common suspicious stories for child fatalities include

- Falls from couches, beds, changing tables, or down stairs
- Falling while being carried, often up stairs or in icy conditions
- Falling and striking the corner of furniture
- Other falls from low heights of less than four feet
- In infants, choking on food or stopping breathing and being shaken by the parent to be revived
- An attempt by an inexperienced person to resuscitate the child
- An alleged traumatic event one day or more before death
- An injury inflicted by a sibling or an older child
- An object that fell onto the child

SOURCE: Kirschner, R. H., & Wilson, H. L. (1997). Fatal child abuse: The pathologist's perspective. In R. M. Reece (Ed.), *Child abuse: Medical diagnosis and management* (pp. 325, 329). Philadelphia, PA: Lea & Febiger.

1. Skin and Soft Tissue Injuries

Injuries to the skin are the most frequent manifestations of abuse. Skin injuries consist of abrasions, lacerations, burns, bruises, scratches, and petechia (small red spots in the skin caused by a tiny hemorrhage). The distribution of these injuries is characteristic in cases of accidental injury and usually can be distinguished from inflicted injury on the basis of their location. Children experience accidental injuries to their shins, on the skin over the bony projections of the hips and spine, on their lower arms, on their foreheads, and under their chins. Inflicted injuries occur more frequently on the upper arms, the trunk of the body, the upper anterior legs, the sides of the face, ears, neck, genitalia, and buttocks.

The source of skin injuries can often be determined by the injury pattern. Some injuries suggest tying, binding, or tethering. Other patterned injuries include strap or belt marks, punctures, looped cord marks, or imprints from coat hangers, shoes, spoons, knives, appliances, or other household items. Other patterns suggest hand marks from grabbing, pinching, squeezing, slapping, or repeated poking. Hair pulling can leave the child with patchy hair loss or bald spots. Adult bite marks can be distinguished from child bite marks by their size and configuration.

Inflicted burns can also be identified by their location and pattern. Burns on the palms and soles or in the genital or anal regions are much more likely to have been inflicted than accidental. These locations are not typical burn locations on children. Children are often burned as a result of their curiosity when they touch hot objects (burns to the fingers) and when they pull hot foods off the stove onto themselves. Burns from immersion in hot liquid are characterized by sharp demarcation lines between the burned area and the unburned area and by the absence of associated splash marks. These characteristics indicate forcible restraint because a child who, for example, steps into a hot tub of water will immediately thrash or pull back, causing splash burns. Immersion burns also display a uniform depth from one edge of the burn to the other. Burns of this type are often called sock or glove burns because of the uniform pattern of the burn. Certain kinds of burns are identifiable by their configuration: round, small burns may have been caused by a lighted cigarette; donut-shaped burns may have been caused by a cigarette lighter. Other appliance patterns may be identified as having caused a burn: irons, heating appliances, stove parts, curling irons, waffle irons, or grills.

Burns have the potential for causing long-term disability. Not only are the scars from burns disfiguring, but there can be severe shortening of the muscle or scar tissue that results in distortion or deformity (called contractures) and can cause mobility problems. The psychological effects of both the disfiguring and the disabling features of this form of inflicted injury make this form of abuse especially cruel.

2. Internal Injuries

Inflicted injuries to the internal organs of the chest (thoracic injuries) or of the abdomen are relatively uncommon, but when they do occur they are extremely serious. The mortality rate attributable to these kinds of injuries is close to 50%. The types and severity of internal injuries from abuse are more severe than those encountered in children who have been run over by the wheels of motor vehicles. In addition, the caregiver often delays seeking treatment for inflicted injuries. Several characteristics separate children who have thoracic-abdominal injuries from accidental causes and children who sustain inflicted injuries. Inflicted injuries tend to involve younger children; the histories for the injuries are often discrepant; medical treatment is often delayed; and the organs usually involved are the hollow organs such as the stomach and small and large intestine rather than the solid organs such as the liver, spleen, and kidneys. The pancreas, when injured, is more likely to be injured by a deep, blunt blow to the upper abdomen, common when a foot, fist, or blunt instrument is thrust into the midline area just beneath the rib cage. This injury is often seen with impalement accidents involving handlebars or sledding injuries, or with inflicted injury. When this injury is accidental, it is almost always witnessed. Injuries to the hollow organs or pancreas require great, blunt force, and flat falls off furniture such as beds, couches, and the like—or even long falls onto flat surfaces—cannot produce such injuries.

3. Head Injuries Caused by Abuse

Intracranial injury is the most common cause of death in physical abuse victims. The terms *shaken baby syndrome* and *shaken impact syndrome* (SBS/SIS) refer to the violent shaking and/or slamming of a child against a surface. It is diagnosed through clinical, radiographic, and sometimes autopsy findings. There are no accurate, carefully tabulated statistics regarding the incidence of SBS/SIS, but based upon the clinical experience of many emergency department physicians and pediatricians, the incidence probably lies between 600 and 1,400 cases in the United States per year. The usual victim age is between birth and two years of age (average 3–8 months), with the majority of abuse occurring during the first year. Some isolated cases occur in older children.

The usual trigger for shaking a baby is inconsolable crying. Frustrated by failed attempts to console the baby, the perpetrator loses control and grabs—either by the chest, under the arms, or by the arms—and violently shakes the baby. The time of shaking varies, usually ranging from around five seconds to 15 or 20 seconds. The number of shakes per second is between two and four. During shaking, the head rotates wildly on the axis of the neck, thus creating multiple forces inside the head. The infant stops crying and stops breathing, causing a decreased oxygen supply to the body and particularly the brain. The infant brain is much softer than an adult brain because it has a higher water content. The absence of myelination, the "insulation" of the nerve cells that is acquired during further development of the nervous system, contributes to the relative softness of the infant brain. These factors make the brain more gelatinous, and during shaking it is more easily distorted and compressed within the skull. The shaking and the sudden deceleration of the head at the time of impact causes

- The veins that bridge from the brain to the dura mater (the fibrous membrane covering the brain and lining the inner surface of the skull) to stretch beyond their elasticity causing them to tear open and bleed. This creates subdural hematoma, subarachnoid hemorrhages, or other characteristics of the syndrome.
- The brain to strike the inner surfaces of the skull, causing direct trauma to the brain substance itself
- The axons located deep in the brain to be broken during the shaking
- Irreversible damage to the brain, owing to the lack of oxygen during shaking
- Damaged nerve cells to release chemicals that add both to oxygen deprivation and direct damage to the brain cells

The combined effect is massive traumatic destruction of the brain tissue that leads to immediate brain swelling, which in turn causes an enormous increase in the pressure within the skull. The swelling compounds the problem, since swelling causes compression of the blood vessels and decreases the oxygen supply to the brain. It is these injuries to the brain, not the bleeding under the dura or the arachnoid membranes, that cause the signs, symptoms, and course of the SBS/SIS.

Other injuries also occur. The most significant of these injuries are retinal hemorrhages. There are a number of theories to explain retinal hemorrhages. One theory is that they are the result of transmitted pressure within the skull. The argument against this as a single cause of the injury is that retinal hemorrhages occur with much less frequency in infants whose brain injuries are due to accidental causes with similar increased intracranial pressures such as those resulting from motor vehicle accidents. Another theory is that retinal hemorrhages occur because shaking causes disruption to the layers of the retina. There are 10 layers of the retina, all richly supplied with blood vessels. Proponents of this theory state that when these layers are subjected to the force associated with shaking, they slide across one another, stretching these vessels so that they shear and bleed.

A number of other injuries may be present in SBS/SIS cases. These include skull fractures when the infant's head strikes a hard or soft surface, fractures of the posterior arcs of the ribs near the spine owing to the perpetrator's fingers holding the baby during shaking, fractures of the clavicles, and fractures of the long bones owing to the flailing action of the arms during shaking. It is uncommon to see injuries to the bones, interspinous ligaments, and muscles of the neck, most probably owing to the underdevelopment of these structures in infants. Spinal cord injuries are also uncommon in SBS/SIS cases.

There are other traumatic injuries to the head owing to inflicted injury. These include injuries to the external eye (hyphema, periorbital ecchymoses [black eyes]); soft tissue or cartilaginous injuries to the ear (bruising, abrasions, "cauliflower ear") or nose; trauma to the oral cavity such as torn frenulum inside the lips or under the tongue; fractured or dislodged teeth; injury to the tongue, throat, or gums; bruises or lacerations to any part of the external surfaces of the head; or hair loss from hair pulling.

4. Skeletal Injuries

Certain factors indicate a higher likelihood of an abusive origin rather than an accidental origin for fractures. The child's age is the most important single factor: Up to 80% of all inflicted skeletal trauma occurs in infants age 18 months or younger, while only 2% of all accidental skeletal trauma to children is seen in this age group. Developmental handicaps and premature birth are also considered to increase the risk of inflicted skeletal trauma. It is common to see trauma to the head or internal organs when there is skeletal trauma. In the absence of easily identified mechanisms of injury such as motor vehicle accidents or falls from heights, Paul K. Kleinman divides fractures into three groups in terms of their specificity for abuse. (Kleinman, P. K. [1990]. Diagnostic imaging of infant abuse. *American Journal of Radiology, 155,* 703). Highly specific for abuse are metaphyseal fractures (ends of long bones), posterior rib fractures, shoulder fractures, and vertebral body fractures. Highly suggestive patterns include fractures at multiple sites, fractures that are bilateral or symmetrical, fractures of different ages, fractures of the hands or feet, complex fractures of the skull, and nonskeletal injuries to the head or internal organs along with fractures. Nonspecific fractures include fractures to the shafts of long bones, clavicular (collarbone) fractures, and linear skull fractures. The type of fracture does not tell much about the origin of the fracture. For instance, a spiral fracture can be of accidental or inflicted origin. This is because a spiral fracture depends upon a mechanism of twisting and it is not specific for abuse per se. It is the history given for a fracture that is critical in distinguishing accidental from abusive fractures in the young child.

D. Medical Indicators of Sexual Abuse

There are three distinct domains to be investigated in child sexual abuse allegations. The first is the disclosure by the alleged victim. The second is the specific behaviors the child may exhibit and that are observed by the nonperpetrating caregiver or a professional caring for the child. The third domain is the presence of medical findings.

Cases of alleged sexual abuse come into a variety of systems from a variety of referral sources. How these referrals are handled becomes critical in the prosecution of the case. When a child discloses possible sexual abuse, a person skilled in the techniques of interviewing children must then interview the child. Inept, unskilled, or inexperienced interviewers, or the use of questionable interview techniques, must be avoided to protect the welfare of the family and to ensure the viability of a case.

An analysis of the behavioral signs and symptoms should be undertaken. Nonspecific behavioral symptoms include sleeping or eating disturbances, nightmares, aggressive behavior, anxiety, depression, changes in school performance, peer problems, bed-wetting, fecal soiling, or temper tantrums. These may be symptoms secondary to sexual abuse, but they are not specific for sexual abuse. Specific sexualized behaviors are often the byproduct of inappropriate sexual exposure and are associated with sexual function in some way. Thus, unexpected knowledge in young children about sexual matters, unusual curiosity about sexual or excretory functions, asking others to engage in sexual acts, acting out sexually with other children, or abnormal masturbation activities, such as masturbating with an object, are examples of specific behaviors suggestive of sexual abuse.

There are also specific and nonspecific physical symptoms and signs that must be taken into account when evaluating a child for possible sexual abuse. A child can present with an innocent injury to private parts caused by play, such as straddle injuries, or have pain on urination, abdominal pain, irritation in the genitalia or anus, or have a skin disease suggesting trauma to the genital and anal region. On the other hand, children who come to the clinic with vaginal discharge, vaginal or rectal bleeding, or injury to the penis or scrotum need careful evaluation to ensure a proper diagnosis.

The determination of normal versus abnormal in an examination for sexual abuse has evolved over the past few years, and a consensus about abnormal findings among child sexual abuse specialists has developed. It must be pointed out, however, that most children with documented sexual abuse, either through conviction or confession of the perpetrator, will not have *any* specific genital or anal findings. Specific findings are present in only 20%–25% of known sexually abused children. The following classification has been established and adopted by many sexual abuse examiners:

Class 1: Normal. Variations in the appearance of the hymen, peri-hymenal, and peri-anal tissues that have been documented in more than 10% of the subjects in studies of nonabused children.

Class 2: Nonspecific. Findings that may be the result of sexual abuse but may also be due to nonabusive causes.

Class 3: Suspicious. Findings that are rarely seen in nonabused children and have been noted in children with documented abuse but have not been clearly proven to occur only as a result of abuse.

Class 4: Suggestive of abuse or penetration. Findings that can be reasonably explained only by sexual abuse.

Class 5: Clear evidence of penetrating injury. Findings that can have no explanation other than penetrating trauma to the hymen or peri-anal tissues.

SOURCE: Adams, J. K., et al. (1992). A proposed system for the classification of anogenital findings in children with suspected sexual abuse. *Adolescent and Pediatric Gynecology, 5,* 73.

These physical findings, when added to other information derived during a medical examination, lead to the overall assessment of the likelihood of sexual abuse, categorized as follows:

Category I. No evidence of sexual abuse
- Normal exam, no history, no behavioral changes, no witnessed abuse
- Nonspecific physical findings with another known etiology and no history or behavioral changes
- Child considered at risk for sexual abuse, but gives no history and has nonspecific behavioral changes
- Physical findings consistent with history of accidental trauma

Category II. Possible abuse
- Class 1, 2, or 3 findings in combination with significant behavioral changes, especially sexualized behaviors, but the child is unable to give history
- Presence of *Condyloma acuminata* (genital or anal warts) or genital herpes infection in the absence of a history of abuse, with an otherwise normal physical examination
- Statement by the child, but no detailed or consistent history provided
- Class 3 findings with no disclosure of abuse

Category III. Probable abuse
- Clear, consistent, detailed description of molestation from child, with or without other findings present
- Class 4 or 5 findings in a child, with or without a history of abuse, in the absence of any convincing history of accidental penetrating injury
- Culture-proven infection with *Chlaniydia trachomatis* (child over 3 years age) or herpes Type 2 or Trichomonas (in prepubertal child)

Category IV. Definite evidence of abuse or sexual contact
- Finding of sperm or semen in or on a child
- A witnessed episode of sexual molestation
- Nonaccidental, blunt penetrating trauma to the vaginal or anal orifice
- Positive, confirmed cultures for *Neisseria gonorrhoeae* in a prepubertal child or serologic confirmation of acquired syphilis
- Pregnancy

Few cases of alleged sexual abuse follow a smooth course from the chief complaint to a firm and unassailable diagnosis. Even children who provide clear and convincing information, exhibit behavioral signs and symptoms known to be induced by sexual abuse, and demonstrate definitive anatomic changes secondary to the trauma of sexual abuse, may not have their cases supported by social services, law enforcement, and the judicial system. Therefore, it is incumbent on the evaluators to gather meaningful information and to analyze and synthesize it so that a balanced, accurate, and holistic appraisal of the case is accomplished.

E. Interview of Caregivers

1. Generally

When the law enforcement agency receives a report of possible abuse, the first step in the investigation is to collect information about the injury leading to the report. This may include medical records, brief interviews with the medical personnel attending to the injured child, explanations offered by the caregivers, interviews with all persons who had access to or custody of the child during the period the injuries occurred, and a thorough investigation of the scene. It may be some time before doctors can offer an explanation of the injuries or sort out their chronology, especially if the child's life is in jeopardy. However, interviews with the child's caregivers should not be delayed, since their *initial* statements are critical to the treating physicians, to the medical examiner if the child dies, and to the prosecutor.

Abusive caregivers generally have no explanation for critical injuries to the child, or explanations that do not account for the severity of those injuries. For example, caregivers may explain that the child was completely healthy all day, ate normally, suffered no falls or trauma, and then suddenly stopped breathing. While such a situation is possible, it is so rare as to be immediately suspect.

Head injuries are the leading nonaccidental cause of death in children. Any head injury should be investigated to see if it is consistent with the caregivers' explanation and the scene. Abusive parents often claim that the child fell from the couch or was dropped, causing the injuries. Studies show, however, that falls from normal household heights are neither fatal nor the cause of severe head injuries in young children. (See Helfer, et al. [1985]. Injuries resulting when small children fall out of bed. *Pediatrics, 60,* 533; Weber, W. [1985]. Zur Biomechanischen fragilität des Säuglingsschädels. *Rechtsmed, 94,* 93.)

It is also common for abusive caregivers to change their story over time, conforming explanations to information received from doctors about the child's condition during treatment. Rather than a single interview at the beginning of an investigation, it may be better to conduct several or wait until the conclusion of the investigation to confront the caregivers about the inconsistency of their initial story with all the other information gathered. Consider asking suspects to reenact the incident on videotape. This not only helps to lock in their version of events but gives medical experts a better opportunity to judge the plausibility of their account.

Failure to seek immediate care is another indication of culpability. Note any time lag between the injury and the call to a doctor or ambulance. Listen to any 911 tape at the beginning of the investigation; statements as well as reactions of the caregivers in the background may give clues about the identity of the perpetrator.

2. When There Are Two Caregivers

a. Determining culpability. When the child has been abused in a setting with two caregivers who have had access to the child, the investigator must try to determine which of the two is responsible or whether both are culpable. Investigators should immediately take individual recorded or written statements from each caregiver, making sure to interview the caregivers separately. *Miranda* warnings generally should be given to both at this early stage. If one cooperates and the other does not, investigators should take a statement from the cooperative person as soon as possible. Be aware of local hospital policies that require staff to attend caregiver interviews. It is often helpful to have a third party witness in order to respond to later defense claims of inappropriate conduct, inaccurate recording, or coercive behavior by the police.

Ask for a detailed account of the child's entire health and medical history, as well as the caregiver's version of events leading to the child's injuries. It is often useful to construct a written time line of the few days preceding the child's injury or death, including the child's feeding and sleeping schedule, activities, and demeanor during that time. Ask the caregiver to describe the relationship between the uncooperative caregiver and the child, as well as all those who had access to the child. Ask whether either caregiver has parented or cared for other children and obtain any information you can about the well-being of those children. This could provide important clues about culpability. In most states, husband-wife privilege and spousal incompetency do *not* bar testimony of one spouse against the other in situations involving child abuse. (See Chapter IV, Section III.E on marital privilege.) In any event, there is no such prohibition on interviews. This should never be used as a reason not to seek a statement.

Depending on the reactions and forthrightness of the cooperative caregiver, you may conclude that that person did not inflict the abuse. It is not uncommon, however, for such a person to have difficulty believing that the other partner is capable of such behavior. The caregiver may struggle to find some innocent explanation and may feel extremely guilty about not preventing the child's injuries. The cooperative caregiver may also have been abused by the uncooperative caregiver. Do what you can to involve such caregivers in counseling and supportive services so they can provide honest testimony and protect themselves and their children. Your understanding of the household dynamics will also be critical at trial so you can present an accurate picture of the child's environment and establish who should be held responsible.

b. Accomplice liability. Your investigation may reveal that both caregivers participated in abusive behavior or that one caregiver covered for the other or actively assisted in making the abuse possible. Accomplice liability in such cases should be clear.

A more difficult circumstance is presented when it appears that one person was responsible for inflicting the child's injuries, but the other stood by and did nothing. Some states allow prosecution under a "failure to protect" theory. Your decision to prosecute the nonparticipating partner may depend on the severity of the case. (See Chapter III.)

F. Interviews of Initial Medical Personnel

The investigator should interview all caregivers, doctors, nurses, admitting personnel, EMTs, ambulance drivers, emergency room personnel, and others who had contact with the child. Explanations they heard about what happened to the child should be compared to what the caregivers say later. The demeanor of the caregivers during treatment of the child should be noted, but appropriate reactions of grief and concern are common even from the abuser and can be misleading if given too much weight. Those who injure a child are likely to be genuinely upset at the prospect that they will be held responsible for their behavior or that the child might actually die as a result.

It is essential to take photographs of the child as soon as possible after presentation to the treatment facility. Most clinics and hospitals have a protocol for photographing injuries in obvious cases of abuse, but when the injuries are more subtle, there may be nothing preserved. The investigator should ensure that medical personnel either take such photographs and preserve them or allow the investigator to take photos. See West, M., & Barsley, R. (1992), Selected forensic and physical evidence experts, *NDAA Bulletin, 11*(4), 8, for new techniques using ultraviolet photography to increase the degree of detail in photographs of bitemarks and other types of wounds.

Conduct interviews with nurses and doctors involved in the care of the child as soon as possible to determine the medical condition of the child and initial impressions of the doctors regarding the cause of injuries. Medical evaluations can then be compared to the caregivers' account, which may differ markedly. For instance, doctors may conclude the child is suffering seizures because of fresh blood in the subarachnoid fluid, which they attribute to recent severe shaking, whereas the caregiver says the likely cause is a fall down the stairs three days ago. In another instance, the caregiver may say the baby's fall from a bed caused difficulty in breathing, but doctors may find that early X-rays and CT scans show a skull fracture and subdural bleeding along with significant edema (swelling) of the brain, injuries unlikely to result from simple trauma or an accident.

Keep in mind that initial interviews with the treating or emergency room physicians are likely to be very brief, and initial impressions about the child may change with time. It is vital that the investigator keep in touch with the doctors regarding the child's prognosis. If the child is dead on arrival at the hospital, investigators must maintain contact with the coroner or medical examiner and seek appropriate consultation with experts concerning injuries found at autopsy.

A knowledgeable investigator may ask the treating physicians about special examinations, such as having an ophthalmologist examine the child for retinal hemorrhages. Physical examinations by nonspecialists may miss the findings essential to solving a case. Although some medical professionals resent suggestions from outsiders, most want to cover every diagnostic base, especially when the cause of injury to the child is elusive. If the treating physician or medical examiner is not experienced in pediatrics and/or child abuse–related injuries, do not hesitate to seek an expert opinion. Contact the National Center for Prosecution of Child Abuse for further information. It is not uncommon for the first physician involved with the child to have little training in the recognition of abuse-related injuries. Therefore, an interview with the initial treating physician should not end the medical investigation.

G. Crime Scene Investigation

Many cases of child physical abuse and homicide occur at a location where a suspect has a constitutionally recognized expectation of privacy, such as the suspect's home. There is no homicide or child abuse crime scene exception to the constitutional protections afforded by the Fourth Amendment. (See *Mincey v. Arizona,* 437 U.S. 385 [1978]. Exploratory searches for evidence of a crime at the scene of a homicide have been invalidated by the United States Supreme Court; see *Thompson v. Louisiana,* 469 U.S. 17 [1984].) Much case law has followed *Mincey* and *Thompson,* refining and distinguishing those cases. Consult the applicable law of search and seizure when planning a search of the crime scene. Prosecutors need to ensure that collection and preservation of evidence is conducted within constitutional parameters lest the evidence be inadmissible at trial.

1. Responding to the Scene

If a police officer or detective arrives at a scene to find an injured or deceased child, the police officer is generally permitted to do a limited search for the purpose of locating other victims and the perpetrator. Evidence in plain view may be seized, but the items must clearly be evidence of a crime. The officer can also conduct a search consistent with ensuring public safety, the safety of those in the immediate area, and the officer's safety.

While the child is taken to the hospital, at least one officer should remain at the scene to prevent tampering with or destruction of evidence. Caregivers of the child are often eager to cooperate early in the investigative process. Officers, therefore, should carry consent-to-search forms that can be quickly completed, signed by the caregivers, and used later in court should the defendant challenge the validity of the search. If the caregivers refuse consent, one officer can remain at the scene while another obtains a search warrant. A methodical search should then be conducted.

2. Responding to the Hospital

Police may be called directly to the hospital when the alleged victim is already hospitalized. As soon as it is apparent that a child has been seriously injured or may die, an officer should immediately be dispatched to the crime scene. Consent-to-search forms may be completed by the caregivers at the hospital. Again, if caregivers refuse consent, the scene where the crime occurred should be secured and a warrant obtained immediately.

3. Searching and Documenting the Scene

A well-documented and photographed crime scene is essential to the trial of most child physical abuse and fatality cases. A scale diagram and photographs or videotapes of the child's residence help explain movements of individuals and are useful in cross-examining the defendant on activities before, during, and after the child's injuries or death. Explanations by the caregivers provide an indication of physical evidence for the investigator to photograph and, if possible, seize. Examples include the crib, couch, or table the child allegedly fell from; the iron, stove, or microwave if the child was burned; any objects the child allegedly landed on; soiled diapers, bedding, or clothing; weapons used to discipline the child, including wires, belts, or ropes. The investigator should photograph in detail the location in the house where the child was hurt. In a house or apartment, investigators should photograph all areas and note pertinent features such as carpeting on floors and stairs.

The general cleanliness and state of repair of the residence can be important. Often the living area will provide evidence of alcohol or drugs—both legal and illegal—that help direct the prosecution's case. For example, evidence that a child was taking medication for colic, together with photographs of the bottle at the child's bedside, can assist the prosecution in developing a possible motive for inflicting injury or identifying a triggering event for the defendant's behavior.

If the caregivers found the child unconscious or not breathing in the crib, carefully photograph and analyze items in the crib and surrounding area, and, if possible, seize the crib and bedding. If the child was burned by hot water, the investigator should photograph the sinks, bathtub, and all spigots in the home and test the spigots to determine whether a child could have accidentally turned on the hot water. It is also critical to test the temperature of the water coming from the water heater, the setting of the water heater, and the temperature at each tap. Water temperature determines the length of time necessary to inflict burns of different degrees and may help to prove or disprove a suspect's account of how the burn occurred. Investigators should also document other sources of heat in the home, regardless of the caregivers' initial explanation of what burned the child. With a contact burn, look for objects the shape of the burn or that may have tissue from the child on them. All investigators need to become familiar with the difference between an intentionally inflicted burn and one that may be from accidental causes. (See Asser, S. [1992]. Assessment of suspicious burn injuries. *APSAC Advisor, 5*(1), 6; Peltier, P. [1992]. Criminal investigation of suspicious burn injuries. *APSAC Advisor, 5*(1), 7 [Winter 1992].)

Trace evidence may be found on walls and floors away from the area where the child was killed. For example, blood spatters may be found some distance from the child's body as a result of the child's being hit repeatedly or thrown or struck against an object. Important evidence such as the child's hair, blood, or diapers may be thrown into wastebaskets and trash receptacles. Evidence that a child's hair was forcibly removed can prove hostility toward the child. Blood spatter patterns in different parts of the apartment may confirm a history of brutal behavior. (See, e.g., *People v. Forsha*, 542 N.Y.S.2d 847 [App. Div. 1989]). This type of evidence might also help distinguish accidental or sudden infant death syndrome (SIDS) cases from homicide.

H. Laboratory Analysis of Physical Evidence

Investigators should obtain training from their local crime laboratory personnel on the types of evidence that can be processed and preserved. Usually, the identity of persons in the child's household is not disputed; thus, fingerprint evidence and the like are usually not particularly helpful. However, if the child appears to have suffered cigarette burns, collecting cigarette butts found in the home may allow analysis of the pattern of the burns. If identification of the perpetrator is an issue, contact your local lab or the F.B.I. lab to determine whether fingerprinting or saliva analysis on the cigarette butts can be conducted.

If the case involves a combination of sexual and physical abuse, collecting the child's clothing and bedding may allow identification of what happened and who was involved. If the child shows evidence of bite marks, have the bites thoroughly photographed. Saliva swabbing should be done to allow an association to be made with the biter. If the child has suffered a depressed skull fracture or has distinct patterns of marks or scars, seize objects consistent with these patterns for analysis.

DNA testing in physical assault or child homicide cases can be effective in identifying blood found at a crime scene that is not the child's or confirming the identity of a dead victim. In the latter case, DNA from the suspected abuser can be analyzed to determine if that person is the child's parent. DNA may, in fact, be extracted from samples that are five to ten years old, and it is sometimes possible to extract DNA from skeletal remains. DNA testing can be performed on hairs with roots attached, partially decomposed tissue and bone, teeth, and envelopes and postage stamps previously moistened with saliva. (For further information, see Stolorow, M., & Clarke, G. [1992]. Forensic DNA testing: A new dimension in criminal evidence gains broad acceptance. *The Prosecutor, 25*(4), 13.)

I. Interviews With Physicians

1. Medical Evaluation

The treating physician should be able to express an opinion about whether the caregivers' explanations are consistent with the nature and severity of the injuries. The investigator should not be satisfied talking to only the attending physician if other specialists such as neurologists, radiologists, gastroenterologists, or ophthalmologists were consulted. Each may supply a needed piece of the puzzle, and not all attending physicians can adequately explain the specialists' opinions. Medical input—usually from several specialists—during the investigation and trial of physical abuse and homicide cases will often be essential to the prosecution and can be costly. Consultation between investigators and prosecutors should take place early in the investigation to assess the need for and ability to pay for expert review.

Most doctors, though extremely busy, recognize their duty to assist in evaluating potential child abuse situations. Be prepared so that you can minimize the amount of time they must spend; such courtesy will yield greater willingness to work with you in the future. The prosecutor supervising the case should be notified if a physician is uncooperative and demands a subpoena or other court order before consulting on a case. Sometimes a phone call from the prosecutor will solve the problem. If not, appropriate subpoenas can be obtained. Do not give up because physicians are initially hesitant—they may unknowingly hold the key to the case.

2. Medical Records

Obtain complete medical records regarding current and prior treatment of the injured child. The nonabusive caregiver, if any, may need to sign a release for the records. When both caregivers are suspects, normal confidentiality provisions are overridden in most states for child abuse investigations. Investigators and prosecutors should consult with one another if subpoenas or court orders are necessary.

While one may expect a simple request or subpoena to produce all relevant hospital records pertaining to the child's death, rarely is the acquisition of hospital records simple or perfunctory. For example, radiological records of X-rays, CT scans, and MRIs (magnetic resonance images) sometimes must be separately obtained. All radiological studies of a child during life, as well as after death, should be reviewed by a qualified pediatric radiologist for evidence of prior abuse. A patient's counseling records, family services or social work department records, and the notes of individual caseworkers involved with the families of deceased children, are ordinarily part of the subpoenaed "hospital records." Such records often indicate histories and statements of individuals involved in the child's death, including the defendant's statements. These statements can be extremely probative at trial and possibly inconsistent with the defendant's statements to law enforcement and trial testimony. Hospital correspondence pertaining to the child, morgue logs, and radio communications between ambulance personnel and a regional emergency network are usually not part of the hospital records. Also, medical records may not be complete when initially requested, particularly soon after hospitalization or death. Continue to check for the official hospital records to ensure that all laboratory reports, radiology reports, discharge summaries, and physician entries have been completed and obtained.

Interview the child's pediatrician to determine the child's general health since birth in order to place the suspected abusive injury in context. A family doctor who does not suspect that the caregivers are child abusers may still be able to provide information that turns out to be pivotal to the overall investigation. Ask the doctor for facts rather than an opinion about the general character of the child's caregivers.

Another frequently overlooked source of relevant information about the family and the alleged victim is EMT records or 911 dispatch tapes. If families have had several emergencies with their children, their bad luck may actually be a pattern of abuse. Check all hospitals in the area, since abusers will often use different hospitals to avoid suspicion.

3. Medical Terminology

During investigative interviews, have the physician explain medical terms so prosecutors, investigators, and doctors share a common understanding. This will save time and effort later on and help in putting together a case that judges and juries will understand. Beware of physicians or other experts who cannot explain things in lay terms, since they are not likely to be good witnesses.

J. Autopsies

In a child homicide investigation, there *must* be an autopsy of the child before the body is prepared for burial. Most states mandate autopsies of children below certain ages who die under unexplained or suspicious circumstances. In states without such a mandate, the medical examiner or local prosecutor usually has the authority to order an autopsy. This authority should be used whenever there is an unexplained or suspicious death of a child. Preferably, the autopsy should be performed by a competent forensic pathologist knowledgeable about child abuse, and with access to experts such as neuropathologists, ocular pathologists, and others. Since bruising is not always readily observable at the time of death, it is helpful to hold the body in the morgue for 24 hours after autopsy to determine if further bruising becomes apparent. This also allows adequate opportunity for X-rays and radiologic studies to be interpreted by such experts as pediatric radiologists to determine whether further examination of the body is warranted. For an excellent book discussing the medicine of radiology and child abuse, see Kleinman, P. [1987]. *Diagnostic imaging of child abuse*. Baltimore, MD: Williams and Wilkens.

During an autopsy, special attention should be paid to the child's mouth and eyes. More than one-half of battered infants have some form of eye lesion such as vitreous hemorrhage (bleeding inside the eye) or detached retina. Retinal bleeding is often associated with subdural hematomas caused by violent shaking of a child. The inner lips may show evidence of bruising due to impact with the teeth. A torn frenulum (thin tissue that connects gum to the lips) can result from a blow to the mouth and is considered a significant finding suggestive of child abuse in infants. The tongue may also show injury due to violent contact with teeth during a blow to the mouth. Observation of the child's stomach contents can be very helpful in framing the time of death. By determining how well digested the food is and comparing that with information gathered concerning the child's last meal, an expert pathologist can often estimate time of injury or death.

1. Exhumation

An exhumation may be required if an autopsy is not done at the time of death or if it is incomplete or fails to preserve needed evidence properly. Most jurisdictions permit the family of a deceased to disinter a body for further medical examination without any legal intervention. However, should the family refuse to consent, a court order is essential. It is important to note that an autopsy after burial will yield far less information owing to decomposition and the likely presence of substances such as embalming fluid.

2. Second Expert

Medical findings must be adequately documented and preserved, and it may be advisable to have a second doctor available at the autopsy. If this is not possible, prosecutors should still consider having a second physician review the initial autopsy report and findings. This second expert can serve as an additional witness at trial. The two experts should consult and work together as a team so that opinions are based on the same information. The State of Illinois has drafted an excellent *Protocol for Child Death Autopsies,* which is available from the National Center.

3. Cause and Manner of Death

The pathologist's interpretation of findings will be more accurate if the investigator shares what is known about the caregiver's explanations, actions, and medical history, along with crime scene analysis, and any preliminary conclusions reached. Most autopsy reports set forth two ultimate findings: cause of death and manner of death. Cause refers to the physiological reason for death, e.g., heart attack or embolism. Manner of death reflects the mechanism of death: natural, accidental, suicide, homicide, or undetermined.

Even when able to pinpoint the cause of death, the pathologist may be unable to specify the manner of death based on autopsy findings alone. For example, massive internal injuries may be the obvious cause of death, but the pathologist might not be able to determine whether they resulted from an accident or a homicide. If more than one mechanism of death is possible, ask the pathologist to identify the different possibilities. Follow-up investigation will often clarify what actually happened.

Successful prosecutions are possible even where the *cause of death* is deemed "natural" or "undetermined" at autopsy; there are ways people can kill children, such as suffocation, that leave no obvious signs. In such situations, the investigator's work is the key to determining the circumstances of the child's death. Spontaneous causes of death are extremely rare, at least when children are more than 18 months old. Most spontaneous causes of death of young children can be discovered at autopsy; those that leave no sign at all are exceptionally rare. Particularly when there is evidence of prior abuse of the dead child or siblings, investigators should check with several medical experts, and confront the suspect with all possible means of causing the child's death. In almost every case, expert physicians will have some plausible explanations of what could have happened to the child.

If it becomes apparent during the course of the investigation that the original cause of death listed on the death certificate is incorrect, request that the medical examiner file an amended death certificate. At trial, this will make it obvious to the jury that the investigation of a child homicide is an ongoing process and never closed. (See transcripts of trial testimony of a medical examiner and pathologist in Appendixes V.14 and V.17.)

K. Child's Medical History

1. Review of Records

Records from the child's prior doctor visits, including checkups, emergency room visits, and any hospitalizations, will be necessary to evaluate a claim that the child's injuries were caused by a preexisting medical condition. A careful review of the records may provide evidence of prior abuse that can be used as prior bad acts. Any injury should be carefully looked at if the story given does not match the pattern of injury. Even if the defendant cannot be tied exclusively to the injury, the prosecutor may be able to introduce prior injuries to the child to show the charged injury is not an accident. (*Estelle v. Maguire,* 502 U.S. 62 [1991]). The medical records of all the child's siblings should be reviewed to determine if the other children have been abused and if there are any other genetic reasons for the child's condition. The prosecutor should obtain the entire medical record including all X-rays, CT scans, and nursing notes. The prosecutor should also obtain the paramedic's report to determine the condition of the child upon arrival, the drugs that were administered, if CPR was performed, and what explanation for the injuries was given by the suspect or caregiver. Often, the explanation of how the injuries occurred changes from what the paramedic was told, what the doctor was told, and what the detective was told since the caregiver keeps getting feedback that the injury could not have happened as described.

The complete set of medical records should be discussed with an expert prior to trial. Ask caregivers and relatives for the names and addresses of all doctors and institutions who treated the child. Subpoena medical records, including birth records, from all health care providers, including hospitals, schools, and health care agencies or clinics. A notice of obtaining medical records must be given in most states to the parent or guardian prior to obtaining the records. The prosecutor may consider subpoenaing all records from the local hospitals in an area since the family may not be truthful about all the facilities where the child was treated. A review of insurance claims may reveal physicians or hospitals that treated the child that the family did not disclose. When reviewing the prior records, the absence of previous injury may be just as important to the case as the presence of injury. In the case of a stepparent who has lived with the family only for a few months, a child's having lived accident-free may help to show the identity of the abuser.

By reviewing the medical records, an expert can find characteristics, physical conditions, or disabilities that make the child more vulnerable to abuse. The expert can rule out defenses such as ostiogenesis imperfecta (brittle bone disease) and other genetic disorders. The expert can determine the possibility that the injuries were caused by birth trauma or an earlier physical condition. The expert can also exclude the explanations the caregiver gave as the cause of the injury, such as the child falling from a changing table.

2. SIDS Deaths

More than 7,000 deaths annually are attributed to sudden infant death syndrome (SIDS), a term describing the sudden unexplained death of an infant under one year of age in which a full autopsy has been performed and no cause of death has been found. SIDS, often called crib death, is a general term adopted to cover unexplained deaths rather than an explicit cause of death such as a disease or injury. The classic features of SIDS cases are children less than one year of age in previous good health, the lack of any apnea episode, and no evidence of SIDS in the family history. SIDS deaths usually occur in children from the age of 2 months to 6 months. Children who are 2 and 3 years old cannot be accurately diagnosed with having died of SIDS.

In cases of possible SIDS, the investigator should review with a medical expert the mother's medical records related to prenatal care and all records related to the child's birth to determine whether there were medical problems that support a conclusion that the child died from SIDS or respiratory failure. A review should also be done of all siblings' medical records since some families have increased risk for multiple SIDS deaths, although recurrent SIDS is believed to be more an environmental problem than a genetic one. However, a review of the autopsy and medical records may prove that the child was a victim of suffocation and not SIDS where there have been multiple deaths of siblings. There have been numerous cases involving multiple deaths of siblings that were believed to be SIDS that proved to be homicide. (See, e.g., *State v. Tinning*, 536 N.Y.S.2d 193 [1988]). If other siblings have been diagnosed as having died of SIDS, a motion to exhume the body for another autopsy should be considered.

A complete autopsy including metabolic studies must be done prior to diagnosing SIDS. A full autopsy may reveal injuries not observed by the treating physician, such as internal injuries or shaking that caused death. Metabolic disorders to rule out are medium chain acydlehydrogenase deficiency, type 1 glycogen storage disease, and carnitine disease. Note that suffocation may cause petechial hemorrhages. However, suffocation can result in brain damage and death without any physical findings. In determining whether it is SIDS or suffocation, the prosecutor should determine if the child is over 6 months of age, or had recurrent apneic episodes, previous unexplained disorders, and a dead sibling. Recurrent apneic episodes in a child with no cardiac, respiratory, metabolic, or neurologic abnormality are rare.

L. Child Protective Services Records

Early in the investigation the records of child protective services (CPS) should be obtained. These records include psychological reports, medical reports, witness statements, and suspect statements. Prior reports of abuse on all members of the family should be obtained, including out-of-state reports from places the family once lived. In reviewing CPS records, the investigator can determine if there is a pattern of abuse or neglect in the family. If siblings have been abused, this may be admissible as prior bad act evidence to show an injury was not accidental. Even if the CPS investigation resulted in an "unfounded" or "unsubstantiated" determination, the investigation records may show a pattern of abuse or include witness statements, suspect explanations, or other information useful in evaluating the current case. Be on the lookout for families who move frequently during abuse investigations to avoid CPS suspicion.

Although these records are confidential, most state statutes require CPS to share them with law enforcement and prosecutors. However, obtaining these records is not always easy, and an investigative subpoena may be needed. A cooperative agreement between law enforcement, prosecution, and CPS is one way to ensure the exchange of records and information. In cases involving death or serious injury, a cooperative multidisciplinary team reviewing the investigation is needed. The investigator may determine that CPS can obtain out-of-state CPS records easier than law enforcement.

M. Interviews of Other Potential Witnesses

Anyone who has contact with the child may have important information for the investigation. A child's siblings, relatives, teachers, neighbors, and babysitters should be interviewed. Siblings may have the most information when the parents or caregivers are suspects. In some states, siblings can be interviewed without parental consent. In other states, parental consent or a civil child protective petition filed in juvenile or family court is required. The sibling may have witnessed the abuse, observed other acts of abuse, observed injuries, and be able to describe the treatment of the sibling in the family. The victim may have confided in the sibling about the abuse. Often, the sibling will be afraid to discuss the abuse for fear of retaliation or fear that the family will be broken apart. The investigator should first determine whether the siblings are victims of abuse. The same kind of careful interviewing and efforts to corroborate their accounts should be undertaken if additional abuse is revealed. Evidence of sibling abuse may be admissible, whether it is charged separately or remains uncharged, to prove the identity of the perpetrator or lack of accident.

Close relatives, neighbors, and family friends often see physical evidence of abuse such as bruises or burns. The family members may have questioned the perpetrator about the care of the child or may have actually observed the perpetrator assaulting the child. They may be able to provide details on the care and treatment of the child that can be used to counter the caregiver's explanation for the child's injuries. Neighbors and relatives may have observed subtle clues regarding abuse, such as harsher treatment and using the child as a scapegoat, unusual anxiety, and other behavioral signs of abuse.

Teachers, day-care providers, church members, and others who play a role in the child's life on a regular basis should be interviewed to determine if they have observed injuries to the child, lengthy or unexplained absences from activities, excessive "clumsiness" on the part of the child, unexplained changes in the child's behavior (such as refusal to take her coat off during the day or wearing long sleeves), volatile behavior toward other children or adults, or unexplained fear of a particular person. All of this may be circumstantial evidence of abuse. The child may have confided in the teacher or made statements that may assist the investigator in learning what occurs in the family home. Schoolteachers and counselors are the leading reporters of physical abuse to children. These witnesses also may help pinpoint the timing of injury by being able to testify about the lack of injury when the child was last seen and the child's overall physical well-being.

N. Prior Contact With Law Enforcement

Obtain all police reports relating to the family from law enforcement agencies in the jurisdictions where they have lived. Because of the connections between child abuse and domestic violence, substance abuse, and other criminal activity, even apparently unrelated arrests may be helpful in determining the family environment. Be sure to request all police reports, including arrests, home visits, and brief contacts with the police. Determine who called the police in prior incidents and interview them regarding their knowledge of the family. The suspect's statements in all cases should be carefully reviewed to determine past drug abuse, alcohol abuse, defenses to crimes, and knowledge of the criminal justice system. Determine if the arrest resulted in prosecution, obtain a copy of the prosecutor's file, and speak to the prosecutor about his or her knowledge of the defendant.

O. The Suspect's Background

In addition to reviewing all prior criminal history, investigators and prosecutors should learn as much as possible about the suspect's background. A wonderful source of information may be the defendant's mother. Information about the suspect's background will be useful in cross-examining character witnesses and may illuminate possible motives for severe physical abuse or killing. Evidence of prior bad acts may be used to impeach character witnesses. Prosecutors should consider the use of an investigative subpoena or investigative grand jury to obtain information outside the reach of investigators.

Look for information regarding prior acts of abuse by the defendant against the deceased child. Evidence of similar abuse of other children is also important, although admissibility varies from jurisdiction to jurisdiction. Evidence of prior abuse may be admissible to show knowledge or the intent of the defendant, a common scheme or plan, the absence of mistake or accident, or motive to cover up the prior abuse of the child or silence the child or to identify the person who inflicted the fatal injuries.

Obtain the records of divorce and family court proceedings, employment records, school records, military records, and welfare records that may contain valuable information, including incidents of domestic violence or abuse. A follow-up interview with the victims of the domestic violence or abuse should be completed. In family court proceedings and employment records, the investigator may be able to obtain psychological records that will give great insight into the defendant even if the records cannot be used in court owing to doctor-patient privilege. Employment records and school records may reflect a substance abuse problem. Indications of animal abuse should be noted and are helpful in analyzing a suspect's background and psychological characteristics. (See *People v. Wood*, 463 N.Y.S.2d 101 [N.Y. App. Div. 1983] [analyzing the relevance of evidence of defendant killing dog]). Abusing pets is also a common method of silencing victims or terrorizing family members. Consider obtaining veterinary records if there appears to be a history of animal maltreatment.

Other sources of information include local police, church members, shelters, employers, coworkers, neighbors, and individuals who have had past relationships with the suspect. Older children who may have lived with the suspect, especially if they no longer do, may provide critical information. Explore the suspect's relationship with family members during interviews with relatives, friends, the family pediatrician, and others with information about the relationship. Previous experience raising children and dealing with the related stressors can provide insight into the suspect's behavior. What disciplinary methods did the suspect use? Was the suspect aware of the risk of serious injury or death? In circumstances endangering the child, did the suspect fail to act? What stressors is the family currently under, such as financial or marital problems or unemployment?

Ask the family pediatrician or clinic workers what education they may have given the suspect about child care such as proper discipline, the appropriate age for potty training, and the danger of shaking a baby. A suspect may have been warned by the doctor or may have heard in a parenting class how to deal with the frustrations of a colicky, disabled, or hyperactive child. Public health nurses or social service workers may have advised a suspect about resources such as counseling and medical care that were ignored. Such knowledge is relevant to the suspect's mental state and may indicate recklessness or a disregard of a known risk, rather than simple negligence. Such information may not appear in records, so the professionals involved with the child and defendant must be interviewed.

P. Munchausen Syndrome by Proxy

Munchausen syndrome by proxy (MSP), or factitious disorder by proxy, is a form of physical child abuse in which adults induce or fabricate illnesses in children. The child is forced to undergo unnecessary and painful medical tests. The inducing of illnesses may put the child at risk of serious illness or death. In 95% of the cases, the mother is the perpetrator, although fathers, babysitters, and other caregivers can also be perpetrators. The perpetrator typically has a void in her life. In placing the child in the hospital, she fulfills her own emotional needs by gaining attention and interacting with the doctor. The perpetrator is often in an emotionally distant marriage and is overly involved with the child. It is also not unusual for the perpetrator to have some type of medical training and appear extremely knowledgeable about her child's illness.

When investigating a suspected MSP case, a multidisciplinary team approach is necessary. Team members should include the treating physician, a consulting specialist such as the gasteroentologist, a pediatrician with knowledge about MSP, the charge nurse, the hospital administrator, law enforcement, a prosecutor, and a child protection worker. The physicians will make a diagnosis of exclusion, that is, no other disease can explain the child's symptoms. The nurses can give insight on the family dynamics, and their notes may document who had access to the child. The hospital administrator can assist in details such as movement of the child and installing surveillance equipment. Law enforcement can interview witnesses, serve search warrants, and confront the suspect. The prosecutor can give legal advice on the collection of evidence, oversee the investigation, and assist in obtaining court orders and search and arrest warrants. The child protective worker can seek an order to remove the child from the perpetrator's care and ensure that the child is protected.

All of the child's medical records should be reviewed in a suspected MSP case. Because many perpetrators "doctor shop," a subpoena should be sent to all local hospitals and any hospital where the family used to live. Notice of obtaining medical records must be given in most states to the caregiver of a child. However, CPS may be able to get these records as part of their investigation without advising the parent. The treating physician may be able to ask the parents to sign a release to obtain the prior medical records to assist in determining what disease the child has. Since the child may be at greater risk for another episode if the perpetrator knows she is a suspect, caution should be taken to prevent the perpetrator from knowing until CPS is ready to remove the child.

MSP should be considered as a diagnosis if the perpetrator claims that the child has an unusual medical condition such as periods of apnea (interrupted breathing), unobserved seizures, infections that appear at the intravenous site, fevers with no evidence of a disease, and other unexplained symptoms. MSP can be divided into two categories: First, there are those perpetrators who induce the illness by injecting feces or urine into the child, administering poisons, suffocating the child, or performing any other means of affirmative acts to make the child sick; second, there are those perpetrators who fabricate the illness by false reports of fevers, seizures, bleeding, apnea, and other false symptoms.

There are many factors to look at in determining whether the child is a victim of MSP. The team should carefully review the medical records, school records, and social service records and ask the following questions:

- Does the child have an unexplained illness or undiagnosed disease in which the symptoms of the illness conflict with the physical evidence?
- Does the child have seizures, fevers, or apnea spells that only the perpetrator observes?
- Is the disease resistant to treatment that should cure the child, such as when antidiarrhea medication fails to stop the diarrhea or when the child is given anticonvulsants and the child is reported to continue to have seizures?
- Does the child have a long medical history of different hospitals and different doctors?
- Is there a family history of siblings or relatives with unknown rare disorders or siblings with unexplained deaths?
- Is the relationship between the perpetrator and the child unusually close?
- Is the perpetrator overly involved in the child's care, such as feeding the child, taking care of the gastric feeding tube, spending all her time in the hospital, while the nonoffending spouse seems to be distant and emotionally unattached?
- Does the perpetrator seem unconcerned over even the most invasive medical procedures done to the child?
- Does the parent have training in the medical field or has she done research on the child's alleged illness?

The team may consider separating the child from the perpetrator to determine if the child becomes healthy when there is no contact with the perpetrator. One way to do this is to remove the child from the private or semiprivate room and place the child on a ward with more supervision and/or not allow visitors for 24–48 hours. As part of the investigation, the team may also consider placing covert video surveillance in the child's room. Some hospitals have written into their consent for treatment forms permission to videotape and photograph the patient as part of the child's diagnosis and treatment. Despite this consent, however, a court order can also be obtained and is the recommended approach. When using video surveillance, wiretap laws should be consulted to determine if sound can be recorded. In many states, sound cannot be recorded unless specific crimes are alleged. If video surveillance is used, the camera should be monitored at all times for the protection of the child. By focusing the camera on the bed, the family's privacy rights can be respected. In cases in which the injection of foreign material is a consideration, a camera might also be placed in the bathroom, remembering, however, to ensure the child's privacy rights. Investigators must be careful to make sure that the placement of the camera is not well known throughout the hospital so the perpetrator does not become aware of its presence. Once the camera is in place, the team should consider notifying the perpetrator that the child will be discharged. The chance of the perpetrator inducing or fabricating a new episode may increase if she believes the child will be released.

When collecting specimens such as urine, feces, and gastric contents, the chain of custody must be protected. Rather than using the usual hospital channels, one nurse should collect the specimen, mark it, and deliver it to the lab. Specimens should also be collected at random, unannounced times. The perpetrator should not be allowed to assist in the collection of the evidence. Perpetrators have gone to great lengths to alter specimens, for example, by adding fat to a stool sample, salt to a sweat specimen, and obtaining sputum from a true cystic fibrosis patient to fabricate cystic fibrosis in her child.

A search warrant should be issued for the hospital room and perhaps the perpetrator's home. The search warrant affidavit will need to include information from the physicians on what MSP is and why MSP is the diagnosis in this case. The search warrant will need to specify what the investigator is looking for, such as syringes, Saran wrap (suffocation), medicine, ipecac (induces vomiting), medical literature, formula that may contain foreign materials, and other items that could be used to create the child's symptoms. When the search warrant is served, the hospital staff should assist in removing the perpetrator from the hospital room while ensuring that she leaves her purse, diaper bag, or luggage behind.

Confronting the perpetrator is the responsibility of law enforcement. The relationship the perpetrator has developed with the hospital staff may make it difficult for them to confront her. As the perpetrator is confronted, a social worker should be on hand to discuss placement issues. Law enforcement needs to talk to the perpetrator before CPS so there can be no claim that the perpetrator was given any promises, such as regaining custody if she confesses. It will be easier to obtain a confession if video surveillance was used. However, it is still possible that some perpetrators caught on tape will continue to deny their actions. If an arrest is to be made, the perpetrator should not be arrested in front of the child.

As part of the investigation, the child should be interviewed. MSP usually occurs with children under the age of five. Children over the age of five may assist or be passive participants in MSP. Siblings should also be interviewed about how the mother takes care of the child (mommy always fixes his medicine). The nonoffending spouse should be interviewed to determine what he knows and where he stands in the prosecution. Some fathers will categorically deny any abuse has occurred, while others may recount having observed certain strange behavior. Remember that the relationship between the perpetrator and the nonoffending spouse is part of the MSP dynamic, and marital problems such as domestic violence may have contributed to the perpetrator's actions.

An expert in the area of MSP should be consulted. A pediatrician with knowledge of MSP should be used. Experts can assist in interpreting the medial records and can explain MSP at trial. The case can be tried without evidence of the syndrome as straightforward physical abuse if the perpetrator is caught on videotape, foreign material is found in the formula, or the child has an infection at the intravenous site that is consistent with fecal matter being injected. Expert testimony about MSP may be necessary in cases in which the evidence is mostly circumstantial. Each physician who has treated the child should be contacted. Many physicians may have suspected MSP in the past and obtained samples or gathered evidence on their own.

The prosecutor and investigator should educate themselves on MSP. (See Schreier, H., & Libow, J. [1993]. *Hurting for love: Munchausen by proxy syndrome.* New York: Guilford; Levin, A. V., & Sheridan, M. S. [1995]. *Munchausen syndrome by proxy: Issues in diagnosis and treatment.* San Francisco: Jossey-Bass; Parnell, T. F., & Day, D. O. [1997]. *Munchausen by proxy syndrome: Misunderstood child abuse.* Thousand Oaks, CA: Sage; see also Dawn, W. [2001]. Munchausen syndrome by proxy: The ultimate betrayal. *Update, 14*(8).)

Q. Consultation With Experts

The investigation of a serious physical abuse or child homicide case often requires consultation with experts beyond those who treated the child or performed the autopsy. Special training will help investigators and prosecutors know what type of expertise is needed, but there is also no substitute for experience. Every case presents new and challenging problems.

In severe head injury cases, a pediatric neurologist, neurosurgeon, or neuropathologist may help determine the likely cause of injury. A radiologist may help determine if the child has fractures and the time frame in which they occurred. This would help to show a pattern of injury. In cases involving SBS, an ophthalmologist may examine the child and provide vital clues. Medical examiners and coroners may have little experience performing autopsies on children and thus not be able to identify injuries accurately. Plan to consult with a pediatrician or physician experienced in recognizing child abuse any time a child dies with suspicious injuries and the pathologist is unsure whether it is an accidental or deliberate death. The National Center for Prosecution of Child Abuse can help identify experts. The prosecutor should meet with the pediatrician and the medical examiner to review each potential explanation of the injuries and how to refute it. During this meeting, the expert can provide medical literature and treatises that support the expert's opinion and refute the defense theory.

Meet with the proposed defense experts prior to trial, along with a detective or third party should it become necessary to have someone testify at trial regarding statements made during the meeting. Request a copy of the defense expert witness's report prior to the meeting and go over the report with your own expert. The prosecution's expert can provide questions to ask along with the medical literature that supports the prosecution expert's opinion. Ask defense experts what medical literature they are relying on, what expertise they have, how they reached their conclusions, and what evidence they have reviewed. After this meeting, meet again with the prosecution's expert to strategize how to rebut the defense case.

R. Child Death Review Teams

When a child dies under suspicious circumstances, there are often many agencies and individuals that have information that is relevant and necessary to determine the cause and circumstances of the death. Unfortunately, the lack of coordination among agencies often results in a failure to recognize and report abuse-related child homicides. Concerned that many child abuse deaths were being ruled accidental, SIDS, or natural, prosecutors and other professionals in a growing number of jurisdictions have convened child death review teams to exchange information about the deaths of children.

The value of interagency child death review teams to coordinate information on cases, track child deaths, and improve investigation procedures is evident. The core death review team members include the prosecutor, the coroner or medical examiner, a pediatric trauma specialist, and representatives of law enforcement and CPS. Additional members may include staff from schools, preschools, probation and/or parole, mental health professionals, child advocates, the fire department, paramedics, health department staff, and emergency room staff. Peer review of cases builds accountability and increases the information available to involved agencies so they can make better individual decisions. It also develops a framework for more competent management of nonfatal cases and multiagency prevention programs. Cases are generally drawn from coroners or public health records. Most involve the very young, with half the victims under 1 year of age. For further information on child death review teams, contact the National Center for Prosecution of Child Abuse.

X. REFERENCE MATERIALS

Sudden Infant Death Syndrome

Monteleone, J. A., & Broedeur, A. E. [1998]. *Child maltreatment: A clinical guide and reference.* St. Louis, MO: G.W. Medical Publishing.

Munchausen Syndrome by Proxy

Levin, A. V., & Sheridan, M. S. [1995]. *Munchausen syndrome by proxy: Issues in diagnosis and treatment.* San Francisco: Jossey-Bass.

Schreier, H., & Libow, J. [1993]. *Hurting for love: Munchausen by proxy syndrome.* New York: Guilford.

Parnell, T. F., & Day, D. O. [1997]. *Munchausen by proxy syndrome: Misunderstood child abuse.* Thousand Oaks, CA: Sage.

Southall, D., et al. [1997]. Covert video recordings of life threatening child abuse: Lessons for child protection. *Pediatrics, 100*(5), 735–760.

III

Charging, Plea Negotiation, and Disposition

Some of the most important, yet under-emphasized, aspects of the child abuse prosecutor's responsibilities relate to filing appropriate charges, maintaining a proper policy relating to plea negotiations, and achieving proper sentencing when offenders are convicted of a crime. Child abuse cases focus a prosecutor's attention upon factors not even considered in many other types of crime. Appropriate decision making requires a basic understanding of the underlying dynamics of child abuse. The prosecutor must understand why abusers act the way they do, the difference between a single act of abuse and a pattern of abuse, the effects of abuse on the victim, the effectiveness of treatment in changing an offender's behavior, and the recidivism rates for child abuse offenders.

The prosecutor's power to file criminal charges, or to refrain from filing charges, is considerable. Competing considerations include the needs and desires of the victim and the victim's family, the need for accountability and punishment for the offender, the public desire for justice and safety from future criminal acts, and the aspiration that the criminal justice system will operate in a way that deters future criminal behavior by others. It is impossible to please every contingent in every case. In the field of child abuse prosecution, it is even more likely than in other types of cases that public attitudes will affect how the charging and disposition of criminal cases is perceived. Public opinion concerning child abuse is often swayed by high-profile criminal cases and whatever spin the media chooses to place upon the issues in such cases. The prosecutor's overriding duty to achieve justice should always take precedence over the public's demands or other pressures.

Underlying all child abuse prosecutions is a public desire to disbelieve what studies show to be a high prevalence of sexual and physical abuse of children. It is common for the general public to refuse to believe that a parent or caregiver would intentionally cause harm to a child, especially serious or life-threatening injury. Most members of the general public have been stressed themselves by child care responsibilities and feel some sense of sympathy for the abuser, who is seen as having lost control. In addition, there is still a general public belief that it is appropriate to use at least some corporal punishment when disciplining children. Thus, the public often understands and forgives a person who goes a "bit too far" when punishing a child. Most jurisdictions continue to have an affirmative defense of "reasonable discipline" for acts toward children that would otherwise be considered abusive.

Similarly, public attitudes toward those who sexually abuse children continue to be shaped by abhorrence of the act itself and the general belief that anyone who would use a child for sexual gratification must be "sick." Such attitudes prevail, even though studies have established the nature of pedophilia and that offenders exhibiting this behavior are generally not mentally ill. It becomes the prosecutor's duty to educate the trier of fact as to the underlying dynamics of child abuse in each case. To some extent, prosecutors can also help get accurate information to the general public so that attitudes are informed not by media sensationalism but by scientifically accurate knowledge about child abuse, victims, and perpetrators.

When formulating policies and procedures for a prosecuting office, it is important that the decision-making process is perceived as not only fair but as consistent and driven by a cogent understanding of child abuse and child abusers. If the decision-making process is seen as well informed and consistent across cases, there is a better chance that decisions in individual cases will be seen as appropriate. The lack of such informed decision-making guidelines will often be criticized as resulting in arbitrary or capricious handling of cases, and the public respect essential for operation of a public prosecutor's office will be lacking.

A. The Establishment of Policies and Standards

Every prosecutor's office has its own policies governing the manner in which decisions related to charging and disposition of criminal cases are made. In many offices, these policies take the form of clearly articulated guidelines. Some are fairly detailed written guidelines specifying the procedures for charging and sentencing different crimes, while others express only general principles. It can be difficult to delineate decision-making criteria, as no objective formula can determine appropriate action in every case. Prosecutors must have flexibility to exercise discretion and make decisions that take into account unique circumstances. They must also maintain an ongoing assessment of the strengths and weaknesses of the case. Nonetheless, written standards can provide guidance in an effort to build consistency and guard against arbitrariness.

The establishment of guidelines promotes uniformity within a prosecutor's office by helping to ensure that similarly situated defendants are treated consistently no matter who handles their particular case. Guidelines will also improve the efficiency of new staff members who are learning to make such decisions. Some offices have published their guidelines, increasing defendants' understanding of the reasons for their treatment, allowing the public to better appreciate the way in which criminal cases are charged and negotiations are carried out, and providing the opportunity for community feedback on policies. Since the prosecutor's duty is to serve the community, this kind of accountability makes sense. A procedure for seeking supervisory approval for exceptions to policies and standards can also be specified, such as requiring written justification for the departure and review and approval by the elected prosecutor or another supervisory prosecutor. Since published guidelines cannot anticipate every fact situation, they should not be overly detailed or "set in stone." There should be room for flexibility and deviation. Written standards that are not followed may become the basis for civil liability claims that may not fall within the "absolute" or "qualified immunity" historically granted to prosecutors.

In the area of child abuse, guidelines should call for vertical prosecution and can emphasize the need to prosecute crimes against children or within families with the same vigor as crimes against adults or involving strangers. Guidelines should also clearly state that the race, ethnicity, marital status, sex, creed, religion, sexual preference, or economic class of the defendant or victim shall not influence the manner in which a case is handled. They can specify what should be considered when deciding how many counts to charge, what crime should be charged when a choice among crimes exists, and the process for plea negotiations. Plea negotiation guidelines should include when and if charges will be reduced, components of sentence recommendations, a requirement to consult with victims and their families, and other factors. (See National District Attorneys Association. [1991]. *National prosecution standards* [2nd ed., Ch. 42, 43]. Alexandria, VA: National District Attorneys Association.)

General standards for filing child abuse charges have been adopted in some jurisdictions. These standards are often the same as those used for all crimes against persons, reflecting a more aggressive stance than that taken with property crimes. For example, Wash. Rev. Code § 9.94A.411(2) (2001) provides that crimes against persons, including all child abuse cases, may be filed "if sufficient admissible evidence exists, which, when considered with the most plausible, reasonably foreseeable defense that could be raised under the evidence, would justify a conviction by a reasonable and objective fact finder." The same statutory section indicates that property crimes can be filed "if the admissible evidence is of such convincing force as to make it probable that a reasonable and objective fact finder would convict after hearing all the admissible evidence and the most plausible defense that could be raised." Such standards recognize that the emphasis in child abuse cases should be on seeking justice even though the case may be difficult to prove. Although the public, judges, and even juries may not have a good understanding of what makes a case strong or appropriate for prosecution, the prosecutor's office must strive to educate and not give in to the opinions of others as to what cases should be pursued and what cases should be dropped or resolved. Child abuse cases are some of the most difficult of all criminal cases to prove, but the degree of difficulty should not discourage prosecutors from rising to the challenge to seek justice on behalf of the most helpless members of society.

B. The Interdisciplinary Process

The development of interdisciplinary teams means that prosecutors, who regularly staff cases with a group of professionals, are no longer alone in making decisions about which cases should be charged and what should happen to the case once it is charged. The prosecutor retains the final discretion as to what charges to file, which cases to pursue, and which cases cannot be pursued, but the exercise of such discretion is easier when the prosecutor has been fully informed by members of other disciplines.

An example illustrates the proper functioning of the process. A 9-month-old baby has been shaken at her home. She is now on life support and is not expected to survive. A staffing of the case is held with the treating pediatrician, the pediatric director of the Children's Hospital, a pediatric neurosurgeon, social workers from the hospital and from CPS, a psychologist, the victim-witness advocate from the prosecutor's office, the child protection attorneys, a guardian *ad litem* for the child, the criminal investigator, and the prosecutor.

Criminal investigators have examined the scene and have determined that the caregivers, the mother and her live-in boyfriend, contend that the baby tumbled down the stairs when one of the other children left the gate unlocked. The criminal investigator explains the caregivers' account that the baby tumbled down the stairs at approximately 10:30 A.M. while they were both in another room, getting dressed. They heard the baby screaming at the bottom of the stairs and ran to find out what happened. They claim the baby cried for a few minutes and rubbed her head, but she was otherwise "fine" within about 15 minutes. She ate baby food and drank a bottle before playing with her older siblings. She went down for a nap at about noon. The boyfriend then said he went in to check on her and to change her diaper at 2:30 P.M. He woke her from her nap, placed her on the changing table, when she suddenly started stiffening and her eyes rolled up into her head. He noticed that she was not breathing well and her color was gray, so he yelled at the mother to call 9–1–1. He gently shook her to start her breathing again, which seemed to work for a few minutes; then she got worse. When paramedics arrived, they described the baby as comatose, blue in color, with skin cool to the touch. They believed that she had been in distress for more than the 10 minutes that had elapsed since the distress call was received.

The physicians explain that the victim's life-threatening injuries were caused by being violently shaken and possibly hit or slammed against something. The child's injuries include bilateral retinal hemorrhages, subdural hematoma, severe brain swelling consistent with widespread brain damage, and a focal area of bleeding at the back of the skull. The baby also has bruises at various stages of healing. The physicians further advise the group that there is no accidental mechanism that would explain this collection of injuries, including a fall down stairs. The physicians explain that the caregiver's discrepant story is a good indicator that the baby is a battered child. The doctors also explain that the delay in seeking medical attention for this critically injured child is common among child abusers. The neurosurgeon explains that a child with such a serious head injury would not have a lucid interval between the infliction of the injury and the onset of symptoms; rather, she would almost immediately have become unconscious, had difficulty breathing, and possibly also would have had seizures. The neurosurgeon also explains that it is extremely uncommon for a child with such severe injuries to be described as "fine," then suddenly go into arrest in the presence of the caregiver with no other injury inflicted.

The CPS agency has removed the two older siblings from the home while the investigation proceeds. CPS workers and the hospital social worker notify the group that there is a history of several prior referrals of this family for abuse and neglect involving the baby and her older siblings. Interestingly, it is noted that all of the referrals are dated after the boyfriend moved in with Mom and her children. The victim-witness advocate indicates that there is a history of Mom reporting domestic violence perpetrated against her by the boyfriend, but each time Mom has recanted her account of what happened and asked that charges not be pursued. Both the advocate and the psychologist explain the effects of battering on women in general and encourage consideration of whether Mom was capable of protecting the baby from the live-in boyfriend's apparent abuse. They also point out the unusual nature of the boyfriend's claim that he went in to "wake the baby up" at 2:30 P.M. to check on her and change her diaper, noting that it is not common for caregivers to awaken a sleeping and content child.

The prosecutor has gained much by participating in this interdisciplinary team meeting. This meeting gives the prosecutor the opportunity to consider the collective experience of all the diverse professionals when deciding what crime was committed and who is likely to have committed it. The prosecutor has also learned that although Mom is not likely to have committed the severe injury, there are other considerations to look into prior to deciding whether Mom should be charged either with being an accomplice to the boyfriend or with failure to protect the victim from abuse.

C. The Involvement of Victims, Their Families, and Others

Decisions regarding whether to file charges, what to offer, if anything, during plea negotiations, and what to recommend at sentencing should be made only after considering all available information and consulting with other professionals involved in the case. In addition, victims, their families and therapists, and the investigating officer(s) may have competing interests in the charging process and may also be consulted. These parties should be consulted before reaching a final charging decision. Not only will this consultation ensure that a prosecutor has all the information needed to make a decision, but it will also give those affected or involved an opportunity to express their concerns and reaction. Most likely it will increase their level of support for the final decision. This two-way communication should continue throughout the process. While it is important that victims, their families, and others involved in criminal child abuse cases understand that their wishes will be taken into account, they should also recognize they will not necessarily determine whether charges are filed. Many people do not realize that the prosecutor represents the collective community rather than a single individual and must make an independent and objective determination. It is best to explain this concept at the outset, not only to those directly involved in cases, but also when setting up a multidisciplinary team review process.

II. THE CHARGING DETERMINATION

A. Who Should Make Charging Decisions?

1. Consultation With Experienced Prosecutors

The good news concerning the increase in the prosecution of child abuse cases is the development of a network of experienced child abuse prosecutors throughout the country who are willing to consult on cases and offer the benefits of their many years of experience. The National Center for Prosecution of Child Abuse has senior attorneys who are available to discuss cases and put the prosecutor in touch with other prosecutors throughout the country. This network can offer insight into everything from standards for prosecuting abuse cases to charging decisions to recommended guidelines for entry of plea bargains and disposition of cases. Although every jurisdiction has a statutory scheme that is somewhat unique, the same issues and concerns seem to be common in child abuse prosecutions nationwide. By seeking such consultation, even smaller prosecutor's offices can dramatically expand their "staff" and obtain expert assistance and guidance.

It is difficult for prosecutors handling their first cases of child abuse in any form to make appropriate decisions without consulting with others with more experience. Filing decisions are best made by, or in consultation with, prosecutors who have training and experience in child abuse cases. It is difficult, if not impossible, for the novice prosecutor to competently evaluate a child abuse case alone. This is not to say that experience alone equates expertise. New prosecutors are encouraged to use their creativity and expand the horizons of effective prosecution. On the other hand, an understanding of the underlying dynamics of child abuse takes some time to acquire, and such a basic comprehension should underlie virtually all decisions made in child abuse cases.

2. Vertical Prosecution

Vertical prosecution occurs when the same prosecutor who makes the charging decision handles all subsequent phases of the case, including pretrial motions, witness preparation, trial, and sentencing. This process is highly recommended in child abuse cases. In jurisdictions where grand juries are used or preliminary hearings are required, the same prosecutor should handle those phases of the case as well. If the prosecutor's office handles both juvenile civil court dependency/neglect/removal actions and criminal child abuse prosecutions, consideration should be given to using the same prosecutor in both the criminal and the civil court proceedings. (See Coordinating criminal and juvenile court proceedings in child maltreatment cases. In *National Institute of Justice Research Preview*. Washington, DC: U.S. Department of Justice, Office of Justice Programs. Oct. 1996, p. 2.) At the very least, there should be active communication and sharing of information between the attorneys handling child protection actions and those handling criminal prosecution involving the same victim or the same family.

The advantages of vertical prosecution of child abuse are numerous. The family of the victim obtains confidence in the prosecutor's skill and understanding by developing a long-term trust. All the input provided by the family about the background of the victim and the perpetrator is lost if prosecutors are switched midstream. It is inefficient to force a prosecutor to get up to speed on a case in the middle of the process. When prosecutors are switched, there is always some difference in the approach taken on a case. Even where office policies and procedures are clear, each prosecutor takes a different view of how to prove a case, what plea bargain to consider, and how to resolve the case. Changing prosecutors can be very disconcerting to the victim and the victim's family, especially if it causes a continuance of an important hearing or trial.

One approach to resolving the sometimes conflicting aims of having experienced prosecutors involved in charging decisions and using vertical prosecution is to create a system in which experienced prosecutors supervise newer ones. Regular training should also be required for all prosecutors handling child abuse cases. The best approach is to create a specialized unit or have prosecutors who specialize in child abuse prosecution vertically prosecute these cases. If your jurisdiction cannot use vertical prosecution, some effort should be made to provide continuity for the child. One way is to provide a single victim-witness advocate to accompany and support the child through every stage of the process and assist each prosecutor involved in the case. In addition, procedures should be instituted to ensure that the prosecutor who charges the case communicates with others involved.

3. Handling Sensitive Cases

Some cases are particularly sensitive because they have generated or have the potential of generating substantial publicity. Such cases may involve well-known members of the community (police, clergy members, teachers), large numbers of child victims (day-care or school settings), novel issues (prenatal drug ingestion leading to injury or death of the child, severe neglect such as starvation), or bizarre circumstances (ritual abuse). In these situations, consult with the elected prosecutor or another individual at an appropriate supervisory level. High profile cases must be carefully managed so that office policies are consistently applied and those in charge are aware of how the case is handled. (For general information on media relations, see Fisher, D. [1992]. Child abuse and the media: Twelve tips for dealing with the press. *APSAC Advisor, 5*(1), 5; see also National District Attorneys Association. [1991]. *National Prosecution Standards* (2nd ed., Ch. 33, 34) Alexandria, VA: National District Attorneys Association.)

B. Charging Child Sexual Abuse Cases

1. Understanding the Basic Considerations

The child abuse prosecutor faced with deciding whether to file child sexual abuse charges must have a basic understanding of the type and quality of evidence that makes a case strong or weak. It is rare to have medical evidence that allows a qualified physician to give an opinion that the child was definitely sexually abused. Only about one third of sexual abuse cases involve a medical finding that is consistent with the child having been sexually abused. The lack of medical evidence means that the allegations made by the child and the surrounding detail provided in the child's disclosures of abuse are the most important features of a child sex abuse prosecution. That does not mean, however, that a case must be reduced to the word of the child victim against the denial of the adult perpetrator. Investigators and prosecutors must be creative in finding other forms of corroboration for the child's statements. This may include evidence of the child's behavioral changes and expert testimony explaining the dynamics of victimization. Prosecutors must become familiar with the developmental levels of children in order to apply appropriate expectations of the quality of a child victim's testimony.

The primary issue in most child sexual abuse cases is not the identity of the perpetrator, since most child sexual abuse is perpetrated by someone who is either a family member or well known to the child and family. (Finkelhor, D. [1994]. Current information on the scope and nature of child sexual abuse. *The Future of Children, 4*(2), 31 [concluding, based upon retrospective surveys, that no more than 10%–30% of abusers were strangers]. Instead, the main issue tends to be determining what happened and what crime was committed based upon the child's allegations and the surrounding circumstances. Studies and experience establish that it is common for child victims to disclose in a piecemeal fashion, and only when the interviewer has obtained the trust of the child. (See, e.g., Bradley, A. R., & Wood, J. M. [1996]. How do children tell? The disclosure process in child sexual abuse. *Child Abuse & Neglect, 20,* 881; Sorensen, T., & Snow, B. [1991]. How children tell: The process of disclosure in child sexual abuse. *Child Welfare, 70,* 3.) It may take time and patience to determine what exactly happened to the child victim. Sometimes it appears that the child is inconsistent when in fact it is the adult interviewer who is confused about what the child is saying. Interviews with children must proceed slowly and cautiously to make sure the child is being understood.

Most individuals who develop a sexual interest in children have an extensive history of sexual acts with children, even if they have not been arrested or prosecuted. It is important to realize that the black-and-white distinctions between "preferential pedophiles," who prefer sexual relationships with children and do not have adult relationships and "regressed pedophiles," married heterosexual males not ordinarily attracted to children who relate to their young female victims in an adult manner, and between offenders who fit the category of incest and those who offend against children outside of their family are being blurred by modern research. (See Salter, A. C. [1995]. *Transforming trauma: A guide to understanding and treating adult survivors of child sexual abuse.* Thousand Oaks, CA: Sage; Becker, J. V. [1994]. Offenders: Characteristics and treatment. *The Future of Children, 4,* 176–177 [noting "it used to be assumed that incest offenders could be clearly separated from other child molesters, but current evidence indicates that a substantial percentage of child molesters offend in both spheres."] A person who has sexual relations with a child was aroused by that child at that time. Alcohol or drug abuse does not cause pedophilic interest in sex with children, although it may weaken normal inhibitions. Once a person has developed a sexual interest in children, such an interest cannot be simply altered with mental health treatment. It has been said that

> Treatment is *not* a cure—rather, it provides new understanding, options, and motivations for the individual to manage that risk and avoid further abusive behavior. For some, the risk remains high despite vigorous interventions, even when the individual is motivated to change, due to the habituated nature of the pattern and/or persistent sexual arousal to children. For others, the risk may be significantly moderated by the treatment process and their own commitment to changes in lifestyle. (Ryan, G. [1997]. The sexual abuser. In M. E. Helfer et al. [Eds.], *The battered child* [5th ed., p. 342]. Chicago: University of Chicago Press.)

A great majority of those who sexually abuse children were themselves sexually or otherwise abused as children. That, of course, does not mean that all victims of childhood sexual abuse will become offenders, but the trend of creating new offenders who were once victims is disturbing. This phenomenon means that the system will continue to see geometric increases in the number of sexual offenses against children until the system effectively intervenes to eliminate the development of new offenders. Research also establishes that intervention with juvenile sex offenders tends to have a much better chance of rendering permanent changes than does treatment of adult sex offenders. (See Ryan, G. D., & Lane, S. L. [1991]. *Juvenile sexual offending* [p. 191]. San Francisco: Jossey-Bass [noting, "It is clear to treatment providers in this field that the court's involvement is crucial in supporting the development of effective treatment resources as well as in facilitating the treatment process."]) Thus, criminal prosecution of juvenile sex offenders may be a focal point to ensure that juveniles receive the treatment they need, since perpetrators must understand that there is a consequence for abusing younger children, even if the deviant cycle began with their own victimization. (See Vieth, V. [2001]. When the child abuser is a child: Investigating, prosecuting and treating juvenile sex offenders in the new millennium. *Hamline Law Review, 25,* 48.)

2. Determining the Suspect's Factual Guilt

Deciding whether charges can or should be filed requires an objective evaluation of existing evidence as well as an understanding of the dynamics of victimization and common behavioral patterns of offenders and victims. (See *National Prosecution Standards* [2nd ed., Rule 1.1]. Alexandria, VA: National District Attorneys Association.) The prosecutor must consider all available evidence, whether admissible or inadmissible, when determining what happened to the child victim, whether it constitutes a criminal act, and what crime was committed. The evidence includes all the statements made by the child, including any statements made to family, friends, teachers, therapists, counselors, and any other person; statements made in formal interviews with CPS workers and criminal investigators; the age-appropriateness of the child's statements; evidence of the defendant's opportunity to commit the crime(s); evidence of the defendant's history of sexual acts even if uncharged; family dynamics; therapist evaluations of the victim and the defendant; admissions or confessions, including partial admissions such as, "I touched her, but I had no sexual intent"; prior CPS history; polygraph or psychosexual evaluations of the defendant; evidence of the child's behavior and symptoms following the abuse; and any corroborative medical evidence. When the prosecutor is satisfied that the identity of the perpetrator is established and that the acts described constitute a crime, the next question to answer is whether the admissible evidence meets the standard established for filing a charge of sexual abuse of a child.

Cases should not be declined solely because of inadequate investigation. A prosecutor who is unsatisfied with the quality or quantity of investigative work performed should become actively involved in seeing that additional steps are taken. The best prosecution models in the country involve a team approach in which the prosecutor takes an advisory role in the criminal investigation from the beginning. This ensures that legal standards of proof are considered and the legal requirements for actions such as search warrants and interrogation of suspects are followed. A joint investigation by CPS and law enforcement has been shown to be the most effective. (Tjaden, P. G., & Anhalt, J. [1994]. *The impact of joint law enforcement-child protective services investigations on child maltreatment cases: Executive summary for Grant Number 90-CA-1446 from the National Center on Child Abuse and Neglect.* Washington, DC: National Center on Child Abuse and Neglect [detailing the authors' study of three locations over a 4-year period and their finding of a distinct benefit to joint investigations in both child protection actions and criminal prosecutions].)

Child abuse investigations are time-intensive and often demand unique skills and additional time and patience. The process is inefficient and insufficient if the investigator conducts the entire investigation, then presents the case to the prosecutor, who decides whether to file charges based solely on the investigation already performed. A collaborative approach yields more complete and appropriate results, even if the prosecutor's office does not employ its own investigative staff. Prosecutors must not shirk their responsibility to see that justice is done by blaming their inaction on an incompetent or inadequate investigation. Achieving justice for children demands that the prosecutor ensure the quality of the investigation, including obtaining specialized training for criminal investigators and providing professional guidance as to the standards expected prior to filing charges in a case.

3. The Standard for Charging a Case

Although different prosecutors' offices use different standards for filing criminal cases, there are good reasons in child sexual abuse cases to establish a standard that exceeds probable cause to believe a crime was committed and that the defendant committed it. It is clear that even filing such a charge causes damage to the defendant's reputation. A person should not be charged when the prosecutor knows the case is not likely to survive a preliminary hearing or pretrial motions to dismiss. The prosecutor should be convinced that the admissible, credible evidence, considered in light of the defenses likely to be raised, is sufficient to warrant a conviction by a reasonable trier of fact. A prosecutor who is not convinced that the evidence meets that standard should either suggest more investigation to shore up weaknesses in the case or, where additional investigation is not likely to be helpful, decline to prosecute and give an appropriate explanation. The prosecutor should also consider from the beginning whether the statute of limitations has run or was tolled by other circumstances.

Most experienced child abuse prosecutors realize that a conviction can be obtained based solely upon the credible statements and/or testimony of the child victim. As law enforcement officers and prosecutors have obtained more and more experience, they have successfully handled cases involving very young victims who would have been considered incompetent witnesses just a couple of decades ago in America. Although it was assumed in the 1980s that child sexual abuse victims would be extremely traumatized by having to testify in court, recent research shows that the opposite reaction by children is sometimes true. Children are often assisted in their recovery from the offense by the experience of testifying, and that is true regardless of whether there is a conviction. (Henry, J. [1997]. System intervention trauma to child sexual abuse victims following disclosure. *Journal of Interpersonal Violence, 12*(4), 499, 510 [finding 72% of children reported positive experience with system intervention].) Most researchers agree that children provide more, and more accurate, information when the stress of testifying is minimized. This stress is minimized when the child is prepared in advance for testifying, when the child has an understanding of the process, when age-appropriate questions are asked, and when accommodations are made in the courtroom for the child. (See Whitcomb, D. [1993]. Techniques for improving children's testimony. In *Child victims as witnesses*. Washington, DC: U.S. Department of Justice.)

There is a general public abhorrence for the crime of child sexual abuse, and that translates into juries who would rather believe anything other than a seemingly normal person gratifying his sexual desires at the expense of a helpless child victim. Public education about the general dynamics of child sexual abuse can help to overcome this public attitude of disbelief. It is important to also recognize that the public attitude has been in large part shaped by sensationalized and often inaccurate or one-sided media accounts of high-profile cases. Such cases have led people to believe that children can be coached or coerced into lying about being sexually abused. Again, prosecutors can educate the public about the reality of child sexual abuse and should make it clear that false statements are extremely rare. (Jones, D. P. H., & Melbourne McGraw, J. [1986]. Reliable and fictitious accounts of sexual abuse to children. *Journal of Interpersonal Violence, 2*(1), 27; Thoennes, N., & Tjaden, P. D. [1990]. The extent, nature and validity of sexual abuse allegations in custody/visitation disputes. *Child Abuse & Neglect, 14,* 151.) In addition, prosecutors should attempt to overcome the all too common belief that sexual abuse allegations that arise during a divorce or custody battle should be discredited. Again, common sense and the literature explain why valid accusations may be raised for the first time when the offender is out of the home and the victim is faced with visits alone with the perpetrator. (Goldstein, S. L., & Tyler, R. P. [1998]. Sorting out allegations of child sexual abuse in divorce cases. *The National Child Advocate,* Summer, 4; see also Burkhart, M.-A. R. [2000]. Child abuse allegations in the midst of divorce and custody battles: Convenience, coincidence or conspiracy? *Update, 13*(10).)

Legitimate and legally sufficient cases should be aggressively pursued. Where the best efforts to investigate a case still leave little chance of success or a slim chance of obtaining a conviction, filing charges may not be in anyone's best interest. If appropriate education of the public is done and the prosecutor spends time explaining to the victim and her family why the case cannot be pursued, including making the victim aware that the decision does not mean her statement about abuse was not believed, the chances of an appropriate resolution are better. Some families will never be satisfied with a declination to prosecute, even if they logically understand why the case is legally insufficient. The prosecutor must realize that making everyone happy is not possible in many cases.

4. Deciding What Crime to Charge

Child abuse prosecutors must become thoroughly familiar with the entire criminal code so that all options can be considered in every case. Each case presents a slightly different twist to the factual and legal issues, and charging sometimes demands creativity and logic. The guiding principle should be to charge the crime that accurately indicates both the nature and the seriousness of the criminal conduct, including whatever mental state is required to obtain a conviction. In general, the most serious offense possible should be filed, without overreaching or extending the charge beyond what the credible evidence will support. Many jurisdictions require that if two statutes apply equally to conduct of the defendant and one is more specific in its elements than the other, or one involves a lesser punishment, the more specific or lesser crime must be charged. In jurisdictions where judges generally do not allow evidence of prior uncharged sexual offenses, charge all offenses that meet the charging standards and are within the statute of limitations. It is important to be able to prove the entire context of the pattern of conduct between the offender and the victim, not just a few isolated and apparently unrelated actions that may not make sense when taken out of context.

Offenses that specify the age of the victim or are specific to children are often categorized as more serious than analogous crimes in which the victim's age is not an element. If such statutes are available, consider implementing a policy that requires the charging of, and pleas to, crimes that are age- or child specific, except in unusual situations. For example, statutes may exist that define sexual contact between relatives, regardless of their ages, as one crime (incest) and sexual abuse of a child under the age of 10 regardless of the parties' relationship as another more serious crime. Charging under the sexual abuse rather than the incest statute would be more appropriate in a case involving a father's sexual abuse of his 8-year-old daughter. Charging under both statutes would be preferred. Consistent with filing and pursuing the most serious charge, however, egregious crimes like first-degree murder or first-degree rape are usually most suitable when a child has been the victim of force and violence. Often the victim's young age will serve as an aggravating factor at sentencing for these crimes. It is also good practice to add a child endangerment charge in jurisdictions where the primary offense such as assault, rape, or murder does not have a child-specific label.

In every jurisdiction, children under a certain age are legally presumed incapable of consenting to sexual contact. (See Phipps, C. A. [1997]. Children, adults, sex and the criminal law: In search of reason. *Seton Hall Law Journal, 22,* 1.) Most states still retain a version of statutory rape where the victim is under a particular age and the offender is more than a certain number of years or months older than the victim. Where the victim is above the statutory age of consent, issues relating to force and resistance necessary to establish lack of consent must be considered prior to filing charges. Some legislatures have enacted statutes that recognize that adolescent victims need not resist in the same way as an adult victim. (See, e.g., Utah Code Ann. § 76–5–406(11) [lack of consent in a sexual offense occurs where the victim is between 14 and 17 years of age and the actor is more than 3 years older than the victim and "entices or coerces the victim to submit or participate, under circumstances not amounting to the force or threat" that is required for other victims].)

Prosecutors should scrupulously avoid overcharging a child sexual abuse case hoping to gain leverage for a plea bargain. Such a practice is not only unethical, but it is dangerous and it risks losing credibility with the public, the courts, and other attorneys. A consistent pattern of overcharging may lead defense attorneys to expect that the charge is inflated to allow broad room for negotiating a plea to a lesser offense. Cases that go to trial after being overcharged may result in consistent jury verdicts on the lesser, more appropriate charges. This can give the appearance that the prosecutor's office is not being aggressive in obtaining convictions.

Undercharging cases, including charging offenses that do not contain elements of sexual conduct with children, such as simple assault or endangering the welfare of a child, causes a similar problem. If such a charge is chosen, even though the facts of the case indicate that an illegal sexual act with a child occurred, the prosecutor may be seen as not being willing to prove sexual conduct against children. Alternatively, the public may interpret the prosecutor's decision as a signal that sexual abuse of children is not important enough to justify the use of felony prosecution resources in the office. Failing to charge sexual offenses also has implications for the defendant's obligation to register as a sexual offender or to provide a DNA sample.

Child sexual abuse prosecutions may evolve as cases move through the sometimes painfully delayed criminal justice process. Victims age and often feel more comfortable making additional disclosures as time goes on. If the jurisdiction allows unfettered amendment of charges up through trial, the prosecutor can easily accommodate these common changes. On the other hand, if the statutory scheme or judicial practice puts strict limits on amending the charges, it is important to build in as much flexibility as possible by filing as many charges as are warranted once the case is ready for charging. This may require filing charges based upon alternate theories of the case or charging lesser-included offenses. The prosecutor must also be familiar with sentencing enhancements or other statutory provisions that increase the level of crime, since many of those matters require charging and adjudication before they can apply. Habitual criminal statutes, the use of weapons, and other enhancements fit within this category. If the state has a sexual predator statute that allows for the civil commitment of sexually violent predators based upon proof of a specified number of predicate offenses, the prosecutor must make sure to charge the predicate offenses whenever the evidence justifies. Keeping valid records of arrests and convictions for child sexual offenses has been difficult in the past, and prosecutors can assist by charging the appropriate offenses and refusing plea bargains that change the nature or category of the offense.

5. The Counts Used in the Charging Process

When charges are based upon the child's ability to remember and relate what has happened, the decision of which and how many counts to charge is never as easy as it is with crimes involving adult witnesses. Children are rarely sexually abused in a single episode. Much more commonly, they are abused frequently over a long period of time. Children, especially younger children, simply are not capable of separating the acts into individual memories. This is not surprising, since even adults have a difficult time compartmentalizing memories for routine matters, such as what they ate for breakfast every day for the past three weeks. Children up to about age nine or ten are not developmentally capable of fixing past events into any sort of chronological sequence, since time concepts for them are not very meaningful. (Myers, J. E. B., et al. [1996]. Psychological research on children witnesses: Practical implications for forensic interviews and courtroom testimony. *Pacific Law Journal, 28*, 3.) It is common for investigators to ask younger children how many times they were abused, but most of the time the answer given is a guess. It is also common for investigators to ask young children whether something happened a day before, a week before, a month before, or a year before the interview. Most children are simply incapable of answering such questions and often provide the interviewer with only a guess.

Fortunately, most courts in the country recognize the limitations of a child's ability to separate events into memories and to fix events in time. Courts allow some flexibility when child molestation extends over a long period of time and when the victim is young. Many courts have held that as long as the acts are proven to have occurred during the period of the statute of limitations, such proof comports with due process since time is not an element of most child sex offenses and, in addition, children are not capable of being more specific. (See Myers, J. E. B. [1997]. *Evidence in child abuse and neglect cases* (3rd ed., pp. 137–139.) In *In re K.A.W.*, 515 A.2d 1217, 1220 (N.J. 1986), the New Jersey Supreme Court observed,

> We need no battery of experts to convince us that a child of the age of five to seven years . . . cannot recall precise dates or even approximate times the way a normal adult can do. Children of that age do not think in terms of dates or time spans. Unlike adults, their lives are not controlled by the clock or the calendar.

Often the best a prosecutor can do in charging individual counts in a sexual abuse case involving a young victim is to charge the first event and the last event, assuming the child can even recognize what happened the first or last time. Other times, the best that can be done is to charge one count for each type of conduct committed against the child, such as one count of rape, one count of sodomy, one count of molestation, even though the child indicates that each of those actions occurred more than one time. Sometimes the best young children can do in identifying time is to indicate that the conduct occurred while they were in kindergarten, or during the summer, or while they lived in a certain house or apartment. In other cases, the child may have been in the defendant's company only on occasions that can be identified by adults, such as during visitation, and this allows for more specificity. If possible, charge actions that occurred "on or about" a certain date, or "between X date and Y date."

a. The number of counts. It is appropriate to allege multiple counts against a defendant in a single charging document when a defendant has committed several separate acts in the course of a single behavioral incident. Different jurisdictions define "behavioral incident" differently. Usually, multiple acts against several different children, if connected together in time or purpose and if relatively coterminous, may be filed in the same complaint. In almost every jurisdiction, multiple crimes against the same victim can be combined into one complaint.

Prosecutors are cautioned, however, about filing a large number of counts of sexual abuse with the concomitant necessity to prove the elements of each of those crimes beyond a reasonable doubt. For instance, if the victim says that the defendant raped her 3 times a week for 3 years, filing a complaint containing 468 individual counts of rape of a child may present several difficulties. If the victim does not repeat the same number of events, the trier of fact will be left to speculate how many times the crime occurred. Second, filing so many counts may necessitate a trial that lasts many months, rather than just a few weeks, which causes confusion with juries. Third, there is a point of saturation beyond which the trier of fact may become sympathetic to the defendant and beyond which the sentencing authority is not likely to enhance punishment. A good rule of thumb is to honestly and objectively assess the culpability of the defendant's conduct, the likely punishment, and the number of counts that reflect the seriousness of the crimes.

b. Separate counts for each victim. In a case with multiple victims, file separate counts naming only one victim per count. In most jurisdictions, it is unwise or not permitted to file a single count naming multiple victims. This could create obvious difficulties at trial if the evidence regarding only one or two of multiple victims named in a count convinces the jury. In some places, it may be possible to amend charges later and combine several victims in a single count (especially for acts occurring during a single incident) for purposes of the defendant's entry of a guilty plea. This would also ensure restitution for each victim and still reflect the fact that more than one child was abused.

c. Multiple acts with a single victim. While it is often difficult to differentiate individual instances of misconduct when a child has been abused over a long period, some effort should be made to represent accurately the seriousness of the defendant's conduct. Look for ways to distinguish one incident from another by establishing different behaviors, different times, or different locations. For example, if the victim can describe the first and last act of abuse, each could be the basis for a separate count. Individual counts could also be filed reflecting

- The nature and progression of acts recalled by the child, such as a count representing the beginning stage of fondling, another to represent the middle stage of oral sex, and another to represent vaginal intercourse
- The child's age when the abuse occurred. For example, file five counts, one for each year of abuse, if the victim was continuously sexually abused from age six to age ten.
- Different factors associated with separate incidents of abuse such as locations or times of day at which abuse happened; clothing worn by the defendant or victim during different incidents; things said by the child or offender at different times; holidays, sporting events, and other significant occasions such as births, deaths, hospitalizations, vacations, moving, graduations, visits; and any other detail that distinguishes one incident from another
- Injuries deemed by a medical expert to have been inflicted at different times or by different methods.

California's legislature creatively addressed the problem of charging ongoing sexual assaults. According to Section 288.5 of the California Penal Code, the crime of "continuous sexual abuse of a child" is committed if the offender lives with or has recurring access to a child under 14 and engages in sexual conduct with that child at least three times during a period of three months. Under this statute, the prosecutor need charge the defendant only with one count. The statute further reads that the jury need find that only three or more acts occurred to return a guilty verdict. It does not have to agree on which particular acts constituted those three or more acts.

New York amended its penal law in 1996 with two new "course of conduct" offenses. Under section 130.75 of the New York Penal Code, a person is guilty of a course of sexual conduct against a child in the first degree when, over a period of time not less than 3 months in duration, he or she engages in two or more acts of sexual conduct that include at least one act of sexual intercourse, deviate sexual intercourse, or aggravated sexual contact with a child less than 11 years old. Under section 130.80 of the New York Penal Code, a person is guilty of a course of sexual conduct against a child in the second degree when, over a period of time not less than 3 months in duration, he or she engages in two or more acts of sexual conduct with a child less than 11 years old. Under both New York sections, a person may not be subsequently prosecuted for any other sexual offense involving the same victim unless the other charged offense occurred outside the time period charged under this section.

6. The Name of the Victim

In many jurisdictions, there are statutes that allow prosecutors not to use the victim's name in the charging documents. (See, e.g, 18 U.S.C. § 3509[d] [1990]; NYS Civil Rights Law § 50-b.) The victim's name can be replaced with "Jane Doe" or "a female child." Even if there is no specific statute providing this protection, the prosecutor should request the court's permission to use such procedures in appropriate cases.

Table III.1   Statutes Protecting the Identity of a Child Victim

Alaska	ALASKA STAT. § 12.61.110, -140
California	CAL. PENAL CODE §§ 293 TO -.5
Connecticut	CONN. GEN. STAT. § 54–86E
Florida	FLA. STAT. ANN. § 119.07(3)(F)
	FLA. STAT. ANN. § 794.03
Georgia	GA. CODE ANN. § 16–6-23
Illinois	725 ILL. COMP. STAT. ANN. 190/1 TO 190/3
Iowa	IOWA CODE § 915.36
Louisiana	LA. REV. STAT. ANN. § 44:3(A)(4)(D)
Maine	ME. REV. STAT. TIT. 30-A, § 288
Massachusetts	MASS. GEN. LAWS. CH. 265, § 24C
Michigan	MICH. COMP. LAWS § 750.520K
Minnesota	MINN. STAT. ANN. § 609.3471
New York	N.Y. CIV. RIGHTS LAW § 50-B
North Dakota	N.D. CENT. CODE §§ 12.1–35–03
Ohio	OHIO REV. CODE § 2907.11
Pennsylvania	42 PA. CONS. STAT. ANN. § 5988
Rhode Island	R.I. GEN. LAWS § 11–37–8.5
South Carolina	S.C. CODE ANN. § 16–3-730
South Dakota	S.D. CODIFIED LAWS § 23A-6–22
Texas	TEX. CODE CRIM. PROC. ANN. §§ 57.02 TO -.03
Vermont	VT. STAT. ANN., TIT. 13, § 5431
Washington	WASH. REV. CODE ANN. § 7.69A.030(4);
	WASH. REV. CODE ANN. § 10.52.100
Wyoming	WYO. STAT. ANN. § 6–2-310
	WYO. STAT. ANN. § 14–3-106
U.S. Code	18 U.C.S.A. § 3509(D)

NOTE: This table includes all legislation passed through March 2002, as verified through Lexis Nexis.

7. *The Statutes of Limitation*

Virtually every jurisdiction limits the time within which criminal charges may be filed. Several jurisdictions have no limit within which felony child abuse charges must be commenced. Still other jurisdictions extend the statute of limitations when the crime involves sexual misconduct against a child victim. The statute of limitations generally does not begin to run until the crime is reported to law enforcement authorities or until the crime is discovered. In other cases, the statute of limitations does not begin until the child reaches the age of 18. Although state courts have upheld these special statutes of limitations for offenses against children within the proscribed statutory limits, the Nevada Supreme Court in *Houtz v. State*, 893 P.2d 355, 357 (Nev. 1995), stated that just because the defendant, "commit[s] a crime in a secret manner does not mean that the statute of limitations under the [special statute] is tolled indefinitely" and found that the statute of limitations had run for a 25-year-old who was molested in his early teens because the statute was tolled only until the victim's eighteenth birthday, as outlined in the statute. The supreme court opined that

> an example of an extreme result under such an interpretation is that, based on the testimony of a sixty-year-old person, the State could choose to initiate prosecution of an offense that occurred more than five decades ago. The interpretation of a statute should be reasonable and avoid absurd results. (*Id.* p. 358 [citations omitted])

It remains to be seen how other states will interpret those statutes based upon recovered memories of sexual abuse that occurred decades earlier. Due process issues will be raised in those cases if there are any that are successfully charged. (See Table III.2 for a list of individual state statutes of limitation.)

In most jurisdictions, issues relating to the statute of limitations are construed strictly against the prosecution. Generally, the State must prove that the crime occurred within the period of the statute of limitations, and the trier of fact must find that the crime occurred within that time frame beyond a reasonable doubt. When prosecutors are reviewing a case, it is important to identify exactly which statute of limitations applies to child sexual abuse cases and whether there are any tolling provisions that might apply. For instance, in some states, the running of the limitations period is tolled if the offender leaves the jurisdiction. It is assumed that if the defendant left the jurisdiction, charges could not be filed because the investigation could not be completed. Other jurisdictions may have a provision that recognizes the common delay in reporting child abuse matters and the effect of threats on the victim.

In *Crider v. State,* 531 N.E.2d 1151 (Ind. 1988), the statute of limitations was considered tolled because intimidation by the defendant caused the victims to delay reporting his criminal actions. In contrast, the Minnesota Court of Appeals held that the statute of limitations was not tolled where there was no evidence of psychological coercion by the defendant on a day-to-day basis that would have constituted "active coercion" of the victim. (*State v. French,* 392 N.W.2d 596 [Minn. Ct. App. 1986]). Courts differ as to whether a victim's failure to understand the criminal nature of sexual abuse tolls the statute of limitations. (See, e.g., *State v. Hensley,* 571 N.E.2d 771, 713 [Ohio 1991] ["the statute of limitations begins to run when any competent person other than the wrongdoer . . . has knowledge of both the act and its criminal nature."]; see *contra,* Conn. Gen. Stat. Ann. §54–193, Iowa Code Ann. § 802.6, Miss. Code Ann. § 99–1–5 [statutes that impose statutes of limitation for child sexual abuse and have no statutory or common law provisions for tolling the statute as of January 2002]).

A recent statutory amendment to the statutes of limitation should apply to any crime not already barred at the time the statutory extension took effect. (*State v. Hodgson,* 740 P.2d 848 [Wash. 1987], *cert. denied,* 485 U.S. 938 [1988] [finding new period of limitation applied to offenses not already time-barred when new enactment was adopted and became effective]; *People v. Gordon,* 212 Cal. Rptr. 174 [Cal. Ct. App. 1985] [noting defendant may be prosecuted within period extended by amendment to existing statute of limitation if amendment was adopted prior to expiration of original period of limitations]).

Table III.2   Statutes Extending or Removing the Statutes of Limitation for Offenses Against
Children

Alabama	ALA. CODE § 15-3-5(4) (sexual abuse)
Alaska	ALASKA STAT. § 12.10.010(a)(4), -.020 (sexual abuse)
Arkansas	ARK. CODE ANN. § 5-1-109(h) (sexual and physical abuse)
California	CAL. PENAL CODE § 803(f) (sexual abuse)
Colorado	COLO. REV. STAT. § 16-5-401 (sexual abuse)
	COLO. REV. STAT. § 18-6-401.1 (physical abuse)
Connecticut	CONN. GEN. STAT. § 54–193a (sexual abuse)
Florida	FLA. STAT. ANN. § 775.15(7) (sexual abuse)
Georgia	GA. CODE ANN. § 17-3-1(c) (sexual and physical abuse)
Hawaii	HAW. REV. STAT. ANN. § 701–108(6)(c) (sexual abuse)
Idaho	IDAHO CODE § 19-402 (sexual and physical abuse)
Illinois	720 ILL. COMP. STAT. § 5/3–6 (sexual abuse)
Indiana	IND. CODE § 35–41–4–2(e) (sexual abuse)
Iowa	IOWA CODE § 802.2 (sexual abuse)
Kansas	KAN. STAT. ANN. § 21-3106 (sexual abuse)
Louisiana	LA. CODE CRIM. PROC. ANN. art. 571.1 (sexual abuse)
	LA. CODE CRIM. PROC. ANN. art. 573 (physical abuse)
Maine	ME. REV. STAT. tit. 14, § 752-C (sexual abuse)
Massachusetts	MASS. GEN. LAWS ANN. ch. 277, § 63 (sexual and physical abuse)
Michigan	MICH. COMP. LAWS § 767.24 (sexual abuse)
Minnesota	MINN. STAT. § 628.26 (sexual abuse)
Mississippi	MISS. CODE ANN. § 99–1-5 (sexual abuse)
Missouri	MO. REV. STAT. § 556.037 (sexual abuse)
Montana	MONT. CODE ANN. § 45-1-205 (sexual abuse)
Nebraska	NEB. REV. STAT. § 29-110(2) (sexual and physical abuse)
Nevada	NEV. REV. STAT. § 171.095 (sexual abuse)
New Hampshire	N.H. REV. STAT. ANN. § 625:8 (sexual abuse)
New Jersey	N.J. REV. STAT. § 2C:1-6(b) (sexual and physical abuse)
New Mexico	N.M. STAT. ANN. § 30-1-9.1 (sexual and physical abuse)
New York	N.Y. CRIM. PROC. LAW §§ 30.10(3)(e) & (f) (sexual abuse)
North Dakota	N.D. CENT. CODE §§ 29-04-03.1, -03.2 (sexual abuse)
Oklahoma	OKLA. STAT. ANN. tit. 22, § 152(C) (sexual abuse)
Oregon	OR. REV. STAT. § 131.125 (sexual and physical abuse)
Pennsylvania	42 PA. CONS. STAT. ANN. § 5552(C)(3) (sexual abuse)
	42 PA. CONS. STAT. ANN. § 5554 (sexual and physical abuse)
Rhode Island	R.I. GEN. LAWS § 12-12-17(a) (sexual abuse)
South Dakota	S.D. CODIFIED LAWS §§ 22–22–1, -7, -19.1 (sexual abuse)
Tennessee	TENN. CODE ANN. § 40-2-101(d) (sexual abuse)
Texas	TEX. CRIM. PROC. CODE ANN. § 12.01 (sexual abuse)
Utah	UTAH CODE ANN. § 76-1–303.5 (sexual abuse)
Vermont	VT. STAT. ANN. tit. 13, § 4501(c) (sexual abuse)
Washington	WASH. REV. CODE § 9A.04.080(c) (sexual abuse)
Wisconsin	WIS. STAT. § 939.74(2) (sexual abuse)

NOTE: This compilation lists all state statutes that toll, extend, or eliminate time limitations for charging criminal offenses relating specifically to child victims. General statutes of limitation that apply for "all felonies" or "all crimes" without specific reference to the age of the victim or children as a class of victims are omitted. When a statute extends or tolls a general statute of limitation, reference must be made to this general provision to determine the applicable time limitations. Kentucky, North Carolina, South Carolina, Virginia, West Virginia, and Wyoming have no statutes of limitation for all criminal felony prosecutions. This table includes all legislation passed through March 2002, as verified through Lexis Nexis.

8. When to File Charges

Child sexual abuse prosecutions should not be commenced until the investigation is complete. The prosecutor must be satisfied that the investigation has produced sufficient admissible and credible evidence to justify a reasonable fact finder to convict the defendant. This type of crime should never be charged with the assumption that additional facts will be discovered during preparation for a preliminary hearing or trial that will make the case stronger. Premature charging decisions tend to create difficulty later. The general rule, often embodied in victim's rights legislation or rules of court, is that child sexual abuse cases should be filed and pursued as expeditiously as possible. Most prosecutors would agree that delay generally assists the defendant. Unnecessary delay between the report of the crime and commencement of the criminal process may put further tension on the family; cause the victim and/or the victim's family to decide that pursuing the charges is not worth the cost; and allow memories to fade, both those of the victim and those of other witnesses.

The prosecutor must never file child sexual abuse charges just to provide some strategic advantage to the custodial parent who is concerned that the abuser may obtain visitation or custody of the child. The prosecutor should maintain communication with the nonabusing parent and that parent's attorney, but should not make decisions based solely upon giving the custodial parent an advantage in juvenile or family court. Similarly, charging decisions should not be made simply because of media pressure. News reporters seem to develop their own timetable for how long an investigation should take, but those expectations are rarely grounded in the real world. Child sexual abuse cases are complex, and the charging decision, if it is taken as seriously as it should be, may take time to make.

9. The Charging Method

Charging methods vary by jurisdiction and depend on statutes, case law, court rules, and custom. There is no single best method to use when charging child abuse cases. There may be no choice about whether the grand jury is used to indict, whether preliminary hearings to establish probable cause are required, or whether the child victim must testify at either or both of these proceedings. In a jurisdiction where there is an option, individual circumstances should determine the choice.

It is important to carefully evaluate whether having the child testify at the preliminary hearing is in the best interests of the case. While it may be appropriate to spare the victim a difficult cross-examination and the trauma of testifying, it may also be wise to take the opportunity to preserve the victim's testimony should she later become unavailable for trial. Some jurisdictions permit videotaping of the preliminary hearing. Having the child testify at the preliminary hearing may also boost the child's confidence for trial and dispel some of the mystery of testifying. In jurisdictions that require the use of indictments, the child will testify without cross-examination before a large number of people. This can be advantageous to gauge how well the victim testifies before a jury and how the jury will accept the child's testimony. Preliminary testimony may also induce a plea, as the defense attorney will see how well the child testifies.

10. Declining to File Child Sexual Abuse Charges

Deciding not to file criminal charges in a child abuse case may be more difficult than the decision to file. Many cases involve situations in which the prosecutor believes abuse has occurred but criminal charges cannot be filed because of insufficient admissible evidence, unavailability of necessary witnesses, the expiration of the statute of limitations, and many other reasons. Whatever the reason, a decision to decline prosecution should not be made without a thorough investigation and consideration of all available information.

Let victims and their families know of the decision as soon as possible. Victims' rights legislation in an increasing number of states mandates such notification. If at all possible, the victim and the victim's family should be notified in person as well as in writing. Although it may not be what the family wants to hear, an honest, sensitive explanation may help them understand why the case cannot be prosecuted. It may also provide resolution to a traumatic situation. Prompt communication is essential to prevent a victim or family from feeling ignored or uninformed. It is important that everyone involved understand that the decision not to file charges does not mean the prosecutor has decided that abuse did not occur or that the child was lying. Children should be commended for truthful disclosures of abuse, but the prosecutor should also give an explanation to the child if the case is not going to trial.

Even when there is a decision not to file charges, the prosecutor should make suitable referrals and encourage contact with counseling resources or victim advocacy and support services. The prosecutor might also indicate other options available to the victim or family such as a civil lawsuit or an action in family court, where there are lower burdens of proof. Victim advocates can also provide this information. Care should be taken, however, not to counsel them on the feasibility of pursuing these options but simply to inform them of other options.

The prosecutor should take whatever steps are necessary to ensure the child's safety in appropriate cases, such as intrafamilial abuse cases or licensed daycare cases by following up with the juvenile court, child protective services, and licensing authorities. It may be possible to seek revocation of an offender's child care license, pursue a civil dependency case, provide services, or otherwise mandate conditions such as supervised visitation and therapy for the child or parent(s). Whoever represents the state or local social services agency in civil abuse and neglect proceedings should be able to coordinate such measures and discuss juvenile court involvement directly with the victim and family. Otherwise, the prosecutor should take the initiative and work with those responsible to elicit their cooperation.

C. Charging Physical Abuse and Homicide Cases

1. Understanding the Basics

A prosecutor must have a good working knowledge of medical science, the timing of injuries, and the violence involved in different types of abusive acts committed against children to make an appropriate charging decision in physical abuse and homicide cases. In most cases, physicians can provide a good explanation of what happened to the child and a time frame during which the injuries were inflicted, rule out natural or accidental causes of the injuries, and explain the significance of a pattern of past injuries through opinions relating to the battered child syndrome (BCS). (See Kempe, C. H., et al. [1962]. The battered-child syndrome. *Journal of the American Medical Association, 181,* 17.) Most state appellate courts have affirmed the trial court's decision to allow expert testimony on the topic of BCS.

(*State v. Moorman*, 670 A.2d 81 [N.J. Super. Ct. App. Div. [1996] [Testimony of expert's opinion, along with slides of the 3-year-old victim's injuries were admitted in support of the theory that the victim had suffered from BCS.]; see *State v. Tanner*, 675 P.2d 539 [Utah 1983] [discussing cases allowing testimony on BCS]; *State v. Mulder*, 629 P.2d 462, 463 [Wash. App. 1981] ["The diagnosis is dependent on inferences, not a matter of common knowledge, but within the area of expertise of physicians whose familiarity with numerous instances of injuries accidentally caused qualifies them to express with reasonable probability that a particular injury or group of injuries to a child is not accidental or is not consistent with the explanation offered therefore but is instead the result of physical abuse by a person of mature strength."])

The challenge in most physical abuse and homicide cases may be determining the identity of the perpetrator of the abuse, especially when several people may have had access to the child during the applicable window of time. In some cases, more than one caregiver may be inflicting injury upon the child. In others, there could be a mixture of accidental injury and inflicted trauma. In still other cases, there are natural conditions that complicate the determination of whether the child's injuries were in fact caused by abusive trauma. Conditions such as osteogenesis imperfecta (brittle bone disease), though rare in children, complicate efforts to determine whether a child was abused. Not surprisingly, a great majority of abusers who break their infants' or toddlers' bones raise osteogenesis imperfecta or coagulopathy of some nature to explain away an extended pattern of torturous abuse to a child.

Most medical journals recognize the significance of a "discrepant history" offered by a child's caregivers to explain serious or fatal injuries. "A significant discrepancy between the physical findings and the history is the cardinal sign of abuse." (Monteleone, J. A., & Brodeur, A. E. [1994]. Identifying, interpreting, and reporting injuries. *Child Maltreatment,* 6.) Equally important is the evolving story told by many abusers. As they are told by medical professionals or investigators that their story does not match the severity of the injuries, abusers suddenly remember other accidents that were a little worse than the previously offered explanation but that were still accidents. "In one series, over 95% of the initial histories supplied by the caretakers of abused children were false . . . [t]he specious history often features a fall or choking event, rather than the true cause." (Smith, W. L. [1994]. Abusive head injury. *APSAC Advisor,* 7(4), 16.) When a discrepant history is given, it may help to identify the likely perpetrator, solidify the perpetrator's awareness of the severity of the abusive conduct, and reveal that the caregiver who did not cause the trauma was aware of what happened and is assisting the perpetrator to cover it up.

Many cases are never prosecuted, and some are never even presented to a prosecutor's office, because of a perceived inability to determine who committed the abuse. Some of those cases are truly unresolvable, yet many could be filed after a little extra investigative work or an additional awareness of the common patterns of conduct among child abusers. Prosecutors who are new to this field should not hesitate to contact and consult with others who have handled more cases to become familiar with the common patterns present in virtually every case. There are ways of proving who committed abuse even when an initial assessment shows that several people could have committed the acts.

Prosecutors must be aware prior to charging a case that serious injuries to children require serious force. A baby who has been shaken and who is not expected to survive, or who will have permanent brain damage and blindness if he does live, was not subjected to minor trauma or "a little rough treatment." "There is no disagreement among professionals in the field that the violent shaking, whether or not it is accompanied by an impact, is not a casual act but rather one that would indicate to a rational observer that severe injury was being inflicted upon the child." (Smith, W. L. [1994]. Abusive head injury. *APSAC Advisor, 7*(4), 16; American Academy of Pediatrics, Committee on Child Abuse and Neglect. [1993]. Shaken baby syndrome: Inflicted cerebral trauma. *Pediatrics, 92,* 872.) Infants and toddlers do not suffer life-threatening or fatal injuries in common household falls, even falls down stairs. In fact, in study after study of free falls of children, death has not resulted until the height of the fall exceeds two to three stories. (Chadwick, D. L., et al. [1991]. Deaths from falls in children: How far is fatal? *Journal of Trauma, 31,* 1353; Barlow, B. A., et al. [1983]. Ten years of experience with falls from a height in children. *Journal of Pediatric Surgery, 18,* 509 [noting that all children who fell three or fewer floors survived].) Further, the onset of a serious or fatally injured child's symptoms would be immediate, which assists in narrowing down the list of possible perpetrators. Milder head injuries to children that do not result in brain damage or death may cause less clear findings and may result in symptoms such as irritability, lethargy, eating difficulties, and sleepiness.

People use a variety of methods to abuse a child, from burning to fracturing bones, from hitting them with objects to slamming their bodies into an object or a surface, from squeezing or grabbing to pinching or hitting with hands. Medical professionals are becoming very adept at identifying the cause of injuries and differentiating those caused by accident and those that were inflicted. The collective clinical experience of pediatricians worldwide is helping to recognize common patterns and causes of injury to children.

2. Determining What Happened to the Child

It is vital to consult with the appropriate expert medical personnel to determine exactly what happened to the child victim, what violence or force was required to cause the injuries, why the injuries are not consistent with accidental or natural causes, and when the injuries were likely inflicted. In some cases, the prosecutor may not want to rely solely on the experience of the local physician, emergency room doctor, or the child's pediatrician. It can be very helpful to consult with physicians who have significant experience treating both intentional and unintentional injuries. The injury causation is the basis for determining what crime was committed. Severely violent acts are consistent with the defendant having at least been aware of the likelihood of causing serious injury to the child. A pattern of abusive injuries over time helps to determine whom to charge and that individual's mental state.

The medical professionals also need to provide the initial information concerning when the injuries were likely inflicted. However, the ultimate determination also depends on the facts provided by those who were around the child during the time the injuries were inflicted. Though caregivers often misrepresent the facts concerning having abused the child and make up stories concerning alleged accidents the child sustained, they often tell the truth about the time when the child was "fine" and the time when the child was not "fine." It is important to recognize that there are limits to the physicians' ability to date an injury. Bruises can be identified as being of different ages as compared with each other, but experts usually are not able to date bruises with exact days or hours. Fractures are even more difficult to date radiographically and sometimes do not even show up when they are new. Usually the most the radiologist can say is that the fracture is more recent than 3 days old or older than 3 days and up to 10 days old. This dating is based solely upon the degree of healing. When the child dies from the abuse, a pathologist can sometimes be more certain as to the age of injuries based upon a microscopic examination of tissues and bones. Some mechanisms used to abuse or kill children leave no medically identifiable signs, such as manual suffocation accomplished with a blanket, pillow, or other soft object. This does not mean, however, that convictions cannot be obtained in cases of suffocation. (See *United States v. Woods,* 484 F.2d 127 [4th Cir. 1973], *cert. denied,* 415 U.S. 979 [1974]; *People v. Eveans,* 660 N.E.2d 240 [Ill. App. 1996]; *State v. Lumbrera,* 891 P.2d 1096 [Kan. 1995]; *State v. Reed,* 676 A.2d 479 [Me. 1996]; *People v. Tinning,* 536 N.Y.S. 2d 193 [N.Y. 1988]; *State v. Allen,* 839 P.2d 291 [Utah 1992].)

Once the mechanism of the injury or injuries is known, a prosecutor can develop a theory as to what the defendant did to cause the injuries. For instance, the expert may explain that a 7-month-old baby has bilateral spiral fractures of the tibia and that the only way that could occur is if one end of the bone was immobilized while violent twisting force was applied to the other end. The prosecutor's theory may be that the caregiver was stressed by having to change the baby's diaper and the baby was trying to crawl away. The caregiver grabbed the baby by one ankle and turned the baby over, putting the entire weight of the baby's body onto the ankle and twisting. This theory can also be supported by testimony from other people who witnessed the defendant's low frustration threshold.

Although jurisdictions with a "reasonable discipline" defense may differ in how much corporal punishment may be legally inflicted upon a child, most draw the line at acts that leave marks on the child or cause injury. What constitutes reasonable discipline depends on the child's age, the type of discipline inflicted, the behavior being punished and the discipline chosen in response to that behavior, the use of an object, and the degree of injury or pain inflicted upon the child. (See, e.g., Myers, J. [1997]. *Evidence in child abuse and neglect cases* (3rd ed., pp. 299–303). New York: Aspen; Vieth, V. [1994]. Corporal punishment in the United States: A call for a new approach to the prosecution of disciplinarians. *Journal of Juvenile Law, 15,* 22.)

Be aware of community standards regarding acceptable discipline and use common sense to assess whether the conduct was criminal. The following factors are useful to consider when making a charging decision:

- The placement of injury
- The instrument used to inflict the injury
- The number of blows inflicted
- Prior injuries to the child or other children
- The reasonableness of any explanation offered by the defendant
- The amount of force used
- The statements made by the defendant during the conduct
- Any inconsistent explanations by the defendant regarding what happened
- Any relevant cultural practices of the defendant

Courts generally hold that discipline is excessive if it involves hitting the child with an object such as a whip or a belt, when the child is burned or scalded, when spanking leaves extensive bruises, and when it is seen that the true intent of the perpetrator was not to correct behavior but merely to inflict pain or was motivated by anger at the victim. Check applicable jurisdictional case law for fact scenarios that courts find to be unreasonable punishment or discipline. (See, e.g., *People v. Sambo*, 554 N.E.2d 1080 [Ill. App. Ct. 1990] [finding evidence sufficient to support conviction for battery when defendants took turns hitting and kicking their 16-year-old daughter in face, back, hips, and buttocks with plastic bat and belt; girl's father dragged her down stairs; tried to pull out her teeth; threw liquor in her eyes; and told her that he was going to kill both her and her boyfriend "by knocking their heads together and taking out their intestines or stomach" if he found them together at school]; *People v. Sykes*, 504 N.E.2d 1363 [Ill. App. Ct. 1987] [finding the beating of a 2-year-old child on the upper body with a piece of rolled cardboard from a coat hanger, causing bruises and red marks, to be clearly beyond reasonable bounds of disciplinary force]; *People v. Johnson*, 479 N.E.2d 481 [Ill. App. Ct. 1985] [finding the use of an extension cord to whip victim was not reasonable discipline]; *People v. Lee*, 405 N.E.2d 860 [Ill. App. Ct. 1980] [finding beating 10-year-old child with extension cord, causing welts and bleeding, was not reasonable discipline]; *State v. Arnold*, 543 N.W.2d 600 [Iowa 1996] [finding that discipline that is corrective "rather than to satisfy passions of enraged parent" may fit the defense of reasonable discipline]; *State v. Spencer*, 486 So.2d 870 [La. Ct. App. 1986] [concluding evidence of beating and spanking of handicapped student by a teacher to be too severe to constitute reasonable discipline]; *State v. Probert*, 719 P.2d 783 [Mont. 1986] [finding hitting a child's buttocks and legs 20 times unreasonable and unnecessary to restrain or correct the child]; *State v. Dodd*, 503 A.2d 1302 [Me. 1986] [finding that taping victim's ankles and hands, covering her mouth with tape, and twice hanging her by her ankles from doorknob for at least 10 minutes was far beyond "reasonable degree of force" to discipline]; *Commonwealth v. Rochon*, 581 A.2d 239 [Pa. Super. Ct. 1990] [concluding evidence that defendant struck 17-month-old son with sneaker, then with a belt, and forcibly and repeatedly immersed him in water while saying, "swim, bitch, swim," along with proof that child had experienced other physical violence, justified conviction for aggravated assault]; *State v. Keser*, 706 P.2d 263 [Wyo. 1985] [containing a discussion of the common law defense of reasonable parental discipline]; but see *Moakley v. State*, 547 So. 2d 1246 [Fla. Dist. Ct. App. 1989] [spanking daughter on buttocks and right hip with leather portion of belt insufficient to support conviction for aggravated child abuse without evidence of great bodily harm, permanent disability, or permanent disfigurement]). The key element in most justification defenses is that the discipline must be reasonable in light of the child's alleged misbehavior.

Neglect of a child's basic needs may also constitute a crime in several jurisdictions. Infants need not only nutrition, but also stimulation in order to develop normally. Babies who are diagnosed with weight loss or failure to thrive when there is no organic explanation for this condition generally have been severely and chronically neglected. Failure to thrive can result in both neurological and physiological delay that may impair the child's condition for a lifetime. Thus, failing to recognize neglect as a crime may allow a great deal of child maltreatment to go unpunished. (See Cantwell, H. B. [1997]. The neglect of child neglect. In M. E. Helfer et al. [Eds.], *The battered child* [5th ed., p. 347]. Chicago: University of Chicago Press [noting that neglect seriously harms children, often causing lifelong impairment, and further noting that of the 1,271 child maltreatment deaths documented in America in 1994, 42% were a result of neglect or a combination of abuse and neglect].)

3. Deciding Who Committed the Crime

Once the method of injury is determined, it is often difficult to determine who inflicted the abuse to make an appropriate charging decision. A prosecutor may use the approach articulated by the United States Supreme Court in *Estelle v. McGuire*, 502 U.S. 62 (1991) to narrow the list of potential suspects. In that case, 6-month-old Tori was killed by abuse while being cared for by her mother and father. The Supreme Court affirmed the trial court's allowing battered child syndrome evidence to show that the child was not hurt by accident, but by someone's intentional actions. The Court said this about proving who committed the abuse:

> When offered to show that certain injuries are a product of child abuse, rather than accident, evidence of prior injuries is relevant even though it does not purport to prove the identity of the person who might have inflicted those injuries. Because the prosecution had charged McGuire with second degree murder, it was required to prove that Tori's death was caused by the defendant's intentional act. Proof of Tori's battered child status helped to do just that; although not linked by any direct evidence to McGuire, the evidence demonstrated that Tori's death was the result of an intentional act by *someone,* and not an accident . . .
>
> The proof of battered child syndrome itself narrowed the group of possible perpetrators to McGuire and his wife . . . Only someone regularly caring for the child has the continuing opportunity to inflict these types of injuries; an isolated contact with a vicious stranger would not result in this pattern of successive injuries stretching through several months. (502 U.S. at 68, 74 [quoting *People v. Jackson,* 19 Cal. Rptr. 919, 921 (Cal. Ct. App. 1971)])

Proof of the likely perpetrator begins with this common sense notion. It is unlikely that a child with repeated inflicted injuries of differing ages just happened to have suffered several different accidents or just happened to have been intentionally harmed by several independent persons over time.

As children who suffer serious, life-threatening, or fatal head injuries begin to suffer symptoms almost immediately after the injury was inflicted, the search for who committed the crime is often as simple as determining who was present when the child became symptomatic. Generally, abusers offer a fairly detailed explanation of the condition of the child when they "found" him in distress, but leave out the details of what they did that put the child in that condition. This "partial admission" assists in identifying the person as the likely perpetrator. This is often seen in statements that the defendant found the baby "not breathing" and shook him to wake him up or revive him. The defendant admits to shaking the baby but attempts to make it appear as though the severely violent act was just an accident or was motivated by a desire to assist the child. It is a rule of thumb among medical professionals that the person who finds the child in distress is usually the perpetrator of the abuse. Of course, that rule does not always work in the forensic world, since it is always possible that one caregiver harmed the baby and immediately turned the matter over to the other to discover the baby in distress.

One method that may be used to prove who committed the abuse is to focus on who has offered the discrepant history to explain serious or fatal injuries. Who explained that the injuries were the result of an accidental fall such as from a bed, couch, high chair, or changing table? These stories are so commonly offered that Dr. Robert Kirschner and Dr. Harry Wilson, two nationally prominent pathologists, have sarcastically called them "killer couches." (See Kirschner, R., & Wilson, H. [1994]. Fatal child abuse: The pathologist's perspective. In R. M. Reece [Ed.], *Child abuse: Medical diagnosis and management* [pp. 325, 345–46]. Baltimore, MD: Williams and Wilkins.) It is important to note that sometimes both caregivers offer the same discrepant story to cover for each other. These discrepant stories help establish knowledge of what really happened to the child, since the story is intended to account for the anticipated injuries but still allege that the injuries were accidental. When the initial story is challenged, the story evolves into something completely new before the suspects are told how serious the injuries are. (See, e.g., *People v. Noble*, 635 P.2d 203 [Colo. 1981].) A variant of discrepant history is the caregiver who alleges the injuries were self-inflicted (the accident-prone toddler) or caused by young siblings of the victim (the murderous 2-year-old). Once again, these unlikely stories are so common among abusers that who tells them becomes one factor to consider in deciding who abused the victim.

Another method that might be used to identify the abuser is to determine who among the several potential suspects has a history of inflicting trauma upon either the same victim or upon other children. Some courts also allow evidence of abuse toward adults, especially if it fits the category of domestic violence. Studies also have established a connection between the abuse of pets and animals and child abuse. An appropriately qualified expert can educate the jury about that connection. (See Lockwood, R., & Ascione, F. R. [1998]. *Cruelty to animals and interpersonal violence: Readings in research and application.* West Lafayette, IN: Purdue University Press.)

A related consideration is who among the possible perpetrators was once a victim of child abuse. Studies indicate an approximate 30% transmission of abusive behavior from one generation to the next. Thus, a caregiver's statement, "I would never do that to my child, because that's what my stepfather did to me," may be a partial admission that the perpetrator resorted to a learned behavior when dealing with her own child. (See Steele, B. F. [1997]. Further reflections on the therapy of those who maltreat children. In M. E. Helfer et al. [Eds.], *The battered child* [5th ed., p. 566] Chicago: Chicago University Press.)

The recently recognized forensic "rule of three" may come into effect if a family or caregiver has had more than one infant or toddler die without an apparent abusive cause. Contrary to the historic and now debunked theory that SIDS runs in families, most experts now feel that the second medically unexplained death in a family is suspicious and the third should be certified as a homicide. (See Kirschner, R. H. [1997]. The pathology of child abuse. In M. E. Helfer et al. [Eds.], *The battered child* [5th Ed., pp. 248, 279]. Chicago: Chicago University Press [noting "if a previous unexplained infant death, including SIDS, has occurred in a family and no further evidence of metabolic disorder is forthcoming, the unexplained death of a second infant should be classified as undetermined . . . Should a third infant death without an obvious natural disease process occur in the same family, the cause of death should be identified as asphyxiation, and the manner of death classified as homicide."])

If one caregiver has shown age-inappropriate expectations of the child or other children, that may also help identify the perpetrator of the abuse. When a person is suddenly thrust into the unfamiliar and possibly unwanted role of child care provider and when that person expects things of the child that are unreasonable for the child's age, stress is often the trigger for the abusive conduct. Thus, a person who expects that a child will be potty trained by age 13 months, or the person who spanks a 6-month-old in the name of discipline, may well be the one who inflicted serious injuries upon the child.

A very common feature in physical abuse cases is a delay in seeking medical care for a seriously or fatally injured child. (See *People v. Northrop*, 182 Cal. Rptr. 197, 200 [Cal. Ct. App. 1983] [involving a live-in boyfriend perpetrator who asked the mother to "avoid doctors for fear that they would be charged with child abuse."]) Commonly, one of the caregivers tries to convince the other that the child is not that badly hurt until the symptoms become undeniably serious. (See *State v. Gardiner*, 898 P.2d 615 [Idaho 1995] [involving a defendant who encouraged the mother to delay calling 911 although child was "unresponsive."]) Caregivers who are alone when the abuse happens often do not call for medical assistance right away but watch as symptoms worsen until they have no choice and have a story concocted. Sometimes the abuser will call someone else rather than dial 911. The first EMTs on the scene often notice that the child is worse than reported during the 911 call or that the child has been in distress longer than reported by the abuser. When more than one caregiver is participating in the abuse of the victim, it is common to see either a failure to seek medical attention or a pattern of taking the child to different hospitals to avoid any one place maintaining documentation of a pattern of suspicious injuries or to prevent the medical personnel from reporting their suspicions of abuse.

4. The Failure to Protect a Child From Abuse by Another Person

In both child physical abuse and child homicide cases, prosecutors may consider filing assault or murder charges against the caregiver who was aware of the abusive conduct by another but took no steps to protect the child. Another approach involves charging both caregivers under the traditional theories of aiding and abetting or accomplice liability. Under this theory, the one who actually administered the blows, as well as the other person who was aware of the abusive conduct and covered for the other caregiver, are both charged. As the West Virginia Supreme Court noted, "the rights of children to be free from abuse require that a parent's first loyalty be to the protection of his or her children." (In re *Brianna Elizabeth M.*, 452 S.E.2d 454, 458 [1994].)

Some states have enacted specific child abuse statutes that create culpability if an individual intentionally or knowingly allows someone else to harm a child. Appellate courts also accept this theory. (See *Boone v. State*, 668 S.W.2d 17 [Ark. 1984] [affirming conviction of mother for second-degree murder when she failed to stop the beatings of her 4-year-old son by her live-in boyfriend]; *Lane v. Commonwealth*, 956 S.W.2d 874 [Ky. 1997] [concluding that a mother has a legal duty to protect her child from injury]; *LaBastida v. State*, 931 P.2d 1334 [Nev. 1996] [affirming second-degree murder conviction of mother who failed to protect 7-week-old baby]; *State v. Williquette*, 385 N.W.2d 145 [Wis. 1986] [finding a common law duty to protect children from abuse by other parent]; but see *People v. Wong*, 619 N.E.2d 377 [N.Y. Ct. App. 1993] [husband and wife were both home when 3-month-old was violently shaken, and both were charged with homicide on the theory that one committed the act and the other failed to obtain medical care; court reversed both convictions for failure to prove who committed

Table III.3	Statutes Creating Culpability for Failure to Protect a Child From Abuse
Arizona	ARIZ. REV. STAT. §§ 13–3619, -3623
California	CAL. PENAL CODE § 273a
Colorado	COLO. REV. STAT. § 18–6-401
District of Columbia	D.C. CODE § 22–1102
Florida	FLA. STAT. ANN. § 827.03
Illinois	720 ILL. COMP. STAT. ANN. § 150/5.1
Indiana	IND. CODE ANN. § 35–46–1-4
Kansas	KAN. STAT. ANN. § 21–3608
Maine	ME. REV. STAT. tit. 17-A, § 554
Massachusetts	MASS. GEN. LAWS. ch. 265, § 13J
Michigan	MICH. COMP. LAWS §§ 750.135, -.136b
Minnesota	MINN. STAT. § 609.378
Mississippi	MISS. CODE ANN. § 97–5-40
Missouri	MO. REV. STAT. § 568.045
Nevada	NEV. REV. STAT. § 200.508(2)
New Hampshire	N.H. REV. STAT. ANN. § 639:3
New York	N.Y. PENAL LAW § 260.10
Ohio	OHIO REV. CODE ANN. § 2919.22
Oregon	OR. REV. STAT. § 163.205
Pennsylvania	18 PA. CONS. STAT. ANN. § 4304
Texas	TEX. PENAL CODE ANN. §§ 22.04 to -.041
Utah	UTAH CODE ANN . § 76–5-109
Virginia	VA. CODE ANN. § 63.1–248.2
Washington	WASH. REV. CODE ANN. § 9A.16.100
	WASH. REV. CODE ANN. §§ 9A.42.030 to -.035
Federal	18 U.S.C. § 3509(d)

NOTE: These statutes include both misdemeanor and a felony liability for failure to protect a child from abuse. This table includes all legislation passed through March 2002, as verified through Lexis Nexis.

the violent act.]) Note that failure to protect a child from *sexual abuse* may also give rise to criminal charges. (See, e.g., *People v. Stanciel*, 606 N.E.2d 1201 [Ill. 1992]; *Commonwealth v. Cardwell*, 515 A.2d 311 [Pa. Super. Ct. 1986] [concluding that the mother knowingly endangered the welfare of her child by violating a duty of care, protection, and support when she was fully aware that her husband had sexually abused her daughter and impregnated her daughter twice but took only feeble and meager actions such as writing her husband letters, moving some of her daughter's clothing to a different residence, and registering her daughter in a different school, which could not reasonably be expected to protect the child's welfare].) A duty to protect usually applies to a child's parent or someone who has assumed parental obligations. (See *Leet v. State*, 595 So.2d 959, 963 [Fla. Ct. App. 1991] [concluding, "the jury could decide that a reasonable person, living with this child and the mother, would not have accepted three suspicious explanations for physical injuries to the child in the span of a few days."]; *People v. Salley*, 544 N.Y.S.2d 680 [N.Y. App. Div. 1989].)

A decision to charge on this basis will depend upon the extent and nature of the abuse, the willingness of the caregiver to admit wrongdoing and testify for the prosecution against the abuser, any attempts the caregiver made to protect the child, and the reasons for the caregiver's failure to act. Charging the nonabusive caregiver is definitely a difficult decision and one that must be made carefully after considering all the particular facts of each case. Experts on the effects of battering may express an opinion that a battered spouse was not capable of protecting children from abuse. Such a defense should not be successful if the battered partner actively participates in the abuse, covers up for the abuser by telling lies, or does other clearly volitional actions concerning the abuse. (National Institute of Justice. [1996]. *Battering and its effects,* report of the National Institute of Justice; Enos, V. P. [1996]. Prosecuting battered mothers: State laws' failure to protect battered women and abused children. *Harvard Women's Law Journal, 19,* 229; Tanck, N. A. [1987]. Commendable or condemnable? Criminal liability for parents who fail to protect their children from abuse. *Wisconsin Law Review, 1987,* 659.)

It is important to find out if the nonabusive caregiver ever saw the victim being assaulted by the abuser. Investigators can interview neighbors and family members to determine this. Determine whether the nature, extent, age, and location of the victim's injuries were such that the caregiver should reasonably have been aware of them. Failure to protect and remove the victim from the abusive environment may be sufficient evidence of *mens rea* to convict of murder. (See, e.g., *Boone v. State,* 668 S.W.2d 17 [Ark. 1984] [concluding that evidence that defendant-mother stood by and repeatedly exposed her 4-year-old son to eventually fatal beatings by her boyfriend was sufficient to sustain second-degree murder conviction]; *State v. Morrison,* 437 N.W.2d 422 [Minn. Ct. App.], *cert. denied,* 493 U.S. 858 [1989].) If murder does not apply in a particular jurisdiction, the prosecutor should consider other charges such as manslaughter, endangerment, or neglect. (But see *People v. Wong,* 619 N.E.2d 377 [N.Y. 1993] [concluding that before a "passive defendant" can be held criminally liable for failing to seek emergency medical aid for a seriously injured child, it must be shown that the passive defendant was personally aware that the shaking occurred and that such abusive conduct created a risk that the infant would die without prompt medical treatment"].)

Consider calling the less culpable caregiver to testify in the grand jury proceeding or at the preliminary hearing. If the caregiver's testimony is untruthful, it may be appropriate to charge the caregiver with perjury.

D. Charging Considerations: Physical Abuse and Homicide Cases

As with sexual abuse cases, the most serious potential charge should be chosen, although the prosecutor should feel confident of the ability to prove all the elements of the crime beyond a reasonable doubt. The nature of the conduct is significant. Was this a sudden loss of control resulting in a single blow to the child or was this the culmination of a pattern of abuse? Did the perpetrator immediately admit to the abuse and was the perpetrator remorseful from the very beginning? Even in the latter circumstance, the infliction of serious or fatal injuries upon a child is not completely excusable and still deserves punishment.

1. Intentional Homicide

When a child is murdered, it is often difficult to prove the perpetrator intended to kill the child. The prosecutor's challenge is to make the trier of fact understand that the life of a child is just as important as that of an adult, and conduct that is directed against a helpless child victim is, if anything, *more culpable* than the same assaultive conduct directed against an adult. A charge of intentional homicide may also raise defenses such as extreme emotional disturbance and intoxication, not otherwise available to a defendant, which opens the door to psychiatric or psychological testimony in an attempt to negate the element of intent.

Intent can be inferred from the act itself as well as surrounding circumstances. For example, forcibly immersing a struggling, screaming infant in a tub filled with scalding water long enough to cause second-degree burns over one third of the baby's body demonstrates "glaring" intent to cause serious injury and supports an intentional manslaughter charge (*People v. Hayes*, 577 N.E.2d 58 [N.Y. 1991]).

Some courts conclude that a pattern of torture leading up to the child's death is evidence of premeditation and intent to kill. (See *Hern v. State*, 635 P.2d 278 [Nev. 1981] [concluding that evidence of the severity of the beating allowed an inference of willfulness, premeditation, and deliberation where defendant beat to death the 3-year-old son of his girlfriend]; but see *Midgett v. State*, 729 S.W.2d 410, 413 [Ark. 1987] [concluding that the evidence that the defendant had beaten his 8-year-old son over a long period of time, finally causing the son's death, was not evidence of a preconceived intent to kill because "the jury could well infer that the perpetrator comes not to expect the death of the child, but rather that the child will live so that the abuse may be administered again and again"].) Most abuse is committed either in the name of discipline or because the perpetrator cannot handle the child, and ultimately removing the child from existence is the conscious choice of the abuser. Many courts simply refuse to find premeditation despite a long pattern of abusive and torturous injuries inflicted upon a child. (See, e.g., *State v. Brown*, 836 S.W.2d 530 [Tenn. 1992] [reducing first-degree murder conviction to second-degree murder and finding evidence insufficient to show premeditation and intent to kill where defendant inflicted massive head injuries, multiple internal injuries, broken bones, bruises to the genitals and extremities, and several other injuries upon a 4-year-old child].)

Interview family and friends of the caregivers. Evidence that the caregivers argued about the child, blamed the child for interfering with their relationship, or sought ways to have the child removed from the household may support a charge of intentional homicide. This evidence is especially helpful if death occurs in proximity to such discussions or fights. Also check to see if there is evidence of other previous charged or uncharged acts of abuse with the same or different victims.

There also may be facts to support an intentional homicide charge, for instance, when death results from the failure to feed a child. (See, e.g., *Zessman v. State*, 573 P.2d 1174 [Nev. 1978]; *Harrington v. State*, 547 S.W.2d 616 [Tex. Crim. App. 1977].) Similarly, the failure to obtain medical attention for a child, an act of omission, can form the basis for an intentional homicide charge as occurred in the highly publicized case of Lisa Steinberg (*People v. Steinberg*, 584 N.Y.S.2d 770 [N.Y. 1992]). The defendant's awareness that a particular result will occur from a course of conduct is only one factor for the jury to consider and not a prerequisite of intent. The court in *Steinberg* noted that parents cannot delegate their affirmative statutory duty to provide their children with adequate medical care.

Be alert for information regarding substance abuse by the defendant. Check applicable case law to determine when voluntary intoxication can be used to negate intentional, premeditated, or knowing conduct.

2. Knowing Murder

If the fatal injuries to the child cannot be said to evidence an intent to kill the child, it may be an option to establish that the nature of the injuries alone show that the perpetrator must have known to a reasonable certainty that death or serious injury would result. In the case of *State v. Broseman*, 947 S.W.2d 520, 524 (Mo. Ct. App. 1997), the Missouri Court of Appeals recognized, "The serious nature of Carlos' brain injury is, in and of itself, a basis for inferring that Broseman knew that his actions would be practically certain to result in Carlos' death." If the trier of fact accepts the medical opinion that the only way to cause such fatal injuries to a child's brain is to apply extremely violent forces, such a charge is appropriate when a child is killed by severely violent abuse. Suffocation cases, when there is sufficient proof to charge them, also fall within this concept. It takes from 3 to 5 minutes to deprive a child of oxygen and cause death, certainly enough time to realize the danger of the action and to stop. Although suffocation generally leaves no medically identifiable clues, cases have been successfully prosecuted. (See, e.g. *People v. Eveans*, 660 N.E.2d 240 [Ill. App. Ct. 1996]; *State v. Allen*, 839 P.2d 291 [Utah 1992 [finding sufficient evidence to corroborate the confession of defendant that he suffocated 3-year-old victim, though there was no conclusive medical evidence of suffocation]; *People v. Tinning*, 536 N.Y.S.2d 193 [N.Y. App. Div. 1988]; *People v. Biggs*, 509 N.W.2d 803 [Mich. Ct. App. 1993] [involving a defendant who admitted to smothering the child with a pillow].)

3. Depraved Indifference to Human Life

Some statutory schemes allow charging a child abuser with an act that evidenced depraved indifference to the value of human life, even if the conduct cannot be said to fit the elements of intentional or knowing murder. Under most schemes, the difference between depraved indifference murder and the recklessness involved with manslaughter is simply the degree of risk of death associated with the defendant's conduct. An example of depraved indifference murder might be a situation in which the perpetrator is beating his wife, who is holding their child, and in the course of the beating, the offender also delivers severe blows to the child, killing the child. The defense may be lack of intent to harm the child, but such actions clearly establish lack of concern about a serious risk of severe harm or death to the child. In some jurisdictions, extreme indifference is part of the murder statute; in others it is part of the definition of manslaughter.

In Utah and New York, depraved indifference supports a finding of murder where the actor was aware of a grave risk of death to the victim. (See *People v. Pope*, 660 N.Y.S.2d 466 [N.Y. App. Div. 1997] [affirming conviction where 2-year-old child suffered from BCS and there was additional evidence that the child was beaten with boards and an antenna wire, punched, and stomped upon]; *People v. Basir*, 578 N.Y.S.2d 603 [N.Y. App. Div. 1992] [upholding conviction where defendant beat the child repeatedly before strangling her]; *State v. Watts*, 675 P.2d 566 [Utah 1983] [upholding murder conviction were 18-month-old infant was struck in head and abdomen with hand-held shower massager]; *State v. Blubaugh*, 904 P.2d 688, 696 [Utah Ct. App. 1995] [concluding evidence that defendant hit 14-month-old victim repeatedly and folded her body in half to make her stop crying supported a jury finding of depraved indifference murder, showing "unmitigated wickedness, extreme inhumanity or . . . a high degree of wantonness."]; *State v. DeMille*, 756 P.2d 81 [Utah 1988] [finding evidence sufficient to support murder conviction where 3-year-old boy was killed by a severe blow to the head equivalent to fall from three-story height].)

It is interesting to note that the New York State Court of Appeals has held that the only culpable mental state required for depraved indifference murder is recklessness (*People v. Roe*, 544 N.Y.S.2d 297 [N.Y. 1989]; *People v. Gomez*, 478 N.E.2d 759 [N.Y. 1985]; *People v. Register*, 457 N.E.2d 704 [N.Y. 1983]). The phrase "under circumstances evincing a depraved indifference to human life" is not a *mens rea* element focusing on the subjective intent of the defendant, but rather involves "an objective assessment of the risk presented by the defendant's reckless conduct" (*Gomez*, 489 N.Y.S.2d at 158).

4. *Felony Murder Statutes*

Even where it is difficult to prove intentional, knowing, or depraved indifference murder, felony-murder may be a viable option. The classic concept of felony-murder is that a defendant is held responsible for a death that results during the commission of a felony. Many jurisdictions specifically designate felony child abuse or felony assault or battery as a predicate felony for application of a felony-murder statute. Some such definitions fall within the first-degree murder category, some within the general second-degree murder category. Even if the jurisdiction does not specify by statute a felony-murder theory, the common-law concept dates back to English law and should be applied in an appropriate case. Under a felony-murder theory, it is unnecessary to establish that the defendant intended the victim's death, only that in the course of committing a dangerous or violent felony, the victim's death resulted. The idea is that intent to commit the underlying felony is substituted for the normal requirement of showing an intent to kill, and the culpability is considered equal in both scenarios. A good discussion of the felony-murder doctrine applied to a child abuse homicide is found in *People v. Northrop* (182 Cal. Rptr. 197, 200 [Cal. Ct. App. 1983]):

> The felony murder rule allows the implication of malice as an element of murder from the committing of an inherently dangerous felony . . . but justification for the rule is found in the need to discourage the commission of felonies inherently dangerous to human life by holding for murder those who kill, either intentionally or unintentionally, during the course of such felonies.

In *Bethea v. State* (304 S.E.2d 713 [Ga. 1983]), a felony-murder conviction was upheld when the defendant killed a 2-year-old by inflicting blows to the stomach. The court held that the underlying felony of cruelty to children applied (*Id.* at 714). (See *Leet v. State*, 595 So.2d 959 [Fla. Ct. App. 1991] [involving a third-degree felony-murder conviction under a Florida statute making it a felony to permit child abuse by culpable negligence, for a live-in boyfriend's failure to stop or report the abuse that ultimately resulted in the death of a 1-year-old child at the hands of the child's own mother].)

The general felony-murder statutory requirements are that the underlying felony be a violent or dangerous felony and that it be sufficiently distinct from the homicide that it constitutes a separate criminal offense. Even in those jurisdictions that generally hold that the underlying felony may merge into the homicide charge, if there is evidence of infliction of prior injuries to the child other than the final, death-causing injury, it is appropriate to charge, convict, and sentence as to all the injuries. Other jurisdictions do not apply the concept of merger in felony-murder cases or in felony-murder cases involving child abuse as the underlying dangerous felony. (See, e.g. *State v. Rhode*, 503 N.W.2d 27 [Iowa Ct. App. 1993] *cert. denied*, 117 S.Ct. 232; *Contra State v. Lucas*, 759 P.2d 90 [Kan. 1988] [concluding that the crime of felony child abuse was not sufficiently distinct from the acts resulting in death to avoid merger].) After the Kansas legislature passed an act clarifying its intent to allow felony-murder prosecutions with child abuse as the underlying crime, the Kansas Supreme Court held that separate punishments for the same conduct is still inappropriate under the double jeopardy concept (*State v. Smallwood*, 955 P.2d 1209 [Kan. 1998]). In *Smallwood,* the 3.5-month-old victim died from brain damage that resulted from a violent shaking, but there was evidence introduced of another series of head injuries committed 2 weeks earlier. The Kansas Supreme Court decided that since a single incident of shaking was both the basis for the underlying felony of child abuse and the cause of death, the defendant could not be punished for both child abuse and felony-murder (*Id.* at 1225–26).

A new theory of felony-murder may be supported when there is evidence of a series of nonfatal injuries inflicted upon a child that reduced the child's immunity levels sufficiently that the child became more susceptible to infection or illness that is the ultimate cause of the child's death. (See Wilson, H. L., & Kirschner, R. H. [1994]. Fatal child abuse: The pathologist's perspective. In R. M. Reece [Ed.], *Child abuse: Medical diagnosis and management* [pp. 325, 345–346]. Baltimore, MD: Williams and Wilkins.) In such cases, it is possible to have an expert pathologist express an opinion that although the technical cause of death is pneumonia, the child abuse preceding the child's death was in fact the cause of the pneumonia and thus also the cause of death. (See *People v. Northrop*, 182 Cal. Rptr. 197, 201–02 [Cal. Ct. App. 1982] [noting, "Felony child abuse can be, and often is, committed without infliction of fatal injuries, so that application of the felony-murder doctrine serves its deterrent function by holding those who commit felony child abuse strictly responsible for deaths that occur either intentionally or accidentally from the commission of the underlying felony."]; *State vs. Widdison*, 28 P.3d 1278, 1280 Utah 2001] [affirming a conviction where a baby died as a result of pneumonia, but experts testified she would not have contracted pneumonia without the suppression of her immune system caused by 2 months of severe torture].)

5. Homicide by Abuse Statutes

One barrier to obtaining the severe penalties that are imposed with first-degree capital murder charges in many states is the requirement that prosecutors prove a defendant intended to kill a child victim. The Arkansas Supreme Court reversed a first-degree murder conviction of a parent who had brutally beaten his 8-year-old child, Ronnie, for this reason (*Midgett v. State*, 729 S.W.2d 410 [Ark. 1987]). At his death, Ronnie weighed only 38 pounds and had multiple bruises and abrasions. The cause of death was an internal hemorrhage caused by blunt force trauma. Ronnie's 10-year-old sister testified that Ronnie's father would "bundle up his fist and hit Ronnie Jr. in the stomach and in the back" (*Id.* at 411). One time, the

Table III.4   Felony Murder Statutes

Alaska	ALASKA STAT. § 11.41.100
Arizona	ARIZ. REV. STAT. § 13–1105
California	CAL. PENAL CODE § 190.2 (a)(17)(E)
Colorado	COLO. REV. STAT. § 18–3-102(1)(b)
Delaware	DEL. CODE ANN. tit. 11, § 633
Florida	FLA. STAT. ANN. § 782.04
Idaho	IDAHO CODE § 18–4003(d)
Illinois	720 ILL. COMP. STAT. ANN. 5/9–1
Indiana	IND. CODE § 35–42–1-1(2)
Kansas	KAN. STAT. ANN. §§ 21–3401 to–3436(a)(7)
Louisiana	LA. REV. CODE § 14:30.1(A)(2)(b)
Michigan	MICH. COMP. LAWS § 750.316(6)
Minnesota	MINN. STAT. § 609.185(5)
Mississippi	MISS. CODE ANN. §§ 97–3-19, -27
New Jersey	N.J. REV. STAT. § 2C:11–3(b)(3)(a)
North Dakota	N.D. CENT. CODE § 12.1–1-16–01(1)(c)
Ohio	OHIO REV. CODE § 2903.01(c)
Oregon	OR. REV. STAT. § 163.115(1)(b)
Rhode Island	R.I. GEN. LAWS § 11–23–1
Tennessee	TENN. CODE ANN. § 39–13–202
Utah	UTAH CODE ANN. §§ 76–5-202, -203(2)(d)
Wyoming	WYO. STAT. § 6–2-101(a)

NOTE: References have been made to the felony murder statutes in jurisdictions that specifically designate felony child abuse as a predicate felony for application of a felony-murder statute. This table includes all legislation passed through March 2002, as verified through Lexis Nexis.

defendant choked Ronnie. The court reduced the father's first-degree murder conviction to second degree after finding the prosecutor failed to prove the father intended to kill Ronnie. The court concluded,

> In a case of child abuse of long duration the jury could well infer that the perpetrator comes not to expect the death of the child, but rather that the child will live so that the abuse may be administered again and again. (*Id.* at 413)

Ironically, if Ronnie's father had shot him with a gun, the court could have inferred an intent to kill, since people generally do not shoot a gun unless they intend to kill the target. Since the state could not prove Ronnie's father intended to kill him, the court reduced the sentence from 40 years to life to 20 years, the maximum imprisonment for second-degree murder (*Id.* at 415).

Recognizing the difficulties in proving intent to kill, premeditation, or willfulness in a child abuse-related homicide, many jurisdictions have enacted special child abuse homicide statutes. Generally, these statutes dispense with the necessity of proving intent to kill or an awareness of the risk of death. Instead, the mental state required for the crime of child abuse is substituted for the intent requirement, or the circumstances must evidence a depraved indifference to human life. If death results during the commission of the child abuse, the homicide statute is triggered. The theory and justification for such statutes is that a person who engages in a dangerous act such as child abuse against a helpless victim is held responsible if death is likely from the pattern of conduct. The historical reduction of murder to some lesser offense in cases involving child victims is another reason that is often articulated for the enactment of such special statutes. Generally, such statutes result in increased punishment for those who kill children during acts of abuse as compared to statutes charging just the acts of abuse as separate crimes.

While most homicide-by-abuse statutes have been upheld by appellate courts, Tennessee's Supreme Court struck down their statute because the Court decided it allowed acts of misdemeanor child abuse that result in death to be elevated to first-degree murder. (See *State v. Hale,* 840 S.W.2d 307 [Tenn. 1992] [Tennessee Supreme Court reversed defendant's first-degree murder conviction and death sentence for beating his live-in girlfriend's son to death upon finding that the statute was unconstitutional by permitting the jury to decide the defendant's guilt or innocence based on his prior uncharged misdemeanors].) Tennessee's legislature amended the statute following that decision to allow a first-degree murder conviction where death of a child results from a protracted pattern of abuse or the infliction of multiple acts of bodily injury. The Supreme Court of Oklahoma upheld that state's homicide-by-abuse statute in *Drew v. State,* 771 P.2d 224 (Okla. Crim. App. 1989). Under Oklahoma's law, the normal requirement of intent to kill is satisfied by showing that the defendant committed child abuse in a willful or malicious manner and the child's death resulted. (See Okla. Stat. tit. 21, § 701.7 [1989].)

6. Murder by Torture

Some states have enacted "murder by torture" statutes, which are classified as a first-degree murder charge (see Table III.5). Rather than requiring a specific intent to kill, a showing that the defendant had a willful, deliberate, and premeditated intent to inflict extreme and prolonged pain is sufficient to convict. (See, e.g., *People v. Mincey,* 827 P.2d 388 [Cal.], *cert. denied,* 113 S. Ct. 637 [1992] [concluding that evidence was sufficient to support conviction for murder by torture when defendant's son died of massive blunt force injuries; shock from repetitive injuries and tearing of tissues led to chemical imbalances that resulted in a cessation of the intestinal tract functioning and swelling of brain; victim's body had hundreds of injuries, virtually all of which could have been inflicted within 24 to 48 hours of death; victim experienced prolonged pain before death; amount of time between onset of injuries and loss of sensation or ability to feel pain as result of physiological effects of injuries was more than few minutes, perhaps an hour or more; metabolic changes caused by injuries and onset of death would have taken hours to develop; and victim's loss of pain sensation would have occurred 15, 30, or possibly 60 minutes before death]; *People v. Mills,* 2 Cal. Rptr. 2d 614 [Cal. Ct. App. 1991] [finding evidence sufficient to sustain conviction of first-degree murder by torture where defendant regularly used obscenities when speaking to his 25-month-old stepdaughter, forced her to sit in erect fashion for hours with hands held on top of her head and fingers locked together, and, if she did not hold position, would curse her, slap her head, or strike her with either spoon or plastic baseball bat; defendant would strike her on the head or face when she refused to eat; defendant had been investigated by CPS several times; in last 3 weeks of the victim's life, she walked as though drunk, and defendant would poke her as she walked, and if she walked too slowly, he would kick her]; *State v. Lee*, 501 S.E.2d 334, 344 [N.C. 1998] [affirming murder-by-torture conviction and concluding that "the presence or absence of premeditation, deliberation and specific intent to kill is irrelevant" where live-in boyfriend inflicted week-long abuse upon the 2-year-old victim, who died of a massive head injury]; *State v. Crawford*, 406 S.E.2d 579 [N.C. 1991] [concluding defendant's past pattern of punishing his 6-year-old son and expert testimony that boy's stomach was painfully distended owing to forced drinking of large quantities of water, fluid that filled child's lungs would have created sensation similar to suffocation, and swelling of brain created tremendous headache followed by blindness sufficient evidence of torture]; *People v. Porterfield*, 420 N.W.2d 853 [Mich. Ct. App. 1988] [finding defendant's single act of fracturing child's skull sufficient to sustain conviction for child torture regardless of defendant's motive]; *State v. Lopez*, 769 P.2d 1276 [Nev. 1989] [finding evidence supported conviction of murder by torture and implementation of the death penalty where the victim died from peritonitis from a perforated ulcer related to the stress of the torture when defendant beat the 4-year-old victim with a belt twice a day, hung her by her hair for an entire night, put her in the bathtub filled with either cold or extremely hot water, and forced her to eat her own feces]; see generally Williams, J. C. [2001]. What constitutes murder by torture. [Annotation] *A.L.R., 83*, 3d 1222.)

In *People v. Walkey* (223 Cal. Rptr. 132 [Cal. Ct. App. 1986]), however, the appellate court held that there was insufficient evidence of torture. In that case, the 2-year-old victim was severely beaten and covered with new and old bruises. An autopsy revealed 17 different bruises, abrasions, and lacerations as well as facial injuries caused by a blunt object applied with relatively severe force. The victim also had upper body abrasions and bruises, including two bite marks. His abdomen was tense and distended owing to a large hemorrhage from a severe blow that crushed and tore open the intestines. The victim had experienced extreme pain and additional injuries inflicted weeks before he died. The appellate court reasoned that one could not infer torture, as the beatings were a misguided, irrational, and totally unjustifiable attempt at discipline, but were not, in a criminal sense, willful, deliberate, or premeditated (*Id.* at 136).

Acts of omission such as the failure to protect a child can support a finding of torture. (See *Nicholson v. State*, 579 So. 2d 816 [Fla. Dist. Ct. App. 1991], *aff'd*, 600 So. 2d 1101 [Fla.], *cert. denied*, 506 U.S. 1008 [1992] [finding defendant had the requisite intent to act as principal in willful torture or malicious punishment of child who died of starvation because defendant exercised complete control over child's diet, directed mother's punishment of child, and prohibited child from eating when offered food by third persons].) At least one state has held that child torture is not a specific-intent crime, and thus voluntary intoxication is not a defense. (See *People v. Kelley*, 446 N.W.2d 821 [Mich. 1989].)

7. Manslaughter

In many jurisdictions, manslaughter is divided into two types, voluntary and involuntary manslaughter. Since voluntary manslaughter is usually defined to include killing committed in the heat of passion or as a result of provocation, voluntary manslaughter should rarely be used in child homicide situations. Most courts have recognized that a child's behavior can never provoke a reasonable person to kill the child. (See *Isaac v. State*, 440 S.E.2d 175 [Ga. 1994]; *Patterson v. State*, 532

Table III.5	Murder by Torture Statutes
Alabama	Ala. Code § 12–15–65(m)(1)
Alaska	Alaska Stat. § 12.55.125
Arkansas	Ark. Code Ann. § 5-4-604(8)(B)
California	Cal. Penal Code § 189, 190.2
Idaho	Idaho Code § 18–4003(a)
Illinois	720 Ill. Comp. Stat. Ann. 5/9–1
Kansas	Kan. Stat Ann. § 21–4636
Nevada	Nev. Rev. Stat. § 200.033
New Jersey	N.J. Rev. Stat. § 2C:11–3
New York	N.Y. Penal Law § 125.27(1)(a)(x)
North Carolina	N.C. Gen. Stat. § 14–17
Oregon	Or. Rev. Stat. §§ 163.095(1)(e), -.115
Pennsylvania	42 Pa. Cons. Stat. Ann. § 9711
South Dakota	S.D. Codified Laws § 23A-27A-1
Utah	Utah Code Ann. § 76-5-202

NOTE: These do not include felony-murder statutes or statutes that use torture as an aggravating factor to murder. This table includes all legislation passed through March 2002, as verified through Lexis Nexis.

N.E.2d 604 [Ind. 1988] [concluding that wetting the bed was not provocation within meaning of manslaughter statute]; *State v. Broseman*, 947 S.W.2d 520, 527 [Mo. Ct. App. 1997] [noting, "We hold categorically and emphatically that an infant's crying is not 'adequate cause' to incite a sudden passion voluntary manslaughter" where defendant violently shook his 4-month-old son to death because he could not cope with his crying any other way]; *Powers v. State*, 696 N.E.2d 865 [Ind. 1998] [concluding that the crying of 5-month-old could not create "sudden heat of passion" to justify giving voluntary manslaughter instruction].) Other jurisdictions define voluntary manslaughter to include "wanton disregard for the value of human life." (See *Baker v. State*, 455 So.2d 770 [Miss. 1984] [concluding "wanton disregard standard" met in case involving the killing of a 5-week-old baby by inflicted severe head trauma].)

Involuntary manslaughter is often defined as causing death while acting with "recklessness" or with "criminal negligence." Under the standard of the Model Penal Code, recklessness is the mental state for manslaughter, while criminal negligence is the mental state for the crime of negligent homicide (Model Penal Code § 210.4 [1985]). Generally, the distinction between reckless manslaughter and murder is the degree of risk of death from the defendant's conduct. When the defendant acts recklessly as to the risk of death, he is aware of a substantial and unjustifiable risk that death will result but acts in disregard of that risk. One of the benefits of a specialized child abuse homicide statute is the shift from having to prove a *mens rea* that relates to the risk of death to proving a *mens rea* relating to the risk that injury to the child will occur from the offender's conduct.

Factors to consider in evaluating whether the defendant's conduct should be considered reckless include the age of the child, any delay in seeking medical attention, and the nature and extent of the child's injuries. These factors should be set forth in charging documents and developed at trial, and their significance should be explained to the jury. (See, e.g., *McClaskey v. State*, 540 N.E.2d 41 [Ind. 1989] [concluding evidence that a 9-month-old child was found in filthy condition with severe diaper rash and sores on his body, extreme dehydration, numerous bruises, and brain and spinal cord injuries typical of shaken baby syndrome was sufficient to warrant a conviction for reckless homicide and neglect]; *State v. Williams*, 497 So. 2d 333 [La. Ct. App. 1986] [affirming conviction for negligent homicide where 1-year-old child was left to sleep in bathtub with sheets and blankets while defendant left house for 45 minutes, was later found in tub filled with scalding water, then resuscitated, and left unattended on the front porch until fire department personnel arrived]; *Simpkins v. State*, 596 A.2d 655 [Md. Ct. Spec. App. 1991] [finding evidence sufficient to support second-degree murder conviction when parents of 2-year-old left her alone for up to 5 days without food, drink, or attention]; *People v. Tinning*, 536 N.Y.S.2d 193 [N.Y. App. Div. 1988] [finding that evidence of defendant's admission she smothered her 3-month-old daughter to stop her from crying supported jury's finding that child's death was recklessly caused under circumstances evidencing depraved indifference to human life]; *People v. Neer*, 513 N.Y.S.2d 566 [N.Y. App. Div. 1987] [concluding defendant should have realized the seriousness of his daughter's injuries and sought medical assistance, notwithstanding defendant's argument that injuries were not visible because they were covered by clothing]; but see *People v. Osburn*, 508 N.Y.S.2d 746 [N.Y. App. Div. 1986] [concluding that failure to obtain medical attention for 9-year-old victim for several hours after striking her in the abdomen did not constitute "depraved indifference," as victim was conscious, ambulatory, and able to eat during the hours following the blow].)

Juries or judges commonly reduce murder to manslaughter in many child abuse homicides. (See, e.g., *State v. Teuscher*, 883 P.2d 922 [Utah Ct. App. 1994] [involving a jury reduction from murder to manslaughter where a daycare provider violently shook a 2-month-old baby by the head, causing transection of the spinal cord and immediate death].) Quite often, shaken baby cases are reduced to manslaughter, apparently when the trier of fact believes that the perpetrator did not intend harm to the child but merely lost control and hurt the baby. Most jurors and judges have been in the situation in their own lives when they were stressed by an inconsolable infant and thus tend to empathize with those who shake babies. Prosecutors must overcome this "there but for the grace of God go I . . ." feeling with evidence of the extended and violent nature of shaking when death or permanent injury to the child is the result.

8. Child Abuse or Child Endangerment Statutes

In cases of abuse or neglect of children when death is not the result, it is important to file charges that accurately reflect the nature of the injury, the mental state of the perpetrator, and the result of the conduct to the child. Many jurisdictions recognize that neglect of a child's basic needs may result in severe developmental delays, physiological difficulties, and even psychological problems and should result in criminal punishment (Utah Code Ann. § 76–5–109[1][d][vii]). Most statutes recognize that failure to provide medical assistance to a child may be criminal. (See, e.g., *State v. Eversley*, 706 So.2d 1363 [Fla. Ct. App. 1998].) Debates still rage around the country as to whether mothers who harm their children before birth by drug abuse should be subject to criminal prosecution. (See *Whitner v. State*, 492 S.E.2d 777 [S.C. 1997] [holding that the definition of "child" did not include a viable fetus where the mother entered guilty plea to criminal child neglect for causing her baby to be born with cocaine metabolites in its system].)

Table III.6   Specialized Child Homicide Statutes

State and Offense	Mental State(s) or Underlying Felony	Past Pattern	Care or Custody	Under Age	Felony Murder
Alaska 11.41.100(a)(2): 1° murder	Knowingly engages in conduct directed toward a child; acts w/criminal negligence	Yes	No	16	Yes
Arizona 13–1105(A)(2): 1° murder	Underlying felony of child abuse; no specific mental state other than that required to prove the underlying felony	No	No	18	Yes
Arkansas 5–10–101(a)(9): capital murder	knowingly causes the death under circumstances manifesting extreme indifference to value of human life	No	No	15	No
5–10–102(A)(3)	Knowingly causes the death	No	No	15	No
California Penal 273ab: assault resulting in death of a child under 8	Assault by means of force that to a reasonable person would be likely to produce great bodily injury	No	Yes	8	No
Colorado 18–3–102(1)(b): 1° murder	Underlying felony of child sexual assault	No	No	15	Yes
18–3–102(1)(f)	Knowingly causes the death and in a position of trust with the child	No	No	12	No
Delaware tit. 11, § 633: 2° murder by abuse or neglect	Criminal negligence	Yes	No	14	No
tit. 11, § 634: 1° murder by abuse or neglect	Recklessness	Yes	No	14	No
Florida 782.04 (1) (a)(2)(h): 1° murder	Underlying felony of aggravated child abuse	No	No	18	Yes
Idaho 18–4003(d): 1° murder	Underlying felony of aggravated battery of a child under 12	No	No	12	Yes
Indiana 35–42–1-1	Underlying felony of child molestation	No	No	14	Yes
Iowa 707.2(5): 1° murder	Killing a child while committing child endangerment or assault upon a child; circumstances manifest extreme indifference to human life	No	No	18	No
Kansas 21–3401(b): 1° murder	Underlying felony of abuse of a child	No	No	18	Yes

(Continued)

Table III.6   (Continued)

State and Offense	Mental State(s) or Underlying Felony	Past Pattern	Care or Custody	Under Age	Felony Murder
Louisiana 14:30(5): 1° murder	Specific intent to kill or inflict great bodily harm	No	No	12	No
14:30.1(A)(2)(b): 2° murder	Expressly applies even if there is no intent to kill or inflict great bodily harm Underlying felony of cruelty to juveniles	No	No	18	Yes
14:32: negligent homicide	Criminal negligence (penalty for negligent homicide is enhanced if a person kills a child committing battery upon the child)	No	No	10	No
Michigan 750.316	Committed in the perpetration of child abuse in the first degree	No	No	18	Yes
Minnesota 609.185(5): 1° murder	Causing death of a child while committing child abuse; circumstances manifest extreme indifference to human life	Yes	No	18	No
Mississippi 97–3-19(2)(f): capital murder	Underlying felonies of felonious child abuse or battery of a child With or without any design to effect the death of another	No	No	18	Yes
New Jersey 2C:11–3(b)(3)(a)	Underlying felony of child sexual assault	No	No	14	Yes
New York Penal, 125.25(4): 2° murder	Recklessly engaging in conduct that creates a grave risk of serious physical injury or death; circumstances evincing a depraved indifference to human life	No	No	11	No
North Dakota 12.1–16–01(1): murder	Underlying felony of abuse or neglect of a child	No	No	18	Yes
Oklahoma tit. 21§701.7: 1° murder	Willful or malicious injuring, torturing, maiming, or using unreasonable force; willfully causing [10.7115] be done upon a child	No	No	18	No
Ohio 2903.01	Purposely causing death	No	No	13	No
Oregon 163.095(1)(f): aggravated murder	Mental state required for murder; intentional	No	No	14	No

(Continued)

Table III.6   (Continued)

State and Offense	Mental State(s) or Underlying Felony	Past Pattern	Care or Custody	Under Age	Felony Murder
163.115(1)(b)(J): murder	Underlying felonies of first or second degree assault of a child under 14	No	No	14	Yes
163.115(1)(c): murder	Reckless and extreme indifference to human life	Yes	No	14	No
163.118(1)(c): 1° manslaughter	Reckless	Yes	No	14	No
163.125(1)(c): 2° manslaughter	Criminal negligence	Yes	No	14	No
Pennsylvania tit. 18 § 2504: involuntary manslaughter	Recklessness or gross negligence; involuntary manslaughter is raised from a misdemeanor to a second-degree felony if the victim is under 12	No	No	12	No
Rhode Island 11–23–1	Committed in perpetration of any degree of sexual assault or child molestation	No	No	15	Yes
South Carolina 16-3-85: homicide by child abuse	Underlying circumstances manifesting an extreme indifference to human life; knowingly aiding or abetting another to commit child abuse that results in the death of the child	No	No	11	No
Tennessee 39–13–202(a)(2): 1° murder	Underlying felony of aggravated child abuse	No	No	18	Yes
	No mental state need be proven other than that required by the underlying felony				
Texas 19.03(8)	Intentionally or knowingly causing death	No	No	6	No
Utah 76–5-202: capital murder	Intentionally or knowingly causing death underlying felony of child abuse	No	No	18	Yes
76–5-203: murder	Underlying felony of child abuse	No	No	18	Yes
76–5-208: child abuse homicide	Degree of felony depends on the mental state of the actor	No	No	18	No
	Causing death of a person under 18 resulting from child abuse				

(Continued)

Table III.6   (Continued)

State and Offense	Mental State(s) or Underlying Felony	Past Pattern	Care or Custody	Under Age	Felony Murder
Washington 9A.32.055(1): homicide by abuse	Circumstances manifesting an extreme indifference to human life	Yes	No	16	No
West Virginia 61–8D-2a: death of a child by a parent	Maliciously and intentionally inflicting substantial physical pain by other than accidental means	No	Yes	18	No
Wyoming 6–2-101(a)	Underlying felony of kidnapping or abuse	No	No	16	Yes

SOURCE: Phipps, C. A. [1998]. *Responding to child homicide: A statutory proposal.* Children's Law Project, University of South Carolina, June 1998.

9. Charging Inconsistent Mental States

Crimes involving inconsistent mental states such as intentional or reckless murder/manslaughter can be charged in a single indictment for the jury to consider. However, convictions for both intentional and reckless murder are generally not allowed to stand. (See *People v. Gallagher,* 508 N.E.2d 909 [N.Y. 1987] [concluding that intentional and reckless murder counts must be submitted to jury in the alternative].) When proceeding with two alternative mental states, the prosecutor has greater leeway to argue to the jury based on the evidence that develops at trial. For example, should defense witnesses provide evidence that the defendant disliked the deceased child, the prosecutor may then use that testimony to argue for conviction of intentional, rather than reckless, homicide.

10. Charging Prior Instances of Abuse

An additional factor to consider is whether there is evidence of prior abuse by the defendant or prior injuries involving the deceased child. Such evidence may be admissible to negate the defense of accident or mistake, to establish the identity of the abuser, or to establish mental state. However, if uncharged, such evidence may be inadmissible as evidence of uncharged crimes. Charging the prior abuse, even at the misdemeanor level, avoids this problem, assuming the other charges can properly be joined and are not severed before trial. A good example of this method is to file a charge of endangering the welfare of a child and include the defendant's course of conduct wherein he is responsible for other injuries to the child, however minor, over the course of a specified time frame.

11. Declining to File Child Physical Abuse or Homicide Charges

The decision not to file charges when a child has been injured by abuse or neglect should be made only after a complete investigation and after all possible sources of information have been discovered. The lack of an opinion from an expert as to the cause or mechanism of the injury to the child should not be a basis to decline prosecution unless the right expert has been consulted. A prosecutor should not decline charges based on a discrepant story to account for abusive injuries to a child. If a decision not to file charges is based upon a reasonable discipline defense, it should be made only after an honest assessment of whether the trier of fact would determine that the nature of the injury to the child truly was the result of a reasonable attempt at discipline.

If there is concern about who committed the abuse of the child, the legal questions set out above should be considered. If the statutory scheme allows for charging both a person who knowingly permits abuse as well as the person who commits the abuse, appropriate charges should be brought against more than one caregiver. Usually, careful scrutiny of the facts and an understanding of the experts' opinions as to the timing of the injuries and the onset of symptoms allows for identification of the abuser. In some cases, evidence including evidence of prior acts of abuse will support charging more than one caregiver as coperpetrators of the abusive injuries to the child.

Charges should not be declined simply because it is undetermined exactly what mechanism an abuser employed to cause the child's injuries. Most statutes do not demand this certainty in charging or proof, and appellate courts have recognized that it is not necessary to specify exactly what happened when injuries are consistent with more than one possible mechanism or cause, as long as all of those mechanisms fit within the definition of the crime. (See, e.g., *State v. Fee*, 1991 Ohio App. LEXIS 2423, 20 [Ohio Ct. App. 1991] [noting, "The exact method by which appellant inflicted the injuries need not be shown. And the fact that there are several methods to inflicting the type of harm that was suffered by the baby in this case does not give rise to a reasonable theory of innocence when the perpetrator may have employed only one method."].)

The prosecutor should consult with all members of the interdisciplinary team working on the investigation. The team should also receive an explanation as to why the evidence is insufficient to file criminal charges. The prosecutor should personally meet with the victim's family members and explain why charges are not possible, explaining that everything that could be done in the investigation was done and considered prior to making the difficult decision. If the parents or caregivers of the victim are also the suspected perpetrators of the abuse, declination reasons should be discussed with CPS workers and child protection attorneys so that appropriate decisions can be made to protect the victim and other children from the risk of additional abuse.

III. PLEA NEGOTIATION

Once a decision has been made to file criminal charges, and sometimes even before charges are formally filed, the prosecutor may begin the process of negotiating with the defense attorney. Usually this occurs at the same time as trial preparation. Plea negotiation is an area in which the prosecutor is potentially subject to the greatest scrutiny, criticism, and misunderstanding from outside sources. Consequently, great care must be taken in the manner in which plea negotiations are conducted.

A. The Approach

Each prosecutor's office undoubtedly has a philosophy that guides the approach to plea negotiation in all criminal cases. Some offices routinely reduce the number or seriousness of charges in order to encourage guilty pleas, while others have a policy of requiring pleas to the charges as originally filed or to the top count of the indictment. Statutes, case law, local practice, defense attorneys, and judges vary across jurisdictions. No matter what the approach, it is especially important to know what result is desired with the particular offender—prison, local jail time, probation, treatment, or some combination of these—when prosecuting a child abuse case. After reviewing the investigation, there should be an assessment of whether the case is likely to go to trial and how much effort should go into the negotiation process.

Except in extremely rare cases when a defendant proceeds *pro se*, plea negotiation will be conducted through the defendant's attorney. The setting in which negotiations occur is crucial. Negotiating should be conducted in a business setting, preferably the prosecutor's office, and there must be a scrupulous effort to avoid acting in any manner that could be interpreted as giving preferential treatment to selected defendants. It is also good practice, and in some places a requirement, to put offers and agreements in writing, with an understanding that nothing is binding until a written accord is reached. This will produce clear understandings and help to avoid later claims of misinterpretation or broken promises.

It is also good practice to solicit input from the victim and victim's family prior to making an offer to the defendant. Some jurisdictions require this to occur before a negotiated plea can take place. Advise the victim of all the sentencing options, including the maximum and minimum term of incarceration. This will hopefully diffuse unrealistic expectations. It will also help them feel that they have had some say in the defendant's punishment. These steps also help ensure victim satisfaction when the case is finally over.

Then, once a plea agreement has been reached, make sure the victim, the victim's family, and any others particularly interested are notified. They may wish to be present when the plea is entered and should be given that opportunity in most situations. Do not, however, tell very young children or witnesses about anticipated guilty pleas in the event the plea falls through. It is especially important not to have victims present in court in cases in which identity is an issue in case the defendant withdraws the plea at the last minute or the judge does not accept the plea. In such circumstances, it is better not to advise the child victim until the plea has been accepted. Once accepted, witnesses and support people should be notified, so they know not to appear for trial and can plan on attending the sentencing if interested.

B. The Benefits of Early Guilty Pleas

Guilty pleas are certainly desirable since they provide public acknowledgment of the defendant's responsibility for the crime, spare the child the possible anxiety associated with trial, prevent costly and time-consuming appeals, and encourage finality of judgment. Further, a defendant who admits criminal conduct may be more amenable to, and likely to benefit from, treatment. Guilty pleas also save time and resources that can then be devoted to other pending cases. All of these advantages are magnified when guilty pleas occur early in the process.

One way the prosecutor can hasten the process of obtaining a guilty plea is by preparing an offer at the earliest opportunity, perhaps to present to the defense attorney at the time of the defendant's first court appearance or shortly thereafter. It is sometimes appropriate and beneficial to attempt to negotiate before the case is formally charged. This might be appropriate when the prosecutor wants to avoid having the victim testify before the grand jury or at the preliminary hearing. If the police arrested the defendant, an attorney may have already been appointed or retained, and contacting counsel to initiate negotiations should pose no problem. Otherwise, the prosecutor should explore options for early appointment of counsel if it is anticipated there will be a need to engage in early negotiations.

The offer should specifically describe the terms of the plea, such as a reduction of the charges and a particular sentencing recommendation. It should also contain a reasonably early expiration date after which the particular offer will no longer be available. It is important to adhere strictly to that deadline to establish and maintain credibility with the defense bar. This will encourage the defense attorney to confer promptly with the defendant and not wait until the day before trial. In some areas, prosecutors will face judicial pressure to keep offers open longer. If a negotiation policy requires early expiration dates and they are applied consistently, it will be easier to resist such pressure. Written standards, especially if published, citing the benefits of early guilty pleas as mitigating factors justifying more favorable plea offers will promote judicial support for the prosecutor's position.

Success in encouraging early guilty pleas depends on the prosecutor's organization, readiness to try the case, and projection of confidence in the trial's successful outcome. Always prepare the case as if it were going to trial. Contact and subpoena witnesses early. Provide discovery to the defense as soon as possible so they have the information necessary to negotiate. Work with others in the community to support and prepare the victim. These steps will ensure readiness for trial. Demonstrating a coordinated approach with other professionals can also help convince the defense that the prosecution has a strong case.

C. The Use of Sentencing Recommendations as a Negotiating Tool

Any plea offer should be based upon the evidence and circumstances of the case. If appropriate, consider using a sentencing recommendation rather than a charge reduction to negotiate a plea. This avoids the resentment often felt by victims and others in the community when the charges are reduced but retains a powerful incentive for a defendant to plead guilty. Realism demands knowledge of the judge presiding over the case and an awareness of how much weight the prosecution's recommendation will carry. The defense attorney will almost certainly be sure to know. Some judges will give serious consideration to the prosecutor's sentencing recommendations if the recommendations are thoughtful and well reasoned. Others will not and may even reject an otherwise agreed-upon disposition.

Several sentencing recommendation options are available and can be combined in most jurisdictions to encourage guilty pleas. These recommendations can include a recommendation that the defendant receive reduced jail or prison time structured so that the lowest amounts of time are recommended for early guilty pleas, a recommendation for probation with a suspended or deferred sentence, a recommendation for treatment of the defendant as a condition of the sentence, and a recommendation of lowered or waived fines. A defendant who refuses a plea offer and exercises his right to trial may not be penalized for doing so by the sentencing court. If the defendant continues to refuse to accept responsibility for his crime, the prosecution will have a convincing sentencing argument that probation and treatment are inappropriate and greater jail or prison time is warranted, as the defendant may pose more risk to the community. Furthermore, the trial will have forced the victim to go through an emotional ordeal on the witness stand. Many facts and details were related to the court that were probably not related to the judge at the pretrial conference. These additional facts can be used as a basis for enhanced sentencing.

D. Factors to Consider in Plea Negotiations

In determining the best disposition for a case, neither a relationship with the defense attorney nor media pressure should affect the prosecutor's decision. However, a number of factors should be considered, many of which are involved in the initial decision regarding whether to file charges, what crime, and how many counts to charge. No one factor is controlling, but all of these factors should be balanced to achieve a just result in terms of the number and seriousness of crimes pled to and the sentence imposed. Input from others involved in the case can be very helpful in determining an appropriate plea offer, but it is critical that the prosecutor retain ultimate responsibility for such decisions so as to ensure fairness, accountability, and consistency in the plea negotiation process.

1. An Accurate Reflection of the Seriousness of the Crime and the Dangerousness of the Offender

a. The severity of the crime. In order to evaluate the severity of a child abuse crime appropriately, knowledge about the dynamics of abuse is invaluable. For instance, it may be tempting to assess a long-term incest situation as less serious than other categories of child sexual abuse because of the offender's nonthreatening outward appearance, the victim's mixed feelings about the abuse and abuser, and a reluctance by the family to cooperate. Incest crimes are, however, especially serious because of the offender's destructive emotional manipulation, the chronic nature of the offense, its lifelong effects on the victim, and the offender's potential for abusing other children. The fundamental presumption of any assessment must be that child abuse is a crime regardless of whether it happened inside or outside of the family.

A primary consideration in plea negotiations should be the severity of the abuse. Obviously, the greater the violence or duration of criminal acts, the greater the number of victims involved, and the greater the impact of the crime on the victims, the more reasons there are to require greater accountability and a more severe punishment. Allowing offenders to plead guilty to reduced charges that fail to reflect or that even misrepresent the true nature of their crimes can be misleading and foster a lack of confidence and faith in the justice system. This is particularly true in jurisdictions with determinate, mandatory, or presumptive sentencing. In those jurisdictions, the sentence range is determined by the specific crime and number of counts for which a defendant is actually convicted, and a prosecutor cannot ask a judge to go beyond that range on the basis of what the defendant really did. Later, if a defendant commits new crimes, the number and specific nature of prior convictions determine the criminal history used to calculate the range of punishment available for new crimes.

Even in jurisdictions without determinate sentencing, proper labeling of the defendants and their conduct is crucial since defendants will be sentenced on the basis of the crimes for which they have been convicted and not on the basis of the more serious crimes they may have in fact committed. In sexual abuse situations, prosecutors should always insist that defendants plead to sexual offenses since appropriate sentencing, including treatment options, may be dependent on accurate labeling. If and when new crimes are committed, the defense can be expected to argue that the prior convictions accurately represent the full extent of prior crimes, and it is unlikely a judge will assume otherwise.

Another factor that is important to consider during plea negotiations is the sex offender registration statute. This type of statute is commonly known as Megan's Law and requires a convicted sex offender to register with law enforcement authorities. The offender may also be rated with a risk level assessment determined in part by the convicted offense. Risk level assessments determine what information can be publicly disseminated. It is important for a prosecutor to know what crimes are registration offenses and, if appropriate, ensure the defendant pleads to a mandatory registration offense.

Aside from practical consequences, persistent undercharging or charge reduction in child abuse cases can lead to the perception by offenders and others, including victims, police officers, and the public, that child abuse is deemed less serious than other crimes and that people who commit these crimes can expect deals. The message that *must* be communicated is that child abuse is a serious crime and it will be treated as such.

b. The dangerousness of the offender. Before plea negotiations, the nature and extent of the defendant's prior criminal history must be known. Defendants with prior criminal convictions or a history of abusive behavior present a greater risk to the community and should not receive offers similar to those given to defendants with no prior record. Further, the defendant's current offense or prior criminal history may be so serious that it may be inappropriate to offer anything, let alone a recommendation of reduced jail time or treatment in exchange for a guilty plea. In such cases, determine what sentence the offender deserves and plan for trial.

If probation is to be considered, the prosecutor should consider probation conditions that will protect the victim, other children, and the community. For instance, if the defendant is a daycare provider, a condition that he not engage in any business that involves taking care of children or just a flat prohibition from being in the presence of children under a certain age may be in order. In such cases, the big issue tends to be whether the prohibition should also apply to the defendant's own children. That can be answered only by an assessment by the child protection agency. Child physical abusers are not automatically dangerous to all children. There are a number of factors to be considered, including what stressors caused the abuse in the first place, the offender's attitude toward a certain child, the offender's practice of singling a child out for unique treatment, and the offender's amenability to successful behavioral modification. If the defendant has been psychologically evaluated, either during the criminal justice process or as a result of the child protection process, the results may be very helpful in determining future risk, although there is no scientifically reliable way to predict who will be dangerous to children and who will not.

Check to see whether the defendant is facing other charges. If so, assess all the open cases to determine if a consolidated plea offer would be appropriate. Keep in mind that many defendants are willing to admit to burglaries and robberies but may be reluctant to acknowledge abuse of a child.

It is inappropriate to offer a plea agreement requiring treatment in lieu of jail or prison time if the defendant denies responsibility for the abuse and offers to enter an *Alford* plea or admits the abuse but denies the need for treatment, or if there is no suitable therapy available for the defendant. *Alford* pleas or no-contest pleas can be especially troublesome. The defendant may attempt to appeal his conviction following such a plea, arguing that the facts outlined by the prosecution are insufficient to support the charges. A defendant who refuses to accept responsibility for the abuse is almost always an unacceptable candidate for treatment and will be far less likely to complete therapy successfully. Moreover, an *Alford* plea may cause further emotional harm to the victim by permitting the perpetrator to maintain his innocence.

Responsible decisions about whether to recommend probation conditioned on successful completion of specialized treatment and whether and how much jail time to recommend often cannot be made quickly. Even when treatment is recommended as a condition of probation, some time in jail is also appropriate. Many sex offender treatment specialists agree that some period of incarceration is necessary to demonstrate that this conduct has consequences. In most cases, conclusions can be reached only after a full evaluation of the offender by a qualified therapist. Rather than delay a case unnecessarily, the prosecutor could consider making an offer and having the defendant enter a guilty plea with the understanding that the treatment recommendation will be conditioned upon the results of a particular therapist's evaluation. Care must be exercised to avoid becoming committed to a recommendation prematurely. An example follows:

> Upon a plea of guilty to [specified charges], by [specified date], the prosecutor agrees to recommend a sentence of _____ days/months/years in jail/prison and will consider recommending said sentence be suspended/deferred for _____ years upon receipt of an evaluation regarding the defendant's amenability to treatment for sexual deviancy from Doctor X. A recommendation for suspension/deferral of sentence will be made only if Doctor X concludes that the defendant is amenable to treatment in his program and that such treatment could be completed in _____ years and if the prosecutor concludes that the defendant does not present an undue risk of harm to the victim or community. The conditions of such suspension/deferral would include serving _____ days/months in jail with work release if the defendant qualifies, successful completion of and full cooperation with and participation in Doctor X's treatment program, compliance with any and all conditions of Dr. X's treatment program, no contact with the victim, no contact with children under _____ years of age, payment of restitution for the costs of counseling for the victim. . . .

The foregoing illustrates one approach. It is important to have an evaluation prior to committing to a specific type of treatment. For example, a recommendation for community-based treatment would be inappropriate when the therapist's report concludes that "in-patient treatment is the best option for the defendant because he presents a danger of re-offending, but I would be willing to work with the defendant in a community treatment setting on a trial basis." Nor would a prosecutor want to be committed to recommending a community treatment alternative if the proposed treatment provider was not qualified.

Appellate courts are divided as to whether a defendant's probation can be revoked after the defendant fails to be accepted into a treatment program or to successfully complete treatment when that failure is due to the defendant's unwillingness to admit guilt to the treatment provider. (See *Russell v. Eaves*, 722 F. Supp. 558 [E.D. Mo. 1989], *appeal dismissed*, 902 F.2d 1574 [8th Cir. 1990]; *People v. Ickler*, 877 P.2d 863 [Colo. 1994]; *State v. Welch*, 671 A.2d 379 [Conn. Ct. App. 1996]; *Henderson v. State*, 543 So. 2d 344 [Fla. Dist. Ct. App. 1989]; *People v. Taube*, 702 N.E.2d 573 [Ill. Ct. App. 1998]; *State v. Gleason*, 576 A.2d 1246 [Vt. 1990].) The U. S. Supreme Court recently refused to consider this issue, dismissing the original writ of certiorari in *State v. Imlay* (813 P.2d 979 [Mont. 1991], *cert. dismissed*, 506 U.S. 5 [1992]). This issue is very specific to each jurisdiction, and the applicable law should be considered prior to plea negotiations. The wisest course is never to agree to recommend probation conditioned on the defendant's participation in and completion of treatment, unless the defendant admits and accepts full responsibility for the crimes. Otherwise, the condition that the defendant receive therapy while on probation may be unenforceable.

2. The Disclosure of Additional Crimes During Treatment

Prosecutors should consider what action to take regarding previously unreported sexual offenses that may be disclosed by a defendant who is allowed to participate in treatment as part of a probationary sentence. Some defendants will seek an agreement that there will be no additional charges filed for any such admitted acts, then proceed to admit literally hundreds of additional acts with scores of victims who never came forward to report those offenses. Effectively granting immunity in advance of those admissions is not only embarrassing to the prosecutor but it creates a great injustice. Defendants will argue that it puts them in a "Catch-22" situation to have to admit to all their other sexual offenses in order to succeed in treatment, while subjecting them to additional criminal charges for any conduct they admit during treatment. The best approach to such arguments is to encourage a full and complete admission of the entire history of sexual misconduct up front, so that all of those offenses can be considered in the plea agreement. At the least, there should be a provision in the agreement that any disclosure made by the defendant during treatment must be immediately reported to the prosecutor's office and the court and that the patient-therapist privilege does not apply to such admissions during treatment.

3. The Victims' Wishes and Well-Being

It is vitally important that the prosecutor obtain input from the victim and victim's family. Find out the expectations of victims and their families. When victims are old enough to express their wishes, they should be asked early in the process what they would like to see happen since early reactions are less likely to be influenced by others. Any misperceptions can then be corrected. For instance, a victim may believe the offender will go to jail for life and may carry a tremendous amount of guilt from that belief. A victim may be relieved to know this is unlikely and should know there will probably be some combination of punishment including possible jail time but also help in the form of treatment. Children need constant reassurance that they were not the ones at fault. Assure the victim that the offender is responsible for his actions and their consequences, the prosecutor is responsible for whether charges are filed and the outcome of trial, and the judge is responsible for deciding how to punish an adult who has done something wrong.

Sometimes children will describe in graphic detail how offenders should be punished. Other times, children may simply indicate they want the abuse to stop. If sentencing options are limited and the child's recommendation is not possible or probable, e.g., keeping the offender from going to jail, explain why this preference may be overruled.

In determining the impact of trial on the child, talk to the family, therapist, or any other professionals involved to form an opinion as to how well the child will do. If the child has already testified before the grand jury or during a preliminary hearing, the child's ability to withstand the pressures of a trial will be known to a certain extent. Probably the single most important variable influencing a child's ability to testify successfully will be the anxieties and expectations of adults. If the child expects the worst, the trial process is bound to affect the child negatively. It is important, therefore, to make sure individuals in the child's support network have a realistic understanding of the trial process.

One of the most common misperceptions is that going through trial is so traumatic for a child that it should be avoided if at all possible. If the defense senses this in any way, their strategy may be to make the child uncomfortable and the prosecutor desperate to negotiate a plea agreement. The horrific trial, however, is usually a myth, as research and practice are increasingly showing. A well-prepared child and prosecutor, especially if supported by a coordinated network of professionals, can make the trial experience not only less stressful but in many cases positive and empowering, almost cathartic. Discomfort is unavoidable, but experience has shown that the child's distress can be minimized and indeed must be weighed against the threat posed by the defendant to current and future victims.

4. Knowledge of the Forum and the Adversary

It is important for a prosecutor to consider what judge will hear the case and what kind of adversary represents the defendant. In other words, a prosecutor should know the attitudes and opinions the judge has about child abuse cases as well as the capability and skills of the defendant's attorney. It is helpful to know, for example, if the judge considers charges involving child abuse as serious. Does the judge understand the dynamics of intrafamilial abuse and other children's issues? Be aware of the judge's past rulings on crucial issues such as a child's credibility or competency to testify. Does the judge have any biases or predisposition that will help or hurt the case? What kind of sentences has the judge given in similar cases, either as part of a plea negotiation or after trial? All this knowledge will be extremely helpful as the prosecutor considers what kind of offer to make.

Similarly, a prosecutor must know whether the defendant's attorney is really willing to take the case to trial. Does the defense attorney normally try cases or avoid trials at all costs? Does the attorney wait until the day of jury selection before agreeing to a plea offer or try to strike a deal prior to formal indictment or pretrial motions? Does the defense attorney have any experience defending or prosecuting child abuse cases? Does the attorney understand the key issues in the case? These are all questions that should be answered before any plea negotiations begin.

Some jurisdictions limit or prohibit a diversionary arrangement or holding a plea in abeyance for crimes involving sexual offenses against children under a certain age. (See, e.g., California Penal Code § 1000.13; [2002]. *U.S. Attorneys' Manual* § 9–75.410. Washington, DC: Dept. of Justice.) Be aware of such restrictions, and if there is no such restriction, it might be appropriate to seek enactment of such a provision. The repetitive nature of pedophilic conduct and the time sensitivity of child abuse cases dictate against taking the risk of the defendant's failure to comply with the conditions of diversion and having to reinstate a prosecution several years after the crime was committed. In addition, it is generally more difficult to maintain control over the defendant during such a diversionary period than if a conviction is entered and the defendant is being supervised by the corrections department.

5. Legal or Evidentiary Problems

Evidentiary or legal problems may develop after cases have been filed, presenting legitimate reasons for altering or reducing charges during plea negotiations. Issues such as speedy trial requirements may arise and form the basis for a defense motion to dismiss. Crucial witnesses may become unavailable, change their testimony, or be too traumatized to go through trial. A victim may recant, making it far more difficult to prove the abuse. Important evidence may have been suppressed or new exculpatory evidence discovered. Prior rulings of the judge assigned to the case may also affect a plea negotiation. These situations require an educated judgment about the wisdom of risking a complete dismissal or acquittal on the original charges or allowing a defendant to plead guilty to a lesser offense.

On occasion, aggravating evidence will surface, such as the revelation of more victims or more extensive abuse of previously known victims, justifying filing additional or more serious charges. Investigate the new facts fully and either amend the original charges or file new ones. Even if the defendant is willing to plead guilty as originally charged, new charges should be pursued unless they are without merit, cannot be proven, or would have no practical effect on the defendant's status or sentence.

Other factors unrelated to evidentiary and proof considerations may warrant the reduction or dismissal of charges. Reducing charges may be appropriate when the defendant offers information or testimony that could reasonably lead to the conviction of others who have committed more serious crimes or represent a greater threat to the community. Negotiating a plea to reduced charges or providing immunity for these reasons should be approached with extreme care and only after consultation with the elected prosecutor or an appropriate supervisor. A defendant who has physically or sexually abused a child is likely to do so again; therefore, the negotiations should allow some provision for control.

Restitution to the victim, covering at least medical and treatment costs, and probation should be minimum conditions of the plea in all but rare cases.

6. Special Considerations in Child Physical Abuse or Homicide Cases

If the defendant has been forthcoming since the beginning of the investigation, admitting the nature of the conduct that resulted in injuries to the child and providing a plausible explanation of the events or circumstances that led up to the abusive conduct, there may be good reason to allow a resolution of the charges early in the process. A "charge agreement" may be appropriate when a defendant admits to the elements of a lesser offense and does not minimize what he did to cause the injuries. On the other hand, most defendants minimize or provide only partial admissions of what occurred, and a plea agreement based upon such a partial admission may be unsatisfying to both the victim's family and the general public in an egregious case. Consider conditioning the plea agreement on the defendant's providing an acceptable explanation of the conduct to the doctors who are acting as experts in the case. If the explanation given is rejected as implausible, charges can then be filed as appropriate. If the explanation given is plausible, the lesser charge can be filed and a guilty plea entered without forcing the family to endure a lengthy preliminary hearing or trial. The same process may be effective if the defendant has a change of heart following a preliminary hearing or grand jury indictment but prior to trial. Videotaping the explanation may make the defendant's admission helpful to medical and legal professionals to obtain a further understanding of what types of conduct result in various degrees of injury to children. The perpetrator's explanation also provides insight as to motivations, what preceded and triggered the abuse, what stressors led the perpetrator to lose patience with the victim, the onset of symptoms after the abuse was committed, and other matters.

Prosecutors must consider the effect of any clearly diagnosed mental illnesses on the defendant's culpability. However, behavior or personality disorders are common, though not universal, among child physical abusers and child murderers. The prosecutor should review such a diagnosis with a consultant whom the prosecutor trusts. If the defendant's mental condition did not preclude understanding the nature of the conduct and the fact that it was wrong or preclude forming the mental state necessary to sustain a conviction, there is no reason to allow a plea agreement to a lesser offense. On the other hand, if it appears that the defendant suffered from a delusion that the child was in fact Satan at the time the fatal blows were struck, there may be some room for a negotiated plea to some alternative such as "guilty but mentally ill" or "not guilty by reason of insanity" if that will result in civil commitment of the dangerous offender. If there are concerns about a defendant's mental competency from the beginning of a case, it is wise for the prosecutor to obtain an early assessment of whether the defendant is even competent to stand trial.

E. Conclusion

Plea negotiations in child abuse cases are not simple. While they may become easier with experience, it is not always possible to predict what defendants and their attorneys will do. Sometimes defendants will plead guilty without any concession by the prosecutor or without an agreement for a particular sentence recommendation. Sometimes, the defendant will refuse to plead guilty no matter how lenient the offer. In any event, a prosecutor must be prepared to proceed to trial if the plea negotiations fall through or if the defendant is allowed to withdraw the plea. Plea negotiation should be conducted from a position of strength. That position can come only from the prosecutor's willingness to try difficult cases. Cases with good evidence and good witnesses are more likely to plead out. Apparently weaker cases tend to get tried more often. A prosecutor who has a reputation for plea bargaining every case will have no credibility for negotiation.

IV. SENTENCING

Sentencing is of critical importance in determining the effectiveness of the criminal justice system's response to child abuse. When decisions are made about what charges to file and during the course of plea negotiations, the prosecutor must always be aware of the impact these actions will have on the sentencing options the judge is likely to use. If the outcome of sentencing seems inconsequential, victims, professionals, and the public at large will feel it is not worthwhile to participate in the criminal justice process.

For some prosecutors, the sentencing hearing seems anticlimactic after overcoming the hurdles necessary to obtain the offender's conviction. Prosecutors who are allowed to participate in the sentencing hearing may spend little time preparing, relying on the notion that sentencing is the exclusive prerogative of the judge. However, without responsible advocacy by the prosecutor at sentencing, a judge cannot be expected to have either the desire or ability to make knowledgeable and sensitive decisions. In recommending sentences to the court and responding to defense recommendations, prosecutors have an obligation to be well prepared and take advantage of the opportunity to educate judges about the realities of child abuse. Prosecutors should, if at all possible, submit a written sentencing memorandum detailing their recommendations. In jurisdictions that allow prosecutors a very limited role in sentencing, they should advocate for the victim to be heard. Victims have the right to make victim impact statements in many jurisdictions.

A. The Components of Sentencing Recommendations

The criminal sentencing process serves multiple objectives including the protection of the community, punishment of offenders, restitution for victims, deterrence of offenders from future crimes, retribution for the victim and the family of the victim, deterrence of others from similar crimes, and achievement of uniformity in sentencing. While all these goals are important, community safety should always be paramount for the prosecutor.

1. Incarceration Recommendations

The imposition of jail time or prison time for a defendant is intended to serve several objectives of the sentencing process, including community safety by preventing the defendant from committing new crimes during the incarceration period, punishment, and deterrence of the defendant and others from committing crimes in the future. Opinions differ about how well incarceration accomplishes these aims, but a prosecutor's recommendation must address the issue. If jail or prison is recommended, the prosecutor must give reasons to support the recommendation. Similarly, if no incarceration is recommended, a prosecutor must be able to articulate why. Prosecutors should typically recommend some jail time, as even a few days of confinement underscores the idea that child abuse is a serious crime and that punishment is important to the victim and to society.

Recommendations for incarceration can be combined with recommendations for offender treatment. Most jurisdictions have work release programs, allowing defendants to continue working and go to therapy but also providing for some degree of incarceration or other restrictions. Many therapists experienced in treating child abusers contend that some incarceration is essential to successful therapy because it clarifies to the offender that society will not tolerate child abuse and provides incentive for the offender to take advantage of treatment to avoid future incarceration.

For too many years, the first thing mentioned at sentencing proceedings following a conviction of a child sexual offender has been the defendant's amenability to treatment, with the issue of punishment only a secondary consideration. Given the questionable efficacy of the treatment of pedophiles, the severe and often long-lasting effects on victims, the helplessness of the victim, and the reprehensibility of gratifying one's sexual desires at the expense of a child, treatment of the offender should not be the first thing to be discussed but should be considered only after appropriate punishment for the crime has been meted out. The first thing to be discussed at the sentencing of a child molester should be the effect of the abuse on the victim, both short term and long term, and the need to punish the offender. Prosecutors must know the effects of abuse on victims in general and must consult with the child's therapist or family to determine what the effects of this crime were on the victim. (See McCauley, J., et al. [1997]. Clinical characteristics of women with a history of childhood abuse: Unhealed wounds. *Journal of the American Medical Association, 277,* 1362 [noting that adults who were sexually abused reported higher rates of nightmares, back pain, headaches, pelvic pain, eating difficulties, and somatic complaints]; Swanston, H. Y., et al. [1997]. Sexually abused children 5 years after presentation: A case-control study. *Pediatrics, 100,* 600 [finding that sexually abused children were significantly more depressed, showed lower self-esteem, and exhibited more behavioral difficulties than a nonabused control group]; Finkelhor, D., et al. [1989]. Sexual abuse and its relationship to later sexual satisfaction, marital status, religion and attitudes. *Journal of Interpersonal Violence, 4,* 379.) The prosecutor should spend most of the time in a sentencing argument making the sentencing authority understand the dynamics of the abuse, the effect of the crime as viewed from the perspective of the victim, and the behavior and background of the defendant.

In some jurisdictions, jail or prison time can be suspended or deferred with the defendant's probation conditioned on successful completion of treatment. In some jurisdictions, special sentencing options exist for sex offenders, including treatment as part of probation, with the possibility of some jail time as well.

If the defendant is placed on probation, build in protections in the event the defendant fails treatment and it becomes necessary to revoke probation. For instance, consider a recommendation that the suspended period of incarceration be rather lengthy to give the defendant the greatest incentive to succeed in treatment. If the defendant fails to take advantage of treatment and is therefore more likely to re-offend, community safety will be maximized by isolation for a longer period. Recognizing the desirability of monitoring defendants over a long period, many jurisdictions have sought statutory revisions that authorize longer, rather than shorter, probationary periods (Minn. Stat. § 609.109[7]). Lifetime probation may be an option. (See, e.g., Ariz. Rev. Stat. Ann. § 13–604.01I.) A prosecutor may also ask the court to schedule review hearings at regular intervals to monitor the defendant's progress in therapy.

If the defendant refuses to acknowledge wrongdoing even in the face of a guilty verdict, incarceration is the only sentence that makes sense. One of the most basic requirements of successful treatment is that the client acknowledge a problem and exhibit a willingness to change. Child abusers who refuse to admit they have done anything wrong or show no remorse are not appropriate candidates for treatment. (See Amicus Brief of American Professional Society on the Abuse of Children, p. 10, in *Montana v. Imlay*, 506 U.S. 807, *cert. dismissed*, 506 U.S. 5 [1992]; Becker, J. V. [1994]. Offenders: Characteristics and treatment. *The Future of Children*, 4(2), 176.) Professionals who claim otherwise should be challenged to establish how treatment can be provided to someone who will not admit to having a problem.

In jurisdictions with determinate sentencing, specific statutes and case law will control the recommendations of the prosecutor and options of the judge. However, when aggravating factors such as extremely young age of the child, especially cruel behavior, repeated assaults, an egregious abuse of trust, multiple forms of penetration, and other aggravating factors exist, the prosecutor should consider recommending an exceptional sentence beyond the standard range of punishment provided for the crime.

2. The Treatment Issue

There is very little agreement or data on the long-range effectiveness of treatment for child abusers, especially sex offenders. However, treatment obviously aims to rehabilitate the offender, teaching ways to control and monitor abusive behavior and thus ensuring that the community will be safe from future crimes the defendant might commit. The therapeutic community is devoting increasing attention to developing effective treatment programs, and judges are routinely ordering defendants convicted of sexual abuse crimes to complete therapy. It is therefore important for prosecutors to become educated about treatment options in their jurisdictions. Inpatient treatment programs are available in some prison systems. Normally available only for the most serious offenders, these programs typically evaluate a defendant before accepting him.

Although some treatment programs have shown promise by reducing the recidivism rates of sexual offenders, the longer offenders are followed, the higher the percentage of recidivism. (Prentky, R. A., et al. [1997]. Recidivism rates among child molesters and rapists: A methodological analysis. *Law and Human Behavior*, *21*, 635 [finding that of child molesters followed over a 25-year period, 32% committed new offenses].) The authors note that "child molesters are at risk to reoffend sexually throughout their lives" (*Id*. p. 652). It is likely that the actual rates of recidivism are much higher, since many offenses are never reported. Experts are reaching consensus that among child molesters, the number of victims and offenses, the number of different paraphilias or aberrational sexual interests, and the degree to which children are the preferred sexual partner for the defendant are the highest risk factors for future abuse.

More often, the prosecutor will be faced with a decision about the defendant's entry into a community outpatient treatment program. While increasing numbers of therapists are offering such treatment, the prosecutor should try to determine whether these therapists are truly qualified before endorsing them. There are generally no special licenses or certifications qualifying therapists to treat child abusers, especially sex offenders, and prosecutors should not assume that all psychiatrists, psychologists, or counselors have special expertise in this area. Note, however, that some states have statutory certification requirements for sex offender treatment providers. (See, e.g., Wash. Rev. Code § 18.155.010, Colo Rev. Stat. § 16–11.7–105, Minn. Stat. § 241.67, Tex. Rev. Civ. Stat. Ann. art. 4413[51].) Review the therapist's approach and practical experience, and ensure that those offering this treatment recognize their obligation to the community as well as to the offender. (For more information, see O'Connell, M. A., et al. [1990]. *Working with sex offenders: Guidelines for therapist selection.* Newbury Park, CA: Sage; Jensen, S. H., & Jewell, C. A. [1988]. The sex offender experts. *Prosecutor, 22,* 13.)

a. The evaluation of treatment amenability. Before recommending that a defendant enter therapy as a sentencing condition, the prosecutor should require the therapist to do a thorough written evaluation of the defendant's amenability to treatment. In order to avoid a potential conflict of interest, some jurisdictions require that an experienced and independent evaluator, and not the treating therapist, conduct a psychological or psychiatric evaluation. A good evaluation will be objective and include the following components.

• *An Accurate Description of the Offense.* While the therapist should present the defendant's perspective of the crime, it is important that the description not be confined solely to the defendant's version. The victim's statement and other available information such as police reports and reports from the victim's therapist should be reflected so the therapist has a full perspective of the crime. The evaluation should indicate the degree to which the defendant accepts responsibility for the crime(s) and whether he shows signs of remorse.

• *A Description of the Defendant's History.* This review includes the defendant's medical, psychiatric, and treatment history and military, vocational, educational, and criminal background. When a sex offense is involved, other instances of abusive behavior by the defendant should be described, with particular attention to other sexually deviant, violent, or abnormal behavior. A description of the defendant's social, marital, and family history is also important. In cases of physical abuse and homicide, ascertain whether the acts for which the defendant was convicted follow a pattern of abusive behavior toward children. A recommendation for sentencing may vary depending upon whether the defendant is a life-long abuser or a caregiver who apparently acted criminally on an isolated occasion.

• *Description of Tests and Results.* Different therapists use different measures to assist in evaluating a defendant's amenability to treatment. Some of these include personality assessments, psychological instruments such as the MMPI, polygraph examinations, and the penile plethysmograph. The penile plethysmograph is a physiological recorder that records changes in the circumference of the penis through a sensor attached to it. The male defendant is presented with different audiovisual sexual stimuli, and his penile erection response is recorded to determine the degree of arousal from deviant and appropriate sexual behavior. Not all men respond to the plethysmograph, and it should be used only in conjunction with other evaluation tools and by someone with training and experience in its operation. In many cases, the results from the plethysmograph will help the therapist understand a defendant's arousal pattern, and the results are not generally admissible as evidence in court. Treatment experts agree that no single tool can reliably evaluate a child abuser and his amenability to treatment. The most effective programs rely on a variety of mechanisms to reach the most informed evaluation.

• *Conclusions and Recommendations.* A good evaluation should end by spelling out a defendant's amenability to treatment, the danger posed to the community at large, and the treatment plan proposed if the defendant is ordered to participate in community-based treatment. Pay attention to the therapeutic methods proposed for the defendant. Common components of plans include behavior modification therapy, cognitive restructuring therapy, group therapy, individual therapy, anger management, relapse prevention, use of the polygraph and plethysmograph to monitor a defendant's compliance and progress, restrictions on the defendant's use of alcohol or drugs, restrictions on contact with the victim and/or other children, the use of "chemical castration" (depo-provera), regular reports to the prosecutor and court by the therapist, and immediate notice to the court and prosecutor of any violations of treatment conditions by the defendant. The specific mode of therapy depends on the defendant's needs. The prosecutor should not support the defendant's participation in treatment with a therapist who is unwilling to provide regular written progress reports or immediate reports about violations.

b. The background of the treatment provider. Before endorsing a therapist as acceptable to the State, a prosecutor must know as much as possible about her credentials and background. The prosecutor should use the same approach to evaluate treatment providers as used with trial experts. Be alert for therapists who have been fired from prior positions or who have criminal records. Try to obtain prior evaluations of the defendant or suggest the court seek copies of prior evaluations before imposing sentence. Some defendants shop for therapists until they find one who will do a favorable evaluation. While treatment specialists may disagree in their conclusions, a reputable therapist is interested in knowing what the defendant said to prior evaluators.

If there is no qualified therapist or outpatient program in your community, encourage local mental health professionals to consult with outside experts. It is a good idea to consult with prosecutors in nearby communities to become educated on these issues. Be aware of other expert resources. Guidance on offender treatment is also available from national organizations and professional publications. (See O'Connell, M. A., et al. [1990]. *Working with sex offenders: Guidelines for therapist selection.* Newbury Park, CA: Sage; Jensen, S. H., & Jewell, C. A. [1988]. The sex offender experts. *The Prosecutor, 22,* 13; McGovern, K., & Peters, J. [1988]. Guidelines for assessing sex offenders. In L. Walker [Ed.], *Handbook of sexual abuse of children* [pp. 216]. New York: Springer.) The Association for Treatment of Sexual Abusers (ATSA), P.O. Box 866, Lake Oswego, Oregon 97034–0140, has developed ethical principles to serve as guidelines for professionals working in sex offender treatment and maintains an ethics committee to deal with violations.

3. Other Conditions of the Sentence

In addition to requiring incarceration and/or treatment for a defendant, other conditions are often appropriate. It is always a good policy to require the defendant to pay restitution for the victim's medical or counseling expenses. Also, as a condition of sentence, the court usually can and should prohibit or restrict the defendant's contact with the victim, additional children who may be at risk, and other persons such as witnesses. In an intrafamilial abuse case, emphasize that after the sentence expires in criminal court, it will be up to the family court to assess whether the defendant may have contact with the victim. The possibility of future contact may affect the victim's wishes concerning the length and conditions of the defendant's sentence.

If the offender's crimes involved the use of alcohol or drugs, the court should prohibit the defendant's use of these substances and require random urinalysis, Antabuse, or blood tests. Completion of a substance abuse treatment program might also be a requirement. If the defendant is involved in a dependency or family court proceeding regarding the victim, cooperation with family court orders and the social services department can be mandated as a condition. With a recommendation of a suspended or deferred sentence and a period of probation, the defendant should be subject to regular supervision by a probation officer. Depending on the case and the defendant's financial resources, consider recommending that the defendant pay a fine (possibly to child abuse prevention and victim support efforts or to a fund established to provide the victim with treatment and educational funds), court costs (including the filing fee, witness fees, expert witness fees, subpoena service fees), and in some jurisdictions, reimbursement based upon ability toward the cost of the court-appointed attorney.

Any conditions, whether part of a plea negotiation or a sentence fashioned by the court, are effective only if the defendant actually complies with them. Take an active part in checking with the defendant's parole or probation officer to ensure the defendant is following sentence conditions. Request that the parole or probation officer forward regular reports from the defendant's therapist to the court, the defense attorney, and to the prosecution. If the defendant violates probation, especially ceasing treatment or living in a home with children, a violation hearing should be requested before the judge who originally sentenced the defendant. If a violation is found, request immediate punitive measures. Ensure that the victim's family understands the importance of promptly reporting any violations of the sentence conditions. The parole or probation officer, the judge, and the prosecutor should all receive notification of the violations.

a. The involvement of others in the sentencing process. Victims and their families should receive prior notice of the defendant's sentencing date. Encourage them to attend, if they wish, and to communicate the impact of the defendant's crimes on their lives. Victim advocates, therapists, police investigators, and others affected by the defendant's crimes should also be notified and given the opportunity for input. Knowing that others are interested in the case's resolution and hearing additional input should help the judge reach a more sensitive and informed decision. The use of a victim impact statement allows victims to communicate the impact of the crime directly to the judge for consideration at sentencing. Victim-witness advocates can assist victims in preparing these statements. A less formal yet effective alternative to a victim impact statement is a letter from the victim and the family to the court prior to sentencing.

Victim impact information should, if possible, also be provided to the person preparing a presentence report or investigation. These reports are critical, not only to the sentencing judge but to prison, probation, and parole officials and judges in subsequent proceedings, since they generally describe the crime(s) as well as the defendant's personal, educational, social, employment, and criminal history. Prosecutors should provide information to the author of the presentence report to ensure a balanced portrayal of the defendant and crimes. Many prosecutor's offices give the agency responsible for preparing the presentence report full access to their files.

Prior to sentencing, let the victim and the family know what to expect, including the process, the judge's options, and the maximum possible sentence, to avoid misunderstandings. If the victim is present at the sentencing, the resolution of the case should be apparent, although there may still be questions that need to be answered.

Table III.7   Statutes Addressing Victim Impact Statements

Alabama	ALA. CODE §§ 15–23–72(2)(c) to -.74
Alaska	ALASKA STAT. § 12.55.022
Arizona	ARIZ. REV. STAT. § 13–4424 to -703
Arkansas	ARK CODE ANN. § 16–90–1112
California	CAL. PENAL CODE § 679.02
Colorado	COLO. REV. STAT. § 24–4.1–302.5(1)(g)
Connecticut	CONN. GEN. STAT. §§ 54–91c, -220(a)
Delaware	DEL. CODE ANN. tit. 11, §§ 4331, 9415
District of Columbia	D.C. CODE § 23–1904
Florida	FLA. STAT. § 921.43
Georgia	GA. CODE ANN. § 17–10–1.2
Idaho	IDAHO CODE § 19–5306
Illinois	725 ILL. COMP. STAT. ANN. 115/3
Indiana	IND. CODE § 35–35–3-5
Iowa	IOWA CODE 915.21, -.26
Kentucky	KY. REV. STAT. ANN. § 421.520
Louisiana	LA. REV. STAT. § 46:1844
	LA. CHILDREN'S CODE ANN. art. 890(A)(2)
Maryland	MD. CRIM. PROC. ANN. CODE § 11–402 to -403
Massachusetts	MASS. GEN. LAWS. ch. 258B, § 3(p)
Michigan	MICH. COMP. LAWS § 780.763 to -765, -.823 to -.825
Minnesota	MINN. STAT. § 611A.038
Mississippi	MISS. CODE ANN. §§ 99–19–151 to -161
Missouri	MO. REV. STAT. § 217.762
Montana	MONT. CODE ANN. § 46–18–112
Nevada	NEV. REV. STAT. § 176.015
New Hampshire	N.H. REV. STAT. ANN. § 21-M:8-k
New Jersey	N.J. REV. STAT. § 2C:44–6
	N.J. REV. STAT. § 52:4B-36
New Mexico	N.M. STAT. ANN. § 31–26–4
North Carolina	N.C. GEN. STAT. § 15A-825, -832
North Dakota	N.D. CENT. CODE § 12.1–34–02
New York	N.Y. CRIM. PROC. LAW § 440.50
Ohio	OHIO REV. CODE § 2929.14, 2947.051
Oklahoma	OKLA. STAT. § 215.33
Oregon	OR. REV. STAT. § 137.013
Pennsylvania	18 PA. CONS. STAT. ANN. § 11.201(5)
Rhode Island	R.I. GEN. LAWS § 12–28–4
South Carolina	S.C. CODE ANN. § 16–3-1515, -1535
South Dakota	S.D. CODIFIED LAWS § 23A-28C-1
Tennessee	TENN. CODE ANN. § 40–38–201 to -208
Texas	TEX. CODE CRIM. PROC. ANN., art. 56.03
	TEX. FAM. CODE ANN. § 57.02 to .03
Utah	UTAH CODE ANN. § 64–13–20
Vermont	VT. STAT. ANN. tit. 13, § 5321
Virginia	VA. CODE ANN. § 19.2–11.01
Washington	WASH. REV. CODE § 7.69.030(13)
West Virginia	W. VA. CODE § 61–11A-2, -3
Wyoming	WYO. STAT. § 7–21–103
U.S. Code	18 U.S.C. § 3509(f)

NOTE: This table includes all legislation passed through March 2002, as verified through Lexis Nexis.

A victim who is not present at the proceeding should be advised of the sentence and any relevant conditions.

   b. Countering common defense arguments. Certain defense arguments are common at sentencing in child abuse cases. The following list summarizes some of those arguments with ideas for responses. New arguments and effective responses should be noted for future reference in sentencing presentations.

Argument. The defendant should not be sent to jail because he will lose his job and be unable to support his family.

Response. Work release may be an option that will allow the defendant to continue working and earning a living. Even if work release is not available, this was a consequence the defendant brought on himself when he committed his crimes and is no different from the consequences of other serious criminal behavior. If the victim of his crimes is within the family, does the defendant's financial support outweigh the risk to the victim? Most criminal defendants have families that suffer when the defendant is incarcerated. The defendant should not be exempted from a jail sentence simply because he chose someone within the family as his victim.

Argument. This was only a one-time incident and it will not happen again. The defendant does not need treatment.

Response. This argument asks the court to ignore extensive research and experience pointing to the prevalence of recidivism, especially for untreated offenders. Without an evaluation by a competent therapist, the court should not take the risk that the defendant will not victimize again.
   Research indicates that although many child molesters escape detection and intervention by the criminal justice system for many years, the first time an offender is arrested and prosecuted is rarely the first time that he has ever acted on sexual desires for children. Most investigations disclose some information from other family members, other children, neighbors, and others that there has been a pattern of abuse over a long period of time. Each act of molestation is a separate crime, which means that even if the defendant has had only one victim, his crime "spree" was much more egregious than most burglars' or robbers'. Society should not reward the defendant for avoiding detection after his first offenses.

Argument. The defendant is an upstanding citizen, a successful professional, a respected community leader and therefore should not be treated like a common criminal.

Response. Someone of the defendant's background and advantages should have fewer excuses for engaging in behavior that he certainly knew was wrong. Further, the defendant betrayed the public's trust by committing the crime. The wealth or status of the defendant does not alter the amount of trauma suffered by the victim.

(Continued)

(Continued)

Although the defendant may not look or act like most people's concept of a common criminal, the effect of his behavior on the victim and on society is actually more egregious, more reprehensible, less excusable, and more deserving of incarceration and punishment than many who commit common crimes. The fact that the defendant led a dual life, leading people to think he was beyond reproach, is an aggravating factor.

Argument. This offense is a family matter and should not be treated as a crime.

Response. Assaulting a child is a crime: Children are not property or objects to be used for the pleasure of adult caregivers. Family offenses are even more devastating to the child because of the violation of trust and resulting confusion inherent in such crimes.

Argument. If the defendant is punished, the child will feel guilty.

Response. It can be made clear by the judge and others that the child was not at fault. Children are generally taught that when people do wrong, punishment results. If the defendant is not punished, the child's interpretation is likely to be that the defendant did not really do anything bad, that the child was at fault, and that the defendant's actions were O.K.

Argument. The defendant has already suffered enough by having lost his job, his family, the respect of others, and many other consequences.

Response. Such consequences are the common result of a conviction for criminal acts. Criminal sanctions are society's way of communicating disapproval for violations of the law. The defendant committed the crime and must be held accountable for his actions. Moreover, his victim's suffering is likely to continue for life.

Argument. The defendant cannot afford to pay for therapy, restitution, court costs, and the other costs of the sentence.

Response. These costs are the defendant's responsibility and no one else's. Some treatment agencies and providers operate on a sliding scale designed to accommodate differing abilities to pay. It is presumed that some hardship will be imposed by criminal financial sanctions. The defendant may have to make some sacrifices in order to pay these obligations, but that is an intended consequence of requiring him to assume this responsibility.

Argument. The defendant was drunk or under the influence of drugs. He would never even think of committing a sexual act against a child if his inhibitions were not lowered. All he really needs is substance abuse treatment in an outpatient program.

Response. Research shows that alcohol or drug abuse alone does not cause a person to be sexually attracted to children, although it may be true that inhibitions are lowered. Committing a sexual offense against a child while intoxicated is

(Continued)

(Continued)

still motivated by the aberrational interest in sex with a child. (See Salter, A. C. [1995]. *Transforming trauma: A guide to understanding and treating adult survivors of child abuse* [pp. 25, 60–61]. Thousand Oaks, CA: Sage.) Voluntary intoxication does not excuse sexual abuse of a child.

Argument. The defendant is mentally ill and needs treatment; therefore, he should not be punished.

Response. Many criminals have mental health problems and need treatment. Punishment can give the defendant incentive to participate and succeed in treatment, and many therapists recognize imprisonment as a valid component of treatment.

Argument. The defendant was just disciplining the child, and the child's death/injury was an accident.

Response. The defendant took advantage of the child's vulnerability in size, strength, and dependence. The extent of the child's injuries (show photographs) are not indicative of reasonable discipline. In addition, if the victim of this assault were an adult, there would be no question about this behavior. The defendant's responsibility should not be minimized simply because the victim was a child.

Argument. The defendant's religious/cultural beliefs call for parents to discipline or forgo medical care for their children in this manner.

Response. Religious belief allows parents to make martyrs of themselves but not of their children.

Argument. The defendant's failure to provide a safe supervised environment or sufficient food/medical care for the child was caused by ignorance or poverty.

Response (if applicable). The defendant was warned repeatedly that she was endangering the child and was offered services but instead concealed her neglect of the victim's needs.

Alternate response. If we accept poverty as an excuse, what we are really saying is that poor children are less entitled to justice and protection than rich children.

Argument. The defendant suffers from the disease of addiction and could not control her behavior.

Response. The defendant had various opportunities to get help for her drug problem. The defendant chose to use drugs or alcohol. Her choice resulted in harm to a child and cannot excuse her from responsibility.

(Continued)

(Continued)

Argument. The defendant has no prior criminal record. This is her first offense.

Response. The defendant molested the victim over the course of several months. Each act was a separate crime. The defendant engaged in a crime spree more egregious than most burglars' or rapists'. Society should not reward the defendant for avoiding detection and not getting caught after the first incident.

Argument. The defendant was abused as a child and so is less culpable.

Response. Accepting this as an excuse implies that the cycle of abusive behavior automatically continues generation after generation. A strong message to the defendant and the community is necessary to stop this cycle. Further, the vast majority of victims do *not* become offenders.

Argument. The victim was not damaged by the sexual abuse, according to his current therapist. Little kids are flexible and get over things easily. He certainly did not understand the significance of the sexual abuse.

Response. The current impact of the abuse is not a very good predictor of what the long-term impact might be. Although it is generally true that young children bounce back from trauma, abuse is more than that, as it involves betrayal by a trusted and loved adult. The defendant should be responsible for any future adverse effects, such as paying for future therapy for the victim.

4. Release Pending Appeal

Once the defendant has been convicted and sentenced, it is not uncommon to face a motion for release pending an appeal. This occurs most often when there has been a jury verdict finding the defendant guilty and the defense contends that errors during trial warrant reversal. It is important that prosecutors vigorously oppose a defendant's release pending appeal for several reasons. Once the defendant has been convicted, there is no longer an entitlement to the presumption of innocence and the right to bail. The conviction should be presumed valid unless and until an appellate court reverses it. This is particularly true when the trial judge has heard the defendant's postverdict motions and has found that no reversal of the conviction is warranted. If the defendant is released while the appeal is taking place, accountability will be further delayed, and the offender will have an opportunity to reoffend and to flee, since there is no way, short of 24-hour monitoring, to guarantee otherwise.

If the judge deems it appropriate to release the defendant despite objections, several conditions should be suggested. The first of these is an appearance bond to guarantee the defendant's reappearance before the court once the appeal has concluded. If the conviction is affirmed, it should be the defendant's responsibility to report to serve the sentence as soon as the appellate court's judgment is final. Other conditions to decrease the risk posed by the defendant might include supervision and regular reporting to someone such as a probation officer, participation in treatment, and restrictions on the defendant's contact with the victim, witnesses, and other children.

B. Conclusion

The sentencing stage of the case is important for a number of reasons. It is usually the final proceeding in which the victim and the victim's family will have input, and it should bring some closure to a traumatic time in their lives. It is also the time for ultimate accountability for the perpetrator. It is an opportunity to fashion a punishment that is appropriate for the defendant's conduct. The sentencing outcome will send clear messages, intentional or unintentional, to the defendant, the victim, the victim's family, and the community at large. It is fundamental in any child abuse prosecution that the defendant's conduct be treated as a serious crime. Nowhere else is this more essential than at the punishment stage. The prosecutor should, therefore, always be prepared for the sentencing hearing, using it as an opportunity to educate and advocate.

The victim and the family should also be provided with any relevant information regarding the conditions of the sentence. For example, if the defendant has been sentenced to probation, the victim should know the probation officer's name and telephone number. If the defendant was sentenced to incarceration and will someday be eligible for parole, the victim should be provided with information making it possible to give input to the parole board prior to the defendant's release to parole supervision. The prosecutor should make it a practice to contact or write a letter to the parole board recounting any particularly horrific facts or what effect the defendant's actions had on the victim. This information should be useful to the parole board. A copy of this correspondence should be sent to the victim to help maintain a continued sense of security or, at the very least, the sense that there is still assistance and support available from the prosecutor's office.

Finally, a prosecutor should be knowledgeable about any referral resources or agencies available that may assist with the victim's physical, mental, or emotional recovery.

V. AN EVALUATION OF THE PROSECUTOR'S OFFICE BY THE VICTIM

As public servants, prosecutors need feedback from victims and their families. A simple evaluation form completed by the child, depending on age, or supportive family members can provide valuable information for improving the handling of child abuse cases (See Appendix III.14).

VI. RESOURCE LIST

A. Charging and Disposition

1. Generally

Arthur, L. G. (1986). Court procedures, sentencing and dispositions in child sexual abuse cases. In *Legal advocacy for children and youth: Reforms, trends, and contemporary issues* (p. 24). Chicago, IL: American Bar Association.

California District Attorneys Association, Uniform Crime Charging Standards. (1974).

Dawson, S. (1985). *Criminal charging and disposition standards of the office of the Snohomish County Prosecuting Attorney.* Washington: Snohomish County Prosecuting Attorney's Office.

Dinsmore, J. (1992). *Pregnant drug users: The debate over prosecution.* Alexandria, VA: American Prosecutors Research Institute.

National District Attorneys Association. (1991). *National prosecution standards* (2nd ed.). Alexandria, VA: National District Attorneys Association.

U.S. Department of Justice. (1980). Principles of federal prosecution. *Criminal Law Report, 27,* 3277.

Washington Association of Prosecuting Attorneys, Charging and Disposition Policies. (1980).

2. Religious Exemptions From Child Abuse Statutes

Horton, A. L., & Williamson, J. A. (1988). *Abuse and religion: When praying isn't enough.* Lexington, MA: D.C. Heath.

American Academy of Pediatrics (Committee on Bioethics). (1988). Religious exemptions from child abuse statutes. *Pediatrics, 81*(1), 169.

Brenneman, R. J. (1990). *Deadly blessings: Faith healing on trial.* Amherst, NY: Prometheus Books.

Bross, D. C. (1986). Court-ordered intervention on behalf of unborn children. *Children's Legal Rights Journal, 7*(2), 11.

Lanning, K. V. (1992). *Investigator's guide to allegations of "ritual" child abuse.* Alexandria, VA: National Center for the Analysis of Violent Crime.

B. Sex Offender Treatment

Barnard, G. W., et al. (1989). *The child molester: An integrated approach to evaluation and treatment.* New York: Brunner-Mazel.

Horton, A. L., et al. (1990). *The incest perpetrator: A family member no one wants to treat.* Newbury Park, CA: Sage.

Jensen, S. H., & Jewell, C. A. (1988). The sex offender experts. *The Prosecutor, 22*(2), 13.

Knopp, F. H. (1985). *Remedial intervention in adolescent sex offenses: Nine program descriptions* (Rev. ed.). Brighton, NY: Safer Society Press.

Knopp, F. H. (1984). *Retraining adult sex offenders: Methods and models.* Brighton, NY: Safer Society Press.

Knopp, F. H., et al. (1988). *Report on nationwide survey of juvenile and adult sex-offender treatment programs and models.* Brighton, NY: Safer Society Press.

Maletzky, B. M. (1991). *Treating the sexual offender.* Newbury Park, CA: Sage.

Mayer, A. (1988). *Sex offenders: Approaches to understanding and management.* Holmes Beach, FL: Learning Publications.

Mayer, A. (1985). *Sexual abuse: Causes, consequences and treatment of incestuous and pedophilic acts.* Holmes Beach, FL: Learning Publications.

McGovern, K., & Peters, J. (1988). Guidelines for assessing sex offenders. In L. E. A. Walker (Ed.), *Handbook on sexual abuse of children* (p. 216). New York: Springer.

O'Connell, M. A., et al. (1990). *Working with sex offenders: Guidelines for therapist selection.* Newbury Park, CA: Sage.

Prendergast, W. E. (1991). *Treating sex offenders in correctional institutions and outpatient clinics: A guide to clinical practice.* Binghamton, NY: Haworth Press.

Laws, R. D. (1989). *Relapse prevention with sex offenders.* New York: Guilford.

Salter, A. C. (1988). *Treating child sex offenders and victims: A practical guide.* Newbury Park, CA: Sage.

Sgroi, S. M. (1988). *Vulnerable populations: Evaluation and treatment of sexually abused children and adult survivors,* Vol. 1. New York: Lexington Books.

Sgroi, S. M. (1989). *Vulnerable populations: Sexual abuse treatment for children, adult survivors, offenders and persons with mental retardation,* Vol. 2. New York: Lexington Books.

Pre-Trial Motions

I. INTRODUCTION

Pre-trial motions are filed by the defense and prosecution in almost every criminal case. Ostensibly, these motions concern legal issues that must be decided prior to or during trial, but in many cases, particularly child abuse, the defense has tactical reasons such as wearing down the prosecutor with required responses, creating anxiety in child victims by subjecting them to repeated and/or confrontational pre-trial hearings, or fishing for information that might discredit the victim.

The prosecutor should use pre-trial motions to force the defense attorney to reveal the defense to be used at trial. Motions *in limine* are effective tools for preventing potentially harmful and irrelevant information from coming before the jury. Pre-trial motions may also allow prosecutors to ease the way for the victim at trial. It is important to be aware of potential defense and prosecution motions throughout the preparation of your case.

II. DISCOVERY

Discovery issues tend to be unique in child abuse cases because the investigation process involves other public agencies and systems such as foster care, social welfare, and child protective services. School records, juvenile court records, psychological and medical records, and many other sources of information may be sought in the discovery process. While these records often contain information helpful to the prosecution, prosecutors must also consider legitimate privacy rights of the victim.

Establish careful control over the discovery process but do not prevent properly discoverable information from being disclosed to the defense. If there is a question about the appropriateness of disclosure, retain the information until a court rules on the issue after a hearing at which both sides have the opportunity to present arguments.

A. Protecting Privacy of Victims

1. Addresses and Telephone Numbers

Protecting the rights of victims can start with something as simple as not disclosing the victim's address and telephone number to the defense. Although requirements vary as to what information must be turned over, most discovery statutes or rules of criminal procedure mandate that the prosecutor disclose the name and address of any witness who will be called to testify at a hearing or trial. However, these same rules often contain provisions precluding disclosure of the victim's address when circumstances suggest a risk of harm to the victim or when the victim is a child. Several states have statutes that address the privacy rights of child victims (see Table IV.3). (See also Victims of Child Abuse Act, 18 U.S.C. § 3509[d] [2002].) Still other jurisdictions have reached agreements with local media that they will not disclose identifying biographical information about child victims of sexual offenses.

Even in jurisdictions without protection for victims, many prosecutors are able to satisfy discovery obligations by making the witness *available* to the defense as opposed to disclosing the victim's current address and telephone. This is often done by indicating on the witness list that the victim can be contacted through the prosecutor, the victim-witness advocate, or some other person—a procedure that also makes it easier for the victim to consult with the prosecutor and child advocate regarding an interview with the defense, the location of the interview, and whether the prosecutor will be present during the interview.

2. Enlisting Police Cooperation

Protecting the victim from disclosure of personal information in the discovery process may require the cooperation of local law enforcement agencies. In many states, police reports are public documents. Personal information on the child victim thus may need to be kept separately from publicly available documents. Advise law enforcement agencies not to provide the defense or media with personal information on the victim unless ordered by the court or approved by the prosecutor handling the case. Some jurisdictions already do this routinely or include such provisions in written protocols on child abuse cases.

If your jurisdiction does not yet have such agreements, verify statutory requirements regarding accessibility to police reports. Since investigating agencies can normally determine the type of information contained in offense reports, their content can be regulated by agreement between the prosecutor and law enforcement agency.

3. Enlisting Child Protective Services (CPS) Cooperation

Defense attorneys or their investigators often contact CPS agencies directly for information, so protocols and agreements regarding release of information to the defense should also be sought with your local CPS agency. Speak with the CPS worker, the CPS supervisor, and/or the attorney who represents the CPS agency in your jurisdiction. You may wish to set up a procedure by which defense attorneys are referred to the CPS attorney if they contact the CPS agency directly. Again, no information should be given to defense attorneys, including the victim's whereabouts, unless required by law or the court. CPS should provide the prosecutor with copies of anything given to the defense. Following these guidelines will force defense counsel to seek discovery via proper channels—through you or through court-ordered disclosures—and you will not be caught off guard by CPS information obtained by the defense (see this chapter, Section II.B.7).

Any correspondence between the CPS attorney and the agency or social workers should be kept in a separate file marked "attorney-client correspondence." Many social workers unwittingly place attorney correspondence in the child's file, where the attorney for the parent perpetrator can access it. This is harmful not only to the civil child protection case but also to the criminal case if the correspondence contains trial strategies that may be applicable to both cases.

4. Enlisting Physician and Hospital Cooperation

Whether the victim was examined by a private physician or emergency room doctor, the defense may subpoena the physician or the hospital's custodian of records for the medical reports. Contact the physicians involved and voice your concern for the privacy of the victim. Reach agreement, preferably in a written protocol, about the procedure to be followed for release of medical records. For example, if your jurisdiction does not require release of the victim's telephone number, seek deletion of the telephone number from medical records before sending them to the defense attorney. *In camera* review of records prior to disclosure should be sought when they include arguably privileged information, and it might be appropriate to involve the victim's guardian *ad litem* or an appointed attorney to represent the victim's interests. These issues are best addressed by a multidisciplinary team. If you do not have an active team in your community, approach health care professionals directly. (See Appendix IV.10 for a sample order to produce a protective order issued on hospital staff for a videotaped forensic interview of a child victim.)

5. Enlisting Therapist Cooperation

Immediately upon receipt of a case, determine whether the victim is or has been in therapy. If so, contact the therapist to warn of the inevitable phone call from the defense. Be aware of confidentiality provisions in your state statutes and regulations governing therapeutic relationships. More likely than not, the therapist is well aware of confidentiality provisions. Remind the therapist, however, of your role and the procedures defense counsel must follow, and request notification of any information obtained by the defense (see this chapter, Section II.B.2).

6. Enlisting Child Advocacy Center Cooperation

Child victims are often interviewed by forensic interviewers in Child Advocacy Centers (CACs). Defense attorneys will often subpoena CAC records pertaining to the forensic interview. In particular, defense attorneys will seek a copy of any videotaped interview with the child. In the event of a subpoena, the CAC should immediately contact the prosecutor.

Although the prosecutor must allow defense counsel to view the videotape, under no circumstances should a copy of this tape be given to defense counsel. Defense attorneys have used these tapes in defense bar training courses, displayed them to the media, and have otherwise used copies to further embarrass or intimidate children.

In rare cases, a defense attorney may articulate a plausible reason for obtaining a copy of the videotape. The attorney may, for example, have a defense expert in another state who will need to have a copy mailed to him. In such cases, have the defense counsel sign a stipulation governing use of the tape and turn the stipulation into a court order. The order should provide that the tape will be used only in preparation of trial and that, after trial, the copy will be returned to the prosecutor. A sample motion and court order is contained in Appendix IV.10.

B. Defense Discovery Motions

1. *General Considerations*

A prosecutor's response to traditional defense discovery motions will be based on whether the jurisdiction makes discovery mandatory or discretionary. Many statutes and rules preclude discovery in certain areas if disclosure could result in substantial harm or embarrassment to other individuals.

Some jurisdictions require disclosure of materials only in the control of the prosecutor, while others require disclosure of information "within the possession, knowledge, or control" of the prosecutor. Prosecutors do not normally control school records, child protective records, juvenile court records, therapy records, or CAC records and should not seek such control. Once the records are made available to prosecutors, defense attorneys have a much stronger case for discovery.

You should request *in camera* examination of any records about which you have questions when it appears the court is going to order disclosure. A court's review of material to determine what is relevant is certainly better than a blanket disclosure of records that could expose irrelevant personal information to unwelcome defense scrutiny. For example, social service records containing information related to a child's abuse may include information about food stamp applications and other irrelevant material. (See *Pennsylvania v. Ritchie*, 480 U.S. 39 [1987] [submitting state child protective agency's files to trial judge for *in camera* review sufficiently protects defendant's right to a fair trial].)

When materials are provided to the defense during discovery, seek restrictions on the defense attorney's dissemination of these materials. Consider asking the court for a protective order prohibiting the defense attorney's (1) disclosure of witness identities, (2) disclosure of the content of witnesses' statements, and (3) duplication of discovery materials. Alternatively, require the defense attorney to sign an agreement not to duplicate discovery material or allow it out of his or her office. If discovery materials are given to the defense without restriction, they are likely to be copied for the defendant, who may have them in jail or his home, destroying the security of this sometimes sensitive material.

Finally, discovery provided to the defense should be accompanied by a documenting letter with a copy placed in the prosecutor's file. Each page of discovery should be numbered so that there can be no dispute later regarding what was turned over and when.

Keep in mind that even when the court orders disclosure of information, it is not automatically admissible at trial. File motions *in limine* to exclude irrelevant, prejudicial (i.e., its probative value is substantially outweighed by the danger of unfair prejudice to the fact-finding process), or otherwise inappropriate evidence.

2. Mental Health Records

Psychological, psychiatric, or other therapeutic records may include information concerning prior events as well as information concerning treatment of the victim after the abuse. Evaluations generally include social history information and personal data about the daily life and problems of the child for treatment purposes. Much of this information has no relevance to the trial of a criminal case.

a. Existence of privileges. In most jurisdictions, the doctor-patient privilege (and in some jurisdictions the social worker–client privilege) may preclude the defense from obtaining some or all of these records through the discovery process. In addition, some state legislatures have created a rape counselor–victim privilege. (See, e.g., Cal. Evid. Code §§ 1037 to 1037.7 [2001]; Mass Gen. Laws Ann. Ch. 233, § 20k [2002].) Statutes defining privileges will usually dictate the appropriate response to a defense motion for discovery in this area, but there is often confusion and sometimes reluctance by the court to deny the defense access to these records in child abuse cases.

Most privilege statutes are designed to allow for effective diagnosis and treatment by encouraging a patient to disclose information to a doctor or therapist without fear of public exposure. Statutes usually state the circumstances under which the privilege does not apply. An express or implied waiver by the patient or client makes the privilege inapplicable. Despite the arguable existence of privilege, physicians are often required to report matters affecting public health and safety, including suspected child abuse and incidence of venereal disease. (See Cal. Penal Code § 11166 [2001]; Mich. Comp. Laws Ann. § 722.631 [Supp. 2001]; [1985]. Comment: Developments in the law: Privileged communications. *Harvard Law Review, 98,* 1450, 1538.)

b. Defense assertion of confrontation rights. A common defense argument in support of a motion to disclose privileged information is that the defendant's right of confrontation overrides any privilege. The right of cross-examination, however, is not absolute. (See *Chambers v. Mississippi,* 410 U.S. 284 [1973].) The prosecutor can point out that privilege statutes reflect a strong public policy entitling certain communications to be kept confidential. This policy is especially valid when it concerns sexual assault victims. Argue to the court that routine overriding of these privileges would place a sexual assault victim in the untenable position of choosing between testifying against her assailant or retaining her right of confidentiality. Consider asking the court to appoint counsel, a child advocate, or guardian *ad litem* immediately to represent the child's interests and argue against the disclosure of such records. (See *State v. S.H.,* 465 N.W.2d 238 [Wis. Ct. App. 1990] [psychologist-patient privilege asserted by guardian *ad litem* on behalf of children superseded defendant's authorization as parent for release of children's treatment records].)

If the request for a child advocate is denied, you will have to prepare arguments to avoid disclosure. Before responding to the defense motion for disclosure of treatment records, make sure the author of the records is actually covered by a statutory privilege. For example, records of a rape crisis center volunteer who is not a certified social worker may not be privileged under a social worker privilege statute. (See, e.g., *People v. Bridges*, 538 N.Y.S.2d 701 [Crim. Ct. 1989].) If a member of the clergy counsels the victim, a therapist's privilege may not apply; a clergy member's privilege, however, may prevent the defense attorney's access to the information.

If the author of the records is covered by a privilege, check your jurisdiction's case law to see whether that privilege has been found absolute despite a defendant's due process claim. Some jurisdictions have found certain privileges absolute and denied even an *in camera* review by the judge. (See *Commonwealth v. Smith*, 606 A.2d 939 [Pa. Super. Ct. 1992] [statutorily privileged confidential psychotherapeutic records are subject to absolute privilege and defendant's rights of confrontation is not violated by denial of access to those records]; *State v. Reynolds*, 792 P.2d 1111 [Mont. 1990] [victim's psychotherapeutic records protected from disclosure by unqualified privilege for confidential communications between psychologist and client]; see also *Dill v. People*, 927 P.2d 1315 [Supreme Ct. of Colo. 1996].) This is particularly true if

1. No issue regarding the victim's postassault mental condition is raised by the prosecutor or victim. (See *People v. Pressley*, 804 P.2d 226 [Colo. Ct. App. 1990].)

2. Defense counsel cannot show that the victim's records would provide a source of impeachment. (See *People v. Foggy*, 521 N.E.2d 86 [Ill.], *cert. denied*, 486 U.S. 1047 [1988]; *People v. District Court*, 719 P.2d 722 [Colo. 1986].)

Keep in mind that the usual purpose behind defense discovery motions is to find something in the records that can be used to embarrass or discredit the victim, regardless of its relationship to the abuse. In most instances, the defense attorney has no idea whether the records contain any relevant information and is simply "fishing." Prosecutors faced with such motions should insist that defense attorneys provide the court with facts establishing a basis for believing the records contain relevant information. If the defense subpoenas privileged material, the subpoena usually directs the records be sent to the court under seal. You should contact the record holder and ensure that "courtesy copies" are not sent to the defense at their request. (See Appendix IV.11 for a sample memorandum in opposition to defendant's motion to compel psychological evaluation and disclosure of private records.)

c. Request for *in camera* review. Most courts confronted with a defense motion for statutorily protected records will conduct an *in camera* hearing to determine if any information should be disclosed to the defense. (See *People v. Stanaway*, 446 Mich. 643 [1994]; *Commonwealth v. Two Juveniles*, 491 N.E.2d 234 [Mass. 1986] [defendant must have a legitimate need to get *in camera* review].) In practice, courts will often conduct the *in camera* hearing without a showing by defense counsel that material information is contained in the records. Upon review, the court may disclose information to defense counsel and the prosecutor. Prior to disclosure, ask the judge to identify the subject of information to be disclosed; then argue against disclosure if the information is not material (e.g., would not change the outcome at trial) or is inadmissible (e.g., violates a rape shield statute). (See *Pennsylvania v. Ritchie*, 480 U.S. 39, 58 [1987]; see also *State v. Scheffelman*, 820 P.2d 1293 [Mont. 1991] [defense may examine psychological records after *in camera* examination by court if state introduces testimony from qualified expert that behavior of child victim was consistent with abuse; defense may have access to only those records that show or tend to show other reasons for such symptoms or behaviors].)

A minority of courts require direct disclosure of records to the defense attorney when there is no explicit privilege outlined by the legislature. (See *Commonwealth v. Lloyd*, 567 A.2d 1357 [Pa. 1989].) Other courts allow the defense to have complete access to the records on the grounds that the privilege is only a qualified one that must give way to the defendant's rights to confrontation. (*See Commonwealth v. Stockhammer*, 570 N.E.2d 992 [Mass. 1991]; see also *Commonwealth v. Sheehan*, 435 Mass. 183 [2001].) If defense counsel makes these arguments, be prepared to show that unfettered disclosure is the minority view and that an *in camera* inspection more equitably balances the interests of the victim and the defendant.

If the judge allows defense counsel to look at the entire record, ask the judge to require that (1) you and the defense attorney remain in the courtroom until the review is completed, (2) the defense attorney refrain from photocopying or removing any of the documents, and (3) the defense attorney return the records to the judge before leaving the courtroom. Such instructions will ensure some vestige of confidentiality.

d. When to disclose. Quite often, treatment records will contain valuable evidence that the prosecutor will want to introduce at trial. These records should then be made available to the defense as part of discovery. This is particularly true if the child is exhibiting changes in behavior thought to be due to the abuse. Normally, someone other than the child's therapist, including the child's mother, guardian, or foster parent, will also have seen these behaviors. They can be called as witnesses and provide the foundation for expert testimony if desired. (See Chapter V, Section IV.E. regarding expert psychological testimony.)

Inculpatory and exculpatory statements made by the defendant and known to the prosecutor must usually be disclosed, including statements made to a therapist. Whether those statements will be considered privileged and inadmissible at trial is a separate issue. In some jurisdictions, disclosure may be accomplished simply by sending a letter to defense counsel summarizing the substance of the statement, the date the statement was made, and the identity of the person to whom it was made. Make sure to disclose inculpatory statements well in advance of trial to preclude any requests for postponement by the defense due to surprise.

Obviously, if the prosecutor is aware that any records actually do contain exculpatory information (e.g., indications that the child told the therapist she lied or was mistaken about the identity of her assailant), the prosecutor must expeditiously disclose this information to the defense. A prosecutor's responsibility is to seek justice while protecting the legitimate privacy rights of the victim.

3. School Records

Privileges are rarely attached to school records. (But see 20 U.S.C. § 1232[g] [2002] [recognizing right of privacy in children's school records].) School records are not normally within the control of the prosecutor unless for some reason they have specifically been made a part of the case. The prosecutor is thus under no obligation to obtain them for the defense. The defense may nonetheless seek school records for information concerning the child's grades or behavior problems occurring at school and to locate bad character witnesses to testify on issues such as the victim's reputation for truthfulness.

If the child is very young, the defense often argues that school records are needed to assess competency to testify. Another argument used to gain access to school or psychological records is that refusal to turn over relevant information relating to the child's developmental level would deny the defendant effective assistance of counsel, since his lawyer would be unable to communicate effectively with the child. Many courts are reluctant to deny requests couched in these terms. Request that judges who consider disclosure based on this reasoning review the records *in camera* and allow the defense access only to those portions relating directly to competency or developmental and communication issues. (But see *Zaal v. State*, 602 A.2d 1247 [Md. 1992] [defense counsel is entitled to review school records; court's *in camera* review of school records is insufficient].) If the court allows defense counsel access to the school records, make sure the access is "controlled"; request the judge's or school board attorney's presence during defense counsel's review of the records and request a ban on photocopies.

Since the defense does not have to go through the prosecutor to acquire school records, they may attempt to obtain them using a subpoena *duces tecum* or its equivalent. When the prosecutor or school opposes disclosure, a court hearing should be held. Be aware of any defense attempts to get such records. If you know of records they have already obtained, make sure you receive copies. Otherwise you may find yourself in the unpleasant position of being surprised with new information during the trial.

On occasion, the judge (perhaps in spite of contrary discovery rules or statutory privileges) may indicate that unless certain records are disclosed, the child or family members will have to be produced for a pre-trial defense interview or a pre-trial hearing. If this occurs, assess which alternative—disclosure of records or production of the witness for an interview or to testify—would be least intrusive to the child and most beneficial to the case. Since you should know the child and have some idea of the content of requested records, you should be able to make an educated determination. If the child witness is strong and fairly articulate, you may prefer a pre-trial interview or hearing instead of disclosure of school records.

4. Juvenile Records

Juvenile court records related to child victims and involving delinquency or criminal wrongdoing are more likely to be available to the prosecutor and thus discoverable by the defense. On the other hand, juvenile court records, because they deal with minors, are often accorded a degree of confidentiality. Find out the juvenile court administrator's position on the status of the court's records and explore applicable statutes or case law. Like any request for records of a child victim, consider court intervention before authorizing their release.

Be aware that the defense may cross-examine the victim concerning open juvenile criminal charges or prior juvenile convictions for which the victim is on probation. In *Davis v. Alaska* (415 U.S. 308 [1974]) the Court reasoned that such impeachment was probative to show the victim's possible reason for giving testimony "favorable to the prosecution." If defense counsel attempts to access juvenile records, present them with a computer printout of the victim's criminal record. That should obviate the need to see the juvenile record itself.

If the court allows the defense to see the juvenile record, make sure you review it too, and make appropriate motions *in limine* prior to trial. If the defense is trying to use these records to suggest the child is of bad character and therefore should not be believed, the evidence should not be admissible. (See Fed. R. Evid. 404[b].) Encourage the judge to reject such evidence unless it can be shown to have probative value outweighing its prejudicial impact.

If you are unsuccessful in convincing the court to prohibit this evidence, determine the best approach for dealing with its admission. For example, juvenile records may indicate the child was involved in an assault at school. Although such behavior alone has no rational connection to the reliability of a child's account of abuse, the trial judge may decide to allow its introduction as evidence. It might be wise in this case to bring up the subject yourself, rather than waiting for the defense to do so. In response to defense arguments demeaning the child because of the assault, acknowledge that assault and other acts of delinquency are often associated with troubled children who have been abused. You could further point out that the defense seems to suggest that a child who has been involved in an assault at school deserves less consideration and protection from abuse than other children.

5. Motions for Psychiatric or Psychological Examination of the Victim

Motions for psychological examinations of the victim occur frequently in child abuse cases, purportedly to determine the competency of the victim. Often the actual purpose is to harass the victim and seek evidence suggesting that the child has the ability or motivation to fabricate. These examinations are intrusive and constitute an extreme invasion of privacy. Since, in almost all cases, their purpose is to diminish the victim's credibility, oppose requests for examinations of this sort. The prosecution's standard response should be that the credibility of witnesses is a matter for the jury to consider and the competency of witnesses a matter for the judge to decide. Since requirements for testimonial competency are fairly straightforward legal requirements, the trial judge should be able to determine the child's competency without using experts or psychological examinations that could cause additional stress and trauma. (See Appendix IV.12 for sample brief in opposition to defendant's motion for psychological evaluation of child victim.)

Most states leave the granting or denial of a motion for psychological examination to the judge's discretion. However, at least four states prohibit, with certain exceptions, a court from ordering a sexual assault victim to undergo a psychological or psychiatric examination. (Ariz. Rev. Stat. Ann. § 13–4065 [2001]; Cal. Penal Code § 1112[2001]; Idaho Code § 19–3025 [2002]; Ill. Ann. Stat. Ch. 725, § 5/115–7.1 [2002].) The Arizona and California statutes both prohibit this kind of examination if requested for purposes of assessing the witness' credibility. California's law applies to any witness in a sexual assault prosecution, while Idaho's and Illinois's statutes apply only to the victim. The Arizona provision also pertains to victims of other child abuse–related crimes. Other states preclude courts from ordering psychiatric examinations of sexual abuse victims because there is no constitutional, statutory, or common law authority allowing for such an order. (See, e.g., *State v. Gabrielson*, 464 N.W.2d 434 [Iowa 1990]; see also *State v. Lanford*, 764 S.W.2d 593 [Tex. Ct. App. 1989]; *State v. Robinson*, 835 S.W.2d 303 [Mo. 1992].)

In *People v. Lucero* (724 P.2d 1374 [Colo. Ct. App. 1986]), the defense argued that an examination of the child victim was necessary to determine her competency. The defendant made an offer of proof that the child was currently residing at the state hospital and had been found incompetent to testify in a related case. The trial court denied the motion. The Colorado Court of Appeals noted that, despite the showing made by the defendant, the trial court had balanced all pertinent factors and had not abused its discretion in denying the motion. This attitude is shared by other state courts that indicate the trial judge must balance possible emotional trauma, embarrassment, or intimidation of the victim against the likelihood of the examination producing relevant evidence.

In most jurisdictions, the defense must show a "compelling reason" to force psychiatric evaluation of the child victim—a difficult standard for the defense. (See *People v. Chard*, 808 P.2d 351 [Colo.], *cert. denied*, 112 S. Ct. 186 [1991]; *People v. Passenger*, 572 N.Y.S.2d 972 [App. Div. 1991]; *Newsome v. State*, 782 P.2d 689 [Alaska Ct. App. 1989]; *State v. Ballard*, 714 S.W.2d 284 [Tenn. Crim. App. 1986].) The court should require more than "mere allegations of a disorder or an unusual condition bearing upon competence" (*State v. R.W.*, 514 A.2d 1287, 1292 [N.J. 1986]). (See also *United States v. DeNoyer*, 811 F.2d 436 [8th Cir. 1987] [defense request to determine victim's "mental state" found insufficient]; *People v. Visgar*, 457 N.E.2d 1343 [Ill. App. Ct. 1983] [child's past stay in psychiatric ward and previous allegations of sexual misconduct by defendant not evidence of compelling need]; *Holder v. State*, 396 N.E.2d 112 [Ind. 1979] [child victim's use of slang terms for genitals and sexual relations found insufficient]; *People v. King*, 581 P.2d 739 [Colo. Ct. App. 1978] [defendant's affidavit alleging victim to be "mentally immature," with vivid imagination and subject to flights of fancy and sexual fantasies found insufficient].)

The court should similarly deny a request for a psychological exam when the defense is simply attempting to explore the victim's motive to fabricate. (See *State v. Tharp*, 372 N.W.2d 280 [Iowa Ct. App. 1985] [defendant failed to demonstrate necessity for exam by alleging victim's hostility toward defendant].) The victim's youth, the seriousness of the charges involved, and the element of surprise in the proposed exam have also not been found "compelling." (See *State v. Ballard*, 714 S.W.2d 284 [Tenn. Crim. App. 1986].) The defense's assertion that the exam is needed to provide a foundation for challenging the victim's credibility on the stand or preparing for cross-examination of prosecution witnesses is similarly insufficient. (See *Gale v. State*, 792 P.2d 570 [Wyo. 1990].)

If the compelling reason given by the defense merely states that the child is mentally unstable, hallucinating, or delusional, without providing facts supporting these conclusions, the court should deny the request. In *People v. Chard* (808 P.2d 351 [Colo.], *cert. denied*, 112 S. Ct. 186 [1991]) an affidavit and testimony that the victim had distorted past occurrences, had been exposed to deviant behavior on television that could have prompted false accusations, and was unduly influenced by her mother and other adults were rejected as lacking a factual basis. The proposed testimony was found insufficient to show a defense exam would produce material evidence. If the defense counsel claims the need for an exam based on behaviors that you know are typical in cases of child sexual assault, resist the request and provide expert testimony, affidavits, or articles to support your position. (See, e.g., *State v. Cain*, 427 N.W.2d 5 [Minn. Ct. App. 1988] [victim's recantation and lack of fear of the defendant or alleged suggestive methods of interviewing children do not constitute compelling reason for exam]; *State v. Gilpin*, 756 P.2d 445 [Mont. 1988] [defendant is not entitled to psychiatric examinations of victims because prosecution is not required to prove psychological trauma, and absence of evidence of psychological trauma would not prove offense did not occur].)

The court is less likely to order a psychiatric or psychological exam if one has already been done (e.g., by the treating therapist), if the results are available to the defense, and if the defense will have the ability to cross-examine the therapist. (See *People v. Woertman*, 786 P.2d 443 [Colo. Ct. App. 1989], *rev'd on other grounds*, 804 P.2d 188 [Colo. 1991].) If the initial exam was not requested by the prosecution specifically for the purpose of obtaining and offering expert testimony, the court may deny a request for a defense exam. The more the prosecution relies on mental health expert opinion to prove its case, the more likely the defense will be entitled to present similar expert evaluation and testimony. A court will also be reluctant to force the victim to undergo an exam if the prosecution can show that the victim may suffer emotional harm as a result. (See *State v. LeBlanc*, 558 So. 2d 507 [Fla. Dist. Ct. App. 1990]; *State v. Ballard*, 714 S.W.2d 284 [Tenn. Crim. App. 1986].) If the purported goals of the exam—examining the victim's credibility or the effects of suggestive methods of interviewing—can be accomplished through cross-examination of the victim at trial, the court may not order an exam. (See *State v. Lanford*, 764 S.W.2d 593 [Tex. Ct. App. 1989]; *In re State ex re Robinson* [2002 Tex.App.] Lexis 4802.) When the request for the exam is years removed from the incidents of sexual abuse, it is also unlikely the court will compel an exam. (See *LeBlanc*, 558 So. 2d 507.)

In extreme circumstances, courts have ordered psychiatric exams of victims. (See *State v. Cain*, 427 N.W.2d 5 [Minn. Ct. App. 1988] [court allowed exam because victim made prior allegations of sexual assault that were viewed "with suspicion" by child welfare workers and mother had "perceived obsession with sexual abuse"]; *State v. Stacy*, 371 S.E.2d 614 [W. Va. 1988] [defense request for exam granted after victim was repeatedly unresponsive or incoherent during competency hearing].) If the court does order a psychiatric exam, request limitations in order to prevent intimidation of the victim. (See *Cain*, 427 N.W.2d at 10 [appellate court ordered trial court on remand to issue protective order limiting time of exam and imposing other applicable restrictions].) See Appendixes IV.12 through IV.13b for sample motions and memoranda opposing psychological evaluation.

6. Motions for Second Physical Examination of Victim

Defense attorneys may request the trial court to order a second physical exam of the victim by a doctor of the defendant's choice. Because of the trauma and embarrassment of additional examinations, oppose the motion.

Consider asking the court to appoint a child advocate or guardian *ad litem*. If that request is denied, argue for the protection of the victim's privacy interests, emphasizing the detrimental impact of an additional physical exam. Consider requesting that the court hear testimony about the physical and psychological intrusiveness of the proposed exam.

Most important, ask the victim how she feels about going through a second medical examination. In a California case, the defense requested an exam mid-trial when the victim revealed penetration had sometimes occurred. The victim told his child advocate that the proposed exam—a rectal exam involving insertion of a finger into his anus—would cause him to relive the sexual assaults. Based primarily on the child advocate's testimony, the court found the anal exam offensive to the victim's privacy, particularly in light of its similarity to the sexual assault, and denied the motion (*People v. Nokes*, 228 Cal. Rptr. 119 [Ct. App. 1986]).

The defendant must show a compelling need for the exam (*State v. Farr*, 558 So. 2d 437 [Fla. Dist. Ct. App. 1990]). A simple assertion that the jury would give more weight to an expert who examined the child is not a compelling reason, absent allegations that there was anything improper about the previous examination (*State v. Drab*, 546 So. 2d 54 [Fla. Dist. Ct. App. 1989]). The prosecutor can rebut the defendant's argument by showing that a second exam is unlikely to produce results that would exculpate the defendant. Further, owing to the lapse in time between the first exam and the motion for a second, injuries seen originally by a doctor may have healed, making a second examination futile. (See *Commonwealth v. Chard*, 808 P.2d 351 [Colo.], *cert. denied*, 112 S. Ct. 186 [1991]; see also Finkel, M. [1989]. Anogenital trauma in sexually abused children. *Pediatrics, 84,* 317.) Similarly, if the original examination showed no injury or seminal deposits, further examination could produce no greater exculpatory evidence (*State v. Filson*, 613 P.2d 938 [Idaho 1980]). It is extremely helpful to have the initial physical examination of the victim documented with photographs. If photographs were taken at the first exam, argue that they can be reviewed by a defense expert and obviate the need for a second exam.

The prosecutor may also be able to show that a defense request for a physical exam is irrelevant to the charges. For example, when the defendant is charged with fondling the victim's breasts or exposing himself, requesting the victim's hymen be examined is unnecessary. (See *Commonwealth v. Visgar*, 457 N.E.2d 1343 [Ill. App. Ct. 1983].) Recognize, however, that appellate decisions should be consulted to determine when the trial court's denial of a second physical exam will be upheld. An error by the trial court may very well result in a reversal of the conviction. (See, e.g., *State v. Barone*, 1991 WL 194148 [Tenn. Crim. App. 1991], *aff'd in part, rev'd in part*, 852 S.W.2d 216 [Tenn. 1993] [trial court's failure to grant defendant's motion for independent medical examination, combined with court's admission of statements made by victim to psychologist, resulted in error necessitating remand for new trial].)

If the court orders a second exam of the victim over the State's objection, speak to the victim and her family, therapist, doctor, and child advocate. Find out whether a second exam is feasible. If so, determine what provisions will make her feel most comfortable, perhaps having her mother or therapist in the room. Ask the court to make those conditions part of the order.

7. Child Protective Services Records

In most states, CPS records enjoy a large degree of confidentiality by statute. Defense attorneys, however, often request access to the CPS records compiled during the investigation. In *Pennsylvania v. Ritchie* (480 U.S. 39 [1987]), the United States Supreme Court held that the interest of a defendant charged with child abuse in securing a fair trial could be fully protected by requiring CPS to submit their records to the judge for *in camera* review.

In most states, the defense attorney (or the court upon a motion from the defense attorney) subpoenas CPS records. Remind the CPS agency or its attorney to submit records only to the court when a subpoena is received and never to deliver records directly to the defense attorney. Some jurisdictions expunge the names of reporters prior to the court's *in camera* review.

After the review, the judge provides any material information deemed appropriate to the prosecutor and defense attorney. Have the judge place reasons for these disclosures on the record. Is the information exculpatory? Would it change the outcome of the trial? Would the information be admissible at trial? Check your case law to assess the standard used. For example, in *Ritchie* (480 U.S. at 39), the Court defined evidence as "material only if there is a reasonable probability that, had the evidence been disclosed to the defense, the result of the proceeding would have been different" (*Id.* at 57, quoting *United States v. Bagley,* 473 U.S. 667, 682 [opinion of J. Blackmun]).

The *in camera* review and disclosure decision should be made by a judge who will not be the fact finder at trial. As in motions regarding rape shield materials (see Section III.D of this chapter), information seen during *in camera* review and then deemed nondiscoverable may prejudice the fact finder. If the trial is to be a bench trial, have another judge rule on such motions.

When the judge delivers the material deemed discoverable from the CPS file, ask for a ruling that no photocopies of the material be made and that the information go no farther than the attorneys' trial files. This way, you can ensure some level of continued confidentiality.

If the defense attorney seeks direct review of the files, check your state's case law to see if the *Ritchie* standard has been adopted. If the defense attorney has direct access to the file, ask the judge to review the file *in camera* first to make sure reporters' names are expunged and to determine whether other privileges bar the discovery of included materials (e.g., psychiatrist's reports). Again, make sure CPS delivers the files to the judge. The judge then should hand the file to the defense attorney and the prosecutor to be reviewed in the courtroom. No CPS file should be allowed out of the courtroom, no document should be removed from the file or photocopied, and all files should be returned to the judge. These steps will help protect the confidentiality and integrity of the CPS file to the greatest extent possible.

Because CPS files are so integral to child abuse investigation and prosecution, some prosecutors remind defense counsel to file motions for exculpatory evidence. This is particularly important when you plan to call a CPS worker as a prosecution witness. A defense attorney's failure to file such motions may later become a claim of ineffective assistance of counsel on appeal. Do not do defense counsel's job but be mindful that egregious defense errors could jeopardize the conviction down the line.

8. DNA Test Results

Discoverable material involving DNA testing conducted in a child abuse case should be given to the defense as early as possible to preclude continuances. Provide all the discovery required and oppose requests for discovery by the defense that are too far-reaching. Be prepared to provide at least

1. All the reports of the testing laboratory in connection with the case
2. A complete copy of the laboratory's working file, lab notes, logs, and photographs

3. All chain of evidence documents

4. Duplicates of all autorads (visible DNA "prints" produced during the testing procedure)

5. Laboratory protocols and procedures

6. Database information from which the statistical analysis is drawn, together with studies supporting this statistical information

Be careful that the defense does not attempt to harass the laboratory with requests for discovery material that is overly burdensome, involves trade secrets, or is merely an attempt to get the prosecutor (or the laboratory) to do their homework for them.

Also pay particularly close attention to chain of evidence documents. The chain of evidence is more critical in DNA cases than in any other kind because of the possibility of cross-contamination of samples. Be prepared to bring in as witnesses everyone who processed the tested materials. Remember, however, that chain of evidence generally needs to be proven only for items that can be tampered with.

C. Prosecution Discovery Motions

1. Motions for Physical Evidence

Many jurisdictions have statutes permitting some form of discovery on behalf of the prosecutor. All states permit a prosecutor to obtain relevant physical evidence from an accused such as fingernail scrapings, blood, or other body fluid samples; handwriting samples; voice tapes; photographs; and fingerprints. The importance of this type of discovery is obvious, and it is essential that prosecutors take advantage of any applicable discovery provisions and file appropriate motions as early as possible. Otherwise, crucial evidence might be lost, altered, hidden, or destroyed.

In child abuse cases, it is not unusual for additional evidence to be discovered after the initial investigation and filing of charges. Consequently, a prosecutor should file for supplemental discovery as soon as a need for additional evidence becomes obvious. For example, pedophiles often keep personal diaries with victims' names, descriptions of their activities, and sometimes even dates and locations of their experiences. If such a diary is discovered, a handwriting sample should be sought so that a comparison can be obtained. Likewise, a child victim may contract a venereal disease that is not detected right away from the abuser. If you learn that the victim has a venereal disease, move to have the defendant tested for that disease immediately. (See Appendixes IV.14a through IV.15d.) Your investigator or police agency should also attempt to discover evidence indicating the defendant has sought treatment or taken medication. Subpoena medical records from jail or prison (if the defendant spent any time in custody before trial), public health centers, or any doctor or pharmacy the defendant used. Some institutions or professionals may refuse to send records because of privacy constraints, and you may need to litigate this issue before trial. Many states, however, will not allow the defendant's privacy interests to preclude a prosecutor's access to medical records in the context of a child abuse allegation. (See *Commonwealth v. Nieves,* 582 A.2d 341 [Pa. Super. Ct. 1990] [statutorily privileged confidential medical records must be disclosed to prosecutors in sexual abuse cases when presence or absence of venereal disease is relevant to issue at trial]; *State v. Bellard*, 533 So. 2d 961 La. 1988] [permissible for CPS to obtain defendant's medical records pursuant to investigation of sexual assault of 5-year-old daughter and turn them over to prosecuting attorney]; *State v. Efird*, 309 S.E.2d 228 [N.C. 1983] [physician-patient privilege inapplicable to medical records of county health department when records offered to corroborate testimony of 7-year-old girl who contracted gonorrhea and records showed defendant was treated for gonorrhea at time of rape].)

2. Motions for Disclosure of Witnesses and Other Information

Some jurisdictions require the defense to notify the prosecutor of names, addresses and statements of potential defense witnesses, including alibi and expert witnesses. As soon as charges are filed, the prosecutor should file a demand or motion for information to which he or she is entitled, as well as a motion to be apprised of the general nature of the defense, if allowed by local court rule. Requests for this information should be pursued persistently until the defense complies.

Further, promptly seek an order setting forth a continuing obligation by the defense to disclose subsequently discovered witnesses or information. Urge the court to make discovery obligations truly reciprocal. Having this information early in a child abuse case is especially important, since it will allow you to obtain statements from witnesses and check their background, employment, and other relevant information.

To prepare properly for a defense expert, you must have time to review résumés and reports, consult with prosecution experts, and research and brief legal issues raised by the proposed expert testimony. An early ruling by the court on admissibility of defense expert testimony could be sought as well.

3. Motions to Depose Defense Witnesses

If the investigator or police are unable to locate defense witnesses or if they refuse to be interviewed, the prosecutor should move to take depositions, assuming this is allowed by local rules. Pinning these witnesses down early can yield a wealth of material for cross-examination at trial and will decrease the chances of testimony changing to conform to the needs of the defense as trial approaches. Further, the better and earlier prepared the prosecutor is to try the case, the greater the chance of obtaining a conviction, whether by guilty plea or verdict.

4. Motions for Order to Compel Blood Testing for HIV Infection

Consider, depending upon the wishes of the child and her family, filing a pre-trial motion to compel the defendant to undergo testing for the human immunodeficiency virus (HIV) infection. Regardless of whether the defendant tests positive or negative, it may be desirable to test the victim. She may not have contracted the disease even if he tests positive; a negative test can only mean that the infection is too recent to detect. Retesting may be advised.

Testing of sex offenders for HIV is now authorized in 47 states. The legislation in these states typically mandates testing whenever a sex offense is committed or bodily fluids pass between an offender and a victim. Most of the laws require the testing to be conducted by court-authorized personnel and allow the results of the test to be released to the defendant and the victim. The information remains otherwise confidential, and a few states specifically prohibit the results of the test from being admitted in the prosecution of the offense.

One important difference among the statutes is whether testing is mandatory or discretionary. Another difference is whether testing is ordered before or after conviction. Of the states providing for testing after conviction, most make the testing mandatory at that time, although a few states leave postconviction testing to the discretion of the judge. Other states make testing mandatory at the request of the victim or prosecutor.

Of states allowing testing at the time of arrest or indictment, a significant number require testing immediately. Other states leave the decision within the discretion of the court, require a finding of probable cause of guilt or of exposure to AIDS, or require the victim to receive the defendant's consent to submit to a test. See Table IV.1 for statutory authority for HIV testing of a defendant. (See Appendix IV.15 for examples of motions to compel HIV testing, supporting briefs, and a sample order.)

Table IV.1   Statutes Authorizing HIV Testing of Sex Offenders

Alabama	ALA. CODE . § 22–11A-17
Alaska	ALASKA STAT. § 18.15.300
Arizona	ARIZ. REV. STAT. ANN. § 13–1415
Arkansas	ARK. CODE ANN. § 16–82–101
California	CAL. PENAL CODE § 1202.1
	CAL. PENAL CODE § 1524.1
Colorado	COLO. REV. STAT. § 18–3-415
Delaware	DEL. CODE ANN. tit. 10 § 1077
District of Columbia	D.C. STAT. § 22–3902
Florida	FLA. STAT. ANN. § 960.003
	FLA. STAT. ANN. § 775.0877
Georgia	GA. CODE ANN. § 15–11–66.1
	GA. CODE ANN. § 17–10–15
	GA. CODE ANN. § 31–22–9.1
Hawaii	HAW. REV. STAT. ANN. § 325–16.5
Idaho	IDAHO CODE § 39–601, -604
Illinois	ILL. REV. STAT. CH. 730, § 5/5–5-3(G)
Indiana	IND. CODE § 35–38-1-10.5
	IND. CODE § 35–38-1-10.6
Iowa	IOWA CODE ANN. § 915.42
Kansas	KAN. STAT. ANN. § 38–1692
Kentucky	KY. REV. STAT. ANN. § 529.090
	KY. REV. STAT. ANN. § 510.320
Louisiana	LA. REV. STAT. ANN. § 15:535
Maine	ME. REV. STAT. ANN. tit. 5 § 19203-F
Michigan	MICH. COMP. LAWS § 333.5129

(Continued)

Table IV.1   (Continued)

Minnesota	MINN. STAT. § 611A.19
Mississippi	MISS. CODE ANN. § 99–19–201, -203
Missouri	MO. ANN. STAT. § 191.663
Montana	MONT. CODE ANN. § 46–18–256
	MONT. CODE ANN. § 50–18–101
Nebraska	NEB. REV. STAT. § 29–2290
Nevada	NEV. REV. STAT. § 441A.320
New Hampshire	N.H. REV. STAT. ANN. § 632-A:10-B
New Jersey	N.J. STAT. ANN. § 2C:43–2.3
New Mexico	N.M. STAT. ANN § 24–1-9.1
New York	N.Y. CRIM. PROC. § 390.15
North Carolina	N.C. GEN. STAT. § 15A-534.3
North Dakota	N.D. CENT. CODE § 23–07–07.5
Ohio	OHIO REV. CODE ANN. § 2907.27
	OHIO REV. CODE ANN. § 3701.243
Oklahoma	OKLA. STAT. tit. 63, § 1–524, -525
Oregon	OR. REV. STAT. § 135.139
	OR. REV. STAT. § 137.076
Pennsylvania	35 PA. CONS STAT. § 521.11A
Rhode Island	R.I. GEN. LAWS § 11–37–17
South Carolina	S.C. CODE ANN. § 16–3-740
	S.C. CODE ANN. § 16–15–255
South Dakota	S.D. CODIFIED LAWS § 23A-35B-3
Tennessee	TENN. CODE ANN. § 39–13–521
Texas	TEX. CRIM. PROC. CODE ANN. § 21.31
Vermont	VT. STAT. ANN. tit. 13 § 3256
Virginia	VA. CODE ANN. § 18.2–62
Washington	WASH. REV. CODE § 70.24.340
	WASH. REV. CODE § 70.24.105
West Virginia	W. VA. CODE § 16–3C-2
Wisconsin	WIS. STAT. § 968.28
Wyoming	WYO. STAT. ANN. § 7–1-109
Federal	42 U.S.C.S. § 14011

NOTE: This compilation includes all statutes (excluding military and tribal statutes) that authorize or mandate HIV testing of persons arrested, detained, charged, or convicted of a sexual offense. This table includes all legislation passed through June 2002, as verified through Lexis Nexis.

III. ADDITIONAL DEFENSE PRE-TRIAL MOTIONS

A. Specificity, More Definite Statement of Charges, or Request for a Bill of Particulars

1. Difficulty of Specifying Dates

In both physical and sexual child abuse cases, the prosecutor often cannot specify in the charging document the precise date(s) on which the crime(s) occurred.

The complaint or indictment commonly alleges that crimes took place within a particular period—anywhere from a few days to a number of years, depending on the nature of the offense.

Because children are often abused on multiple occasions over time and generally do not reveal abuse immediately, they may have difficulty recalling on what days abuse occurred. Young children are also simply unable to specify dates in the way adults do. (See Chapters I and II.) As a rule, children are better able to recall significant events such as holidays, the beginning or ending of school, or a younger sibling's birth but cannot necessarily attach a date to them. A child who has been repeatedly abused may have difficulty distinguishing one incident from another, leaving the prosecutor with no option except to allege that the abuse occurred sometime over a rather lengthy period. Inability to pinpoint a date may lead to a defense motion for a more definite statement or bill of particulars. Anticipate this type of motion from the outset and attempt to minimize problems by seeking information at the initial victim interview that would identify incidents or narrow down a time frame.

In child sexual assault cases, the abuse will often escalate in number and severity of acts. The defendant will often progress from relatively less intrusive acts (such as touching the victim outside and then inside her clothing) to more intrusive acts (such as exposing his penis to the victim, having her touch his penis, and finally having oral, vaginal, and/or anal intercourse). This gradual escalation allows the defendant to slowly introduce the victim to sexuality and to secure her compliance through threats, bribes, and/or a sense of isolation.

When physical or sexual assaults involve a continuous course of conduct, most states agree that an exact date is not a material element of charges. There is no consensus among the states, however, as to the degree of specificity required in charging documents. Generally, courts require prosecutors to fix the dates of the offenses within a "reasonable" period of time. Your own jurisdiction's case law should be consulted for guidance. (See Section 3, below.) If, after charging, you find that the dates alleged in the charging document are incorrect, seek an appropriate amendment to the dates in the charging document. (See this chapter, Section V.B.)

2. Defense Request for a Bill of Particulars and Prosecutor's Response

Whether or not the prosecutor files a motion to broaden the dates alleged in the original charging document, the defense attorney may file a request for a bill of particulars. Such requests generally demand that dates, times, and locations of the assaults be stated with greater specificity than set out in the charging documents. In determining how to respond, the prosecutor should consider information gleaned from the investigation and interview the victim again if that would be helpful in ascertaining more precise times. However, extreme care should be taken that the response be as general as allowed by case law in the particular jurisdiction, since the state will be bound by the answer at trial. A bill of particulars constitutes an amendment to the dates alleged in the original charging document. The prosecutor will then be required to prove that the incidents occurred on those dates. *If the state's proof at trial fails to establish those dates specifically, or indicates different dates, an acquittal is likely.* If the prosecutor cannot comfortably provide any further information than alleged in the original charging document, inform the court and defense counsel that no greater specificity is possible. The prosecutor's response *must* be based on what the victim and other witnesses will be able to testify to at trial to determine dates. If, for example, the victim is *certain* that the assaults happened only on weekends, the prosecutor may indicate that in the bill of particulars. (See Appendix IV.6a-c for an example of prosecution response to a request for a bill of particulars and to defendant's subsequent motion to dismiss.)

3. Defense Motion to Dismiss and the Prosecutor's Response

The defense may file a motion to dismiss for lack of specificity, claiming denial of due process. Most courts will deny such a motion, particularly if the case involves a long period of continuous sexual assault of a young victim. (See *State v. Corbin*, 809 P.2d 57 [Ct. App.], *cert. denied*, 809 p.2d 634 [N.M. 1991] [assault occurring over 4-month period]; *State v. Hoyt*, 806 P.2d 204 [Utah Ct. App. 1991] [indictment charging defendant with sexual abuse of child at a particular motel where defendant registered at four well-defined times over course of 4 months was sufficient]; *People v. Mendoza*, 561 N.Y.S.2d 183 [App. Div. 1990] [counts in indictment designating four distinct periods was reasonable]; *State v. Spigarolo*, 556 A.2d 112 [Conn.], *cert. denied*, 493 U.S. 933 [1989] [allegation that defendant sexually abused two girls, ages six and nine, on various dates between October 1984 and January 3, 1985, was sufficient]; *State v. Mulkey*, 560 A.2d 24 [Md. 1989] [indictment stating offenses occurred over three consecutive summers was sufficient]; *Commonwealth v. Fanelli*, 547 A.2d 1201 [Pa. Super. Ct. 1988], *appeal denied*, 565 A.2d 1165 [Pa. 1989] [*en banc*] [6-year-old's testimony establishing one-time sexual assault occurred within two years was sufficient]; *State v. Hoban*, 738 S.W.2d 536 [Mo. Ct. App. 1987] [allegation of multiple sexual assaults over 15-month period was sufficient]; *Commonwealth v. McClucas*, 516 A.2d 68 [Pa. Super. Ct. 1986] [indictment charging ongoing sexual assault over 5-year period was sufficient]; but see *State v. Beermann*, 436 N.W.2d 499 [Neb. 1989] [allegations in four indictments that defendant committed sexual assault on unnamed victim at four unspecified occasions during 3-year period were insufficient].) Check the case law in your jurisdiction to find out what response satisfies due process requirements.

4. Election of Act or Unanimity Instruction

Several states have rejected a continuous course of conduct approach and devised other ways to handle specificity. (See *People v. Beauchamp*, 539 N.E.2d 1105 [N.Y. 1989] [charges dismissed because bill of particulars alleging "continuous course of conduct" over 9-month period was duplicitous, as each count encompassed more than one offense and the period was unreasonably excessive].) Although a precise date is not required in the indictment, the prosecutor must elect an act on which to rely for conviction and/or the jury must be instructed that it must unanimously agree on a specific act for conviction. In *Woertman v. People* (804 P.2d 188 [Colo. 1991]), the court found that the bill of particulars alleging ongoing sexual assault over a 55-day period was sufficiently specific to allow the defendant to prepare his defense; it was an error, however, not to require the prosecution to elect a specific act of sexual assault on the victim or provide the jury with a unanimity instruction. In *People v. Estorga* (612 P.2d 520 [Colo. 1980]), the court held that when evidence of a number of acts that could constitute the offense charged was presented, the prosecutor could be compelled to elect a transaction on which to rely for conviction, though the state need not identify the exact date of the offense. In *State v. Petrich*, 683 P.2d 173 (Wash. 1984), the state was not required to elect a particular incident or specify the times that various incidents occurred when such could not reasonably be done, but the court did require the jury to reach unanimous agreement on the particular act constituting the offense.

Failure to elect a specific act or to give a unanimity instruction may not be reversible error when the evidence could convince a reasonable person beyond a reasonable doubt that the defendant committed the charged offense during the alleged period. (See *State v. Altgilbers*, 786 P.2d 680 [N.M. Ct. App. 1989]; see also *State v. Bailey*, 475 A.2d 1045 [Vt. 1984] [when testimony presented that conduct occurred on at least six occasions in a one and a half–hour period, court's failure to require election of acts relied on or to issue special jury instruction was not reversible error].)

5. The Single Incident of Abuse

When the victim describes only a single incident of abuse, confirm that no other incidents actually occurred. Because victims often need time before feeling comfortable enough to disclose long-term abuse, the victim's initial statements may not reflect the full extent of the abuse. If you are satisfied the abuse happened only once, try to determine the date of the occurrence as closely as possible. If the defense files a request for a bill of particulars, follow the guidelines set out above.

With a one-time incident, courts are often less flexible about the time alleged, particularly when the defense wants to present an alibi defense. Consult case law in your jurisdiction to ascertain how much specificity is required. If the victim is young, has been threatened by the defendant, and/or reported to a family member who then took no action, the court will probably require less specificity. (See *Commonwealth v. Fanelli*, 547 A.2d 1201 [Pa. Super. Ct. 1988], *appeal denied*, 565 A.2d 1165 [Pa. 1989] [*en banc*] [6-year-old's testimony that mother's boyfriend sexually assaulted her once within 2-year span was sufficient to withstand due process challenge, given victim's age, threatened harm, and apparent lack of support from her family]; *Johns v. State*, 352 S.E.2d 826 [Ga. Ct. App. 1987] [indictment alleging that crime occurred between March 1981 and September 1981 sufficiently showed time when offense occurred, given evidence defendant committed offense during March 1981 and offense was within statute of limitations period].)

Granting or denying a motion for a bill of particulars or related motions is usually left to the court's discretion. Generally, the law requires that charges be sufficient to give the defendant fair notice to prepare an adequate defense. It is difficult to predict what a young child will say during trial regarding dates or other details not directly related to the nature of the obtrusive acts. Prosecutors should not be any more specific than absolutely required by law or by the trial judge. This will help to avoid problems if the child provides different or additional details during trial.

B. Continuance Motions

1. Disadvantages of Continuances

Continuances are a plague of the criminal justice system—exasperating to the courts and frustrating to victims and their families. Continuances are especially detrimental to the success of child abuse prosecutions. Pressures on the child and the child's supporters are magnified when accompanied by the emotional rollercoaster of repeated changes in schedule. (See 18 U.S.C. § 3509[j] [2002] [requiring court to take into account potential adverse impact delay may have on child's well-being].)

Once a determination has been made that enough evidence exists to file a child abuse case, most prosecutors find that the typical case only becomes weaker as time passes. When the prosecutor and child are prepared for trial, delays can decrease the likelihood of conviction by discouraging victims from cooperating, causing all witnesses to remember less, and reducing any sense of urgency by putting more time between the offense and the trial. Defense attorneys are well aware of this and often seek continuances in child abuse cases for these reasons. Therefore, oppose defense requests for continuances aggressively unless they are somehow advantageous to the prosecution. (See Appendix IV.19 for a sample motion to deny defendant's motion to continue.)

2. Opposing and Avoiding Continuances

Most states require a showing of good cause to justify a continuance. Prosecutors objecting to continuance requests should insist that the defense present legitimate reasons warranting a delay and point out defense failures to exercise due diligence to the court. For example, if the defense requests a continuance shortly before trial to investigate using an expert witness, point out their lack of diligence by waiting until the last minute. The prosecutor might also argue that there is no basis to believe the expert could offer testimony admissible at trial.

Keep a detailed record and make judges aware of the negative effects of postponing the trial on the victim and the victim's family. Traditionally, courts have leaned over backward in deferring to defense motions for continuances, while failing to take into account the detrimental impact on victims and cases. Though prosecutors may find it discouraging to see judges consistently granting continuances over their objections, perseverance is needed to change this trend. Detailed affidavits or actual testimony from family members or therapists can be submitted to show how difficult it is for the victim to deal with delay.

Individuals who support the prosecution in opposing a continuance can express their concern by appearing in person at the hearing at which the motion will be argued. Many state legislatures have enacted statutes requiring greater consideration to child victims, specifically referring to the need for speedy disposition of criminal proceedings involving child victims (see Table IV.2). If your jurisdiction has such a statute, cite it as authority to the court and emphasize the public policy behind the statute. Also see 18 U.S.C. § 3509(j) (2002), which requires federal judges to expedite criminal trials in which a child will be a witness.

A number of jurisdictions now have victims' rights legislation requiring that victims receive notification of hearings and case status. Use such legislation to your advantage and insist on victim input when continuances are ruled on.

Defense continuance requests are often based on claims that they have not received timely or complete discovery and are sometimes accompanied by motions for psychological evaluations of the victim premised on purportedly recently acquired information. To prevent continuances granted for these reasons, comply fully with discovery requirements. Provide timely discovery along with a verification letter listing the items defense counsel was supplied with or given an opportunity to

Table IV.2   Statutes Mandating Speedy Disposition of Criminal Cases Involving Child Victims or Witnesses

Alabama	ALA. CODE § 15–25–6
California	CAL. PENAL CODE § 1048(b)
Colorado	COLO. REV. STAT. § 18–3–411(4)
Delaware	DEL. CODE ANN. tit. 11, § 5133
District of Columbia	D.C. CODE § 23–1903(d)
Florida	FLA. STAT. § 918.0155
Hawaii	HAW. REV. STAT. § 706–606.3
Idaho	IDAHO CODE § 19–110
Illinois	725 ILL. REV. STAT. § 5/114–4(k)
Indiana	IND. CODE ANN. § 35–36–7-3
Kentucky	KY. REV. STAT. ANN. § 421.510
Massachusetts	MASS. ANN. LAWS ch. 278 § 16F
Michigan	MICH. COMP. LAWS ANN. § 780.759(1)(a)
Minnesota	MINN. STAT. ANN. § 630.36
Missouri	MO. REV. STAT. § 491.710
Nevada	NEV. REV. STAT. ANN. § 174.515(3)
New Hampshire	N.H. REV. STAT. ANN. § 632-A:9
New Jersey	N.J. REV. STAT. § 2A:163–4, -5
New York	N.Y. EXEC. LAW § 642-a(3)
North Carolina	N.C. GEN. STAT. § 15A-952(g)(3)
North Dakota	N.D. CENT. CODE § 12.1–35–05
Oregon	OR. REV. STAT. § 44.545
Rhode Island	R.I. GEN. LAWS § 11–37–11.2
Utah	UTAH CODE ANN. § 77–37–3(h)
Washington	WASH. REV. CODE ANN. § 10.46.085
Wisconsin	WIS. STAT. ANN. § 971.105
U.S. Code	18 U.S.C. § 3509(j)

NOTE: This compilation includes all statutes (excluding military and tribal statutes) that specifically mandate the speedy disposition of criminal cases that involve child victims or witnesses. The citation date indicates the year of passage or latest amendment. This table includes all legislation passed through June 2002, as verified through Lexis Nexis.

review. Make sure to give written notice well in advance of trial of motions to amend dates, proposed expert witnesses, or other bad acts of the defendant to be introduced in the case in chief. Expeditious notifications will also cause the court to scrutinize last-minute requests for psychological evaluations of victims more critically. If the court grants the defense motion, ask that the court file indicate no further continuances will be granted at defense's request and defense must be ready for trial on the new date.

Prosecutors should not seek continuances in child abuse cases unless absolutely necessary because of missing witnesses, opportunities for additional evidence, incompetence of the victim (which often changes in a relatively short time), or similar valid considerations. Caseloads and trial schedules may tempt you to agree to continuances, but every effort should be made to move expeditiously on these cases.

C. Severance Motions

In cases in which there are multiple defendants, victims, or offenses, a common defense strategy is to move for severance. Severance of defendants allows the defense to reduce the amount of negative information considered by a jury about a particular defendant and diverts culpability from the defendant to others not on trial. Severing counts regarding victims confines jury deliberations to the crime committed upon one victim as opposed to crimes against all. Severing offenses involving the same victim diminishes the seriousness of the defendant's victimization of the child and allows a defendant to mislead the jury about the extent of criminal behavior. Multiple trials, moreover, increase the potential for inconsistent statements, providing the defense with a second chance at cross-examination of key witnesses. Defense counsel will often attempt to parlay advantages associated with successful severance motions into better plea offers from the prosecutor, particularly when the offender is charged with multiple offenses against several victims.

Prosecutors should oppose severance motions in child abuse cases in all circumstances in which joinder can be legally justified, unless severance is considered beneficial. There is normally little tactical advantage to agreeing to severance unless, in the case of multiple defendants, joinder prohibits you from using helpful admissions of one of them. (See *Bruton v. United States*, 391 U.S. 123 [1968].) In limited circumstances, the prosecutor may also find severance beneficial if it is likely to increase the chances of longer sentences for serious or violent offenders. This may be more likely in states with determinate sentencing. If appellate courts in your jurisdiction generally disapprove of multiple victim trials because of perceived prejudicial impact on the defendant, weigh the risk of reversal associated with joinder of counts involving multiple victims and be able to articulate persuasive reasons to merit joinder. Your approach will obviously depend on the facts of your cases and applicable law and practice.

1. Multiple Defendants

Joinder of defendants is generally allowed if each defendant is charged with responsibility for the crime(s) or if the charged crime(s) are so closely connected that it would be difficult to separate proof of one from proof of the others. Joinder of defendants will usually occur in child abuse cases when defendants such as a husband and wife or father and mother are jointly responsible for the abuse, or when different abusers victimize a child together or in the same setting, such as a school or daycare facility.

Legal principles governing joinder and severance of defendants are the same for child abuse cases as other crimes. Generally, it is much easier for a child victimized by more than one person to go through only one trial. Moreover, one trial makes better use of the time and resources of the court, juries, witnesses, police, and prosecutors and will prevent the jury from wondering why only one of the culpable actors is being pursued. (See *State v. Cassey*, 543 A.2d 670 [R.I. 1988] [denial of motion to sever was not abuse of discretion, particularly considering age of victim and burden imposed upon victim by being required to testify concerning shocking subject matter in two separate trials, that evidence in case was relatively simple, and that jury would have no significant difficulty in separating evidence against each defendant, that there were no antagonistic defenses, and that neither defendant made statements implicating another defendant]; *State v. Jenkins,* 351 S.E.2d 299 [Ct. App. 1986], *cert. denied,* 356 S.E.2d 791 [N.C. 1987] [trial judge did not abuse discretion in joining cases of husband and wife charged with taking indecent liberties with children since joinder could have been based on reasoned decision that there was a common plan or scheme to gratify their sexual desires on children they baby-sat, defenses were not antagonistic, and instructions were adequate]; but see *State v. Brown,* 586 A.2d 1085 [R.I. 1991] [denial of motion to sever trials of brothers charged with separately and independently committing sexual assault on niece was reversible error in that it resulted in restriction of one brother's ability to defend himself; niece testified second brother's assaults may only have been bad dream, second brother's counsel suggested dream was caused by first brother's conduct, and first brother was precluded from impeaching niece's testimony regarding second brother].)

In the relatively rare cases involving large numbers of defendants, it may be easier for the children not to face cross-examination in one proceeding by several defense attorneys. The prosecutor in such cases may wish to seek separate trials. Further, in the event of guilty verdicts at the beginning, the remaining defendants may be more likely to plead guilty.

2. Multiple Offenses Involving Different Victims

Joinder and severance are controlled in each jurisdiction by statutes or rules. Rule 8 of the Federal Rules of Criminal Procedure is typical. Rule 8(a) provides that two or more offenses may be charged in the same indictment if the offenses charged "are of the same or similar character, or are based on the same act or transaction, or on two or more acts or transactions connected together or constituting parts of a common scheme or plan."

Rule 14 of the Federal Rules of Criminal Procedure provides that, if a defendant or the prosecution is prejudiced by joinder of offenses, the trial court may order separate trials of counts. Case law suggests that joinder may be prejudicial when (1) the defendant may become embarrassed or confounded in presenting separate defenses, (2) the jury may use the evidence of one of the crimes charged to infer a criminal disposition on the part of the defendant and infer his guilt of the crime or crimes charged, or (3) the jury may cumulate and find guilt as to all charges when, if considered separately, it would not do so.

Even when multiple offenses are properly joined, defendants may argue that severance is necessary to avoid violating restrictions such as Federal Rule of Evidence 404(b), which prohibits use of other crimes, wrongs, or acts to prove the defendant is a person of bad character and acted in conformity with his character. However, Rule 404(b) allows evidence of other crimes to be introduced to prove the defendant's motive, opportunity, intent, preparation, plan, knowledge, identity, or absence of mistake or accident. Since the rules vary from jurisdiction to jurisdiction, and appellate courts in some states tend to review joinder of sex offenses critically, the prosecutor should make a clear and persuasive record of the need to join offenses.

When a defendant is accused of similar crimes involving several victims, the prosecutor often has a valid basis for joinder. For example, child molesters frequently follow a standard method of operation—the use of threats, candy, presents, money, alcohol, drugs, pornographic magazines, photographs, or films to lure and then persuade children to participate in sexual activities. Peers or older children the defendant has victimized are often manipulated into pressuring or lessening the inhibitions of new victims. Many child molesters seek employment in organizations that put them in contact with children. Often, therefore, sufficient links exist between a group of victims and the offender's pattern of exploitation to make a convincing argument to allow a single trial. (See *State v. Chandler*, 376 S.E.2d 728 [N.C. 1989] [trial court properly consolidated charges against defendant involving seven minor victims, as all crimes were committed against children in his exclusive care while he transported them to and from their homes and daycare center during 5-month period]; *State v. Fultz*, 373 S.E.2d 445 [N.C. Ct. App. 1988] [trial court properly consolidated charges involving three victims, as each offense occurred in Boy Scout environment, defendant was each victim's Boy Scout leader during entire 11-month period, three offenses occurred at a single campsite and remaining offenses occurred at troop's meeting place, and evidence demonstrated a plan or scheme in which defendant used his position as troop leader to commit acts]; *Langham v. State*, 494 So. 2d 910 [Ala. Crim. App. 1986] [indictments properly consolidated when similar crimes charged; victims were girls 9–12 years old, crimes occurred in same room of defendant's residence over relatively short period, crimes involved similar lure and activities with victims, and offenses were committed as part of common plan or scheme]; *Commonwealth v. Zigler*, 509 A.2d 389 [Pa. Super. Ct. 1986] [three separate indictments charging defendant with sex offenses against three children in three different episodes held properly consolidated under *modus operandi* theory when all crimes occurred within 6-month period and involved anal sex with young children, and none of the fact situations were so complicated as to confuse jury or make it incapable of separating offenses]; *State v. Effler*, 309 S.E.2d 203 [N.C. 1983] [consolidation of rape and sexual offense charges were proper when defendant engaged in sexual acts with both of his children within 1-month period, taking advantage of his position of authority when alone with them during visitation].)

Often the defense will provide justification for joinder at trial as illustrated by the following examples. If the defendant claims to have been wrongly identified, joinder is appropriate so the jury can consider the similarities between crimes and identifications of all victims in deciding the identity issue. If the defendant claims that touching a victim was accidental or (in sex offense cases) not sexually motivated, joinder to show the repeated accidental touches or unintended injuries is necessary to refute these claims. If the defendant claims to have never been alone with a victim and thus had no opportunity to commit the charged crimes, joinder will give the jury relevant information about the existence of opportunities.

In cases involving the defendant's recurring abuse of a number of victims under nearly identical circumstances, such as within a daycare center and using the same approach (grooming, abuse, and intimidation), the existence of a common plan or scheme can be demonstrated by allowing joinder. The more similarities between both victims and characteristics of assaults, the better the prosecutor's chances of persuading the court to deny severance.

3. Multiple Offenses Involving Same Victim

Multiple offenses involving a defendant's abuse of a single victim should rarely if ever be severed. These situations clearly involve a continuous course of conduct, and it is difficult to imagine a convincing argument that could justify severance. In many jurisdictions, even evidence of remote uncharged sexual misconduct involving the same victim is deemed admissible to show the defendant's lustful disposition or inclination toward the victim. (See Section IV.A. of this chapter regarding admissibility of prior bad acts involving the same victim.)

D. Motion to Permit Evidence of Victim's Prior Sexual Conduct

Children who have been victimized by sexual abuse are often at great risk for revictimization at the hands of other offenders. There are several reasons for this common phenomenon:

- The betrayal of trust implicit when a family member, friend, or respected adult takes sexual advantage of a child can leave the victim unable to make reasonable judgments about others. When children distrust their own ability to judge others or completely misjudge them, they are vulnerable to further manipulation.

- Inability to rebuff unwanted sexual behavior can leave the child resigned to the role of victim. Powerlessness breeds futility and compliance.

- Sexual abuse, usually accompanied by emotional assaults, makes many children feel they are damaged goods. Their experience can instill and constantly reinforce the notion that their only value to others is as a sexual object. This damaged self-image can lead to involvement in drugs, promiscuity, and prostitution—thereby increasing vulnerability to victimization.

- Potential offenders who suspect or know of a child's previous sexual abuse can find such victims more provocative. Their inhibitions against sexually assaulting a juvenile are lessened, and their efforts to force the child into repeating the experience are increased. Offenders are often experts in discerning which children are likely to be vulnerable to their attempts.

For further information on revictimization, see Russell, D. E. H. (1986). *The secret trauma: Incest in the lives of girls and women.* New York: Basic Books.

Increasingly, defense counsel will attempt to cross-examine or present extrinsic evidence regarding the victim's past sexual conduct. Such evidence is not only hurtful for the victim to recount and an intrusion on her privacy, but highly prejudicial when put before a jury. Jurors often have a hard time believing a child may have been sexually assaulted once; it is even harder for them to believe that children are serially abused. When the victim is a sexually active adolescent, the prejudicial effect of the intrusive questions about relationships with peers is obvious.

Every state has enacted statutes to preclude introduction of prior sexual conduct of victims involved in sex crime cases. Commonly referred to as "rape shield statutes," they were initially intended to protect adult victims. Case law in many states has extended their application to child victims. Prior sexual conduct usually is defined to include past consensual and assaultive conduct. (See *State v. Wright,* 776 P.2d 1294 [Or. Ct. App. 1989]; *State v. Muyingo,* 171 Ore. App. 218, 15 P.2d 83 [2000].) Defense counsel must thus comply with procedural requirements and show that the evidence proffered falls into an exception to the rape shield statute before presenting such evidence.

1. Preparation

During pre-trial investigation of a child sexual assault case, find out if the victim has ever been sexually assaulted by someone other than the defendant or is sexually active. Check with the CPS worker and police for prior reports of sexual abuse of the victim. Reassure the victim that you need to know everything so that you can be effective in countering possible defense arguments in court.

If you discover that the victim was sexually assaulted in the past, get details. Find out approximately when and where the abuse happened, who the perpetrator was, and how it differed from circumstances in your case. You will need to know if the abuse was reported, to whom, and what action was taken. If the case was reported, find out if an arrest was made and what happened. Get the old prosecution files on the case and check court files since you will need as much information as possible. If the abuse was not previously reported, report it as mandated by state law. Most important, find out if the victim is currently being sexually assaulted. If so, the first concern will be the victim's safety; contact CPS and the police to allow them to separate the offender and the victim.

If the prior assault on the victim is arguably admissible under any of the following exceptions, disclose the prior assault to the defense attorney as potentially exculpatory evidence. Should the prior assault appear inadmissible, your obligation to disclose it becomes less clear. One alternative is to submit the information to the court *ex parte* and ask for a ruling on whether it is discoverable. It is best to err on the side of disclosure and then prepare a strong pre-trial argument to bar admission of the prior assault at trial.

2. Mechanics of the Pre-Trial Motion

Under most rape shield statutes, defense counsel must file a written pre-trial motion with the court in order to present evidence at trial of prior sexual conduct. The motion must be accompanied by a detailed offer of proof and reasons justifying admissibility. The court then schedules an *in camera* hearing for argument and presentation of evidence. In a jury case, the judge who will preside should hear the motion. If the case will be a bench trial, a different judge should hear the motion since the prejudicial impact of the arguments and/or evidence is far too great to allow the motion to be heard by the fact finder. If a bench trial is ordered following the rape shield hearing, request assignment of the trial to another judge.

In many cases, the defense bypasses the written motion and required hearing and proceeds, in front of the jury, to question the victim about third-party sexual contact. Although unlawful and unethical, such questions as, "Isn't it true your uncle did this to you too?" will have made a prejudicial impact on the jury before the prosecutor has a chance to object. Consequently, prosecutors should routinely file a motion *in limine* to preclude the defense from introducing evidence of prior sexual contact at trial. Even if unaware of any allegations of prior sexual activity, filing a motion *in limine* allows the prosecutor to "smoke out" the defense. Defense counsel will have to acknowledge on the record that there is no intent to raise the issue of other sexual contact or be forced to comply with the law and make a pre-trial offer of proof, revealing the defense in the process.

The court's ruling on admissibility of prior sexual conduct of the victim should be recorded by the court stenographer and in the court file, thus limiting defense counsel's questioning of the victim at trial. Should defense counsel raise issues deemed impermissible, the court's oral or written ruling can provide a basis for contempt sanctions.

3. Rape Shield and the Exceptions

Although rape shield statutes generally prohibit admission of the victim's prior sexual conduct as well as opinion or reputation evidence regarding the victim's sexual conduct, certain exceptions have been recognized by statute or case law. Defense counsel must demonstrate the proffered evidence is otherwise admissible *and* fits into one of the narrowly delineated exceptions.

Before considering whether exceptions to the rape shield statutes apply, determine if the proffered evidence is inadmissible for other reasons. In *Commonwealth v. Johnson*, 566 A.2d 1197 (Pa. Super. Ct. 1989), defense counsel proffered the victim's 6-year-old friend to testify the victim told her that in the past a neighborhood boy had fondled the victim. The friend believed the statement was made several years ago but could not remember any details about the statement other than the boy had "touched" the victim. The victim denied any prior assault, never reported any prior assault, and denied making the statement. This statement was deemed classic hearsay, lacking in probative value, and not competent evidence, regardless of the rape shield statute.

If, on the other hand, competent evidence is proffered, evaluate whether rape shield exceptions apply. (See Appendix IV.36 for a sample brief in opposition to defendant's motion to admit victim's prior sexual history.)

a. Consent. Evidence of the victim's prior sexual conduct with the defendant is admissible if the defense of consent is available and being claimed. In cases of young children, this exception is not available since many statutes define sexual contact with a child under a particular age as a crime no matter how willing the victim. Likewise, sexual contact between a child and his parents or other relatives is generally criminal, regardless of consent. As victims enter adolescence, the consent defense becomes more plausible to a jury in a nonincest case. Consult with the victim to determine if what was initially reported as a one-time occurrence actually was a continuing course of conduct. Assess whether prior sexual conduct with the defendant reveals a pattern of abuse that began when the victim was a young child, is truly and legally a consensual relationship, or is some hybrid.

b. Alternative explanation of objective signs of intercourse or behavioral symptoms. The defense may wish to present evidence at trial of the victim's sexual contact with someone else as an alternative explanation for semen, pregnancy, sexually transmitted disease, vaginal or anal trauma, or other objective signs of intercourse. Defense counsel will argue that, although the victim was abused, it was not by the defendant. (See, e.g., *Saylor v. State*, 559 N.E.2d 332 [Ind. Ct. App. 1990] [reversible error to exclude evidence of victim's prior sexual assault, as defendant was entitled to use such evidence to explain corroborating medical evidence]; *State v. Douglas*, 797 S.W.2d 532 [Mo. Ct. App. 1990], explained in *State v. Sales*, 58 S.W.3d 554 [Mo.Ct.App. 2001] [rape shield statute no bar to defendant's cross-examination of complainant with respect to alleged sexual activity with her boyfriend; defense contended complainant's sexual activity with boyfriend took place after alleged assault but before examination by pediatrician and was admissible to explain alternative cause for victim's condition].)

In order to avoid evidence coming under this exception, consider whether to offer testimony regarding the condition the defense plans to explain. Review medical records with the state's expert; e.g., "redness" documented by the examining physician can be consistent with causes other than intercourse, including infection or normal irritation, and you may decide not to introduce it in your case-in-chief. In that case, there would be no basis to allow in allegations of a third-party assault as an alternative explanation for such medical findings.

Determine whether the state's medical expert can tell anything about the timing of intercourse based on the evidence. Was the anal tear fresh? How many days old was the observed injury? Can the expert tell how long the victim had gonorrhea? If the defense proffers a sexual contact with a third party predating the injury, that third-party sexual contact would not be relevant and should be excluded.

When pregnancy results from a sexual assault, the defense may attempt to show that someone other than the defendant caused it. If the victim had or will be getting an abortion, contact the doctor performing the abortion to ascertain whether tests were or can be done on fetal material to determine the approximate time of conception or paternal characteristics (e.g., blood type). Check with the state laboratory, F.B.I. laboratory, or a private laboratory to determine if DNA testing can be conducted on fetal material. Have the state's investigator interview defense witnesses who will be called to testify concerning other sexual contact. The earlier in the process they are interviewed, the less likely they will have tailored their testimony. Use all this information to block the defense offer of proof if the third-party sexual contact does not correspond to the date of conception.

If the victim had a baby as a result of the abuse, use blood and DNA tests to determine paternity. Allowing evidence of third-party sexual contact will depend on how conclusively tests establish paternity (i.e., excluding or including both the defendant and the third party).

Some jurisdictions will not allow questions about third-party sexual contact when the victim has a sexually transmitted disease unless the defense can actually show (1) the other person had the disease at the time the victim contracted it and (2) the other person had access to the victim at that time. You may need to investigate the other individual's medical background to be properly prepared. (See *Commonwealth v. Nieves*, 582 A.2d 341 [Pa. Super. Ct. 1990].)

Finally, some jurisdictions allow a prior sexual assault of the victim to come into evidence to provide an alternative explanation for her behavioral symptoms. (See *Hall v. State*, 396 S.E.2d 271 [Ga. Ct. App. 1990] [evidence of prior unrelated sexual assaults of child victim admissible to establish other possible causes for behavioral symptoms described by state's expert witness as typical of child sexual abuse accommodation syndrome].) If considering calling a behavioral expert in your case in chief, be sure to review the rape shield case law. Benefits of expert testimony may be outweighed by the dangers of opening the door to admission of prior sexual assault.

c. Bias. Prior sexual conduct with a third party is admissible to prove bias against the defendant if

- The evidence is relevant to show bias or attack credibility
- Its probative value outweighs its prejudicial value
- There is no alternative means to prove bias or attack credibility

The defense must, under this exception, logically show that third-party sexual relations caused the victim to have a "specific bias" against the defendant that would prompt a fabricated report of abuse. For example, a Pennsylvania court found that evidence of an incestuous sexual relationship between the victim and her brother was admissible, because the defendant/father of the victim had attempted to end that relationship and throw the brother out of the home directly prior to the victim's allegation of sexual abuse by her father. (See *Commonwealth v. Black*, 487 A.2d 396 [Pa. Super. Ct. 1985].)

Specific bias against the defendant as a result of prior sexual conduct is difficult to show. When, for example, the victim accused the defendant after her mother questioned her about a possible pregnancy, any reference to the pregnancy was found inadmissible since no specific bias against the defendant was shown. (*Commonwealth v. Simmons*, 513 A.2d 453 [Pa. Super. Ct. 1986]; see *State v. Wright*, 776 P.2d 1294 [Or. Ct. App. 1989] [evidence that victim had motive to accuse defendant falsely given her independent basis of knowledge of sexual matters and sympathy and praise she received for reporting sexual molestations not admissible because defense counsel did not show particularized motive or bias that would lead victim to fabricate charge]; but see *People v. Gray*, 568 N.E.2d 219 [Ill. App. Ct. 1991] [defendant's right to confront victim by cross-examining her about fear of pregnancy by another man as her motive to falsely accuse him superseded rape shield statute]; *State v. Finley*, 387 S.E.2d 88 [S.C. 1989] [evidence of victim's alleged intercourse with neighbor in defendant's presence and defendant's belief regarding her resulting motive for allegedly fabricating charge was not within purview of rape shield statute].)

Argue that the prejudicial value of a prior sexual assault far outweighs its probative value, particularly if the defense has other ways to attack the victim's credibility. This argument appeals to the court's sense of fairness, and the judge can protect the victim's privacy while allowing the defense to pursue a permissible line of impeachment. In *Commonwealth v. Poindexter* (539 A.2d 1341 [Pa. Super. Ct.], *appeal denied*, 549 A.2d 134 [Pa. 1988]), the victim reported that her father (the defendant) had sexually abused her. Defense counsel wished to produce evidence at trial that the victim was having sex with her boyfriend and that her father found out and filed criminal charges against the boyfriend for corrupting the morals of his daughter. As a result, according to the defense, the victim fabricated the sexual abuse charges against her father. The trial judge allowed defense counsel to ask the victim about the fact that the defendant brought charges against her boyfriend, but disallowed under the rape shield statute any reference to the *type* of charges or the fact the victim had a sexual relationship with her boyfriend. (See also *Commonwealth v. Purcell*, 589 A.2d 217 [Pa. Super. Ct. 1991] [trial court did not abuse discretion by removing explicit sexual material from victim's love letters to her cousin, despite defendant's claim that court's ruling prevented him from establishing victim had bias against him for breaking up her relationship with her cousin; court permitted defendant wide latitude in attempting to prove victim's testimony was influenced by bias].)

d. Source of sexual knowledge. Some jurisdictions have created an exception that admits evidence of third-party sexual assault to show an alternative source of sexual knowledge on the part of young victims. Under this exception, defense attorneys argue that the victim's graphic testimony about sexual acts results from an earlier sexual assault by someone else. (See *State v. Budis*, 593 A.2d 784 [N.J. 1991] [evidence of 9-year-old victim's prior sexual abuse by her stepfather, described in language almost identical to her description of incidents involving defendant, relevant and admissible to show alternative source for child's sexual knowledge]; *State v. Jagielski,* 467 N.W.2d 196 [Wis. Ct. App. 1991] [4-year-old's allegation of prior assault admissible to explain sexual knowledge and provide alternative explanation for her changed behavior and fear of returning home; prior acts by third party nearly identical to those with which defendant charged; some occurred at the same place and time, and allegations were all made at same interview].)

To combat admission of third-party sexual contact under this exception, show the differences between the prior assault and current case. For example, if the prior abuse involved fondling the victim's vagina on top of her clothing and the case at hand involves penetration of the victim's mouth with the defendant's penis, it is clear the prior experience did not provide the victim with her source of knowledge of oral intercourse. The prior assault should thus be excluded.

If the sexual acts are similar, differentiate for the judge the two experiences with other details. Did the first assault occur in a different location? Was the prior assault a one-time violent incident as opposed to an ongoing escalation of sexual abuse? When appropriate, argue that the victim's life experience and exposure to peers and older siblings also serves as an alternative basis for sexual knowledge. This argument will be most persuasive with an older victim.

If the judge rules that prior sexual contact is not admissible to show an alternative source of sexual knowledge, be careful in your closing argument not to give the jury the impression that the victim was never assaulted prior to the defendant's act. Emphasize the details of the victim's testimony but do not add, "How else would she have known all of the details of sexual assault if not from the defendant?"

e. Attack on victim's credibility. Using prior sexual assaults as evidence to attack the victim's credibility has been resisted by most courts. When attempted, the defense will argue that the victim's past reports of sexual assault were false and part of a pattern of fabricating sexual abuse claims. Such efforts serve to put the victim "on trial" rather than the defendant and should be strenuously opposed. Some courts hold that evidence of prior false accusations is relevant to the victim's credibility and conduct pre-trial evidentiary hearings to determine if the contention is supportable. (See *State v. Kobow,* 466 N.W.2d 747 [Minn. Ct. App. 1991] [victim not subject to impeachment concerning prior allegations of sexual abuse because she did not refer to allegations during direct examination and defendant could not show that prior allegations were false]; *People v. Passenger,* 572 N.Y.S.2d 972 [App. Div. 1991] [there was no basis for believing prior unrelated claims false]; *Shelton v. State,* 395 S.E.2d 618 [Ga. Ct. App. 1990] [failure to hold hearing on alleged false accusations of sexual misconduct is error; error could be cured by post-trial hearing to determine whether reasonable probability of falsity existed]; *State v. Boiter,* 396 S.E.2d 364]S.C. 1990] [17-year-old victim's prior allegation of sexual abuse at age eight too remote and thus inadmissible]; *State v. LeClair,* 730 P.2d 609 [Or. Ct. App. 1986] [since court balanced probative value with prejudicial effect before disallowing evidence, the decision to prohibit defendant from cross-examining victim regarding earlier incidents did not violate defendant's right to confrontation]; but see *United States v. Stamper,* 766 F. Supp. 1396 [W.D.N.C. 1991], *aff'd sub nom. In re One Female Juvenile Victim,* 959 F.2d 231 [4th Cir. 1992] [introduction of evidence that victim had admitted in writing to falsely accusing her mother's boyfriend of sexual molestation on prior occasion and accusing two others under circumstances tending to show ulterior motives was admissible to show motive or scheme of fabrication by victim]; *Clinebell v. Commonwealth*, 368 S.E.2d 263 [Va. 1988] [victim's prior false claims of pregnancy created reasonable probability that prior claims of sexual misconduct against grandfather and uncle were false; fact finder could infer defendant-father's alleged sexual acts with daughter also fabrications; therefore, prior allegations of sexual behavior were admissible to impeach victim's credibility].)

Check the status of each prior sexual assault your victim experienced. If the case was reported, find out what happened. Obviously, if the case went to trial and the offender was convicted, the contention that the accusation was false cannot be supported and the victim should not be subjected to inquiry about it. If the prior assault resulted in an acquittal or the victim recanted, investigate why it happened and consider presenting testimony during the pre-trial hearing to explain it. Get information about the acquittal from the prosecutor who tried the prior case; you may find that there was overwhelming evidence, but the victim froze on the stand.

4. Dealing With Admission of Prior Sexual Assault

If, despite your best efforts, evidence of a prior sexual assault is deemed admissible, discuss the ruling ahead of trial with the victim. Offer reassurance that the judge's decision is no reflection on the victim and is part of the trial process. In preparing your case, consider introducing the prior sexual assault during direct examination of the victim. This will show the jury you are not attempting to hide anything. Through expert testimony and/or closing argument, turn the prior sexual assault evidence to your advantage. If the victim was previously sexually assaulted, did not report it, and the assaultive behavior continued for years, but she immediately reported the current assault, you can argue that the victim learned from past experience that she had to tell someone to make the abuse stop. Or perhaps the victim did report the previous abuse, but nothing happened to the perpetrator; the victim's perception that no good comes from reporting explains the delay in disclosing the present offense. A child victim who has had sexual contact with more than one adult may have been taught that sexual contact was acceptable or may have learned that sex was the only way to gain affection or attention. If the defendant knew that others had sexual contact with the victim, he may have viewed her as an easy target. Do not minimize the prior sexual assault; determine how it affected the victim and turn it to your advantage.

E. Defense Motion to Preclude Defendant's Spouse From Testifying: Marital Privilege and Spousal Immunity

In most child abuse cases, the defendant's spouse is often an essential witness; e.g., as an eyewitness, a charged codefendant, or the person to whom the defendant admitted his assault. When defense counsel learns the state will call the spouse of the defendant as a witness, the prosecutor can expect a motion to preclude her testimony.

There are two bases for prohibiting spousal testimony: spousal immunity and the confidential marital communication privilege. Traditionally, spousal immunity bars testimony by one spouse against another in any criminal proceeding, and some states do not allow a defendant's spouse to be called as a witness by the prosecution.

(See, e.g., *People v. Hamacher*, 438 N.W.2d 43 [Mich. 1989].) Federal courts have ruled that a spouse cannot be compelled to testify but may choose to testify (*Trammel v. United States*, 445 U.S. 40 [1980]). Some states, such as California, follow this rule. Spousal immunity, however, ends when the marriage is terminated by death or divorce. (See, e.g., *Chadwick v. State*, 335 S.E.2d 674 [Ga. Ct. App. 1985], *aff'd*, 339 S.E.2d 717 [Ga. 1986].)

More and more states, however, limit spousal immunity to a few situations and exclude child abuse cases. (See, e.g., *State v. Willette*, 421 N.W.2d 342 [Minn. Ct. App. 1988]; *Daniels v. State*, 681 P.2d 341 [Alaska Ct. App. 1984]; Myers, J. E. B. [1997]. *Evidence in child abuse and neglect cases* [3rd ed., pp. 30–31]. New York: John Wiley.) Check case law, statutes, and evidence rules regarding the status of spousal immunity in your state.

The privilege regarding confidential communications prohibits a person from testifying against the defendant in a criminal proceeding about statements made in confidence during the marital relationship. (See, e.g., *State v. Holmes*, 412 S.E.2d 660, 664 [N.C. 1992].) The privilege can be invoked by either spouse even after the marriage is dissolved if the discussion took place while they were legally married. The privilege does not apply if the communication was made in the presence of a third party, including siblings, parents, and children capable of understanding. (See, e.g., *Commonwealth v. Skibicki*, 586 A.2d 446 [Pa. Super. Ct. 1990].) It also does not apply to acts performed in front of the spouse or to ordinary daily exchanges. Testimony regarding threatening communications (e.g., letters, verbal threats, or attempts to force the spouse to give false testimony) are not barred by this privilege. (See, e.g., *People v. Mohammed*, 470 N.Y.S.2d 997 [Sup. Ct. 1984].). Again, in many states, the privilege of confidential marital communications does not apply in legal proceedings involving children. (See Myers, *supra*.) Check your jurisdiction's case law, evidence rules, and statutes.

IV. MOTIONS REGARDING SIMILAR ACTS

Both prosecutors and defense attorneys may make motions related to similar acts by a defendant. These could include uncharged misconduct or prior convictions. Ordinarily, the defense moves *in limine* to exclude such evidence, and the prosecution moves to allow it.

Whether responding to a defense motion *in limine*, arguing in support of your own motion, or simply going ahead with a plan to introduce such evidence, it is essential to research the applicable law thoroughly and brief the issue in advance. This is an area in which jurisdictions have differing rules and that appellate courts scrutinize carefully. Unless well thought out and properly supported by appropriate reasons and authority, use of such evidence could endanger an otherwise valid conviction. Evidence of similar acts can, if used properly, go far toward strengthening a case and obtaining a guilty verdict.

Federal Rule of Evidence 404(b) states,

> *Other Crimes, Wrongs or Acts.* Evidence of other crimes, wrongs or acts is not admissible to prove the character of a person in order to show that he acted in conformity therewith. It may, however, be admissible for other

purposes, such as proof of motive, opportunity, intent, preparation, plan, knowledge, identity, or absence of mistake or accident.

Most states have comparable rules, and in child abuse cases, many states have distinct case law dealing with acceptable uses of similar acts evidence.

A. Prior Bad Acts Involving Same Victim

1. Sexual Misconduct

Evidence of the defendant's uncharged acts of sexual misconduct involving the *same victim* is permitted in most, but not all, states. Generally, the purpose of such evidence is to prove the defendant's motivation by showing his sexual desire for a particular child. The reasoning would be the same for evidence of prior convictions for sexual crimes against the same victim. While remoteness in time is a factor considered by appellate courts, 7 years between the charged acts and prior incidents has been allowed (*State v. Ferguson*, 667 P.2d 68 [Wash. 1983]). In *United States v. Hadley*, 918 F.2d 848 (9th Cir. 1990), prior offenses evidence was allowed despite a 10-year gap. New York is among the jurisdictions that precludes the admission of uncharged prior bad act evidence. (See *People v. Lewis*, 506 N.E.2d 915 [N.Y. 1987].) One alternative is to charge all instances of the defendant's past abuse of the victim. (See Chapter III.)

Most sexual offenses require an intent to arouse or gratify the sexual desires of the defendant or the victim. When the accused clearly places intent in issue, prior sexual abuse of the same victim is probative of the defendant's mental state. For example, the accused will occasionally admit touching the victim but deny it was done with sexual intent; e.g., he was teaching the victim about sex or was bathing her. The court will decide the admissibility of this evidence by weighing its probative value against its prejudicial effect. (See, e.g., *State v. Tecca*, 714 P.2d 136 [Mont. 1986] [probative value of prior acts evidence was not outweighed by prejudicial effect to defendant where evidence established continuing course of conduct and helped in determining opportunity, intent, and identity].)

As a practical matter, it makes sense for the prosecutor to try to use evidence of any uncharged misconduct by the defendant with the victim. There are a number of reasons why such misconduct might not be charged. It may be beyond the statute of limitations. It may have occurred outside your jurisdiction. It may not have been revealed by the victim in time to include it with the original charges. Or, because of repeated and long-standing abuse, the victim may be unable to identify dates and incidents with enough precision to file charges on each incident.

When pointing out the relevance of such evidence to the court, stress that it will provide the jury with a comprehensive framework within which to evaluate the charged offenses. When victims have been repeatedly abused, their testimony about its extent and how it began can help to explain their difficulty recalling and differentiating incidents, why seemingly inconsistent descriptions of abuse are offered, and how fear of the defendant or other factors caused reluctance in revealing the abuse. Testimony concerning the prior acts will help the jury understand escalation of the molestations. (See *People v. Wright*, 411 N.W.2d 826 [Mich. Ct. App. 1987].)

Some courts allow evidence of uncharged conduct only on the condition that the jury is given a limiting instruction. (See *State v. Catsam*, 534 A.2d 184 [Vt. 1987] [conviction reversed on other grounds].) If a standard instruction does not exist, be prepared to submit a suggested draft. One court approved the following instruction:

Evidence has been received that the defendant has been involved in offenses other than that charged in the information. This evidence has been received solely on the issue of the defendant's intent or design. This evidence may be considered by you only for the limited purpose for which it was received. (*People v. Gaither*, 582 N.E.2d 735, 741 [Ill. App. Ct. 1991])

2. Physical Abuse

In physical abuse cases, evidence regarding uncharged incidents or prior convictions involving the same victim has been allowed. Such evidence can explain why a medical doctor diagnosed a past injury as consistent with the battered child syndrome or refute the defendant's claims that the child's injury resulted from an accident rather than a deliberate assault. Depending on the case, such evidence may also be relevant to such issues as intent, opportunity, or identity, particularly when the child has multiple caregivers. In a U. S. Supreme Court case, the Court held that evidence the victim was a battered child and suffered prior injuries was admissible in the defendant's trial for murder of the child. The prior injury evidence, although not linked specifically to the defendant, was probative on the issue of intent since it demonstrated that her death was not an accident. (*Estelle v. McGuire*, 112 S. Ct. 475 [1991].) The premise in *Estelle v. McGuire* has generally been accepted in most, if not all, jurisdictions in the country. Prosecutors should, through thorough investigation, attempt to link the prior injury to the defendant in order to strengthen the argument for admissibility. Finally, prior events, although not necessarily criminal, may be admissible to prove the defendant's knowledge of a dangerous condition and to establish reckless intent of the defendant. (See *People v. Harris*, 580 N.E.2d 185 [Ill. App. Ct. 1991] [evidence of prior similar incident was admissible to prove recklessness in prosecution for involuntary manslaughter for the death of infant left unattended in bathtub]; *People v. Turner*, 249 Ill.App.3d 474, 619 N.W.2d 781 [1993].)

B. Prior Bad Acts Involving Different Victims

1. Sexual Abuse

Evidence of uncharged acts of misconduct or prior convictions for crimes against children other than the victim falls into a different category and is not as readily admissible as prior acts against the same victim. When uncharged acts can be used to prove preparation, plan, intent, opportunity, knowledge, or absence of mistake/accident, the prosecutor has a basis for urging their admission. (See, e.g., *State v. Stephens*, 466 N.W.2d 781 [Neb. 1991] [finding evidence of defendant's prior sexual contact with child relevant to show identity of assailant and absence of accident or mistake].) If similarities among offenses are so striking they can be classified as "signature crimes," the evidence should be admissible.

The following four elements will usually be evaluated to determine admissibility: similarity between current charged crimes and other acts, nearness in time of other acts to the charged crimes, tendency of the other acts to establish a common plan, and probative value of evidence of the other acts. (See *George v. State*, 813 S.W.2d 792 [Ark.], *opinion supplemented on denial of reh'g*, 818 S.W.2d 951 [1991] [defendant's conviction for first-degree sexual abuse 2 months before his trial for sexual abuse of two and a half-year-old girl admissible to show intent, motive, or plan]; *State v. Moore,* 819 P.2d 1143 [Idaho 1991] [testimony of defendant's stepdaughter and daughter that he sexually assaulted them 11 and 3 years ago was admissible at trial for abuse of 6-year-old granddaughter; testimony demonstrated plan to exploit and abuse identifiable group of young females living in household]; *State v. Jendras,* 576 N.E.2d 229 [Ill. Ct. App. 1991] [evidence of sexual misconduct that occurred 9 and 15 years prior to trial demonstrated an ongoing plan when all three victims were male seventh and eighth grade students in defendant's class who went alone to his apartment, were provided swimming suits, and invited to swim and use sauna]; *State v. Moore,* 404 S.E.2d 695 [N.C. Ct. App. 1991] [evidence that defendant previously abused 7-month-old stepson and 15-year-old sister-in-law was admissible at trial for sexually assaulting 5-year-old daughter to show common plan; continuous execution of similar acts throughout a long period tended to show probability of ongoing plan]; *State v. Crane,* 799 P.2d 1380 [Ariz. Ct. App. 1990] [prior conviction for sexual conduct with minor properly admitted since other acts took place within same time span as act performed upon current victim and sufficiently similar—both involved vaginal intercourse with underage females; difference in victims' ages was unimportant].)

Though not admissible in all jurisdictions, some courts allow evidence of prior sexual offenses involving other children to prove "propensity," "lustful disposition towards children," or "depraved sexual inclination." (See *State v. Lopez,* 822 P.2d 465 [Ariz. Ct. App. 1991] [evidence of defendant's previous acts of sexual misconduct with other boys admissible to show continuing propensity for sexual aberration]; *State v. Lachterman,* 812 S.W.2d 759 [Mo. Ct. App. 1991], *cert. denied,* 112 S. Ct. 1666 [1992] [evidence of repeated acts of sexual abuse of children demonstrates, *per se,* propensity for sexual aberration and depraved sexual instinct, is distinct exception to rule against admission of evidence of uncharged crimes, but is limited to sexual abuse of children of same sex as victim occurring near in time to acts charged]; *State v. Charles L.,* 398 S.E.2d 123 [W. Va. 1990] [unrelated sexual acts and tendencies of defendant admissible to show lustful disposition toward children].) Unless your jurisdiction clearly recognizes the validity of this reasoning, try to establish additional, more widely accepted reasons to justify admission of evidence of other sexual misconduct.

Never ignore allegations of misconduct against other victims. The defendant may open the door for admission of misconduct against other victims. (See Chapter V, Section VII.B.) Even if inadmissible in your case-in-chief, this evidence could be used to cross-examine a defense expert who testifies that the defendant did not engage in grooming behavior. See Federal Rule of Evidence 405, which allows cross-examination of a witness who offers opinions about the defendant's character or a particular trait concerning their knowledge of the defendant's past conduct. Finally, evidence of misconduct against other victims is also helpful to the judge at sentencing.

2. Physical Abuse

a. Admissibility

i. Lack of accident. Evidence of prior physical assaults against children other than the current victim may be admissible to prove absence of accident or mistake in a prosecution for physical abuse. (See *Commonwealth v. Donahue,* 549 A.2d 121 [Pa. 1988] [evidence of prior acts of child abuse was admissible in homicide prosecution of another victim to show lack of accident, since both victims were being toilet trained at time defendant was caring for them, both were seriously injured or killed while under his care, and a similar pattern of injuries evidenced over children's bodies]; *State v. Ostlund*, 416 N.W.2d 755 [Minn. Ct. App. 1987] [other bad acts against victim and other children was admissible to show absence of accident in child death case]; *State v. Holland*, 346 N.W.2d 302 [S.D. 1984] [evidence defendant grabbed 10-week-old baby by throat and hit 1-week-old baby with his fist was admissible to show absence of mistake or accident in trial for murder of 23-month-old child].)

ii. Intent of defendant. In homicide and physical abuse crimes, the prosecutor must usually prove that the defendant acted in a particular state of mind. The defendant's state of mind can often be shown through circumstantial evidence, including prior acts of violence toward other victims. (See *People v. Summers*, 559 N.E.2d 1133 [Ill. App. Ct. 1990] [evidence defendant struck deceased's 2-year-old stepbrother about the head at approximately same time defendant struck fatal blows to 18-month-old victim's head was probative of his state of mind as he performed these acts].) In *State v. Coffey*, 389 S.E.2d 48 (N.C. 1990), the court permitted evidence of the defendant's sexual assault of another child to prove his felonious intent in the kidnapping/murder of a 10-year-old. (See also *Rhodes v. State*, 717 P.2d 422 [Alaska Ct. App. 1986] [evidence that defendant's first child died of skull fracture when 5 weeks old and alone with defendant was admissible to show defendant acted with extreme indifference to human life when assaulting his 6-week-old daughter]; *State v. Powers*, 645 P.2d 1357 [Mont. 1982] [in prosecution for deliberate homicide, evidence of defendants' acts against other children showed common design of disciplining children by beatings pursuant to their church's policy and provided proof of their motive].)

iii. Identity of defendant or instrument of crime. Prior bad acts may also be admissible to prove the identity of the defendant or the instrument used in the assault. For example, in *Rivera v. State*, 561 So. 2d 536 (Fla. 1990), the court held that evidence of a prior assault was admissible in a murder trial because the similarities between the two crimes were sufficient to be probative of the identity of the defendant. Both victims were female, 11 years old, Caucasian, blond, and petite; both were alone, approached from behind in daylight, and located within 4 miles of the defendant's home; after each incident, individuals received phone calls from a man who identified himself as "Tony" and stated he was wearing pantyhose and leotards and had fantasized about raping young girls. (See also State v. Hudgins, 810 S.W.2d 664 [Mo. Ct. App. 1991] [testimony that witness recognized electric extension cord allegedly used to strangle victim because defendant had used same cord to beat her and her children was relevant and admissible, even if testimony amounted to proof of another, unrelated crime].)

b. Proof of prior bad act. Some states require the prosecutor to establish by clear and convincing evidence that a prior bad act was actually committed by the defendant. (See *State v. Wilson*, 513 A.2d 620 [Conn. 1986]; *People v. Summers*, 559 N.E.2d 1133 [Ill. App. Ct. 1990]; *Commonwealth v. Donahue*, 549 A.2d 121 [Pa. 1988].)

In *Estelle v. McGuire*, 112 S. Ct. 475 (1991), the Court ruled that when the state attempts to prove injuries are a product of child abuse rather than accident, evidence of prior injuries is relevant even though it does not purport to prove the abuser's identity, which paves the way for greater admissibility. The prosecutor should attempt to demonstrate some connection between the other bad acts and defendant (e.g., the other victims were also in his care when they were injured) to strengthen the inference at trial that the defendant is responsible for the abusive acts. (See Myers, J. E. B. [1997]. *Evidence in child abuse and neglect cases* [3rd ed.]. New York: John Wiley; Myers, J. E. B. [1988]. Uncharged misconduct evidence in child abuse litigation. *Utah Law Review, 1988, 479.)

c. **Pre-trial investigation and motions.** Check with the CPS agency, police, and family members to determine whether they know or have records of the defendant physically assaulting any other child. If you discover prior incidences, obtain all available paperwork, including a transcript of proceedings. Locate reports of prior uncharged physical abuse and interview witnesses for further details. Obtain a search warrant if necessary to examine and document a scene and collect evidence.

Find out as much as possible about the defendant's statements regarding the current case. If the defendant (or anyone) called 911, get the tape immediately. If someone called for an ambulance, find out what was said to those who answered the phone and responded to the call. Have your investigators interview anyone to whom the defendant may have offered an explanation for the child's injuries. Look closely at medical records of the victim; every entry is potentially valuable. If the defendant told anyone, including the triage nurse, emergency room doctor, social worker, or any hospital personnel that the victim was injured accidentally, the door has been opened to present prior acts of child abuse to rebut the allegation of accident. Even if the accident defense is abandoned at trial, you should be allowed to present the evidence. You can argue that the defendant first claimed the injury was accidental but realized the infeasibility of the accident claim when prior acts of child abuse and other evidence were discovered and switched defenses mid-stream, demonstrating consciousness of guilt. It is essential to file a pre-trial motion to permit admission of prior assaultive behavior involving the victim or others. Outline the similarities between current charged crimes and other acts: the nearness in time of the other acts, the tendency of other acts to show a common plan or scheme, and the probative value of these acts. Be careful about presenting testimony in the pre-trial motion that creates a transcript the defense may later use for impeachment. If possible, make legal arguments based on the factual averments in your motion. If the court denies the motion, listen carefully to the defendant's testimony at trial. He may yet open the door to evidence of prior acts of child abuse by claiming he would never harm a child. (See Appendix IV.29 for an example of a prosecution motion for admission of prior acts of physical abuse and Chapter V, Section VII, on rebuttal evidence.)

V. ADDITIONAL PROSECUTION PRE-TRIAL MOTIONS

Motions *in limine* or other pre-trial motions may be filed for traditional purposes or to seek advance permission of the court to arrange special courtroom configurations or use special procedures in child abuse cases. Though available to both prosecution and defense, these motions are more likely to be useful to prosecutors. In addition, prosecutors have become more aggressive in urging courts to exercise responsibility toward victims and the community when ruling on pre-trial release of defendants.

A. Motions *In Limine*

It is important for the prosecutor to anticipate defense questions, comments, arguments, or tactics that may be objectionable. Motions *in limine* that encourage court rulings in advance on such matters will give the state a better idea of how to prepare for trial. Favorable rulings should decrease the incidence of objectionable defense behavior and prevent some of the harm of statements that the jury is then instructed to disregard. (See Appendixes for Chapter IV for sample motions *in limine*.)

For example, it has become increasingly common for defense attorneys in *voir dire,* opening statement, or closing argument to refer to child abuse cases that have received a great deal of negative publicity. Most jurisdictions disallow such references, but once made, a prosecutor has little recourse but to ask the judge to instruct the jury to disregard the reference, to declare a mistrial, or to allow the prosecutor to respond in closing. Since these approaches may be ineffective or undesirable, a court ruling in advance on the issue is preferable as a means of preventing improper remarks. On issues that may not be as clear cut, motions *in limine* will at least permit the prosecutor to argue the issue prior to trial. Favorable rulings can reduce or eliminate problems, while unfavorable rulings at least provide the prosecutor with opportunities to plan the best strategy for dealing with problems.

Other common uses of motions *in limine* are to prevent defense witness hearsay statements, exclude defense expert-witness testimony, obtain a ruling requiring attorneys to ask age-appropriate questions of the victim, limit character witness testimony to permissible questions and answers, and prohibit reference to negative opinion or character evidence about victims, including evidence that may be covered by rape shield laws. (See Section III.D., this chapter.)

Many prosecutors will be familiar with opposing counsel who appear frequently and often employ improper personal tactics. Motions *in limine* can bring such matters to the attention of the trial court before the defense lawyer has a chance to repeat objectionable behavior. Providing the court with transcripts of hearings or trials demonstrating inappropriate behavior is an especially effective response to protests that the prosecutor's concern is unfounded.

B. Motions to Amend Dates

If you find after interviewing the victim and completing other investigations that the dates alleged in the original charging document are too narrow, amend them following your jurisdiction's rules of criminal procedure. If, for example, the original document states crimes occurred "on diverse dates from July 1999 through August 2001," and the victim later says incidents continued until the defendant left the home (in November 2001 according to the victim's mother), move to amend that the incidents occurred "on diverse dates from July 1999 through November 2001" or add a count naming an incident or incidents occurring "on a date separate and distinct from the dates in counts (all others)." Check your case law and consult with experienced child abuse prosecutors from your jurisdiction to determine the appropriate charging language.

Inform defense counsel in writing of your intention to amend dates in the charging documents well in advance of the trial date. If the court does not rule on the issue until the day of the trial, you can counter any claim of surprise and argue against a continuance by showing that the defense had adequate notice.

Charging documents must reflect, as accurately as possible, the full period of the abuse to avoid defense cross-examination aimed at showing the victim's trial testimony does not match allegations in the charging documents. Your explanation to the jury that the law allows amendments of dates because it recognizes victims disclose slowly will help educate the jury about the disclosure process.

C. Motion for Admissibility of DNA Evidence (*Frye/Daubert* Hearing)

All states permit admission of DNA evidence, and many, if not all, have appellate court rulings on DNA admissibility requirements.

A National Academy of Sciences (NAS) report recommends that courts take judicial notice that DNA is accepted within the scientific community for purposes of *Frye* hearings. (National Research Council, Committee on DNA Technology in Forensic Science. [1992]. *DNA technology in forensic science* [p. 145]. Washington, DC: National Academy Press.) The report noted that judicial inquiry should be limited to whether "appropriate standards have been followed, that tests were adequately performed by a reliable laboratory, and that the appropriate protocols for DNA typing and formulation of an opinion were fully complied with . . . so long as the safeguards we discuss in this report are followed, admissibility of DNA typing should be encouraged."

Despite these decisions, findings, and the NAS Report, a prosecutor may be required to establish the reliability of scientific principles used by a local DNA laboratory at a pre-trial hearing in order to introduce DNA comparison evidence at trial. The first task will be to determine the legal standard of admissibility for new scientific principles in the local jurisdiction. Some states have adopted the standard set forth in *Frye v. United States*, 293 F. 1013 (C.A.D.C. 1923). The scope of *Frye* is typically limited to determining whether there is general acceptance within the scientific community of the principles of DNA identification. (See, e.g., *State v. Ford*, 392 S.E.2d 781 [S.C. 1990]; *Cobey v. State*, 559 A.2d 391 [Md.], *cert. denied*, 565 A.2d 670 [Md. 1989].)

Several states do not subscribe to the *Frye* analysis but adopt a more lenient standard of admissibility: Scientific evidence must be shown to be reliable, probative, and relevant, but general acceptance need not be proven. (See, e.g., *Andrews v. State*, 533 So. 2d 841 [Fla. Dist. Ct. App. 1988].) A hearing may still be required outside the presence of the jury to determine whether evidence is relevant, reliable, and "helpful" to the fact finder, and even if admissible on this basis, DNA evidence may be excluded if the court determines it would have a propensity to mislead the jury. (See *Kelly v. State*, 824 S.W.2d 568 [Tex. Crim. App. 1992].) Other states have refined the *Frye* rule with additional requirements. For example, California requires not only that scientific procedures are generally accepted but that the correct scientific procedures were used in the case. (See *People v. Kelly*, 549 P.2d 1240 [Cal. 1976].)

To persuade a judge at the pre-trial hearing that the DNA science proposed for the courtroom is sufficiently accepted within the scientific world, you must first understand the material yourself. Question lab personnel, local experts, or other prosecutors who have tried these cases. Read cases and articles discussing DNA evidence. Once you master the material, do not wait until testimony starts. Prepare a brief for the judge setting forth legal standards to be applied. Use the brief as a starting textbook on DNA analysis with a glossary of terms, general science articles, copies of cases and law review articles. (See, e.g., Beeler, L., & Weibe, W. R. [1988]. DNA identification tests and the courts. *Washington Law Review, 63,* 903.) Generally, the Rules of Evidence do not apply to the *Frye* hearing. The judge can therefore consider classic hearsay information as substantive evidence. Consider attaching expert testimony or letters from experts to your brief. (Be aware that the opposing side might opt to do this as well.) (See the Resource List at the conclusion of Chapter III for further references.)

Give an opening statement when the hearing begins. Explain the appropriate legal standard, the science, the process for analyzing DNA, and how any error would work to the defendant's benefit. Both at the hearing and at trial, use as many exhibits as possible: charts, models, and slides of relevant pieces of laboratory equipment used in this process. Have scientists bring in some of the smaller pieces of equipment. Get a quality light box for viewing the autorads.

While it is important to use your scientists as expert witnesses, do not overlook local experts. Independent experts eliminate the financial interest argument that might be used against your laboratory experts and allow you to show that procedures used in this case are performed in the community every day. You can find scientists using DNA analysis at almost any hospital or medical research facility.

D. Motions for Special Courtroom Configurations or Seating Arrangements

1. Adjustments to Accommodate Children

If you foresee a need to use closed circuit television testimony, close or limit attendance of observers in the courtroom, rearrange the courtroom, utilize support persons for the victim, or use special furniture (such as a smaller chair for the child victim or an additional chair for a support person) and other aids, consider a pre-trial motion for such authorization. Chapter VI discusses these issues in detail. See also 18 U.S.C. § 3509 (1990), calling for federal courts to make the same kind of adjustments for child witnesses as many state courts. (See Appendixes for Chapter VI for samples of motions for special accommodations for children.)

2. Pro Se (In Propria Persona) *Defendants*

In those rare instances when facing a *pro se* defendant in a child abuse case, it is especially important to consider courtroom configuration issues and prepare appropriate pre-trial motions. If a defendant has decided to proceed *pro se,* this decision is very possibly motivated by a desire to intimidate the child victim. Most defendants realize self-representation is not in their best interest since they usually lack the legal knowledge necessary to conduct a viable defense and are likely to antagonize jurors in a child abuse case.

Do everything in your power to ensure the *pro se* defendant does not succeed in intimidating the child. If the defendant attempts to disrupt proceedings or threaten witnesses, the trial court has the power to stop such harassment and can even terminate self-representation if the defendant engages in serious misconduct. (See *Faretta v. California,* 422 U.S. 806 [1975].) The court can also take steps to ensure that abuse of witnesses does not occur. It can require that the defendant not approach the child and remain behind counsel table at all times, as with any attorney. The court can also clearly admonish the defendant in advance that improper or argumentative questions will not be tolerated and the defendant will be held to the same standards as an attorney, with no leeway because of self-representation.

During cross-examination of the child victim, most courts recognize that the rights of the child outweigh the right of the defendant to conduct his own cross-examination. In those instances where the defendant is proceeding *pro se,* one of two options should be utilized: An attorney should be appointed for the limited purpose of conducting cross-examination of the child victim or the judge should conduct the cross-examination on the defendant's behalf. In both instances, the questions should be those of the defendant but merely be posed through another party. In addition, bear in mind that the defendant should have immediate access to the questioner in order to preserve the defendant's right to confront witnesses against him.

E. Motions to Exclude Witnesses

Motions to exclude witnesses are made in many criminal cases and can be especially beneficial in child abuse litigation.

F. Motions to Restrict Media Access or Seal Records

Motions for courtroom closure generally stem from fear that the child will be identified by name, picture, or otherwise by the media. While many reporters acknowledge the harm of unwanted publicity to child abuse and sexual assault victims and agree to suppress identifying information, others may not share that view. Prosecutors who expect difficulty may want to file pre-trial motions to close the courtroom, seal records, or restrict media access. (See Appendix IV.9.) Motions and orders to seal portions of discovery or court documents available to the public but possibly traumatizing to victims may be appropriate in some circumstances. Statutes in some jurisdictions prohibit use of the victim's name or other identifying information in documents available to the public. (See Table IV.3.)

Blanket closure of child abuse proceedings is not realistic at this time, and case-by-case evaluation is required. The United States Supreme Court in two cases, *Richmond Newspapers, Inc. v. Virginia,* 448 U.S. 555 (1980), and *Globe Newspaper Co. v. Superior Court,* 457 U.S. 596 (1982), overturned statutes excluding media and the public from criminal trials because of such overall exclusions.

Tailor your motions and, if possible, fashion court orders in the least restrictive way so as not to violate First Amendment rights or the defendant's right to a public trial. If cameras are allowed in the courtroom, a motion and order not to photograph the victim or use the victim's name and to distort the victim's voice in any broadcast may be adequate. Excluding the public and press only during the child victim's testimony would be another carefully tailored closure order. (See, e.g., *Mosby v. State,* 703 S.W.2d 714 [Tx. Ct. App. 1985] [proper to exclude public from courtroom during child's testimony to protect child witness from harassment or undue embarrassment resulting from his sexually explicit testimony].)

Table IV.3 Statutes Limiting the Release of Identifying Information Concerning Child Abuse Victims in Criminal Proceedings

Alabama	ALA. CODE § 15–1-2(b)
Alaska	ALASKA STAT. § 12.61.110–140
Arizona	ARIZ. REV. STAT. ANN. § 13–4401(18), -4434 +
Arkansas	ARK. CODE ANN. § 16–90–1104
California	CAL. EVID. CODE § 352.1 +
	CAL. PENAL CODE § 293, -.5
Colorado	COLO. REV. STAT. § 4.1–303(2)
	COLO. REV. STAT. § 14–13–20 (5)
Connecticut	CONN. GEN. STAT. ANN. § 1–210
	CONN. GEN. STAT. ANN. § 54-86d, -86e +
Delaware	DEL. CODE ANN. tit. 11, § 9403
District of Columbia	D.C. CODE § 16–2316
Florida	FLA. STAT. ANN. ch. 119. 07(3)(f)
	FLA. STAT. ANN. ch. 794.024, -03 +
Georgia	GA. CODE. ANN. § 16–6-23 +
Illinois	725 ILL. COMP. STAT. ANN. § 190/1 et seq.
Indiana	IND. CODE § 35–37–4-12 +
Iowa	IOWA CODE § 915.36
Louisiana	LA. REV. STAT. ANN. § 44:3(A)(4)(d) +
Maine	ME. REV. STAT. ANN. tit. 30-A, § 288
Maryland	MD. ANN. CODE art. 27, § 772 -78
Massachusetts	MASS. ANN. LAWS ch. 258B, § 3 +
Michigan	MICH. STAT. ANN. § 28.788(11)
Minnesota	MINN. STAT. ANN. § 609.3471
	MINN. STAT. ANN. § 611A.035 +
Nevada	NEV. REV. STAT. § 48.071
New Hampshire	N.H. REV. STAT. ANN. § 21-M:8-k
New Jersey	N.J. STAT. ANN. § 2A:82–46
New York	N.Y. CIV. RIGHTS LAW § 50-b +
North Dakota	N.D. CENT. CODE § 12.1–34–02(10) +
	N.D. CENT. CODE § 12.1–35–03
Ohio	OHIO REV. CODE ANN. § 2907.11 +
Pennsylvania	42 PA. CONS. STAT. ANN. § 5988
Rhode Island	R.I. GEN. LAWS § 11–37–8.5
South Carolina	S.C. CODE ANN. § 16–3-730 +
South Dakota	S.D. CODIFIED LAWS § 23A-6–22
Texas	TEX. CODE CRIM. P. ANN. §. 57.02, -.03 +
Virginia	VA. CODE ANN. § 19.2–269.2
Washington	WASH. REV. CODE ANN. § 7.69A.030(4)
	WASH. REV. CODE ANN. § 10.52.100
Wisconsin	WIS. STAT. ANN. § 904. 01, -13 +
Wyoming	WYO. STAT. ANN. § 6-2-310, -4–403 +
	WYO. STAT. ANN. § 14–3-106 +
U.S. Code	18 U.S.C.A. § 3509(d)

NOTES: This compilation includes all statutes (excluding military and tribal statutes) that require the identity of a child victim/witness in a criminal proceeding to be withheld from the record or the public. The citation date indicates the year of passage or latest amendment. This table includes all legislation passed through June 2002, as verified through Lexis Nexis.

+ Applies to victims generally.

G. Motions Regarding Bail and Pre-Trial Release

Defendants who are arrested or charged and summoned to court will normally appear before a judge for decisions on bail and pre-trial release. Only in extremely rare and unusual cases will a defendant be ordered held in custody without bail, and those situations should be easy to recognize. Child abuse cases commonly require the prosecutor to take a position regarding amount of bail and conditions of pre-trial release.

1. Considerations

Request bail whenever reasons justify it. Jurisdictional practices about setting bail may not be identical, but factors such as a defendant's prior criminal record, ties to the community, employment and mental health history, stability, reputation, prior history of compliance with court orders, dangerousness, threat to victim, and seriousness of current offense(s) are commonly taken into account. The Bail Reform Act of 1966, 18 U.S.C. § 3141 (2002), indicates circumstances that could result in the defendant's detention prior to trial. In *United States v. Salerno*, 481 U.S. 739 (1987), the U. S. Supreme Court, ruling on pre-trial detention of suspects considered dangerous, determined that provision of the 1984 Bail Reform Act did not violate a defendant's Fifth Amendment due process rights or the Eighth Amendment's excessive bail clause. Since the Bail Reform Act applies only to cases prosecuted in federal courts, check your state's statutes concerning the possibility of pre-trial detention of a defendant pending trial. (See, e.g., Ariz. Rev. Stat. Ann. § 13–3961 [2001].) Make every effort to obtain criminal history information from local, federal, and military authorities by the time of the bail hearing. If necessary, request a postponement of the hearing until you have this information.

The same factors mentioned above should determine conditions set by the court on a defendant's release. Even when bail is set and the defendant is in custody, conditions should be set in the event he eventually posts bail and is released. In addition to conditions discussed below, consider such conditions as continued employment, random urine testing for drugs/alcohol, etc. Release conditions should be clear, specific, and in writing.

2. No-Contact Orders

a. Prohibiting contact with victim. In almost every child abuse case, the prosecutor should request and the court should order that the defendant have no contact with the victim. Written orders are best, stating the defendant is to have no personal, phone, written, or computer contact. These conditions are necessary to protect the child from additional abuse and block the defendant from trying to influence the child's testimony.

In cases involving abuse of the child at home, the defendant should not be allowed to stay or visit. Point out that it is unfair for courts to punish the victimized child by removing her from familiar surroundings when it is the defendant who is accused of violating the family and the law. If necessary, present affidavits or testimony regarding threats to the child by the defendant and detailing negative consequences of removing the child from home. As adults, defendants can usually find another place to go prior to trial and are better able to handle disruption. The National Council of

Juvenile and Family Court Judges formally recognized the importance of removing offenders rather than children from the home in its August 1986 report, *Deprived Children: A Judicial Response—Seventy-Three Recommendations* (recommendations 20, 31, 33, and 34). (See also National Legal Resource Center for Child Advocacy and Protection, *Recommendations for Improving Legal Intervention in Intrafamily Child Sexual Abuse Cases* [October 1982].)

Professionals who have handled intrafamilial abuse cases know removal of the offender may not always be possible. Problems often arise when the nonoffending spouse refuses to support the child and chooses instead to believe the offender. Here, the potential pressure on a child to recant is great, and the only viable option may be to place the child in a safe, neutral environment. If a judge refuses to prohibit a defendant from contact with the victim, the prosecutor should vigorously advocate for supervision of any contact by a responsible adult, such as the child's caseworker. The nonoffending spouse is not an appropriate choice for supervision of visits. If the spouse is supportive of the victim, it invites trouble between the spouses. If the spouse is supportive of the offender, it magnifies pressure on the victim to recant.

If the state's case is also the subject of a juvenile or family court proceeding, advise the child protective services worker or victim's attorney of the no-contact order in the criminal case and ask for notification of any violation of the order. Coordination will help to ensure consistent orders out of both courts.

b. Prohibiting contact with other children. In addition to seeking an order prohibiting contact between the defendant and victim, prosecutors may want an order prohibiting contact with other children. The scope and nature of abuse as well as the number of victims will often determine the state's success in persuading the court to issue such an order. In a case involving allegations of repeated sexual abuse of students at school, there is little question about the appropriateness of such an order. A single incident of physical abuse or fondling in the home may not be as clear-cut to the judge and could simply result in an order not to engage in unsupervised contact with the victim.

3. Compliance With Therapy as a Condition

On occasion, the defense attorney will tell the court at the pre-trial release hearing that his client is in treatment and thus presents no risk to reoffend or act improperly. If such a representation is made, ask the court to condition the defendant's release on continuing compliance with therapy. In addition, the prosecutor should request the judge to order a regular report from the therapist to the court on the defendant's treatment progress and risk to the child. It is unlikely a reputable therapist would contend that the child's contact with the offender is free of risk. In fact, most therapists insist that the courts issue an order directing the defendant to have no contact with the victim. Appropriate safeguards in the court's conditions of pre-trial release protect the child and remove potential obstacles to the prosecution of the case.

4. Motions to Revoke Pre-Trial Release

If, at any time prior to trial, a prosecutor learns of a defendant's failure to abide by release conditions, the State should take immediate steps to have the release revoked. In some jurisdictions, violation of conditions is a basis for a probable cause arrest. It is especially important to take immediate action if the condition violated is the no-contact order. While defendants may offer creative rationalizations for their behavior, neither courts nor prosecutors should tolerate these manipulations. Every effort must be made to structure clear directives that leave no room for a defendant's erroneous interpretation. (See Appendix IV.1 for sample motion to revoke conditional release.)

5. Motions Regarding Children's Testimony

a. Developmentally appropriate oath. If questioned appropriately, even young children can articulate that they know the difference between the truth and a lie and that there are negative consequences for lying in court. In every case involving testimony from a young child, the prosecutor should educate the court about the research on developmentally appropriate oaths and then ask the court to administer an oath the child can understand.

b. Linguistically and developmentally appropriate questions. Just as the court will not allow a witness who can speak only Spanish to be questioned in English, the court should not allow children to be questioned in a manner that is difficult for them to understand. In support of this motion, the prosecutor can attach myriad research articles concerning the developmental and linguistic capacities of young children. The prosecutor may also wish to support the motion with an affidavit or testimony from a child psychologist, educator, or other professional familiar with the child who will be testifying at trial and who can give the court insight into the particular child's developmental and/or linguistic capacity. When properly educated, courts can do a better job requiring both the prosecutor and the defense attorney to ask questions the child witness can understand. In general, court and counsel should limit the use of pronouns, double negatives, "isn't it true" questions, and questions asking the child for estimates of weight, measurement, or distance. For more information regarding proper interviewing techniques for children, see Chapter II.

c. Silent objections. Children have egocentric personalities and often take raised voices and animated speech personally. The prosecutor can educate the court about this issue and ask that, during the testimony of young children, neither attorney be allow to shout objections. Instead, the attorneys can simply raise their hand if they have an objection. The judge will then recognize the attorney and quietly argue the objections outside the presence of the child. If the court rules against a prosecutor bringing the motion, the prosecution should renew the motion at the first sign that a defense attorney is making the child uncomfortable. If, for example, the defense attorney shouts "Objection!" and the child jumps, the prosecutor should immediately seek a protective order.

d. Time certain and recesses. In preparing children for court, prosecutors must ascertain the time of day when the child is at her best and ask the court to grant a "time certain" for the taking of the child's testimony. If the court denies this motion, the prosecutor must do everything possible to call the child to the witness stand when the child is functioning at her best. Generally speaking, young children are freshest in the morning. The prosecutor should verify this with a parent, teacher, or other person familiar with the child. The prosecutor should also inquire as to the child's nap times, use of medications, and any other relevant factors.

The prosecutor should also ascertain the child's attention span. The attention span of a typical preschool child is no longer than 15 minutes, and for a kindergarten child is no more than 30 minutes. The prosecutor can alert the judge about these facts and support the motion with affidavits about this child's typical attention span. The court should grant frequent recesses reflecting the child's need to stay fresh and focused. It is not sufficient for the judge to instruct a young child to alert the court if a break is needed. It is unrealistic, if not cruel, to expect a young child to tell a courtroom full of adults that he needs a break. It is not the job of the child but rather of the adults in the courtroom to ensure the comfort of young witnesses. For further information regarding this motion, see Chapter VI.

VI. CONCLUSION

The foregoing review of pre-trial motions does not cover all possible motions a prosecutor might raise or encounter in a child abuse case, but does give an overview that can serve as a starting point. Do not hesitate to use pre-trial motions in creative ways to achieve greater justice in the criminal system. Success at this stage can mean the difference between a positive or negative experience for the victim as well as between conviction or acquittal.

VII. RESOURCE LIST

Beeler, L., & Wiebe, W. R. (1988). DNA identification tests and the courts. *Washington Law Review, 63,* 903.

[Block, Comment] Defining standards for determining the admissibility of evidence of other sex offenses. (1977). *UCLA Law Review, 25,* 261.

[Comment] Developments in the law: Privileged communications. (1985). *Harvard Law Review, 98,* 1450.

Donner-Froelich. (1985). [Comment] Other crimes evidence to prove the *corpus delicti* of a child sexual abuse case. *University of Miami Law Review, 40,* 217.

Mendez, M. A. (1984). California's new law on character evidence: Evidence Code Section 352 and the impact of recent psychological studies. *UCLA Law Review, 31,* 1003.

Myers, J. E. B. (1997). *Evidence in child abuse and neglect cases* (Vols. 1 & 2). New York: John Wiley.

Myers, J. E. B. (1988). Uncharged misconduct evidence in child abuse litigation. *Utah Law Review, 1988,* 479.

Necessity or permissibility of mental examinations to determine competency or credibility of complainant in sexual offense prosecution. [Annotation] (1986). *A.L.R., 45,* 4th 310.

Potential problems may disallow DNA evidence. (1993). *The Prosecutor, 27*(2), 11.

Protecting child rape victims from the public and press after Globe Newspaper and Cox Broadcasting [Note]. (1983). *George Washington Law Review, 51*, 269.

Quigley. (1978). [Comment] Admissibility of evidence under Indiana's "Common Scheme or Plan Exception". *Law Journal, 53*, 805.

Stolorow & Clarke. (1992). Forensic DNA testing: A new dimension in criminal evidence gains broad acceptance. *The Prosecutor, 25*(4), 13.

Storing evidence may make DNA tests suspect. (1993). *The Prosecutor, 27*(1), 11.

Validity and construction of constitution or statute authorizing exclusion of public in sex offense cases. [Annotation] (1971[1986]). *A.L.R., 39*, 3d 852.

Wallendorf. (1978). Evidence: The emotional propensity exception. [Note] *Arizona State Law Journal, 1978*, 153.

Whitcomb, D. (1992). *When the victim is a child: Issues for judges and prosecutors* (2nd ed.). Washington, DC: National Institute of Justice.

V

Trial

I. PRE-TRIAL PREPARATION

Preparation involves not only assembling and knowing the facts of the case, but also thinking about the case and developing a strategic message of what the case is about. Think about the most effective arguments that could be raised on behalf of the accused and then determine what can be done at each stage of the trial to counter them. The following sections are areas to consider as you organize your trial file and focus on the issues and potential problems in your case.

Theme and Closing Argument Ideas. Long before you enter the courtroom, think about the theme of your case and the form of your closing argument. While you cannot anticipate everything that may surface during trial, your theory of the case will help you to assess the strengths and weaknesses of your case, formulate appropriate *voir dire* questions, and develop a strong opening statement. (See this chapter, Section III.) Advanced development of the theme of your case will allow you to develop a profile of who on a jury might be most receptive to such a theme. The theme will also help structure direct and cross-examinations and closing argument. For more information on the importance of developing a theme, see this chapter, Section II.B.

Review of Statements. Carefully review all pre-trial statements or testimony given by the victim, the defendant, and witnesses to be called at trial. A key concern is to make sure that the investigators have turned over all witness statements to the prosecution. Chart the statements, looking for inconsistencies, cross-corroboration, and impeachment material. Some prosecutors make skeletal outlines of prior statements with page notations, while others use plastic tabs to signal crucial portions. Whatever system you develop, make sure the content of prior statements is easily accessible during trial. As the statements are reviewed, consider the legal arguments that will allow these statements into evidence, such as spontaneous declarations, prompt complaints, and other hearsay exceptions.

Period of Abuse. Chart the victim's ages, school grades, or other identifying factors such as prior addresses or prior teachers during the period the abuse occurred. This will help you present that information clearly to the jury. In some situations, a chart may be used as demonstrative evidence.

Applicable Case Law and Pre-Trial Motions. Consider the legal issues likely to come up during trial and gather relevant statutes and case law. You should keep memoranda of law or files on issues that arise on a regular basis in child abuse cases. It is much easier to update previous work as you prepare for the next trial than to start from scratch each time. If at all possible, prepare a trial brief regarding the issues most crucial to your case. A brief statement of facts will help you organize your thoughts and theories. It can also go far in convincing the court to rule in your favor. Determine what motions *in limine* should be made. The list may include motions to amend the dates contained in the charging documents, rape shield motions, and motions to allow jurors to take notes in a complex case, as well as many other issues. (See Chapter IV for a more detailed discussion of motions *in limine*.) For example, it is often wise to bring a motion to preclude any evidence of a complainant's sexual history before jury selection and to further request an offer of proof. This avoids unanticipated testimony regarding allegations of a child's sexual contact with other individuals. Knowing whether such testimony will be produced before the trial begins allows both the prosecutor and the complainant to prepare for such testimony. The American Prosecutors Research Institute's National Center for Prosecution of Child Abuse provides legal research and other technical assistance.

Discovery and Notice to Defense. Verify that the State has given all discovery to defense counsel. Make sure the defense has complied with any obligations to provide reciprocal discovery. If necessary, file motions to compel. Double check to ensure that all required notices were given to the defense. For example, in some jurisdictions, the State must provide notice of intent to seek the mandatory minimum prison sentence, expert witnesses, intent to proceed under a special statutory hearsay exception, intent to present prior bad acts of the defendant, and physical evidence to be presented. It is important to check jurisdictional statutes, as the requirements vary greatly from state to state.

Defendant's Statements. Most jurisdictions require that the prosecution give notice to the defense of statements made by the defendant to law enforcement officials. While most prosecutors recognize this requirement, prosecutors must take numerous steps to obtain these statements. For example, some oral statements by a defendant may not be considered significant by a police officer and not be included in a report. One way to ensure that all the statements made by the defendant are known is to interview all officers who had contact with the suspect before the filing of charges. Prosecutors should also seek to obtain all statements the defendant may have made about the allegations to persons other than law enforcement. The defendant may have made statements to friends, neighbors, siblings of the complainant, to the news media, or in the course of family court proceedings. Sometimes inconsequential statements become excellent impeachment material. If the defendant gave a multitude of statements, you should index them much as you would the victim's statements.

Prior Bad Acts and Convictions of Defendant. Make sure you have obtained information concerning the defendant's prior arrests and convictions. Information concerning a defendant's prior criminal history such as the underlying acts and statements made by the defendant in the course of those proceedings may require a subpoena for court records or files, presentence reports, parole records, or probation records. The details of the prior bad acts will enhance the effectiveness of prior acts or convictions when used during cross-examination. Investigation into a defendant's prior bad acts may uncover information that is not admissible at trial but may be helpful in plea negotiations, precluding character witnesses, or during a sentencing argument.

The State should note harassment or threats made by the defendant to the victim or the victim's family. The prosecutor should aggressively pursue motions to revoke bail or obtain a warrant for the defendant's arrest on charges of witness intimidation or tampering. These threats may be admissible not only on cross-examination but also during the State's case-in-chief. Appropriate notice must be given when these acts are going to be presented during the State's case-in-chief.

Subpoenas and Record Checks. Make sure you have subpoenaed all necessary witnesses and documentary material, including serving a subpoena *duces tecum* for the files documenting prior arrests and convictions of other witnesses for possible impeachment use. You must disclose prior convictions of your witnesses to the defense. If any of your witnesses are on probation or parole, prepare the witness for that fact to come out regardless of whether you decide to bring it out during direct examination or leave it to the defense during cross-examination. If television or radio stations covered your case, subpoena and review the relevant tapes. Reviewing newspaper and other articles regarding the case can lead to additional witnesses. You may locate additional statements that can be used to impeach witnesses at trial. Newspaper articles and television or radio tapes may also be useful for motions for change of venue owing to pre-trial publicity.

Work Records of the Defendant. Subpoena the defendant's or parent's work records to show when the defendant had access to the victim. The records should show vacation or sick time, work hours, and other information showing access. Work records may also reveal information concerning a defendant's prior bad acts. In addition, work records may lead to witnesses from the defendant's workplace to rebut defense character witnesses at trial.

Military Records of the Defendant. A defendant's military records may provide information concerning the defendant's education, training, prior bad acts, or the circumstances of the defendant's discharge from the military. The records may also provide useful information for purposes of bail. For example, a defendant's history of being AWOL is a factor to argue in setting a defendant's bail.

The Elements of the Offense and Jury Instructions. Review the statutory definitions of the charged crimes. Their language may be incorporated in opening and closing statements. A concise list of the elements of each crime and evidence you will use to prove each one can be extremely helpful. Make sure that essential elements, such as the age of the victim and the defendant, are covered during the case-in-chief. Submit any special jury instructions in accordance with local procedure.

Witness List. Organize the case-in-chief by jotting down a list of the ideal witness line-up. Your list should include their schedules and phone numbers so that you or your assistants can contact them to arrange for their appearance. Rather than specifying questions, consider outlining important issues or elements you wish to cover. Also, set out the exhibits to introduce through each witness so they can be checked off as the trial proceeds.

Cross-Examination Checklists. Outline the areas you want to cover on cross-examination of the defendant and defense witnesses. This list should include details that the victim or other prosecution witnesses mention that can be corroborated by defense witnesses.

Investigation of Defense Witnesses. The State should insist on compliance with applicable defense obligations to give notice of witnesses. Check the court file for indications of potential defense witnesses such as return of service of defense subpoenas, or *ex parte* orders for payment of expert witness fees. Contact defense witnesses, or have an investigator do so, to interview them about their testimony and knowledge of the case. If you conduct the interview, make sure to have a detective or other investigator with you. If stories change at trial, the detective can testify concerning prior inconsistent statements. Contact the National Center for Prosecution of Child Abuse for information on defense experts.

Preparation of Prosecution Witnesses. Prepare *all* your witnesses for trial, including doctors and social service personnel, regardless of whether they have previous experience testifying in a criminal trial. Do not assume that a witness who has testified in other cases will necessarily be well prepared to testify in your case. Review with the witness areas to be covered during direct examination, possible cross-examination questions, and the documents either side might introduce. Make sure you are aware of any notes or documents your witnesses may use to refresh their recollection or notes they have made that must be disclosed to the defense. The witnesses should be told what information or documents regarding their testimony have been provided to the defense.

Physical Evidence and Exhibits. Carefully review evidence seized by the police or other investigators with an eye to both the helpful and damaging use of that evidence in the case. Read through all documents, such as the victim's diary. Provide defense counsel with the opportunity to review physical evidence if this is required but make sure the detective is present. List the exhibits you plan to introduce at trial, necessary chain of custody witnesses, and the witnesses through whom you will authenticate and offer each exhibit. Note potential objections to admissibility and your responses. Consider pre-marking exhibits if they are numerous and this is permissible in your jurisdiction.

Demonstrative Evidence. Be creative in designing charts, graphs, diagrams, models, or other visual exhibits to illustrate important points and simplify complicated information. In a multiple-victim, multiple-defendant case, a chart can be particularly helpful during closing argument. Medical illustrations of the genitals can help explain "negative evidence" such as how there can be sexual intercourse without disruption of the hymen. Models and diagrams are often quite useful to explain the mechanism of injury in a physical abuse or fatality case. Time lines can clarify the periods when the defendant had exclusive custody of the child. Prepare exhibits such as photographs of injuries in different sizes and in black and white as well as color.

Scientific Testing. If bodily fluids such as semen or blood were found on the victim's clothing, bed sheets, or elsewhere, ensure appropriate laboratory tests were ordered, the results were received and forwarded to defense counsel, and the State's expert is prepared to testify concerning the meaning of the test results. In addition, make sure the expert has provided, and the State has disclosed, all of the notes that were made in connection with this work.

Victim Support and Therapy. Arrange for someone—usually a trained victim-witness advocate—to provide support for the victim before, during, and after the trial. If your jurisdiction lacks such resources, determine which family members, friends, or other professionals will have a calming influence on the victim. If possible, choose a support person who will not be subject to a sequestration order. Ensure that the victim is involved in therapy, which is usually critical to a victim's well-being and ability to testify, especially if caregivers are not supportive. Let the therapist know the status of the case and consider working together to prepare the child for trial. Carefully document statements made by the child prior to commencing therapy in order to counter defense suggestions that the child's account is the result of ideas "planted" during therapy. Beware that notes and records of a support person or counselor may be obtained by the defense.

Photograph of Victim. Obtain a picture showing the victim's appearance at the time of the abuse. When there has been a long delay between the abuse and trial, photos may illustrate the victim's state of mind and the lack of consent in view of her youth at the onset of the abuse. Photographs of victims in multivictim cases help to keep each child separate from the others in the jurors' minds.

Family Court Records and Transcripts. If your case involves a divorce or custody dispute, obtain relevant court records and transcripts. Check to see whether the defendant violated restraining orders when gaining access to the victim. Review family court records for any findings of fact that may be relevant to the criminal trial. Also, be aware of any neglect and abuse proceedings. Review court orders to see if the defendant or any other trial witness violated those orders. Read all signed affidavits or testimony of the defendant or other witnesses and be alert for prior consistent or inconsistent statements.

Plea Offer. Consider whether plea negotiation is appropriate and, if so, formulate an offer. Whether initiated by you or the defense attorney, it is important to know the type of sentence you will seek when plea negotiations begin.

II. JURY SELECTION[1]

A. Introduction

Facts do not determine the outcome of a trial. Jurors determine the outcome of a trial. While there are many principles that can be applied during jury selection, it is an area of litigation that calls for tremendous judgment.

As a general rule, the State will want jurors who will identify with the key witnesses and the issues in the case. Thus, it is important to determine what the issues of the

---

[1]Sections b, c, f, h(4)(5)(6)(7)(8)(9)(10)(11) are reprinted by permission of Lexis Law Publishing from *Sexual Assault Trials,* Second edition (1998). Copyright 1995, The Michie Company. Copyright 1998, LEXIS Law Publishing. Reprinted with permission from *Sexual Assault Trials,* Second Edition by Paul DerOhannesian II. Lexis Law Publishing, Charlottesville, VA. (800) 446-3410. All Rights Reserved.

case are, as presented by the case theme. Developing an effective case theme will guide the attorney through jury selection. As noted below, jurors use themes and stories to unravel the facts of a case. Just as the most successful commercial products do not appeal to everyone, the most persuasive facts do not appeal to all jurors. The better the message, the more likely it will appeal to jurors. Knowing your message will also help you focus on those jurors who may be most receptive to it. Traditional tools of jury selection, such as demographic factors, are among the poorest in determining who is an ideal juror for one's case.

It is also helpful to have an understanding of the research and studies of jurors in sexual assault and child abuse cases to help focus not only on issues to address in jury selection but also to assist in the development of case themes and stories.

B. The Importance of Establishing the Theme of a Case

Before selecting the jury, it is important to have a theme of the case. Research indicates that jurors process testimony, facts, and pieces of information by composing a story that allows them to make sense of what they are hearing. (Pennington, N., & Hastie, R. [1991].) A cognitive theory of juror decision making: The story model. *Cardozo Law Review, 13,* 519. Jurors need a story or theme to explain events and a person's behavior to help them put together what may appear to be disconnected evidence. As might be expected, jurors also bring certain assumptions with them. The theme or story line of the trial also helps the juror to fill in gaps in the evidence and provides the motives or reasons for behavior.

Research has helped to identify what constitutes a good theme. The three most important components to a good theme are consistency, plausibility, and completeness. Pennington and Hastie write,

> A story is consistent to the extent that it does not contain internal contradictions either with evidence believed to be true or with other parts of the explanation. A story is plausible to the extent that it corresponds to the decision maker's knowledge about what typically happens in the world and does not contradict that knowledge. A story is complete when the expected structure of the story "has all of its parts." . . . Missing information, or lack of plausible inferences about one or more major components of the story structure, will decrease confidence in the explanation. (p. 528)

The authors note that once jurors determine what happened, or establish a story, it is difficult for them to change their opinions (p. 556). This supports the proposition that a convincing theory of the case should be presented as early as possible in the opening statement, having already laid the foundation for that theme during *voir dire.*

Establishing a theme of the case will help guide the jury selection, opening statement, and the examination of witnesses. Themes are not found in law books. They are developed from life experiences. More important, they are developed from the facts of the case and the interactions between the attorney and witnesses. A theme should be short and simple, explain the testimony, and tie diverse pieces of testimony together. A good theme should deal with both constraints and weaknesses.

To establish a theme, write down the important points in your case, the negative factors in your case, and any response to the weaknesses in your case. The lists should then be synthesized. Then think about unifying traits, characteristics, or expressions that tie various thoughts together.

A common theme for prosecutors in child sexual assault cases is the "betrayal of trust," or the "family secret." Either theme can explain how the abuse began, how it continued, why the victim did not report at first, and why the victim may have recanted her allegations. Themes should be tested on friends, family, and office staff for effectiveness and for suggestions for improvement or modification.

Use the theme statements during jury selection. The theme can help identify issues, characteristics, and traits of preferred jurors. Determine who best understands your theme. To whom does the theme's message make the most sense? Establishing a theme helps identify those jurors who will be most sympathetic to your case. If the theme involves the "lost innocence" of a child victim, ask yourself what type of juror is most likely to identify with the child's innocence and who would be least sympathetic to that claim.

C. Research and Studies of Jurors in Sexual Assault and Child Abuse Cases

There has been some research on jury selection and jurors in rape cases. Harry Kalven and Hans Zeisel, authors of the classic and frequently cited *The American Jury,* published in 1966 by the University of Chicago Press, studied 106 forcible rape cases involving adult victims. Kalven and Zeisel found that the jurors' feelings about a victim's behavior were crucial in determining whether to convict or acquit a defendant. These were the authors' conclusions:

> The law recognizes only one issue in rape cases other than the fact of intercourse: whether there was consent at the moment of intercourse. The jury, as we come to see it, does not limit itself to this one issue; it goes on to weigh the woman's conduct in the prior history of the affair. It closely, and often harshly, scrutinizes the female complainant and is moved to be lenient with the defendant whenever there are suggestions of contributory behavior on her part. (*Id.,* pp. 249)

> Where it perceives an assumption of risk the jury, if given the option of finding the defendant guilty of a lesser crime, will frequently do so. It is thus saying not that the defendant has done nothing, but rather that what he has done does not deserve the distinctive opprobrium of rape. If forced to choose in these cases between total acquittal and finding the defendant guilty of rape, the jury will usually choose acquittal as the lesser evil. (*Id.* p. 254)

More recently, the National Center for Prevention and Control of Rape, a division of the National Institute of Mental Health, reviewed 37 sexual assault trials in Indianapolis from July 1978 through July 1980. Despite the perceived changes in attitudes about proper behavior for women in cases of adult rape, the authors of the study found,

> If the case does come to court, the jurors are as likely to be influenced by the behavior of the victim as by the factors of the assault. They treat more seriously the rape of a woman who appears chaste or is traditional in her life

style. They are more likely to exonerate men charged with raping women who reputedly are sexually active outside of marriage or women who knew the assailant. (Brozan, N. [1985]. Jurors in rape trials studied. *New York Times,* June 13, p. C13.)

As for defendants, the study found,

If they came across as losers, scruffy, held no job and were unmarried, they tended to be biased against him [sic]. But if they were attractive, had evidence of having a girlfriend or were married and thus had access to a woman, the jurors could not believe that they would commit rape. More often than any other statement, we heard, "But he doesn't look like a rapist." (*Id.*)

A 1980 study of jurors in sexual assault cases found that of those surveyed

1. Two thirds (66%) agreed with the statement, "Women provoke rape by their appearance and behavior."

2. Forty-one percent thought "a charge of rape two days after the act has occurred is probably not rape."

3. One third (34%) stated, "In order to protect the male, it should be difficult to prove that rape has occurred."

4. One third (34%) reported that "a woman should be responsible for preventing her own rape."

5. Nearly one third (32%) felt "the degree of a woman's resistance should be the major factor in determining if a rape has occurred."

6. Nearly one third (29%) felt "most charges of rape are unfounded" and that rape of a woman by a man she knows can be defined as a "woman who changed her mind afterward."

(Field, H. S., & Bienen, L. B. [1980]. *Jurors and rape* [pp. 50–530]. Lexington: MA: Lexington Books.) The study also looked at several other factors in jurors' backgrounds that might affect their decisions, but there was, as might be expected, a significant amount of unpredictability. While there appears to be gradual movement away from the stereotypes and beliefs reflected in the earlier studies, these stereotypes are resilient and still present.

A 1992 study surveyed 50 child abuse experts and 150 jurors using a 40-item questionnaire. (Morison, S., & Greene, E. [1992]. Juror and expert knowledge of child abuse. *Child Abuse & Neglect, 16,* 595.) Jurors differed from the experts on 22 of 28 questions. Over half of the jurors believed that children are easily manipulated into making false reports and over half of the jurors expected physical trauma as a result of the abuse (p. 603). More than one third of the jurors believed that allegations are frequently proven false. Still another third of the jurors believed victims resist, run, and tell after being sexually abused. There was a high level of agreement between jurors and experts that children do not invite abuse (86%) and that moral and legal responsibility rests with the adult (88%). Jurors between 53 and 83 years of age were less knowledgeable about the dynamics of child sexual abuse than younger jurors (p. 605). Jurors 18–31 years of age believed that allegations of child sexual abuse are usually not false, that allegations are often retracted, and that children do not invite abuse. The study also indicated that those jurors with more education scored better on knowing that most abuse does not involve intercourse; that violence, resistance, and crying are atypical; and that the lack of physical trauma is common in these cases (p. 606).

A 1993 study by the Illinois State Attorney General of jurors in 23 sexual assault trials found that the jurors' attitudes regarding victims were better predictors of the trial outcome than the strength of the case. (Maroules, N., & Reynard, C. [1996]. *State's Attorney's Appellate Prosecutor Child Witness Project, voir dire in child victim sex trials: A strategic guide for Illinois prosecutors* [p. 33, 2nd ed.]. Attorney General's Office of Illinois.) This is a significant finding and likely true in both adult and child sexual assault cases. This survey concluded that approximately 80% of jurors found children credible and approximately 88% had empathy for the victims (pp. 30–31). Interestingly, the survey found that jurors held a negative attitude toward a case that utilized special child hearsay statutes (p. 36). This study, too, found that more-educated jurors were more receptive to abuse allegations (p. 37).

Another study of child sexual assault jurors found that corroborating testimony of a child victim increased the victim's credibility. (Bottoms, B. L., & Goodman, G. S. [1994]. Perceptions of children's credibility in sexual assault cases. *Journal of Applied Social Psychology, 24,* 702.) It also found that exposure to a defendant's criminal acts or other negative defendant-character evidence heightened the perception of the victim's credibility and a defendant's guilt.

D. The Approach

Before jury selection begins, familiarize yourself with the jury orientation process in your jurisdiction so you know what jurors have been told before you speak with them. If they receive a juror handbook, read it. If they are routinely shown a video, watch it. If juror questionnaires are available prior to the *voir dire* process, look at them. In a case with pre-trial publicity, review the media coverage to determine the type of information potential jurors may already possess.

First impressions have a major impact on potential jurors. Be conscious of your dress and appearance, remembering that you want jurors to perceive you as a trustworthy professional. Potential jurors are evaluating you just as much as you are evaluating them. During jury selection, many lawyers agree it is best to sit or stand facing the jurors as opposed to turning to observe each individual as he or she is called. No one appreciates averted glances and whispered discussions while singled out by name. Similarly, jurors remember the manner in which they are challenged or sworn. An abrupt or sarcastic "challenge" or "excuse the juror" without mention of a name can leave a negative impression with the juror or anyone else listening. "Please challenge/excuse Mrs. Jones, Your Honor. Thank you, Mrs. Jones," may lessen the indignity of being excused. Similarly, a clear-cut, "Swear Mrs. Jones," or "Pass Mrs. Jones for cause, Your Honor," politely nodding in her direction is better than a mere, "Swear the juror" or "Pass for cause." It is important to gain rapport with prospective jurors as soon as possible. Also, jurors will notice whether you look organized and ready to proceed during jury selection. Be prepared to challenge, accept, or excuse jurors quickly and politely. Avoid consulting with others, whispering, or gesturing during *voir dire*. Be courteous to your adversary but refrain from participating in friendly or whispered discussions with defense attorneys.

E. Procedures and Mechanics

Approaches to *voir dire* differ greatly according to the controlling statutes, court rules, and practices of each jurisdiction. In almost every jurisdiction, the judge will pose questions at the beginning of jury selection. Some jurisdictions allow attorneys to ask the majority of questions themselves, while in others the judge asks all or a majority of the questions. Still other jurisdictions use written juror questionnaires along with questions from the judge, the attorneys, or both.

Along with variations in the way information is elicited, there are differences in exercising challenges for cause and peremptory challenges. If allowed in your jurisdiction, exercise challenges out of the presence of the jury, *in camera*, at side bar, or in writing. Otherwise, you may embarrass or alienate people on the jury, especially if the judge denies a challenge for cause.

Know the law in your jurisdiction regarding resisting a challenge for cause. You have the right to ask questions or have the judge initiate further questions to reha-bilitate a juror who has been challenged. It is common for jurors in child abuse cases to be challenged and excused for cause if they indicate any knowledge about the subject of child abuse or contact with people who have been victims. However, such factors alone are normally an insufficient basis for a challenge for cause. To prevent a successful challenge for cause and thus prompt the defense to use a peremptory challenge, consider asking that the judge inquire whether the juror would be able to base a decision solely on the evidence produced in court and whether the juror would not vote guilty unless convinced beyond a reasonable doubt of the defendant's guilt. Most jurors will answer such questions appropriately, demonstrating that their knowledge or experience does not automatically mean they cannot be fair.

At the prosecutor's request, some courts will allow jurors to respond to sensitive questions in chambers with only the judge and the attorneys present. This allows prospective jurors to answer questions candidly but in confidence. Remember then to remind the jury in closing argument how difficult it was for jurors to discuss sensitive topics in front of the panel and not to expect more from a child witness than one would from an adult. It is important for prosecutors in child abuse cases to resist challenges for cause based solely on the prospective juror's discomfort with the subject matter. Careful questioning of uncomfortable prospective jurors can prevent the stampede of otherwise fair and conscientious citizens requesting to be excused for cause. Remind the prospective jurors that we expect them to have emotional reactions to the charges, but as jurors they need to put their feelings aside.

1. Individual Questioning by Counsel

In states that allow attorney-conducted *voir dire,* some practical issues include whether to question prospective jurors from counsel table, sit or stand, use a podium or move around, ask more general questions of the entire panel than individual questions, or ask all questions orally or use a questionnaire. Decisions depend on your style, judgment, and preferences.

Jurisdictions that allow attorneys to talk with jurors individually during *voir dire* provide the greatest flexibility and the best opportunity to learn the most about the jurors and exercise the greatest influence. Give careful thought to your questions, keeping in mind the strengths of your case and the type of person you would most like to have on the jury. Questions suggested in this chapter suit this kind of juris-diction best, but they should be kept in mind in other systems as well.

One way to elicit a juror's true feelings and impressions during individual questioning is to ask open-ended questions that force the person to reflect before responding. Try to get the juror to do the talking. Questions that are easily answered "yes" or "no" will not necessarily expose the juror's biases. "What" questions reveal factual data. "Why" questions reveal a juror's reasoning. "How" questions usually reveal a juror's true feelings. For example:

> "Have you ever discussed with your children what they should do if someone touches them in an inappropriate way? If so, what have you suggested for them to do?"

> "How do you feel about personal safety programs in the elementary and middle schools dealing with child abuse?"

> "Could you explain why?"

Jurors are more responsive when they believe the attorney is paying close attention. Find ways to phrase questions so you are not using the same words with every juror. Rapport can be established between jurors and attorneys when the juror feels the attorney is disclosing information about himself or herself. Take the time to introduce yourself and be a model for candid disclosure. Most jurors appreciate your taking the time to learn their names. It is important to listen sincerely to jurors' responses and try to empathize with their difficulty in answering some of the questions. Thanking individuals for their candor and expressing understanding, such as, "I know that talking about sexual matters involving children is difficult, and I appreciate your doing so," provides positive reinforcement and establishes a tone for the other prospective jurors. Do not hesitate to object if the defense attorney asks questions that are clearly improper. If you know ahead of time that the defense attorney uses objectionable inquiries, make a motion *in limine* to prevent the particular behavior.

2. *Court-Conducted* Voir Dire

Prosecutors in jurisdictions where the judge conducts *voir dire* have very little ability to communicate directly with the jurors during jury selection. Generally, both the defense and prosecution submit a list of potential questions to the court. After review and approval or disapproval of the questions, the judge proceeds. It is therefore important to submit a complete list of desired questions. In many of these jurisdictions, the judge has discretion to allow attorneys to participate in follow-up inquiries if a juror has affirmatively responded or visibly reacted to a potentially embarrassing question. By and large, it is more difficult for prosecutors in these jurisdictions to establish an early relationship with jurors, but there is still some opportunity to make an impression and establish a theme that will carry over into the trial.

Follow-up inquiries from participating attorneys must usually be approved in advance by the court. They are allowed most often in cases of an exceptional nature, such as child abuse. If the judge does not permit the attorneys to participate in follow-up questions, jurors' impressions of child abuse should be fully explored in the judge's questions. Consider submitting the questions in the subsequent sections to the judge.

3. Juror Questionnaires

Jurisdictions throughout the country use juror questionnaires. Some courts routinely mail a general juror questionnaire to all prospective jurors months in advance of their jury term and use the information provided to narrow the questions that need to be asked during *voir dire*. However, there is still an opportunity to judge the demeanor of the juror when answering specific questions during *voir dire*.

In some jurisdictions, detailed juror questionnaires are used only in cases considered exceptional or generating a great deal of pre-trial publicity such as capital cases, highly visible murder or rape cases, and child abuse cases, particularly those involving institutional or child care settings. Usually the questionnaire focuses on issues relevant to the case and is intended to replace major parts of the *voir dire* process. Those who favor their use argue that they save valuable time in a usually lengthy process and encourage candor by eliminating the embarrassment involved in public disclosures. For example, some prosecutors report success in using questionnaires to find out if potential jurors ever engaged in behavior similar to that involved in the charged crime. A question such as, "Have you or anyone you know ever had a sexual encounter/experience, as an adult, with a person under 16 years of age?" may generate affirmative responses and give you extremely valuable information you are unlikely to discover in any other way.

The drawbacks of questionnaires are that they limit the time the attorneys talk with the jurors, and jurors may have difficulty remembering answers given weeks before. Further, nonverbal reactions of jurors responding to sensitive questions on the questionnaire cannot be assessed. (See Appendixes V.1 through V.2 for examples of juror questionnaires.)

F. Basic Areas of *Voir Dire*

In most trials, there is certain basic information that should be gathered during *voir dire*. This basic information includes

- Age (as estimated based upon circumstantial factors, from the juror questionnaire data, or asked directly)
- Education
- Family status and household makeup
- Past and present employment of self, spouse, and children; supervisory responsibility; what the juror likes or dislikes about his or her job
- Location of past and present residences
- Ownership of home or other property
- Prior civil, criminal, or grand jury service
- Military service
- Hobbies, organizations, leisure activities
- Any knowledge of the parties, attorneys, or witnesses involved in the case
- Jurors' awareness of publicity surrounding the case and its source
- Physical problems that will prevent that person from sitting on the jury
- A preference not to serve on this case
- Acquaintance with any other jurors on the panel
- Interest in the legal system or law-related organizations or legal employment
- Prior accusations of criminal conduct by or against the juror
- Prior victimization

- Law enforcement relationships
- Relationship with other individuals accused of a crime

This list offers some basic criteria to evaluate in formulating a model of the ideal juror in a particular case. Subsequent sections provide more detailed discussion of some of these. Some areas may require extensive probing or questioning depending on the juror's initial response.

In addition, prosecutors should include, as basic *voir dire*, questions concerning reasonable doubt and the burden of proof. Quite often, jurors misunderstand these principles. The jurors may believe that the prosecution must prove a case beyond all possible and conceivable doubt. For example, consider the following questions:

- If the court instructs that the prosecution's burden is to prove these charges beyond a reasonable doubt but not beyond all possible or conceivable doubt, could you accept that?

- I have the duty to prove beyond a reasonable doubt that the defendant did X. You've probably heard the phrase "beyond a reasonable doubt". It is the standard of proof in criminal trials. As the phrase implies, it is a *reasonable* standard. It simply means that we must show or prove to you beyond a reasonable doubt that the defendant is guilty. It is reasonable that we must remove any *serious, well-founded* doubt that you may have about the defendant's guilt. And this we will do. However, I should remind you that the standard *is not* "beyond an *unreasonable* doubt." As the judge will instruct you later, we are not held to the extreme position of having to remove all possible or conceivable doubt. That is what is meant by beyond a reasonable doubt. You wouldn't require more than a reasonable doubt?

G. General Considerations in Child Abuse Cases

Listed below are some very general observations about selecting jurors in child abuse cases. As there are so many variables, the presentation of universally accurate generalizations is not possible.

- Getting along and working with other jurors is important. Look for jurors who have been involved in large organizations or establishments that require working in harmony with others. Avoid those who appear to be odd, loners, or incompatible with other jurors. Contentious and argumentative jurors should be excused.

- Unkempt individuals may have a tendency to dislike and distrust authority figures. Their approach to any criminal case may be to find fault with the prosecutor or police department as opposed to the defendant.

- Older, single people who have no experience with children should usually be avoided. People who are parents or who regularly interact with children may have more realistic expectations of children. On the other hand, parents may have a tendency to compare their children with the victim. Single, mature individuals may have a more objective perspective. Also, some individuals who work with children regularly, such as teachers and Boy Scout leaders, may identify with the fear of an accusation of abuse.

• The prosecution wants someone whose main interest will be to make the right decision and determine the truth. Be careful of anyone who might be more interested in the process and focus on issues that have no bearing on the factual matters in the case.

• Avoid individuals who have unstable or transient lifestyles. Also, persons who appear very naïve or those who have led sheltered lives may not be good prosecution jurors. They may find it difficult to believe that a defendant or one of his witnesses would deliberately lie. They may find it even more difficult to believe that anyone is capable of the conduct described in a child abuse case.

• Stay away from jurors who appear to have engaged in or been accused of similar acts or arrested for other crimes even if they were not prosecuted.

• Jurors of deep religious convictions or theologians may not want to sit in judgment on the conduct of others. A good question for potential jurors is whether anyone has difficulty with judging someone else, either for religious or other reasons. Very introspective or indecisive jurors may also have trouble making a decision in child abuse cases.

• Consider how prospective jurors are likely to react to the victim, the defendant, and key witnesses. Note how the jurors look at the defendant, if at all. Try to get some idea of how harshly they will judge him compared to the victim and other witnesses. If the juror seems likely to identify with or sympathize with the defendant, you should obviously avoid that person.

• The type or extent of evidence that you intend to present may influence the type of person you want sitting on your jury. According to some juror studies, professionals with scientific training should generally be avoided for cases with bizarre evidence, cases in which the evidence is not logically foreseeable, and cases in which there is an absence of thorough investigation or lack of scientific evidence. Technical and scientific fields emphasize balance and symmetry. Their training and logic do not accept "loose ends." Therefore, these professionals are more difficult to convince of guilt in cases in which everything does not fall precisely into place. They may be good jurors, however, for cases with strong scientific or circumstantial evidence.

H. Subject Areas for Specific Inquiry

The following topics are not meant to cover all of the subjects that might be raised during *voir dire*. Questions on areas such as reasonable doubt should also be asked. Family composition, residence, and occupation are usually covered in the initial inquiry by the court. Having this information gives you some insight into the person's lifestyle and, one hopes, about how he or she will react to the case. The following areas are important for child abuse cases. Your focus will vary considerably from case to case according to the issues and actors. The prosecutor must also keep in mind that the types of questions allowed vary from jurisdiction to jurisdiction and from judge to judge.

1. Jobs

The longer a person has worked or resided in one location, the larger stake he or she may have in the area and community. You can expand on these questions to show interest in the juror and also help educate a juror. For example,

- You said your job involves working with other people. Do you have supervisory duties?
- Do you hire or fire people?
- Have you had occasion to discuss a plan of action to take with other employees?
- Under what circumstances?
- Did you listen to other employees' points of view?
- Did you express your point of view? How?
- Were you able to work together to reach a decision?
- How did you feel about that process?
- Can you apply those same skills to sitting as a juror? . . . to the deliberation process?
- Have you had to investigate or evaluate an employee's or colleague's conduct or work?

2. Residence

Where a juror resides is also important. As a general rule, jurors are less tolerant of defendants charged with crimes that have occurred in their immediate community. The thought of a potential child abuser living near them may be an important consideration.

In a multiple-victim daycare or school case, however, be more cautious with people living in the same community as the facility. If the owners or operators have a good reputation and long-standing ties in the community, it may be difficult to convince jurors of the existence of significant abuse. This is particularly true if their own children or children of friends, neighbors, or acquaintances attended the facility without apparent incident.

3. Leisure Time

A juror's leisure activities can speak volumes about his or her feelings and preferences. How we spend the little free time we have indicates what is truly important to us. An individual's activities can give you insight into his or her beliefs and attitudes. Are the leisure activities of a potential juror associated with family? Are they group activities or are they done alone? Do they involve children? Do they involve compassionate activities such as volunteering time to help the homeless or the elderly in nursing homes?

Questions about leisure activity are likely to elicit honest responses from potential jurors, since they allow them to discuss something they feel comfortable about and enjoy doing. Among the questions that may be asked are

- How do you spend your free time or leisure time?
- Do you ever get a chance to spend any time watching TV or reading?
- What type of shows do you like to watch?
- What is your favorite TV show?
- What kind of books or magazines do you enjoy reading?
- How often do you get a chance to do that?
- What hobbies or activities do you enjoy?
- Do you participate in any organized activities with children such as Little League, Girl Scouts, or Boy Scouts?

- Are you involved in the PTA?
- Why do you participate in these activities?
- How do you feel about the media attention given to the subject of child abuse recently?

4. Questions About Family

Questions concerning family composition and relationships provide information about a juror's life experiences. Experiences with and attitudes about family can especially play a role in a juror's evaluation of child sexual abuse allegations. These considerations might be

- Do you have children who are adults?
- Are these children individuals who may have shared experiences similar to those of the victim or defendant?
- Have discord or problems marked the family relationship?
- What is your attitude toward your children or spouse?
- How do you describe the current activities of family members?
- Has the family experience been limited to one geographical area or has there been substantial movement?
- Are those moves unexplained or are they the product of career advancement?

Typically, jurors will express concern about hearing evidence in a case involving a child victim when the juror has minor children or grandchildren. This will not necessarily justify a challenge for cause. Such a juror may ultimately declare, "I would still want to be fair. There is still emotion, but I want to be fair. And I want to hear the whole story." (*People v. Robinson,* 874 P.2d 453, 457 [Colo. App. 1993].)

5. Questions Concerning the Juror's Experience With Children

Jurors who have experience with children on a professional or personal level will bring stronger opinions to a case involving child victims. For example, someone who works with children, such as a teacher, may fear the allegation of sexual abuse. Past work or social experiences with children may be strong factors in an individual's view of children. Experience with children in a family may be important if arguments are presented as to how children would behave in a particular situation. Experience with children may also provide a juror with different insight on either physical or emotional child development. Though important, at least one court in a child sexual abuse trial has found no abuse of discretion in a trial court's failure to ask a juror questions about childcare, child development, child custody, or medical or nursing training (*United States v. Payne,* 944 F.2d 1458, 1475 [9th Cir. 1991] [noting these "questions do not fall within one of the three recognized classes raising a real possibility of bias and are only speculatively related to bias."]). Consider asking the following questions of individuals or of the panel:

- Have you had a job that involved working with infants or young children?
- Do any of you or a close family member baby-sit for children?
- Do any of you or a close friend or family member have an occupation that brings him or her in regular contact with children, such as school teacher, daycare worker, or Little League coach?

- Do any of you have children? Tell me about your children.
- Who has a child, or is close to a child, who is about the age of the complainant in this case?

The court's failure to ask these questions is not necessarily an abuse of discretion. (See, e.g., *United States v. Joe*, 831 F.2d 218, 221 [10th Cir. 1987], *cert. denied*, 484 U.S. 1072 [1988].)

- Has your contact with children ever involved discussing sexual matters or allegations of sexual abuse?
- Has child development been an area of interest to you?
- Have you taken courses in child development?
- Have you read any books or watched or attended programs on the subject? Describe them, please.

The follow-up to many questions is crucial. If the potential juror has had experience with a particular area that might be involved in the trial, allow the juror to honestly express feelings rather than inhibiting disclosure by asking, "Could you still be fair and impartial?" For example, consider the following questions:

Q: Tell us about your experiences working with children in foster care.

A: Well, it's challenging, frustrating.

Q: Were any abused?

A: Yes, many of the children I work with in foster care have been abused.

Q: And how might that affect you?

A: I'm not sure.

Q: You are somewhat uncertain how those experiences might affect you in this case?

A: It's hard to say.

Q: And because it's hard to say, this may not be the case for you?

A: Perhaps not.

Q: And because of that uncertainty, you feel it's best that you not sit on this case?

A: Yes, I'd rather not sit on this case.

Had the juror been confronted immediately with, "Can you be fair and impartial because of that association?" or something to that effect, the juror probably would not have expressed her reluctance to sit on the case. There may be many such issues in a trial that touch emotional experiences or deeply held feelings. Rather than guess about the juror's reactions to those experiences, it is best to let the juror express them as much as possible so that peremptory challenges and challenges for cause can be wisely used.

6. The Juror's Ability to Assess the Credibility of Witnesses

You will want to discuss with jurors their ability to assess the credibility of witnesses and in particular the credibility of a child witness. The following questions may assist you.

- How do you feel about being asked to judge the honesty or credibility of a witness?
- Have you ever been in the position of having to decide whom to believe when told directly conflicting stories?
- Were you able to decide?
- How do you feel about children coming into court and testifying?
- What are your thoughts about a child's testimony compared to an adult's testimony? Would you automatically believe an adult over a child or a child over an adult?
- Do you believe children are necessarily more or less truthful than adults are?
- Do you believe that because children believe in Santa Claus, they cannot be believed about other things?
- Do you believe that you could be more easily fooled by a child who is lying or an adult who is lying?
- Will you consider whether a witness may have a motive to lie?
- Could you give a child's testimony the same consideration you would give to any other witness?
- How do you expect a child victim to act in a courtroom?
- Do you feel all children react in the same way when discussing an embarrassing or upsetting situation?
- Do you realize you will need to judge every child individually?
- Do you expect all children of the same age to have the same personality or abilities?
- Can you imagine how difficult it might be for you to discuss normal sexual activity in a setting such as this?
- Do you feel that you would require more physical proof when a child is the victim as compared to when an adult is the victim?
- Do you believe children deserve any less protection under the law than adults?
- Are you a decisive person? A hard worker?
- Do you stick with something until you have resolved it to your satisfaction or are you likely to give up and throw up your hands when faced with a difficult decision?

7. Questions Concerning Opinions on Rape, Child Sexual Abuse, or Sexual Assault

In sexual assault trials, it is important in *voir dire* to know a juror's attitude, feelings, and opinions about rape and sexual assault. Unlike other background information on jurors, jury research shows that an individual's attitudes about crime in general, and rape in particular, are an important element of juror bias. (Hastie, R., et al. [1983]. *Inside the jury* [pp. 127, 128]. Clark, NJ: The Lawbook Exchange. Ltd. [noting, "In effect, no research has provided evidence that social scientific methods can be a powerful aid to attorneys in the task of detecting juror bias. However, attitudes, particularly case-relevant attitudes, such as toward the death penalty or rape, appear to be the most powerful individual difference predictors of verdict preference that have been studied to date."].) To the extent permitted by the court, attitudes and feelings about sexual assault crimes should be explored.

Many individuals feel uncomfortable listening to testimony involving sexual assault and discussing matters of a sexual nature with 11 strangers. Many potential jurors will readily ask to be excused if given the opportunity. When given the opportunity to forgo sitting on a sexual assault case, a "jury walkout" may result and sometimes necessitate calling multiple panels for jury service.

As a general rule, a court need not excuse for cause a juror who voices misgivings about sitting on a sexual assault case, unless the juror expresses a preconceived notion of the defendant's guilt. (See, e.g., *People v. Zurak*, 571 N.Y.S.2d 577 [1991], *appeal denied*, 588 N.E.2d 112 [1990], *cert. denied*, 504 U.S. 941 [1992].) A juror who has two young granddaughters need not necessarily be disqualified from a case involving the sexual abuse of a young girl if the juror can still state that she will be fair (*Noltie v. Peterson*, 9 F.3d 802 [9th Cir. 1993]). A juror who feels sympathy toward children and commits to follow the law "to the extent humanly possible" is not subject to a challenge for cause since a court is not required to discharge a juror who cannot claim a total absence of bias or prejudice (*People v. Harris*, 669 N.Y.S.2d 355, *appeal denied*, 698 N.E.2d 965 [N.Y. 1998]). However, when a juror has difficulty with, or opinions about, particular aspects of a case, the juror is more likely to be excused for cause. When a juror expresses a strong attitude about an issue in a case and cannot state "with conviction" that such bias will not influence his or her verdict, the juror should be excused for cause (*People v. Webster*, 578 N.Y.S.2d 43 [N.Y. 1991] [holding that the juror's statements that she "thought" or "hoped" that she could put aside her attitudes about gun control and the senseless, "unnecessary" killing of a child were equivocal and uncertain declarations of impartiality on the juror's part]). In considering whether the juror's promise is unequivocal, all the responses of the juror, not just one, must be considered to determine whether the juror can be fair and impartial (*People v. Blyden*, 432 N.E.2d 758, 760 [N.Y. 1982]).

Striking for cause a juror who may have difficulty accepting particular facts of an abuse case can present a different situation. For example, a defendant's conviction was reversed where the trial court granted a challenge for cause of a prospective juror who first said he would have difficulty believing a child who did not promptly complain of sexual assault but later indicated he could be fair and impartial (*Commonwealth v. Lane*, 555 A.2d 1246, 1249 [Pa. 1989]). The court noted,

> A review of this record only reflects that this prospective juror might well place great weight upon the belated accusations against the accused than another serving in that capacity. The record also indicates that the same venire person indicated he would assess that fact with all the other evidence presented. . . . Moreover, it is well established in this Commonwealth that the lack of a prompt complaint is a factor to be considered by a juror in cases involving sexual offenses. Dismissing the juror may have had a prejudicial effect on the jury members who sat in defendant's trial. If the juror's opinion is fixed, a challenge for cause would be appropriate.

The following are some questions to consider in exploring this area:

- Do any of you feel that the presumption of innocence or burden of proof should be higher or lower because this is a case involving child abuse (or rape)?
- What does rape/sexual abuse mean to you?
- Could you accept a different definition if the court told you there was a different definition you had to use in evaluating the issues in this case?

- Do any of you have experience through courses or work with sexual abnormalities?
- Will anyone here have any difficulty in sitting and listening to testimony from a young child or young woman concerning matters of a graphic sexual nature?
- Does the emotional component of these charges cause you to have certain feelings about sitting on this case?
- Will anyone here have difficulty sitting and listening to testimony of a graphic and sexual nature and discussing it with 11 strangers?
- Will anyone here have any difficulty with my asking questions concerning graphic sexual acts of the complaining witness or other witnesses?
- Is there anyone here who feels that because there may be testimony of a graphic and sexual nature you might be inclined to turn off and not listen to the questions or answers concerning such testimony?
- What is it about the topic of sexual assault that might make it difficult for you to listen to the testimony?
- Do you feel that difficulty might make it a problem for you to discuss some of the issues in this case?
- Do you feel that because of that difficulty, this might not be the case for you?

8. Questions About a Juror's Victimization and Relationship With Crime Victims in General or Sexual Assault Victims in Particular

Questions about a potential juror's victimization or relationship with a crime victim are basic *voir dire* questions in criminal trials. So are questions about relationships with alleged offenders. It is important to explore the nature and extent of these relationships as well as the attitudes and feelings developed as a result of the juror's experiences since a relationship with a crime victim does not necessarily justify a challenge for cause. (See, e.g., *Sanders v. Commonwealth*, 801 S.W.2d 665 [Ky. 1990] [holding that the fact that juror has been victim of a similar crime was insufficient basis to challenge a juror for cause]; *State v. Walker*, 577 So. 2d 770 [La. Ct. App. 1991] [upholding trial court's denial in a murder case of defendant's challenge for cause to prospective juror whose brother had been murdered]; *Lattany v. State*, 388 S.E.2d 23 [Ga. 1989] [affirming trial court's denial of a challenge for cause in assault case where juror stated that her father had been assaulted "and for that reason I think I am somewhat biased," but stated she could set aside any prejudices or preconceived notions and determine defendant's guilt solely on basis of evidence]; *People v. Bartell*, 652 N.Y.S.2d 172, *appeal denied*, 678 N.E.2d 1358 [1997] [holding that trial court did not abuse discretion in denying defendant's challenge for cause of a prospective juror whose mother had been a crime victim]; see generally "Fact that juror in criminal case, or juror's relative or friend, has previously been victim of criminal incident as ground of disqualification" [Annotation]. A.L.R., 65, 4th 743.)

It is not necessarily improper for a court to restrict the areas of inquiry concerning personal experiences with child abuse. (*United States v. Payne*, 944 F.2d 1458, 1474-75 [9th Cir. 1991] [noting, "The proposed *voir dire* questions concerning sexual molestation, including whether the venire members had been victims of child sexual abuse, whether they had ever been accused of child molestation, whether they were associated with any group supporting child sexual abuse victims, and whether they had read, heard, or seen anything about child sexual abuse, clearly relate to an area about which the community harbors strong feelings. In such a case we review the trial court's refusal to ask the proffered questions for abuse of discretion."]; see also *United States v. Boise,* 916 F.2d 497, 504 [9th Cir. 1990].) Another court noted that a defense attorney is not ineffective in failing to make specific inquiry of prospective jurors as to whether they or their friends had been sexually abused. "While *voir dire* related to the discovery of grounds for challenges for cause will certainly aid counsel in exercising peremptory challenges, counsel is not entitled under Pennsylvania law to ask questions intended solely to aid the exercise of peremptory challenges" (*Commonwealth v. Slocum,* 559 A.2d 50, 53 [Pa. 1989]). Nonetheless, a defendant's conviction will be reversed when *voir dire* does not adequately address the jurors' past experiences in an area of crime victimization or religious beliefs that may relate to issues of the case that can prejudice a juror against a defendant (*United States v. Shavers,* 615 F.2d 266-68 [5th Cir. 1980]). At least one court has deemed it reversible error to prohibit the defense from asking the following question: "Have you or any member of your family been involved previously with a rape or proceeding involving a sexual crime?" (*Commonwealth v. Fulton,* 413 A.2d 742 [1979]). Counsel should always consider inquiring, if the court does not, about prior victimization with a question such as, "Has anyone here been the victim of sexual abuse or have a close friend or family member who has been?"

A sexual assault victim is not necessarily disqualified from sitting on a sexual assault case (*United States v. Miguel,* 111 F.3d 666, 673 [9th Cir. 1997]; *Gonzales v. Thomas,* 99 F.3d 978 [10th Cir. 1996], *cert. denied,* 520 U.S. 1159 [1997] [noting that rape victims are not as a matter of law incapable of being impartial in a sexual assault trial]; *Whalen v. Commonwealth,* 891 S.W.2d 86 [Ky. Ct. App. 1995] [holding that trial court did not abuse its discretion in a sexual assault trial in refusing to strike a juror who stated she could be objective even though she had been raped by her stepfather]; *People v. Kimbro,* 655 N.Y.S.2d 481, *appeal denied,* 681 N.E.2d 1315 [1997] [concluding, "The trial court properly denied defendant's challenge for cause to a venire person who was questioned extensively regarding her experience as a victim of a sexual assault similar in some aspects to the crime charged herein, and who maintained consistently that she would be able to put aside this experience, which had occurred more than 15 years prior to the time of trial herein, and to determine this case fairly and impartially, based on the evidence adduced at trial."]; *Webb v. Commonwealth,* 397 S.E.2d 539 [Va. 1990].) This is particularly true if the juror's sexual assault is not recent and the juror is not in the process of recovery from the sexual assault experience or otherwise actively influenced by it (*State v. Mundy,* 650 N.E.2d 502, 516-17 [Ct. App. 1994], *rev. denied,* 648 N.E.2d 513 [Ohio 1995]). If the juror is still affected by the sexual assault and has not fully recovered from it, it may be reversible error not to grant a challenge for cause as to this juror (*State v. Zerla,* 1992 Ohio App. LEXIS 1280). If there are significant differences between the juror's sexual assault experiences and the case being tried, this may allow a court to accept the juror's declaration of impartiality. In upholding one trial court's denial of a defendant's challenge for cause of a prospective juror who had been sexually abused a few years earlier, the appellate court explained,

> We hold that no error was committed because the prospective juror's comments did not create an inference of partiality or prejudice against defendant. The juror was not the victim of a crime sufficiently similar to raise

such an inference. The juror indicated her boyfriend sexually abused her after she reached adulthood. In contrast, the State charged defendant with multiple incidents of incestuous child sexual abuse. Moreover, subsequent questioning by both the trial court and defense counsel sufficiently dispelled any inference of bias that may have been raised by the juror's initial response. She unequivocally stated that she would be fair and impartial and believed defendant to be innocent until proven guilty. Her candid admission that she felt uncomfortable with the topic of sexual abuse does not automatically preclude her from objectively evaluating testimony that defendant might offer in opposition to the charges of sexual abuse. (*State v. Saunders*, 893 P.2d 584, 587-88 [Utah Ct. App. 1995])

However, careful questioning about the sexual assault experience and its consequences might develop opinions and attitudes inconsistent with the juror's ability to sit fairly and impartially on a case.

The failure of a sitting juror to disclose the fact that he or she was a victim of child abuse might result in the court's seeking to determine what role the victimization played in the jury's deliberation. (See *Gonzales v. Thomas*, 99 F.3d 978 [10th Cir. 1996], *cert. denied*, 520 U.S. 1159 [1997] [holding that the fact that a juror who convicted defendant was a prior rape victim, a fact she failed to disclose, did not require a finding of actual bias on her part and that there was no showing that she drew upon this experience to bolster her opinions in deliberation]; *State v. Jackson*, 912 P.2d 71, 81–82 [Haw. 1996] [holding that juror's childhood sexual assault, not disclosed during jury selection, did not affect or infringe on defendant's right to a fair trial by impartial jury since juror did not "communicate her recollection" or utilize it in support of the victim's credibility]; *State v. Parsons*, 1997 Tenn. Crim. App. LEXIS 1262 [affirming conviction where juror disclosed during jury deliberations, but not jury selection, that her father had sexually abused her because there was no evidence she was biased against the defendant or exposed the jury to prejudicial information]; *contra State v. Larue*, 722 P.2d 1039, 1042 [Haw. 1986] [holding that juror who was sexual assault victim "was vouching for, and attempting to secure the acceptance by the jury of the reliability of the statements of the minor [child molestation victims] as to their sexual molestation by appellant, based not upon evidence in the record, or their appearance on the stand, but upon her own similar personal experience and recollection thereof"].) One must carefully pose questions seeking to ascertain prior victimization. For example, in one case, the judge asked, "Have you or has any member of your immediate family ever been involved in a similar type of incident?" A rape victim answered "No," and explained later that there were different circumstances in her case (*Gonzales v. Thomas*, 99 F.3d 978 [10th Cir. 1996], *cert. denied*, 520 U.S. 1159 [1997]).

Courts generally do not find a relationship with a sexual assault victim to be sufficient by itself to challenge a juror for cause. Courts have upheld the selection of jurors whose daughters, granddaughters, sisters, nieces, cousins, or other relatives were sexual assault victims (*United States v. Miguel*, 111 F.3d 666, 673 [9th Cir. 1997]; *United States v. Barrow*, 42 M.J. 655 [A.F.C.C.A. 1995], *aff'd*, 45 M.J. 478 [C.A.A.F. 1997]; *Jamison v. State*, 295 S.E.2d 203 [Ga. 1982] [daughter]; *People v. Arredondo*, 642 N.Y.S.2d 630, *appeal denied*, 670 N.E.2d 1350 [1996] [sister]; *People v. Smyers*, 562 N.Y.S.2d 1017 [1990], *appeal denied*, 573 N.E.2d 589 [1991] [niece]; *Commonwealth v. Henderson*, 418 A.2d 757, 761 [Pa. 1980] [granddaughter]; *State v. Percy*, 595 A.2d 248, 253 [Vt. 1990], *cert. denied*, 502

U.S. 927 [1991] [daughter]). In *Barrow*, two jurors stated they had close family members who had been sexually abused as children. The trial judge rejected challenges for cause. The Air Force Court of Criminal Appeals noted,

> An individual is not disqualified from serving as a court member solely because the individual, or a family member, has been the victim of a crime similar to the one charged against the accused. [citation omitted] Instead, the military judge must determine whether an actual or implied bias exists which disqualifies the member. (*Barrow*, 42 M.J. at 660)

Some courts do suggest that excusing jurors whose immediate family members such as a spouse or a child have been crime victims is appropriate (*People v. Smyers*, 562 N.Y.S.2d 1017 [1990], *appeal denied*, 573 N.E.2d 589 [1991]).

As with failing to disclose that the juror was a victim of sexual abuse, the failure to disclose a relationship with a victim of sexual abuse will not necessarily result in reversal. Similarly, a juror's disclosing this information during deliberations will not necessarily result in a reversal of conviction if the relationship does not appear to have affected the juror's impartiality. (See *Fitzgerald v. Greene*, 150 F.3d 357 [4th Cir. 1998] [finding that new trial was not warranted even though juror stated he had no sympathy for a rapist because his granddaughter had been molested as a child, as juror's impartiality not shown to have been affected].)

Some courts have even held that a relationship with the complainant does not necessarily disqualify the juror (*George v. Commonwealth*, 885 S.W.2d 938, 941 [Ky. 1994] [holding that the fact that the juror was sexual assault victim's third cousin did not create a presumption of prejudice where the juror stated that he could be fair and impartial and that the relationship would not affect his judgment]). In many states, a juror will be disqualified for cause if related by a certain degree of consanguinity to the complainant. However, such a challenge may be waived if not made prior to the swearing of the juror. A juror's having met the complainant also may be an insufficient basis to challenge a juror for cause (*State v. Bubeck*, 1997 Wash. App. LEXIS 367 [being related to a witness or having met the complainant are not grounds for a challenge based on implied bias]). The fact that a juror's children go to school with the complainant, without more, is likely an insufficient challenge for cause (*Herrington v. State*, 690 So. 2d 1132, 1139 [Miss. 1997] [noting that during *voir dire* the juror did not know complainant went to school with her children but learned this fact later]). Thus, *voir dire* questioning should include not only, "Do you know the complainant?" but also, "Do your children attend the same school as the complainant?"

Some questions to consider when attempting to determine a juror's exposure to sexual assault are

- Has anyone here been the victim of sexual abuse? Does anyone have a close friend or family member who has?
- Do you know anyone accused of sexual abuse, either officially or informally?
- Do you know anyone who has ever made a false allegation of sexual or physical abuse?
- Has anyone here ever reported a case of possible sexual abuse?

The handling of past sexual abuse allegations or the results of those allegations should be discussed for potential impact upon the juror. The questioning of jurors concerning victimization may be handled in an individual and sequestered fashion. It may also be appropriate to have the Court ask these sensitive questions, allowing the State and the defense to follow up if need be, to avoid the juror's feeling like the attorney is prying into private matters.

9. Questions About Experts: General Questions, Mental Health Experts, Medical Experts

Expert testimony plays a significant role in many sexual abuse trials. If the testimony is significant, a potential juror's contact and experience with that area of expertise should be explored, since it may reveal a bias or prejudice. It also may reveal knowledge that would suggest that the juror has preconceived opinions on topics in that field.

Question the potential jurors about their view of the role of the expert trial witness. The questions utilized and approach taken may depend on whether the other party is also calling an expert witness and how critical of the expert testimony counsel wants the jury to be. Some general questions to consider on expert testimony are

- Have you ever listened to the testimony of an expert witness?
- Are you ever been intimidated by persons who have a higher level of education than you have?
- Would you tend to believe the testimony of an expert witness just because that person is called an "expert" witness?
- Do you think that "expert" witnesses are capable of being incorrect or untruthful?
- If you are instructed to evaluate the testimony of an expert witness as you would the testimony of all other witnesses, do you think that you would be able to follow that instruction?
- Do you think you would be capable of rejecting the testimony of an expert witness if the testimony of that witness did not appear to be reliable or consistent with common sense?
- How do you feel about evaluating the testimony of an expert witness and deciding whether to accept it or reject it?
- Could you reject the testimony of an expert?
- Are you going to accept testimony just because someone with a degree says it?
- Do you think the testimony of an expert witness should be treated differently by you when you consider the evidence?
- Do you agree that an expert can have a bias or motive just like other witnesses?
- Do you think experts are always right?
- Do you think that you would have to like a witness in order to believe his or her testimony?

Many child sexual abuse cases involve mental health or psychological expert testimony. Explore potential jurors' backgrounds and experiences in this area with the following questions:

- Do you have any special training in the area of social work, psychology, or psychiatry?
- Do you have any close friends or relatives who have training in the area of psychology or psychiatry?
- Have you, a close friend, or relatives ever gone to any sort of counseling?

- Has anyone here or a close friend or family member ever had contact with a social worker, psychologist, or psychiatrist?
- Does anyone here have a friend or family member who works in the field of mental health, social work, psychiatry, or psychology?
- Do you, a close friend, or relative work with individuals who have alleged abuse?

While some questions overlap, certain questions may elicit positive responses, while the others do not.

If the case involves medical-opinion testimony, there should be questions about the juror's background and his or her contact with the medical field, medical issues, and medical institutions.

- Do you, a close friend, or family members work in the field of pediatrics or emergency medicine?
- Do you, a close friend, or family members have a background or training in nursing, medicine, or emergency medicine?
- Have you had medical care or contact with the institution where a testifying expert works?
- What kind of experience did you have there?
- Have you ever had a dispute with a physician?
- Do you have a pediatrician?
- Has your pediatrician ever discussed sexual issues or sexual abuse with you or your child?
- Have you ever disagreed with an opinion of your pediatrician?

10. Questions About Intent, Mental State, and the Charges

Certain sexual assault charges such as attempted rape or sexual abuse may have a specific intent requirement. In other words, it may be necessary for the prosecution to establish that the defendant intended to accomplish a certain act or that the defendant intended to engage in sexual contact for sexual gratification.

The prosecutor may wish to emphasize that certain charges do not require a particular mental state. Many sexual assault crimes are "strict liability" crimes, in that the prosecution must simply prove that the act was performed with someone under the age of consent. The following questions may help in this area:

- Do you understand that these charges do not require the prosecution to demonstrate that the defendant forced the child to have sexual contact?
- Do you understand that, regardless of what the defendant may have thought, the law simply requires that the State prove that this defendant had sexual contact with this 15-year-old?

Mental state questions may be important when intoxication is an issue. In some states and situations, intoxication is relevant to the intent element of sexual assault trials.

11. Memberships in Groups and Organizations

Questions about a potential juror's membership in groups and organizations can be particularly revealing about the juror's beliefs and preferences. The fact that an individual takes the time to engage in the activities of an organization represents, in most situations, a significant commitment. Persons active in organizations often have strong feelings about certain criminal justice issues, particularly organizations that have legislative or political agendas. Memberships in organizations that deal with any of the issues that might arise in a sexual assault trial, such as rape crisis or victim counseling, are particularly significant. The following are some questions dealing with this area:

- What social, neighborhood, professional, political, or religious groups do you or your spouse belong to?
- Do you hold a leadership position in any of these groups or organizations?
- Is there anyone here who is a member in any group or organization that advocates on behalf of crime victims?
- Is there anyone here who is a member of any group or organization that advocates on behalf of domestic violence or sexual abuse victims or is a member of a rape crisis organization or victim counseling program?
- Do any of you belong to any groups or organizations that are active in civic or political matters or legal issues such as Mothers Against Drunk Driving, ACLU, or Common Cause?
- Is there anyone here who is a member of any group or organization that advocates on behalf of those accused of crimes or those in our correctional system (such as prisoner rights, legal services, ACLU)?
- Is there anyone here who is a member of a group or organization that has as its goal or purpose, or as part of its agenda, changing the laws of our criminal justice system or the laws in the area of sexual assault, the law on the age of consent, or the operation of our correctional system?

Also find out if potential jurors belong to any organizations that advocate positions on government and the family, corporal punishment, unwed mothers, public assistance, family values, or similar issues that might come up during testimony and trigger a reaction in a particular juror who has strong feelings in these areas.

The failure of a court to permit questions about a potential juror's association with rape crisis or victim centers is not necessarily an abuse of discretion (*United States v. Joe,* 831 F.2d 218, 221 [10th Cir. 1987]). For example, one court concluded that a prospective juror may not be challenged for cause because of membership in a rape advocacy program since opposition to rape is a widely shared sentiment and expressing that opinion by "[joining] an organized group of persons who share the same sentiment does not necessarily render a person incapable of weighing evidence impartially to determine whether a rape has occurred in fact or whether the person accused is in fact the person who committed the act" (*Commonwealth v. Myers,* 545 A.2d 309, 312-13 [1988], *rev. denied,* 561 A.2d 741 [Pa. 1989]). The same court held that a trial court need not permit an attorney to ask about membership in a rape advocacy organization. A court need not necessarily question a rape crisis worker about whether that experience would make her treat a rape victim the same as any other witness, as long as the court inquires whether her experience as a rape crisis volunteer would affect her ability to be impartial (*State v. Walden,* 905 P.2d 974, 987 [Ariz. 1995], *cert. denied,* 517 U.S. 1146 [1996]). More detailed questioning may be requested when a rape crisis center is involved in the case or where testimony is expected from a rape crisis center employee who is a fact witness or expert witness. Any proposed questions that the court forbids should be recorded for appellate review.

12. *The Media*

It may be important to determine the impact the media have had on a juror's impressions of child abuse. Prosecutors disagree, however, on whether it is a good idea to initiate general questions about media coverage. Those who recommend against it believe that doing so may prompt jurors to think about negative messages. Others feel it is important to bring the subject up in order to try to neutralize impressions jurors already have formed or to gain information for making wise decisions about peremptory challenges. If you wish to elicit a juror's feelings on this subject, you might ask the following questions:

- Have you seen any movies or shows concerning child abuse?
- Have you seen programs or read literature concerning child abuse?
- What are your reactions to these kinds of programs?
- Do you think that they should be on television? Why or why not?
- How about newspaper coverage of child abuse?
- Do you feel that the attention the subject receives is good or bad?
- What do you think the overall effect of this media attention is on the public?
- Do you believe that the individual sensational cases that receive a lot of publicity are representative of all cases?

If a potential juror indicates no awareness of media coverage of child abuse, this may signal an inability or unwillingness to accept the existence of child abuse.

13. *Stereotypes and Biases*

The next series of questions should help you determine whether prospective jurors have stereotyped the child abuser or whether they may be biased.

- When you first heard that the charges involved child abuse/molestation, what were your thoughts?
- Did you wonder what the defendant would look like?
- Are you able to describe what a bank robber might look like? Do you think it is any easier to describe a typical child abuser?
- Do you think you can tell just by looking at someone whether he is capable of doing something like this?
- Do you think it would be fair to conclude that someone did or didn't do something simply based on his appearance?
- If, during the course of jury deliberations, one of your fellow jurors said he didn't care about the evidence—he just couldn't believe such a nice looking man could do something like this—would you be able to point out that this was stereotyping and that he was refusing to consider the evidence with an open mind?
- Do you have trouble believing that there are adults in our society who physically abuse children or use children for sexual gratification?
- How do you feel about having to hear a child talk about explicit sexual matters?
- Will you be so embarrassed or offended that you cannot consider these charges with an open mind?
- Will you be offended if I ask the child to describe embarrassing and explicit sexual activity in detail?

- Would you be able to discuss these matters openly with your fellow jurors and objectively evaluate the evidence?
- Have you ever known anyone who was accused of, or a victim of, anything like this?
- Have you ever known anyone who made a false accusation of abuse?
- Have you ever known anyone who was falsely accused of abuse?
- Have any of your friends, acquaintances, or relatives ever talked about situations like this?
- Have you, a close friend, or a relative ever been involved with Family Court? Divorce proceedings? Domestic violence? Child abuse?

14. Educating the Jury and Dealing With Red Flag Issues

Take advantage of any opportunity during *voir dire* to build rapport, develop your theme, and transform weaknesses of a case into strengths. Jurisdictions and judges vary considerably in the extent to which they allow lawyers to educate the jury by explaining common dynamics of abuse or applicable legal principles. Many prosecutors recommend disclosing and attempting to diminish potential problems ("red flag issues") during jury selection. It is generally best that the prosecution present potential problems first in the trial. Some believe that in certain situations you should not ask these types of questions unless the defense does so first. Whatever you do, always convey confidence in your case and do not put too much emphasis on the difficulties. The following are examples of some questions used by prosecutors in jurisdictions where this kind of inquiry is permitted.

When the victim is a "problem" child or comes from a family with a different lifestyle than most of the jurors:

- Is your family like families on TV, such as the family on *The Cosby Show,* with simple answers to all of life's problems?
- Do you believe that a child should not be worthy of belief simply because she comes from a troubled family?
- There may be evidence in this case that the victim has mental, emotional, or behavior problems. Would that cause you to be prejudiced against the child, or would you be able to consider whether the problems might have been caused, or made worse, by the alleged abuse by the defendant?
- Even if you do not like the victim, his family, or his lifestyle, can you put aside your personal feelings and decide this case based only on the facts presented in court?
- Would you agree that it is important not to judge other people on the basis of whether they acted in the manner you feel you would have under the same circumstances?
- Do you believe that even a child with problems has the same right to protection under our laws as anyone else?

Be careful not to overemphasize the prospect of either trauma or composure from the child. If her demeanor on the stand is different than you have described, jurors may

(Continued)

(Continued)

question her credibility. It might be wise to preface your questions in this area with a simple statement that you do not know how the complainant will react to having to testify because she has never had to do so before.

When you do anticipate either the victim's nervousness or lack of emotion when recounting the abuse:

- Have you ever been involved in a traumatic incident and had to relate it to someone else? Was that difficult?
- Do you recall how you felt about appearing in public as a young child?
- Are you more comfortable talking with adults or talking with children? Do you believe children are more comfortable with other children or with adults?
- Can you understand why the victim of a traumatic situation, especially a child, might be nervous coming into a courtroom full of strangers?
- Do you have any preconceived ideas about a child's demeanor while testifying?
- Have you ever had to describe something that happened to you to a number of people? Did it become easier as you told it to more people?
- Can you understand how a person who has had to repeat an account might show less emotion each time?
- It may be necessary for me to use leading questions when the child testifies. Can you understand why that might be so with a very young child?

When the case involves lack of consent owing to age, a lack of physical force by the defendant, and a lack of resistance by the victim:

- Do you agree or disagree with the laws that make it a crime for an adult to have sexual contact with any child under a certain age?
- Do you believe that a child should be required to resist sexual advances in order to hold the adult accountable for his behavior?
- Were you aware that it is a crime to have sex with a child even if the child complies or even participates? How do you feel about that?
- As a child, were you taught to respect authority and obey adults?

When disclosure follows presentation of a personal safety program at school or elsewhere:

- Recently many schools as early as the elementary level have started education programs to teach children about abuse with themes such as good touch and bad touch. How do you feel about that?
- Have you done anything to educate your children or grandchildren about this problem?

(Continued)

(Continued)

When the child is your only source of direct evidence—no eyewitnesses or definitive physical or medical evidence:

- Were you aware that sexual abuse of a child usually causes no lasting physical injury?
- Would you expect there to be conclusive medical evidence even when such evidence is not always possible or plausible?
- Would you expect a person who sexually abuses a child to do so in front of other witnesses?
- Would you be able to follow an instruction telling you that the testimony of one witness whom you believe is sufficient to decide an issue?
- Would it make any difference to you if that witness was a child?

When there has been a delay in disclosure:

- Were you aware that it is not unusual for a child to wait some time before reporting having been sexually abused?
- Do you understand why a child who has been sexually abused by one adult might not immediately trust another adult enough to tell what happened?
- If the evidence shows that the child delayed in reporting these incidents, will you listen to and consider her reasons?
- As a child, did you have any experiences with bullies? How did you handle those situations? Did you ever tell your parents? Why not?

When the victim has given inconsistent statements, or if there are multiple victims with some inconsistencies in their accounts:

- When talking about something that happened to you, do you always tell it exactly the same way each time you talk about it?
- Do you ever forget or leave out details one time and include them when you talk about it at a different time?
- Do you believe that different people might have different memories of the same event?
- Do you believe they might perceive things differently and that what is important to one person might not be as important to another?

Similar questions can be used to deal with other problems, such as a victim's recantation or use of drugs or to give jurors information about legal requirements, e.g., that penetration occurs upon any intrusion, however slight, and that touching over the clothing can constitute sexual touching. Use questions designed to fit the case, that suit your style, and comply with restrictions in your jurisdiction.

I. Considerations When the Victim Is Physically or Mentally Disabled

Voir dire is an excellent opportunity to educate the jury about any disability the victim might have. Question the jurors about their own experience and contact with persons who have physical, mental, or developmental disabilities. Ask whether persons with disabilities in general, or the victim's specific disability, make them feel uncomfortable. Perhaps the disability will make the witness difficult to understand or watch. This is important because these factors are used when jurors evaluate testimony. Ask about the believability of persons with mental disabilities and whether they are more or less believable than those who are not disabled. Compare the victim's mental age with a child of the same chronological age. Ask if jurors equate mental disability with mental illness.

J. Special Considerations in Child Physical Abuse and Child Homicide Cases

In cases involving physical abuse, particularly if the defense will argue it was accidental or reasonable discipline, learn about jurors' attitudes toward use of physical punishment. Any indication that the potential juror is likely to envision himself in the defendant's position or feel sorry for the defendant should be a signal to eliminate that juror from consideration. Jurors familiar with children have a better basis for assessing the story regarding what happened to a child, including how the defendant says a child behaved. Since the juror who was abused by a loved one may identify with the defendant or the victim, the emotionally charged nature of such an experience must be carefully evaluated before allowing the individual to serve as a juror. Consider the following questions:

- What kinds of discipline do you use or have you used with your own children?
- How do you feel about the state intervening in situations involving how a parent disciplines his or her child?
- Do you agree with laws that make it a crime to assault another person? How about if the other person is your own child?
- Would you be willing to determine the appropriateness of the defendant's method of physically disciplining his child?
- Do you believe people should be allowed to use greater physical force with their children than we allow them to inflict on an adult?
- If you found yourself feeling sorry for the defendant or for someone associated with him, would you let that influence your verdict? Could you set that aside and decide the case solely on the facts presented?
- Do you feel that a parent who uses excessive force to discipline a child has committed a crime?
- Do you think the criminal courts should get involved in such situations?
- Do you believe that it is okay to cause bruises, swelling, or other types of injury when disciplining a child?
- Have you, a friend, or relatives ever experienced the serious injury or death of a child?

In child homicide and physical assault cases, it is important to educate and question potential jurors about a fundamental bias: that a parent or guardian would never intentionally injure or kill his or her own child and therefore the injury or death must have been an accident. Many people find it hard to believe that a mother could abuse her child. Ask whether anyone would have difficulty convicting the victim's mother regardless of proof. Stress the *mens rea* required by the charges in the *voir dire* questions:

- Would you have any difficulty with an instruction from the judge that states a defendant can be guilty of murder by recklessly killing someone?
- Could you consider whether a parent had recklessly, rather than intentionally, killed/injured a child?
- Can you accept that the reckless killing of a child is a crime?
- Are you willing to consider the relative differences in size, strength, and responsibility between the defendant and victim in judging the reasonableness of his conduct?

Ask questions to expose possible attitudes about the caregiver that you plan to call as a witness against the defendant. This is particularly important if the nonoffending caregiver was present at or near the scene of the child's injury or death and may be considered partially responsible for the child's death.

- Have you known a single mother whose circumstances caused her to receive public assistance?
- How do you feel about single mothers on public assistance living with men?
- Can you put aside feelings about public assistance recipients and base your decision solely upon the evidence?
- Do you understand that, in this trial, you are only being asked to judge the guilt of one person, the defendant?
- Will you be able to do so, even if you believe someone else bears some responsibility for the situation?

Find out about jurors' experiences with professionals associated with the death of children, especially pathologists, hospitals, and protective workers.

- Have you taken any courses related to law or legal issues, medicine, nursing, emergency rescue, medical technology, or child development?
- Have you, a close friend, or relatives ever called upon one of these professionals?
- What was your experience in dealing with this professional?

If the case is based heavily on medical testimony, further exploration of experiences with doctors and hospitals is required. Even if the jurors' biases cannot be ascertained during jury selection, your exploration of these issues may cause fellow jurors to reprimand the juror who expresses such biases during jury deliberations.

Since you seldom have an eyewitness in a child abuse case, it is important to cover that in *voir dire*:

- Do you believe that a confession or an eyewitness to a crime is necessary in order to conclude that the State has proved its case beyond a reasonable doubt?
- Would you be surprised to learn that few criminal cases have eyewitnesses?

If you are dealing with a single incident, particularly if it results in death, ask potential jurors how they define child abuse. Most people readily identify a repeatedly battered child as abused. Then ask whether the jurors would be able to find a defendant guilty if the State proved the charged crime beyond a reasonable doubt even though the child was hit only once.

What motivates people to act is fascinating to everyone, and jurors often expect you to explain why the defendant abused a child. Acknowledge that although we would all like to know the "why" of someone else's behavior, especially when deciding if that person committed a crime, it is not necessary to prove the "why." You might ask,

- Does everyone realize that the State does *not* have to explain to you *why* the defendant beat/killed the victim? We just have to prove that he did it?
- How do you feel about that?

If you have charged an adult who knew the abuse was occurring and did nothing to prevent it, discuss that with your panel. Ask whether they agree with the proposition that a parent or responsible adult has a duty to protect children from harm. Finally, consider asking questions to dispel juror sympathy for defendants who may appear distraught over the victim's death.

K. Documenting Peremptory Challenges

Prosecutors face increasing demands to justify peremptory challenges that the defense claims are exercised because of group bias or gender bias. (*See Batson v. Kentucky*, 476 U.S. 79 [1986].) The Constitution also prohibits a criminal *defendant* from engaging in purposeful discrimination on the basis of race when exercising peremptory challenges. (See *Georgia v. McCollum*, 502 U.S. 42 [1992].) Gender, like race, can be an improper basis on which to exercise a peremptory challenge (*J.E.B. v. Alabama ex rel J.B.*, 511 U.S. 127 [1999].) Thus, striking older women in a sexual assault case can be an improper exercise of peremptory challenges. (See *Riley v. Commonwealth*, 464 S.E.2d 508 [Va. 1995].)

Become familiar with the laws and practices in your state. Make a habit of documenting your reasons for excusing prospective jurors. Familiarity with a crime scene, prior crime victimization, or a relationship with an accused or convicted person may be a race-neutral reason. A potential juror's demeanor, lack of attention, weakness in responding, or nervousness can be the basis of a race-neutral challenge (See *United States v. Sherills*, 929 F.2d 393 [8th Cir. 1991]; *Brewer v. State*, 932 S.W.2d 161 [Tex. Crim. App. 1996].) Equivocation in responding to questions during *voir dire* may also be a race-neutral reason. (See *Commonwealth v. Caldwell*, 641 N.E.2d 1054 [Mass. 1994].) Certainly, challenges based on the demeanor of a juror should have an articulable basis. Your notes on body language, employment history, lack of familiarity with children, and so on will defend against a challenge should you later be called upon to provide justification. (See, e.g., *Commonwealth v. Smulsky*, 609 A.2d 843 [Pa. 1992] [finding that prosecutor's explanations for exclusion of black panel members were valid and nondiscriminatory].) If you believe the defense is striking jurors based solely on race or gender, the prosecution can insist that the defense attorney cite race-neutral or gender-neutral reasons on the record.

III. OPENING STATEMENT

A. The Purpose and Importance of the Opening Statement

The opening statement develops the theme of the case. Used intelligently, the opening statement will set the tone and pace of the trial, fully establish your courtroom presence with jurors, spur their concern, alert them to potential pitfalls, and interest them in hearing from you again. During the jury selection process, jurors will have formed an initial impression of the defense and prosecuting attorneys. They will also have learned about the nature of the charges and, to some extent through specific *voir dire* questions, about the dynamics of child abuse. A strong opening statement, delivered clearly and confidently, will continue this education process and give them a framework for the evidence to follow. Even though its purpose is to outline the evidence the State intends to present to support the charges, the opening can go far in persuading jurors of the defendant's guilt even though argument is usually not permitted.

Making presentations to juries in opening or closing your case is a highly personal matter. It requires a thorough knowledge of the intricacies of the case and will be dictated in part by the law and custom of the jurisdiction. The following discussion includes some general observations and techniques that may help you formulate an approach to opening statements.

B. Goals of an Opening Statement

Most jurors are anxious to see the selection process end and are eager to find out what the case is *really* about. Their attention will be at a high point as you stand to deliver your opening statement. Be organized and positive, leaving the jury with a clear picture of the defendant's crimes and no doubt about your knowledge of the case and belief in the defendant's guilt. Before the first witness takes the stand, you want the jurors to feel that a conviction is the only result that is consistent with the facts.

To accomplish these goals, present the facts in a sensible way to keep the jury interested. Focus on your theme, avoid getting bogged down in details, personalize the victim, do not overstate your case, and diffuse weaknesses. Many prosecutors approach a trial having developed a theme for the case that they use in *voir dire*, opening statement, presentation of evidence, cross-examination, and closing argument. The theme is generally a message of the case that allows you to characterize all of the evidence as consistent with the conclusion that the child was abused. Because jurors focus so much on the victim and defendant, try to paint as sympathetic a picture as possible of the victim and a negative picture of the defendant. A common belief is that good things happen to good people and bad things happen to bad people. The images of the victim and defendant are filters through which the evidence will be viewed.

A common theme in cases involving abuse within the family is one that describes the abuse as a family secret involving a betrayal of the child's trust. Such a theme can simply and eloquently indicate why a child did not disclose ongoing abuse by a parent and kept the secret from others for years. It explains the dominance of the parental offender in a child's world and lets the jury know why the child kept silent. The explanation for the silence might be that the child was threatened with physical harm or removal from the home, or that the child was fearful that the mother would be unwilling to acknowledge the abuse because of the companionship and financial security afforded by the offender. Or the child may have kept the family secret because she was ashamed or felt responsible for the abuse. The child might have loved the father who "trusted" the child not to reveal their "special relationship." The abuse may have been the only perceived bad thing in an otherwise loving relationship. This theme can illustrate the pressures brought to bear on the victim by the family after the abuse was discovered and thereby explain later inconsistencies, reluctance, or recantation by the victim.

In many physical abuse cases, a defendant lies about what happened to a child. A theme in such a case is "lies told to save oneself rather than truth told to save the child." In many cases, especially those involving a mental health defense, the theme is "actions speak louder than words." This focuses attention on facts and the defendant's conduct or failure to act rather than on the defendant's mental state.

The facts and evidence in your case will dictate the nature of your theme. With older children as victims, particularly troubled adolescents, you may choose to portray the case as one in which the offender took advantage of a troubled child's vulnerability and made her problems worse. The idea to be communicated would be that the defendant was able to get away with his crimes because he chose a victim who was less likely to be believed and encouraged her to become dependent on him by providing her with affection, money, drugs, or alcohol. A prosecutor can set the stage for the theme during the opening statement without being too detailed. Wait until closing arguments to see what has emerged from the testimony and *then* become specific.

Consider the case of a teenage runaway who engages in repeated sexual activity before being raped by the defendant. (See DerOhannesian, P. II. [1998]. Establishing victim credibility in acquaintance rape case. *Practical Prosecutor, 1998,* 12–13.) While initially the 14-year-old girl's sexual relations with the defendant were not forcible, they became forcible when the defendant sought to have her engage in prostitution. In this case, it is likely that a rape shield law would not prevent evidence of the complainant's sexual activities with numerous men prior to the defendant. However, the jury's view of this teenager's need to engage in such activity can be influenced by the use of a "survival sex" theme. In the context of survival sex, the complainant's repeated sexual activity on the streets is seen as a necessity for survival rather than strictly promiscuous behavior.

Let the jury know in the opening statement that the child who has been victimized is a real person. Try to present her in a way that will cause the jury to care about and feel protective toward her. Use her first or full name and describe her daily routine, some of her likes and dislikes, and the problems she may have recounting what happened to her. For instance, you might begin in the following manner:

> Lori Jones is a 6-year-old child who has a dog named Buster. Buster is her buddy, and Kim is her best friend who lives next door. She likes her house—particularly her room, which has all of her things, including the bed her Mom made for Buster in the corner. But she does not like her Dad's office with all of the books on the second floor. We expect her to tell you, *very reluctantly,* that although she loves her Dad, she does not like going into that room with him. In that room, Lori's Dad, the defendant, made her promise to keep secret what happened there. But Lori eventually did tell, revealing the secret of sexual abuse that she endured.

Using these kinds of simple statements personalizes the victim. It can help the jury better appreciate some of the problems she may have in telling them what happened and, at the same time, does not over dramatize the issues.

To the extent possible, a prosecutor should prepare the jury for the demeanor expected from the victim, such as nervousness, fear, or a lack of emotion.

Adolescents may be more fearful and self-conscious about appearing in court than young children. They may demonstrate their embarrassment by giggling, becoming sullen or antagonistic, or crying. The turmoil and pressures of adolescence are usually difficult enough without the additional burden of describing abuse in a public trial. Jurors are less likely to sympathize with the adolescent victim, who may appear tough, have an unusual hairdo, wear odd clothes, or have a history of delinquent behavior. Anticipate these reactions and explain the pressures the victim is undergoing as a result of her experience and disclosure. Suggest the difficulties she faces in describing a sexually abusive relationship, particularly one of long duration with an immediate family member. Emphasize the importance of peer acceptance to an adolescent and the shame and ridicule she has endured. If the victim has recanted on previous occasions, explain the reasons, such as family or peer pressure, fear of the criminal justice process, or an unwillingness to risk a negative trial outcome.

Revealing and explaining potential case weaknesses in your opening statement, rather than waiting for the defense to bring them out, allows you to cast them in the proper light so that the jury understands and is not surprised when they come up in testimony. This will also prevent any later implication that the State was hiding something. Do not give away all of your arguments, however, during opening statement. If all the State's arguments are revealed, the defense attorney will have the opportunity to consider how to counter these arguments during the trial.

C. Content and Organization

Many prosecutors begin their opening statements by briefly introducing themselves and thanking the jurors for their patience during the *voir dire* process. If you are part of a specialized child abuse unit in your office, consider telling the jury that you work in that unit. This will educate the jurors about the prevalence and seriousness of abuse. Avoid belaboring the length of time you have prosecuted child abuse or the number of cases. Not only should personal details be limited owing to their prejudicial nature, but you do not want to appear self-congratulatory. Some prosecutors avoid this personal approach entirely.

The law in some jurisdictions requires that the facts related in opening statement cover all elements of the crimes with which the defendant is charged. A prosecutor in those jurisdictions could start by indicating, in legal terms, what the evidence is expected to show by listing the elements of the crimes. The prosecutor could then follow with a more interesting and understandable account of the evidence of abuse.

Telling a story in opening is more effective than a recitation of what each witness is expected to say in testimony. While a prosecutor wishes to present the account from the victim's testimony, children, particularly young ones, will not always realize the significance of some details and may even freeze. Be prepared for the child to relate less or describe the abuse in a different way than previously. You are safer using particular facts from the child's prior statements when it is known in advance that they fit a hearsay exception and other witnesses will be allowed to present these statements.

Avoid overstating the evidence or specifying dates, times, and locations of abuse, particularly in chronic abuse situations, unless they can be established through witnesses other than the child. It may be best to let these facts come out naturally through evidence during the course of the trial. Also remember that lay witnesses and even professionals may overlook details or vary slightly from factual recitations provided earlier to investigators and prosecutors. Defense attorneys may later exploit a failure to present the evidence promised during opening statement.

It often makes sense to start the account with the child's disclosure, explaining how the case first came to light. If other witnesses will be testifying about what the child said, describe the child's words and emotions to convey what the abuse involved. Watch the jurors carefully to see how they react as you describe the abuse. A graphic description, especially of sexual abuse, is often shocking to them. Summarize the corroborating evidence, giving the jurors the results of the investigation process such as searches and medical and scientific tests rather than lengthy explanations of the mechanics involved. It may be wise to give the jurors an idea of what the child has been through so far, such as how many people she has talked to, medical exams, and disruptions in her living situation and relationships with friends and family.

Finally, if the defendant has made admissible statements that you plan to present in testimony, tell the jury what those statements were, especially if you can prove them wrong or use them in support of your theory of the case. This will make any change in defense tactics immediately obvious to the jury as well as provoke questions regarding the reasonableness of the defense's explanations from the beginning. Be brief without sacrificing any important information you want to relay. By this time, the jury is anxious to hear from the witnesses.

Reasonable doubt and the burden of proof should be acknowledged in a positive way. For example, "When you hear and see all the evidence, we will have proven the defendant guilty beyond a reasonable doubt, not all possible or conceivable doubt, since that is not our burden." End your opening with confidence, perhaps indicating that at the end of the trial you will ask the jury to return their verdicts consistent with the evidence. At this time, consider pointing out that the defense also has the option of making an opening statement, and ask that they listen as carefully to it as they have to yours. Doing so shows you are playing fair and have nothing to fear from the defense. It also invites the defense to respond. If they choose to reserve their opening statement, it will appear that they have nothing to say to contest the facts that you have outlined. If, on the other hand, the defense attorney gives an opening, you will have some advance warning of their plan of attack and any changes in tactics.

Pay careful attention to the defense opening. If anything especially helpful to your case emerges, or if it later becomes apparent that the defense was unable to produce what was described, consider having the court reporter transcribe the relevant portions of the opening to provide you with a verbatim account. Always remember, though, that the defense attorney can do the same with your opening. Once opening statements are completed, you should be ready to present the evidence now expected by the jury. Giving them even more than you promised can never hurt your case, but delivering less will weaken your case considerably.

IV. THE STATE'S CASE

A. The Child Victim's Testimony

1. The Order of Testimony

The order of testimony is an important tactical decision. In a child abuse case, the child is often the most critical witness. This does not mean, however, that the victim should necessarily testify first. You must evaluate the entire case to determine when the victim's testimony will be the most effective.

The order of witnesses will likely depend upon their availability. If your case involves expert testimony, inform jurors during jury selection and your opening statement that you may need to call the expert out of turn. Explain that an expert such as a pediatrician or child therapist, who is in the business of treating children, will testify when able to take time away from a busy hospital or clinic.

The time of day the victim testifies may be significant in determining witness order. Occasionally, the best made plans must give way to placing a young child on the stand when she is having a good day and ready to go. If, for example, you know that the child victim naps in the afternoon, plan to have her testify in the morning rather than the afternoon when she will be less alert.

In general, the prosecution's case should start strong and end strong. When the child is a strong witness, you may have the option of presenting such testimony either at the beginning or end of the case. In contrast, the testimony of a child who may have difficulty testifying can be strengthened by first presenting corroborative evidence to establish numerous facts prior to the child's testimony. This may include introducing photographs or other exhibits before the child testifies so that foundation questions for the photographs or exhibits need not be asked of the child witness. Other strong pieces of evidence with which the prosecutor may begin or end a case involve medical testimony indicating abuse or admissions of a defendant. A weak witness can be supported by strong evidence such as medical evidence of abuse or a defendant's confession.

If the child has difficulty testifying it may be helpful to call witnesses who can place the child's behavior in context. For example, in a case where the 8-year-old victim disclosed to a favorite aunt repeated sexual assault by a stepfather, you may call a relative to testify that the child became withdrawn and depressed in recent months. This lends some corroboration to the reported abuse while preparing the jury to be sympathetic and understanding when the child has difficulty testifying.

If you know the victim will recant and are able to impeach her through prior testimony and statements, you may want to set the stage by having the relative who pressured the victim to recant testify first. On the other hand, you may want the jury to observe the victim's demeanor first and then present witnesses who created the environment that forced her to recant. If the relative is highly articulate and may seriously undermine your case, you may decide against presenting that testimony in your case-in-chief.

When the victim is mentally or physically disabled, you may want to present background information about the victim before she testifies. The jury is then more likely to understand her behavior and allow the court and defense counsel to formulate appropriate questions for the victim.

Whenever the prosecution anticipates potential difficulties with a victim or key witness, it is important to prepare the jury for such testimony. Otherwise, the jury may anticipate that the victim, even a child, will clearly and directly testify and accuse the defendant.

2. Preparation for Testimony

a. Courtroom visit. A trip to the courtroom is essential not only for young children but also for older victims. As with many decisions, when to take that trip to the courtroom presents conflicting considerations. It should not be so early that the child is forced to stay "keyed up" for a long period. On the other hand, fear of the unknown can be substantial, and familiarizing the child early can allay some fears. Consider the advice of caregivers and advocates for the child in deciding which course to take.

The first step in the process could be a short visit to a trial in session. Let the child see a judge in a robe. Select a calm, low-key trial with few, if any, spectators. You can sit in back of the courtroom with the child and explain who sits where and does what. Do not select a trial that may have emotionally charged testimony or other factors that may increase the child's stress. If possible, select a trial with the same judge that will be presiding in the victim's case. If identity is an issue in your case, you should *not* tell the child where the defendant will be seated. Rather, you can tell the child that you will ask her to look around the courtroom and point to the person who abused her if he is present. Explain that it is important for the jury to know who did it so that they are sure they have the right person. Let the victim know where court personnel will be stationed to prevent the defendant from approaching her. If possible, introduce the child to the bailiff and the court clerk and explain their responsibilities.

The child should be taken to an empty courtroom as well and, if at all possible, to the courtroom where the case will be heard. Let the child walk around and learn the layout of the courtroom. Encourage the child to sit in the witness chair, test out the microphone, and practice answering innocuous questions. This may be the first time a child has heard her voice amplified. Have the child sit up straight, not chew gum, and speak loudly enough to be heard. Explain the importance of looking at and communicating to the jury.

Explain that when the prosecutor, defense attorney, and judge move from the courtroom to chambers that they are simply discussing points of law that the jurors are not supposed to hear. You should also explain witness sequestration to prepare the victim for the fact that family members and others will be outside the courtroom while she testifies. Make sure anyone who will be sequestered at trial steps out of the courtroom during this visit. If possible, have the support person who will accompany the victim to court present to reassure the child that there will be another familiar face in the courtroom when she testifies. This is also a good time to tell the child that she can focus her eyes wherever she wants to while answering questions. Prosecutors should reassure the child they will be close the whole time the child is in the courtroom. Also, be sure to tell the child that she can request a bathroom break if necessary. If a court school program is available to the victim, it should cover these points as well.

b. Blind victims. If the victim is blind, describe the courtroom as accurately as possible. Walk with the child around the courtroom to give her an opportunity to touch things and orient herself to the room's layout. Ask the victim how she prefers to be helped in the courtroom. Many blind persons opt for their hand on your arm, which gives them greater control, rather than you holding their arm or hand. Familiarize the child with where the defense attorney, the prosecutor, the judge, and any others who will be talking during the trial will be seated by speaking from each location while the child sits in the witness chair.

Because a blind person's sense of smell and hearing are acute, she will often be aware of things that you are not. Have the child describe the sounds she hears during the courtroom tour such as the steno machine so that you can explain them. Inform the child of anything that might be unusual or frightening to someone who cannot see what is happening.

c. Deaf victims. When your case involves a deaf victim, educate yourself about the deaf victim's abilities and the procedures that will allow you to communicate with her more effectively. Do not make assumptions regarding the child's intellectual capabilities based on her deafness. Deafness does not correlate to intelligence or the lack thereof. Deaf children also vary in their ability to read lips and to understand what is being said around them. Contact the deaf victim's school. Ordinarily, a school counselor or teacher will be able to talk to you at length about the victim's abilities.

Find an appropriate sign interpreter to accompany the child to trial and involve the interpreter throughout the preparation process to allow the child to become comfortable with that interpreter. You cannot assume that a sign interpreter who is routinely provided by the court will be adequate, as deaf children have different levels of proficiency in signing. Each school may even teach a slightly different signing idiom. School officials can educate you about the child's language level, signing idiosyncrasies, and name signs for particular people.

A deaf child who attends a mainstream school often has an interpreter who accompanies her to class. The interpreter and the child may become good friends, and the child may actually first report the abuse to the interpreter. If the interpreter is a potential witness at trial, the defense may make a motion to use another interpreter in court. Be prepared with options for alternate interpreters should the judge grant the defense motion.

Find out from the child's teacher or counselor a name sign that you can use to introduce yourself to the child. Making that small effort will reassure the child that you have taken the time to find out something about her world.

When you take the child on a courtroom visit, orient the child to the physical layout of the courtroom, to the individuals who will be in the courtroom, and to the procedures to be followed in court. It is particularly important to educate the child about what may be going on outside her line of sight. Explain sequestration thoroughly, as the deaf child may become extremely anxious when her caregiver leaves the courtroom and goes into the hallway. You should show the child exactly where sequestered witnesses will wait, in order to reassure the child that they are close by.

During pre-trial interviews and court school, encourage the deaf victim to sign clearly and slowly, holding her hands away from the body. If the child becomes nervous during testimony, she may tend to curl up or sign in a less precise fashion. The interpreter should inform you or the judge that the child needs a break to allow the child to relax and be reminded to sign clearly.

Ask a teacher or interpreter for advice regarding the best way to frame questions for the deaf child. Generally, as with many child witnesses, keep questions short, concise, and concrete. File a pre-trial motion asking the court to instruct the defense attorney to adhere to appropriate questioning techniques delineated by the child's teacher, interpreter, or counselor.

Always look at the deaf victim when asking her questions. Do not look at the interpreter. Maintaining eye contact with the child is essential in establishing rapport even if the child looks primarily at the interpreter. Consider positioning the interpreter beside you as you question the child. As you speak to the deaf victim, do not use a lot of hand gestures, as the child will find them distracting.

Finally, recognize that the deaf victim may be frightened and wary of people who can hear. Do all that you can to reassure the deaf child that you will educate yourself about deafness and about her special needs.

d. Mentally disabled victims. Insight into the mentally disabled victim's abilities and strengths can be gained through contact with teachers or counselors. These children may be easily intimidated and very fearful of the defendant. Reassure the victim repeatedly about her safety in the courtroom. Inform the child that angry outbursts in the courtroom may occur but will not be directed at her. Repetition of simplified explanations of the courtroom arrangements and procedures is helpful. The prosecutor should help the victim realize that she does not need to answer questions that she does not understand and that she has a right to say she does not understand a question.

e. Preparation for direct examination. Prosecutors vary significantly in their approach to preparing the child for direct examination. Some do not review specifics of the abuse ahead of trial, while others prepare the child as they would any adult witness. Most agree that practicing specific questions and answers is not desirable, as it can lead to the child sounding rehearsed and flat. On the other hand, reviewing the facts essential to proving the elements of the crime and reminding the child of the statements she has made before can help set the child at ease about what to expect. It also ensures that crucial evidence will be covered.

Explain why the jury needs to hear from the child about what happened even though she has previously spoken about the abuse. Use the child's words and emphasize how important it is to tell the truth and tell everything, no matter how difficult or embarrassing. Ask the child to correct you if you get something wrong. Consider going through some nonleading questions with the victim just prior to trial to elicit the most important and embarrassing details such as penetration of her vagina, anus, or mouth. Go over what, if anything, the defendant said to the victim. It is important to review the child's reasons for complying with the defendant, the delay in reporting, or other factors that may be of concern to the jury. However, do this in a way that does not blame the child for a delay in disclosure. Do not ask, "Why did you wait so long to tell?" Instead, ask, "What made you decide to tell?"

Often, the prosecutor may wish to question the child on direct examination about possible prior inconsistencies. It is not unusual that at some point during the initial investigation a child may have denied the sexual assault. Ask how the child felt at the time. Was the child scared or embarrassed at the first interview? Was the child in an intimidating environment such as a police station where officers with guns were present? Were the perpetrator, his friends, or relatives present?

f. Preparation for cross-examination. Child witnesses 10 years of age and older should review all of their prior statements, including statements made to caseworkers, hospital personnel, and others. With very young children, some prosecutors feel that it is best not to have the child review the prior statements to avoid the suggestion that the victim was rehearsed. Indeed, a young child may not understand that reviewing a prior statement is about refreshing her memory as opposed to teaching her the right answer.

Prepare the child for the manner in which inconsistencies are developed. A child witness may feel uncomfortable and not understand the traditional format in which prior testimony is utilized such as, "Do you recall testifying at a prior proceeding?" and, "At that time do you recall being asked the following questions and making the following answers . . . ?" Such legal ritual can be befuddling to any witness but particularly to a child.

Prepare the child for the key issues of the case. While no witness can be expected to recall all details and facts, the witness should be prepared to deal with questions about crucial issues. If force is an element of the crime, it is essential that the child be prepared to answer questions about the force involved. For example, if the child is asked: "Did you scream at the time the defendant asked you to perform this act?" the child should be prepared to state that she did not scream because she was too scared, intimidated by the defendant's size, or because of past physical abuse.

The child should be made aware that it is very possible that there may be questions she does not understand, and that she may say that she does not understand the question. Explain that it is all right to disagree with something that is incorrect as long as it is done politely. The child should understand that many questions will be leading and suggestive, and that it may not be possible to answer a question yes or no. Reinforce that the child should not guess at an answer and that there is nothing wrong with saying, "I don't know" when she does not know. Practice the concept with the child by asking a question such as, "What did I have for breakfast this morning?" When the child says she does not know, tell her that is the right answer because she was not there when you ate breakfast. Tell her to do the same if she is asked a question in court for which she does not know the answer.

Explain to the child that you may object to some of the defense attorney's questions. Ask the child to take a breath, pausing for a short time after each of the defense attorney's questions. That pause will then give you time to object. Tell the child that if there is an objection during her testimony, she should stop talking and wait until the judge or lawyer says it is okay to continue. Emphasize that the child should ask for the question to be repeated or for clarification if she is unsure what to do. The child should also be told that one lawyer objecting does not mean that she did anything wrong. It merely means that one lawyer thinks the other lawyer broke the rules of court.

Ask some questions the defense attorney is likely to ask and see how the child responds. Include questions that you expect the child to disagree with to let her get used to listening carefully and speaking up if she is confused or does not agree.

Consider yourself successful if a very young child retains any of these points. Indeed, when preparing young children, be careful not to present them with too many rules they cannot understand or may not remember. Too many rules may heighten a child's anxiety. Hope the defense attorney will at least ask the question: "Didn't the prosecutor tell you what to say?" Answer: "Yes." If defense counsel does not follow up, on redirect you can ask, "What were you told to say?" Answer: "The truth." Avoid telling the child what the defense attorney will try to make her say, because most 5-year-olds cannot outwit defense attorneys. Most jurors, however, understand a child witness's limitations and will give the child the benefit of the doubt if she appears confused by cross-examination.

g. Redirect examination. The child witness should be prepared for redirect examination. Explain that you may ask questions to articulate or clarify issues raised on cross-examination. For example, you may ask the child to provide the rest of a conversation when only a portion of it was elicited on cross-examination.

It is very important that the child be prepared to discuss prior uncharged acts that were precluded by the trial court's ruling but are now permissible because of questions during cross-examination. For instance, cross-examination about the child's failure to report or delay in reporting may open the door to the complainant's explanation that the report was delayed because of prior assaults upon her or a third person. It may be appropriate to request a recess to inform the child that an area of testimony that the child was previously told was off limits is now permissible.

h. Court school. Court preparation programs, or court schools, educate child victims or witnesses and their caregivers about trial procedures. Such programs are acceptable as long as they prepare the child for courtroom protocol and procedure and do not result in coaching the child with respect to facts or issues of the child's particular case. (See *People v. McNeil,* 613 N.Y.S.2d 302 [1994].) While individual cases are not discussed, the child's attendance at a court school helps to allay the child's fears about court proceedings.

Since role-playing is a particularly effective way to familiarize children with court, have the children act the parts of the judge, prosecutor, defense attorney, sheriff, court reporter, and jury member. Have the child portraying the prosecutor ask questions that elicit "I don't know," "I don't understand," or "I don't remember" answers. One of the lawyers can "object" to a question and the judge can remind the witness not to answer. Explain "overruled" and "sustained" and have the child judge use those terms. In a large group, two children can be witnesses with one excluded from the courtroom during the other's testimony as a way of explaining sequestration.

Because identity of the perpetrator may be an issue, court school staff should not tell children that the person who committed the crime will sit in a particular place. Some court schools leave the defendant's presence in the courtroom to the prosecutor to discuss with the child on an individual basis. Others indicate that, during trial, the child may be asked to point to the person who committed the crime if that person is in the courtroom.

Defense challenges regarding the appropriateness of court schools provide an opportunity for you to rebut the inference of coaching by calling a court school staff member to describe the program and why it is needed. Jurors can then learn about the fearfulness of children faced with testifying in court and the sensitive, fair, and creative procedures designed to reduce their fears. Your witness can also educate the jury that child abuse is common enough to warrant development of court school sessions and keep them filled month after month.

Trial judges are sometimes willing to help in role-play during court school. Some prosecutors refrain from using judges in court school since defense attorneys have been known to file motions to recuse those judges from hearing child abuse cases owing to alleged prejudice in favor of child victims. If you do enlist the help of judges, resist defense motions for recusal. Press defense attorneys to show *actual,* not merely potential, prejudice. Judges often speak at functions to educate the public about the criminal justice system, and court schools simply educate children who are entering the system. Moreover, court schools should be available for all child witnesses in any civil or criminal trial, including children defense counsel may call to testify. Unless the judge discussed the allegations with a specific child, no actual prejudice could result. The defense may argue that the judge has seen the child outside the courtroom and must have formed certain opinions. However, the judge, like any juror, is sworn to set aside bias in criminal cases and base decisions on the evidence presented in court. Judges have an ethical duty to inform attorneys should they feel impartiality is impossible. Finally, in a jury trial where the judge does not function as the fact finder, a motion for recusal is completely frivolous.

Materials on establishing a court school are available from the National Center.

B. Courtroom Procedures to Assist the Child While Testifying

1. Courtroom Seating Arrangements

The trial judge has wide discretion over courtroom seating arrangements. "Nothing in the law or the Constitution preordains that courtrooms be configured in a particular way, and, so long as the defendant's rights are protected, minor alterations to accommodate children are proper" (*Hicks-Bey v. United States*, 649 A.2d 569 [D.C. 1994]). Generally speaking, positioning the child so that the defendant is not in the direct view of the child does not deny the defendant his right to a face-to-face confrontation as long as a defendant can view the witness. (See, e.g., *Commonwealth v. Sanchez*, 670 N.E.2d 377 [Mass. 1996].) Totally blocking the defendant's view of the child is likely to raise constitutional issues.

The trial judge may have some discretion in where attorneys stand while questioning the child. For example, counsel may be directed to stand at a neutral place in the courtroom while questioning the child.

A miniature chair may be provided to a child so that the child's feet can reach the floor. Sitting in a large chair where her feet cannot reach the floor can be intimidating to a child. If a child wants to sit in the witness box, make sure she can see over the railing of the box. A simple solution is to place an extra cushion on the witness chair.

2. The Use of a Support Person During the Child's Testimony

Many courts follow the provisions of the Child Victims' and Child Witnesses' Rights Act and allow a child to be assisted by another person to provide "emotional support to the child" (18 U.S.C. § 3509[e]). For additional statutes, see Table VI.6.

Sometimes, as with many procedures designed to assist children while testifying, a showing of a "compelling necessity" should be made prior to using a support person. Otherwise, the defense may argue that the support person unfairly bolsters the child's credibility and denies the defendant a fair trial. (See *State v. Suka*, 777 P.2d 240 [Haw. 1989].) Although not all statutes require a showing of necessity, it is certainly prudent to establish on the record a factual predicate and need for a support person. The court can also instruct the jury that no inference should be drawn from the fact that the child has a support person.

A parent may be a poor choice as a support person since it may be difficult to reveal the nature and extent of the abuse in front of a parent. The child's testimony may also be upsetting to the parent. The parent is also likely to be a witness.

If the support person is a prospective witness, most courts will hold that a sequestration order does not preclude the support person from testifying. This is likely a matter of a court's discretion, although some statutes specifically address the issue. It may still be wise to have the support person testify before the child to prevent any issue of prejudice.

It is important to instruct any support person not to lead or prompt the child witness during testimony. Any effort to encourage or affect the child's testimony may well be a basis for mistrial or an appeal.

3. Comfort Items for the Child Witness

Most courts will allow a child to hold a doll, teddy bear, blanket, or some other object that comforts the child. Once again, some courts may require some showing of necessity before permitting the procedure. However, be careful about having the child hold something that may be distracting, as you do not want the child playing instead of testifying. Also keep in mind that any deviation, however slight, from what you told the child to expect may cause problems. Not being allowed to hold the teddy bear while testifying as you promised may totally disrupt the child's ability to concentrate. Accordingly, file a motion and get the judge to agree that the child can bring a comfort item before pronouncing this to the victim.

4. The Timing of the Child's Testimony and Breaks

Alert the trial court to the possible necessity of frequent breaks or the need to present a child's testimony at a particular time. Prearranged breaks, every 15 minutes for children under five and at longer intervals for older children, relieve the child of the responsibility of asking for breaks. Schedule testimony early in the day instead of during the afternoon session if possible. For young children, it can make the difference between no testimony and great testimony. If the child must wait, try to arrange for someplace other than the courtroom hallway where she can color, play a board game, or read. A calm victim-witness advocate can make waiting much easier.

As the attorney questioning a child, one must be very sensitive to signs that a child is tired, hungry, or needs a comfort break. Be sensitive that the child may have a limited attention span and that direct examination should be limited for that reason. Also, consider asking the judge to take a break before the child is cross-examined so that the child has an appropriate period to rest.

One issue that surfaces during recesses or breaks is the permissibility of the prosecutor discussing the case or testimony with the child or witness. While generally this is permitted, it is appropriate for a defense attorney to cross-examine the witness about the nature of any contact with the prosecutor during the recess or break. If at all possible, a break should be a true break for the child, an opportunity to relax and rest. The purpose of the recess or break should not be to prepare the child for the next round of questioning.

5. Developmentally Appropriate Questions, Oaths, and Silent Objections

With young children, it is appropriate to ask the court to administer an oath the child can understand and to require both the prosecutor and defense counsel to ask questions the child can understand. It may also be wise to have both attorneys object silently by raising their hands instead of their voices. For further information on these motions, see Chapter IV and Appendixes Chapter IV.

C. Competency

1. The Necessity for Competency Hearings

Federal Rule of Evidence 601 states, "Every person is competent to be a witness except as otherwise provided in these rules." Many states follow this rule. See Table V.1 for a list of state statutes regarding competency.

Challenges to a child victim's testimonial competence are frequently raised in child abuse cases. Since a judicial finding of incompetence prevents the child from testifying, this threshold determination can have a decisive impact. Often there is no direct evidence of abuse other than the child victim's account, making that testimony indispensable.

The 1990 Child Victims' and Child Witnesses' Rights Act presumes a child competent and that a competency exam is conducted by the court only "upon written motion to offer proof of incompetency by a party" (18 U.SC. § 3509[c][2][3]). Many states presume a child competent above a particular age and require a determination of a witness's competency only if the witness is under a specific age. Some statutes provide that a child below a particular age is incompetent unless it is shown that the child understands the nature and obligation of an oath. Nonetheless, competency hearings are the norm in many jurisdictions, regardless of the Child Victims' and Child Witnesses' Rights Act and other court rules.

Prosecutors dealing with child witnesses should be aggressive in objecting to competency hearings when there is no reason to believe a child cannot meet minimal requirements. Children may become confused, and their testimony before the jury may have less impact when they are required to answer the same questions twice in the courtroom, once in the competency hearing and again before the jury. Often, defense attorneys insist on competency hearings in hopes of intimidating the victim and reducing the child's effectiveness before the jury. On the other hand, prosecutors sometimes welcome the usually innocuous questioning involved in a competency hearing as a way of building the child's confidence before having to answer more upsetting questions about the abuse. If you do not wish to object to the competency hearing, be sure to limit it to its purpose and prevent the defense from turning it into a discovery mechanism.

Prosecutors can argue that the trial judge should adopt the approach of the Federal Victims of Child Abuse Act of 1990, 18 U.S.C. § 3509(c), which requires a written motion and affidavit from the defense setting forth reasons apart from age to justify a competency hearing. Under the Act, the court may permit the hearing to take place outside the presence of the defendant. The Act further requires the use of age-appropriate questions and that the questions be related solely to determining competency and not to fact issues. The Act was the result of the case of *Kentucky v. Stincer*, 482 U.S. 730 (1987), which held that the defendant does not have a constitutional right to be present during a competency hearing. For further discussion on this issue, see Section C.4., below.

If the competency hearing involves a young child, be sure to educate the court about the growing body of literature concerning the developmentally appropriate way to question children about the difference between a truth and a lie and their obligation to testify truthfully. Ask the court to question the child consistent with this research.

2. Competency and Hearsay

Most jurisdictions do not require that a hearsay declarant's competency be established. However, some jurisdictions do require that the declarant's competency be established as a prerequisite to admissibility of the hearsay statement. Compare *State v. Said*, 644 N.E.2d 337, 339–41 (Ohio 1994) (excepting excited utterances competency rule) with *People v. Sullivan*, 504 N.Y.S.2d 788 (1986) (applying competency rule to spontaneous utterances). Prosecutors offering hearsay statements of children should verify that their jurisdiction does not require a showing of competency before the hearsay statement is offered.

Table V.1 Statutes Regarding the Competency of Child Witnesses to Testify in Criminal Proceedings

Alabama	ALA. CODE § 15-25-3(c)
	ALA. R. EVID. 601
Alaska	ALASKA R. EVID. 601
Arizona	ARIZ. REV. STAT. ANN. § 13–4061
Arkansas	ARK. R. EVID. 601
California	CAL. EVID. CODE § 700 to 701
	CAL. EVID. CODE § 710
	CAL. PENAL CODE § 1321
Colorado	COLO. REV. STAT. § 13–90–106
	COLO. REV. STAT. § 13–90–117.5
	COLO. R. EVID. 601
Connecticut	CONN. GEN STAT. ANN. § 54–86h
Delaware	DEL. CODE ANN. tit. 10, § 4302
	DEL. R. EVID. 601
Florida	FLA. EVID. CODE § 90.601, .603, .605(2)
	FLA. STAT. ANN. § 914.07
Georgia	GA. CODE ANN. § 24–9–1, -5
Hawaii	HAW. REV. STAT. § 601
	HAW. REV. STAT. § 603.1
Idaho	IDAHO CODE § 9-202
	IDAHO CT. R. 601
Illinois	725 ILL. COMP. STAT ANN. § 5/115–14
Indiana	IND. CODE § 34-37-4-1
	IND. CODE § 35-45-2-1
Iowa	IOWA R. EVID. 601
Kansas	KAN. STAT. ANN. § 60–417
Kentucky	KY. R. EVID. 601
Louisiana	LA. CODE EVID. ANN. art. 601
Maine	ME. R. EVID. 601
Maryland	MD. CODE ANN. CTS & JUD. PROC. § 9–103
	MD. R. EVID. 5–601
Massachusetts	MASS. GEN. LAWS ch. 223, § 20
Michigan	MICH. R. EVID. 601
Minnesota	MINN. R. EVID. 601
	MINN. STAT. ANN. § 595.02(1)(m)
Mississippi	MISS. R. EVID. 601
Missouri	MO. REV. STAT. § 491.060(2)
Montana	MONT. CODE ANN., CH. 10, R. 601
Nebraska	NEB. REV. STAT. § 27–601
Nevada	NEV. REV. STAT. ANN. § 50.015
New Hampshire	N.H. R. EVID. 601
New Jersey	N.J. R. EVID. 601
New Mexico	N.M. R. EVID. 11–601
	N.M. STAT. ANN. § 30–9–18
New York	N.Y. C.L.S. C.P.L. § 60.20
North Carolina	N.C. GEN. STAT. § 8C-1, RULE 601
North Dakota	N.D. R. EVID. 601

(Continued)

Table V.1   (Continued)

Ohio	OHIO REV. CODE ANN. § 2317.01
	OHIO R. EVID. 601
Oklahoma	OKLA. STAT. ANN. tit. 12, § 2601
Oregon	OR. REV. STAT. § 40.310
Pennsylvania	42 PA. CONS. STAT. ANN. § 5911
Rhode Island	R.I. R. EVID. 601
South Carolina	S.C. R. EVID. 601
South Dakota	S.D. CODIFIED LAWS § 19–14–1
Tennessee	TENN. R. EVID. 601
Texas	TEX. R. EVID. 601
Utah	UTAH CODE ANN. § 76–5–410
	UTAH CODE ANN. § 78–24–2
Vermont	VT. R. EVID. 601
Virginia	VA. CODE ANN. § 8.01–396.1
Washington	WASH. REV. CODE ANN. § 5.60.020, .050
	WASH. R. EVID. 601
West Virginia	W. VA. CODE § 61–8–13(e)
	W. VA. CODE § 61–8B-11(c)
	W. VA. R. EVID. 601
Wisconsin	WIS. STAT. ANN. § 906.01
Wyoming	WYO. R. EVID. 601
U.S. Code	FED. R. EVID. 601
	18 U.S.C.A. § 3509(c)

NOTE: This compilation includes all statutes regarding the competency of child witnesses to testify in criminal proceedings. This table includes all legislation passed through January 2002, as verified through Lexis Nexis.

3. Competency at Time of Trial and/or at Time of the Abuse Event

Most jurisdictions will allow a child who is competent to testify at trial to recall events that may have occurred many years earlier. (See, e.g., *Commonwealth v. McMaster*, 666 A.2d 724 [Pa. 1995].) In contrast, some jurisdictions may require that a child witness be competent at the time of the event, not just at the time of testifying, before the child may testify. (See, e.g., *Simmers v. State*, 943 P.2d 1189, 1199 [Wyo. 1997].) Prosecutors may argue that the ability of any witnesses to recall events about which they are testifying is a matter of *credibility*, not of competency. The competency issue has traditionally involved issues pertaining to a witness' status at the time of trial and not prior to trial.

4. Competency Hearing Procedures

Judges are responsible for determining competency. The judicial test for competency in most jurisdictions involves determining whether the child possesses the ability to perceive, recall, and relate facts accurately; understands the obligation to tell the truth; and understands the difference between truth and falsehood. The test of a child's competency derives from the United States Supreme Court decision in

Wheeler v. United States, 159 U.S. 523 (1895). Since few jurisdictions continue to have presumptive ages below which children are considered incompetent, children as young as three have qualified and testified before juries.

Mental health experts should have little, if any, role in determining competency of child witnesses. Whether a child can perceive and relate facts accurately must be tested against objective facts. On occasion, courts want to turn this function over to someone else, and may require a psychological evaluation to determine if the child is competent. This is usually in response to a defense motion. In practice, the result is that evaluators decide whether they think the child was abused. If they decide the abuse did not occur and the child persists in saying it did, they testify that the child clearly cannot perceive or relate facts accurately. This must be avoided, and prosecutors should vigorously resist efforts by the defense or the court to require such evaluations.

The United States Supreme Court in *Kentucky v. Stincer*, 482 U.S. 730 (1987), held that the defendant does not have a constitutional right to be present at a competency hearing. The Court found that excluding the defendant did not interfere with defense opportunity for later cross-examination of the child witness at trial. The Court further found that the defendant's Fourteenth Amendment due process rights were not violated because of the nature of the competency hearing, which excludes questioning about substantive trial issues. As a practical matter, however, some prosecutors prefer the defendant be present during the competency hearing to acclimate the victim to the defendant's presence and demonstrate that the defendant cannot harm her.

5. The Timing of Competency Hearings

Competency examinations should be held at the time of trial since they relate to the child's ability to testify at that time, not weeks or days earlier. You should have a fairly good idea beforehand whether the child will be deemed competent and should resist efforts to have pre-trial competency hearings. Not only does a pre-trial competency hearing mean an extra trip to the courtroom with added trauma for the child, but the variations in the child's day-to-day abilities may necessitate a second competency hearing at the time of trial.

If, on the day of trial, you are unsure whether the victim will be deemed competent by the trial judge, have the court conduct the competency exam before jeopardy attaches. In most jurisdictions, this is before the jury is sworn. If the victim is deemed incompetent before the trial has begun, you can dismiss without prejudice and may consider whether, after the passage of time and additional therapy, the victim has become competent. If so, you have the option of reopening the case. In some cases, the child's incompetence to testify may strengthen the state's case by opening the door for admission of statements that could not otherwise be presented to the jury.

Competency hearings are conducted outside the hearing of the jury. After the victim has been declared competent and is called to testify, consider repeating the competency examination in front of the jury. It is important for the jury to know that the victim understands the duty to tell the truth. Answers to competency questions can also be used effectively in closing arguments. When you question the victim in front of the jury, vary your questions slightly from those previously asked so the jury will not mistakenly infer that the victim was rehearsed.

6. *Who Should Question the Child?*

It is debatable who should actually conduct the competency exam—the judge or the prosecutor. If you have a sensitive judge who knows the law and can ask questions likely to get answers, it may be reasonable to have the court do the questioning. If the judge is unable to get the child to respond, the prosecutor must step in and try to get the child talking. If given the choice, many prosecutors prefer to do the initial questioning themselves. One obvious advantage is that the child is familiar with the prosecutor and more likely to be responsive. The prosecutor is also more likely to know how to question that particular child effectively. Moreover, a kind, thorough prosecutor whose questions are tailored to the child's personality and level of development will often cause the judge to bar a defense attorney's cross-examination in areas already covered.

7. *Sample Questions*

Whether the judge, prosecutor, or defense attorney is doing the questioning, inquiry should be limited to determining whether the child meets the minimum requirements of competency. Questions related to the facts of the case should not be permitted or should be severely limited if absolutely required under the law. The child's answers to fact questions will not reveal whether she can relate facts "truthfully" since that is the issue for the jury to decide and the reason for trial. Questions about *uncontested* facts occurring around the same time as the abuse can be asked to demonstrate the child's ability to recall accurately and relate pertinent facts. Ask adults who are involved in the victim's life to supply information about such events. For example, the victim may have gone on a trip to Disneyland at some time during the period of the abuse and may remember details from the trip.

Questions should be chosen based on the child's age and circumstances. Stay away from philosophical questions like, "Explain the difference between a truth and lie," or "What is the difference between right and wrong?" These questions confuse adults, let alone children. Some case law requires that the child demonstrate an understanding of the oath, including the concept of promising to tell the truth "before God." Be sensitive to cultural and religious differences and be creative in your questioning. Some children may come from families that do not believe in God.

There is nothing wrong with educating the child about the obligation to testify truthfully in court. What matters is that the child understands this obligation. Make sure the child does not simply parrot what she has been told in a court school program or seen in court preparation materials such as the coloring books used in many areas. Vary your questions in order to demonstrate the child truly understands the concept of testifying truthfully. Otherwise, the defense will suggest you have merely trained the child to repeat what she has been told. The following are examples of appropriate questions to establish competency, but they must be tailored to the child's age and developmental level:

- What is your name?
- How old are you?
- When is your birthday?

- Did you have a party on your last birthday?
- Who was there?
- Did you get any presents?
- What presents did you get?
- Do you go to school?
- What is the name of your school?
- What is the name of your teacher?
- Did you go to school last year?
- What was your teacher's name last year?
- What grade are you in now?
- Do you know anybody in this room?
- What are their names?
- Do you know your ABCs?
- Who lives in your house right now?
- Does anybody else live there?
- What color is your house?
- What is your telephone number?
- Do you have any brothers and sisters?
- Where do they live?
- Do you have any friends who you play with?
- What are their names?
- Do you do chores around the house?
- What kind of chores?
- Do you remember last Christmas?
- Where were you living?
- Do you have any grandparents?
- What are their names?
- Who is your mother?
- Where does she live?
- Who is your father?
- Where does he live?
- What street do you live on?
- Did you ever live anywhere else?
- Where did you live before? What street? Who lived there? Where did you sleep? Did you have any pets?
- Do you promise to tell the truth today?

Defense attorneys frequently ask whether the child believes in Santa Claus or the Easter Bunny and then later argue she does not know what is real versus what is make believe. Point out that Santa Claus and the Easter Bunny are made real by people who dress up like them and leave presents and baskets, setting them apart from fantasy. Other defense strategies involve having the child admit playing make believe or pretend games. This can be used to your advantage to illustrate that the child knows fantasy from fact and can talk about the difference. Moreover, even adults engage in fantasy when they watch movies, play video games, or play with their children. Defense attorneys will often ask if the victim *ever* told a lie. Make sure you prepare the child for this, that it is all right to admit to lying in the past, and that most children and adults have told "white" lies. The child's candor will highlight her truthfulness to the jury.

8. The Competency of Mentally Disabled Witnesses

Individuals with mental or developmental disabilities are not automatically disqualified as witnesses. (See *Wagner v. State*, 562 N.E.2d 421 [Ind. Ct. App. 1990] [finding mildly mentally disabled girl competent to testify even though her limited mental ability caused her testimony to be confusing and contradictory at times]; *People v. Lawler*, 536 N.E.2d 1283 [Ill. 1989] [upholding finding that a mildly mentally disabled child sexual abuse victim was competent to testify even though she gave ambivalent answers to questions about truth and falsity, when she eventually responded she would tell the truth, which she defined as "to tell what happened"]; *State v. Gonsalves*, 706 P.2d 1333 [Haw. 1985] [concluding mentally disabled victim was competent to testify when ability to testify involves understanding nature of duty to tell the truth].) The trial court may consider as part of its decision the testimony of physicians or other persons, such as a teacher, who have information relevant to the witness's capacity or intelligence. (See *People v. Parks*, 359 N.E.2d 358 [N.Y. 1976].) Such information may also be presented to the trial jury.

Mentally disabled victims often have a well-developed sense of right and wrong even though they find it difficult to explain *why* a particular action is right or wrong. Prior to the competency hearing, discuss the importance of telling the truth. Use concrete examples and explanations to establish competency. Also, do not confuse competence to testify and competence to give consent. The judge determines whether a witness is legally competent to testify. Competence to consent to sex is a factual determination for the jury. A victim can be incompetent to consent but capable of testifying truthfully.

D. Direct Examination of the Child Victim

1. Introductory Questions of the Child Witness

The initial questions to a child witness should help the child relax. The questions should be easy for the child to answer. They may include biographical information as well as questions often utilized during competency proceedings. These questions should also help the jury to assess the witness and develop confidence in the witness's intelligence. For example, the child's discussion of her school activities and studies should include questions that a child should be able to answer. At the same time, the answers will demonstrate for the jury the child's level of intelligence. With a very young child or a preschool child, the questions may involve having the child recite the alphabet.

Most children have contact with television or movies. Perhaps the child can discuss a favorite program or movie and what the program or movie is about. In some situations, the theme or message of a program or movie may later be referenced during the examination to explain the child's understanding of right and wrong or why the child came forward. Introductory questions may involve well-known TV characters.

Introductory questions can also involve background information about the witnesses. The child may be able to discuss who the defendant is and how long the child has had a relationship with the defendant. The testimony can include positive aspects of the relationship as well as information explaining helpful background information. Even if some of this information is repetitive, it is helpful for the child witness to develop some comfort in responding to questions.

Do not ask questions that are not age appropriate and will undermine the child's confidence. For example, avoid pinning the child down to times and dates, which may be beyond the developmental abilities of the child. Pay careful attention to the vocabulary of the question since the child witness will have particular difficulty with new or strange words and may be uncomfortable in stating that she does not understand the question. Questions should also be short and direct. The child's confidence is immensely aided by well-formed questions. Avoid using pronouns, legalese, double negatives or "isn't it true?" questions. Attend a forensic interview and training course, such as APRI's Finding Words program. One way to practice is by asking questions of young children. If you do not have young children of your own, practice on the children of a relative or neighbor or volunteer.

2. Leading Questions

Courts generally permit leading questions with a child witness who may have difficulty communicating details of a sexual assault or may be reluctant to testify. Unlike many other special accommodations for child witnesses, the court does not need to make special case-specific findings before permitting leading questions. Nonetheless, it is often preferable to minimize the use of leading questions since a child's credibility can be enhanced if the child can readily testify about the assault.

Often, leading questions can be avoided by using questions that a child understands and that are direct and simple. Leading questions are often less necessary when the child is comfortable.

There are alternatives to leading questions. For example, in the following section, the use of photographs is discussed as a technique to encourage the child to discuss a person, place, or event. A child can also be given choices in the question, such as, "Did he touch you in the bedroom, the den, or someplace else?" Another option is to be specific without leading, for instance, by asking, "Were you standing up?" when you know that the child was lying down. Then the witness can disagree and correct the questioner. The obvious problem with such a question is that the child may not feel comfortable about correcting the questioner.

3. The Use of Photographs or Other Real Evidence

A good technique during the direct examination of a child witness is to use photographs or other real evidence. Prior to a child's testifying, a prosecutor can introduce into evidence photographs depicting relevant persons or places. If the photograph of a house or bedroom where the incident occurred is in evidence, the child can be asked to discuss the exhibit. "What is this room? Did you ever go in this room? Who would be in the room? Do you ever sit anyplace in the room? When you sat on the bed, would anyone else be on the bed with you?"

If the child viewed pornographic videos, the child can be asked about the television shown in a photograph of the room and what type of videos the defendant would show on the television. In general, photographs and other real evidence relating to the crime assist all witnesses. The photographs can act as cues and stimulate the child's memory.

4. The Use of Dolls or Drawings

Some children may feel more comfortable drawing to illustrate an act or event or may feel comfortable utilizing a doll to assist in testifying. However, it is important that the questioner not use dolls in a suggestive fashion.

Dolls or drawings may be helpful when a witness does not have the vocabulary to describe an act such as penetration. They may also be helpful to those witnesses who are uncomfortable verbalizing matters of a sexual nature. If a child witness utilizes a drawing, the drawing should be marked and identified as a record of what the witness described. Remember that drawings or the use of dolls may be subject to ambiguous interpretations. However, when a witness uses dolls, it is important to have the record reflect what the child has demonstrated with the dolls. This can be very important when the issue of legal sufficiency, such as whether penetration was sufficiently described by a witness, is an issue on appeal. The questioner should ask the witness to describe what is being demonstrated in order to establish the record. If the child cannot verbalize the description, the prosecutor may have to do this and then ask the court to have the record reflect that the prosecutor's description is accurate.

Many states have provisions similar to the federal law that specifically authorizes the use of anatomical dolls during a child's testimony (18 U.S.C. § 3509[l]). For further information on this issue, see Holmes, L. S. [2000]. Using anatomical dolls in child sexual abuse forensic interviews. *Update, 13*(8); Holmes, L. S., et al. [2002]. The use of anatomical diagrams in child sexual abuse forensic interviews. *Update, 15*(5).

5. Establish the Relationship Between the
Child and Defendant and the Lack of a Motive to Fabricate

As part of establishing the relationship between a child and defendant, it is also helpful to establish the child's lack of motive to lie by asking questions that establish a close relationship between the defendant and the child. This is important even if it existed prior to disclosure of the abuse. Questions such as, "Did your Daddy ever do anything nice for you?" or "Did your teacher ever do things that you liked?" will help describe the relationship. Some children may describe shopping sprees, gifts of jewelry or makeup, or even alcohol or drugs as items they received from the defendant.

Another way of approaching the issue of motive is to talk about the consequences of disclosure. Children will often describe their embarrassment over the disclosure or their fear that others will learn about the abuse. Let the child explain some of the consequences of disclosure: the loss of a family relationship, placement out of the home, repeated questioning by strangers, isolation, suicidal impulses, disruption in school and social activities, and hospitalization. This is a foundation for a closing argument about the negative impact of disclosure and why the victim has no motive to fabricate the abuse.

6. Utilization of Narrative by the Child and Interrupting the Child

As a general rule, narratives are less effective as a form of direct testimony. However, it is possible that the child may give one long explosion of an answer that may include ambiguities such as "he touched me here and there." In such a situation, it is best to let the child provide the narrative without interruption. Interrupting the child may diminish the information received from the child. It is best to make notes of the child's answer or listen carefully and then go back and ask the child for details by using follow-up questions. Follow-up questions are more effective when they utilize the exact language the child used. However, to follow up a child's answers effectively and use the language of the child requires concentration and attention by the questioner.

7. Questioning the Child About the Sexual Act and Collateral Details of the Sexual Act

The most important area of the child's direct examination is testimony concerning the sexual act and details surrounding the act. This testimony is very important since it must legally establish the elements of the offense(s) charged. It also helps convince the jury that the child's ability to recall details, especially those one would not expect a child to know, means that the child must have actually experienced the abuse.

For example, ask the victim to describe the positions she and the defendant were in when the abuse occurred. She may indicate that the defendant was on top of her with his chest on her face. If the defendant forced the victim to perform fellatio, the child may describe a kneeling position. You might ask whether the defendant moved during the act. The victim may explain how the defendant's buttocks moved up and down, or how the child used her hands to masturbate the defendant. If the child has difficulty describing positioning, the use of anatomical dolls will often elicit this important testimony. To this end, prosecutors should receive training on the proper, legally defensible uses of the dolls. For information on this type of training, contact the National Center for Prosecution of Child Abuse.

Determine whether the defendant made any sounds or comments before, during, or after the sexual activity. He may have commented, "I love you, does it feel good?" or given such explanations as, "I want to teach you about boys," or "This is what you should not let boys do to you." The victim may describe the defendant's panting or groaning noises. This is especially persuasive from a young victim.

If the victim saw the defendant's penis, have the child describe it. She may be able to tell the jury what the penis looked like. The child may be able to describe that the penis changed in size or in the direction it was pointing. The victim may be more comfortable drawing a picture or pointing to something in the courtroom that is approximately the same shape.

Find out if the victim noticed hair around the defendant's penis. The following is an example of a nonleading approach to presenting this detail:

- Did Uncle Bob have hair on his head?
  "Yes."

- What color was the hair on his head?
  "Brown."

- Did Uncle Bob have hair anywhere else?
  "Yes."
- Where else did Uncle Bob have hair?
  "On his pee-pee."
- What color was the hair on his pee-pee?
  "Brown."
- Can you see the pee-pee on this doll?
  "No."
- What would you have to do to see the pee-pee on the doll?
  "Pull down the pants."
- Could you pull down the pants and show me the pee-pee?
  Victim does so.
- Can you show me where Uncle Bob's hair was on his pee-pee?

Victim points to a semi-circular area at the stomach side of the penis—more convincing if the doll lacks pubic hair.

Testimony that demonstrates the victim's knowledge of an erection may be helpful.

- Which way was his pee-pee pointing?
  "It was pointing straight at me."
- Can you show me what you mean with this doll?
  Victim takes the penis and holds it out straight.
- After the white stuff came out, what happened to his pee-pee?
  "It fell down," or "It got soft."

It is also important to determine whether ejaculation occurred. The following questions will help elicit this information:

- What happened after he moved back and forth?
  "Something came out of his pee-pee."
- Did you see it?
  "Yes."
- Where did you see it?
  "On the floor."
- What did it look like?
  "White and slimy goo."
- Did the goo stay on the floor?
  "No, Daddy wiped it up with a towel."
- What did Daddy do with the towel?
  "He put it in the washing machine."

If the defendant ejaculated in the victim's mouth, ask her how it tasted and how the defendant's penis felt in her mouth. Answers such as "salty," "yucky," "slimy," or "it made me cough" undermine defense suggestions that the victim learned about fellatio from pornography or an X-rated movie.

In a case involving penetration, or attempted penetration, careful descriptive questioning is critical. Careful questioning is critical since eliciting testimony that establishes penetration, or attempted penetration, can mean the difference between a conviction or an acquittal. For example, testimony that a defendant touched the child's "behind" may be insufficient to establish contact between the penis and anus. (See, e.g., *United States v. Plenty Arrows*, 946 F.2d 62, 65 [8th Cir. 1991].) It may be helpful to explain to the witness the importance of clearly explaining the nature of the sexual contact, however difficult or unpleasant this may be for the witness. Dolls or drawings can be very helpful for younger children who may have difficulty explaining penetration. Older children are more likely to say that the defendant put his penis "in the hole" or something similar.

- Where did his pee-pee go?
  "It went down here."—pointing to vaginal area.

- How did it feel when his pee-pee went down there?
  "It hurt."

- Where did it hurt?
  "In my pee-pee."

- Can you show me where his pee-pee went on this doll?
  Child puts her finger into the vaginal opening of the doll.

Make sure to describe for the record exactly what the child demonstrates if the child cannot.

Have the victim tell the jury what, if anything, the defendant did after the sexual act. Elicit information that answers the questions of, Did he wipe up the semen in an attempt to hide the signs of the abuse? Go to the bathroom? Wipe the child's vaginal area? Aside from these actions immediately after the sexual act, the perpetrator may have taken her shopping, to a fast food place, or to the zoo to help her "forget" the incident. The defendant may also have said something to the victim to persuade her not to tell others, ranging from outright threats to subtle intimidation. To elicit such statements, ask

- Did he want you to tell other people about what he did?
  "No."

- How do you know?

8. *Establish the Child's Feelings or State of Mind*

In discussing the sexual acts, it may be helpful to ask the child how she felt at the time of the act. This question, and variations of it, may help explain certain behaviors of the child such as the delay in reporting or continuing to have contact with the perpetrator. For example, if the child felt confused, scared, or threatened, this may explain the child's reactions. Perhaps the child felt helpless because of the relationship with the accused. The child's state of mind may also be relevant to establishing the element of force. It is also possible that the defendant's past statements or conduct affected the witness's feelings. For instance, a sexual assault complainant may feel vulnerable or coerced into complying with the defendant's request for sexual activity because of past statements or threats from the defendant. (See, e.g., *People v. Thompson*, 530 N.E.2d 839 [N.Y. 1988].)

9. *Questions Concerning Disclosure*

The prosecutor should ask the victim whom she first told about the abuse. Ask to whom else the witness may have disclosed the abuse. In some jurisdictions, the testimony of the first person the child told about the sexual abuse may be limited to the fact of the disclosure and not the details. It may be possible to establish through the child witness additional details of the disclosure. Likewise, the child may be able to provide additional details concerning a medical history that the health care professional may not be able to testify about.

Elicit testimony to explain delays in reporting and discuss thwarted attempts to disclose. Perhaps the child tried to tell a family member that she did not want to be around the defendant any more without being asked why. Family members may have rebuffed the child's attempts at disclosure. Have the victim describe the reactions of those persons she told or tried to tell, particularly if the victim has recanted.

The child's testimony about who she has talked to about the abuse, including the names, the number of times, and the length of the conversations, serves several functions. If the child has been consistent and not impeached, it shows a number of consistencies. It may also set the stage for prior consistent statements. If the child is inconsistent about details, a large number of interviews can help explain it. Furthermore, such testimony provides the foundation for a persuasive argument that no one would put herself through such an ordeal if nothing happened.

10. *Sample Questions for Children*

The following examples suggest how to phrase typical questions for child victims.

Do Not Ask

- Do you remember testifying at the preliminary hearing?

Do Ask:

- Did you ever talk to another judge?
- Was it a man or a woman judge?
- What did the judge wear?
- What/who did you talk to the judge about?

Do Not Ask:

- Were you interviewed by the social worker from the Department of Social Services?

(Continued)

(Continued)

Do Ask:

- Do you remember talking to Chris?
Have Chris brought into the courtroom for identification by the victim.

- Where were you when you talked to Chris?
- What did you talk about?
- How did you feel when you were talking to Chris?

Do Not Ask:

- How did the doctor examine you at the hospital?

Do Ask:

- Did you go to the doctor's?
- What happened at the doctor's?
- What part of you did the doctor check?
- Did the doctor check your ears? Your eyes? Other parts?
- Where was your mommy when the doctor checked you?

Write down the questions that seem to trigger the victim's memory during your preparation and use them at trial. With some victims, an open-ended question may be a good way to start: "Do you know why we're in court today? Can you tell me about it?" You can then use the victim's words to fill in details by incorporating them into nonleading questions. For example,

- Where were you when your Daddy "freaked" you?
- Did your teacher do something bad one time or more than one time?
- Was anyone else there when your teacher did something bad?
- Did you tell anyone that your Daddy "freaked" you?

11. Additional Areas for Questioning

Because sexual abuse is a secret crime, there are rarely eyewitnesses. If someone caught the defendant in the act, have the victim describe what happened. You then set the stage for upcoming eyewitness testimony or the recantation by the eyewitness who now supports the defendant. Ask the victim what the eyewitness said and did. Ask whether the police came to the house the same day.

During direct examination, present evidence of circumstances surrounding the abuse and its aftermath that you can independently corroborate. For example, the child may be able to describe furnishings in the bedroom or the defendant's underwear. She may be able to describe what the doctor did, if a doctor saw the child, with descriptions such as, "He put a Q-tip in my privates, not in my ear." The doctor can later corroborate that detail. The prosecutor must be cautious here because peripheral details are more easily forgotten. If you can corroborate the description, however, it is a strong practical demonstration of the child's abilities. Use physical evidence whenever possible, such as drawings by the victim, photographs of the scene, or clothes worn by the defendant or the victim during the abuse. Juries respond well to visual exhibits.

The prosecutor should bring out information about the victim's prior bad acts or sexual history if pre-trial motions *in limine* were lost. Eliciting potentially damaging evidence allows for minimization of its harmful effect and shows the jury that the State is not hiding anything. You will also be able to put the evidence into perspective and turn it to your advantage. For example, if an older victim has been adjudicated in juvenile court, ask the child whether she discussed the conviction with you, and if she was promised any special treatment in exchange for testimony in this case. Ask the victim about other sexual abuse incidents and how she distinguishes those incidents from the defendant's actions. If the victim did not report the earlier abuse, ask why, because the jury will want to know the reason. Since you will have discussed these issues with the child well before trial, you can phrase them in a way that does not make her feel defensive. If you are nonjudgmental and explain how important it is for you to know the truth, the child will have an easier time answering.

E. Other Potential State's Witnesses

Additional witnesses can provide information to the jury that can go a long way to strengthen your case in the absence of physical evidence. Be creative. Some witnesses can be called to dispel prejudices a jury may have. For instance, if most of the witnesses—the victim, child protective services worker, and teacher—are female and the jury is overwhelmingly male, consider calling a male police officer to testify to demonstrate that the case is not a "female conspiracy." The jury will also infer that the male police officer clearly believed the victim sufficiently to arrest the defendant.

Question each witness who dealt with the child about the child's demeanor. Testimony about the child's withdrawn, sad, or numb behavior can educate the jury about the victim's trauma following the disclosure.

1. School Teachers

Some jurors want to hear from the child's teacher. If the teacher is to testify, determine whether she will be supportive. A teacher's testimony may be admissible for a variety of reasons. If the teacher is part of the chain of disclosure, simply have her testify about the disclosure and also the details of the disclosure, if this is permissible. Another reason for calling a teacher to the stand is to elicit testimony about emotional and behavioral changes in the victim. If the victim's grades have dropped since the onset of the abuse, the teacher can testify about this change. Some caution is necessary here because some victims of child abuse escape the turmoil of their situations by throwing themselves into schoolwork and becoming straight "A" students. Make sure to explain that dynamic to the jury in your closing argument if that describes the victim.

Defense attorneys may attack the child's character by asking direct or indirect questions about the victim's reputation for truthfulness. If the judge determines that the issue of the victim's character has been raised during your case-in-chief, call a supportive teacher as a good-character witness. If the defense attorney has the defendant or other defense witnesses testify to the victim's bad character, call a teacher to testify about the victim's good character on rebuttal. Most defense attorneys, however, will attack the child indirectly to negate the opportunity for this type of rebuttal. By calling the victim's teacher, you subtly show the jury that the teacher believes the victim. It also helps the child feel that there are more people on her side. The teacher may also help rebut a claim that the child is unduly suggestive and offer examples from school of the child's resistance to misleading or inaccurate information.

2. Daycare Providers

The daycare provider will often be a witness to whom the abuse was disclosed and can sometimes testify regarding behavioral changes. Daycare people can serve much the same function as teachers: They strengthen your case, they show the child that more people are testifying for her, and they give a subtle stamp of legitimacy to the case. The daycare provider may have information on the child's development, injuries, or lack of injuries at a particular time. A daycare worker may also have had interactions with the defendant. The prosecutor must be on guard that the defense attorney may try to shift the blame for the victim's assault to the daycare provider in cases of physical abuse. If that is the case, it is especially important to produce the daycare provider to refute this suggestion.

3. Child Protective Services Caseworkers

If a child protective services (CPS) caseworker is involved in your case, make sure that you know as much as possible about that file on the case. CPS caseworkers can be crucial witnesses in your case-in-chief, although they may also provide important ammunition for the defense. As part of pre-trial preparation, make sure that the caseworker has carefully reviewed the file and knows that you, the defense attorney, and judge (if applicable) have seen it.

In some jurisdictions, the CPS worker can testify about the child's out-of-court statements, and if the child's statements are not admissible under an exception, at least establish that the child told the worker what happened. You can also use the fact that the victim had to recount the abuse repeatedly to assert that no child would fabricate and maintain a false claim of abuse, given the ordeal she has been put through. Children lie to get themselves out of trouble, not into it. Moreover, the CPS worker can outline the actions he took, such as asking the defendant to leave or removing the child from the home. The prosecutor can then point out in closing that the disclosure caused multiple problems for the child and that the easy response for the child would have been to recant the statements.

The CPS worker will be a major witness if there has been a recantation, since he can describe his knowledge about the pressures placed on the child. In many cases, the CPS worker will have also spoken to the defendant. If the defendant's statements early in the investigation ascribed a ludicrous motive to the victim or one that is different than the motive asserted at trial, you can address the discrepancy in your case-in-chief or on rebuttal. The defendant may have also admitted or corroborated aspects of the victim's testimony in statements to the CPS worker.

Always assess the community attitude toward the child protective agency before calling the worker. The agency is often the scapegoat, as defense attorneys paint a picture of an overzealous child welfare system. If it appears that the defendant was wrongfully forced from his home, the caseworker's testimony may do more harm than good. On the other hand, a skilled, experienced social worker who handled the case professionally and is a polished witness may do much to reduce, if not eliminate, community biases against the child protective system.

4. Police Officers

In many jurisdictions, the police are likely to have talked to the child. Establish that the officer made a report, talked to the victim, and took some action. The officer should explain how, when, and where the statement was taken; the victim's demeanor during the interview; and who else was present during the interview. The police officer should then relate the content of the statement to the jury if it is admissible as a hearsay exception or prior consistent statement. Make sure you have been provided with all notes and reports of the police officer.

Elicit information about the results of searches, photographs of the scene, interviews with the defendant, evidence of flight or use of aliases, and the arrest process. The officer should explain the chain of custody of evidence unless the defense attorney stipulates to the chain of custody regarding physical evidence recovered, including samples taken from the victim at the hospital and submitted by the police officer to the police laboratory. Be as detailed with the police officers in their testimony as is dictated by their helpful observations of the child and resulting investigative action. The officer and CPS worker should detail their training and experience handling child abuse cases, including the number of cases investigated. This is relevant to give the jury background on the witness's qualifications and will allow you to combat the common defense argument that "overzealous" investigators were on a "witch hunt." You can point out that the witnesses have more than enough cases to keep them busy and it makes no sense to conclude they have nothing better to do than try to encourage children to describe abuse when none occurred. The officer may also have sufficient expertise and qualifications to testify as an expert witness. (See, e.g., *People v. Turner*, 608 N.E.2d 906 [Ill. 1993]; *Commonwealth v. Richardson*, 667 N.E.2d 257 [Mass. 1996]; *State v. McMillan*, 590 N.E.2d 23 [Ohio 1990].)

5. Other Victims

During the investigation and preparation of the case, you may have become aware of other victims. If the defense opens the door or the judge grants your pretrial motion to present uncharged victims' testimony, have them ready to testify. Interview, prepare, and present prior victims using the same techniques you used for the child victim in the present case. Emphasize the similarities of the assaults. A checklist or chart of similarities can be extremely helpful.

6. The Forensic Interviewer

It is the best practice to have the child interviewed by a well-trained forensic interviewer. The interviewer can be a social worker, police officer, or employee of the local child advocacy center. Every community must have an interviewer who is well trained. At a minimum, the forensic interviewer should complete a 5-day course that teaches the science and art of interviewing. It is also wise that the interviewer receive continuing education, have his interviews subject to peer review, and stay abreast of the research on interviewing. The interviewer should utilize a protocol consistent with the research that is defensible in court. Interviewers trained through Cornerhouse, Finding Words, or a similar well-established forensic interview–training program should testify about their credentials, the development of the protocol, the necessity of asking a variety of questions in an interview, and the interview itself. A well-trained interviewer is essential to dispel the myth that most children are so suggestible they can be easily led into making and believing assertions against their best interests. Sample direct examinations of forensic interviewers are contained in Appendixes V.11 through V.13.

7. Other Corroborating Witnesses and Evidence

Most criminal cases have witnesses whose reliability will be called into question. This is particularly true in the typical child abuse case in which a young child, perhaps with mental, emotional, or learning difficulties, is called upon to provide the only direct evidence against a mature, articulate adult abuser. The need for corroborative evidence is more pronounced and, because of the nature of these cases, more difficult to obtain.

There is always a need for corroborative evidence despite the fact that most legislatures have enacted laws eliminating the legal need for corroboration. Before deciding to use this type of evidence, consider how consistent the child has been in her recitations and beware of calling witnesses who will highlight inconsistencies.

a. Corroborating the details of the child's account. Anything a child witness says that can be proven through independent and objective evidence should be pursued and presented as evidence. For example, if the child says she was assaulted on a blue cot located in a classroom closet by a teacher who always wore white clothing, the cot could be seized pursuant to search warrant and photographs should be taken of the closet. The photographs not only show that the cot and closet exist but also help the jury understand what happened from the child's perspective. Locate photographs of the defendant in white. Witness testimony about the cot's location or the dressing habits of the defendant could be sought if photographs cannot be obtained. Photographs of the crime scene, including items the child described and/or the items themselves, should be offered as exhibits at trial. These objects may include sexual literature or implements, weapons, drugs, or alcohol. Children may also accurately remember distinctive furnishings such as pictures, wall colors, locks, windows, shades, or bedspreads.

b. Photographs. If you have photographs of injuries to the child, use them as exhibits. Make sure they accurately portray the location of injury, color, and other descriptive aspects of the injury. Likewise, if you have pictures of the child taken by the offender in a sexual abuse case, use them. You may need to lay a foundation for their admission through the child. If this is the case, do so in a way that minimizes the child's discomfort. If the photos are at all embarrassing, do not display them to the judge and jury while the child is still in the courtroom. If you are using the child's possessions or clothing as exhibits, treat them with respect.

Other corroborative evidence might include photographs of the defendant prior to his arrest and photographs of any unique physical characteristics of the defendant described by the victim. The former can often be obtained from the defendant's colleagues and will show his appearance before he is "manicured" for trial. A search warrant or court order might be used to obtain the latter. Consider presenting evidence about the vital statistics, such as height and weight, of the defendant and victim to show size and strength differences. This will help explain why the child did not resist or was fearful. It will also allow the jury to better evaluate the reasonableness of physical discipline in a physical abuse case.

In a case involving ongoing abuse over a period of years, introduce a picture of the victim at the time the abuse began to remind the jury how young the victim was when the defendant first used his authority and superior knowledge to ensure compliance and secrecy. (See *Mahoney v. State*, 388 N.E.2d 591 [Ind. 1979] [finding no abuse of discretion for admission of photograph of victim, as victim's appearance changed greatly during the 3 years between the time of offense and trial, and photograph may aid jury in formulating more accurate reconstruction of offense].)

In every child abuse case, there is a crime scene that needs to be photographed. The photos may help the child testify as he describes different aspects of the abuse. The photographs also introduce the child's world to the jury. If the abuse took place in the child's bedroom and that room is cold and desolate, the jury may get a sense the child was not treated well. If, on the other hand, the child's room had all the trimmings and trappings of a child's room, the jury may get a sense of the innocence that was destroyed.

c. Out-of-court statements. Hearsay and other evidence of out-of-court statements are discussed in detail in Section IV.F of this chapter. Make sure the investigators have interviewed others to whom the child may have spoken about the abuse. The child may have confided in friends or siblings, asking them to keep the secret, prior to the disclosure that set the investigation in motion. Such statements, if admitted as substantive evidence under a hearsay exception, might provide the *corpus delicti* to allow admission of a defendant's confession or qualify as prior consistent statements to rebut an implication of fabrication by the child. Witnesses from related juvenile court proceedings or transcripts of testimony from these hearings might provide corroborative evidence. If the child testified in juvenile court, that prior testimony may be admissible under nonhearsay rules of evidence. (See Fed. R. Evid. 801[d][1].) If the child is unavailable at the criminal trial because she refuses to testify, testifies to a lack of memory, cannot be located, or for other reasons, the testimony may be admissible as prior sworn testimony. (See Fed. R. Evid. 804[b][1].) Evidence of prior out-of-court statements will strengthen the allegation of abuse, and these witnesses may be able to provide observations of behavioral changes in the child that correspond to the time when the abuse began. Whether the corroborative evidence directly and obviously relates to the facts of the crime should not be controlling. It should be admissible if it meets the relevancy standard; that is, it has any tendency to make the existence of a fact or consequence to the case more or less probable. (See Fed. R. Evid. 401.)

d. Corroborating other events. The child's accuracy in recalling other events occurring during the same period is important to demonstrate the child's reliability in recalling details of the crime. If the child recalls other incidents from that day, witnesses and even photographs may be located to demonstrate the validity of the recollection. For example, if the child went with a neighboring family to the zoo following an episode of abuse, those who accompanied her would be good witnesses.

Photographs of the excursion may, however, cause as many problems as they solve. Juries can be troubled by the image of a happy, smiling face so soon after the alleged abuse. The defense may also be able to elicit from the witnesses who accompanied the child to the zoo that they did not notice any unusual behavior on the part of the child victim. The value of this evidence in enhancing the child's credibility must therefore be weighed against its "defense value."

e. The child's relationship with the abuser. As already touched upon, the relationship between the child and abusing adult may be important testimony to elicit from other witnesses. The testimony of witnesses familiar with the positive relationship between the child and abuser should defeat any attempt by the defense to persuade the jury that the child had a motive to lie.

f. The location of the abuse. Often, a child has been abused in a house occupied by many people unaware of what was occurring, despite defense claims that such abuse could not have occurred without the knowledge of someone in the home. This may be possible because of the location of the room or its uniqueness, such as solid onstruction, sound proofing, lack of windows, or other features. If at all possible, go to the site of abuse yourself prior to trial so you can understand the statement and be better able to elicit trial testimony. At a minimum, obtain photographs to illustrate critical facts pertaining to the location, and diagram the site for the jury. You may wish to request that the judge allow a jury to view the scene. Do this only when there is no easier way to ensure that the jury understands the evidence and when you believe it to be necessary to refute a defense theory on a critical point. Because of the time and logistical difficulty in arranging a jury view, judges will be reluctant to grant this.

If the child had a daily routine that allowed the defendant exclusive access to the child, the prosecutor should call witnesses to corroborate that routine. If some unusual event in the child's life explains the opportunity for abuse, secure witnesses to corroborate why the child was at the location where the abuse occurred, e.g., the victim's mom was in the hospital so the child stayed with an uncle.

Investigators can also place themselves in the room where the abuse occurred and in other rooms where family members may have been and determine how easy it is to hear noises from one room to another. The argument that someone would have seen or heard the abuse can be attacked by a common sense closing argument from the prosecutor. For hundreds of years, parents have been engaging in marital relations without children or other household guests seeing or hearing the conduct. If a defendant can have sex with his wife and prevent his children from seeing or hearing the event, he is arguably smart enough to molest his daughter without others being aware of the conduct.

g. The defendant's actions after disclosure. Any attempt by the defendant to encourage the victim or others to change their testimony, leave the jurisdiction, or otherwise undermine the administration of justice or the trial process, is relevant to show the defendant's consciousness of guilt. Present any witnesses who can establish that the defendant threatened the victim or her family after the disclosure.

h. Spouses and others involved with the defendant. Consider calling the defendant's spouse as a witness. Marital privilege and spousal incompetency are not applicable in most states in cases involving familial and/or child abuse. The investigation may have turned up helpful evidence to explore with that spouse. Also, the perpetrator's ex-spouses and/or current and former significant others may provide corroborating information. It may even be possible to use the defendant's therapist as a witness if the applicable state statutes exempt information about child abuse from the relevant privileges. Defense witnesses often know the child, the defendant, their general relationship, and the environment in which the abuse took place. Cross-examination of these witnesses can often corroborate facts provided by the child, such as events of the day or room features and layout. Their observations, too, of a warm relationship between the child and the defendant will add legitimacy to your position that the child had no motive to fabricate. If the case involves physical abuse and a defense claim that the child is "accident prone" or "bruises easily," question these witnesses to show that the child was not always covered with bruises or breaking bones. Use the witnesses in any way you can to cast doubt on the defense explanations.

F. Hearsay Foundations

The words a child uses to describe the abuse to people outside of the courtroom are often compelling and powerful. These words, however, are legally described as hearsay and are inadmissible absent some exception. Nevertheless, hearsay plays an important role in child abuse litigation. The law of hearsay varies in detail from state to state and is enormously complex. This section is not intended to cover the variations of law among the various states. Each prosecutor must master the jurisdiction's hearsay rules and case law. The limited objective here is to discuss the admission of children's out-of-court statements under the most commonly invoked exceptions to the hearsay rule.

This section refers to the Federal Rules of Evidence because the majority of states have adopted the Federal Rules. There are thousands of cases interpreting the hearsay rule and its exceptions. This chapter cites only a few selected cases.

1. Hearsay Defined

Hearsay is "a statement, other than one made by the declarant while testifying at the trial or hearing, offered in evidence to prove the truth of the matter asserted" (Fed. R. Evid. 801[c]).

A "statement" for hearsay purposes is "(1) an oral or written assertion or (2) nonverbal conduct of a person, if it is intended by the person as an assertion" (Fed. R. Evid. 801[a]). Although the Federal Rules do not define the word *assertion*, the meaning is clear. "Nothing is an assertion unless intended to be one" (Fed. R. Evid. 801[a] advisory committee's note). A speaker makes an assertion, and thus a statement, when the speaker intends to communicate some fact or opinion.

a. Verbal and written words. A declarant's oral or written words are hearsay if three requirements are fulfilled:

1. The words were an assertion of fact or opinion.

2. The words were stated out of court (spoken or written prior to the hearing at which the words are repeated by the declarant or someone else).

3. The words are offered in evidence to prove the truth of the matter asserted.

If one or more of the three requirements is absent, the words are *not* hearsay.

b. Nonverbal conduct as hearsay. Nonverbal conduct can be hearsay if the conduct is assertive. The conduct is considered assertive if the conduct is intended to communicate some fact or opinion. In other words, the conduct is a substitute for words. *Non*assertive nonverbal conduct is not hearsay unless the jurisdiction recognizes the doctrine of implied assertions. The law regarding implied assertions is so arcane and so seldom used in practice that it is not discussed in this section. For further discussion on implied assertions, see Myers, J. E. B. (1997/Suppl. 2002). *Evidence in child abuse and neglect cases,* Vol. 2, Sect. 7.9–7.11.

c. The trial judge determines whether out-of-court utterances are hearsay: The burden of persuasion. The trial judge decides whether an out-of-court utterance, whether verbal, written, or conduct, is hearsay and, if so, whether an exception applies (Fed. R. Evid. 104[a]). When an out-of-court utterance is offered, which party bears the burden of persuading the court that the utterance is or is not hearsay? In many cases, the answer depends on whether the out-of-court utterance is composed of words (oral or written) or nonverbal conduct.

i. Verbal and written words. When a hearsay objection is interposed against spoken or written words, the hearsay quality of the words is usually obvious. For example, the statement, "The man touched my pee-pee," is clearly offered to prove that the defendant touched the child's genitals. If the proponent of oral or written words claims the words are not hearsay, the proponent has the burden of persuading the court by a preponderance of the evidence that the words are not assertive or, if assertive, are not offered to prove the truth of the matter asserted.

If the objected-to words *are* hearsay, the proponent of the statement has the burden of persuading the judge by a preponderance of the evidence that the statement falls within one of the hearsay exceptions. (See *United States v. Bartelho,* 129 F.3d 663 [1st Cir. 1997].) As the court stated in *Cofield v. State,* 891 S.W.2d 952, 954 (Tex. Crim. App. 1994), "Since [defendant] preserved error by raising an objection to the hearsay, the burden then became the State's to show that the evidence was admissible pursuant to some exception to the hearsay rule."

ii. Nonverbal conduct. Some nonverbal conduct is obviously assertive and is hearsay when offered for the truth of the assertion. Consider, for example, a case in which a child nodded her head up and down in response to an interviewer's question. The head shaking is a substitute for words and is hearsay when offered to prove the child's nonverbal answer.

The assertive quality of most nonverbal conduct, however, is less obvious. Suppose, for example, that a young child is playing by herself with dolls. The child positions the dolls in sexual poses. Is the child intending an assertion of fact? Would it be hearsay to describe the child's nonverbal conduct with the dolls? When a hearsay objection is made to nonverbal conduct that is not obviously assertive, who has the burden of persuasion? Does the proponent of the nonverbal conduct have the burden to convince the court that the conduct was nonassertive and thus not hearsay? Or does the opponent have the burden to persuade the court that the conduct was assertive and thus hearsay? There is little case law on this point. Some light is shed on the issue by the Federal Rules of Evidence 801(a) advisory committee note, which states, "When evidence of conduct is offered on the theory that it is not a statement, and hence not hearsay, a preliminary determination will be required to determine whether an assertion is intended. The rule is so worded as to place the burden upon the party claiming that the intention existed; ambiguous and doubtful cases will be resolved against him and in favor of admissibility."

The case of *People v. Roberto V.*, 113 Cal. Rptr. 2d 804 (Cal. Ct. App. 2001), provides useful information on a young child's play as hearsay. In *Roberto V.*, two victims, 3-year-old Maria and 7-year-old Stephanie, were sexually abused by their father. Maria was observed by her mother, Martina, engaging in developmentally unusual sexual play. The court wrote,

> Martina saw three-year-old Maria inappropriately kissing a toy and attempting to insert it into her vagina. Martina asked Maria what she was doing. Martina understood from Maria's answer that Maria was playing, and wished her to play along. Maria told her mother to lie on the bed. Maria sat on top of Martina's pelvic area, moved in a manner that simulated sexual intercourse, and attempted to kiss Martina on the mouth. Martina asked Maria who had taught her to play that way. Maria said, "ella ["she" in Spanish] and Poppy." Martina asked who "ella" was, and Maria pointed to a picture of Stephanie. Martina also stated that Maria had placed her prone on the bed and said "Poppy would get in that position." On one or two other occasions thereafter, Maria attempted similar conduct, including attempting to disrobe Martina, kiss her, and touch her. During those incidents, Maria stated that she wanted to "play like Daddy plays." (at 808–9)

The defendant argued that

> Maria's sexual behavior was equivalent to an out-of-court declaration that Maria had learned sexual behavior, and thus should have been excluded as hearsay under Evidence Code section 225. (at 815 n. 9)

The California Court, however, rejected this claim and noted,

> We find this contention specious. Section 225 defines a "statement" as, inter alia, "nonverbal conduct of a person intended by him as a substitute for oral or written verbal expression." Three-year-old Maria's conduct cannot fairly be characterized as intended by her to substitute for oral or written expression. (citation omitted). The record suggests Maria believed she was playing a game, not attempting to non-verbally communicate. Appellant cites no authority or argument persuading us otherwise. Thus, Martina's testimony regarding Maria's conduct was not barred by the hearsay rule.

2. Nonhearsay Uses of Children's Out-of-Court Utterances

In most cases, the prosecutor offers out-of-court statements for the truth of the matter asserted, thus making the statement hearsay. However, the hearsay is often offered under an exception to the hearsay rule. In some cases, however, the prosecutor offers an out-of-court utterance as *non*hearsay. An out-of-court utterance is not hearsay if

1. The utterance was not a statement.

2. The utterance was a statement, but the statement is offered to prove something other than the truth of the matter asserted.

    3. The utterance was a verbal act or a verbal part of an act.

    4. The utterance was a fresh complaint of rape or sexual assault. In a few jurisdictions, fresh complaints are hearsay within an exception.

a. Nonassertive utterances. An out-of-court utterance is hearsay only if it is an assertion of fact or opinion. Nonassertive words are not hearsay. Exclamatory utterances are sometimes nonassertive. Thus, a child's utterance "Ouch!" or "Owie!" may be nonassertive and thus not hearsay. Even if "ouch" and "owie" are assertions, they may be admissible as statements of then existing physical or mental condition under Fed. R. Evid. 803(3) or as excited utterances under Fed. R. Evid. 803(2).

b. Assertions offered to prove something other than the truth of the matter asserted. There are at least six situations in which an out-of-court assertion may be admissible to prove something other than the truth of the matter asserted:

i. Precocious sexual knowledge. A young child's description of sexual abuse is hearsay when offered to prove the truth of the child's words. If, however, the child's words are offered not for the truth of the matter asserted, but for the alternative purpose of establishing the child's precocious sexual knowledge, the words are non-hearsay circumstantial evidence of abuse. (See *In re Jean Marie W., 559 A.2d 625* [R.I. 1989].)

ii. Effect on the listener. In some cases, the victim's fear of the defendant is relevant. In such cases, the defendant's statements, such as threats, to the child may be admissible to prove the effect of the threat on the listener. The defendant's threats are also admissible against the defendant as admissions or verbal acts.

iii. When the child's out-of-court statement links child to defendant. When a child is abducted by a stranger, the identity of the perpetrator may be disputed. A child's out-of-court statements to parents or police may describe attributes of the perpetrator's home, car, or body that could have been acquired only if the child witnessed the home, car, or body. In such cases, the child's description of the home, car, or body is hearsay if it is offered for the truth of the matter asserted. Alternatively, however, the child's description may be offered as nonhearsay circumstantial evidence linking the child to the defendant. (See *Bridges v. State, 19 N.W.2d 529* [Wis. 1945].)

iv. The timing and circumstances of report or investigation. A child's out-of-court statement may be offered to establish when a report was made or when or why an investigation was commenced. It should be noted, however, that the timing and circumstances of a report and the reason for beginning an investigation are often irrelevant. (See *United States v. Cass, 127 F.3d 1218* [10th Cir. 1997] [providing a useful discussion of the use and abuse of out-of-court statements to establish why the police became involved in a case]; *State v. Emmons, 528 A.2d 1266* [Me. 1987]; *State v. Pettrey, 549 S.E.2d 323, 330* [W. Va. 2001] [noting, "we are convinced Ms. Akers' testimony was offered solely to explain the reasons she discussed the child's behavior with his grandmother and referred him to a therapist for treatment. Because the statements were admitted not to prove the truth of the matter asserted but rather to show why the teacher reported the incident, the statements were not hearsay by definition.

Statements which are not offered for the truth of the matter asserted do not implicate the Sixth Amendment right to confrontation."]; *People v. Roberto V.*, 113 Cal. Rptr. 2d 804, 816 [Cal. Ct. App. 2001] [concluding 3-year-old victim's statements to her mother, implicating the child's father, were not admissible even though the prosecutor offered the child's out-of-court statement for the nonhearsay purpose of establishing why the child's mother had questioned the child and why the mother then questioned the other victim. The Court of Appeals concluded the child's "statement possessed very little probative value apart from its truth."].)

v. Verbal acts. In some cases, words have legal significance whether or not the words are true. What is important is that the words were spoken, not that the words are true. The term *verbal acts* describes such words. Verbal acts are nonhearsay because the words are not offered to prove the truth of the matter asserted. The most common illustration of verbal acts is words creating a contract. Words of offer and acceptance create a contract whether or not the words are true. When a defendant is charged with making threats, the threats are admissible as verbal acts. Of course, the defendant's threats are also admissible as statements against interest.

vi. Fresh complaint of rape or sexual assault. In most jurisdictions, fresh complaint evidence is admissible nonhearsay. (See discussion below.)

3. Exceptions to the Hearsay Rule

This section briefly discusses the hearsay exceptions most frequently applicable in child abuse litigation. If a statement falls into one of the exceptions, the statement is admissible as substantive evidence even though it is hearsay.

a. Present sense impression: Fed. R. Evid. 803(1). A present sense impression is admissible hearsay under Fed. R. Evid. 803(1). A present sense impression is described as "a statement describing or explaining an event or condition made while the declarant was perceiving the event or condition or immediately thereafter."

i. Foundation elements

1. The declarant perceived an event or condition. The declarant must have personal knowledge of the event under Fed. R. Evid. 602. The event or condition need *not* be startling.

2. The statement must be made while the declarant is perceiving the event or condition, or immediately thereafter.

3. The statement must describe or explain the event.

ii. Sample foundation. Consider the prosecution of a defendant for physically abusing his 6-year-old daughter by hitting her repeatedly in the face and stomach. While the defendant was assaulting his daughter, the defendant's 10-year-old son watched from the next room. The son (declarant) telephoned 911 to report the assault, and the prosecutor offers the audiotape of the son's 911 call as a present sense impression. The witness on the stand is the 911 operator who received the son's call.

In addition to laying the foundation for the present sense impression exception, the 911 operator will authenticate the audiotape to fulfill the best evidence rule. The son's voice will have to be identified. Foundation questions by the prosecutor:

Q: By whom are you employed?

A: I work for the city as a 911 operator.

Q: Were you on duty on July 6, 2002?

A: Yes.

Q: Did you receive a 911 call at 5:11 P.M. on July 6, 2002?

A: Yes, I took a call on July 6, 2002 at 5:11 P.M. from a person who identified himself as the defendant's 10-year-old son.

Q: What did the son say during the 911 call?

Defense   I object. This is hearsay not within an exception.
counsel:

Prosecutor: Your honor, the boy's statement is hearsay, but the statement meets the requirements of the present sense impression exception. If I may question this witness further, I will lay the foundation for the exception.

Court: Proceed with the foundation.

Q: Thank you, your honor. Now, when the boy was on the phone with you, did he say he was witnessing anything at that moment?

A: Yes.

Q: Did the boy indicate whether he was witnessing this event with his own eyes?

A: Yes. He said he could see his dad beating on his sister in the next room.

Q: Did the boy indicate whether the beating was going on as he was talking to you on the phone?

A: Yes. He said he needed help because his dad was hitting his sister at that moment.

Q: Did the boy describe what was happening?

A: Yes.

Prosecutor: Your honor, I believe I've laid the foundation for admission of the boy's call to 911 as a present sense impression.

Court: Yes. The objection is overruled. You may play the tape for the jury.

The foregoing hypothetical involves only *one* layer of hearsay: the 10-year-old boy's description of what the defendant was doing to the victim. The audiotape is *not* a second layer of hearsay. A tape recorder does not make statements for hearsay purposes; people make statements. Since the audiotape is not a second layer of hearsay, the prosecutor does not have to find a hearsay exception for the audiotape itself. Thus, there is no occasion to consider the business records exception or the public records exception since the audiotape is not a second layer of hearsay. If the boy's statement is a present sense impression, the boy's statement is admissible. (See *State v. Ballos*, 602 N.W.2d 117, 122 [Wis. Ct. App. 1999] [noting, "In this case, the trial court admitted the 911 evidence as present sense impressions. The trial court was correct; it is undisputed that the 911 callers were describing the events they were perceiving or had just observed."]; *Commonwealth v. Chamberlain*, 731 A.2d 593 [Pa. 1999] [concluding statement made over the phone by a murder victim identifying her killer was admissible as present sense impression and as dying declaration].)

b. Excited utterance: Fed. R. Evid. 803(2). An excited utterance is defined as "a statement relating to a startling event or condition made while the declarant was under the stress of excitement caused by the event or condition" (Fed. R. Evid. 803[2]).

i. Foundation elements

1. The declarant was a participant in or witnessed a startling event. The declarant may be, but does not have to be, a participant in the startling event. Statements by bystanders, even anonymous bystanders, can be excited utterances. The declarant must have personal knowledge of the event.

2. The hearsay statement must relate to the startling event.

3. The statement must be made while the declarant was under the stress or excitement induced by the startling event. Factors relevant to determining whether a statement was made while the declarant was under the stress induced by the event include:

   a. The nature of the event

   b. The spontaneity of the statement

   c. The type of questioning eliciting the statement

   d. The lapse of time between the startling event and the statement

   e. The declarant's emotional condition: crying, shaking, sobbing

   f. The declarant's physical condition

   g. The content of the statement

   h. The declarant's speech pattern

   i. The age of the declarant

For numerous cases on each of these factors see Myers, J. E. B. (1997/Suppl. 2002). *Evidence in child abuse and neglect cases*, Vol. 2, Sect. 7.33.

In the normal case, hearsay is admissible only if the declarant was competent to testify *at the time* the out-of-court statement was made. Excited utterances, however, are an exception to this rule. An excited utterance is generally admissible even though the declarant lacked testimonial competence at the time the statement was made.

ii. Sample foundation. The defendant is being prosecuted for sexually abusing a 6-year-old neighbor. The defendant, Bill, denies any wrongdoing. He lives with his wife and daughter next door to the victim. The defendant acknowledges that the victim was in his home on the day in question, playing with his daughter. At 2:00 P.M., the victim ran into her own home crying, and blurted out, "Mommy, Mommy, Bill hurted me. He took off my panties and put his finger in my pee-pee, and it hurt! He said not to tell or he'd hurt me really bad!" At trial, the prosecutor calls the victim's mother. The prosecutor's foundation questions follow:

Q:	When your daughter ran into the house, what was her emotional condition?
A:	She was very upset. She was crying uncontrollably, and she was frightened. She ran to me and hugged me around the legs, burying her face in my apron.
Q:	What time did she run into the house?
A:	Right at 2:00 P.M.
Q:	How is it that you remember the precise time she ran in?
A:	Well, I had just looked at the clock. It was time for me to pick her up from the defendant's home, where she had been playing, so that I could drive to my son's school and pick him up at 2:25 P.M.
Q:	Where was your daughter just prior to running into the house at 2:00 P.M.?
A:	She was at defendant's house next door. I had walked her over there a little before 1:00 P.M. to play with defendant's daughter.
Q:	So, your daughter arrived at the defendant's house at approximately 1:00 P.M.?
A:	Yes.
Q:	Was the defendant home when you delivered your daughter?
A:	Yes, he was there.
Q:	Apart from going to the defendant's house, had your daughter been anywhere else that day?
A:	No. Just the two of us were at home until 1:00 P.M., when I walked her over to defendant's.
Q:	When your daughter ran into your house at 2:00 P.M., did she say anything to you?
Defense counsel:	Objection, hearsay.
Prosecutor:	Your honor, the child's statement to her mother is hearsay, but it is an excited utterance. I have laid the foundation for the exception, but I can add further to the foundation by having the witness repeat what the child told her.
Court:	Proceed.

Q: When your daughter ran into your house at 2:00 P.M., what did she say to you?

A: She said, and these are her exact words, "Mommy, Mommy, Bill hurted me. He took off my panties and put his finger in my pee-pee, and it hurt! He said not to tell or he'd hurt me really bad!"

Q: When you took your daughter to the defendant's house at 1:00 P.M., did she have underwear on?

A: Yes.

Q: Did she have underwear on when she ran into the house at 2:00 P.M.?

A: No.

Q: What happened to your daughter's underwear?

A: Well, she said the defendant took them off. All I know is I never found the underpants.

Q: What was your daughter's emotional condition when she said what she said?

A: She was crying and frightened. She was shaking she was so scared.

Q: Apart from the defendant, does your daughter know any other men or boys named "Bill"?

A: No.

Prosecutor: Your honor, I believe I have established that the child's statement to her mother was an excited utterance.

Defense counsel: Your honor, I disagree. My client denies anything happened. The only evidence of the so-called startling event is the hearsay statement itself. The statement cannot constitute evidence of the event the statement is offered to prove. To permit the statement to serve as evidence that the event occurred is an example of circular reasoning and improper bootstrapping. Therefore, the prosecutor has failed to prove there was any kind of startling event.

Prosecutor: Your honor, defense counsel is wrong on two counts. First, there is evidence apart from the child's statement that a startling event occurred. The child's emotional condition—crying, shaking, rushing to her mother for comfort—is strong evidence of a startling event. Moreover, the child's underpants were missing. Second, modern decisions hold that the statement can constitute evidence of the startling event.

Court: The objection is overruled. The witness may repeat the child's statement as an excited utterance.

c. Fresh complaint of rape or sexual assault. When a victim of rape or sexual assault testifies, it is usually proper to admit evidence that the victim revealed the crime within a reasonable time thereafter. With the apparent exception of Tennessee, states apply the fresh complaint doctrine to child sexual abuse cases. Under this exception, the State does not need to show that the child was competent to testify at the time the statement was made. In the majority of states, the fresh complaint doctrine is a product of case law rather than statute or rule. Thus, the practitioner should consult applicable case law for the parameters of fresh complaint evidence.

In most jurisdictions, fresh complaint evidence is not hearsay because the victim's statement is not offered for the truth of the matter asserted. Rather, the statement is admitted to corroborate the victim's trial testimony. In a few states, a fresh complaint of rape is considered an exception to the hearsay rule. (Or. R. Evid. 803[18a]; La. R. Evid. 801[D][1][d]; Tex. Code. Crim. Proc. ann. art. 38.072.)

In most states, the victim must testify at trial. In rare cases, fresh complaint evidence may be admissible when the victim does not testify. (See *People v. Meacham*, 199 Cal. Rptr. 586, 597 [Cal. Ct. App. 1984] [noting, "while it is generally true that evidence that a complaint was made is inadmissible where the prosecutrix does not take the stand, an exception is made where, as in the present case, the child is too young to testify."].) Fresh complaint evidence is admissible during the State's case-in-chief, and impeachment of the victim is *not* required before the State can offer the statement.

The complaint must be fresh. A complaint is fresh if it is made within a reasonable time after the assault. Delayed reporting may be explained and justified. (See *Brown v. Commonwealth*, 554 S.E.2d 711, 712 [Va. Ct. App. 2001] [affirming the admissibility of the statement, noting, "The record in the instant case explains the victim's [two-year] delay in reporting and is consistent with the occurrence of the offense. The child testified that she did not tell anyone about the incident because her grandfather told her not to tell and she 'didn't think anybody was going to believe me.' Further, on cross-examination, she answered affirmatively that she felt scared and threatened by appellant."].)

In most states, the victim may repeat her own fresh complaint during direct examination. Alternatively, anyone who overheard the victim's fresh complaint may testify and repeat the complaint, subject to the court's authority to limit cumulative evidence. Most jurisdictions limit the amount of detail that is admissible under the fresh complaint doctrine. Generally, courts allow enough detail to identify the particular incident, including the time and place of assault, the number of assaults, the circumstances of the report, and the condition of the victim at the time of the report. Some decisions state that a fresh complaint may include the identification of the perpetrator. (*Battle v. United States*, 630 A.2d 211, 223 [D.C. 1993]; *State v. Twyford*, 186 N.W.2d 545, 548 [S.D. 1971].) Other decisions state that the report may not identify the perpetrator. (*State v. Grady*, 183 N.W.2d 707, 718 [Iowa 1971]; *State v. Tripp*, 634 A.2d 1318, 1321 [Me. 1994]; *State v. Ferguson*, 667 P.2d 68, 72 [Wash. 1983].)

Prosecutors use fresh complaint evidence less often today than they did a few years ago. The decline is the result of the widespread adoption of residual and child hearsay exceptions that allow statements to be admitted provided the statement is sufficiently reliable, even if it does not meet a traditional hearsay exception. The fresh complaint doctrine arose at a time when residual and child hearsay exceptions did not exist. The disadvantage of fresh complaint evidence, of course, is that in most states a fresh complaint is not admissible for the truth of the matter asserted. Generally, a prosecutor would prefer to offer a child's out-of-court statements for the truth of the matter asserted under a residual or child hearsay exception or, following impeachment, as a prior consistent statement.

d. The declarant's state of mind: Fed. R. Evid. 803(3). Under Fed. R. Evid. 803(3), the following type of statement is not excluded as hearsay: "A statement of the declarant's then existing state of mind, emotion, sensation, or physical condition (such as intent, plan, motive, design, mental feeling, pain, and bodily health), but not including a statement of memory or belief to prove the fact remembered or believed unless it relates to the execution, revocation, identification, or terms of declarant's will."

i. Foundation elements. Although the state of mind exception can be complex, the foundation is easy. The elements are when, where, and to whom the statement was made, plus the contents of the statement.

ii. Use of the state of mind exception in child abuse cases. Although the state of mind exception is not used very often in criminal child abuse litigation, it comes up in three scenarios. First, the state of mind exception clears the way for admission of a child's statement of a then-existing physical condition, such as, "My leg hurts." Note that the state of mind exception does not allow admission of, "My leg hurt yesterday" because that is a statement of memory offered to prove the thing remembered. The exception also does not allow for the admission of statements of identification of the perpetrator, such as, "My leg hurts because Mommy hit me." (See *State v. Hazard*, 785 A.2d 1111 [R.I. 2001] [making the distinction that "Rule 803(3) must be limited to those declarations of condition—'I'm scared'—and not belief—'I'm scared because Galkin threatened me.'"])

Second, the state of mind exception allows hearsay statements describing the declarant's then-existing feelings or emotions, such as "I love him," "I hate him," and "I'm afraid of him." In some child sexual abuse cases, the child's sexual arousal is relevant. The state of mind exception can be used to admit the child's statements indicating then-existing sexual interest or arousal.

Third, the state of mind exception authorizes admission of hearsay statements of intent or plan to do something in the future. (See *Mutual Life Ins. Co. v. Hillmon*, 145 U.S. 285 [1892].) Thus, the state of mind exception allows statements such as, "I intend to go to Bill's house" and "I'm going to Chicago tomorrow."

The defendant may use the state of mind exception to admit his own hearsay statements negating *mens rea*. For example, the defendant might offer his out-of-court statement to a child whose pants he is removing, "I need to get these pants off you so I can see whether the dog bit you."

e. Statements for purposes of medical diagnosis or treatment: Fed. R. Evid. 803(4). A statement is admissible as an exception to the hearsay rule if it was "made for purposes of medical diagnosis or treatment and describing medical history, or past or present symptoms, pain, or sensations, or the inception or general character of the cause or external source thereof insofar as reasonably pertinent to diagnosis or treatment." (Fed. R. Evid. 803[4].)

i. Foundation elements

1. The statement was made for the purpose of obtaining a medical diagnosis or treatment. Courts generally require a showing that the child-declarant had some understanding of the clinical importance of being truthful with the health care provider.

2. The statement describes medical history, past or present symptoms, pain or sensations, or the cause of injury or illness.

3. The statement is pertinent to the professional's ability to diagnose or treat the child. Statements identifying the perpetrator are admissible in most jurisdictions *if* knowledge of the identity of the perpetrator is pertinent to diagnosis or treatment.

ii. Sample foundation. The defendant is being prosecuted for sexually abusing his 7-year-old daughter, Mary. The child disclosed the abuse to her mother. The mother took Mary to the hospital emergency room. At the hospital, Mary was examined and questioned by Dr. Mosk. The witness on the stand at trial is Dr. Mosk. The prosecutor's foundation questions follow:

Q: What is your profession?

A: I am a physician licensed to practice medicine in this state. My specialty is emergency medicine.

Q: Where do you practice medicine?

A: I am an emergency room physician at Mercy Hospital here in the city.

Q: Were you on duty in the emergency room on July 2, 2002?

A: Yes.

Q: And while on duty, what are your responsibilities?

A: At our hospital, there is a physician in the emergency room at all times. When I'm on duty, I am in charge of the emergency room. I see all patients that come into the emergency room, and I provide appropriate diagnostic and treatment services.

Q: While you were on duty on July 2, 2002, did Mary Dobbs and her mother come to the emergency room?

A: Yes, they arrived at 5:00 P.M.

Q: What happened when they arrived?

A: Mary and her mother were escorted into a private examination room. The mother provided admitting information to the admitting clerk, and I entered the room about 10 minutes after they arrived.

Q: What was your purpose in seeing the child?

A: My purpose was to question the child about why she was there and to conduct a physical examination for possible sexual abuse.

Q: What did you do first when you entered the examination room?

A: I followed my usual practice in cases like this. I introduced myself to the mother and to Mary. Then I made sure the child knew I was a doctor and that my job was to talk to her and examine her to ensure she was in good health. I told the child that it was important for her to tell me the truth—"only things that really happened"—so I could do my job as a doctor.

Q: Did it appear to you that Mary understood your professional role and the importance of telling you the truth?

A: Yes. The child knew she was in the hospital. I was in my white coat, and the child knew I was a doctor.

Q: Did you question the child about why she was there?

A: Yes.

Q: What, if anything, did the child tell you?

Defense Counsel: Your honor, I object. This is hearsay.

Prosecutor: Your honor, the child's statements to the doctor are hearsay, but they meet the requirements of the medical diagnosis or treatment exception. I've laid the foundation for the exception and would like to follow up with a few more foundational questions.

Court: Proceed.

Q: Thank you, your honor. Now, Dr. Mosk, what is a medical history?

A: A patient's medical history includes the chief complaint, that is, what brought the patient to the hospital. The history also includes information about the patient's past medical problems or illnesses. It is standard medical practice to take a patient's medical history.

Q: Did you take Mary's medical history?

A: Yes. Mary was able to tell me why she was in the hospital. She described sexual abuse by her father as the reason her mother brought her to the emergency room.

Q: In order for you to diagnose and treat the child, did you need to know whether the child was sexually abused?

A: Certainly, that's why she was there, to see if there was evidence of sexual abuse, and to decide what treatment to advise.

Q: You stated a moment ago that Mary identified her father as the person who sexually abused her. As a physician, was the identity of the perpetrator pertinent to your ability to diagnose or treat the child?

A: Absolutely. In the emergency room, I have to know the identity of the abuser so that I can decide whether to order laboratory tests for possible sexually transmitted diseases. I also have to know the identity of the perpetrator when I make the report of suspected abuse that I am required by law to make to child protective services. Finally, I need to know the identity of the perpetrator so that I can decide whether it is safe to send the child home. Deciding whether to send children home, admit them to the hospital, or recommend foster care is a critically important aspect of treatment in child abuse cases.

Prosecutor: Your honor, I offer the child's statements to the doctor under the medical diagnosis or treatment exception.

Court: The objection is overruled. The doctor may repeat as much of what the child said that was pertinent to diagnosis or treatment, including the identity of the perpetrator.

iii. Statements identifying the perpetrator. There is a split of authority concerning whether a child's hearsay statement identifying the perpetrator is admissible under the medical diagnosis or treatment exception, with a clear majority holding that statements of identity are admissible under the exception. As the West Virginia Supreme Court stated in *State v. Pettrey,* 549 S.E.2d 323, 334 (W. Va. 2001), "Statements which attribute fault to a member of the victim's household may reasonably be pertinent to treatment because these statements are relevant to prevention of recurrence of injury."

iv. Statements made during psychotherapy. There is a split of authority concerning whether statements made during psychotherapy are admissible under the medical diagnosis or treatment exception. The majority position is that statements made during psychotherapy can be admissible under this exception.

v. Do young children understand why it is important to be truthful with medical professionals? The medical diagnosis or treatment exception should apply only when a child understands to some degree the clinical importance of candor. The premise of statement admissibility under the medical diagnosis exception is that people tell doctors the truth because of the importance to do so to receive a proper diagnosis. But do young children understand the clinical importance of telling the truth to doctors or nurses? It depends on the child. Some children possess the necessary understanding, while others do not. Age alone is not a reliable marker, although it is more difficult to imagine a 2-year-old with the necessary understanding. A case-by-case assessment is required.

The medical and psychological literature contains information on children's understanding of illness and the role of medical professionals. As one would expect, a child's understanding of this concept follows a developmental progression. (See generally Au, T. K.-F., et al. [1999]. Considering children's folkbiology in health education. In M. Siegal & C. C. Peterson [Eds.], *Children's understanding of biology and health* [p. 209]. Cambridge, U.K.: Cambridge University Press; Genevro, J. L., et al. [1996]. Young children's understanding of routine medical care and strategies for coping with stressful medical experiences. In M. H. Bornstein & J. L. Genevro [Eds.], *Child development and behavioral pediatrics* [p. 59]. Hillsdale, NJ: Lawrence Erlbaum.)

An illustration from the writing of psychologists Margaret Steward and David Steward provides insight into young children's limited understanding of the role of medical professionals. (Steward, M., & Steward, D. [1981]. Children's conceptions of medical procedures. In R. Bibace & M. E. Walsh [Eds.], *New directions for child development: Children's conceptions of health, illness, and bodily functions* [pp. 67, 72–72]. San Francisco: Jossey-Bass). Steward described 3-year-old Sammy, who was knocked off his tricycle by a passing car, causing a concussion and skull fracture. When Steward visited Sammy in the pediatric ward he was a solemn little boy. Steward talked with Sammy about being in the hospital, and asked, "Are the doctors helping you get well?" Sammy replied, "No, the doctors are berry mean" (p. 67). For Sammy, nurses, not doctors, were "helpers." Sammy's confusion is understandable. The pediatric nurses were ever-present, kind, and nurturing. Sammy had a warm relationship with his nurses. Doctors, by contrast, tend to rush in, poke and prod, ask questions, and dash away without forming much of a relationship. Little wonder Sammy viewed the nurses as his only helpers. Sammy did not demonstrate an understanding of the importance of the physician's role.

A young child might mistakenly conclude that the doctor actually *caused* the child's illness. Redpath and Rogers wrote that "because of the tendency of preschoolers to confuse cause and effect, clinicians or teachers working with them should be prepared to help these youngsters understand that body state, germs, and/or accidents, not the doctor, may be the cause of illness." (Redpath, C. C., & Rogers, C. S. [1984]. Healthy young children's concepts of hospitals, medical personnel, operations, and illness. *Journal of Pediatric Psychology, 9,* 29.)

Steward offers another illustration of the limits of young children's understanding. In a study of kindergartners and third-graders, the kindergartners knew that a hypodermic syringe was used to give shots, but many of the kindergartners did not understand *why* shots were given. By contrast, most third-graders, that is, 8- and 9-year-olds, knew shots were given to prevent or cure illness. (Steward, M., & Regalbuto, G. [1975]. Do doctors know what children know? *American Journal of Orthopsychiatry, 45,* 146.)

Some 3- to 6-year-olds believe medical procedures are administered as punishment. (See Burbach, D. J., & Peterson, L. [1986]. Children's concepts of physical illness: A review and critique of the cognitive-developmental literature. *Health Psychology, 5,* 307; Bibace, R., & Walsh, M. E. [1981]. Children's conceptions of illness. In R. Bibace & M. E. Walsh [Eds.], *New directions for child development: Children's conceptions of health, illness, and bodily functions* [p. 31]. San Francisco: Jossey-Bass; Brewster, A. B. [1982]. Chronically ill children's concepts of their illness. *Pediatrics, 69,* 355.) Ellen Perrin and Susan Gerrity wrote that "children's ideas regarding illness frequently involve punishment, guilt, and self-blame. . . . Hospitalized children often ascribe the cause of their illness to disobedience of parental commands and interpret their hospitalization as rejection or punishment." (Perrin, E. C., & Gerrity, P. S. [1981]. There's a demon in your belly: Children's understanding of illness. *Pediatrics, 67,* 841.)

Daniel Burbach and Lizette Peterson observed that "older, less anxious, and cognitively mature children seemed to reject the notion that illness and misbehavior are related. Younger, highly anxious, and less cognitively mature children did perceive of illness in a moralistic way and, furthermore, exhibited more self-blame for the etiology of illness." (Burbach, D. J., & Peterson, L. [1986]. Children's concepts of physical illness: A review and critique of the cognitive-developmental literature. *Health Psychology, 5,* 307.) John Taplin and his colleagues studied children's understanding of pain and wrote that for children as young as five, "pain is less likely to be regarded as a form of punishment for wrongdoing than as due to a biological or physical/ behavioral cause, even by younger children." (Taplin, J. E., et al. [1999]. Children in pain. In M. Siegal & C. C. Peterson [Eds.], *Children's understanding of biology and health* [pp. 131, 134]. Cambridge, U.K.: Cambridge University Press). Taplin concluded that "from a relatively young age [children] have acquired a basic understanding of pain as a biological phenomenon and already know a little about how it may be caused" (p. 151).

In a study that reflects positively on children's developing understanding, Pamela Kato and her colleagues wrote,

> When children as young as 4 years of age are asked to recognize the causes of illness rather than to generate explanations, they show impressive understanding. . . . As in many contexts, children can recognize what they cannot articulate. (Kato, P. M., et al. [1998]. Reasoning about moral aspects of

illness and treatment by preschoolers who are healthy or who have chronic illness. *Journal of Developmental and Behavioral Pediatrics, 19,* 68.)

In this study, with a simplified interview technique, 3-year-olds, especially healthy 3-year-olds, showed impressive abilities to distinguish illness concepts from moral concepts: 4-year-olds showed even more impressive abilities. This is not consistent with a large body of research that documents a developmental progression in children's understanding of causal mechanisms and moral blame. This research claims that children as young as 3 and 4 years of age are unable to understand causal mechanisms and to assign moral blame. The children in our study displayed these abilities when asked to distinguish illness and treatment from moral transgressions. (*Id.* p. 74)

Children who show immanent justice reasoning believe that Nature is capable of seeking retribution for misdeeds, and they might also think that Nature intends to punish "naughty" children with illness. (*Id.* p. 68)

Our data *do not* support the claim that children think that illness and treatment are a form of imminent justice. Our data *do* support the claim that children have difficulty distinguishing illness and treatment from punishment. (p. 74)

Consistent with other research that uses a simplified interview methodology, we found that significant numbers of young children were able to show sophisticated reasoning skills concerning illness and immorality when they are asked to *recognize* rather than *generate* reasons for illness and treatment. (p. 18)

In addition, our findings do not support the current theory that claims that very young children have a primitive understanding of the concepts of illness and treatment. . . . Children as young as 3 and 4 years old in our study who were given simplified tasks and asked to distinguish between immoral and ill characters were surprisingly proficient at doing so. (p. 75)

Melody Herbst and her colleagues gathered information about the medical knowledge of 3- to 6-year-old children. (Herbst, M. R., et al. [1999]. Young children's understanding of the physician's role and the medical hearsay exception. In M. Siegal & C. C. Peterson [Eds.], *Children's understanding of biology and health* [p. 235]. Cambridge, U.K.: Cambridge University Press.). Herbst describes the 3- and 4-year-olds as the "younger children." The 5- and 6-year-olds are the "older children." Herbst wrote,

Our data indicate that young children are more likely to report painful than benign touch and that they understand the necessity to provide an accurate narrative to persons in authority. This suggests that, compared to younger children, older children were better able to distinguish what kinds of events merit possible concern and need an adult's attention and acknowledgment. They often mentioned the presence of blood as a reporting requirement. The older children, in determining whether or not to tell a doctor, also made the discrimination between self-inflicted injury and injury caused by another—and were more likely to report the latter. These findings parallel research on children's highly accurate reports of painful medical procedures and suggest that even some very young children have the capacity to meet the medical hearsay exception. (pp. 247–248)

Herbst also asked the children about lying to a doctor:

> Characteristics of the younger children were vague negative responses such as "You're in big trouble now" or punishments such as a time-out or a loud reprimand from the doctor. Older children often thought that the doctor would become angry; eight [out of 20 older] children understood that the doctor would not be able to be helpful or would prescribe inappropriate treatment. . . . Younger children's responses were characterized by centration and showed concern with possible punishment for lying. Older children [5 and 6 years old] were beginning to express a discriminated perception wherein lying prevents the physician from being helpful or results in possible harm from inappropriate treatment. (p. 250)

Herbst concluded,

> Both the 3–4 year-olds and the 5–6 year-olds could concretely describe what a physician does: older children were better able to describe concepts such as treatment and prevention functions and to identify the special knowledge associated with the physician's role than younger children. Neither group expected that the physician would know the cause of an injury without being told. Both age groups identified the truth as positive and older children tended to more reliably identify lying as negative. Older children were significantly better than younger children at describing the concepts of truth telling and lying and could also better understand potential consequences of lying to a physician. (p. 253)

This brief review of the psychological literature yields tentative conclusions. As would be expected, children do not possess adult-like knowledge of health and illness. Nor do children fully comprehend the roles of medical professionals. On the other hand, many children as young as 3 and 4 years of age have a developing appreciation of the doctor's role and of the importance of telling the truth. As Herbst wrote, "even some very young children have the capacity to meet the medical hearsay exception" (p. 248). It seems clear that with children under the age of roughly seven, a case-by-case assessment is needed to evaluate the child's understanding of the clinical importance of candor.

When considering children and the medical diagnosis or treatment exception, it is appropriate to consider the analogous situation of children's testimony in court. Children do not have adult-like knowledge of the legal system and the roles of legal professionals. Ask a child the meaning of "court," and the reply is likely to be, "A place to play basketball." (Saywitz, J. [1989]. Children's conceptions of the legal system: "Court is a place to play basketball." In S. J. Ceci [Ed.], *Perspectives on children's testimony* [pp. 131, 136]. New York: Springer.) When asked the meaning of an "arrest," a 5-year-old answered, "It means you're lying down." (Aldridge, M., et al. [1997]. Children's understanding of legal terminology: Judges get money at pet shows, don't they. *Child Abuse Review, 6,* 141.) When the court clerk told a child he could "take the witness stand," the youngster thought he was allowed take it home with him (*Id.*). A child's incomplete, and sometimes mistaken, understanding of the legal system does not mean the child is incompetent to testify. By the same token, a child's incomplete and sometimes mistaken understanding of the medical system does not mean a lack of the incentive to tell the truth to the doctor. The important question is whether a particular child had the incentive to be truthful on a particular occasion.

f. Prior inconsistent statements: Fed. R. Evid. 607, 613, 801(d)(1)(A). A witness may be impeached with the witness's prior inconsistent statements. When an out-of-court inconsistent statement is limited to impeachment, and is *not* offered for the truth of the matter asserted, the statement is not hearsay. When a prior inconsistent statement is offered *both* to impeach and for the truth, the statement is hearsay.

i. The foundation to impeach with prior inconsistent statements:

Prior Oral Inconsistent Statement. When the prior inconsistent statement is oral, the cross-examiner asks the following foundation questions:

1. Did the witness make the statement at a certain place?

2. Was the statement made at a particular time (exact time generally not required)?

3. To whom was the statement made?

With this foundation in place, the cross-examiner confronts the witness with the oral inconsistent statement.

Written Prior Inconsistent Statement. When the prior inconsistent statement is in writing, the foundation is similar: where, when, and to whom. Prior to the widespread adoption of the Federal Rules of Evidence, many states imposed an additional requirement when the inconsistent statement was in writing: The cross-examiner had to hand the writing to the witness *before* asking the witness about the inconsistency. This requirement was derived from *Queen Caroline's Case,* 129 Eng. Rep. 976 (1820).

A witness impeached with a prior inconsistent statement must have an opportunity to deny the inconsistency, explain away the impeachment value of the earlier statement, or put the out-of-court statement in context. In most cases this opportunity comes on redirect.

ii. Rule 613 of the Federal Rules of Evidence. Rule 613 provides,

(a) Examining witness concerning prior statement. In examining a witness concerning a prior statement made by the witness, whether written or not, the statement need not be shown nor its contents disclosed to the witness at that time, but on request the same shall be shown or disclosed to opposing counsel.

(b) Extrinsic evidence of prior inconsistent statement of witness. Extrinsic evidence of a prior inconsistent statement by a witness is not admissible unless the witness is afforded an opportunity to explain or deny the same and the opposite party is afforded an opportunity to interrogate the witness thereon, or the interests of justice otherwise require. This provision does not apply to admissions of a party-opponent as defined in rule 801(d)(2).

Rule 613 does not govern all aspects of impeachment with prior inconsistent statements. For example, the rule does not state what, if any, foundation must be laid to impeach with an inconsistent statement, and many judges require the cross-examiner to lay the foundation described above—when, where, and to whom. Nor does Rule 613 govern when a prior inconsistent statement is admissible for the truth of the matter asserted. Substantive use of prior inconsistent statements is governed by Rule 801(d)(1)(A).

The purpose of Rule 613(a) is to eliminate the rule established in *Queen Caroline's Case,* which required the cross-examiner who wished to impeach with a written inconsistent statement to first show the statement to the witness. Rule 613(a) "abolishes this useless impediment to cross-examination." (Fed. R. Evid. 613[a] advisory committee note.) The cross-examiner can spring the written inconsistency on the witness without first giving the witness an opportunity to read the statement.

Rule 613(b) limits extrinsic evidence of inconsistency. The rule provides that extrinsic evidence is admissible only if the witness has an opportunity to explain or deny the inconsistency. In most cases the opportunity to explain or deny comes while the witness is still on the stand during cross- or redirect examination. On rare occasions, an impeaching attorney does not mention a witness's prior inconsistent statement while the witness is on the stand. In this case, the attorney may decide to present another witness to repeat the out-of-court inconsistency of the witness to be impeached. When this happens, how does the witness to be impeached have an opportunity to explain or deny the inconsistency? The Advisory Committee note to Rule 613(b) provides that "the traditional insistence that the attention of the witness be directed to the statement on cross-examination is relaxed in favor of simply providing the witness an opportunity to explain and the opposite party an opportunity to examine on the statement, with no specification of any particular time or sequence." Thus, the witness to be impeached may be recalled and provided an opportunity to explain or deny.

Rule 613(b) provides two exceptions to the rule that extrinsic evidence of inconsistency is admissible only if the witness is afforded an opportunity to explain or deny the inconsistency. First, the opportunity need not be provided when the inconsistency is offered against a party as an admission. Second, in rare cases, the interests of justice dictate that a prior inconsistent statement be admitted to impeach despite lack of an opportunity to explain or deny. A third exception is found in Rule 806, the rule governing impeachment of hearsay declarants. Rule 806 provides that "evidence of a statement or conduct by the declarant at any time, inconsistent with the declarant's hearsay statement, is not subject to any requirement that the declarant may have been afforded an opportunity to deny or explain."

iii. Offering prior inconsistent statements for the truth of the matter asserted. Under Rule 801(d)(1)(A) of the Federal Rules of Evidence, certain inconsistent statements are admissible for the truth of the matter asserted as well as to impeach. Rule 801(d)(1)(A) provides,

> A statement is not hearsay if the declarant testifies at the trial or hearing and is subject to cross-examination concerning the statement, and the statement is inconsistent with the declarant's testimony, and was given under oath subject to the penalty of perjury at a trial, hearing, or other proceeding, or in a deposition.

Rule 801(d)(1)(A) has five requirements: (1) The declarant must testify at the hearing where the prior inconsistent statement is offered for the truth of the matter asserted;

(2) the declarant must be subject to cross-examination concerning the statement; (3) the out-of-court statement must be inconsistent with the declarant's trial testimony; (4) the out-of-court statement must have been under oath subject to perjury; and (5) the out-of-court statement must have been given at a trial, hearing, proceeding, or deposition.

In a number of states, prior inconsistent statements are defined as hearsay within an exception. In California and Utah, for example, prior inconsistent statements are admissible for the truth of the matter asserted whether or not they were made under oath. State evidence rules regarding prior inconsistent statements vary greatly and the prosecutor must be aware of these differences.

It is important to keep in mind that regardless of the rule governing substantive use of prior inconsistent statements, *all* jurisdictions allow prior inconsistent statements—whether or not under oath—for purposes of impeachment.

g. Prior consistent statements: Fed. R. Evid. 801(d)(1)(B). A witness who has been impeached may, in limited circumstances, be rehabilitated with the witness's prior consistent statements. When an out-of-court consistent statement is limited to rehabilitation, the statement is not hearsay because the statement is not offered for the truth of the matter asserted. When an out-of-court statement is offered for the truth of the matter asserted as well as for rehabilitation, the statement is hearsay.

Rule 801(d)(1)(B) of the Federal Rules of Evidence governs prior consistent statements offered for the truth of the matter asserted. When a prior consistent statement is *not* offered for the truth of the matter asserted, but is offered for the limited purpose of rehabilitation, some courts hold that Rule 801(d)(1)(B) does not govern admissibility. Rule 801(d)(1)(B) provides,

> A statement is not hearsay if the declarant testifies at the trial or hearing and is subject to cross-examination concerning the statement, and the statement is consistent with the declarant's testimony and is offered to rebut an express or implied charge against the declarant of recent fabrication or improper influence or motive.

In some states, prior consistent statements are hearsay within an exception. (See, e.g., Cal. Evid. Code § 1236.) Some states have eliminated the provision that the statement must be offered to rebut a charge of fabrication or improper influence or motive and simply state that the statement is admissible as a prior consistent statement if it is consistent with the declarant's testimony and helpful to evaluate the witness's credibility. (See, e.g., Minn. R. Evid. 801[d][1][B].)

i. Foundation elements. The proponent of a prior consistent statement under Fed. R. Evid. 801(d)(1)(B) must fulfill four requirements:

1. The declarant testifies at trial.

2. The declarant is subject to cross-examination about the prior consistent statement.

3. The declarant is impeached in a way that triggers rehabilitation with prior consistent statements. An express or implied charge of recent fabrication triggers rehabilitation under Rule 801(d)(1)(B).

4. The out-of-court statement is consistent with the trial testimony of the declarant.

ii. What is the meaning of "consistent"? An out-of-court statement does not have to be identical to trial testimony to be consistent with the testimony. Some sexually abused children disclose the abuse progressively over time, gradually revealing more detail. In such cases, a child's trial testimony may be more detailed than earlier statements. Nevertheless, the child's earlier statements may be consistent with, albeit less detailed than, the child's trial testimony. Christopher Mueller and Laird Kirkpatrick write that Rule 801(d)(1)(B) "should reach a statement that repeats important parts of what the witness says at trial even if trial testimony goes further and provides more detail, for successive statements on a single subject almost inevitably vary in some ways." (Mueller, C. B., & Kirkpatrick,, L. C. [1994]. *Federal Evidence*, Vol. 4 [2nd ed., p. 405].)

iii. Who repeats the prior consistent statement? A prior consistent statement may be repeated by the witness who made the statement. Alternatively, a prior consistent statement may be repeated by a witness other than the declarant. Note that Rule 801(d)(1)(B) requires the declarant to be subject to cross-examination about the prior consistent statement.

iv. What is "recent" fabrication? Rule 801(d)(1)(B) speaks of "recent" fabrication. The word *recent* does not mean temporal proximity to trial. Michael Graham aptly described the requirement when he wrote that "a 'fabrication' is 'recent' if the in-court testimony is expressly or impliedly charged to have been consciously fabricated at any time after the event." (Graham, M. H. [1979]. Consistent statements: Rule 801(d)(1)(B) of the Federal Rules of Evidence, critique and proposal. *Hastings Law Journal, 30*, 575.)

v. Types of impeachment that trigger rehabilitation with prior consistent statements

Charge of Recent Fabrication. The most common way to open the door for rehabilitation with prior consistent statements is to impeach the witness with a charge that the trial testimony is a recent fabrication. There are innumerable ways for a cross-examiner to charge that a witness's testimony is fabricated. The cross-examiner does not have to come right out and say, "Isn't it true you are lying?" Sometimes the sheer length and intensity of cross-examination amounts to an implied charge of fabrication. (*United States v. Cherry*, 938 F.2d 748 [7th Cir. 1991]; *United States v. Andrade*, 788 F.2d 521, 533 [8th Cir. 1986].) Asserting bias may imply fabrication. With children, the cross-examiner often suggests that trial testimony is a result of coaching, thus triggering the ability to use prior consistent statements. (*State v. Bass*, 535 A.2d 1 [N.J. Super. Ct. App. Div. 1987].)

The Premotive Rule: *Tome v. United States*. The majority rule is that prior consistent statements are admissible to rebut a charge of recent fabrication only if the statements were uttered before the motive to fabricate arose. This is the so-called premotive rule. In *Tome v. United States*, 513 U.S. 150 (1995), the U.S. Supreme Court adopted the premotive rule for the federal courts. The *Tome* majority wrote that "the introduction [under Rule 801(d)(1)(B)] of a declarant's consistent out-of-court statements to rebut a charge of recent fabrication or improper influence or motive [is permitted] only when those statements were made *before* the charged recent fabrication or improper influence or motive" (at 167) (emphasis added). Although the *Tome*

Court's interpretation of Rule 801(d)(1)(B) is not binding on state courts, most post-*Tome* state court decisions adopt *Tome*'s interpretation of Rule 801(d)(1)(B).

Prior Inconsistent Statements. Impeachment with a witness's prior inconsistent statements sometimes amounts to a charge of fabrication, paving the way for rehabilitation with prior consistent statements. (*State v. Gardner,* 490 N.W.2d 838 [Iowa 1992].) In *United States v. Ellis,* 121 F.3d 908, 919 (4th Cir. 1997), *cert. denied,* 522 U.S. 1068 (1998), the court wrote that "even before the adoption of the federal rules, this court recognized that where a cross-examiner has endeavored to discredit a witness by prior inconsistent statements, it is sometimes permissible to offset the damage by showing prior consistent utterances."

Lapse of Memory. A cross-examiner may hope to undermine a witness's credibility by implying that the witness's memory is faulty. The cross-examiner may emphasize inconsistencies between the witness's trial testimony and earlier statements, on the theory that the earlier statements were true, and that the witness's memory has faded in the interim. Faced with impeachment that focuses on memory, courts often admit prior consistent statements uttered close in time to the event, when the witness's memory was fresh. (*Applebaum v. American Export Isbrandsten Lines,* 472 F.2d 56, 61–62 [2d Cir. 1972]; *State v. Bruggeman,* 779 P.2d 823, 825 [Ariz. Ct. App. 1989]; *State v. Altergott,* 559 P.2d 728 [Haw. 1977]; *Slater v. Baker,* 301 N.W.2d 315, 319–20 [Minn. 1981].

Contradiction. Impeachment by contradiction may or may not trigger rehabilitation with prior consistent statements. In some cases, the impeachment carries an insinuation of recent fabrication, opening the door to rehabilitation. (*United States v. Cherry,* 938 F2d 748 [7th Cir. 1991].)

Untruthful Character. A cross-examiner may impugn a witness's character for truthfulness with evidence that the witness has been convicted of a crime or that the witness has committed untruthful acts. (Fed. Rule Evid. 608[b], 609.) McCormick opined that impeachment going to untruthful character should not open the door to rehabilitation with prior consistent statements. (Strong, J. W. [1992]. *McCormick on evidence* [4th ed., p. 47]. West Wadsworth.) Christopher Mueller and Larid Kirkpatrick, on the other hand, wrote that "an attack suggesting untruthful disposition (bad character for truth and veracity) can similarly suggest" recent fabrication. (Mueller, C. B., & Kirkpatrick, L. C. [1994]. *Federal evidence,* Vol. 4 [2nd ed., p. 406]. New York: Aspen.)

h. Residual and child hearsay exceptions. A majority of states have a residual exception to the hearsay rule modeled after Federal Rule of Evidence 807. In addition, a majority of states have a special child hearsay exception. Although child hearsay exceptions differ slightly from state to state, all the child hearsay exceptions contemplate the admission of certain out-of-court statements that do not meet the requirements of one of the traditional hearsay exceptions. Whether hearsay is offered under a residual or a child hearsay exception, the critical issue is usually whether the hearsay is sufficiently reliable to gain admission in evidence.

When assessing the reliability of hearsay offered under residual or child hearsay exceptions, judges consider the totality of the circumstances pointing toward and away from reliability. In *Idaho v. Wright,* 497 U.S. 805 (1990), the Supreme Court

Table V.2   Statutes Regarding the Use of Special Hearsay Exceptions in Criminal Child Abuse
                    Cases

Alabama	ALA. CODE § 15–25–30 to–40
Alaska	ALASKA STAT. § 12.40.110
Arizona	ARIZ. REV. STAT. § 13–1416
Arkansas	ARK. CODE ANN. § 16–41–101
	ARK. R. EVID. § 803(25)
California	CAL. EVID. CODE § 1228
Colorado	COLO. REV. STAT. § 13–25–129
	COLO. REV. STAT. § 18–3–411(3)
	COLO. REV. STAT. § 18–6–401.1(3)
Delaware	DEL. CODE ANN. tit. 11, § 3513
Florida	FLA. STAT. ANN. ch. 90.803(23)
Georgia	GA. CODE ANN. § 24–3–16
Hawaii	HAW. R. EVID. § 804(b)(6)
Idaho	IDAHO CODE § 19–3024
Illinois	725 ILL. COMP. STAT. ANN. 5/115–10
Indiana	IND. CODE § 35–37–4–6
Kansas	KAN. STAT. ANN. § 60–460(dd)
Maine	ME. REV. STAT. ANN. tit. 15, § 1205
Maryland	MD. ANN. CODE. ART. 27, § 775
	MD. ANN. CODE ANN., CRIM. PROC. § 11–304
Massachusetts	MASS. GEN. LAWS. ANN. ch. 233, § 81
Michigan	MICH. R. EVID. § 803A
Minnesota	MINN. STAT. ANN. § 595.02(3)
Mississippi	MISS. CODE ANN. §§ 13–1–403
	MISS. R. EVID. 803(25)
Missouri	MO. REV. STAT. § 491.075
Nevada	NEV. REV. STAT. § 51.385
New Jersey	N.J. R. EVID. 803(C)(27)
North Dakota	N.D. R. EVID. 803(24)
Ohio	OHIO R. EVID. 807
Oklahoma	OKLA. STAT. ANN. tit.12, § 2803.1
Oregon	OR. REV. STAT. § 40.460(18b)
Pennsylvania	42 PA. CONS. STAT. ANN. § 5985.1
South Carolina	S.C. CODE ANN. § 19–1–180
South Dakota	S.D. CODIFIED LAWS § 19–16–38
Texas	TEX. CRIM. PROC. CODE ANN. § 38.072
	TEX. FAM. CODE ANN. § 54.031
	TEX. FAM. CODE ANN. § 104.006
Utah	UTAH CODE ANN. § 76–5–411
Vermont	VT. R. EVID. 804a
	VT. R. CRIM. PROC. 26(D)
Washington	WASH. REV. CODE ANN. § 9A.44.120

NOTE: This table includes all legislation passed through March 2002, as verified through Lexis Nexis.

endorsed the totality of the circumstances approach to reliability. In one respect, however, the majority in *Wright* established an odd rule. The majority held that in criminal cases, the Confrontation Clause of the Sixth Amendment dictates that when a judge evaluates the reliability of a hearsay statement, the judge may consider *only* those factors "that surround the making of the statement." (*Id.* at 819.) The judge must *ignore* factors that do not surround the making of the statement, even though those factors corroborate the reliability of the statement. Thus, according to the *Wright* majority, the Sixth Amendment prohibits a judge from considering corroborating evidence such as medical or physical evidence of abuse, the defendant's opportunity to commit the offense, or the testimony of an eyewitness to the abuse. (*Id.* at 826.) *Idaho v. Wright* draws a distinction between reliability factors that surround a statement, which a judge may consider, and reliability factors that corroborate a statement but do not surround it, which a judge must ignore.

Justice Kennedy could not make sense of this distinction. In his dissent, Justice Kennedy wrote,

> The majority errs, in my view, by adopting a rule that corroboration of the statement by other evidence is an impermissible part of the trustworthiness inquiry. The Court's apparent ruling is that corroborating evidence may not be considered in whole or in part for this purpose.
>
> I see no constitutional justification for this decision to prescind corroborating evidence from consideration of the question whether a child's statements are reliable. It is a matter of common sense for most people that one of the best ways to determine whether what someone says is trustworthy is to see if it is corroborated by other evidence. (*Id.* at 828–29)

In cases where the hearsay declarant testifies at trial, it is possible to escape *Wright*'s prohibition of corroborative evidence to assess reliability. This is so because *Wright* is based squarely on the Sixth Amendment Confrontation Clause. If the declarant testifies at trial, however, *California v. Green*, 399 U.S. 149 (1970), indicates the Confrontation Clause is satisfied. Thus, with the requirements of the Confrontation Clause fulfilled, *Wright*'s limits on assessing reliability ought to be inapplicable, allowing the trial judge to consider corroborating evidence as well as factors that surround the statement. This is precisely the position taken by a number of courts, most notably the U. S. Court of Appeals for the Armed Forces. (*United States v. Kelley*, 45 M.J. 275 [C.M.A. 1996]; *United States v. Ureta*, 44 M.J. 290 [C.M.A. 1996], *cert. denied*, 117 S. Ct. 692 [1996].)

A large body of case law discusses factors impacting the reliability of hearsay offered under residual and child hearsay exceptions. These factors are outlined below.

i. Factors that surround the making of the statement

Testimonial Competence When Out-of-Court Statement Was Made. The fact that a child possessed the competence to testify *at the time* of an out-of-court statement may support reliability.

Testimonial Competence at Time of Trial. The fact that a child is incompetent to testify at trial may undermine the reliability of the child's earlier out-of-court statements. The Court noted in *Wright*, however, that incompetence at trial does not necessarily render a child's earlier statements unreliable. It is necessary to ask *why* the child is incompetent. For example, if a child is able but unwilling to communicate at trial, the child's earlier hearsay statements may be reliable. On the other hand, if a child is unable at trial to differentiate truth from falsehood, doubts may arise as to the child's earlier statements.

Spontaneity. Many, many decisions indicate that the more spontaneous a child's statement, the more reliable the statement.

Type of Questioning. The reliability of a child's statement may be influenced by the questions asked during investigative and other interviews. If the questioning was leading or suggestive, the statement is less reliable and more unlikely to meet the sufficient indicia of reliability required under the *Wright* analysis.

Consistency. Reliability may be enhanced when a child is consistent over time. Inconsistency is normal in children, however, especially young children. Moreover, what is to be considered is the child's consistency during the interview, not the child's consistency across statements. Consistency across statements is not a factor surrounding the statement.

Developmentally Unusual Sexual Knowledge or Terminology. When a young child's statement reflects sexual knowledge or terminology one would not expect in a young child, confidence in the statement may rise.

Lack of Motive to Fabricate. Lack of a motive to fabricate bolsters confidence in a child's statement.

ii. Factors that corroborate the statement

Medical or Physical Evidence of Abuse. A child's hearsay statement may be corroborated by medical or physical evidence.

Changes in Child's Behavior. Changes in a child's behavior may corroborate the child's out-of-court statements.

Eyewitness. The testimony of an eyewitness to the abuse may strengthen confidence in a child's hearsay describing the abuse.

Defendant's Opportunity to Commit the Abuse. The fact that the defendant had an opportunity to commit the act described in the child's hearsay statement may increase the reliability of the statement.

Admission by Defendant. An admission by the defendant may corroborate a child's hearsay statement.

4. Conclusion

The law on hearsay and its exceptions is complex and diverse among the states. Prosecutors are encouraged to learn and understand the evidence rules, case law, and individual jurisdiction practices. The use of a child's out-of-court statements can be powerful and may make the difference between a guilty verdict and a not guilty verdict.

V. PHYSICAL ABUSE AND HOMICIDE: SPECIAL CONSIDERATIONS

To the extent that a child's injury is obvious, a physical abuse or homicide case has more physical evidence and is easier to comprehend than many child sexual abuse cases. It is more difficult to argue that nothing happened to the child. However, many physical abuse and homicide cases involve injuries that cannot be seen, or for which there is little *visible* evidence. For example, a child homicide case might involve a serious head injury with little external evidence of any injury. The defense may argue that it is impossible that there was any significant or serious trauma to the child because of the lack of observable injuries. In such cases, the prosecutor's challenge is to establish that significant trauma was inflicted and that the injury was not accidental. It may be necessary to call an expert witness or use a model to show the child's internal injuries.

Many physical abuse cases involve eliminating all other explanations for the child's injuries. When the defendant's responsibility for the injury is established, the level of the crime and aggravating factors surrounding the crime become the crucial issues. Important areas for investigation include a defendant's background, experience with children, the opportunities available for the child to have received medical care, warnings and instructions offered through child care or medical visits, and prior abuse by the defendant.

A. Presenting the Victim

1. When the Victim Is Available to Testify

The victim should be called to testify if available and competent. In physical abuse cases, the child may believe he deserved the punishment for misbehavior. Ironically, the more abusive the child's environment, the more likely the child is to view the abusive behavior as normal and appropriate. Be sensitive to these dynamics and present the child's testimony in as matter-of-fact a manner as possible. Ask the victim to describe the circumstances surrounding the assault, including any "misbehavior" that ostensibly triggered the defendant's conduct. If the defendant used an instrument during the assault, the investigator should recover it. Have the victim identify it and demonstrate how the defendant used it. For example, how did the defendant hold the extension cord in his hands and how did the defendant beat the child with it? Which parts of the child's body did the defendant hit? Such a demonstration usually illustrates the abuse far more graphically and effectively than any verbal description. If prior abusive acts are admissible, have the victim testify about them. Explain their effect on the child's state of mind. Ask the victim about statements that the defendant made before, during, or after the assault to show evidence of intent or to ensure the child would not reveal the abuse or injuries. For example, did the defendant keep the child home from school? Did the defendant delay taking the child to the doctor, or even fail to take the child to the doctor at all? Was the child allowed to see other friends or family? Have the victim describe how the physical assault was discovered and what happened afterward.

Consider showing the jury the child's injuries or scars from the assault if this is not too embarrassing for the victim or uncomfortable for the judge and jury. Otherwise, use photographs of the injuries taken by investigators and/or medical personnel. Handle the photos sensitively if you need to show them to the victim to authenticate them. If the victim is embarrassed, wait until he is off the witness stand before showing them to the jury.

It is generally *not* a good idea to ask the victim to express a judgment about the appropriateness of the defendant's discipline or to imply your own value judgment in questions to the victim. Let the conduct and resulting injury speak for themselves. During closing argument, you can point out that the defendant's conduct is even more reprehensible because he caused the child to believe this clearly abusive assault was deserved. In a physical abuse case where the victim has recanted, use the same strategies you would in a sexual abuse case.

2. When the Victim Is Unavailable to Testify

If the victim is too young to testify, consider having the infant or toddler brought into the courtroom so the jury can evaluate the size difference between the child and defendant. Be prepared for smiles or other signs of affection between the child and defendant should you do this.

If the child is deceased, try to obtain photographs or videotapes of the child prior to the date of the charged abuse. It is important that the child, whose life has ended because of abuse or neglect, become real to the jury. Photos and videos are relevant to illustrate the physical condition and size at a given time and may help to pinpoint the timing of an injury. Videotapes can be especially helpful to show a child's developmental level and motor skills. They can even demonstrate the nature of some of the interaction between the defendant and child.

Photos and videos can also be used by lay witnesses to help them describe the victim, by experts and the jury to evaluate the reasonableness of the defendant's explanation about what happened, by the prosecutor in opening statement if premarked and approved by the trial judge, and in closing argument to remind the jury of the reason for this trial. The videotape can also be helpful to establish a serious and permanent injury from physical abuse for a child too young or too impaired to testify.

If the child was in a coma prior to death, videotape or photograph the child during this time period. Some prosecutors have the child photographed periodically throughout the period of hospitalization to document that the child was not re-injured in the hospital or that hospital treatment did not cause the death, or to document possible changes in the injuries. The photographs also may be relevant to show the child's suffering prior to death.

B. The Order of Witnesses

The order of witnesses in a physical abuse or homicide case may depend on the nature of the injuries, the type of defense you anticipate, and to some extent the availability of medical witnesses. Begin your case-in-chief by calling lay witnesses and investigators to establish the defendant's access to the child and opportunity to inflict injuries. These witnesses can tell the jury about the defendant's statements to explain what happened and present evidence concerning their observations of the child's injuries and the scene.

Recognize that you may need to be flexible to accommodate the demanding schedules of medical experts or other witnesses. Most judges are willing to take physicians out of order, as long as you alert the judge to this need in advance.

Medical experts greatly appreciate your efforts to be sensitive to their schedules and reduce waiting time at the courthouse. In general, it is best to have medical experts testify at or near the end of your case-in-chief, so they can effectively address all the issues raised or evidence presented. The medical expert may answer hypothetical questions that are based on facts and evidence such as photographs showing a child's injuries or lack of injuries at a particular point in time, based upon the defendant's version of events, and based upon photographs of a scene. Placing the medical expert toward the end of the prosecution's case allows the medical expert to review the prosecution's evidence and sum up the prosecution's case.

C. Establishing the Defendant's Opportunity and Responsibility

It is critical that you prove the victim was in the care of the defendant during the period that medical testimony indicated the child was injured. If you can establish the defendant's *exclusive custody* of the child during the relevant time, you can effectively eliminate a defense that someone else did it. Present witnesses—law enforcement, medical, or others—to whom the defendant admitted being alone with the child. Since such admissions are more likely to have occurred early in the case, law enforcement should be sure to interview ambulance and hospital personnel, the first officers on the scene, and obtain 911 tapes.

1. Establishing the Defendant's Exclusive Opportunity and the Timing of Injuries

Call witnesses who can testify that the child was free from injury *prior* to the exclusive contact with the defendant. You must then show that the child sustained injuries during this time. This is usually accomplished by evidence of the defendant seeking medical assistance for the child or someone else arriving at the scene.

When there is proof that the child was healthy and had no injuries prior to being left in the exclusive custody of the defendant, the medical expert can be asked hypothetical questions along the following lines:

Q: Based upon your background, training, and experience in the field of medicine, and assuming this child was seen by his mother at 7:30 A.M. healthy, walking, and eating, immediately prior to the time she left this child alone with the defendant in the apartment, and that at 10:00 A.M. paramedics responded to the apartment and found the child comatose, not breathing, and alone with the defendant, do you have an opinion with reasonable medical certainty as to when the fatal injuries were inflicted upon this child?

A: "Between 7:30 and 10:00 A.M."

Evidence establishing a defendant's exclusive custody of the child, together with medical testimony eliminating other explanations for a child's injuries, is generally sufficient to support a conviction. (See *Kutch v. State*, 807 S.W.2d 602 [Tex. Ct. App. 1991] [affirming conviction where medical testimony established the injuries suffered by a 22-month-old child were nonaccidental and occurred before she was taken to her mother]; *Commonwealth v. Merola*, 542 N.E.2d 249 [Mass. 1989] [upholding first-degree murder conviction where defendant had exclusive custody immediately prior to the victim's loss of consciousness, medical evidence indicated victim lost consciousness moments after injury, and the amount of force used was equivalent to falling from third-floor window onto hard surface]; *Drew v. State*, 771 P.2d 224 [Okla. Ct. App. 1989] [affirming homicide conviction against mother when medical testimony revealed daughter's fatal injury most likely occurred within 12 hours prior to arrival at hospital, consciousness would be lost almost immediately following such an injury, and defendant's husband left for work early in morning and returned home to find mother holding unconscious child]; *Commonwealth v. Earnest*, 563 A.2d 158 [Pa. 1989] [concluding the evidence was sufficient to allow the jury to conclude the defendant inflicted the injuries when the defendant had sole custody of the child for the period during which the child suffered the wounds that unquestionably were neither self-inflicted nor accidental]; but see *Berry v. Commonwealth*, 473 N.E.2d 1115 [Mass.1985] [when evidence showed that *both* defendant and the mother had the opportunity, ability, and disposition to kill the child, no rational trier of fact could have found defendant guilty of murder or manslaughter].)

The injury itself generally cannot be used to pinpoint with precision when it occurred. However, a medical expert can pinpoint the timing of an injury based upon testimony from various witnesses regarding the defendant's exclusive custody and the child's good health prior to the defendant's exclusive custody. It is preferable for the jury to hear this opinion from the expert rather than leaving it to the prosecutor's argument or the jury's common sense. If anyone else, such as baby-sitters, neighbors, and siblings, had access to the child during the critical period, make sure they testify and describe their observations of the child's behavioral changes or symptoms such as vomiting, increased irritability, failure to eat, and any other symptoms. These witnesses may also be able to provide information about when the child last ate, urinated or defecated, appeared awake or alert, and was without signs of injury. For example, the deceased's stomach contents of pizza can be timed to a pizza delivery. Such facts can be referenced during the testimony of your medical expert in narrowing the time the injury was inflicted. A time line illustrating the periods of exclusive custody, the onset of symptoms or abnormal behaviors, and other relevant facts can help the jury organize events prior to death.

2. The Testimony of Emergency Personnel and Paramedics

If the child received emergency medical care such as CPR from paramedics, emergency room personnel, or others, they should testify about the child's condition before they did anything and whether their actions could have caused injury to the child. Establish a chain of custody for the child to show that the emergency or medical personnel are not responsible for the child's injuries. Defendants will often claim the child's injuries were caused by life-saving actions. However, studies show that CPR does not cause the retinal hemorrhaging commonly associated with shaken baby syndrome. (See [1991]. Resuscitation and retinal hemorrhage. *American Journal of Forensic Medicine and Pathology, 12*, 354 [abstract]; Fackler, J. C., et al. [1992]. Retinal hemorrhage in newborn piglets following cardiopulmonary resuscitation. *American Journal of Diseases of Children, 146*, 1294.) Defendants often claim that injuries such as broken ribs resulted from the actions of medical professionals. The medical literature does not support such a claim. (See e.g., Fellman, K. W., & Brewer, D. K. [1984]. Child abuse, cardiopulmonary resuscitation, and rib fractures. *Pediatrics, 73,* 339 [no rib fractures documented in any reviewed cases involving CPR].) Review any reports or notes prepared by these individuals about the case. They should provide a detailed account of their entire time with and care for the child. Mannequins used for emergency medical training can be helpful as demonstrative evidence at trial to allow medical personnel to demonstrate how they treated the child. In some situations, trained paramedics may be used as experts.

3. Other Children or Victims as a Source of Injuries

If the "someone else" alleged to be responsible for the child's injuries is another child or the victim himself, present medical evidence regarding the physical and/or developmental capacity of the child to cause that type of injury. Have the expert use a time line to illustrate for the jury the capabilities of children at particular ages, such as when a child can roll over, sit up, walk, or feed himself. For instance, it is highly unlikely that a 3-year-old would have the ability to hold down his 2-year-old sibling in a tub of scalding water and cause clearly delineated immersion burns. Likewise, a 5-month-old child is probably physically unable to turn on a bathtub's hot water spigot. Falls from beds or couches rarely cause serious injury to children. There are several excellent articles and studies concerning falls and injuries in young children that should be reviewed by a prosecutor whenever there is an issue of whether a fall may have produced an injury. (See Dubowitz, H. [1999]. *Neglected children: Research, practice, and policy.* Thousand Oaks, CA: Sage; Monteleone, J. A., & Brodeur, A. E. [1994]. *Child maltreatment: A clinical guide and reference* [pp. 8–9]. St. Louis: G.W. Medical Publishing; Reiber, G. D. [1993]. Fatal falls in childhood: How far must children fall to sustain fatal head injury? Report of cases and review of literature. *American Journal of Forensic Medicine and Pathology, 14,* 201; Duhaime, A. C., et al. [1992]. Head injury in very young children: Mechanisms, injury types, and ophthalmologic findings in 100 hospitalized patients younger than 2 years of age. *Pediatrics, 90,* 179; Helfer, R. E., et al. [1977]. Injuries resulting when small children fall out of bed. *Pediatrics, 60,* 533; Hall, J. R., et al. [1989]. Mortality of childhood falls. *Journal of Trauma, 29,* 1273.) Further, the kind of subdural hematomas (blood collection on the surface of the brain underneath the covering of the brain) typically found in severe shaking cases does not result from jumping up and down or falling down stairs. (See Joffe, M., & Ludwig, S. [1988]. Stairway injuries in children. *Pediatrics, 82,* 457.)

4. Charging Decisions Involving One or More
Parent or Caretaker and Liability Based on Omission

One of the most difficult cases to prove is that in which more than one person had the opportunity to injure the child, such as the mother and father, and neither has given a statement. Generally, it is insufficient, in the absence of a special statutory scheme, to allege that the child sustained the injuries while with two caregivers, and therefore one of the caregivers must be guilty. For example, in *People v. Wong,* 619 N.E.2d 377 (N.Y. 1993), the defendants' convictions were reversed when there was evidence at trial that both caregiver-defendants were present in the apartment when a child died of shaken baby syndrome, but the prosecution was unable to show which defendant inflicted the injuries and which defendant failed to seek medical attention. However, the court noted that a passive defendant without duty to act, aware of the harm done to the child, may be held criminally liable for failing to seek medical attention. (See also *Berry v. Commonwealth*, 473 N.E.2d 1115 [Mass. 1985] [when evidence showed that both the defendant and the child's mother had the opportunity, ability, and disposition to kill the child, no rational trier of fact could have found the defendant guilty of murder or manslaughter].)

Carefully consider whether both can be charged and successfully prosecuted based on the theory that, no matter who struck the blows, the defendant failed to protect the child, then acted together with the other person to cover it up. Whether you can proceed in this fashion will depend on your jurisdiction's law regarding parental duty and accomplice liability. Some states have statutes specifically based on omission as a basis for legal liability in child homicide or child abuse prosecutions. (See, e.g., Ariz. Rev. Stat. § 13–3623[B] [establishing liability for causing or permitting child to be "placed in situation where its person or health is endangered"]; Wisc. Stat. § 948.03[4] [making it a crime for a person responsible for a child's welfare to fail to take action to protect the child]; *United States v. Valdez*, 40 M.J. 491 [1994]; *State v. Smith*, 935 P.2d 841 [Ariz. 1996].) Thus, a defendant may be responsible for the failure to act, such as seeking medical treatment, even if not present when the harm is inflicted. (*People v. Stanciel*, 606 N.E.2d 1201 [Ill. 1992] [noting not only that one with a parental duty may be liable for failure to act but also that a defendant need not be present to be culpable under this theory].) Beware that liability under this legal theory is based on the parent's or guardian's legal duty and would not apply to someone who does not have such a legal duty. If there is no legal duty to act, liability may not be based on a failure-to-act theory. However, what appears to be a failure to act may actually be acts designed to cause a child's death. Thus, physical neglect is not necessarily conduct by omission. For example, a defendant can "intentionally and knowingly" kill a child by not feeding a child when told to do so or preventing the mother from coming to the aid of a child by threatening and physically abusing her. (*State v. Banks*, 641 N.E.2d 331 [Ill. 1994].)

Some courts also appear willing to expand the duty to care for a child beyond that of a biological or legal parent. Connecticut's Supreme Court has held that a defendant who "established a family-like relationship with the mother and her two children . . . had voluntarily assumed responsibility for the care and welfare of both children, and . . . considered himself the victim's stepfather" had a common-law duty to act to protect and care for the children under his supervision, even if he was not a biological or legal parent. (*State v. Miranda*, 715 A.2d 680 [Conn. 1998].) Some courts will also consider a duty owed by a defendant under an implied contract theory. (See, e.g., *People v. Wong*, 588 N.Y.S.2d 119, *rev'd on other grounds*, 619 N.E.2d 377 [1993] [holding that defendants contracted to care for the child and assumed care for the child, but reversing conviction owing to insufficient evidence]; *Leet v. State*, 595 So. 2d 959 [Fla. App. Ct. 1991] [holding defendant "assumed responsibility for care of the child and could be liable for failing to act"]; *Commonwealth v. Pestinikas*, 617 A.2d 1339 [Pa. 1992] [finding defendant had made an oral contract to provide for the child and thus could be liable for failure to act].)

If a mother is charged for her failure to act, consider what defenses or mitigating factors may be offered on her behalf. If her husband or boyfriend physically abused her, she may be able to offer a claim of battered woman syndrome on the issue of whether she shared in the husband's or boyfriend's intent to abuse the child. (See, e.g., *Commonwealth v. Lazarovick,* 574 N.E.2d 340 [Mass. 1992].) Possible mitigating factors or defenses should be considered when exercising prosecutorial discretion in the charging decision and during plea negotiations.

In contrast, a case involving a defendant who is charged with aiding and abetting will generally require verbal or overt conduct by the defendant together with conscious desire or intent on the part of the defendant to yield assistance. (See *State v. Rundle,* 500 N.W.2d 916 [Wis. 1993] [reversing defendant's conviction for aiding and abetting the intentional and reckless physical abuse of his daughter by his wife but upholding conviction on theory of liability for parent's failure to act].) If it is impossible to identify who injured the child, your case will be lost unless you have a strong accomplice liability theory.

When you have determined that both caregivers are responsible, but that the less culpable caregiver's testimony is essential to convict the more culpable caregiver, you may elect to try the more culpable caregiver using the accomplice's testimony. Before doing so, review the applicable statutes on marital privilege before offering immunity. Be careful not to offer witness immunity or a plea bargain disproportionate to the degree of responsibility for the crime. Many prosecutors have noted a backlash from a jury when a deal is offered to one parent or caregiver. Many jurors feel that the parent or caregiver to whom a deal has been offered is "equally as responsible" as the defendant on trial and may reduce the level of the defendant's culpability so that the defendant is "equally responsible." If you do enter into an agreement to reduce charges, provide immunity, or otherwise negotiate with the less culpable caregiver, the agreement should state that the witness receives no immunity from perjury. The witness should indicate, in writing, that she understands the nature of the agreement. Schedule the sentencing of the witness after she provides testimony against the defendant to encourage truthful testimony at trial.

You should also consider the possibility of offering the witness no immunity or no deal until the investigation and testimony are fully developed. Consider waiting before making this very crucial prosecutorial decision. It is possible that either of the caregivers or suspects may make additional statements to investigators, to other parties, or to each other that may enhance your ability to make an informed decision. It is also possible that the parent or caregiver who did not inflict the injuries has a criminal responsibility for allowing the abuse to occur.

One approach is to charge both defendants so that the jury sees that the prosecution is interested in establishing responsibility for all persons involved. If a codefendant has made a statement implicating another codefendant, thus triggering *Bruton* issues, a trial before two juries is a very effective way of presenting the evidence involving abuse and responsibility of both parties. This also avoids the problem of the absent defendant who has been charged but from whom the jury expects to hear testimony.

The prosecution may offer explanations for a parent's involvement in the abuse, the failure to act, or acquiescence to the child abuse. There may be a history of physical abuse of the parent at the hands of the defendant or a good reason for the parent to fear the defendant. However, juries are often not sympathetic to these explanations in a child abuse case, especially in child homicide cases. The jury is likely to believe that a parent should protect the child first regardless of whatever reasons there are for the parent's involvement or failure to act. Furthermore, presenting reasons for failure to act may deflect the jury's attention from the prosecution's case and lead the jury to debate the caregivers' relationship and the witness's weaknesses in the relationship. If the prosecutor decides to utilize testimony from a parent or caregiver who was involved in the abuse or responsible for the abuse, it is important to focus the jury's attention on the only issue for their consideration, i.e., this defendant's guilt or innocence, and remind them that "no other person and no other institution" is on trial.

In some states, the nonoffending parent or guardian may be considered an accomplice whose testimony must be corroborated. For example, New York law does not permit a conviction based upon accomplice testimony "unsupported by corroborative evidence tending to connect the defendant with the commission of such offense." (N.Y. C.P.L.R. 60.22 [2002].) In states with a corroboration requirement, the prosecutor will have to ensure that there is other evidence connecting the defendant to the child's homicide. Even if there is no legal requirement for such corroboration, the prosecutor should be prepared for the defense to argue that the accomplice's testimony must be corroborated to be believed.

D. The Degree of Injury

In cases of child physical abuse that do not result in death, the defendant may admit to having hit the child but claim that the resulting injury is not severe enough to merit a conviction under the applicable statutory provisions. Courts rejecting this argument have found a variety of injuries to be the product of criminal conduct. (See *People v. Keenan*, 277 Cal. Rptr. 687 [1991] [cigarette burns]; *Commonwealth v. Rochon*, 581 A.2d 239 [Pa. 1990] [hitting the child with sneaker and belt, then immersing the child in cold water, causing hypothermia]; *State v. Dodd*, 503 A.2d 1302 [Me. 1986] [taping 3-year-old's ankles and hands, covering mouth with tape, and hanging her by ankles from doorknob]; but see *Pickering v. State*, 596 S.W.2d 124 [Tex. Crim. App. 1980] [reversing conviction requiring "serious bodily injury" where victim's bruises healed without medication and the burns created neither serious permanent disfigurement nor a protracted loss or impairment of function of any bodily member or organ].)

The fact that children can recover quickly from injuries may make it difficult for the jury to find that the defendant inflicted the degree of injury specified in the statute. To overcome this problem in cases involving serious physical injury defined as involving the risk of death or grave risk of death, the medical expert should explain how the child was at risk of death from the injury because of the nature of the injury, the defendant's lying about what happened to the child and then providing an incomplete medical history, or the defendant's delay in getting medical attention. Emphasize to the jury the child's condition at time of admission to the emergency room. The emergency room doctor should explain how seriously injured the victim was and, if the victim survived, how close to death the child was. Describe permanent injuries. Use photographs to illustrate visible injuries to the child that have healed by the time of trial. If it will be years before the full damage to the child is known, the medical expert must describe the potential for long-term repercussions. If the victim is unable to testify or is deceased, a medical expert should attempt to describe the victim's degree of pain from the injuries.

E. Evidence of the Defendant's Intent and Possible Motive

Child physical abuse and homicide trials usually revolve around the issue of the defendant's intent or mental state. It is an attractive defense strategy since it appeals to the natural reluctance of judges and jurors to believe that anyone would deliberately harm a child, especially one's own child. Some variation of the intent defense is therefore likely whenever the defendant's responsibility for the child's injuries is clear. Common alternatives are that the defendant intended only to discipline, not harm, the child, perhaps in a manner consistent with his cultural background; the defendant had an understandable outburst of anger that accidentally went too far; the defendant was shaking the child for a legitimate purpose such as to wake her, because she was having a seizure, or because she stopped breathing; the defendant did not direct any action toward the child, but the child got in the way of his assault on someone else or in the way of his cigarette.

Many child abuse or assault statutes do not involve "intent" as an element. Typically, the offense will involve a reckless mental state. Each jurisdiction's jury charge pertaining to mental state should be carefully reviewed to make sure that the prosecutor has proof sufficient to establish the requisite mental state, such as recklessness or criminal negligence. When describing the knowing and reckless mental states, the Colorado Supreme Court explained,

> Knowingly in child abuse does not refer to the actor's awareness that his action is practically certain to cause the prosecuted result. Instead, knowingly refers to the actor's general awareness of the abusive nature of his conduct in relation to the child or his awareness of the circumstances in which he commits an act against the well being of the child. (*People v. District Court*, 803 P.2d 193 [Colo. 1990] [*citing People v. Noble*, 635 P.2d 203 (Colo. 1981)])

Charging a crime based on intent may raise certain otherwise unavailable defenses such as intoxication or extreme emotional disturbance. Jurors always want to know the "why" or the motive of someone who seriously physically abuses or kills a child. It should be discussed during jury selection that motive is not an element of the crime. When possible, however, develop a motive or reason for the behavior. Quite often, the triggering event is defecation or crying. Explore the background and relationship of the parties. Were there problems in the relationship? For example, did the defendant abuse the child because the mother was seeing someone else and he was upset with her? Was the child a pawn in the defendant's struggle with the other parent or person? Was the child unplanned or unexpected? (See, e.g., *Commonwealth v. Avellar*, 629 N.E.2d 625 [Mass. 1993] [finding relevant to attitude toward deceased child the defendant's urging of child's mother to undergo abortion].) Were there time demands on the parent?

Short of an outright confession, circumstantial evidence and argument is the only way to establish the defendant's intent. This includes testimony from medical experts who can establish possible instruments of injury as well as the amount of force needed to inflict particular injuries. Other factors providing circumstantial evidence of the defendant's intent are discussed below. Always be prepared to address any argument about lack of intent in your case-in-chief. In particular, the prosecutor should educate the jury during jury selection that the charges do not require the prosecution to establish that the defendant intentionally inflicted injury on the child when the charges do not involve the intentional infliction of injury, but other mental states such as the reckless infliction of injury.

1. Intent Based on a Failure to Act

In many jurisdictions, a defendant's failure to act may be the basis for a charge based on intent. Death resulting from failure to supply food to a child can be the basis of an intentional homicide charge. (See, e.g., *Zessman v. State,* 573 P.2d 1174 [Nev. 1978]; *Harrington v. State,* 547 S.W.2d 616 [Tex. Crim. App. 1977].) Similarly, the failure to obtain medical attention for a child, an act of omission, can form the basis of an intentional homicide charge, as the New York Court of Appeals ruled in the highly publicized case of Lisa Steinberg. (See *People v. Steinberg,* 595 N.E.2d 845 [N.Y. 1992].) Intent is based on the failure to perform a duty imposed by law. The defendant's knowledge or awareness that a result will occur is only a factor for the jury to consider and not a prerequisite of intent. *Steinberg* notes that parents have a nondelegable affirmative duty to provide their children with adequate medical care by statute, and that the failure to fulfill that duty can form the basis of an intentional homicide charge.

2. Intent Based on Acts and Surrounding Circumstances

Intent can be inferred from the act itself as well as surrounding circumstances. For example, when a man forcibly immerses a baby in a tub filled with scalding water and holds a struggling and screaming infant in hot water long enough to cause second-degree burns over one third of the baby's body, the intent to cause serious injury is "glaring" and supports an intentional manslaughter charge. (See *People v. Hayes,* 577 N.E.2d 58 [N.Y. 1991]; *State v. Screpesi,* 611 A.2d 34 [Del. Super. Ct. 1991] [since defendant was alone with 7-week-old son when injury occurred and medical testimony established that broken femur was nonaccidental, jury could use circumstantial evidence to conclude that child's injuries were intentional].)

In some circumstances, an expert may testify that the injury was intentional, not accidentally inflicted. (See *Steggall v. State,* 340 Ark. 184 [2000]; *State v. Forsythe,* 1998 Wash. App. LEXIS 1028.) The expert's opinion may be that the injuries are consistent with trauma and not a fall. (*Porter v. State,* 823 S.W.2d 846 [Ark. 1992]; *Gideon v. State,* 721 P.2d 1336 [Okla. Crim. App. 1986] [allowing expert opinion that injuries occurred through nonaccidental means and injuries were inconsistent with the child falling off the bed].) However, at least one court has reversed a defendant's conviction because a medical expert testified that an infant's cause of death was the result of "homicidal suffocation" given such an opinion "improperly states a conclusion regarding defendant's intent." (*People v. Eberle,* 697 N.Y.S.2d 218 [1999].)

3. Intent Based on the Extent of the Injuries

The nature and extent of a child's injuries can also establish a defendant's intent or callous behavior. Argue, for example, that the nonlethal, nonfatal injuries show that the defendant could have stopped and did not. Each injury and blow is evidence of the defendant's desire to hurt the child.

4. The Defendant's Statements and Expert Opinion Based on the Defendant's Statements

Review every statement made by the defendant, not just those to the police, concerning the injury or death of the victim for possible introduction in your case-in-chief. One of the most crucial and easily overlooked sources of valuable evidence is testimony by emergency medical personnel or emergency room personnel who have information concerning the statements or behavior of the accused at the scene or hospital. Such testimony can establish a defendant's indifference that may be crucial to elevating the defendant's intent or level of criminal responsibility.

Because emergency medical personnel primarily chart only information that is essential to the patient's treatment, their observations of individuals at a scene might not be written in their records. If investigators have not already obtained this unwritten information, ask them to do so as soon as possible or, if appropriate, subpoena these witnesses before the grand jury to provide a full explanation of the events. At trial, ask emergency personnel to explain the significance of the history given by a caregiver to the care and treatment of the child. Omissions or misrepresentations by the defendant may also be important since the failure to describe critical symptoms could affect the medical response or treatment. If a delay occurred between the child's symptoms and the defendant's request for medical attention, ask emergency personnel whether delay is common and the effect of delay in treating the injury. This theme can be further developed through emergency room personnel who treated the child. During closing argument, you can then argue the defendant's callousness by his failure to seek help that would have reduced the severity of the child's injuries or saved the child's life.

The defendant may have made statements that the acts were "to discipline" the child or to "teach the child a lesson." Witnesses who heard the defendant threaten the victim around the time the injuries were inflicted with such statements as, "I'm going to kill you," will help the State convincingly prove intent. Finally, threats and physical intimidation by a defendant toward a child's mother are admissible as consciousness of guilt and intent. (See *State v. Ruiz,* 892 P.2d 962 [N.M. 1995].)

Once the State presents the defendant's explanations to the jury, the medical expert can evaluate the explanation's plausibility through the use of a hypothetical question. (See *State v. Heath,* 957 P.2d 449 [Kan. 1998] [finding permissible a physician's opinion that deceased child's injuries were not consistent with defendant's statement to police]; *State v. Butterfield,* 874 P.2d 1339 [Or. 1994] [finding it acceptable that jury may infer from expert's opinion that defendant is not telling the truth].)

Patently implausible explanations and conflicting statements by the defendant can be used to infer an attempt to hide the actual conduct that caused the victim's injuries and indicate consciousness of guilt. (See *State v. Goble,* 560 N.Y.S.2d 553 [1990] [finding defendant's convictions supported by evidence where she was baby's primary caregiver, she gave numerous contradictory explanations, and stated that she "might as well take the blame" for child's injuries]; *People v. Gordon,* 738 P.2d 404 [Colo. Ct. App. 1987] [affirming convictions where defendant gave discrepant history].)

5. Evidence of the Child's Behavior and the Defendant's Reactions

Present evidence of the context in which the defendant's physical abuse or severe neglect of the child took place. Establish the nature of the relationship between the defendant and child through family members, neighbors, friends, and others. This will be of particular importance when the defense tries to argue reasonable discipline or accidental injury. It may also provide you with the motive for the defendant's loss of temper. Some of the areas to cover include:

- How often and for how long was the defendant responsible for caring for the child?
- What was the defendant's daily routine? Was he unemployed? Forced to take care of the victim for the first time? Uncomfortable dealing with an infant?
- Were there observed displays of anger, affection, or resentment by the defendant toward the child?
- Was the defendant patient or impatient with the child?
- Was the defendant responsible for discipline in the child's household? If not, who was, and did the defendant have permission to, and/or experience with, administering discipline? Is there any reason why the defendant was not allowed to discipline? Explosive temper? Unusual disciplinary measures? If so, what was the usual method of discipline, how often was it used and why, and did any other children in the household experience such discipline at the hands of the defendant?
- Did the child have any special needs, such as a disability or illness, requiring extra attention, effort, or patience? When did the child first need extra attention, effort, or patience from the defendant? If so, how did the defendant react?
- Did the child present behavior problems such as being colicky or having difficulty with toilet training? If so, how did the defendant deal with these problems?
- Was the child clumsy or accident-prone? Who thought so? The defendant? Others?
- Did the child show signs of injury or difficulty prior to being left alone with the defendant?
- Did the defendant have any previous experience caring for children, and if so, what was it?
- Had the defendant talked about the child previously, and if so, how was the child described?
- Were other witnesses aware of any cultural practices of the defendant that could account for the behavior toward the child?
- Did the defendant treat the child the same or differently from other children in the household?
- Was the child the result of a planned or unwanted pregnancy? Was abortion or adoption contemplated?

Explain to the jury why, in some situations, the defendant injured only one child. During your closing argument, ask the jury to draw common sense inferences from the evidence in your case-in-chief. Use the defendant's statements to others regarding his relationship with the victim to establish any animosity the defendant feels toward the victim. The injured child may not be the defendant's natural child or may remind the defendant of the child's other parent.

Another way of establishing the defendant's awareness of and conscious disregard for the risk of injury to the child is to present testimony from medical professionals who may have advised the defendant about the difficulties in raising children or risks presented by the child's behaviors, and the steps the parent could take to deal with those risks. For example, a parent may have been advised of different techniques for dealing with stressful situations, such as leaving the room, calling a friend, or asking someone else to help with the child. This testimony may come from a physician who had counseled the family or from professionals who provided the defendant with parent education classes as a result of prior interactions with the child welfare system.

6. Dealing With Reasonable Discipline Claims and Intent

Prosecutors must consider community standards as well as their own judgment about what constitutes criminal conduct. The attitude and experience of jurors regarding physical discipline should be apparent from *voir dire*. If the child suffered severe injury or death, argue that no matter what the motive, the conduct was inappropriate and reasonable discipline should not be available as a defense. (See, e.g., *People v. Mincey*, 827 P.2d 388 [Cal. 1992], *cert. denied*, 506 U.S. 1014 [1992] [finding defendant's claims that his acts leading to death of 5-year-old child constitute misguided attempt at discipline was factually based argument directed at negating element of intent and was not a legal defense to murder].) For the most part, the defendant, an adult, will be far superior to the child in physical strength and size. The greater the disparity in the defendant's and victim's relative size, strength, age, intelligence, and communication skills, the more likely the use of force may not be seen as a reasonable effort to discipline the child. The following areas can be explored to argue that the defendant's behavior could not be considered reasonable discipline.

Placement of the Injury. Evaluate the location of the injury. For example, injury to a child's face rather than buttocks will undermine the defense assertion that the injury was appropriate discipline. Head injuries and certain bone fractures, such as a fractured femur, are usually caused by abuse, not discipline. The more vulnerable the location of the injury, the less likely it was caused by thoughtful, measured doses of parental discipline.

Instrument Used. Evaluate the instrument used to inflict the injury. Did the defendant use an open hand or a fist? A board with nails protruding from it? Many people view the use of a foreign object in disciplining a child as unreasonable. Some instruments leave impressions, often referred to as pattern injuries, on the body of a child. Physicians can sometimes identify the instrument used based on the pattern on the child's body. Make sure the police recover the instrument that was used and present it as an exhibit at trial. Determine whether the victim is afraid of the instrument and whether the instrument was used to abuse other individuals such as the spouse or siblings.

Repetitive Nature of Conduct. If the defendant hit the child repeatedly, argue that the repetitive nature of the blows differentiates the charged conduct from reasonable disciplinary measures. For example, striking a child once may be discipline, but striking a child multiple times may be abuse. However, the prosecutor should also recognize that one blow, when combined with other factors, may render the conduct criminal.

Prior Injury to the Child and Other Children. Evidence of prior injuries inflicted by the defendant on the victim or other children may undermine a defense of reasonable discipline. Evaluate the nature of the conduct of the defendant; the purported reason for beatings, blows, or other physical force; and the nature of the injuries inflicted. Argue that such a pattern shows a deliberate use of force to inflict harm by the defendant.

Reason Offered by Defendant. Evaluate any reason offered by the defendant for his conduct. Was the defendant's response commensurate with the situation? Is it appropriate to hit a young child because she opened a detergent bottle? Is it appropriate to hit or kick a child repeatedly for coming home 5 minutes late, eating the cat's food, crying, or for other behavior? Did the defendant's explanation match the child's explanation for the defendant's conduct? Sensitivity to community standards and cultural differences will influence your charging decisions, trial strategy, and final arguments.

Amount of Force Used. Even when the defendant inflicted only one blow, the degree of force may make it clear that this was not reasonable discipline. In closing argument, point out that although there may have been a single blow, it was delivered with an adult's fast-moving fist to a vulnerable area of the child's face, abdomen, lower back, or genitals.

The Defendant's Statements at the Time. Remind the jury of the defendant's explanations when the assault was discovered. Did he tell the child not to tell anyone? Did he tell her he was going to kill her?

Cultural Factors. If the defendant asserts that the charged conduct is reasonable in light of his cultural background, talk to others of the same background. If they indicate that the conduct is not acceptable, call a respected community leader or a sociologist to testify to that fact. Find out if the defendant hid his conduct from other members of the cultural community or anyone else. Has he said or done anything that indicates that he recognized that the community or culture in which he has chosen to live does not approve of the behavior? A defendant who tells the child not to reveal the physical abuse or to wear clothing that conceals the injuries clearly indicates knowledge that the community would not accept the mode of discipline.

Determine whether the defendant followed practices inconsistent with his assertion of a cultural belief, indicating that he, in fact, is not an adherent to general cultural norms. For example, could the defendant, consistent with cultural practice, have chosen to bring the child to a leader of the group for instruction?

Religious Beliefs. Biblical admonishments such as "spare the rod, spoil the child" do not extend to punishment that causes serious injury or death. Determine what the defendant's religious community advocates concerning appropriate parental discipline and demonstrate through witnesses of the same faith the criminal nature of the defendant's actions. Note that religious defenses are often offered in criminal neglect cases when the defendant has failed to seek medical help for a sick child who subsequently dies or is severely impaired.

7. Delay in Seeking Care

Any delay by the defendant in seeking care for the injured child is potentially relevant and useful to prove his intent. If the case involves a genuine accident, the reasonable response would be to seek help for the child immediately. Be alert for indications that the defendant is not being truthful about how soon he called for assistance. Often, a defendant will let time pass, hoping the child will recover and not show obvious signs of the assault, and then desperately summon aid when he realizes that the child is *not* recovering or is getting worse.

Also, consider how the delay in obtaining medical attention illustrates the defendant's intent, recklessness, cruelty, or depravity. Could this child get help or give an accurate history without help? Argue that the child was essentially defenseless in the situation presented and the defendant's behavior was an abuse of power. Only the defendant was in a position to seek help for the child, since the child was not physically or verbally able to communicate the need for help. Argue that the defendant, as an adult, was responsible for the child, who was in distress. Sometimes the defendant will delay seeking medical care, preferring instead to treat the child at home. Be prepared to present expert testimony that the delay in seeking proper medical care increased the chances of serious physical injury, lessened the chance of survival, or increased the likelihood of death.

A defendant with previous experience in child rearing should know how to care for a child and be aware of a child's needs, vulnerabilities, and the demands of parenthood more than a first-time, adolescent parent. The defendant may have received instruction or direction on dealing with the particular problem, such as colic, presented by the child. This knowledge can be used during closing argument to overcome arguments of the defendant being overwhelmed and not certain how to respond to a situation.

8. Prior Injury/Abuse of the Child or Others

An expert should review the child's medical records to determine the existence of prior injuries. A skeletal survey may be important to locate fractures at various stages of healing. Evidence of old injuries in various stages of healing helps establish the defendant's intent to injure and undermine an argument that the current injury was accidental or caused by a preexisting condition. Similarly, investigate and present when admissible evidence of prior injuries to other children in the defendant's care. Prior injuries to the victim or to other children may be admissible to show the defendant's intent, lack of mistake or accident, motive, or plan. Prior injuries may also be relevant to establish the depravity or malice element of a homicide charge. (See, e.g., *United States v. Boise*, 916 F.2d 497, 502 [9th Cir. 1990]; *People v. Biggs*, 509 N.W.2d 803 [Mich. 1993].)

When considering any previous or old injuries, pay particular attention to your jurisdiction's law concerning connecting the defendant with any previous or old injuries. Some courts may view prior injuries as prior bad act evidence and require "sufficient evidence for a jury to reasonably conclude that the defendant was the actor." (See *Huddleston v. United States*, 485 U.S. 681, 689 [1988].) *Huddleston* states that prior bad acts of a defendant should be established by a preponderance of evidence standard under Rule 104(b). There is increasing authority that evidence of a child's prior or old injuries is not admissible against a defendant unless connected to the defendant by clear and convincing evidence. (See, e.g., Neb. Rev. Stat. § 27–404[3] [prosecution must establish by clear and convincing evidence that defendant committed any prior bad act or crime]; *State v. Prieur*, 277 So. 2d 126 [La. 1973] [holding that State should demonstrate by clear and convincing evidence that defendant committed the other crimes]; *State v. Guyette*, 658 A.2d 1204 [N.H.

1995] [finding trial court erred in admitting evidence of child's prior injuries that could not be connected to the defendant and in admitting testimony concerning battered child syndrome]; *State v. Cutro*, 504 S.E.2d 324 [S.C. 1998]; *State v. Pierce*, 485 S.E.2d 913 [S.C. 1997] [reversing defendant's child homicide conviction owing to prosecution's failure to establish by clear and convincing evidence that deceased child's previous injuries were inflicted by the defendant].)

Some jurisdictions allow the evidence connecting the defendant to the prior injuries to be circumstantial and based on a jury's credibility determination. (See *Clemens v. State*, 610 N.E.2d 236, 242 [Ind. 1993] [holding that there must be "sufficient evidence" to support a finding that the defendant inflicted prior injuries upon the child, but proof may be circumstantial and not direct]; *Pavlick v. Commonwealth*, 497 S.E.2d 920 [Va. 1998] [finding the child's rib fractures sufficiently connected to defendant even though defendant's mother had access to the child, as the jury could believe her testimony that she had not struck the child]; *State v. Norlin*, 951 P.2d 1131 [Wash. 1998] [requiring that the child's prior injuries must be connected to the defendant by a preponderance of the evidence and finding that the defendant's role as prime caregiver and description of other incidents of the child falling while in his care, coupled with no evidence that anyone else was alone with child when incidents occurred, were sufficient to establish necessary connection].)

The introduction of testimony concerning prior injuries may require a limiting instruction. Of course, the defendant can be charged with inflicting the prior injuries when there is sufficient proof to connect the defendant to the injuries. The defendant could also be charged with neglect for allowing past injuries to be inflicted or allowing the child to become an abused or neglected child while the child was in the defendant's care. (See *State v. Delgado*, 707 A.2d 1 [Conn. 1998].)

9. Shopping Around for Medical Care

It is not unusual for abusive caregivers to "shop around" for medical care to treat a child's injuries so repeated visits to the same medical professional will not cause suspicion of abuse. A doctor who sees the child is more likely to accept the caregiver's explanation that an accident caused the injury if she is unaware of the child's many previous "accidents." Collecting evidence of shopping around for medical care may require subpoenas for various health care providers and hospitals to establish that the child was taken elsewhere. Remember that the child's primary pediatrician or health care provider may be unaware of other medical treatment sought by the defendant, and thus those treatments may not be included in those records. Sometimes this evidence can be obtained through insurance records. Be aware that the new HIPPA regulations may have some impact on this process.

10. Transferred Intent: The Cross-Fire Defense

A defendant may have inflicted unintentional harm on a child in the course of trying to hurt another person. The victim, for example, may be caught in the "crossfire" when the defendant throws an object at another adult but hits the child with it instead. Review the statutes in your jurisdiction: Check for crimes requiring a *mens rea* of recklessness or negligence and statutes involving transferred intent. Emphasize the factors that made injury to the child predictable or even inevitable:

prior injury to the child in a similar domestic fight; the location of the child in the arms of the adult under attack; the size of the object thrown; actions of the child directly prior to the defendant's conduct, such as running back and forth between the adults, thus making the child very vulnerable to inadvertent injury. (See, e.g., *State v. Cantua-Ramirez*, 718 P.2d 1030 [Ariz. 1986] [applying doctrine of transferred intent to "bad aim" situation where defendant intended to strike the baby's mother but actually struck the baby's face].)

F. Medical Evidence

Successful prosecution in a physical abuse case involves presenting not just some medical testimony, but often presenting medical testimony from multiple medical specialties. For example, the prosecution may have to call the following medical witnesses in a child fatality prosecution: the child's pediatrician to testify about the child's prior condition or health, the emergency room physician to testify about the importance of prompt medical attention and receiving an accurate history, the pediatric intensive care specialist who cared for the child prior to death, a radiologist to explain the significance of fractures in a child, a neurosurgeon to testify concerning the child's brain injury not only in terms of deceased children but also those children who survive and have been treated by the neurosurgeon, and the pathologist to testify as to the cause of death. Identifying the many physicians involved with a child's care and treatment may require a careful review of a hospital chart. Each of these physicians may also have had interaction with the defendant or the defendant's family and may be able to provide additional information such as statements and demeanor that was not charted.

Assessing which medical experts or specialties may be needed at trial may require a substantial investment of time. Meet with medical experts well in advance of trial, perhaps even before making a charging decision, to assess which factual, legal, or medical theories will be employed. Meeting with the different physicians may also reveal possible areas of conflict or gaps in their testimony that should be addressed at trial. It may be unwise, except in unusual circumstances, to rely on one medical expert to address different areas of medicine. A pathologist may be able to give a clear opinion as to the manner of death or rule out certain accidental causes for injuries, but a clinician experienced with child abuse victims or brain injury might be able to add another dimension to the medical testimony. Experts should be viewed as a team, each complementing and adding to the complete picture. Each expert should be aware of the other types of medical evidence that will be presented at trial.

It is becoming more common, probably because of heightened awareness and early detection of abuse, to encounter cases involving a single explosive incident that leads to serious injury or death. The injury often involves head or abdominal trauma. The prosecutor will be able to emphasize, through medical testimony, the type of physical act(s) necessary to inflict the injury and, if possible, the amount of force needed to inflict the injury. Physicians can contrast this child's injury with the many accidental injuries they have seen. Absent such testimony, the jury may be persuaded that the injury was a one-time accident when defense witnesses testify that the defendant is a great parent.

If the victim has multiple injuries of varying ages or to multiple organ systems, the examining doctor or expert should be able to testify that the child was diagnosed with battered child syndrome. (See Appendixes Chapter V.) These cases can be horrifying and present convincing evidence with which to convict defendants. The challenge in these cases is to place the child in the defendant's control at the time the injuries occurred.

The most frequent serious injuries in young children are head and abdominal injuries. Broken bones and bruises are also common. (See Chapter II, Section IX.C for descriptions of injuries often seen in physical abuse cases.) The physician who examines the child must be able to state that those injuries are consistent with abuse and inconsistent with the accidental injury explanation proffered. Long before trial, the prosecutor should meet with the examining physician and assess that doctor's potential strength as a witness. Physicians often do not like to make the firm statements prosecutors would prefer or may lack the training, expertise, or knowledge to do so. Consult experts from a larger community and have the experts consult with the local physician. Both physicians should be called to testify.

1. The Treating Physician

When presenting medical testimony, the prosecutor should consider first calling the treating physician who saw the child at the hospital. Be aware of this doctor's level of expertise. An intern or resident may have seen the child first. If this is the case, the prosecutor may decide to call the treating doctor as a fact witness only. Even if the treating physician is not qualified as an expert, spend some time having the physician describe her experience with child abuse cases to enhance the testimony and give the jury an idea of the broad scope of child abuse. The physician, if possible, should establish who brought the child to the hospital, how the child was dressed, what history was given, and whether this history was consistent with the observed injury. Use any photos of the injuries. If there are no photos, have the doctor locate the injuries on a diagram. If the victim is very young, the physician could point out the location of the injuries on a doll. Establish any medical history of suspicious injuries. The doctor should describe her actions: notified CPS or law enforcement authorities, ordered a more complete set of medical X-rays such as a full skeletal exam, consulted the local physician's child abuse team or expert, or all of the above. Ask *why* the action was taken. Any of these actions imparts a sense of seriousness to the jury.

2. Paramedics and Nurses as Experts

Paramedics and nurses can be experts on certain issues in child abuse cases as long as these issues are within their area of training and expertise. (See, e.g., *State v. Candela*, 929 S.W.2d 852 [(Mo. Ct. App. 1996]; *State v. White*, 467 S.E.2d 841 [N.C. 1995].) For example, a paramedic might be asked the importance of an accurate history or the effect of a delay in treatment for a particular child. However, do not ask for an opinion outside the witness's expertise. (See, e.g., *People v. Davis*, 620 N.Y.S.2d 20 [1994] [finding EMT was not qualified to give opinion on time of death].)

3. The Pathologist

The pathologist who conducts the postmortem examination of the child homicide victim is usually the "eyewitness" to the child's death. The importance of medical testimony and findings in child homicide cases requires that findings be adequately documented and preserved. Sometimes a second doctor can be helpful. When a second pathologist is unavailable for the actual autopsy, prosecutors should consider a second qualified physician to review the initial autopsy report for further suggestions. This second expert is then available as an additional witness at trial. If two pathologists are used, make sure they work as a team to avoid the risk of possible conflicting opinions.

Since bruising is not always readily observable before or at the time of death, it is helpful to hold the body in the morgue for 48–72 hours to determine if further bruising becomes apparent. This also allows adequate opportunity for X-rays and radiologic studies to be interpreted by pediatric radiologists and other experts to determine if any further examination is required of the body for fractures or other findings. Photographs should be taken as soon as the child is discovered and later at the autopsy to document any change in injuries such as bruising. If a proper autopsy was not done or evidence such as hair was not properly preserved, exhumation may be required. Most jurisdictions permit the family of a deceased relative to disinter a body for further medical examination without any legal intervention. However, if the family of the deceased does not consent to disinterment of the body, a court order is essential.

With children, the mouth and eyes present the more likely areas of physical findings. Many murdered infants have died of head trauma. Bruising to the scalp, not visible before death, may be identified only at autopsy, after the scalp is reflected back. Retinal hemorrhages occur in approximately three quarters of children who suffer severe shaking injuries. (Smith, W. L. [1994]. Abusive head injury. *APSAC Advisor, 7,* 16.) In addition to retinal hemorrhages, other injuries often associated with shaken baby syndrome include retinal detachments, vitreous hemorrhages, or optic nerve sheath hemorrhages. Eye injuries may be associated with subdural hematomas and result from the violent shaking of a child. The inner lips may show evidence of bruising caused by impact with the teeth. The frenulum (the thin tissue that connects gum to the lips) may be torn by a blow to the mouth and is considered a significant finding suggesting child abuse when found with other factors. The tongue may also show injury caused by violent contact with teeth during a blow to the mouth. The extent of bruising can be seen under the skin when the pathologist cuts through the child's skin during the autopsy. In framing the time of death in a child homicide case, it may be helpful to observe the deceased's stomach contents and compare them with the factual information concerning the child's last meal to present expert testimony concerning the time of death.

4. The Victim's Medical History

To deal with the suggestion that the child had a preexisting medical condition that led to injury or death, present the child's medical history as part of the prosecution's case-in-chief. This can be done by first obtaining all of the child's previous medical records to offer as an exhibit together with direct testimony about the victim's prior physical condition. The medical expert should then review them for the jury and indicate their significance regarding the expert's opinion about cause of the injury or death.

The victim's pediatric records may be spread among several health care providers, including institutional care, schools, health care agencies, or clinics. Such records should be reviewed for evidence of disposition and any physical conditions or disabilities that make the child more vulnerable to abuse. They may also establish baseline medical data for a medical expert. When sudden infant death syndrome (SIDS) is raised as a defense, it is essential to review the mother's prenatal care records as well as all birth records of mother and child or siblings of the child. Have the medical expert testify whether there were problems at birth or abnormally low Apgar scores that might lend support to an argument that the child died from respiratory failure. Note, however, that many SIDS deaths are not associated with any respiratory or other abnormalities in the infant. Except for the infant who was killed by suffocation, SIDS should not be an arguable defense.

Photographs of the child when healthy are helpful to both the physician and the jury. These pictures can show that the child was free of injury shortly before death or at some other relevant time. They may provide other information critical to the doctor's diagnosis or evaluation of a defendant's explanation. Earlier photographs of the child may be particularly helpful in starvation cases. Likewise, videos of a child will demonstrate motor skills that may assist in analyzing whether the suspect's history of what happened to the child is consistent with the child's developmental level.

5. The Age and Timing of the Victim's Injuries

Use medical experts to date the victim's injuries insofar as they can. Previously taken photographs can help the medical expert time the injury. For example, a subpoena was used in one case to obtain the family court records of a child and his mother in a paternity file. This subpoena produced a photograph of the child taken just days before fatal injuries were inflicted to his head. It revealed no injuries to the face and head that were seen just a few days later upon his arrival in the emergency room. This helps establish that the child was free of injury shortly before his death. Other photographs of the child may be obtained from a nonoffending caregiver or through a search warrant. These photographs may show bruising or injury to the child and may be used in questioning the defendant. In some situations, photo-processing codes may also indicate approximately when a photograph was taken.

Sometimes injuries can be dated in the form of a hypothetical question to the expert. This is essential to provide the window of time during which the injuries had to have occurred. However, a doctor's ability to date bruises, fractures, subdural hematomas, and other injuries, based solely on findings, is somewhat imprecise. Objective medical data rarely can be used to time an injury. For example, a doctor can distinguish between a fracture that is less than 10 days old and one that is weeks old but cannot make distinctions between yesterday and the day before radiographically. Only a physician with training or experience should be asked to date the injuries. For example, the primary care physician may not have any experience reading skeletal surveys or CT scans. For an excellent book discussing the medical aspects of radiology and child abuse, see Paul Kleinman, *Diagnostic Imaging of Child Abuse* (St. Louis, MO: Mosby, 1987). (See also Schwartz, A. J., & Ricci, L. R. [1996]. How accurately can bruises be aged in abused children? *Pediatrics, 97,* 254.)

In many instances, the clinical history of when the child was last observed to be well can be used to support an argument that a serious or fatal injury had not yet occurred. Have the medical experts testify regarding the explanation offered about the child's alleged behavior to determine when the injury occurred. For example, it is logical to assume that a 1-year-old with a femur fracture must have been injured during the 1-hour time period between when the defendant indicated that the child had been playing in the backyard and when the child suddenly could not bear weight on his right leg. Or, if the defendant indicated that the child seemed fine and then started to have seizures, ask the medical expert when the injury was inflicted, given that description of symptoms. Compare the medical expert's opinion about the timing, age, and number of injuries with the defendant's version of events. Any discrepancies will cast serious doubt on the defendant's account.

6. The Possibility of Self-Inflicted Injury

Make sure the medical experts eliminate the possibility that the victim caused the injuries herself. How does the observed injury compare to the physician's experience and training with self-inflicted injuries by a child? Emphasize that the developmental stage of the victim is inconsistent with the ability to inflict the type of injury suffered. Ask about this explanation in advance of trial. Once on the witness stand, have the expert explain the impossibility of self-inflicted injuries in simple, clear language.

7. The Degree of Force

Ask the medical experts for an opinion regarding the degree of force needed to cause the victim's external and internal injuries. It may be difficult to quantify the amount of force required for such injuries. However, analogies to events the jurors can understand, such as auto accidents or falls, can be effective. If the doctor is unable to describe the amount of force used to cause an injury, at least ask for an opinion about the reasonableness of the defendant's explanation and amount of force he describes. If the defendant says the child climbed or rolled off an object, ask the medical expert if such activity is within the child's developmental capacity and whether it would generate the force necessary to cause the injuries. Ask the physician what injuries would be expected from the mechanism of trauma described by the caregiver. Relate this back to what is known about common, accidental childhood injuries. Multiple nonfatal injuries to the child are also helpful to gauge the force, level of recklessness, negligence, or depravity of the defendant's conduct toward a deceased child. A diagram of all injuries—fatal and nonfatal—will make the medical testimony more meaningful and powerful.

8. The Mechanism of Injury

Ask the medical expert for an opinion regarding the possible mechanism of injury. This testimony can be presented in the form of a demonstration. Always have the expert acknowledge whether there is more than one causal possibility and include nonaccidental infliction by an adult as one of those possibilities. If the other causes offered by the defendant are highly unlikely or unsupported by any other history or evidence in the case, you may wish to have the expert so indicate. For example, "In my experience I have never encountered such a case, nor have I seen it documented in any medical journal," or "There was nothing in the history I received or the records I reviewed that would support that possibility in this case." For children with multiple injuries, the expert's testimony should stress that although each *isolated* injury may be explained by a proposed accidental mechanism, all the injuries must be considered together in order to reach the correct diagnosis, and that in this particular case, the totality of the injuries leads only to the diagnosis of child abuse. Review the treatment of the child with the expert, including emergency care at the scene, in the ambulance, and at the hospital to rule out the possibility that the cause of injury or death was the resuscitative or emergency treatment of the child.

9. Battered Child Syndrome

Determine with your medical experts whether the victim suffered from battered child syndrome (BCS). BCS describes a collection of old and new symptoms and injuries widely recognized in the medical community as indicative of nonaccidental injury in children. It is a recognized medical diagnosis. Prior injuries to the victim may be admissible in your case-in-chief to assist in establishing BCS. Make sure the experts emphasize any repeated injuries. Note that the definition of BCS may vary, as some experts use the term to describe children with single, severe injuries, while others reserve the diagnosis for cases involving repeated and severe beatings. BCS has traditionally involved a child under 3 years of age, with some children showing evidence of neglect. See C. Henry Kempe's landmark article, "The Battered-Child Syndrome," ([1962]. *Journal of the American Medical Association, 181,* 17; [1984] *Journal of the American Medical Association, 251,* 3288), for a thorough discussion of these symptoms.

Although the admissibility of expert testimony on this subject is relatively well established, expect the defense to challenge any attempt to identify, through a medical expert, the defendant as the person who caused the injuries, especially old injuries. Many courts require the defendant to be connected to prior injuries by clear and convincing evidence, and the failure to do so will result in a reversal of a defendant's conviction. Furthermore, a limiting instruction may be required on the jury's use of the evidence regarding the prior injuries. The instruction should indicate that prior injuries are offered to help the jury determine if the fatal injury was accidentally inflicted. The instruction must ensure that the jury does not view evidence of prior injuries as propensity evidence or evidence of defendant's bad character. (See, e.g., *State v. Moorman,* 670 A.2d 81 [N.J. 1996].) Because evidence of the child's prior injuries may be admissible, even if not connected with the defendant, caution the doctor not to mention the defendant as the cause of the injuries.

Expert medical testimony regarding the cause of a child victim's injury will still be admissible even if it does not precisely fit BCS. BCS's signs and symptoms are less common in children than are other episodic injuries. Even if several old and recent injuries cannot be deemed evidence of BCS, the injuries may still be explained by an expert to show a history of nonaccidental intentional injury. Courts generally permit medical examiners, pathologists, radiologists, and other doctors to testify regarding the manner of a victim's injuries, whether accidental or intentional. (See, e.g., *People v. Peters,* 586 N.E.2d 469 [Ill. 1991] [allowing medical examiner to render an opinion on whether an infant's injuries were the result of intentional, ongoing abuse based on experience in conducting over 1,500 autopsies, 200 on children under 2 years of age]; *State v. Crawford*, 406 S.E.2d 579 [N.C. 1991] [finding that an expert in pediatric care qualified to testify that a 6-year-old boy would not voluntarily drink such a large quantity of water in a case where the child died of water intoxication]; *State v. Dufrene*, 461 So. 2d 1263 [La. Ct. App. 1984] [permitting doctor to testify as to her opinion on cause of a child's injury based on the type of injury and the age of the child]; *State v. Applegate*, 668 S.W.2d 624 [Mo. Ct. App. 1984] [allowing expert testimony, when corroborated by other evidence, regarding what could and could not have caused abundant external and internal injuries to the child victim, including testimony on the actual cause]; *Bell v. State*, 435 So. 2d 772 [Ala. Crim. App. 1983] [permitting forensic pathologist to testify that injuries were the result of intentional acts based on experience both as a father and a forensic pathologist who had examined many infant deaths, the infant's medical history, the pattern of bruises, and the extent of the child's injuries].) See Appendixes V.14 and V.26 for trial transcripts of expert testimony about the cause of injuries in physical abuse and child homicide cases.

Some prosecutors prefer not to label a victim's injuries as the result of BCS in case the defense raises the argument that the injuries to the victim do not precisely "fit" the syndrome. Instead, medical experts testify as to the nonaccidental nature of the repeated injuries. The prosecutor then argues during closing that this pattern supports the conclusion that the current injury is also nonaccidental.

10. Battering Parent Profile

Experienced prosecutors in child physical abuse and homicide cases frequently conclude that the mother's boyfriend, who was jobless and was left to care for the child, frequently commits the majority of these crimes. This profile, or any similar evidence suggesting that a particular type of defendant is more or less likely to abuse a child, is not admissible evidence in most jurisdictions, regardless of whether it is the State or defense offering the evidence. (See, e.g., *Hoosier v. State*, 612 So. 2d 1352 [Ala. Crim. App. 1992] [finding evidence that the defendant did not fit so-called battering parent profile to be inadmissible]; *People v. Walkey*, 223 Cal. Rptr. 132 [Cal. Ct. App. 1986] [excluding evidence regarding battering parent syndrome because it tends to associate defendant with a group of people who are often abusers, even when expert does not assert that defendant fits profile]; *Sanders v. State*, 303 S.E.2d 13 [Ga. 1983] [deeming battering parent syndrome inadmissible unless the defendant places his character in issue or raises a defense that syndrome can rebut]; *State v. Cheeks*, 853 P.2d 655 [Kan. 1993] [holding prosecution expert discussion of behavioral triggers leading to physical abuse to be improper]; *Duley v. State*, 467 A.2d 776 [Md. App. 1983] [finding child battering profile testimony irrelevant]; *State v. Conlogue*, 474 A.2d 167 [Me. 1984]; *Commonwealth v. Day*, 569 N.E.2d 397 [Mass. 1991]; *State v. Wilkerson*, 247 S.E.2d 905, 911 [N.C. 1978] [rejecting testimony that the victim's injuries, consistent with BCS, were, "in fact, caused by any particular person or class of person"]; *People v. Neer*, 513 N.Y.S.2d 566 [1987]; *State v. Steward*, 660 P.2d 278 [Wash. Ct. App. 1983] [finding error to admit expert testimony that in 18 of 36 serious physical abuse cases the mother's boyfriend was the perpetrator].) It must be remembered that the natural parent may well commit physical abuse and child homicide. Do not focus on one individual too early in the investigation. Carefully evaluate evidence concerning all those who had access to the child during the period in which the injuries were inflicted.

11. Shaken Baby Syndrome/Shaken Impact Syndrome

Shaken baby syndrome (SBS), or shaken impact syndrome (SIS) as it is sometimes referred to, results from the violent shaking of an infant, causing the head to whip back and forth. The action can produce brain injuries, often accompanied by sub-dural or subarachnoid hematomas and retinal hemorrhaging. In some cases, the shaking is coupled with an impact injury when the child is thrown or banged against a surface during or after the shaking. Even with an impact to the head, there may be no observable external injury. The lack of external injury does not rule out that the child was thrown, struck, or hit. The acceleration-deceleration movement of the child's unsupported head tears the vessels of the brain, causing bleeding in and around the eyes and brain. Infants under 1 year of age are particularly vulnerable because of their small size, relatively large head, weak neck muscles, and the frequency with which they cry. Expert testimony regarding whether a child suffered from SBS is generally admissible. Courts generally find that testimony about SBS is acceptable and reliable when presented by a qualified expert. (See *State v. McClary*, 541 A.2d 96 [Conn. 1988]; *State v. Compton*, 701 A.2d 468 [N.J. Super. 1997].).

SBS/SIS has become easier to detect through the use of CT scans and magnetic resonance imaging (MRI). The injuries from SBS/SIS typically include subdural hemorrhage, brain injury, and retinal hemorrhage. (See Duhaime, A. C., et al. [1998]. Nonaccidental head injury in infants: The "shaken baby syndrome." *New England Journal of Medicine, 338,* 1822.) Skeletal injuries may or may not be present. Although retinal hemorrhages are highly correlated with child abuse, they are not independently diagnostic of abuse. However, severe hemorrhages, particularly those with retinal folds or detachments, are typically seen with severe trauma and are virtually diagnostic of injury in the infant. (See Levin, A. [1990]. Ocular manifestations of child abuse. *Journal of Ophthalmology Clinics of North America, 3,* 249; Massicotte, S. J., et al. [1991]. Vitreoretinal traction and perimacular retinal folds in the eyes of deliberately traumatized children. *Ophthalmology, 98,* 1124; Buys, Y. B., et al. [1992]. Retinal findings after head trauma in infants and young children. *Ophthalmology, 99,* 1718.)

Some forensic experts believe that shaking alone does not produce death or severe injury without some blunt trauma from throwing the baby against a surface. (See Dimaio, D., & Dimaio, V. [1989]. *Forensic pathology,* p. 323; Duhaime, A. C., et al. [1987]. The shaken baby syndrome: A clinical, pathological, and biomechanical study. *Journal of Neurosurgery, 66,* 409; see also Dykes, L. J. [1996]. The whiplash shaken infant syndrome: What has been learned? *Child Abuse & Neglect, 10,* 211; Alexander, R. C., et al. [1990]. Incident of impact trauma with cranial injuries ascribed to shaking. *American Journal of Diseases of Children, 114,* 724.) A good interview of the suspect and a careful review of medical evidence will help develop evidence of impact, but do not get sidetracked into a debate over whether shaking alone will be sufficient to produce the injuries in a given child. One article notes that "whether shaking or impact occurred is less critical than concentrating on the presence of lethal inflicted head trauma." (Krous, H. F., & Byard, R. W. [1999]. Shaken infant syndrome: Selected controversies. *Pediatric Developmental Pathology, 2,* 497.) Accordingly, focus on charging and proving the lethal inflicted head trauma rather than establishing that the defendant shook, threw, banged, or struck the child.

Despite the arguments that the shaking must have been accompanied by a blunt force injury, recent studies document the ability of experts to diagnose SBS/SIS when there are retinal hemorrhages and no other adequate explanations. (See Levin, A. [1990]. Ocular manifestations of child abuse. *Journal of Ophthalmology Clinics of North America, 3*, 249; Massicote, S. J., et al. [1991]. Vitreoretinal traction and perimacular retinal folds in the eyes of deliberately traumatized children. *Ophthalmology, 98*, 1124; Buys, Y. M., et al. [1992]. Retinal findings after head trauma in infants and young children. *Ophthalmology, 99*, 1718.)

Some defendants will argue that most individuals are unaware of the dangers of shaking a child so the defendant did not realize the potential consequences. Thus, the defendant will argue that in fact the child did suffer from SBS and this was the result of efforts to revive the child or the result of "innocent" shaking. (*People v. Holmes*, 616 N.E.2d 1000 [Ill. 1993] [reversing defendant's murder conviction based upon insufficient proof that the defendant knew his actions would cause death or serious bodily harm in light of defendant's limited education and testimony that he did not know shaking would kill a child].) In fact, some jurisdictions permit a defendant to present expert testimony that most individuals are not aware of the harm caused by shaking a child to support a defense of SBS. (See e.g., *United States v. Gaskell*, 985 F.2d 1056 [11th Cir. 1993].)

However, other courts have found that a defendant's *mens rea* or intent to cause injury by shaking a baby or afflicting the lethal head trauma can be inferred from the force required to sustain the child's injuries. (*Steggall v. State*, 340 Ark. 184 [2000] [finding evidence of the child's other injuries in a shaken baby case helpful to establish that the defendant acted in a knowing manner]; *People v. Coleman*, 311 Ill. App.3d 467 [2000] [holding that jury "could infer from the numerous, severe, and fatal injuries . . . that defendant knew that his actions created a strong probability of death or great bodily harm"]; *People v. Ripley*, 685 N.W.2d 362 [Ill. 1997] [finding the severity of the child's injuries inconsistent with the defendant's claimed lack of *mens rea*]; *Cunn v. Stat*, 2000 Tex. App. LEXIS 518 [finding that the defendant's intent could be inferred from injuries of the child, who died as a result of blunt force trauma and SBS].)

In responding to a lack-of-knowledge defense, look for evidence of prior injury or abuse that shows the shaking is not an isolated act. There is research suggesting that shaking is usually not an isolated event by the perpetrator. (Alexander, R. C., et al. [1990]. Serial abuse in children who are shaken. *American Journal of Diseases of Children, 144*, 58 [noting that 58% of shaken babies had evidence of prior abuse and 33% had been previously shaken, corresponding to the 33% recidivism rate reported for child abuse in Iowa].) Another response to the argument that the defendant was unaware of the consequences of his actions of shaking is to show the information, instructions, or guidance provided to the defendant such as in parenting classes. Testimony concerning a defendant's prior parenting classes may be relevant to the element of recklessness and the awareness of a known risk. (*Cf. People v. Kenny*, 175 A.D.2d 404 [3d Dept. 1991] [finding evidence of defendant's prior drinking and driving course relevant to the issue of defendant's recklessness in a DWI manslaughter prosecution].)

Examine carefully the suspect's account of what happened to see if it is consistent with the medical findings. Emphasize the degree of force required to inflict the severe injury. Consider having the medical expert demonstrate, with a doll, the type and severity of shaking required to injure or kill a baby. Some courts have found it appropriate for a physician to describe that the force applied to a child is beyond what a normal person would use and what a simple shake can produce. (*People v. Rader*, 651 N.E.2d 258 [Ill. Ct. App. 1995].) Have the expert explain that the injuries seen in the shaken child or child with substantial head trauma are those usually seen in severe motor vehicle accidents or falls from several stories. (See, e.g., Billmire, M. E., & Myers, P. A. [1985]. Serious head injury in infants: Accident or abuse? *Pediatrics, 75,* 342; Smith, W. L. [1994]. Abusive head injury. *APSAC Advisor, 7*(4), 18; Monteleone, J. A., & Brodeur, A. E. [1994]. *Child maltreatment: A clinical guide and reference* [p. 12] St. Louis: Mosby.). If the victim had bruises from the perpetrator's fingers, show where they were placed and exactly how the perpetrator held the victim. The nature of injuries, as well as force applied, suggests inflicted, not accidental, injury.

12. The Lack of External Injury to the Child

Most jurors will find it hard to believe that a severely injured child may have little or no external injuries. Have your expert carefully explain how a brain can be severely damaged without obvious external signs. Use autopsy photographs to show the extent of internal injuries. In a highly regarded textbook on forensic pathology, the author emphasizes a principle that even the defense expert should acknowledge:

> Sufficiently important to justify repetition is the generalization that absence of external traumata does *not* preclude the presence of grave internal injuries. The most common form of "concealed" fatal trauma, whether it involves the head, neck, chest or abdomen, is that caused by blunt force . . . the pathologist must be aware of the frequently encountered combination of minor or absent external injuries associated with internal traumata of sufficient gravity to be fatal. (Adelson, L. [1974]. *The pathology of homicide* [p. 381]. Springfield, IL: Charles C Thomas.)

13. Tin Ear Syndrome

Tin ear syndrome (a term borrowed from boxing) involves trauma to the sides of the head, particularly the ear. The term "tin ear syndrome" describes the clinical triad of unilateral ear bruising, ipsilateral (located on or affecting the same side of the body) subdural hemorrhage with cerebral edema, and retinal hemorrhage. Subdural hemorrhage is found at autopsy. Blows to the ear produce bleeding under the cartilage. These injuries are due to a blunt injury to the side of the head, resulting in rotational acceleration of the head. In other words, the child's head is violently moved from side to side. A medical examination of a child suffering from this syndrome would reveal bruising on the ear, CT radiographic evidence of subdural hematoma with severe cerebral (brain) swelling, and retinal hemorrhaging. Make sure the medical expert explains tin ear syndrome using a model of a child's head or other device to show the amount of force needed to produce such trauma. According to current research, a child will not survive if he experiences such injuries. (See Hanigan, W. C., et al. [1987]. Tin ear syndrome: Rotational acceleration in pediatric head injuries. *Pediatrics, 80,* 618.) This syndrome is more rare than SBS/SIS.

14. Sudden Infant Death Syndrome (SIDS)

SIDS is a term used to describe the sudden unexplained death of an infant under 12 months of age, most commonly under 6 months, that remains unexplained after a full autopsy and review of both the death scene and the family history. The majority of infants who die of SIDS (or from an unknown cause) have died a natural death that has nothing to do with child abuse. In some cases, however, intentional suffocation can be confused with SIDS, as the autopsy of a suffocated child is usually normal. (See Meadow, R. [1990]. Suffocation, recurrent apnea, and sudden infant death. *Journal of Pediatrics, 117,* 351; Southall, D. P., et al. [1997]. Covert video surveillance for life-threatening child abuse. *Pediatrics, 100,* 735.)

Remember that SIDS is a diagnosis of exclusion. It is stating that no cause of death has been found. Some pathologists utilize the designation of sudden undetermined death syndrome when they have been unable to determine the cause of a child's death. In recent years, many prosecutors have aggressively investigated cases involving multiple SIDS deaths in a family and developed evidence to establish that a child (or the children) died as a result of homicide. (See, e.g., *People v. Tinning,* 536 N.Y.S.2d 193 [1988].) For many years, it was believed that many SIDS cases were the result of apnea and that apnea monitors could prevent SIDS. This was based upon an article in a leading pediatrics journal (Steinschneider, A. [1972]. Prolonged apnea in the sudden infant death syndrome: Clinical and laboratory observations. *Pediatrics, 50,* 646.) The basis of Steinschneider's study was the death of multiple children in one family. This study also led to the acceptance that multiple children could die from SIDS in one family. Eventually, it was established that the children who formed the basis of the study were murdered by their mother. An excellent book that explains not only the mistaken basis of Steinschneider's theory but also the investigation and prosecution of a SIDS case is one by Richard Firstman and Jamie Talan (*The death of innocents.* [1997]. New York: Bantam). There are many articles and studies that discuss the diagnosis of SIDS and distinguish it from homicide or accident. (See Bass, M., et al. [1986]. Death-scene investigation in sudden infant death syndrome. *New England Journal of Medicine, 315,* 100; Beal, S. M., & Byard, R. W. [1995]. Accidental death or sudden infant death syndrome? *Journal of Pediatrics and Child Health, 31,* 269; Emery, J. L. [1999]. Child abuse, sudden infant death syndrome, and unexpected infant death. *American Journal of Diseases of Children, 147,* 1097; Reece, R. M. [1992]. Fatal abuse and sudden infant death syndrome: A critical diagnostic decision. *Pediatrics, 91,* 423.)

Some states allow the prosecutor to introduce expert testimony regarding the likelihood that the child would have died of SIDS when SIDS is advanced by the defense as the cause of death. Courts are more likely to permit such testimony should several SIDS-labeled child deaths occur in the same household. (See, e.g., *United States v. Woods,* 484 F.2d 127 [4th Cir. 1973] [allowing evidence of the apparently unexplained deaths of a defendant's nine children, including the death of one child that resulted in an order of dismissal as evidence to prove homicide, even though none of the deaths viewed alone was classified as a homicide]; *State v. Pankow,* 422 N.W.2d 913 [Wis. Ct. App. 1988] [upholding expert testimony regarding mathematical probability that three infants would die of SIDS in the same household during a 5-year period proper to counter defendant's theory of SIDS]; but see *Johnson v. State,* 405 S.E.2d 686 [Ga. 1991] [finding biostatistician's testimony regarding the probability of SIDS harmless error].) However, the cases cited that allowed testimony about statistical probability evidence should be viewed in light of the later cases discussed in Section VII in this chapter that required evidence connecting prior bad acts to the defendant even though the court in *Woods* stated that "evidence of what happened to the other children was not, strictly speaking, evidence of other crimes" (*Woods,* 484 F.2d at 133).

There is also research concerning the mother's use of cocaine and its causal relationship to SIDS. (Bauchner, H., & Zuckerman, B. [1990]. Cocaine, sudden infant death syndrome and home monitoring. *Journal of Pediatrics, 117,* 904; Bauchner, H., et al. [1988]. Risk of sudden infant death syndrome among infants with in-utero exposure to cocaine. *Journal of Pediatrics, 113,* 831.)

15. *Munchausen Syndrome by Proxy*

Munchausen syndrome is a term describing the behavior of people who seek unnecessary medical attention for themselves such as tests, hospitalizations, operations, and treatment by fabricating medical histories, physical evidence, and/or symptoms. Munchausen syndrome by proxy, also known as factitious disorder by proxy, refers to the conduct of adults who fabricate illnesses and/or deliberately induce injurious or life-threatening symptoms in a child, causing the child to undergo sometimes painful and potentially fatal medical tests and treatment. Dr. Roy Meadow first described this syndrome in 1977, and a number of other articles have since been published describing case studies and symptomatology.

Reported cases typically involve a mother fabricating a history of illness in a child under 9 years of age. The range and variety of illnesses that parents have fabricated is astounding. Some of the more common symptoms include recurrent bleeding, seizures, and apnea, but virtually any complaint can be fabricated or induced by a scheming parent. Some of these parents appear to have Munchausen syndrome themselves, and some have prior medical training. Child victims may die or suffer injury as a result of actions to induce symptoms. (*In re Jessica Z.,* 515 N.Y.S.2d 370 [Fam. Ct. 1987] [involving acts of repeatedly administering laxatives, causing severe diarrhea, blood infection, dehydration, and months of hospitalization]; *In re Colin R.,* 493 A.2d 1083 [Md. Ct. App. 1985] [injecting child with diuretics, causing vomiting, dehydration, high urinary output, low potassium levels, and calcium deposits in his kidneys]; *People v. Phillips,* 175 Cal. Rptr. 703 [Ct. App. 1981] [involving repeated administration of sodium bicarbonate to children, eventually causing one to die and another to be hospitalized with vomiting and diarrhea].) The literature also involves cases in which parents have induced seizures or cardiorespiratory arrest by suffocation, injected contaminated fluid into the child's intravenous tubing, applied caustics to the child's skin to cause a rash, and administered various other poisons to the child.

Dr. Jerry G. Jones, in "Munchausen Syndrome by Proxy" ([1986]. *Child Abuse & Neglect, 10,* 33), describes 10 signs of this syndrome. Note that not all signs need to be present in any single case, and that a few of these features can be present in other medical conditions. The 10 signs are:

1. Persistent or recurrent illnesses for which a cause cannot be found
2. Discrepancies between history and clinical findings
3. Symptoms and signs that do not occur when a child is away from the caregiver
4. Unusual symptoms and/or signs or a hospital course that does not make clinical sense
5. A differential diagnosis consisting of disorders less common than Munchausen syndrome by proxy
6. Persistent failure to tolerate or respond to medical therapy without clear cause

7. A parent less concerned than the physician, sometimes comforting the medical staff

8. Repeated hospitalizations and vigorous medical evaluations of parent or child without definitive diagnoses

9. A parent who is constantly at the child's bedside, excessively praises the staff, becomes overly attached to the staff, or becomes highly involved in the care of other patients

10. A parent who welcomes medical tests for her child, even when they are painful

The same article suggests that physicians who suspect Munchausen syndrome by proxy should take the following steps to support the diagnosis: Separate the child from the parent and note whether the symptoms continue, obtain detailed social and medical histories from the family, determine whether the parent was always present when past symptoms occurred and whether other witnesses were ever present, collect specimens, and conduct appropriate tests (*Id.* pp. 36–37). It is also helpful, when appropriate and possible, to conduct covert video surveillance at the hospital of the child's interaction with the parent. There should also be an investigation as to whether the child was admitted to other medical facilities in the region with similar or other hard-to-diagnose symptoms. Changing health providers is one way in which defendants escape detection for long periods. These steps should accompany information gathered from the doctor or other witnesses by law enforcement personnel.

Recognition of this phenomenon is relatively recent, and so far only a modest number of cases have been pursued in civil or criminal courts. However, more cases should be referred to the criminal justice system for prosecution of assault, homicide, or other appropriate charges as doctors gain more experience in recognizing and diagnosing this type of child abuse. Because these offenders are often intelligent and appear to be extremely loving and attentive parents, expert testimony may be necessary to prove motive or overcome the jury's natural reluctance to believe anyone could be capable of such behavior. In *People v. Phillips*, 175 Cal. Rptr. 703 (Ct. App. 1981), the court approved the admission of expert psychiatric testimony generally describing the syndrome in order to establish the defendant's motive to poison her children. General testimony describing the behavior of the defendant may be safer than that which specifically diagnoses the child as a victim of Munchausen syndrome by proxy.

Before offering *any* testimony on this subject, educate yourself fully and be well prepared to persuade the trial judge to allow the evidence. (See Rosenberg, D. [1987]. Web of deceit: A literature review of Munchausen syndrome by proxy. *Child Abuse & Neglect, 11,* 547; Beros, S. [1992]. Munchausen syndrome by proxy: Case accounts. *Law Enforcement Bulletin, 61,* 16; Wilsey, D. D. [2001]. Munchausen syndrome by proxy: The ultimate betrayal. *Update, 14*[8].)

G. The Use of Demonstrative Evidence by Experts

1. Overview

Demonstrative evidence can be crucial to explain complex medical principles, and it is especially important in child abuse cases when injuries are not easily seen or understood. There are many theories that permit the use of demonstrative evidence by experts. Among the theories and arguments for utilizing demonstrative evidence are

• To help an expert explain, clarify, or illustrate testimony (*Kinney v. State*, 868 S.W.2d 463 [Ark. 1994] [allowing odontologist to use picture of another child's penis with no bite marks to help explain his testimony concerning the bite mark on child's penis]; *State v. Padberg*, 723 S.W.2d 43 [Mo. Ct. App. 1986] [allowing autopsy photographs of 10-week-old victim to help jury understand cause of death]; *People v. Wernick*, 215 A.D.2d 50, 54 [N.Y. App. Div. 1995], *aff'd*, 674 N.E.2d 322 [N.Y. 1996] [finding photographs of newborn child admissible to illustrate medical testimony]; *People v. Ellwood*, 205 A.D.2d 553 [N.Y. App. Div.], *appeal denied*, 645 N.E.2d 1224 [N.Y. 1994] [allowing use of photograph of newborn to illustrate expert witness testimony as well as to corroborate the testimony of other witnesses]; *People v. Dogan*, 566 N.Y.S.2d 126 [App. Div. 1991] [finding photographs of infant's vagina admissible].)

• To support an element of the offense such as forcible compulsion or depraved indifference (See *People v. Quinones*, 155 A.D.2d 244 [1st Dept.], *appeal denied*, 551 N.E.3d 117 [N.Y. 1989]; *State v. Brooks*, 684 P.2d 1371 [Wash. Ct. App. 1984] [finding photographs of 10-year-old murder victim relevant to issues of intent and premeditation]; *People v. McNeeley*, 433 N.Y.S.2d 293 [App. Div. 1980] [concluding that photographs of burned baby were admissible to support murder charge]; *Barnes v. State*, 858 P.2d 522 [Wyo. 1993] [allowing 19 autopsy photographs of the child victim to establish defendant's depraved conduct].)

• To demonstrate the defendant's intent (See *Fentress v. State*, 702 N.E.2d 721 [Ind. 1998] [finding photographs of shattered skull relevant to the defendant's intent to kill].)

• To negate a defense or argument raised by the defense such as accident or mistake (*People v. Sims*, 494 N.Y.S.2d 114 [App. Div. 1985].)

• To explain the cause of an injury or how it was inflicted

• To establish the time of an injury by showing the stomach contents or the coloration of a bruise

• To prove or disprove a material fact, illustrate other relevant evidence, or corroborate or disprove other evidence in the case (*People v. Whitaker*, 537 N.Y.S.2d 66 [App. Div. 1989] [finding photographs of victim's body, the murder scene, and bloody footprints leading from victim's bedroom to victim's brother's bedroom and out of victim's apartment admissible].)

• To establish identity (*Poyner v. Commonwealth*, 329 S.E.2d 815 [Va.], *cert. denied*, 474 U.S. 865 [1985] [finding photograph relevant to proving identity of victim and method of killing].)

2. Photographs

As a general rule, photographs of an injury are admissible if relevant to a material issue. Often in child abuse cases, particularly those cases involving death or serious injury, an opponent of the evidence will raise the issue that the photograph, or some other demonstrative evidence, is prejudicial because of the gruesome nature of the photograph. From a practical point of view, some photographs, such as autopsy photographs, may be confusing to the jury since they reflect injuries or views not ordinarily seen. They can also be so powerful as to turn off the jury. Nonetheless, such photographs are generally admissible as long as they relate to a material issue. Even if the defendant admits to killing the child, this does not necessarily defeat the propriety of admitting autopsy photographs, as they may establish other aspects of the crime, such as intent in a first-degree murder case. (See, e.g., *People v. Wood*, 591 N.E.2d 1178 [N.Y. 1992].) Further, stipulating to the facts shown in a photograph does not necessarily defeat the relevancy and admissibility of a photograph. In this regard, the number of photographs, whether they are enlarged, and the significance of the issues for which they are offered, are factors to consider in the admissibility of so-called gruesome photographs.

3. Medical Illustrations[2]

A good way to avoid objections concerning the prejudicial effect of photographs that display the victim's injuries is to use medical illustrations of such injuries. Illustrations not only eliminate the gory aspect of many photos, but they can more clearly focus on and demonstrate the relevant injuries. Medical illustrations are almost always more effective than X-rays, which tend to be difficult for jurors because of the special skills required for their interpretation. Also, comparison illustrations of normal anatomy can be presented when photographs depict injuries that may not be readily understood by a jury. Since many injuries are internal, the use of overlays can show a variety of injuries, such as how an abdominal bruise correlates with a rupture of the liver. This helps the expert explain the findings to the jury. If such illustrations aid the jury in understanding issues, their use should be allowed. (*State v. Ray*, 202 A.2d 425, 432-33 [N.J. 1964]; see also *Joynt v. Barnes*, 388 N.E.2d 1298, 1310 [Ill. Ct. App. 1979] [drawing of the tumor in question by a treating physician was properly admitted as evidence since it was "a reasonably accurate depiction"].)

The principles governing the use and admissibility of medical illustrations are no different than other types of demonstrative evidence such as charts and drawings that display physical facts. (*Van Welden v. Ramsay's, Inc.*, 419, 430 P.2d 298, 301 [Kan. 1967].) With all medical illustrations, however, there must be an adequate foundation for the illustration, and it must be accurate. As noted at 29 Am. Jur. 2d *Evidence* § 805 (1967),

> Medical or anatomical charts showing a human skeleton or a part of a human body have been admissible, in the discretion of the trial court, in a number of cases. The test as to the admissibility of medical and anatomical charts is their capacity to inform the jury, and where they are accurate and fully explained, they are admissible even though abstract.
>
> Both in criminal and civil cases, where the problem of the admissibility of a skeleton or model of a human body or a part thereof has been presented, the

---

[2]Sections IV.G.7(c)(d)(g)(i) are reprinted by permission of Lexis Law Publishing from *Sexual Assault Trials*, Second edition (1998). Copyright 1995, The Michie Company. Copyright 1998, LEXIS Law Publishing. Reprinted with permission from *Sexual Assault Trials*, Second Edition by Paul DerOhannesian II. Lexis Law Publishing, Charlottesville, VA. (800) 446-3410. All Rights Reserved.

courts are in apparent agreement that if the jury or court will be enlightened by the introduction of such evidence, it is admissible within the trial court's discretion. Such a model, if otherwise relevant and admissible, may be received in evidence even though it may be of a shocking or gruesome character.

The best evidence rule applies and it may be important to produce or have available the photographs or X-rays that the medical illustrations depict.

In a child sexual assault case, an illustration may display injuries to a child's hymen. (See, e.g., *State v. Curry*, 1998 Tenn. Crim. App. LEXIS 707 at 7-8 [finding no error in the admission of illustration of hymenal injuries].) A less expensive alternative to an original medical illustration is to utilize an overlay with a commercially available illustration. A medical expert may rely on, and introduce into evidence, illustrations from medical treatises under the principles of the learned treatise exception. (See Fed. R. Evid. 803[18]; *State v. Henry*, 554 N.W.2d 472 [S.D. 1996].)

4. Admitting, But Not Displaying, Photographs to the Jury

When the opposition challenges medical illustrations that show an assault victim's injuries, counsel should be ready to offer into evidence the photos that form the basis for the illustrations but not necessarily present them to the jury. In this situation, the photographs are being offered only to establish the foundation for the illustrations and to establish a record for appellate review. Another situation where photographs may be admitted into evidence but not shown to the jury is where the party wishes to have the photographs available for cross-examination at a later time. This may occur where material in the photographs is challenged or a medical witness is questioned about certain findings that can be supported by the photographs. This obviates the need to call a witness back to the witness stand to identify and establish the significance of the photographs. Also, the photographs can be used for cross-examination of the defendant's witness.

5. Illustrations and Drawings by Witnesses

As with any witness, an expert may illustrate his testimony through drawings. If a chalk board or drawing pad is used, the prosecutor must make sure that the jury can see the illustration and writing. This inexpensive alternative to medical illustrations not only helps the jury understand a witness's findings and opinions but also gets the expert witness off the stand and in a setting where many experts are more comfortable, that is, teaching a small group of individuals.

6. The Use of Models

A model or commercially prepared drawing or mannequin may be helpful to an expert witness to explain his testimony. As long as the witness states that the model or exhibit is a true and accurate representation of what it seeks to depict and that the object would assist the expert in explaining the testimony, the model or prepared drawing should be admissible. However, generic models and drawings lack some of the impact of custom-prepared medical illustrations since they do not depict exactly the injury or case on trial.

When emergency medical or rescue personnel testify, they should use the models or mannequins from their training to show exactly how the child was held or carried. This will vividly show the jury that the care and treatment of the rescue personnel did not injure the child.

7. Radiological Studies: X-Ray, CT Scans, and MRI

In cases of physical injury, particularly serious child abuse cases, there may be radiological studies, such as X-ray examinations, CT scans (computerized axial tomography), or an MRI. While physicians often refer to these studies in the courtroom, they are difficult for the jury to interpret. While they may be a convenient prop for the testifying medical witness, the results of radiological studies are not effective demonstrative evidence. At best, the typical X-ray film simply provides the jury with a fleeting image from an illuminated shadow box. If the X-ray is easily understood, that is, if a lay person can see the findings described by the witness, the exhibit can be made much more effective by obtaining positive prints that can be admitted and distributed to the jurors just like a photograph. MRI and CT scans can demonstrate soft-tissue injury or the lack thereof. This demonstration is not always clear to lay persons. Quite often, they require color overlays, enlargements, or illustrations to explain the findings.

The usual foundation for a photograph does not apply to a radiological study, since no one actually sees what the X-ray, MRI, or CT scan displays. Most courts will accept such studies based on a showing of adequate, identifiable markings on the exhibit or by showing a proper chain of custody. (Imwinkelried, E. J., et al. [1993]. *Courtroom criminal evidence* [2nd ed., p. 412]. Charlottesville, VA: Lexis Law Pub; see also Imwinkelried, E. J. [1989]. *Evidentiary foundations* [2nd ed., pp. 75–78] Mathew Bender [containing sample foundation testimony for an X-ray]; but see *Howard v. State*, 342 N.E.2d 604, 608 [Ind. 1976].)

8. Videotape

Videotape is more accessible and practical in the courtroom because of its increased availability and decreased costs. Videotape can be used to show a scene, explain a theory of how an injury occurred, or show the jury the effect of injury on the victim. The foundation for the use of videotape is the same as with other demonstrative evidence. However, since videotape evidence is more likely to have a powerful impact, it is likely to be reviewed by the court before being presented to a jury.

The audio portion of the videotape may constitute hearsay. However, a witness present in court may make the comments and statements and thus be available for cross-examination. Before videotaping, the prosecution and law enforcement officials should give consideration to whether there will be audio commentary during the tape. If there is going to be commentary, the narrator should be aware that the statements made could be subject to scrutiny by defense counsel.

A good example of the use of videotape is to show a child with a serious and permanent injury from physical abuse. The child may be too young or too impaired to testify. The prosecution may wish to present "a day in the life" videotape of the child that demonstrates the effects and consequences of the child's injuries. This videotape can be made at the child's home or rehabilitation center. The videotape can show not only the limitations of the child but also the special efforts and treatment the child requires during the day, such as physical therapy or tube feeding. The videotape need not be long. In fact, it is best if limited to 10–20 minutes in duration because a lengthy videotape may be difficult to watch, and the impact of the videotape will decrease with a long presentation. A videotape avoids the necessity of presenting the child in court. It also avoids a trial where the jury never gets the chance to see the victim and the effects of the abuse. While the defense attorney may object to such a videotape because it is prejudicial, the response to this objection is to offer to present the profoundly impaired child in person, which would be even more prejudicial.

9. In-Court Demonstrations and Re-Creations

Demonstrations of how a crime occurred are permissible so long as the circumstances surrounding the demonstration are sufficiently similar to those existing at the time in question and so long as the trial court finds that the demonstration plays a positive and helpful role in the ascertainment of truth. (*People v. Estrada*, 486 N.Y.S.2d 794 [1985]; see also *People v. Barnes*, 600 N.E.2d 228 [N.Y. 1992] [upholding demonstration in which court officers played the defendant and victim for purposes of illustrating their relative positions at the time of the shooting].) However, care should be taken to ensure the fairness of a demonstration since "by conveying a visual image of what allegedly occurred, one side can imprint the jury's mind with its version of the facts." (*United States v. Birch*, 39 F.3d 1089 [10th Cir. 1994]; see also *United States v. Wanoskia*, 800 F.2d 235, 238 [10th Cir. 1986] [permitting demonstration that victim could not have inflicted her own wounds, in which prosecution showed that the demonstration was sufficiently similar to the facts of the case by offering testimony that the victim's arm length was comparable to the model's].) Demonstrations or tests relevant to a contested issue can be helpful in finding the truth and should not be lightly rejected. (*People v. Boone*, 575 N.Y.S.2d 393 [1991], *appeal denied*, 588 N.E.2d 760 [N.Y. 1992] [upholding an out-of-court demonstration of a live firing of the weapon in question].) In the well-known murder case of Captain Jeffrey MacDonald, the prosecution offered a demonstration of the similarity between the pattern of puncture holes in the defendant's pajama top and the pattern of ice pick wounds in his wife's chest to rebut his version of events. (*United States v. MacDonald*, 688 F.2d 224, 228–29 [4th Cir. 1982], *cert. denied*, 459 U.S. 1103 [1983].)

In-court demonstrations under circumstances that are different from, or do not purport to replicate, physical characteristics of a scene, the victim, or the defendant can be improper. (*State v. Philbrick*, 436 A.2d 844 [Me. 1981]; *People v. Gregg*, 611 N.Y.S.2d 151, *appeal denied*, 637 N.E.2d 284 [1994] [noting, "The trial court appropriately exercised its discretion in denying defense counsel's application to demonstrate to the jury the sound of a small tin container hitting the ground, for the purpose of challenging the police officer's testimony that a tin container dropped by defendant sounded to him like a small caliber gun being dropped, as it would be impossible to recreate the precise conditions under which the testifying officer heard the sound in question (e.g., the force used in dropping the tin container; the surrounding street noise, or lack thereof) and there was no indication that the members of the jury would be able (as defendant apparently speculated) to compare that sound with the sound of a small caliber gun dropping to the ground."]) The burden of establishing the similarity of conditions or circumstances is on the party offering the demonstration or experiment. The conditions need not be identical but must be sufficiently similar so as to provide a fair comparison. (*Jackson v. Fletcher,* 647 F.2d 1020, 1027 [10th Cir. 1981]; *Barnes v. General Motors,* 547 F.2d 275, 277 [5th Cir. 1977].) The demonstration may, for example, help explain the likelihood of a complainant's or witness' actions. (*Commonwealth v. Impellizzeri,* 661 A.2d 422 [Pa. 1995], *appeal denied,* 673 A.2d 332 [Pa. 1996] [finding an adequate foundation for prosecution's videotape experiment of victim's ability to crawl out of defendant's basement].)

One common demonstration is by a physician demonstrating how injuries were or were not sustained by a victim. If the victim had bruises from the perpetrator's fingers or fists, the medical expert can show where they were placed and exactly how the perpetrator held or struck the victim. (See *People v. Shattell,* 578 N.Y.S.2d 694, *appeal denied,* 594 N.E.2d 956 [1992]; *State v. Schatz-Sousa,* 1998 Wash. App. LEXIS 425 at 15–17 [upholding prosecution's demonstrative videotape of a 2½-year-old child attempting to bathe a 6-week-old who sustained burn injuries allegedly inflicted by defendant to rebut the defense that 2½-year-old was responsible for the 6-week-old's injuries and to demonstrate that the 2½-year-old was not physically capable of inflicting the injuries].)

Another common demonstration is one showing the shaking involved in a child diagnosed with SBS. The appellate court in *Powell v. State,* 487 S.E.2d 424 (Ga. Ct. App. 1997), upheld the use of a doll to demonstrate the force involved to cause the injuries in an SBS case. The court noted, "Obviously, a demonstration of how shaken infant syndrome occurs would have to be done with a mannequin or doll rather than a real infant. Such an object will differ in many respects from a real child. However, any dissimilarity between the conditions of the demonstration and the actual occurrence affects the weight rather than the admissibility of the evidence." (*Id.* at 426). (See also *State v. Candela,* 929 S.W.2d 852 [Mo. Ct. App. 1996] [affirming trial court allowing a demonstration by a physician in which he shook a rag doll to illustrate the type of shaking involved in shaken impact syndrome where defendant was able to show the difference between the doll and the deceased child]; *People v. Shattell,* 578 N.Y.S.2d 694 [App. Div. 1992] [concluding that dolls can be used to show how victim was shaken].) Although some prosecutors ask the expert to demonstrate, with a doll, the type and severity of shaking required to injure or kill a baby, in truth, the biomechanical thresholds for causing the brain injury are not known, and many physicians will not participate in this sort of demonstration.

A prosecution expert could demonstrate that a child was unable to breathe through a pillow found in the defendant's bed, which may have been in a child victim's crib at the time of her death, to support the witness's opinion that the child was suffocated. (*People v. Lane,* 600 N.Y.S.2d 848, *appeal denied,* 627 N.E.2d 524 [1993].) However, when there are substantial differences in the circumstances of the demonstration, it can lead to reversible error, such as when the model used to represent a child in a demonstration varies significantly in its characteristics from the actual victim. (*United States v. Gaskell,* 985 F.2d 1056 [11th Cir. 1993] [disapproving expert's demonstration with rubber doll to show the amount of force necessary to cause injury to an infant who was allegedly a victim of SBS since conditions were substantially dissimilar to the defendant's allegations and not supported by trial evidence, and cautionary instruction was insufficient to negate prejudicial effect of the demonstration].) A defendant's demonstration or reenactment will also be precluded when there are substantial differences between the demonstration and the circumstances at the time of the incident. (*State v. Schatz-Sousa*, 1998 Wash. App. LEXIS 425 [rejecting defendant's reenactment of how the child's injuries were sustained because the differences in the children's sex, size, and weight and use of a step stool gave the reenactment no probative value to the actual physical capabilities of the 2½-year-old child who allegedly, instead of defendant, inflicted injuries to 6-week-old child].)

Some courts may also require a limiting instruction be given to the jury as to the limited purpose for which the demonstration is offered or may be considered, such as helping an expert explain a theory.

10. Documents

When there are significant records, such as entries in a hospital chart, records of emergency rescue personnel, or statements by the defendant, these can be enlarged and mounted on foam core boards for reference as well as use in cross-examination, direct examination, and summation. Documents such as the defendant's statement or a portion of a medical chart can also be photocopied for the jury to follow as the prosecutor or witness reads them aloud. If the defendant's phone call for assistance is used as evidence, provide a transcript for all jurors. Check your jurisdiction's case law first, as it is reversible error in some states to give the defendant's statement in writing or transcript form to the jury during trial or deliberations.

11. Scene Diagrams and Models

Another extremely helpful demonstrative aid in many homicide and physical abuse cases is a scaled diagram of the scene where the abuse occurred. This, too, can be enlarged for jury reference. The drawing can reference photographs of the house and items at issue, such as the couch or crib. Scene diagrams, with dimensions of objects included, can be helpful in explaining why the injury could not have occurred as suggested by the defendant. For example, a diagram can explain why a child who cannot walk or climb could not have "stepped" into a tub of hot water.

12. Charts

In cases involving multiple victims and abuse over a period of time, a time line or chart can help organize and present the evidence. For example, one prosecutor prepared a 2' x 3' chart, half of which applied to each defendant. For each victim of each defendant, there were boxes for each of the charged unlawful acts such as "P-M," "penis to hand." The appeals court held that the prosecutor properly entered a check mark for each item to which a child testified. (See *State v. Olson*, 579 N.W.2d 802 [Wis. 1998].)

Generally, the admissibility of summary charts is within the court's discretion. The summaries may be of three kinds: (1) primary evidence summaries that are admitted in lieu of voluminous evidence and when there is substantive evidence,

(2) pedagogical device summaries or illustrations that summarize testimony or other evidence, and (3) secondary evidence summaries that summarize evidence to assist the jury in understanding complex primary evidence. (See *United States v. Bray,* 139 F.3d 1104 [6th Cir. 1998].) Child abuse cases will usually utilize the third form of summary exhibits. In such an instance the jury should be given a limiting instruction that "the summary is not independent evidence of its subject matter, and is only as valued and reliable as the underlying evidence it summarizes" (*Id.* at 1112).

VI. SPECIAL FACT SITUATIONS IN CHILD PHYSICAL ABUSE AND HOMICIDE CASES

A. The Murder of a Newborn Infant

Complicated issues arise when contemplating charging and prosecuting a case involving the murder of a newborn. In the absence of a special statute, a person cannot be prosecuted for murdering an unborn child. The prosecutor must, largely through medical testimony, establish the *corpus delicti.* Unless the infant was born alive, there may be no "person" for purposes of a murder charge. The main issue in many of these cases is the definition of live birth and whether there is sufficient evidence to show the baby was born alive. Many courts hold that the prosecution must establish that a newborn had the capacity of a "separate and independent existence" before sustaining a conviction. (See, e.g., *United States v. Nelson,* 53 M.J. 319 [2000]; *People v. Hall,* 158 A.D.2d 69 [N.Y. App. Div. 1990]; *State v. Kinskey,* 348 N.W.2d 319, 324, 35 [Minn. 1984].) There may also be statutory definitions of live birth that may apply.

Under the "separate and independent existence" definition, it may be insufficient to simply establish that the child's lungs were aerated. (See *People v. Flores,* 4 Cal. Rptr. 2d 120 [1992] [finding an occasional heartbeat insufficient to support live birth]; *White v. State,* 232 S.E.2d 57 [Ga. 1977]; *Lane v. Commonwealth,* 248 S.E.2d 781 [Va. 1978] [finding that medical evidence that full-term baby's lungs were aerated and three cubic centimeters of air were found in infant's stomach did not constitute an unqualified opinion that child had acquired independent existence from mother even though it showed the baby breathed a few times after birth].) The presence of gas or air in the lungs, often the main evidence of live birth, may be affected by decomposition or resuscitation. (See generally Guthrie, P. G. [1975]. Proof of live birth in prosecution for killing newborn child [Annotation]. *A.L.R., 65,* 3d 413.)

It is often difficult for a pathologist to testify on the issue of live birth based solely on autopsy findings. Additional information and circumstantial evidence will sometimes be helpful when asking the doctor to give an opinion. If the defendant or another witness describes the newborn as moving, this supports the opinion of live birth. (See *State v. Kinsky,* 248 N.W.3d 319 [Minn. 1984] [finding that medical testimony indicating baby's lungs were well aerated and evidence that a bra had been tightly wrapped around baby's neck was sufficient to allow jury to infer infant was born alive].)

In addition to establishing live birth, the cause of death may be at issue. Often the cause of death may be asphyxiation by suffocation, strangulation, or drowning in a toilet. In these circumstances, there may be little or no physical or histological evidence at autopsy. The cause of death diagnosis may require a forensic pathologist to opine on cause of death based upon the circumstances such as the baby being found in a tied plastic bag or a hypothetical question based on a defendant's statements. (See e.g., *State v. Hopfer*, 679 N.W.2d 321 [Ohio 1996] [affirming verdict where jury could reasonably conclude that child died of suffocation after being placed in knotted garbage bag and that defendant's method of disposal caused baby's death].)

Cause of death may be affected if the child has some other medical condition at the time of birth, such as being premature or having an infection or congenital problem. In these cases, it is helpful to have evidence from a neonatal pathologist or pediatric pathologist with specialized knowledge of the issues involved with the death of a newborn. Also, testimony from a neonatologist that the newborn could have been successfully treated at the hospital will rebut defense arguments that the child was never going to survive. As in other areas of child homicide, a clinician can provide an extra dimension to the medical testimony of a pathologist.

Remember that the prosecutor must present evidence to show that the defendant in fact gave birth to the infant and was responsible for the death of the child. Simply establishing that a defendant was no longer pregnant and the newborn was found dead is insufficient to establish a *prima facie* case. (See, e.g., *Graham v. State*, 642 S.W.2d 342 [Ark. 1982] [finding insufficient evidence where baby was retrieved from deserted rural area, autopsy found that baby was born alive and killed by a blow to head, medical examination of defendant revealed substantial likelihood she had recently been pregnant, and witnesses testified that defendant had been pregnant one month before discovery of baby's body]; *State v. Doyle*, 287 N.W.2d 59 [Neb. 1980] [finding insufficient evidence when neighbors and relatives observed defendant pregnant, defendant told witnesses about due date, defendant was not pregnant 3 days before due date, dead infant was found on premises occupied by defendant, and pathologist was unable to state cause of death].)

The investigation of the death of a newborn should include all those who knew that the defendant was pregnant and may have discussed pregnancy or childbirth with the defendant. Coworkers, friends, and neighbors may have such information. The child's father and his family may also have information concerning the defendant's awareness and attitude toward the pregnancy or the child. The defendant's friends, coworkers, or the father of the child may also have received correspondence or communications concerning the defendant's knowledge and feelings about the pregnancy. The defendant may have consulted with individuals or health professionals concerning termination of the pregnancy or adoption.

Examine the defendant's behavior during the pregnancy. Was the defendant preparing for the birth or death of a child? What decisions and choices did the defendant make leading up to the delivery and death of the child? What choices and decisions did the defendant make at the time of delivery?

As in any child homicide prosecution, it is important to develop a motive for a seemingly inexplicable act. All acts of neonaticide are not driven by the same forces. Selfishness is one motive. The child may be an impediment to the defendant's lifestyle or relationship with a significant other. Eliminating the child allows the defendant to continue her life without the responsibilities of raising a child. There may be many possible factors triggering the homicidal act, and it is best to investigate the specific case rather than apply common theories, usually not scientifically validated, about women who kill their newborns.

Sometimes the defendant, usually an adolescent, will claim she did not know of her pregnancy. To undermine a pregnancy denial defense, investigate thoroughly to uncover evidence that the defendant knew she was pregnant, was unhappy about the pregnancy, took steps to hide it, and perhaps intended to kill the child. Did the mother obtain or receive literature on pregnancy or birth? Did the mother discuss abortion or adoption with the father or someone else? Make sure the father of the child is interviewed whenever possible to answer not only these questions but the circumstances regarding the sexual relations leading to the pregnancy. While some may speak of a defendant's denial of a pregnancy, often the proof establishes that the defendant was aware of the pregnancy but does not want to take responsibility for the pregnancy.

A defendant's postbirth behavior may be important. Did the defendant call 911 or seek help for the child? Did the defendant dispose of the body? If so, how was that accomplished? Did the defendant try to cover up the death? What do the defendant's postbirth actions say about her attitude toward the newborn's life? Interview the defendant and others concerning what happened after the birth. Actions such as cutting the umbilical cord, giving inconsistent or nonsensical explanations of the baby's death, or hiding the infant's body indicate an awareness of the birth and intent to kill the infant. As with other child homicide cases, interview the first persons the defendant may have contacted, such as paramedics, nurses, friends, or family members, to see what statements she may or may not have made. (See *People v. Doss*, 574 N.E.2d 806 [Ill. 1991] [finding first-degree murder conviction where evidence showed a deliberate attempt to dispose of unwanted child based upon the defendant giving birth in secret, cutting the umbilical cord, wrapping the baby in a plastic bag, putting it in a garbage can, and giving explanations inconsistent with two stab wounds to the baby's chest].) Remember, too, that a defendant's failure to act may be the basis of a homicide charge against someone with a legal duty to protect the child such as a parent. (See Chapter III, Section II.C.4; Dougherty, F. M. [2001]. Homicide: Sufficiency of evidence of mother's neglect of infant born alive, in minutes or hours immediately following unattended birth, to establish culpable homicide [Annotation]. *A.L.R. 4th*, 724.) The failure to act or delayed medical attention may also be an aggravating factor in charging or sentencing.

Postpartum depression, a mental disturbance that can surface some time after a woman gives birth, may be asserted as a defense. (See *State v. Barsness*, 473 N.W.2d 325 [Minn. Ct. App. 1991] [excluding some evidence of defendant's low IQ and alleged mental illness arising from postpartum depression but allowing evidence of behavioral changes related to the condition].) However, there is also authority that expert testimony concerning "neonaticide syndrome" in support of an affirmative defense of insanity does not meet the threshold of scientific reliability under *Frye*. (See *People v. Wernick*, 674 N.E.2d 322 [N.Y. 1996].) The prosecutor must make sure the expert testimony meets the threshold of scientific reliability and other standards for the admission of scientific testimony. Furthermore, postpartum depression does not necessarily excuse criminal conduct. (See *Commonwealth v. Comitz*, 530 A.2d 473 [Pa. 1987]; see also Gardner, C. A. [1990]. Postpartum depression defense: Are mothers getting away with murder? [Note]. *New England Law Review, 24*, 953.) Remember, too, that a defendant may be required to provide notice of a mental health defense or otherwise be precluded from asserting it. An assertion of a defendant's psychological condition may also open the door to the defendant's mental health records. Make sure that the defense complies with its obligations to supply not only the records, but also an authorization for the State to obtain the defendant's records and interview the defendant.

B. Negligent Homicide or the Injury of an Unattended Child

When children are left alone and are injured or die, prosecutors are faced with the decision of whether to prosecute the caregivers who left the children. In assessing the circumstances, consider the following:

- The length of time the child(ren) was/were left unattended
- The reason stated for leaving the child(ren) alone
- The defendant's knowledge of a dangerous condition at the location where the child(ren) was/were left alone or the obvious nature of the condition
- The age of the child(ren)
- The child(ren)'s access to and capacity to call for assistance

See *United States v. Bald Eagle,* 849 F.2d 361 (8th Cir. 1988) (affirming conviction for involuntary manslaughter where defendant left five unattended children in a house that burned down); *Wayne County Prosecutor v. Recorder's Court Judge,* 324 N.W.2d 43 (Mich. Ct. App. 1982) (finding evidence that defendant previously observed her infant children playing with matches, left children alone in locked room for more than 2 hours, and fire started by children playing with matches sufficient to establish probable cause for defendant's gross negligence); *Commonwealth v. Skufca,* 321 A.2d 889 (Pa. 1974), *cert. denied,* 419 U.S. 1028 (1974) (finding evidence that defendant locked infant children unattended in apartment that burned down sufficient to sustain conviction for involuntary manslaughter). But see *People v. Rodriguez,* 8 Cal. Rptr. 863 (Ct. App. 1960) (finding that evidence did not support inference that defendant knew leaving children locked in a house that burned down would probably produce death).

C. Failure to Provide Medical Care in Furtherance of Religious Beliefs

Some cases of child neglect, endangerment, and homicide involve parents or caregivers who assert that, owing to religious teachings, no medical assistance was provided for an ailing child. If such a defense comes up, check for a statutorily defined religious exemption to the duty to provide medical treatment in either the child endangerment statutes or child abuse reporting statutes. The religious exemption may be buried in statutes that do not deal directly with criminal matters. Check child welfare, juvenile, and child support enforcement statutes. If there is no such exemption, evaluate the case for charging and trial as you would other "failure to protect" or homicide cases. Even when such an exemption exists, the prosecution may be able to argue that it was not intended to excuse a defendant from criminal conduct resulting in a child's death.

If the parent, however, *caused* the severe injury that lead to the child's death, there is no religious justification for that conduct. Not seeking medical care may be statutorily exempted, but actual abuse of a child that *causes* the injuries is not.

If there is no statutorily defined religious exemption to the duty to provide medical care, consider filing a motion *in limine* to prohibit testimony or argument regarding the religious beliefs of the defendant. The defense attorney may attempt to create disagreement among the jurors by raising irrelevant questions about freedom of religious practice. Remind jurors that religious beliefs are not in question.

The issue before the jury is the severity of injury to the victim. The United States Supreme Court held in 1944 that "parents may be free to become martyrs themselves. But it does not follow that they are free, in identical circumstances, to make martyrs of their children before they can reach the age of full and legal discretion when they can make that choice for themselves." (*Prince v. Massachusetts,* 321 U.S. 158, 170, *reh'g denied,* 321 U.S. 804 [1944].)

Keep the injured or deceased victim as the focus: Use photographs of the victim, dwell on the severity of disease symptoms and the obvious suffering they caused the child. Make sure the jury understands that the defendant is free to *believe* the victim could be healed through prayer, but the defendant was not free to act on that belief in a manner that jeopardized the health of the victim. (See, e.g., *State v. Norman,* 808 P.2d 1159 [Wash. 1991].) The defendant-parent may appear distraught that the child has died or is close to death. Make sure to sensitize jurors during *voir dire* that their decision must be based on the parent's failure to prevent avoidable suffering and death, not on sympathy for the child victim or defendant-parent.

As of 2002, 25 states allowed a defendant to present an affirmative defense to criminal child abuse and neglect charges when a parent or caregiver depends on spiritual means to treat a child's illness. The wording in two such statutes is as follows:

> *West Virginia.* W. Va. Code § 61–8D-2 (2001). Crime: Murder of a Child
> *Exemption.* The provisions of this section shall not apply to any parent, guardian or custodian who fails or refuses, or allows another person to fail or refuse, to supply a child under the care, custody or control of such parent, guardian or custodian with necessary medical care, when such medical care conflicts with the tenets and practices of a recognized religious denomination or order of which such parent, guardian or custodian is an adherent or member.

> *Alaska.* Alaska Stat. § 11.51.120 (1978). Crime: Criminal Nonsupport
> *Exemption.* There is no failure to provide medical attention to a child if the child is provided treatment solely by spiritual means through prayer in accordance with the tenets and practices of a recognized church or religious denomination by an accredited practitioner of the church or denomination.

Table V.3 lists state statutes providing a religious defense to criminal child abuse and neglect. If the defendant asserts that the religion is well recognized, the prosecutor should consider arguing that protection of only certain religions violates the Anti-Establishment Clause of the First Amendment. (See, e.g., *Dalli v. Board of Education,* 267 N.E.2d 219 [Mass. 1971] [extending preferred treatment to adherents and members of recognized church or religious denominations while denying exemption to others objecting to vaccination on religious grounds was held unconstitutional].)

Find out if the leader of the religious group or the person providing any relevant spiritual treatment is an accredited practitioner of the religious denomination. If the leader or spiritual healer is not properly accredited, any practices followed should not fit into the religious exemption statute. Interview, if possible, the leader of the group and other members. Ask for documentation regarding accreditation and

Table V.3	Statutes Providing a Religious Defense to Criminal Child Abuse and Neglect
Alabama	Ala. Code § 13A-13-6
Alaska	Alaska Stat. § 11.51.120
Arkansas	Ark. Code Ann. § 5–10–101(a)(9)
	Ark. Code Ann. § 12-12-518
California	Cal. Penal Code § 270
Colorado	Colo. Rev. Stat. § 19–3–103
Delaware	Del. Code Ann. tit. 11, § 1104
Idaho	Idaho Code § 18-1501(4)
Indiana	Ind. Code § 35-46-1-4
	Ind. Code § 35-46-1-5
Iowa	Iowa Code § 726.6(d)
Kansas	Kan. Stat. Ann. § 21-3608
Louisiana	La. Rev. Stat. Ann. § 14:93
Michigan	Mich. Comp. Laws § 722.634
Minnesota	Minn. Stat. § 609.378
New Hampshire	N.H. Rev. Stat. Ann. § 639:3(IV)
New York	N.Y. Penal Law § 260.15
Ohio	Ohio Rev. Code Ann. § 2919.22
Oklahoma	Okla. Stat. Ann. tit. 21, § 852.1
Oregon	Or. Rev. Stat. § 163.11
Rhode Island	R.I. Gen. Laws § 11–9–5
Tennessee	Tenn. Code Ann. § 39–15–402
Texas	Tex. Penal Code Ann. § 22.04(k)(2)
Utah	Utah Code Ann. § 76–5–109(4)
Virginia	Va. Code Ann. § 18.2–371.1
West Virginia	W. Va. Code § 61–8D-2, 4a, 4(d)
Wisconsin	Wis. Stat. Ann. § 948.03(6)

NOTE: This compilation includes all criminal statutes (except military and tribal statutes) that specifically state that an offense is not committed by the failure to provide medical care owing to religious beliefs. The citation date indicates the date of passage or latest amendment. This table includes all legislation passed through January 2002, as verified through Lexis Nexis.

verify that information. If there is an overarching national organization, call it to determine if the leader is actually sanctioned by the central organization. Subpoena documentation describing the religion, its by-laws, and any certification of leaders.

Assuming the religion is recognized and its leader and any relevant spiritual healer are accredited, find out if the practice adhered to by the defendant is actually part of the religion's tenets. If the defendant claims the religion's followers believe in faith healing and do not accept medical intervention, interview others within the religious group or, if they are not cooperative, nonmember relatives or past members of the religion to determine if this is the case. Again, subpoenaing any writings from the religious group may indicate whether faith healing and the exclusion of *all* medical intervention is endorsed. Were such practices taught by the religion or was the defendant shaping an individual version of the religion?

Determine whether the defendant was in fact a true follower of the religion. Evidence that the defendant sought or took advantage of any kind of medical treatment for herself would call the defense into question.

Ascertain whether the conduct of the defendant should be charged as a misdemeanor or felony. In most states, the religious exemption applies only to instances of misdemeanor conduct and does not apply if the child was at risk of serious bodily injury or death. For the most part, statutory religious exemptions were never intended to apply to a case of homicide. (See, e.g., *Walker v. Superior Court,* 763 P.2d 852 [Cal. 1988], *cert. denied,* 491 U.S. 905 [1989] [finding exemption inapplicable to involuntary manslaughter and felony endangerment prosecution]; *Funkhouser v. State,* 763 P.2d 695 [Okla. Crim. App. 1988], *cert. denied,* 490 U.S. 1066 [1989] [finding that religious defense in child neglect statute does not apply to manslaughter charge]; *Hall v. State,* 493 N.E.2d 433 [Ind. 1986] [concluding that prayer in lieu of medical care was not a statutory defense excusing responsibility for death that resulted from reckless acts, regardless of whether acts were conducted pursuant to religious beliefs]; but see *Commonwealth v. Twitchell,* 617 N.E.2d 609 [Mass. 1993] [holding that although the spiritual healing provision did not bar manslaughter prosecution, special circumstances entitled defendant-parents to present affirmative defense that they reasonably believed they could rely on spiritual treatment without fear of criminal prosecution].)

If the religious exemption applies to charges filed against the defendant, check your case law and statutes to assess what standard courts and juries should apply. If the defendant has the burden of proof on the issue, state this burden in jury selection, opening, and closing. An affirmative defense may require the defense to show, by credible evidence, that the defendant-parent had an honest and reasonable belief that the child, although ill or injured, was not suffering from a condition that would endanger the child's life or pose a risk of serious bodily harm. (See *Lybarger v. People,* 807 P.2d 570 [Colo. 1991].) Use expert medical testimony to explain to the jury the obvious nature of the child's symptoms, the ease with which medical treatment could have prevented the death or injury, and the child's decline. Friends and relatives of the defendant may have warned that the child was very ill and should have been taken to the hospital.

States are divided as to the constitutionality of prosecutions for failure to provide medical care to children owing to religious observances and practices when the state has a religious exemption to child neglect in the state's child abuse reporting statute. California found that an involuntary manslaughter conviction of a Christian Scientist who provided her daughter with spiritual treatment alone did not violate the First Amendment. (*Walker v. Superior Court,* 763 P.2d 852 [Cal. 1988], *cert. denied,* 491 U.S. 905 [1989].) In a Florida case, however, the court found that the defendant was denied due process since Florida's reporting statute, which had a religious exemption, failed to give parents notice of the point at which their reliance on spiritual treatment loses statutory approval and they become culpably negligent. (See *Hermanson v. State,* 604 So. 2d 775 [1992]; see also *State v. McKown,* 475 N.W.2d 63 [Minn. 1991], *cert. denied,* 112 S. Ct. 882 [1992] [finding that conviction violated due process because parents had right to rely on religious exemption].) For further general information on the topic of failure to provide medical treatment owing to religious beliefs, contact the National Center for the Prosecution of Child Abuse.

VII. REBUTTAL EVIDENCE

A. General Considerations

Before presenting testimony on rebuttal, carefully assess your case-in-chief and the evidence presented by the defense attorney to determine if rebuttal is necessary. A good rebuttal to tie up an important issue is important. However, a rebuttal witness may open a door to new problems or issues or weaken a case.

Avoid calling a witness who is potentially explosive or unsympathetic. If it is felt that the defense attorney "scored points" with a defense witness, examine exactly what the witness said and look at whether, in the context of the overall case, the points made by the witness are trivial. By presenting rebuttal testimony on an unimportant point, the State may play into the defense attorney's hands and divert attention from the real issues in the case. Check to see whether the point raised by the defense witness was answered adequately by evidence presented during the case-in-chief. If so, do not put on rebuttal evidence and emphasize the testimony that rebuts the defense position in your closing argument.

If it is necessary to present a rebuttal witness, keep the direct examination narrow and succinct. Make sure to tell the rebuttal witness to answer all questions directly and not to volunteer extra information. If the witness's testimony is limited to those issues that must be rebutted, the defense attorney cannot conduct a roving cross-examination.

Some prosecutors find the complainant a good final rebuttal witness. As the final witness, he can remind the jury of the victim, who has been overshadowed by witnesses subsequent to his testimony. It also allows the prosecution to answer one or two points raised by the defense. If the rebuttal is limited in scope, so is the cross-examination.

B. Rebuttal Based on the Defendant Opening the Door

One of the most important rebuttals is evidence of a defendant's prior acts that is now admissible because the defendant, through testimony offered on behalf of the defense, has opened the door. The United States Supreme Court in *Walder v. United States*, 347 U.S. 62 (1954), noted that a defendant who does more than deny an offense can open the door to otherwise improper evidence. For example, if a defendant states that he never had sexual contact with the child, the door is opened to prior uncharged acts involving the child. (See *State v. Banks*, 593 N.E.2d 346 [1991].) Similarly, a defendant's assertion that he was not the sole disciplinarian and did not condition the child's treatment upon performing sexual acts opens the door to otherwise precluded sexual contact. (See *State v. Kholi*, 672 A.2d 429 [R.I. 1996].)

Some defendants assert that they would "never molest a child" or that they "love children and would never harm one." Such testimony may open the door to the admission of prior bad acts with other child victims or signature acts with adult sex partners. Before presenting such evidence on rebuttal, request an opportunity to make an offer of proof outside the presence of the jury to place the reasons for the introduction of such evidence on the record, present the judge with applicable case law, and secure the court's permission to present the testimony. (See *State v. Newman*, 790 P.2d 971 [Mont. 1990] [holding ex-wife's testimony that defendant encouraged her to engage in anal sex with him and she had seen him become sexually aroused by a pornographic movie depicting a father having sex with his preteen daughter admissible to rebut defendant's testimony that he had no interest in anal sex or sexual contact with children]; *State v. Prouse*, 767 P.2d 1308 [Kan. 1989] [finding testimony that the defendant covered the witness's baby's mouth to stop the child from crying and that he was temperamental and became physically violent on one occasion to be admissible to rebut defendant's testimony that he had great self-control and never became angry].)

Some jurisdictions may restrict the use of such rebuttal evidence if the prosecutor elicited a general denial of an interest in sexually assaulting children during cross-examination rather than the defendant volunteering such statements during direct examination. (See *People v. Leo*, 470 N.W.2d 423 [Mich. 1991] [finding that defendant's denial of improper touching on cross-examination did not allow for admission of testimony as to defendant's improper touching of two additional victims on rebuttal, as such denial injected a new issue into the case and could not be used to revive a right to introduce evidence that could have been introduced in prosecutor's case-in-chief]; but see *Commonwealth v. Powers*, 577 A.2d 194 [Pa. 1990] [finding testimony of defendant's grandchild that defendant had shown X-rated movies to her to be admissible to rebut defendant's testimony on cross-examination that he had never shown his movies to any of his grandchildren].)

C. Rebuttal as to the Defendant's Good Character

A defendant may intentionally or unintentionally offer character evidence. For example, a defendant who testifies to medals or other honors received in the military opens the door to character. (See, e.g., *People v. Jones*, 503 N.Y.S.2d 109 [1986].)

If the defense attorney presents good-character witnesses on behalf of the defendant, consider putting on bad-character witnesses. Assess carefully whether the bad-character witnesses appear unbiased against the defendant. It is probably better to present a neighbor who got along well with the defendant until learning of his inappropriate sexual conduct toward children than an angry ex-spouse. Keep bad-character witness testimony narrow and concise. "Do you know the defendant?" "How do you know him and for how long?" "Do you know other people in the community who know the defendant?" "Based on your conversations with those people, what is the defendant's reputation for being a (truthful) (sexually moral) (honest) person?" Make sure to confine the traits you address to those raised by the defendant's character witnesses and do not elicit specific bad acts from the bad-character witnesses you present. Simply have these witnesses testify that the defendant has a bad reputation. A prosecutor eliciting or a witness volunteering specific bad acts on direct examination may result in a mistrial. If the defense attorney cross-examines your witness about the basis for the opinion that the defendant has a bad reputation and elicits examples of rumored prior bad acts, the defense attorney will be stuck with the witness's answer without grounds to complain later.

D. Rebuttal as to the Complainant's Character

If the defense attorney presents witnesses to testify to the victim's bad character, you should have good-character witnesses lined up for rebuttal. Again, try to find unbiased witnesses such as neighbors or teachers rather than relatives. Keep the testimony focused on a series of questions similar to those above. If you are unable to find rebuttal witnesses, address the unrebutted points as creatively and thoroughly as possible in your closing arguments.

E. Other Areas for Rebuttal Evidence

If the defendant or defense witnesses lie on the stand about a detail central to your case, consider all available rebuttal witnesses to refute the testimony. For example, if the defendant testifies that he could not have assaulted the victim because he drove a cab that night, obtain records from the cab company and have a company official present testimony showing the defendant was rarely on night duty. If the victim testifies that the defendant used handcuffs while sexually assaulting her and the defendant ridicules the notion in his testimony, find out whether he restrained other sexual partners with handcuffs. If it is discovered that this was a common practice with the defendant's partner, present that testimony to the jury.

If you did not present expert testimony in your case-in-chief but the defense called an expert, consider using an appropriate expert on rebuttal.

VIII. CLOSING ARGUMENTS

A. An Overview of Closing Arguments

1. The Purpose and Importance of Closing Arguments

The jury has listened to hours or days of testimony in a courtroom that may have been stuffy, too warm, or too cool. The jurors have heard testimony that has been sometimes boring, sometimes painful, from witnesses who were sympathetic, frightened, or abrasive. They have been kept waiting during objections and legal arguments they did not understand, and they have been puzzled over sidebar conferences. Each juror has focused on particular pieces of information during the testimony. Closing argument is the prosecutor's opportunity to draw the pieces together and help the jury see the case as the prosecutor sees it. Closing argument allows the prosecutor to highlight information significant to the State's case, structuring the facts to lead to the inevitable conclusion of the defendant's guilt.

2. The Limitations of Closing Arguments

Closing argument is limited to the confines of the record, although reasonable inferences from the facts may be argued. Each jurisdiction has unique restrictions on closing argument, and the consequences for improper prosecutorial argument range from corrective instructions to mistrial, from harmless error to reversal on appeal. To avoid a mistrial or reversal, the prosecutor must be familiar with applicable rules and case law. Certain general prohibitions apply in most jurisdictions:

- It is improper for the prosecutor to express a personal opinion regarding the credibility of witnesses or the guilt or innocence of the defendant. Avoid saying "I believe (the victim) . . ." Instead, it is generally acceptable to say "The evidence shows that (the victim) is telling the truth" or "(The victim) is telling the truth because . . ."
- It is improper to ask the jurors to put themselves in the place of the victim.
- It is improper to comment on the defendant's failure to testify, call witnesses, or present evidence. In some jurisdictions, the State may be allowed to point out when evidence is uncontroverted, so long as the State does not suggest that the defendant has an obligation to produce evidence. It may be appropriate to state, "There is no evidence before you that suggests (the defendant) was not with (the victim) on December 12, 2001." It would be even safer to say, "All of the evidence before you points to the (the defendant) being with (the victim) on December 12, 2001."
- It is improper for an attorney to "instruct" the jury on the law. In most jurisdictions, attorneys are allowed to discuss the instructions given to the jury by the court.
- It is improper to ask the jury to return verdicts based on sympathy or prejudice.
- It is improper to argue facts not in evidence.
- It is improper to argue matters excluded at trial.

3. Areas to Cover During a Closing Argument

The following argument topics should be covered during closing, depending on the facts of the case and the laws and rules of each jurisdiction.

- Explain that the law does not require the State to prove the specific dates on which the assaults occurred.
- Emphasize the explicit details provided by the victim and tell the jury that such knowledge of explicit details shows the victim experienced abuse.
- Explain the reasons for the victim's delay in reporting the abuse and why the delay does not weaken the victim's allegation.
- Explain the lack of medical evidence, such as no vaginal trauma, no semen or sperm found, by using common sense arguments that no penetration is alleged, there was only oral-genital contact so one would not expect to find trauma. Use expert testimony to do the same.
- Explain that sexual abuse is a secret crime so one would not expect to have eyewitnesses.
- Repeatedly emphasize to the jury that the testimony of the victim does not need to be corroborated. If the jury believes the victim's testimony, it is sufficient on its own to prove the defendant's guilt. Explain that this is the law because it is not expected that there will ever be eyewitnesses to these types of crimes.
- Contrast the lack of motive for the victim to lie with the interest of the defendant in the outcome of the case.
- Discuss that the standard of proof beyond a reasonable doubt is not a magic formula but is based on common sense. Reasonable doubt does not mean guilty beyond all doubt or that the State must prove guilt to a mathematical certainty. It also does not mean that a juror should go fishing for a doubt or go looking for a doubt.

- Highlight and repeat every bit of corroboration the State elicited at trial.
- Emphasize that the defendant's statements to the victim, such as "don't tell" and "this is our little secret," corroborate the victim's allegations.
- Contrast the demeanor of the victim on the witness stand to that of the defendant if the defendant testified.
- Be ready to defend the child's inappropriate behavior or demeanor on the stand, and explain that such behavior is to be expected.
- Explain how little probative value defense character witnesses have and emphasize that there are some things that even our best friends do not know about us.
- If the defendant comes across as an upstanding citizen, remind the jury that it is impossible to identify a child abuser by looks or acts alone. If so, there would be no need for jury trials. One could simply walk down the street, recognize an abuser, and arrest him.
- Emphasize consistencies in the victim's testimony and prior consistent statements. Small inconsistencies do not mean the victim is untruthful. Tell the jury that an account told exactly the same way each time would sound like a memorized script and be far more troubling. Help the jury understand the difference between credibility and memory. For example, if you asked your child what he got for Christmas last year, he could probably tell you. He probably could not tell you, however, what day of the week Christmas fell on. Does that mean the child is wrong about what he got for Christmas? Did he tell you a lie? Credibility and memory are two separate things altogether.

B. Organization

1. Preparation

Since the prosecutor must see the trial as an integrated whole, trial preparation includes identifying themes and issues that will be developed over the course of the trial. The same theme should be the basis for the closing argument, which is built upon predetermined issues highlighted from pre-trial motions through *voir dire*, opening statement, and the trial itself. It is, of course, impossible to anticipate everything. Adjustments to the planned closing are inevitable, and it is important to be open to new issues raised at trial. When preparing the closing argument, consider the State's case as planned and as presented, the defense case as anticipated and as presented, the anticipated defense arguments at closing, and jury instructions. In preparing for trial, it is often best to draft the closing argument first and then simply modify it to reflect any changes or additions to the evidence as the trial unfolds.

Every closing argument should have a structure developed to meet the unique aspects of the case and should flow from the overall plan. The prosecutor may wish to emphasize and develop the entire argument around a particular theme or piece of evidence. If, for example, the family secrets theme was introduced in *voir dire* and opening and then developed through trial testimony, the prosecutor should structure the closing so all the facts, all the physical evidence, all the inferences, and all the expert testimony come back to that theme.

2. Delivery

Closing argument should be presented using notes as little as possible. While it is helpful to draft a closing argument word-for-word to ensure the best possible argument, the prosecutor should be so familiar with the argument that there is only the need to glance at a page to recall the next point. In addition, while an outline is useful and necessary for most prosecutors, it is important to talk to the jurors, maintain eye contact, and let them feel the conviction of the argument. The court may dictate the length of argument. Even without imposed time constraints, be sensitive to the fact that jurors have been sitting for a long time and are tired. In order to keep the attention of the jury, consider using a PowerPoint presentation or other visual aids. In many jurisdictions, the prosecution argues first and again in rebuttal, although in some states and in certain types of proceedings, the defense may argue first followed by the prosecution. Whether the State presents a rebuttal argument or not in the former instance, the prosecution should anticipate the best possible arguments the defense could make and structure the initial closing to deflate them. When the prosecutor has finished making her closing argument, she wants the jury to realize that all the defense will be able to do in closing is rehash issues already rejected as unconvincing and unreasonable.

Use rebuttal argument to again highlight the strengths of case and do not give the defense legitimacy by spending a long time responding to every detail argued by the defense. If the prosecutor appears worried about a defense argument, the jury may think there is good reason for concern. Watch the jurors and focus on exposing those weaknesses in the defense arguments that appear to have been most persuasive. While some prosecutors want to save some especially good points for rebuttal when the defense cannot respond, prosecutors must be careful not to risk being prohibited from doing so because it is not considered responsive rebuttal material. A common defense strategy is to tell the jurors that their decision will affect the defendant for the rest of his life, and if wrongly convicted, the damage can never be undone. The State can turn this argument around in rebuttal by reminding the jury that the decision is equally important to the victim, and the jury's responsibility also extends to the other witnesses and the community. It might be appropriate to point out that the defendant's actions robbed the child of her childhood and innocence. The child will never be able to look back on her childhood without seeing what role she played in carrying out the defendant's lustful desires.

The prosecutor must have decided how to end the closing argument and do so strongly. Assuming the State is allowed to argue that a trial should be a search for the truth, it can be effective to say simply and directly that the State seeks just verdicts, and the truth is obvious from the evidence presented—that the defendant abused the victim and is guilty of the crimes charged. Alternatively, the prosecutor could argue that it is the jury's job to reach a verdict that speaks the truth, a verdict that is consistent with the evidence. A verdict of guilty.

C. Content

1. The Beginning

Prosecutors often fall into a habit of beginning their closing argument with a description of its purpose and cautioning jurors that an attorney's statements do not represent evidence or legal instructions. The judge's instructions will tell the jury that what the attorneys say is not evidence. Avoid falling into this habit—it tells the jury they can ignore what the prosecutor has worked so hard to say. Instead, consider beginning the argument with a statement or image that focuses attention on the theory of the case. For example, if the case involves the family secrets theme, begin with, "Ladies and gentlemen, the secret has been told." Or remind the jury of a particularly strong statement by a witness or description by the victim that highlights the central theme. The beginning of the closing argument should tell the jury the story of what occurred in an interesting manner with the corroborative evidence woven into the story.

The facts of a child abuse case present jurors with information they would rather not have to hear. They are asked to believe that a normal-looking adult has done abnormal things to a vulnerable child. Acknowledge that these are difficult things to consider and believe, but point out that they *do* unfortunately happen, and the jurors have the duty to consider the evidence with an open mind. These are emotional issues, and arguing them emotionally may be tempting. It is important, however, to use facts, analysis, and reasonable inferences so the jury has something more than emotion as a basis on which to convict.

2. *The Facts of the Case, Jury Instructions, and the Elements of the Crime*

The jury instruction conference attended by the prosecutor, defense counsel, and judge is usually held at the close of evidence. Each attorney will know the jury instructions prior to preparing and presenting closing arguments, but some jurisdictions do not allow attorneys to read the instructions to the jury. Careful paraphrasing, however, is generally allowed, and instructions detailing the elements of the crime should be woven into the argument.

Jurors often have preconceived definitions of elements that are different from the applicable legal definitions. Not all juries receive copies of jury instructions, and not all jurors listen carefully as the judge reads the instructions. It is helpful to the jury to place a chart in front of them listing the elements. A prosecutor could also list the elements as part of a PowerPoint presentation. The prosecutor should identify and emphasize any elements that might be misunderstood or resisted by jury members. For example, if the evidence shows that the defendant put his penis in the victim's mouth, the prosecutor should highlight that the legal definition of "sexual penetration" includes oral or genital penetration and penetration is defined as any intrusion, however slight. If the evidence shows the defendant touched the victim's genital area over her underwear, point out that the law defining "sexual contact" includes sexual touching over the clothing.

Prosecutors should take each element of the crime charged and explain how it has been proven with a particular piece of evidence. For example, "One element of child molestation is that the defendant committed these acts with the intent to arouse and satisfy the sexual desires of the accused. To prove intent, the State does not have to show the defendant said, 'Little girl, I intend to molest you.' Intent can be proved by circumstantial evidence. Remember when Susie testified that her daddy told her to 'rub him until he got hard?' That is an example of the defendant's intent."

Emphasize that only the elements of the crime must be proven by the State in order to convict. Jurors are often bothered by not having evidence explaining *why* the defendant would abuse a child physically or sexually. It can help to say that no one really understands why anyone derives sexual gratification from a child. Point out that while the motive for something like robbery *is* understandable, motives for abuse are not, and the defendant's *reason* for the abusive behavior is not an element of the crimes charged.

If there have been discrepancies in testimony that can be explained and do not undermine the credibility of a witness, consider mentioning one to illustrate that it is not an element and that the discrepancy does not mean the State has not proven its case. For example, the victim testifies she has been assaulted numerous times over the past one and a half years and several times in the past 2 months in the presence of her 4-year-old brother. She testifies that her brother saw her dad touch her on Saturday. The brother confirms he has seen his sister touched on many occasions but does not remember whether he saw the Saturday incident. The children's mother says the brother was with her on Saturday and could not have witnessed the assault that day. The victim's statement about her brother's presence on other occasions, however, is confirmed, although the jury may question whether he was actually there on Saturday. Point out that his presence is not an element of the crime, and the discrepancy in testimony is understandable given the number of times the child was assaulted and should not defeat the State's case.

In a complicated case involving multiple victims and counts, consider using a large chart at closing, delineating the crimes, elements, and victims in simplified fashion. As each element is discussed as to a particular victim and related to the evidence, it can be checked off. Exhibits introduced during trial should also be incorporated into the closing to help the prosecutor illustrate key points.

Instructions regarding issues other than the elements of the crime, or the lack of instructions, should be selectively highlighted depending on the needs of the case. This emphasizes that the law supports the facts as the jury has heard and seen them. For example, if the child is unable to testify to the precise date of the assault, point out that the law does not require pinpointing the exact date of the crime in a child abuse case.

3. Argue Strengths, Common Sense, and Credibility

A closing argument must be framed in a positive manner. Focusing on negatives gives the defense an opportunity to respond to these points and focus on them rather than on the elements of the crime. The defendant should be found guilty because the child testified that he abused her and the medical evidence corroborates her testimony, not simply because the defendant says he cannot remember where he was on the day of the assault. This is not to say that these facts should not be pointed out, but, rather, they should be presented as additional evidence supporting the victim's credibility.

Encourage jurors to use their common sense in assessing the witnesses, evidence, and arguments. Use the jury instruction about common sense and good judgment to reinforce your comments. During closing argument, point out the reasonable, common sense inferences that should be drawn from the evidence.

Since many child abuse trials come down to the issue of credibility, it is critical throughout the trial that the prosecutor show confidence in the child. If the child has had trouble testifying, such as appearing nervous, hostile, or angry, the prosecutor should comment on the demeanor of the child. Facts in evidence should include the report of abuse, the professionals involved, the number of times the child has had to describe the abuse to strangers, her family's reactions, and so on. Discussing this process may help explain the child's difficulty in court. Detailing the process the child has gone through, such as multiple interviews, discussions with strangers of sexually intimate details, a physical exam, removal from her home, or other negative impacts, also demonstrates the child's courage in reporting and following through despite the difficulty and discomfort.

If the child says the defendant sexually assaulted her and the defendant denies it, ask the jury who has the most at stake and most to lose. Ask who is best able to fabricate a complicated story designed to sway a jury. Emphasize that their decision should be based on who they believe—the child or the defendant. Be careful, however, not to shift the burden to the defendant. They should feel that an acquittal is justified only if they believe the child is lying and the defendant is telling the truth. Highlight reasons to believe the child and show how her account is corroborated. Point out reasons the defendant is not to be believed.

In nearly every case, a prosecutor can make the following argument as to why the child and not the defendant should be believed:

a. The victim testified under oath. If the child is sworn in as a witness, argue that the oath gives the victim an incentive to be honest. When queried in a developmentally appropriate manner, even very young children can distinguish between a truth and a lie and have an understanding that dishonesty is immoral.

The incentive the oath gives a child to be honest can be contrasted with the impact of the oath on an accused child abuser. Unlike the child, the perpetrator has something to gain by committing perjury. A perpetrator lacks the incentive to tell the truth if doing so will ensure his conviction.

b. Not only does the oath give the child an incentive to tell the truth, but the child has no incentive to lie. A prosecutor can begin to set up this argument in *voir dire* by asking potential jurors if they have ever been lied to. When a juror responds affirmatively, ask whether there was a reason for the lie. Most jurors agree that people lie for a reason. Remind the jury of this in your closing argument and point out that the victim has no reason to lie.

For many children, the aftermath of a disclosure is so painful that recanting the allegation is preferable to telling the truth. In closing argument, point out the negative consequences that the child suffered after disclosure. Argue that if these consequences did not cause the child to alter the allegation, the child must be telling the truth. The following argument illustrates this point:

> Does anyone believe accusing her father of incest has been fun for this child? This girl told a male police officer about sexual conduct most adults cannot speak of candidly. This girl endured an uncomfortable medical examination. This girl was removed from her home and placed with strangers. This girl was ostracized by her family. This girl was required to come to court and, in front of her father, tell twelve strangers what it feels like to be raped. This child endured a cross-examination designed to discredit her. She's having a lot of fun, isn't she? Would any human being endure such anguish unless she was telling the truth?

c. The victim's testimony is corroborated by medical evidence. Sexually transmitted diseases or other positive medical findings obviously corroborate a victim's allegation. Negative medical findings also corroborate the allegation so long as the findings are consistent with the history given by the child. If a child alleges sexual contact, not penetration, or contends the abuse occurred some time ago, a physician can explain that the absence of an injury is consistent with the history. This testimony opens the door for the following argument:

If this six-year-old girl is a liar, she has remarkable foresight. At the time of the original statement to the police, she was able to realize she would no doubt be compelled to undergo a medical examination. Accordingly, she alleged sexual conduct that would not produce medical evidence. Does that make any sense? Do you really believe the child thought that far in advance and with the degree of sophistication necessary to pull off such a lie?

d. The victim lacks the sophistication to lie convincingly. Although children lie, they are not very good at it. Crumbs on the face often give a child denying a theft of cookies away. Jurors experienced with children will understand the unsophisticated nature of childhood lies and will likely find appealing the following argument:

> Anyone, including a child, can be a liar. This does not mean, though, that a little kid is as good a liar as a grown-up. In this case, the defendant wants you to believe the victim is so sophisticated she can tell a lie believable enough to fool the police, social services, and a physician. The defendant wants you to believe this little girl is such a good liar that she can keep a consistent story intact over a period of months. Even when confronted by her assailant's attorney, this child did not wilt. Under this rationale, you are asked not only to believe this four-year-old kid is a liar, but that she is a darn good liar. In the history of childhood, has any kid pulled off such a feat?

e. If the child is lying, why is the lie not exaggerated? In many cases, a victim's testimony is less damning than would be expected of someone making a false accusation. For instance, a victim may allege sexual contact but deny penetration. A victim may deny that her father threatened her with physical harm. Find nuggets like these in a victim's statement or testimony and cite them to the jury as evidence that the child is not on a crusade to crucify the perpetrator. After all, if the child was really out to get the defendant, why not seize every opportunity to falsely accuse him? The answer, of course, is that the victim is telling the truth and is willing to do so whether the truth hurts or helps the accused.

f. The victim's behavior corroborates her testimony. Although bedwetting, nightmares, and sexual behaviors are not diagnostic of abuse, they may be consistent with it. If a behavior such as bedwetting occurs only after visits with the alleged perpetrator, the correlation is even stronger.

g. The victim's testimony is corroborated by other witnesses. Relate to the jury each portion of the child's testimony that is corroborated by other witnesses. For instance, if a child alleges abuse on a camping expedition, other witnesses may corroborate a claim that the victim and the perpetrator shared a tent.

h. The victim's testimony is corroborated by the physical evidence. Police officers and prosecutors often think of physical evidence only in terms of semen, hair, fibers, and the like. While physical evidence of this nature is often not present, other types of physical evidence may be available. For instance, a child says he was abused on a fishing trip with his grandfather. Upon request, the mother may be able to produce photographs of the fishing trip to document the existence of such a trip, and, to this extent, corroborate the victim's testimony. If a victim describes drinking beer with the perpetrator or recalls the color of the room in which the abuse occurred, search the house for the presence of beer and photograph the room to verify the accuracy of the child's memory at least as to color. If denied a consensual search of the house, obtain a warrant. If denied a search warrant, certainly a witness can be found to verify that the defendant drinks beer and that his bedroom is orange. Perhaps the defendant himself will concede this much.

i. The victim's testimony is corroborated by the defendant. Even if a defendant denies the allegation, there is often something to hang your hat on. Perhaps the defendant admits taking the child on a particular outing or being alone with the child at a particular time. A perpetrator may admit to a close, loving relationship with the child and agree there is no reason for the victim to fabricate. Guilty persons often ask few questions about the child's allegations. If you are permitted to play to the jury the suspect's recorded police interview, the jury may realize the defendant is not behaving innocently. You may be able to drive this point home to the jury with the following argument:

> You heard the defendant's interview with the police. Did he speak to the officer in a manner consistent with innocence? If he were falsely accused would he not be demanding to see the child's statements and asking as many questions of the officer as he was answering? Isn't it obvious that the reason the defendant had no questions is because he already knew the answers? He knew he had abused his child. There is no other explanation for his demeanor during the interview.

j. The child's allegation is supported by expert testimony. Some jurisdictions have allowed experts to testify about delayed reporting, child development issues, and a host of other matters that may enhance the credibility of your child victim. If your jurisdiction allows this evidence, it can be cited as an additional reason the child can be believed.

When done citing to the jury the reasons to believe the child, you may wish to summarize them in a way that highlights the absurdity of any claim the child is lying. You might try something like this:

> When you consider that the child testified under oath, when you consider that the child has no reason to lie, when you consider that the child is not sophisticated enough to pull off such a convincing lie, when you consider that some or all of the child's statement is corroborated by medical personnel and other witnesses who also have no reason to fabricate, and when you consider that even the defendant corroborated portions of the victim's testimony, it is clear that the defendant is guilty beyond a reasonable doubt.

4. Corroboration

Though many jurisdictions do not require corroboration in sexual assault cases, most cases will have some facts that corroborate the victim's report. Resist the temptation to characterize the case as the child's word versus the defendant's. With rare exceptions, there will be witnesses other than the victim who testified and thus there will be evidence other than the child's testimony. The evidence need not corroborate the crime itself but may support the child's credibility. Do not assume the jury has seen the significance of the corroborative evidence or drawn desired inferences. That is your job. You should consider creating a chart listing the corroboration and discussing it point by point. Your experience and training allow you to see things much differently from a juror who may have heard about child sexual abuse for the first time.

Highlight the most significant parts of important witness testimony and tie them directly to the case. When arguing the evidence supporting the victim's account, the prosecutor should emphasize the testimony of other witnesses and physical evidence or exhibits, encouraging the jury's consideration of common sense, human nature, and probabilities. For example, the child may have testified that her friend's brother took her to his house and sexually assaulted her in his bed. She testifies his bedspread was blue with green flowers. A photograph of the bedspread or the bedspread itself, seized from the friend's house, is introduced into evidence—corroborating a detail of the victim's account. In another case, an employer's time sheet is admitted into evidence showing the defendant's absence from work on the day that the child testified the defendant molested her. Physical evidence corroborates her testimony; though it does not prove he molested her, it shows opportunity to do so. In another case, the child testifies that the defendant gave her money, earrings, and a radio after he sexually touched her. The child's mother testifies she noticed that her daughter had new clothes, tapes, and a radio, but the child refused to say how she got them.

Emphasize the fact that child abuse is a secret crime. The defendant intentionally chose an isolated and vulnerable child and intentionally sought a time and place when the child was alone. The obvious result is that there are no witnesses besides the child to testify at trial. It can also be helpful to point out that this is not unlike other crimes, such as murder and burglary, that are generally also not committed in front of eyewitnesses.

5. Confessions, Admissions, and Statements of the Defendant

Suspects in child abuse cases are often willing to talk to police. Statements and partial admissions are often useful during closing argument to corroborate the child's testimony. For example, the defendant may admit he was alone with the child at the time and place the child says she was molested. The defendant may state that he knows of no reason the child would lie about him. A defendant may also admit he touched the child but claim it was accidental. Another defendant may admit he assaulted the child but explain it as discipline. Highlight these admissions as supporting the child's account.

As with other portions of the closing argument, the prosecutor may want to use a visual aid to emphasize the defendant's admission. This could be done by writing the words on an overhead, using a PowerPoint presentation, or placing a blowup of the relevant page of the defendant's statement on foam board. Similarly, the defendant's statement may corroborate everything the child said happened except for the sexual touching. Create a chart showing the parallels of the statements. Use the chart to then argue that the child correctly told everything else that happened on that particular day, so it must also follow that the abuse happened.

6. Acknowledge Weaknesses in the State's Case

A prosecutor should directly confront weaknesses in the State's case during closing argument. Assume that the jury is aware of any problems and that the defense is certainly aware of them. If the State raises these arguments, the State can define them and answer the questions as desired. If nothing is said until the defense raises the weaknesses, the defense will frame them to the defendant's advantage. It cannot hurt to admit that no person, case, or investigation is perfect and that mistakes are sometimes made. The State can remind jurors that the purpose of the trial is not to reward or punish investigators for the job they did, but to determine what really happened. (See Appendixes V.33 and V.38 for a closing argument in a child sexual abuse case.)

7. Considerations in Child Physical Abuse and Homicide Closing Arguments

While much of the information in the preceding section on closing arguments applies to sexual and physical abuse and homicide cases, some additional points must be raised. Closing argument may be the only opportunity to distill complicated medical and lay testimony in a physical abuse or homicide case. Visual aids will help the jury during closing argument to see the "whole picture." If the trial was particularly long, photographs of each witness will remind jurors who testified and the substance of what each said. Repeat any demonstrations done by experts. PowerPoint presentations or large charts detailing elements of the crime can focus the jury on exactly what the prosecution must prove.

Remind the jury that the prosecution does not have to *prove* motive, since motive is not an element of any of the crimes charged. It is helpful, however, to offer a motive for the defendant's conduct, since jurors generally do not want to believe that anyone would seriously injure or kill a child. If the jury appears to sympathize with the defendant, the prosecutor may emphasize her compassion for the defendant. If appropriate, characterize the defendant as overwhelmed but out of control owing to her life circumstances. Concede that the experiences of first-time caring for an infant or frustration with toilet training can be trying. Explain to the jury that to find the defendant guilty, they do not need to find that she is a bad person. The defendant is in court, however, because she must be held accountable.

The prosecutor may want to let jurors know that it is understandable to prefer to believe the injuries were accidental to avoid the uncomfortable reality that some individuals can be that brutal. Remind the jury that they took an oath to look at the evidence without prejudice or sympathy. It is not sufficient simply to parrot the State expert's conclusions that the injuries were nonaccidental. Instead, the prosecutor must emphasize that the facts show why the injury or death could not have been an accident. Appeal to the jurors' common sense and ability to be objective.

When reviewing the medical testimony, avoid using technical terminology, but do not patronize or imply that the jurors were unable to understand medical testimony. If there was conflicting medical testimony, show why the prosecution experts are more qualified and why their testimony makes more sense. Discuss any bias the defense medical experts may have.

The prosecutor should review the timing of the injuries and the instrument that caused the injuries. Explain that it is impossible to know the exact series of events, as only the defendant and the deceased or injured child were present. Emphasize that the law does not require the State to prove everything that happened to a mathematical certainty or in a precise order. It is sufficient for the State to show that the act happened, it was not an accident, and the defendant is responsible for the act. (See Appendix V.35 for a sample closing argument in a child homicide case.)

8. Responding to Defense Arguments

Some defense arguments surface regularly in child abuse cases. The State's response will depend on the facts of the case, but certain approaches are useful. If the defense is known before trial, the prosecutor can present evidence during trial and then use that evidence to show the implausibility of that argument during closing.

Defense Argument: If the abuse claim were true, why did the child wait so long to report?

Responses:
- The child's explanation if the child has given one:
  - Threatened with harm or threatened with the breakup of family
  - Feared defendant would go to prison
  - Feared parents or nonabusing parent would be angry
  - The child told her parent, but the parent did not believe her
  - Did not think anyone would believe her, perhaps based on prior attempts to tell and the reaction encountered
- Expert testimony on delayed reporting in child abuse cases
- Facts, common sense:
  - The child was attached to and trusted the defendant
  - The child was taught to obey
  - The child did not know what the defendant was doing was wrong, or that the defendant was committing a crime
  - The child was embarrassed and felt guilty
  - In child abuse cases, delay is the norm, not the exception

Defense Argument: If the abuse claim were true, why is it being embellished over time? Didn't the child really get caught up in a lie she felt compelled to maintain?

Responses:
- The child's explanation:
  - During the police interview, the child did not want to tell a stranger the details about what happened.
  - The child was afraid because of the defendant's threats, but wanted the abuse to stop. The child thought disclosing just a little bit would make the defendant stop.
  - Significant details included in initial disclosure
- Expert testimony on disclosure over time
- Facts, common sense:
  - The child's initial disclosure was not made to report a crime. The child did not know telling teacher would result in police investigation.
  - The child had a natural reluctance to tell strangers about intensely intimate and embarrassing experiences.
  - The child told the least threatening aspects of abuse first to gauge the receiver's reaction. When the child felt more comfortable, she was able to reveal other, more frightening aspects.
  - The interviewer stressed the importance of telling the truth throughout the sessions, and the child maintained a consistent account even during defense cross-examination.

(Continued)

(Continued)

Defense Argument. If the abuse claim were true, why did the child later deny or recant the allegation?

Responses:
- The child's explanation if child has testified about abuse:
  - Pressure from defendant and/or family.
    - The child felt guilty and/or responsible for the disruption caused by the disclosure.
    - The child was removed from home and wanted to return. The child believed that the social worker would allow her to go home if she said it did not happen.
  - Expert testimony on recanting in child abuse cases
  - Facts, common sense:
    - The child was threatened with harm or breakup of family.
    - The disclosure took place when child was safe from defendant or wanted to avoid another assault. When initial aim was accomplished, the child wished to spare everyone from continuing turmoil.
    - The result of the disclosure was painful for the child. The child was removed from home; condemned and pressured by the defendant or family members; mother attempted suicide; friends abandoned or ridiculed the child; etc.

Defense Argument: The child misunderstood/misinterpreted the defendant's actions.

Responses:
- Common sense and facts:
  - Consider what happened according to the child—specific sexual actions, statements, secrecy, and threats
  - The defendant's attempts to conceal incident, including the timing and place of the assault

Defense Argument: The child has a history of poor behavior (runaway, involved in drugs, sexually promiscuous) and cannot be believed.

Responses:
- Expert testimony about impacts of abuse
- Facts, common sense:
  - A troubled child deserves the same protections from the law as anyone else.
  - The behavior began after the onset of abuse, and the child's acting out behavior is a response to the defendant's actions.
  - The defendant intentionally chose a victim who was vulnerable, needed attention, lacked parental supervision, and lacked credibility.
  - The defendant introduced the child to sex and reinforced sexual behavior with affection and gifts. The defendant taught the child that sex is the key to acceptance.

Defense Argument: The child is lying to get the defendant in trouble.

(Continued)

(Continued)

Responses:
- Facts, common sense:
  - The child was threatened with harm or breakup of family.
  - A very young child does not have the ability to make up and maintain a complex allegation.
  - The consistency of the child's account to several professionals and during testimony.
  - Like adults, children lie to get themselves out of trouble ("I didn't break the lamp") or to make themselves look good ("I tied my own shoes"). A child's allegations of abuse accomplish neither purpose. The attention that is generated is generally negative, and the criminal justice process is uncomfortable at best.
  - The child trusted and liked the defendant, according to both the victim and the defendant.

Defense Argument: The child has been coached by the other parent, who is involved in divorce/custody/visitation battle with the defendant.

Responses:
- The child's testimony:
  - The child used her own words, not adult terms, to describe assault. The child was also able to answer questions and elaborate on her prior statements. False accounts should sound memorized.
  - The child used her own words for body parts and sexual acts.
  - The child provided sensory details of the abuse: sights, smells, and sounds. Even if a parent tried to "teach" a sexual abuse allegation, a parent is unlikely to teach a child what it tastes like to perform fellatio.
- Facts, common sense:
  - The disclosure was made before the divorce or custody proceeding was initiated.
  - The disclosure was made in spontaneous manner to someone other than parent.
  - A loving parent would not put her child through this if the report was false.
  - The nonabusing parent did not believe allegation at first.
  - The nonabusing parent testified and refuted the defendant's allegations.
  - The prospect of the divorce made it safer to reveal abuse because the abuser was no longer in the home where he could continue to harm the child.
  - The possibility of being alone with the abusive parent motivated child to report.

Defense Argument: The child was coached or "victimized" by an overzealous police officer, CPS worker, prosecutor, treatment specialist, or other professional.

Responses:
- Facts, common sense:
  - A coached child cannot answer questions convincingly or consistently relate details about an abuse incident.
  - The child's testimony gave no indication that she was coached. For example, the child indicated she was told to tell the truth and used her own words to describe the abuse.

(Continued)

(Continued)

- The procedures followed by professionals who investigated the report are aimed at finding out what really happened. Investigators would welcome the case where a suspicion of abuse was incorrect.
- With the volume of cases requiring extensive follow-up, it does not make sense that professionals would want to create additional cases by coaching a child about abuse.
- The defense theory does not make sense because the child dealt with numerous professionals, and effective coaching would have required them all to conspire to frame an innocent person.

Defense Argument: The child fantasized the sexual abuse.

Responses:
- The child's testimony regarding explicit descriptions of the defendant's activity.
- Expert testimony.
- Facts, common sense:
    - Children do imagine fanciful stories—giving life to a favorite toy, fearing a monster under the bed—but the elements of truth and fiction are generally obvious and distinct.
    - The child's previous unsuccessful attempts to stop the abuse—pleasing the defendant, avoiding contact, feigning illness—are not consistent with fantasy.
    - Sexually explicit details come from direct experience, and sexual abuse is the only source of such information the child was exposed to.
    - Even if a child fantasized about intimate contact, would any child fantasize about sexual contact with a parent?

Defense Argument: The child has seen sexually explicit videos or adults engaged in sexual acts, and therefore the child has the ability to describe sexual activity.

Responses:
- The child's testimony:
    - The child testified she had not seen these things.
    - The child's description of sexually explicit details concerning sensations—taste, smell, texture—can only be accurately described as a result of direct experience.
- Facts, common sense:
    - The other witnesses deny child's exposure to such things.
    - The child is otherwise in touch with reality and not fantasizing about every other incredible thing seen on TV, movies, or videos.
    - The defendant showed the child pornography as part of the grooming process and now he has the audacity to use this grooming as "evidence" of his innocence?

Defense Argument: The defendant is an upstanding citizen, loving parent, and loving husband.

Responses:
- The child's testimony:
    - Defendant used affection and authority to pressure and persuade child.

(Continued)

(Continued)

- Facts, common sense:
  - Child abuse is not a crime limited to a particular class, group, race, occupation, or religion.
  - Defendant's motive is not an element; no one knows why anyone would do such a thing to a child.
  - You cannot tell a child abuser by the way he looks.

Defense Argument: The child is lying about sexual abuse because she thinks discipline at home is too strict.

Responses:
- The child's testimony:
  - The child cared for the defendant and still does.
- Facts, common sense:
  - The child did not want to leave home, only wanted abuse to stop.
  - If the child were going to fabricate in response to discipline, would it be reasonable to fabricate about physical, not sexual, abuse?

Defense Argument: The child's account is full of inconsistencies that prove she is lying.

Responses:
- Facts, common sense:
  - Ask the jury to consider the effect of confusing and intimidating cross-examination, matching the sophistication, experience, and aggressiveness of the defense attorney against the young child.
  - It is difficult for anyone to have a clear memory of all details over time, particularly when the experience was repeated. No person tells something exactly the same way every time the experience is shared unless it is a memorized story.
  - Inconsistencies in account relate to details, not to the central facts of the abuse.
  - The child had no desire to maintain detailed memories of unpleasant, upsetting events and attempted to "block" the experiences as a coping mechanism.

Defense Argument: The child is lying to get attention after participating in a personal safety course at school or following a friend's disclosure.

Responses:
- Expert testimony on disclosures following "safe touching" courses
- Facts, common sense:
  - The halting, embarrassed demeanor of the child during her testimony is inconsistent with someone enjoying the attention the disclosure produced.
  - The negative attention the child received following disclosure, the condemnation and rejection, would not encourage the child to stick to a false statement of abuse.
  - The content of personal safety educational program did not include the explicit details of abuse that the child was able to tell the investigator.
  - The child's friend's experience was different from that of the child in this case.
  - The personal safety course did not teach the child to lie, it taught her how to get help. This is precisely why we have personal safety courses.

(Continued)

(Continued)

Defense Argument: The defendant could not have sexually abused the child because he is impotent.

Responses:
- Facts, common sense:
  - The defendant's claim is not supported by expert medical evidence.
  - Defendant is sexually aroused by children, not adults.
  - An impotent man can nonetheless molest a child with his hands, mouth, and even a penis that is not erect.

Defense Argument: A unanimous verdict on a particular act is impossible because the child has been so unclear. The child described many ongoing activities without being specific about particular acts. All jurors must agree on the same thing, and you cannot convict if one juror believes the defendant did one thing at one time and another juror believes he did something else or the same thing at another time.

Responses:
- Facts, common sense:
  - The critical decision is whether the child or the defendant is telling the truth.
  - If the jury believes everything the child said, the unanimity requirement is satisfied.
  - Follow the judge's, not the attorney's, instructions as to the law.

Defense Argument: The child's injuries were the result of reasonable discipline that accidentally went too far.

Responses:
- Expert testimony from a medical specialist on the nature, location, and extent of injuries
- Facts, common sense:
  - The size and strength differences between the adult and the child gave the adult an advantage and therefore responsibility for controlling the use of force.
  - Assaulting another adult—leaving scars, breaking bones, inflicting burns, other injuries—would not be tolerated under law. Children deserve equal if not more protection under the law because of their complete vulnerability.
  - The defendant was aware of his ability to inflict injury because of past injuries to the child.
  - The defendant's claim that the child "bruises easily" is not supported by medical testimony or by the witness's testimony.
  - The defendant's delay in obtaining treatment shows the defendant realized the act was not reasonable.
  - The defendant's prior history of abuse of children shows the defendant was not disciplining the child, but abusing the child.
  - If the defendant were disciplining the child, why would the defendant give inconsistent explanations for the child's injuries?

Defense Argument: The defendant couldn't have injured the child. He lived with him for years before the injury and never hurt him.

(Continued)

(Continued)

Responses:
- Facts, common sense:
  - The defendant had different levels of tolerance for the child's various behaviors. He could not tolerate the child's "toilet training" stage and began to physically assault the child when he had toileting accidents.

Defense Argument: The defendant is an upstanding citizen and did not intend to cause the child any harm.

Responses:
- Facts, common sense:
  - The defendant may not be an evil person, but he is a person out of control. The defendant lost control because of his problems with debt, marriage, or work and took those problems out on the child.
  - The defendant wrongly focused his frustration on the most vulnerable member of the household and the one who could not fight back.
  - Every child has right to be safe in his home, classroom, or daycare.

Defense Argument: Someone else injured the child, not the defendant.

Responses:
- Expert testimony from medical specialist indicating timing and cause of injuries.
- Expert testimony that siblings and child not developmentally capable of inflicting such injuries
- Facts, common sense:
  - The defendant had exclusive custody of the child at time of injuries.
  - The defendant hid the child's injuries.
  - The defendant fled after the child was hospitalized while other caregivers remained.
  - The defendant gave inconsistent explanations for the child's injuries.

Defense Argument: The State is trying to tell you how to raise and discipline children.

Responses:
- Facts, common sense:
  - Acknowledge that caregivers have a right to discipline their children, set rules, and use corporal punishment.
  - There is a dramatic difference between criminal abuse and corporal punishment.
  - Being a parent does not give that person a license to abuse.
  - Stop cycle of violence.
  - Seventy years ago children worked in coal mines. Children haven't become more deserving, but we understand now that they need more protection.
  - The defendant would not have done this conduct in public. A person's conduct is criminal regardless of whether it is done in public or at home, but the defendant was more comfortable inflicting these injuries at home where her criminal actions would not be scrutinized.

(Continued)

(Continued)

Defense Argument: You must find a reasonable doubt, as the prosecution can't tell you exactly what happened to the child.

Responses:
- Expert testimony from medical specialists regarding the nonaccidental, intentional nature of the act. The injuries were not self-inflicted.
- Facts, common sense:
  - The defendant had exclusive access to child at time of injury.
  - Only two people, the child and defendant, know exactly what happened.
    - You see your mom in the kitchen with mixing bowl and cake ingredients, you leave and return later to see cake cooling on rack. You do not know the order that your mom put the ingredients in the batter, but you do know that Mom made a cake. The State's inability to give the precise order of injuries or events does not mean they did not happen.

Defense Argument: The defendant's discipline of the child was appropriate within his culture.

Responses:
- Expert testimony or lay testimony from individuals of same culture indicating the defendant's conduct is not part of the culture
- Facts, common sense:
  - The defendant hid his conduct or the child's injuries from other members of cultural community.
  - The defendant threatened the child to prevent disclosure.
  - The defendant failed to conform to *other* dictates of his cultural community.

IX. JURY INSTRUCTIONS

A. How to Prepare

During case preparation, a prosecutor should be thinking about what specialized jury instructions might be appropriate. Judges unfamiliar with child abuse cases may be reluctant to deviate from their routine, but there are special jury instructions that should always be considered. Many of these instructions are included in the jurisdiction's standard or pattern criminal jury instructions. Present them to the judge with supporting case law. The judge should rule on proposed instructions prior to closing arguments so the prosecutor can comment on them during closing argument if this is allowed by court rules or local practice.

B. Jury Instructions in Child Abuse Cases

1. Expert Witness Instruction

If an expert testifies for either side, request that the judge give an "expert witness" jury instruction. For example:

8625986767878

A witness who has special knowledge, skill, experience, training, or education in a particular area may testify as an expert in that area. You determine what weight, if any, to give to an expert's testimony just as you do with the testimony of any other witness. You should consider the expert's credibility as a witness, the expert's qualifications as an expert, the sources of the expert's information, and the reasons given for any opinions expressed by the expert. (NJI2d Crim. 5.4 [1992])

2. Uncorroborated Testimony of the Victim

Regardless of whether the case includes corroborative evidence, the prosecutor should ask the judge to give a jury instruction that the uncorroborated testimony of a victim is sufficient to convict the defendant if believed beyond a reasonable doubt. This reinforces what the prosecutor should point out in closing—that the law recognizes that child abuse usually occurs in secret without direct witnesses other than the victim and defendant. It also allows the prosecutor to argue that the case consisted of far more evidence to convict than required under the law. For example,

The testimony of _____ standing alone, if believed by you, is sufficient proof upon which to find the defendant guilty in this case. The testimony of the victim in a case such as this need not be supported by other evidence to sustain a conviction. Thus you may find the defendant guilty if the testimony of _____ convinces you beyond a reasonable doubt that the defendant is guilty. (Pa.SSJI [Crim.] § 4.13B [1995])

3. The Interest of the Defendant in the Case Outcome

If the defendant has testified, ask the court to give a jury instruction indicating that, when assessing the defendant's credibility, they can take into account the fact that this person has a vital interest in the outcome of the trial. Some judges will simply rely on the general "witness credibility" charge. The law and procedure in each jurisdiction will determine whether this instruction can be included. Pennsylvania's standard jury instruction reads as follows:

1. The defendant took the stand as a witness. In considering the defendant's testimony, you are to follow the general instructions I gave you for judging the credibility of any witness.

2. You should not disbelieve the defendant's testimony merely because he is the defendant. In weighing his testimony, however, you may consider the fact that he has a vital interest in the outcome of this trial. You may take the defendant's interest into account, just as you would the interest of any other witness, along with all other facts and circumstances bearing on credibility in making up your minds what weight his testimony deserves. (Pa.SSJI [Crim.] § 3.09 [1995])

Nebraska's standard jury instruction does not specifically address the defendant's interest. Make sure to emphasize the portion of the instruction that describes self-interest as a factor to be weighed.

> You are the sole judges of the credibility of the witnesses and the weight to be given to their testimony. In determining this, you may consider the following:
>
> 1. The conduct and demeanor of the witness while testifying;
> 2. The sources of information, including the opportunity for seeing or knowing the things about which the witness testified;
> 3. The ability of the witness to remember and to communicate accurately;
> 4. The reasonableness or unreasonableness of the testimony of the witness;
> 5. The interest or lack of interest of the witness in the result of this case;
> 6. The apparent fairness or bias of the witness;
> 7. Any previous statement or conduct of the witness that is consistent or inconsistent with the testimony of the witness at this trial; and
> 8. Any other evidence that affects the credibility of the witness or that tends to support or contradict the testimony of the witness. (NJI2d Crim. 5.2 [1992])

4. *The Use of a Witness's Prior Statements as Substantive Evidence*

If the victim recants at trial and the prosecutor has presented prior statements to prove the assault allegations, make sure the judge instructs the jury to consider prior statements as substantive evidence in considering whether to convict the defendant. The following example allows the trial judge to choose the appropriate alternative.

You have heard evidence that a witness, _____, made a statement on an earlier occasion that was inconsistent with his present testimony.

First Alternative

You may, if you choose, regard this evidence as proof of the truth of anything that the witness said in the earlier statement. You may also consider this evidence to help you judge the credibility and weight of the testimony given by the witness at this trial.

Second Alternative

You may consider this evidence for one purpose only, to help you judge the credibility and weight of the testimony given by the witness at this trial. You may not regard evidence of an earlier inconsistent statement as proof of the truth of anything said in that statement. (Pa.SSJI [Crim.] § 4.08A [1995])

---

5. Limiting Instructions

Whenever evidence has been admitted for a limited purpose, an oral instruction regarding the limitation should be given during trial. It may also be appropriate to propose written instructions clarifying the purpose for which selected evidence may be considered, particularly to protect the record on appeal. For example, if several victims' cases were consolidated for trial or if the court allowed the admission of prior bad acts of the defendant, some jurisdictions require that a cautionary instruction be given to the jury that the multiple victim evidence should not be considered as evidence to show the defendant's "propensity" to abuse children. The court should indicate the limited purpose for which the evidence was admitted and caution the jury to consider it for that purpose alone. (See, e.g., *People v. Holder*, 687 P.2d 462 [Colo. Ct. App. 1984].)

6. Character Evidence

If the defendant has presented character evidence, be sure the court instructs the jury how to assess and weigh that evidence appropriately. Check the jurisdiction's standard jury instruction for the applicable charge. The following is an example from Pennsylvania:

1. The defense offered evidence tending to prove that the defendant is a person of good character. I am speaking of the defense witnesses who testified (that the defendant has a good reputation for being a law-abiding, peaceable, non-violent individual) (that _____).

2. [The district attorney called witnesses who in effect denied that the defendant has a good reputation for _____. You may use the Commonwealth's testimony for one purpose only. That is to help you judge whether the defense character witnesses are really familiar with the defendant's reputation and whether in their testimony they gave you an accurate description of his reputation.]

3. The law recognizes that a person of good character is not likely to commit a crime which is contrary to that person's nature. Evidence of good character may by itself raise a reasonable doubt of guilt and require a verdict of not guilty.

4. You must weigh and consider the evidence of good character along with the other evidence in the case. If, on all the evidence, you have a reasonable doubt of the defendant's guilt, you must find him not guilty. However, if on all the evidence, you are satisfied beyond a reasonable doubt that the defendant is guilty, you should find him guilty. (Pa.SSJI [Crim.] § 3.05 [1995])

7. Child Physical Abuse or Homicide Cases

Most pattern jury instructions lack reference to specific legal principles critical to child physical abuse and homicide prosecutions. Prosecutors must draft instructions addressing these issues, using language from case law to supplement standard jury charges. Consider the following example:

> The phrase "under circumstances evidencing a depraved indifference to human life" does *not* focus on the subjective intent of the actor, that is, the defendant, but rather involves an objective assessment evaluation by the jury of the degree of risk presented by the defendant's reckless conduct. (*See People v. Roe*, 542 N.E.2d 610 [N.Y. 1989]; *People v. LaMountain*, 547 N.Y.S.2d 430 [N.Y. App. Div. 1989].)

This language reminds the jury that there is an objective yardstick by which to measure the defendant's conduct. How the defendant felt at the time is not germane. The defense will often seek to minimize the defendant's responsibility for a child's death by focusing on the defendant's mental state and lack of intent to cause death at the time of the act.

The defendant's right to a "circumstantial evidence" instruction must be carefully researched. Some states do not differentiate between circumstantial and direct evidence in jury instructions. Others require an instruction referring to the need for "moral certainty" in a case that is entirely circumstantial. However, "[the moral certainty] legal standard does not apply to a situation where both direct and circumstantial evidence are employed to demonstrate a defendant's culpability." (*People v. Barnes*, 406 N.E.2d 1071, 1073 [N.Y. 1980].) In certain states, this charge need not be given when one element of a crime such as intent is proven by circumstantial evidence. Among the direct evidence that can negate the necessity for a moral certainty charge are the defendant's admissions describing the event and medical evidence testimony about the child's multiple injuries while in the exclusive custody of the defendant. A prosecutor must know the law so the defense does not create the impression of an additional burden of proof associated with a moral certainty instruction.

C. At Trial

When the judge gives the final instructions to the jury, check off each requested instruction as the judge reads it. Make sure the judge gives all necessary and agreed upon instructions. There is nothing more disheartening than to have a conviction reversed because the trial judge forgot to give the jury a required instruction. If the judge garbles a point or misstates an instruction, request that the jury be re-instructed. Make a clear record of any objections the State has to the instructions for purposes of appeal.

Special Courtroom Procedures

I. INTRODUCTION

Testifying in court can be a frightening experience for crime victims, but it is especially so for child witnesses. Courtrooms are large and intimidating, and a child witness must make public an intensely private and shameful experience in the presence of the abuser. Prosecutors have a variety of options to modify the traditional courtroom procedure to reduce the trauma experienced by a child victim. Each case calls for a careful analysis of which procedures would best meet the individual child's needs. Prosecutors should be creative in adapting courtroom procedures to provide maximum comfort for young witnesses.

Congress and the legislatures of numerous states have authorized special protective procedures for child victims. Some statutes authorize the videotape recording of a child's pre-trial interview, statement, deposition, or other sworn testimony. Potential uses for these videotaped interviews and depositions would include pretrial hearings or other matters, thereby preventing multiple court appearances by the child. Other statutes permit the use of closed circuit television to broadcast live testimony of the child from a separate room into the courtroom during trial. The merits of such technology, as well as the logistics and legal requirements, are discussed in Section II.C.

There are also many other mechanisms, in some states, to deal with the special needs of child victims. Some of these procedural mechanisms include closing the courtroom to the public and/or media during the child's testimony, allowing support persons and/or guardians *ad litem* in the courtroom with the child, limiting the length of time of in-court testimony, allowing for periodic recesses for the child, and requiring that questions be developmentally appropriate to the age of the child. Other mechanisms include modifying the physical logistics of the courtroom by allowing demonstrative aids to assist the child in testifying, turning the child's chair slightly away from the defendant, and using child-sized furniture to make the child more comfortable. (See Appendix VI.1 for sample motions to use the foregoing special procedures during a child victim's testimony.)

While these procedures often prove helpful to children and to the court process, they do not guarantee improved handling of child abuse cases. Professional opinion varies on the benefits of such procedures. Before employing any of the techniques described in this chapter, the prosecutor must carefully evaluate each individual case for its unique facts and use the appropriate procedures and available mechanisms that are allowed under the applicable jurisdictional rules and statutes.

II. USE OF ELECTRONIC EQUIPMENT

There is no consensus among prosecutors regarding the desirability of videotape and closed circuit technology in child abuse cases. Common concerns regarding the use of such technology in child abuse cases include the belief that jurors prefer to hear the testimony of the child in person, the fear of defense challenges based on constitutional issues, a lack of training in equipment use, and a lack of training in when the use of such testimonial aids is appropriate. Some prosecutors have found that the detriments of such technology outweigh the benefits and choose not to use it. Others have had positive experiences in the use of videotape or closed circuit technology and advocate its use.

A. Videotaped Interviews and Statements

1. The Advantages and Disadvantages

The opinions on policies to videotape child victim interviews vary widely among states and even within each state. (See Berliner, L., et al. [1992]. Commentary: Should investigative interviews of children be videotaped? *Journal of Interpersonal Violence, 7*(2), 277; Berliner, L., et al. [1992]. Accurate determination of guilt. *Journal of Interpersonal Violence, 7*(2), 277; Stephenson, C. [1992]. Videotaping and how it works well in San Diego. *Journal of Interpersonal Violence, 7*(2), 277.) For example, in some Utah counties, all police and child protective services interviews are videotaped, while in others the policy is *not* to videotape any interviews.

Jurisdictions supporting videotaped interviews usually refer children to central neutral facilities where trained persons conduct a videotaped interview pursuant to a written protocol. In some states, prosecutors introduce these videotapes not in lieu of, but in addition to, the victim's courtroom testimony. In other states, the prosecutor may use this statement even if the child does not testify. Jurors report that the ability to see the child talking about the abuse in a less intimidating setting is very helpful. Prosecutors in these jurisdictions tend to view the introduction of videotaped statements in their case-in-chief as critical to a successful prosecution. Many jurisdictions report considerable trial success with videotaped interviews of child victims. Some prosecutors also attribute high guilty plea rates in part to the use of videotaped interviews.

However, some prosecutors criticize setting requirements to videotape all interviews of child victims when victims of other types of crimes are not routinely videotaped. The implication, they argue, is that children are less reliable, highly suggestible, and their interviews are suspect. Others prosecutors cite cases that have been damaged because of badly conducted interviews. Still others believe that videotaped interviews shift the jury's focus from determining whether the child was, in fact, abused, to deciding the case based on their assessment of the quality of the interview. The videotaped interview invites a defense attorney to call an expert to criticize the interview methods. In fact, a group of such witnesses has emerged in the past two decades. In many other jurisdictions, videotaping is simply not practical since children enter the criminal justice system in a variety of ways, and consistently videotaping the first investigative interview is difficult.

The following figure illustrates the arguments for and against videotaping.

Figure VI.1 Advantages and Disadvantages of Videotaping Interviews

---

A. The Potential Advantages of Videotaping Interviews

1. Videotaping can decrease the number of interviews required of the child. Police officers, prosecutors, victim-witness advocates, and expert witnesses can review the tape and evaluate it without having to conduct redundant interviews with the child. This also limits the number of interviewers.
2. A videotape of an early statement or interview may capture spontaneity, emotion, or detail often absent in a child's later account of abuse.
3. If the interviewer's conduct or the child's exact words later become an issue, the videotape will provide a verbatim account of the interview, including the child's and the interviewer's facial expressions and gestures.
4. The interview is not adversarial and can occur in a comfortable environment so the child may be more relaxed and more communicative than in other settings.
5. The videotape, usually available to defense attorneys with a protective order, may be instrumental in inducing guilty pleas. An early guilty plea is especially desirable in child abuse cases since it spares the child further involvement in the criminal justice system. It also eliminates any incidental trauma or confusion that might result from the possibility of an acquittal.
6. The videotaped interview may be used in grand jury proceedings and in civil child protection proceedings in lieu of the child appearing to testify. It might also be used to support various showings required before trial. For example, a judge could review the videotape to assess the need for special procedures to facilitate the child's trial testimony.
7. The videotape can be used to refresh the child's recollection prior to trial much the same way that adult witnesses are permitted to review police reports and transcripts prior to testifying. This is especially helpful with children too young to read. Although useful, this use of the videotape may be attacked by the defense as coaching. As a result, many prosecutors show videotaped interviews only to victims 10 and older. Children at this age are, as a whole, no more suggestible than adults, and thus the argument of coaching is more difficult to make.
8. The tape may be used to impeach a child who recants the allegations on the witness stand. Showing the videotape to a victim who has recanted may also be useful in breaking through that denial.
9. A videotaped interview, if admissible, might be useful to corroborate the child's trial testimony.
10. Videotapes can be used to help convince nonoffending parents that the abuse did occur. Once convinced, they may be better able to protect the child and help the child deal with the effects of the abuse and also be more supportive during the trial.

(Continued)

(Continued)

11. The videotape may assist in the charging decision if the prosecutor making the decision has not personally interviewed the child.
12. Videotaping child interviews increases accountability for the interview process and serves as a mechanism for effective training to improve interviewing skills.

B. The Potential Disadvantages of Videotaping Interviews

1. The child or the interviewer may be uncomfortable and nervous about being videotaped, resulting in a stilted or unproductive session. Young children reluctant to reveal abuse in the first place may become distracted by the camera and want to play rather than concentrate on the interview.
2. Victims who may have been photographed as part of the abuse can be traumatized by the presence of the camera. Placing the camera behind a one-way mirror out of the child's sight may eliminate this issue. However, professionals almost uniformly agree that the child must be treated honestly and be informed that the interview is being taped.
3. Several interviews may be necessary to elicit a full account of the abuse even when a skilled professional conducts the interview. Videotaping every interview and contact with a child is a practical impossibility. It can also create the impression that the child was inconsistent about what occurred if the disclosure is progressive or details change.
4. A single videotaped interview can be very misleading because it represents only one point in the disclosure process. Yet, the jury and the defense will give it undue weight. Other out-of-court disclosures by the child, which may be *more* compelling, will receive decreased consideration simply because they were not taped. A defense attorney can discredit even a convincing disclosure on videotape by stating it is a product of earlier, untaped, unreliable, and coached interviews.
5. If other professionals such as doctors, social workers, and therapists tape their interviews with child victims, the chance that the recorded statements will appear inconsistent increases, as does the chance of interviewers using so-called improper techniques.
6. Defense counsel can make use of an ineffective interview and more effectively argue that improper and suggestive techniques tainted the child's memory or ability to recount events accurately. It must be remembered that there is no perfect interview. Defense experts are appearing with increasing frequency, ready to criticize *any* interview, thus encouraging distracting battles of the experts. The focus of the trial becomes the quality of the interview rather than the defendant's actual guilt or innocence.
7. If interviews are videotaped only in certain cases, this helps cast unnecessary doubt on those cases where taping was not available or not used.
8. Many children initially deny or minimize sexual victimization and may recant an earlier, truthful allegation of abuse. A recorded denial or recantation has the potential to be replayed for the jury numerous times with obvious damaging repercussions for the prosecution.
9. The costs of acquiring and maintaining high-quality videotapes and videotape equipment, redesigning interview rooms, and obtaining storage facilities with adequate security can be prohibitive. These resources might be better used to train professionals in effective interviewing skills.
10. If only child victims are videotaped, it seems to create a different standard. It implies that children are less reliable and more easily suggestible than adult victims, and that those who interview them are less trustworthy.

(Continued)

(Continued)

11. Videotaping may jeopardize the privacy rights of the child victim if a copy of the tape is obtained by the defense (or anyone else) and later played. This can be mitigated by obtaining a protective order prior to disclosing it to defense counsel and obtaining an order to seal the videotape if admitted as an exhibit at trial.

12. A videotape that can be replayed, stopped, and rewound may take emphasis away from the child's live testimony.

13. A reliance on technology can backfire if the equipment malfunctions, soft voices are inaudible on the tape, the camera is out of focus or positioned incorrectly, the tape is erased or lost, or tape quality is poor. In some states, even inadvertent destruction of evidence can be a basis for dismissal of criminal charges.

2. Practical Considerations

There are several additional issues to resolve if the prosecutor or another agency working with the prosecutor's office determines that videotaping a child victim's statement or interview is desirable.

a. Establish protocols. The prosecutor should take the lead in dealing with affiliated professionals and agencies to develop a protocol to identify cases in which a videotaped interview is appropriate. The protocol must contain procedures to ensure that videotaped interviews fulfill their intended functions. These functions include reducing the child's trauma, minimizing the child's involvement in the investigation and court proceedings, and enhancing the effectiveness of prosecution. Videotaped interviews must not be conducted haphazardly or unilaterally. Contact the National Center for Prosecution of Child Abuse for examples of interview protocols.

Protocols for videotaping should require that interviews be conducted by trained professionals who are both familiar with interviewing techniques and sensitive to the legal issues raised by videotaping. Training materials and articles on interviewing child victims are available and should be used. The protocol should also reflect the statutory prerequisites for the admission of the videotaped interview. It must be remembered that defense counsel will undoubtedly have access to the protocol and will use any deviation from that protocol against the State.

b. When to videotape. Because the child may not disclose a full account of the victimization initially or at any single interview, the prosecutor should be involved in determining which interview, at what stage of the investigation, should be videotaped. As a practical matter, it is impossible to tape every meeting with the child. If a child victim is interviewed prematurely, the statement may be incomplete and even jeopardize a criminal prosecution. In contrast, a videotaped statement made after repeated interviews undermines the purpose of limiting the number of interviews and may also be criticized by the defense as "selective" videotaping. If the child's statement is convincing, the defense will argue that the child was coached and the videotaped statement should be disregarded because the earlier statements were not recorded. Likewise, the defense will argue that evidence derived from unrecorded statements should also be ignored if there are any inconsistencies in the videotaped statement. While the timing of the videotaped interview is an important consideration, it is more important to establish protocols that guarantee consistency in taping procedures. Defense attorneys can use inconsistencies in this practice to cast doubts on the reliability of the interview.

c. **Where to videotape.** The ideal setting for videotaped interviews of children is a room in a central location specifically designed and furnished for interviewing children. It should have a one-way mirror and microphones permanently installed. In lieu of the one-way mirror, some jurisdictions provide a viewing room located away from the interview room and equipped with a closed-circuit television. However, if such a facility is not available, consider using a typical living room arrangement with a comfortable chair, a low table, lamps, and carpeting. There should be enough open space for both the child and the interviewer to sit or lie on the floor comfortably while remaining in camera range. It is important to create a mechanism for other members of the multidisciplinary team to provide feedback and questions to the interviewer prior to the conclusion of the formal interview. Such mechanisms could be an earpiece worn by the interviewer through which the other members of the team can communicate, a telephonic hook-up, or simply having the interviewer take a break and leave the child briefly in order to confer with team members. (See Slicner, N. A., & Hanson, S. R. [1989]. Guidelines for videotaped interviews in child sexual abuse cases. *American Journal of Forensic Psychology, 7*(1), 61.)

d. **Who conducts the interview?** Before determining who should interview the child, the prosecutor and other professionals involved should examine state confidentiality, privilege, and nondisclosure laws. Such laws may prevent agency personnel or professionals such as the child's therapist from disclosing information to other agencies or from testifying unless they first obtain waivers of confidentiality from the child or from the child's parents or guardian. The interviewer is likely to be called as a witness at trial, so the interviewer should be chosen accordingly.

The person chosen to conduct the interview should be the most qualified regardless of which agency the person is from. This person should have training in forensic interviewing of children. Many agencies have, or are developing, training for forensic interviewing of children. This being said, consideration should also be given to cultural considerations that may impact on the interview. (See Victor, V. [2002]. Cultural sensitivity in the forensic interview process. *Update, 15*(1)).

e. **How to videotape.** When videotaping child interviews, use high-quality equipment. A camera operator is preferable over a stationary camera to ensure that the child remains within camera range. The quality and level of sound should be considered when determining where to position the microphone. The interviewer must take care not to let the child roam out of audio range. Consider placing a back-up audiocassette recorder in a strategic location in the event the primary system fails. Visible microphones can distract children, so some investigators and prosecutors use P.Z.M. microphones. These microphones look like small metal plates, usually 4" x 4" in size, and they can easily be located anywhere in the room. P.Z.M. microphones are extremely sensitive, work well with any video or recording equipment, and should be reasonably priced. If the camera used does not have a date/time display, place a clock within camera range to nullify possible charges that the tape was edited or stopped and the child coerced off camera. (See Slicner, N. A., & Hanson, S. R. [1989]. Guidelines for videotaped interviews in child sexual abuse cases. *American Journal of Forensic Psychology, 7*(1), 61.)

f. Privacy issues. Any videotaped interview presents a potential threat to the child's privacy. Prosecutors and other professionals must take immediate steps to limit access to the tape, either by using a protective order or asking that the record be sealed. (See Appendix IV.10 for an example of a protective order regarding videotapes of interviews.) Be aware that videotaped interviews of children have been distributed and used for other purposes despite court orders. One defense expert kept a videotaped interview of a child despite a court order to return the videotape and later used the videotape in public training programs. In another case, a defense witness kept some interview tapes from an interview center and used them for research. To assure maximum protection, the prosecutor may request that defense counsel and expert witnesses be required to view tapes at the prosecutor's office. In states that allow videotaped interviews to be admitted as evidence, ownership of and access to the videotapes are usually governed by statute.

If the jurisdiction requires that a copy of the videotape be turned over to defense counsel, the prosecutor must protect the child's privacy as much as possible through strict protective orders that outline the permissible uses of the tape. The order must also require that the tape be returned to the State at the conclusion of the case.

3. Statutory Authority

Numerous states have enacted legislation that addresses the admissibility of a child victim's videotaped statement during a criminal proceeding. However, the statutes vary widely in their content and application. Some states permit the introduction of videotaped interviews only during a grand jury proceeding. Some statutes apply only to child sexual or physical abuse cases, while others apply to any crime committed against a child or involving a child witness. Child interviews can be videotaped without specific statutory authority. However, they are generally not admissible as substantive evidence of the crime unless they fit within a hearsay exception.

Most statutes authorizing the use of videotaped statements in court contain most or all of the following provisions:

- The tape contains both a visual and audible recording either on videotape or other electronic means.
- The statement was not induced by questioning calculated to lead the child to make a particular statement.
- Every voice on the recording is identified.
- The interviewer is present at the proceeding and available to testify or be cross-examined by either party.
- The recording equipment must be capable of making an accurate recording and not be altered.
- The defendant or defendant's attorney must have an opportunity to view the recording.

Many states require that either the child be available to testify at trial or that the court find the child to be unavailable before a videotaped statement can be introduced. Those states also generally require corroborative evidence of the crime. A few states require a finding that the time, content, and circumstances of the proposed statement or videotape provide sufficient indicia of reliability.

Table VI.1   Statutes Addressing the Admissibility of Videotaped Interviews or
                  Statements in Criminal Child Abuse Proceedings

Arizona	ARIZ. REV. STAT. ANN. § 13–4252 +
Colorado	COLO. REV. STAT § 18–3–413
Hawaii	HAW. REV. STAT. § 587–43
	HAW. R. EVID. § 804(b)(6)
Indiana	IND. CODE ANN. § 31–34–13–2
	IND. CODE ANN. § 35–37–4–6
Iowa	IOWA CODE § 915.38
Kansas	KAN. STAT. ANN. § 22–3433
	KAN. STAT. ANN. §§ 38–1557, -1657
Louisiana	LA. REV. STAT. ANN. § 15:440.5
	LA. CHILDREN'S CODE arts. 322 to 327
Michigan	MICH. COMP. LAWS § 600.2163a
Minnesota	MINN. STAT. ANN. § 595.02(3)
Missouri	MO. REV. STAT. § 492.304
New York	N.Y. CRIM. PROC. LAW §§ 190.25, .30 (grand jury only)
North Dakota	N.D. CENT. CODE § 31–04–04.1
Oklahoma	OKLA. STAT. ANN. tit. 10, § 7003–4.2
Rhode Island	R.I. GEN. LAWS § 11–37–13.1 (grand jury only)
Texas	TEX. CODE CRIM. PROC. ANN. art. 38.071
	TEX. FAM. CODE § 104.002
Utah	UTAH R. CRIM. PROC. 15.5(1)
Virginia	VA. CODE ANN. § 63.1–248.13:3
Wisconsin	WIS. STAT. § 908.08

NOTES: This compilation includes all statutes (excluding military and tribal statutes) that
allow pre-trial videotaped statements of a child victim/witness to be introduced as substantive
evidence in a criminal proceeding. This table includes all legislation passed through March
2002, as verified through Lexis Nexis.

+ Held facially unconstitutional

4. Legal Issues

a. Federal constitutional issues. Even if a videotaped statement is admissible under
a state or federal statute, it must still satisfy the requirements of the federal and state
constitutional confrontation clause. This clause affords a criminal defendant the right
to confront adverse witnesses in open court. The United States Supreme Court has
not ruled specifically on the introduction of a child's videotaped statement. Rather,
the Court has looked at the admissibility of a child's out-of-court statements as substantive evidence. (See *Idaho v. Wright*, 497 U.S. 805 [1990]; *White v. Illinois*, 502
U.S. 346 [1992].) The analysis contained in these decisions is applicable to the admissibility of a child's videotaped interview. For further discussion regarding the introduction of hearsay evidence, see Chapter V, Section IV.F.

b. State constitutional issues. To date, at least eight state appellate courts have
upheld legislation authorizing the introduction of videotaped statements in criminal
trials. These include Georgia, Indiana, Kansas, Louisiana, Minnesota, Missouri,
Texas, and Wisconsin. In Minnesota, the supreme court upheld the introduction of
videotaped statements, even when the child does not testify at trial, under Rule

803(24) of the Minnesota Rules of Evidence, provided the statement contains sufficient indicia of reliability as outlined in *Idaho v. Wright*, 497 U.S. 805 (1990). (See, e.g., *State v. Salazar*, 504 N.W.2d 774 [Minn. 1993].) The Minnesota Supreme Court has specifically rejected reliance on the statute if a rule of evidence can be used to support the statement's admissibility. (*State v. Edwards*, 485 N.W.2d 911, 915 [Minn. 1992].) For further information regarding this issue, see Zehnder, M. M. (1994). A step forward: Rule 803(25), a new approach to child hearsay statements. *William Mitchell Law Review, 20, 3.*

Two states, Kentucky and Tennessee, have found such statutes to be unconstitutional. (See *Gaines v. Commonwealth*, 728 S.W.2d 525 [Ky. 1987]; *State v. Pilkey*, 776 S.W.2d 943 [Tenn. 1989], *cert. denied*, 494 U.S. 1046 [1990].) In Kentucky, the statute was unconstitutional because it permitted testimony from a child who the trial court had not declared competent to testify. The court reasoned that this was an unconstitutional legislative infringement on the inherent powers of the judiciary. The dissent, however, felt the statute would be held to be constitutional if the trial court had determined competency. (*Gaines*, 728 S.W.2d at 528.) In *State v. Pilkey*, the Tennessee Supreme Court deemed its statute unconstitutional under both the state and federal constitutions. (776 S.W.2d at 948–49.) Although the *Pilkey* court concluded that the introduction of an unsworn videotaped statement as substantive evidence was unconstitutional, it left open the possibility of admissibility if the statement otherwise satisfied the requirements of Tennessee's Rule of Evidence. (See also *State v. Deuter*, 839 S.W.2d 391 [Tenn. 1992].)

The Hawaii Supreme Court dealt with this issue in *State v. Apilando*, 900 P.2d 135 (1995). In *Apilando*, the defendant was charged with committing a sexual assault upon his then 5-year-old grandniece. During the first trial, the victim, who was then 7 years old, took the witness stand and testified. At the close of the victim's testimony, the state moved to introduce the videotaped statement that had been taken by police officers 2 days after the incident. The interview was conducted solely by the police, and neither attorney was present for the taping. The trial court refused to allow the introduction of the videotape. The defendant's first trial ended in a hung jury, and he was subsequently retried.

The victim was 9 years of age at the time of the defendant's second trial. Prior to trial, the defendant filed a motion *in limine* to exclude the introduction of the videotaped statement. The trial court, relying on Hawaii Rule of Evidence (HRE) 616, denied the defendant's motion and allowed the introduction of the child's videotaped statement. A redacted version of the videotaped interview was introduced during the detective's testimony. Subsequently, outside the presence of the jury, the victim was called to the stand and underwent *voir dire* concerning her memory of the events that transpired with the defendant. During *voir dire*, the victim testified that she could not remember what she had told the detective, although she remembered being in the interview room. In response to defense counsel's question whether she had seen the videotape "at least once before," she stated, "I forgot."

The jury returned to the courtroom, and the victim underwent cross-examination by defense counsel and redirect examination by the prosecution. The victim essentially testified that (1) she remembered testifying about the incident at the first trial, including her statement that the defendant had taken off all of her clothing by the stream; (2) the defendant had pushed her down by the stream; (3) she did not remember what the defendant did to her after he pushed her down, but she remembered that he touched her; (4) she did not want to say where he touched her, and characterized the touching as "bad"; (5) she pushed the defendant off her and told her mother what had happened; and (6) she did not remember being pinched or feeling sore.

Figure VI.2 Advantages and Disadvantages of Videotaped Testimony or Depositions

---

A. Advantages of Videotaped Testimony or Depositions

1. The testimony may be taken in a relatively informal, less intimidating setting, outside the courtroom, and outside the presence of the public, press, and jury.
2. In states that allow the defendant to be excluded from the room, the child is spared the anxiety of testifying in the presence of the defendant.
3. A pre-trial deposition could potentially be used to refresh the victim's recollection at a later hearing, as a prior consistent statement, or as substantive evidence of abuse. This testimony could be particularly helpful if the child later recants. Some states may not require the child witness to testify in court after a deposition has been taken.
4. As with videotaped interviews, a good videotape of testimony may induce a guilty plea.
5. The child may be unable to testify at trial with the defendant present. The procedure may provide assurances to parents who might not otherwise cooperate. Without the child's testimony, the case may be more difficult if not impossible, to prosecute.
6. If the child does not testify at trial, videotaped testimony can be effectively used to make the victim real to the jury. Videotape captures facial expressions, gestures, pauses, and other aspects of the testimony not available with a written transcript.

B. Disadvantages of Videotaped Testimony

1. A videotaped image of the child victim lacks the immediacy and persuasive impact of a child's live in-court testimony. The jurors are "watching television," thus removing the victim one step farther from reality.
2. Videotaping a child's testimony prior to trial allows the defense to prepare its case better because it knows the content of the crucial testimony.
3. If pertinent evidence comes to light after a deposition is recorded, the defendant may have a right to cross-examine the child victim further in another session. This defeats the intended purpose of recorded testimony, which is to spare the child from having to make repeated statements about the abuse.
4. Some state statutes permit the defendant to be present in the room with the child while she testifies. The defendant's physical proximity may be closer to the victim than in normal courtroom settings and be more intimidating.
5. A child's parent, guardian, or victim advocate may expect the prosecutor to use videotaped testimony in lieu of live testimony. They may become angry, resentful, or uncooperative when the child is required to testify in court even after videotaping the testimony.

In reversing the defendant's conviction for sexual assault, the Supreme Court of Hawaii stated,

> . . . the videotaped interview was presented in lieu of the complainant's direct testimony, as part of the prosecution's case in chief. Further, the complainant's statements, at the time of the interview, were not subject to cross-examination, nor was Apilando present at the interview to face his accuser. The videotape was offered without a determination of necessity; that is, there was no determination whether the complainant would recant, would have insufficient recollection, or would be unable to communicate the events surrounding the alleged assault. The tape was not offered as a prior inconsistent statement to impeach her testimony nor was it offered to restore her credibility on rebuttal. Additionally, the video- taped interview cannot be said to have been offered as a past recollection recorded pursuant to HRE 802.1(4) because the requisite showing that the

declarant "once had knowledge but now has insufficient recollection to enable the witness to testify fully and accurately," HRE 802.1(4), was not demonstrated prior to the introduction of the videotape. (*Id.* at 146)

The Court seemed to indicate that the above situation would have withstood appellate scrutiny had the victim first testified live on direct examination, thus making the prior out-of-court statement not violative of the confrontation clause.

B. Videotaped Testimony

1. The Advantages and Disadvantages

Although less controversial than videotaped investigative interviews, the use of videotaped testimony also has advantages and disadvantages. Some prosecutors believe that videotaped testimony is used too often as a way to avoid preparing a child witness for trial. Others consider videotaped testimony essential for the child witness who is too frightened to testify in court.

2. Practical Considerations

Videotaped testimony requires intelligent planning and the availability of personnel and equipment. It should be utilized only as a last resort. If the defendant is to be excluded from the deposition, the court must find that the defendant's presence would have a severe traumatic effect on the child witness. If, however, the child's fears or anxiety center around testifying in open court, rather than the defendant, the prosecutor should consider other methods to reduce the child's anxiety. Some of these methods are discussed below.

Law enforcement officials may wish to maintain a central or regional facility for conducting videotaped depositions of children. Such a system lends continuity and uniformity to the process, reduces costs and delays occasioned by an ad hoc approach, and can make innovative technologies more accessible to counties without skilled professionals or resources.

3. Statutory Authority

Thirty-eight states and Congress have authorized the use of videotaped testimony at trial in lieu of live testimony. Most statutes refer to videotaping a child victim's deposition and require that the judge, prosecuting attorney, and defense attorney be present. The defense attorney must also have an opportunity to cross-examine the child. Some jurisdictions permit videotaping of testimony only for preliminary hearing purposes.

The statutes that permit the admission of videotaped depositions or testimony in child abuse cases are very jurisdiction specific. Some jurisdictions require the defendant to be present during the child's testimony. These same statutes, however, also include a mechanism for altering the view of the child should the court determine that the defendant's presence creates a severe risk of trauma.

Vermont requires the defendant to be present and situated so that the child can see and hear him, unless the court finds this causes such a high risk of trauma to the child that it would substantially impair the child's ability to testify. If the court makes such a finding, the room must be arranged so that the child cannot see or hear the defendant, but the defendant must be able to confer personally with counsel. (Vt. R. Evid. § 807 [2002].) In Connecticut, the defendant may be excluded or

Table VI.2   Statutes Addressing the Admissibility of Videotaped Depositions or Testimony in Criminal Child Abuse Cases

Alabama	ALA. CODE §§ 15–25–2, -32
Arizona	ARIZ. REV. STAT. ANN. § 13–4251
	ARIZ. REV. STAT. ANN. § 13–4253 +
Arkansas	ARK. CODE ANN. § 16–44–203
California	CAL. PENAL CODE § 1346
Colorado	COLO. REV. STAT. §§ 18–3–413
Connecticut	CONN. GEN. STAT. ANN. § 54–86g
Delaware	DEL. CODE ANN. tit. 11, § 3511
Florida	FLA. STAT. ANN. § 92.53 +
Hawaii	HAW. R. EVID. § 587–43
	HAW. R. EVID. § 804(b)(6)
Indiana	IND. CODE ANN. § 35–37–4–8 +
	IND. CODE ANN. § 31–34–13–2
Iowa	IOWA CODE § 915.38
Kansas	KAN. STAT. ANN. §§ 22–3433 to -3434
	KAN. STAT. ANN. § 38–1557 to 1558
Kentucky	KY. REV. STAT. ANN. § 421.350(3)
Louisiana	LA. REV. STAT. ANN. §§ 15:440.3, .5
	LA. CHILDREN'S CODE arts. 322 to 329
Massachusetts	MASS. GEN. LAWS ANN. Ch. 278, § 16D +
Michigan	MICH. COMP. LAWS § 600.2163a
Minnesota	MINN. STAT. ANN. § 595.02(4) +
Mississippi	MISS. CODE ANN. § 13–1–407
Missouri	MO. REV. STAT. § 491.675 to 491.705 +
Montana	MONT. CODE ANN. §§ 46–15–402, -16–216
Nebraska	NEB. REV. STAT. §§ 29–1925 to -1926
Nevada	NEV. REV. STAT. §§ 174.227 to .229
New Hampshire	N.H. REV. STAT. ANN. § 517:13-a +
New Mexico	N.M. STAT. ANN. § 30–9–17 +
New York	N.M. DIST. CT. R. CRIM. PROC. § 5–504
	N.Y. CRIM. PROC. LAW §§ 190.25, .30, .32 (grand jury only)
North Dakota	N.D. CENT. CODE § 31–04–04.1
Ohio	OHIO REV. CODE ANN. § 2937.11(B)
	OHIO REV. CODE ANN. §§ 2945.48.1 to.49
Oklahoma	OKLA. STAT. ANN. tit. 22, § 753
Pennsylvania	42 PA. CONS. STAT. §§ 5984 to 5984.1
Rhode Island	R.I. GEN. LAWS § 11–37–13.2 -
South Carolina	S.C. CODE ANN. § 19–1–1180
South Dakota	S.D. CODIFIED LAWS § 23A-12–9
Tennessee	TENN. CODE. ANN. § 24–7–117
Texas	TEX. CODE CRIM. PROC. ANN. art. 38.071 +
Utah	UTAH R. CRIM. PROC. 15.5(3)
Vermont	VT. R. EVID. 807 -
Virginia	VA. CODE ANN. § 63.1–248.13:3
Wisconsin	WIS. STAT. § 967.04(7)(a)
Federal (U.S. Code)	18 U.S.C.A. § 3509(b)(2)

NOTES: This compilation includes all statutes (excluding military and tribal statutes) that allow pre-trial videotaped depositions and/or testimony of a child victim or witness to be introduced in lieu of live testimony at a criminal trial. It includes only those states that specifically refer to a child's testimony being taken by deposition, for a preliminary hearing or for a grand jury proceeding, or other sworn testimony. This table includes all legislation passed through March 2002, as verified through Lexis Nexis.

+ Held unconstitutional as applied

- Held facially unconstitutional

screened during the child's testimony only if the State proves by clear and convincing evidence that the child would be so intimidated or inhibited by the defendant's presence that the testimony must be taken privately to ensure its reliability. (Conn. Gen. Stat. Ann. § 54–86g [2002].)

4. Legal Issues

Depositions in criminal proceedings are permitted by Rule 15 of the Federal Rules of Criminal Procedure and other similar state statutes. Fed. R. Crim. P. 15 authorizes the testimony of a prospective witness to be taken and preserved for trial whenever exceptional circumstances such as the witness's unavailability for trial demonstrate that it is in the interest of justice to do so.

Videotaped testimony, like a videotaped interview, is an out-of-court statement and subject to hearsay objections. Therefore, its use must meet the applicable constitutional protections. The United States Supreme Court has not yet specifically considered the use of videotaped testimony or depositions of child witnesses. Traditionally, a deposition is admissible as substantive evidence if the witness is unavailable or gives testimony at trial or a hearing inconsistent with the deposition. (*Ohio v. Roberts*, 448 U.S. 56 [1980]; *Manncusi v. Stubbs*, 408 U.S. 204 [1972; *California v. Green*, 399 U.S. 149 [1970].) In *Green*, the Court stated that the following factors must be considered to determine whether there was substantial compliance with the confrontation requirements of the Constitution:

1. The hearing where the testimony was obtained was conducted under circumstances closely approximating those of a typical trial.

2. The declarant was under oath.

3. The defendant was represented by counsel.

4. The defendant had every opportunity to cross-examine the declarant.

5. Proceedings were conducted before a judicial tribunal equipped to provide a record of the hearings. (*Green*, 399 U.S. at 165.)

It is clear under *Roberts* that the party seeking to introduce prior testimony must either produce the child or demonstrate the child's unavailability at the trial. The Supreme Court of New Hampshire ruled that "once a video tape deposition has been taken pursuant to [this statute], it is not *per se* admissible in lieu of live testimony at trial, but before [it] may be admitted, the trial judge must make a specific finding, at a time of trial, that the victim or witness in a particular case continues to be unavailable to testify at trial." (*State v. Peters*, 587 A.2d 587, 589–90 [N.H. 1991].)

Constitutional problems arise when, pursuant to statute, the defendant is not physically present during the taking of the videotaped testimony. In order to exclude the defendant during the testimony, the court must make a specific finding that the defendant's presence would prevent the child from reasonably communicating what occurred. (See the analysis of *Maryland v. Craig*, 497 U.S. 836 [1990], in this chapter, Section II.C.4.) State courts have consistently held that excluding the defendant during the videotaped testimony without such a finding violates federal and state confrontation clauses. For example, the Supreme Court of Minnesota, while upholding its video statute, ruled that the trial court's failure to make case-specific findings that a child witness would be psychologically traumatized if required to testify in the presence of the defendant, violated the defendant's right of confrontation. (*State v. Conklin*, 444 N.W.2d 268 [Minn. 1989].) The Missouri Court of Appeals held Missouri's statute unconstitutional as applied when the defendant was excluded from the room without a specific finding of trauma to the child victim if the defendant was allowed to stay. (*State v. Davidson*, 764 S.W.2d 731 [Mo. Ct. App. 1989].)

Trial judges have considerable discretion in determining whether witnesses would undergo a sufficient level of trauma to justify exclusion of the defendant. The United States Supreme Court in *Craig* declined to establish prerequisites for proving necessity and instead ruled that the trial court need only make case-specific findings. State appellate courts have upheld trial court findings based on expert testimony, lay person testimony, and the trial judges' observation of the child witness. (See, e.g., *State v. Spigarolo*, 556 A.2d 112 [Conn.], *cert. denied*, 493 U.S. 933 [1989] [holding that the father's and his wife's testimony about the victims' attitude toward the defendant for purposes of determining whether the victims' ability to relate facts truthfully would be impaired or compromised by the defendant's physical presence was sufficient, and expert testimony was not necessary]; *Cope v. State*, 736 S.W.2d 533 [Ark. 1987] [upholding the trial court's reliance on a social worker's testimony that it was in the best interests of the children to allow them to testify before a small group because the girls would be embarrassed in front of several people]; *State v. Twist*, 528 A.2d 1250 [Me. 1987] [upholding findings of trauma based upon the testimony of a pediatric psychiatrist that child victims' placement in court settings on other occasions has caused them to regress and children would suffer psychologically if required to face defendant].)

At least 30 state appellate courts have upheld statutes allowing videotaped testimony in a criminal trial. Many impose additional conditions to satisfy constitutional requirements before videotaped testimony can be admitted as evidence. Courts in Illinois, Indiana, and Massachusetts have found that their videotaped testimony statutes violate state constitutional provisions. These courts struck down the statutes by applying the more restrictive interpretation of their state constitution versus the interpretation of the federal constitution. The individual state constitutions were deemed to grant defendants the right to "face-to-face" confrontation. (See *People v. Bastien*, 541 N.E.2d 670 [Ill. 1989]; *Brady v. State*, 575 N.E.2d 981 [Ind. 1991]; *Commonwealth v. Bergstrom*, 524 N.E.2d 366 [Mass. 1988].) This literal impression of face-to-face remains a minority view, since many other states have identical constitutional language as well as statutes permitting use of videotaped testimony.

C. Testimony by Closed Circuit Television

1. The Advantages and Disadvantages

Closed circuit television allows the child victim's live testimony to be broadcast from another room into the courtroom via television monitors that the judge, jury, and others can observe. Based upon anecdotal information, very few prosecutors throughout the country use this method of presenting testimony. Prosecutors prefer to limit its use to extreme cases where there is no other alternative to present the child's testimony. It should be limited to those cases where the child takes the stand but is unable to testify because it is so traumatic. If the child can tolerate in-court testimony, the prosecutor should not resort to closed circuit television. Closed circuit television, like the other available electronic testimonial aids, has its advantages and disadvantages.

Figure VI.3   Advantages and Disadvantages of Closed Circuit Testimony

A. Advantages of Closed Circuit Testimony

1. The child can testify in a more relaxed environment than the courtroom and outside the physical presence of the jury, spectators, and in most states, the defendant.
2. The risks of memorializing a child victim's testimony before trial, such as giving defense additional preparation time or newly discovered evidence after the videotaped testimony, do not arise.
3. Absent the use of closed circuit television testimony, the child may be unable to testify with the defendant present or in open court.

B. Disadvantages of Closed Circuit Testimony

1. A televised image of the child victim is not as effective as a child's live testimony.
2. If the state statute requires that the defendant be present in the same room as the child, the defendant's close proximity in the smaller room may be more intimidating than if the testimony is taken in the courtroom.
3. A victim's parent, guardian, or victim advocate may expect the prosecutor to use closed circuit television in lieu of live testimony. They may become angry, resentful, or uncooperative when this alternative is not used.
4. Closed circuit television is expensive and may be cost prohibitive.

2. Practical Considerations

As with videotaped testimony, the prosecutor must determine whether closed circuit television is appropriate on a case-by-case basis. The most critical consideration is whether the child's anxiety is caused by the presence of the defendant or the courtroom setting. Closed circuit television may not be constitutionally acceptable if any less restrictive yet effective procedure is available.

The equipment necessary for closed circuit television can also be very expensive. Properly functioning equipment is critical, as problems with the visual or audio transmissions may cause a mistrial. This would only increase system-based trauma for the child. Large jurisdictions might consider equipping one courtroom with closed circuit television to ensure consistency in procedure and properly trained operators.

3. Statutory Authority

By March 2002, 38 states and the United States Congress had authorized the use of closed circuit television to present the victim's testimony in a criminal trial. The various state statutes reflect one of three basic beliefs about the defendant's role and physical location when closed circuit television is used:

1. The defendant is in the room while the child testifies.

2. The defendant can observe and hear the child's testimony, but the child can neither hear nor see the defendant.

3. The defendant can observe and hear the child's testimony, and a television monitor projects the defendant's image into the room where the child is located so that the child sees the defendant while she testifies.

The majority of the statutes exclude the defendant from the room when the child testifies. Some states permit the defendant to remain in the room; however, the judge may exclude the defendant if the child would be intimidated or inhibited by this physical presence.

The majority of the statutes require the State to show that the child witness would suffer severe emotional harm if forced to testify in open court. Other jurisdictions, like Florida, require a stricter showing that the child would become unavailable if forced to testify in the presence of the defendant. Yet other jurisdictions, like Connecticut, focus on the reliability of the testimony that will be obtained from the child as the basis for allowing testimony by closed circuit television.

The Maryland statute upheld by the United States Supreme Court in *Maryland v. Craig,* 497 U.S. 836 (1990), requires the judge to determine whether in-court testimony by the victim would result in such distress that the child could not reasonably communicate. (Md. Code Ann., Cts. & Jud. Proc. § 9–102 [2001].) Mississippi requires a judicial finding based on behavioral indicators that there is a substantial likelihood that the child would suffer traumatic emotional or mental distress if compelled to testify in open court. (Miss. Code Ann. § 13-1-407 [2001].)

4. Legal Issues

The Sixth Amendment to the United States Constitution provides that "[i]n all criminal prosecutions, the accused shall . . . be confronted with the witness against him." This fundamental right is the basis for most defense attacks on the use of closed circuit television, especially when the child cannot see or hear the defendant during his or her testimony.

The United States Supreme Court first began dealing with the Confrontation Clause issue in child abuse cases in *Coy v. Iowa,* 487 U.S. 1012 (1988). In *Coy,* the defendant was convicted on two counts of lascivious acts with a child. During the trial, the court allowed a large screen to be placed between the defendant and the two child witnesses during their testimony. The screen enabled the defendant to dimly perceive the witnesses, but the witnesses were not able to see the defendant at all. Although the convictions were reversed and the case remanded for trial, the Court did rule that "[t]he Confrontation Clause does not, of course, compel the witness to fix his eyes upon the defendant; he may look studiously elsewhere, but the trier of fact will draw its own conclusions." The issue that caused the Court to remand the case was that the defendant was not able to view the witnesses' demeanor. The *Coy* Court stopped short of answering the question of whether the defendant's Sixth Amendment right may be curtailed to protect child witnesses, but it did state that any deviations from face-to-face confrontation must be based on a strong individualized showing of necessity.

A short time later, the Supreme Court was again faced with this Sixth Amendment issue in *Maryland v. Craig,* 497 U.S. 836 (1990). The *Craig* Court found the use of closed circuit television testimony to be constitutional. The Court found that while the federal Confrontation Clause guarantees the defendant a face-to-face meeting with witnesses appearing before the trier of fact, this right is not absolute and "must occasionally give way to the considerations of public policy and the necessities of the case" (at 847) (quoting *Mattox v. United States,* 156 U.S. 237, 243 [1895]). In *Craig,* the public policy consideration was the state's interest in the physical and psychological well-being of child abuse victims.

Table VI.3   Statutes Addressing the Use of Closed Circuit Television in Criminal Child Abuse Cases

State	Statute
Alabama	Ala. Code §§ 15–25–3, -32
Alaska	Alaska Stat. § 12.45.046
Arizona	Ariz. Rev. Stat. Ann. § 13–4253 +
Arkansas	Ark. Code Ann. § 16–43–1001
California	Cal. Penal Code § 1347
Colorado	Colo. Rev. Stat. § 18–3–413.5
Connecticut	Conn. Gen. Stat. Ann. § 54–86g
Delaware	Del. Code Ann. tit. 11, § 3514
Florida	Fla. Stat. Ann. § 92.54
Georgia	Ga. Code Ann. § 17–8–55
Hawaii	Haw. Rev. Stat. Ann. § 616
Idaho	Idaho Code § 19–3024A(1)(b)
Illinois	725 Ill. Comp. Stat. Ann. 5/106B-5
Indiana	Ind. Code Ann. § 35–37–4–8
Iowa	Iowa Code Ann. § 915.38(1)
Kansas	Kan. Stat. Ann. § 22–3434
Kentucky	Ky. Rev. Stat. Ann. § 421.350
Louisiana	La. Rev. Stat. Ann. § 15:283
	La. Children's Code §§ 322 to 329
Massachusetts	Mass. Gen. Laws Ann. Ch. 278, § 16D -
Minnesota	Minn. Stat. Ann. § 595.02(4) +
Mississippi	Miss. Code Ann. § 13–1–405
Missouri	Mo. Rev. Stat. § 561.031
New Hampshire	N.H. Rev. Stat. Ann. § 517.13-a
New Jersey	N.J. Stat. Ann. § 2A:84A-32.4
New Mexico	N.M. R. Dist. Ct. Crim. Proc. § 5–303
New York	N.Y. Crim. Proc. Law §§ 65.00 to 65.30
	N.Y. Exec. Law § 642-a
Ohio	Ohio Rev. Code Ann. § 2937.11
	Ohio Rev. Code Ann. §§ 2945.48
Oklahoma	Okla. Stat. Ann. tit. 22, § 753
Oregon	Or. Rev. Stat. § 40.460(24)
Pennsylvania	42 Pa. Cons. Stat. Ann. § 5985 +
Rhode Island	R.I. Gen. Laws § 11–37–13.2
South Dakota	S.D. Codified Laws §§ 26–8A-30 to -31
Tennessee	Tenn. Code Ann. § 24–7–120
Texas	Tex. Crim. Proc. Code Ann. § 38.071
Utah	Utah R. Crim. Proc. 15.5(2)
Vermont	Vt. R. Evid. 807
Virginia	Va. Code Ann. § 18.2–67.9
	Va. Code Ann. § 63.1–248.13:3
Washington	Wash. Rev. Code Ann. § 9A.44.150
Wisconsin	Wis. Stat. Ann. § 972.11(2m)
Federal (U.S. Code)	18 U.S.C. § 3509(b)(1)

NOTES: This compilation includes all statutes (excluding military and tribal statutes) allowing or mandating the use of closed circuit television testimony in a criminal proceeding. This table includes all legislation passed through March 2002, as verified through Lexis Nexis.

+ Held unconstitutional as applied

− Held facially unconstitutional

The Court concluded, however, that the requisite finding of necessity for closed circuit testimony must meet a three-part test to determine whether the state's interest in protecting a child victim is constitutionally sufficient to overcome the right of confrontation. First, the trial court must make a trial-specific finding that the closed circuit procedure is necessary (*Id*. at 855–56). Second, the state must show that the child's anticipated trauma is due to the face-to-face presence of the defendant (*Id*. at 856). Finally, the trial court must find that "the emotional distress suffered by the child witness in the presence of the defendant is more than *de minimis*, i.e., more than 'mere nervousness or some reluctance to testify'" (*Id*., quoting *Wildermuth v. State*, 530 A.2d 275, 286 [Md. 1987]). All three parts of the test must be based on the case under consideration and not on the general trauma that can come from testifying. The Court did decline to set evidentiary standards such as requiring expert testimony for presenting the prerequisite information to the trial court.

Of the many state appellate courts that have reviewed the use of closed circuit testimony in criminal child abuse proceedings, only Pennsylvania, Massachusetts, and Illinois have held their statutes facially unconstitutional. In *Commonwealth v. Ludwig*, the Pennsylvania Supreme Court acknowledged the *Craig* opinion, but held that the United States Constitution reflects only preference for face-to-face confrontation. In contrast, the Pennsylvania Constitution, Art. I, § 9 "clearly, emphatically and unambiguously requires a 'face-to-face' confrontation" (594 A.2d 281, 284 [Pa. 1991]). Massachusetts also applied a literal interpretation of its state constitutional requirement for face-to-face confrontation. (*Commonwealth v. Bergstrom*, 524 N.E.2d 366, 371 [Mass. 1988].) While it stated a willingness to consider the availability of new techniques to preserve and present evidence at a criminal trial on a case-by-case basis, the Massachusetts court was unwilling to approve a categorical exemption from constitutional mandates.

The Illinois Supreme Court similarly dealt with the issue of face-to-face confrontation in *People v. Fitzpatrick*, 633 N.E.2d 685 (Ill. 1994). In *Fitzpatrick*, the Court declared the use of closed circuit television testimony unconstitutional, as the Illinois Constitution unequivocally stated, "In criminal prosecutions, the accused shall have the right . . . to meet the witnesses face to face" (*Id*. at 687). The Illinois Supreme Court distinguished this language from that considered in *Maryland v. Craig*. The Illinois Constitution was subsequently amended to remove the "face-to-face" language. This language was replaced with language identical to that in the United States Constitution.

Arizona, Colorado, Indiana, Kansas, Kentucky, New Hampshire, Ohio, Oregon, Tennessee, Washington, and Wisconsin have state constitutional provisions identical to those in Pennsylvania and Massachusetts, but the courts in these states have upheld the use of closed circuit television. In *State v. Self*, the Ohio Supreme Court interpreted its confrontation clause language, "the party accused shall be allowed . . . to meet the witnesses face-to-face," to provide no greater right of confrontation than the Sixth Amendment of the United States Constitution. (564 N.E.2d 446, 453 [Ohio 1990] [interpreting Ohio Const. Art. I, § 10].) The court reasoned that "the Confrontation Clauses were written into our constitutions to secure for the opponent the opportunity of cross-examination. The opponent demands confrontation, not for the idle purpose of gazing upon the witness, or of being gazed upon by him, but for the purpose of cross-examination, which cannot be had except by the direct and personal putting of questions and obtaining immediate answers" (*Id*. at 450). Thus, the opportunity to cross-examine the child may satisfy the Confrontation Clause in the absence of an actual physical confrontation between the child and the defendant.

The Supreme Court of Kentucky similarly concluded that the requirement in Kentucky Constitution § 11, to "meet witnesses face-to-face," is basically the same as the Sixth Amendment to the United States Constitution. (*Commonwealth v. Willis*, 716 S.W.2d 224, 227 [Ky. 1986].) The court emphasized that "there is no authority under traditional courtroom procedures which specifically requires any witness to look at the defendant. . . . The testimony of a blind victim would not be invalid. The same is true for the testimony of a witness who refuses to look on the accused. By analogy a defendant would not be denied the right of confrontation when a young victim is so intimidated by his mere presence that she cannot testify unless she is unable to see or hear him" (*Id.* at 231).

The other four state appellate courts upheld their closed circuit television statutes without discussing the impact of face-to-face constitutional requirements. (See *Brady v. State*, 575 N.E.2d 981 [Ind. 1991] [citing use of two-way closed circuit television as an alternative to using videotaped testimony]; *State v. Vess*, 756 P.2d 333 [Ariz. 1988] [upholding statute as constitutional if state shows the atmosphere of the courtroom or the presence of the defendant would traumatize the victim or render the victim unable to communicate]; *People v. Schmitt*, 562 N.E.2d 377 [Ill. App. Ct. 1990], *rev. denied*, 571 N.E.2d 154 [1991] [finding no confrontation violation where defendant and his attorney were in the room when the child testified, and the child's testimony was broadcast live to the jury]; *State v Chisholm*, 777 P.2d 753 [Kan. 1989] [finding that confrontation right was not violated when the child testified via closed circuit television, where trial court made individualized finding that the child witness would suffer trauma as a result of giving in-court, face-to-face testimony].)

III. COURTROOM CLOSURE

A. Statutory Authority

State closure statutes vary significantly. Sixteen states and the United States Code allow trial courts to close the courtroom to the public during the testimony of a child victim or witness during a criminal trial. Five states permit news reporters to remain during testimony while excluding the remaining spectators. Michigan requires and Virginia permits closure only during the preliminary hearing. Eleven states permit courtroom closure during sexual offense trials.

Three states, Florida, Georgia, and Massachusetts, mandate courtroom closure when child victims testify in sex offense cases. In Florida and Georgia, the public must be excluded in all trials when a person under the age of 16 testifies concerning any sex offense. Newspaper reporters and broadcasters may remain. In Massachusetts, the presiding judge must exclude the general public from the courtroom in trials involving rape, incest, carnal abuse, and other sex crimes when the victim is under the age of 18. Only persons who have a direct interest in the case may remain.

Some states, such as Illinois, Louisiana, North Carolina, South Carolina, and Virginia, permit closure without a case-specific showing of necessity. For example, North Carolina permits closure in any trial for rape or a sex offense. In contrast, four states, California, Michigan, Minnesota, and South Dakota, require the trial

Table VI.4   Statutes Permitting Courtroom Closure During Child Victim or Witness Testimony in Criminal Child Abuse Cases

California	Cal. Penal Code § 859.1
Connecticut	Conn. Gen. Stat. Ann. § 54–86g(b)
Florida	Fla. Stat. Ann. Ch. § 918.16 *
Georgia	Ga. Code Ann. § 17–8–54 *
Illinois	725 Ill. Comp. Stat. Ann. § 5/115–11 *
Kansas	Kan. Stat. Ann. § 38–1552
Louisiana	La. Rev. Stat. Ann. § 15:469.1
Massachusetts	Mass. Gen. Laws Ann. Ch. 278, § 16A
Michigan	Mich. Comp. Laws § 600.2163a(10)
Minnesota	Minn. Stat. § 631.045
New Hampshire	N.H. Rev. Stat. Ann. § 632-A:8 +
North Carolina	N.C. Gen Stat. § 15–166
South Carolina	S.C. Code Ann. § 16–3–1550(E)
South Dakota	S.D. Codified Laws § 23A-24–6 *
Virginia	Va. Code Ann. § 19.2–266 +*
Wisconsin	Wis. Stat. Ann. § 970.03(4) -
Federal (U.S. Code)	18 U.S.C.A. § 3509(e)

NOTES: This compilation includes all statutes (excluding military and tribal statutes) that allow or require the judge to close the courtroom to the public in a criminal child abuse trial. This compilation does not include statutes referring to the use of cameras in the courtroom. This table includes all legislation passed through March 2002, as verified through Lexis Nexis.

+ Held unconstitutional as applied

− Held unconstitutional in part. (See *State v. Circuit Court for Manitowoc County,* 414 N.W.2d 832 [Wis. 1987].)

* Statute specifically permits the media to remain in the courtroom

judge to make a case-specific finding of necessity. California prosecutors must show that testifying in public would cause serious psychological harm to the child victim or witness, and that no other alternative procedure is available to avoid that harm. In Minnesota, the state must show that closure is necessary to protect a witness or ensure a fair trial. The court must state the reason for closure on the record. In another variation, New Hampshire victims under the age of 16 may testify *in camera* unless the defendant shows good cause for their not doing so.

B. Legal Issues

1. Federal Constitutional Issues

Closing the courtroom in a criminal proceeding involves three rights protected by the United States Constitution: the First Amendment rights of freedom of speech and the press, and the Sixth Amendment right to a public trial.

a. The First Amendment rights. Under federal constitutional law, the press and public have a qualified First Amendment right to attend a criminal trial. (See *Globe*

Newspaper Co. v. Superior Court, 457 U.S. 596 [1982]; *Richmond Newspapers, Inc. v. Virginia,* 448 U.S. 555 [1980].) In *Press-Enterprise Co. v. Superior Court,* the Supreme Court emphasized that the purpose behind a public trial is to enhance the basic fairness so essential to public confidence (464 U.S. 501 [1985]). Closure may be justified, however, by a compelling governmental interest if the order closing the courtroom is tailored to serve that interest. The Court in *Press Enterprise* reiterated a four-part test for trial courts when closure of a criminal hearing or trial is being considered:

1. The party seeking to close the proceeding must advance an overriding interest that is likely to be prejudiced absent closure.

2. The closure must be no broader than necessary to protect that interest.

3. The trial court must consider reasonable alternatives to closing the proceeding.

4. The trial court must make adequate findings to support the closure. (*Id.* at 510–11)

The Supreme Court first applied this test in *Globe,* where the judge closed a portion of a criminal trial involving allegations of sexual abuse pursuant to a Massachusetts statute that required exclusion of the press and public during the child victim's testimony. (See *Globe Newspaper Co., Inc.,* 457 U.S. at 607–10.) The Court ruled that the statute, which did not require a case-specific showing of necessity, was an unconstitutional infringement on the newspaper's First Amendment right to be present. It concluded that, while the state's interest in safeguarding the physical and psychological well-being of a minor is compelling, "it does not justify a mandatory closure rule" (at 608). The Court did conclude that the trial court can close the courtroom on a case-by-case basis when necessary, after weighing factors such as the victim's age, psychological maturity, and understanding; the nature of the crime; the wishes of the victim; and the interests of parents and relatives.

b. The Sixth Amendment rights. The Sixth Amendment of the United States Constitution guarantees the accused the right to "a speedy and public trial." (U.S. Const. Amend. VI.) In *Waller v. Georgia,* the Supreme Court made clear that the "explicit Sixth Amendment right of the accused is no less protective of a public trial than the implicit First Amendment right of the press and public." (467 U.S. 39, 46 [1984].) The Court stressed that "the requirement of a public trial is for the benefit of the accused; that the public may see that he is fairly dealt with and not unjustly condemned, and that the presence of interested spectators may keep his triers keenly alive to a sense of their responsibility and the importance of their functions" (quoting Cooley, T. M. [1927]. *Constitutional limitations,* Vol. 1 [8th ed., p. 647]. Clark, NJ: Lawbook Exchange). Under *Waller,* the same four-part test must be applied to evaluate Sixth Amendment issues that was set forth in *Press-Enterprise.*

2. State Legal Issues

Several state appellate courts have upheld statutes authorizing courtroom closure. (See, e.g., *Sears v. State,* 356 S.E.2d 72 [Ga. Ct. App. 1987].) If the trial court followed the procedures established in *Globe* and *Waller,* state appellate courts uphold the statute even if it is silent on the procedure itself. For example, the Illinois Appellate Court held that its statute, as applied, violated the defendant's right to a public trial when the trial court failed to make the findings required by *Waller*. (*People v. Holveck*, 524 N.E.2d 1073 [Ill. 1990].) The court, however, did not strike the statute as facially unconstitutional. (See also *Thornton v. State*, 585 So. 2d 1189 [Fla. Dist. Ct. App. 1991] [reversing conviction where trial court failed to apply *Waller* test for closure]; *People v. Priola*, 561 N.E.2d 82 [Ill. App. Ct. 1990], *rev. denied*, 567 N.E. 2d 339 [Ill. 1991] [upholding statute authorizing trial court to exclude nonmedia persons during child's testimony only if the criteria set forth in *Waller* were satisfied]; *State v. Klem*, 438 N.W.2d 798 [N.D. 1989] [reversing conviction where trial court did not conduct hearing to make required findings before ordering closure]; but see *Renkel v. State*, 807 P.2d 1087 [Alaska Ct. App. 1991] [declaring unconstitutional a statute mandating courtroom closure during a child victim's testimony on sexual abuse because a criminal trial is preemptively a public proceeding].)

In *Eversole v. Superior Court*, the California Court of Appeals required the trial court to consider explicit alternatives before closing the courtroom. These alternatives included videotaped testimony or simultaneous testimony through the use of closed circuit television. (195 Cal. Rptr. 816, 817 [1983].)

A trial judge has the inherent power to exercise discretion and close the courtroom in a criminal trial even without specific statutory authorization. (See *Reeves v. State*, 818 P.2d 495 [Okla. Ct. App. 1991] [upholding closure where it was narrowly tailored to accommodate the State's interest during the testimony of an adolescent victim]; *State v. Fayerweather*, 540 A.2d 353 [R.I. 1988] [upholding closure of courtroom to all but the press and the defendant's family because it was tailored to accommodate the defendant's right to public trial and the privacy interest of the 6-year-old victim].) (See Appendix VI.2 for a sample motion to close the courtroom.)

IV. SUPPORT PERSONS AND GUARDIANS *AD LITEM*

The appointment or assignment of a qualified guardian *ad litem* and/or child advocate in civil child abuse cases is required by states receiving funds under the federal Child Abuse Prevention and Treatment Act, 42 U.S.C. § 5106a(b)(6) (1988). These support persons can also be very helpful in criminal cases, in which they can advocate for the child's rights, since children are generally viewed as neutral observers in criminal proceedings. These advocates can also assist the prosecutor in preparing the child witness for court and provide emotional support to the victim and family during the trial. In noncriminal cases, a child's advocate often takes a more active role in investigating the case, sometimes making recommendations to the court and possibly examining witnesses during trial.

A. Statutory Authority

1. Guardian Ad Litem

Sixteen states and the United States Congress require or authorize appointment of guardians *ad litem* for child victims in criminal child abuse proceedings. Some of those jurisdictions require the guardian *ad litem* to be an attorney.

Table VI.5   Statutes Regarding the Appointment of a Guardian *Ad Litem* in Criminal Child
Abuse Cases

Alabama	ALA. CODE § 26–14–11
Alaska	ALASKA STAT. § 12.45.046(a)
California	CAL. WELF. & INST. CODE § 326.5
Connecticut	CONN. SUPER. CT. 44–20
Florida	FLA. STAT. ANN. § 39.822
	FLA. STAT. ANN. § 914.17
Illinois	705 ILL. COMP. STAT. ANN. 405/2–17
Iowa	IOWA CODE ANN. § 915.37
Kentucky	KY. REV. STAT. ANN. § 26A.140
Montana	MONT. CODE ANN. § 41–3–112
North Carolina	N.C. GEN. STAT. § 7B-601
	N.C. SUPER CT. RULE 7.1
North Dakota	N.D. CENT. CODE § 12.1–20–16
Oklahoma	OKLA. STAT. ANN. tit. 10, § 7112
South Dakota	S.D. CODIFIED LAWS § 26–8A-18
Tennessee	TENN. CODE ANN. § 37–1–610
Utah	UTAH CODE ANN. § 78–7–9
Vermont	VT. R. CRIM. PROC. 44.1
Federal (U.S. Code)	18 U.S.C.A. § 3509(h)

NOTE: This compilation includes all statutes (excluding military and tribal statutes) that require or permit the appointment of a guardian *ad litem* in a criminal proceeding. This table includes all legislation passed through March 2002, as verified through Lexis Nexis.

Guardians can play an active role in the criminal proceedings. For example, in Iowa, guardians receive notice of and may attend all depositions, hearings, and trial proceedings and they may advocate for the protection of the child. They may also file reports with the court. They may not, however, introduce evidence or directly examine or cross-examine witnesses. In Florida, the guardian has full access to all evidence introduced during proceedings, can interview witnesses, can make recommendations to the court, and must receive notice of and has a right to appear on behalf of the minor child at all proceedings. A guardian may, if necessary, seek protective orders or initiate placement proceedings on the child's behalf.

Prosecutors may wish to request a guardian *ad litem* to provide representation for the child, even when not specifically called for by statute in criminal cases. The guardian has standing to protect a victim from inappropriate discovery requests, such as attempts to obtain school or counseling records or medical or psychological examinations by defense-selected experts. Prosecutors then cannot be accused of interfering with defense discovery rights.

Duties afforded to guardians *ad litem* under the United States Code include attendance at all depositions, hearings, and trial proceedings; making recommendations to the court; having access to all reports, evaluations, and records; and marshaling and coordinating delivery of resources to the child. The United States Code, at 18 U.S.C. 3509(h), specifically includes a guarantee that the guardian *ad litem* cannot be compelled to testify as a witness in the proceeding.

Table VI.6   Statutes Permitting a Support Person or Child Advocate in the Courtroom in Criminal Child Abuse Cases

Alaska	Alaska Stat. § 12.45.046(c)(2)
Arizona	Ariz. Rev. Stat. Ann. § 13–4403(E)
Arkansas	Ark. Code Ann. § 16–42–102 *
California	Cal. Penal Code § 868.5
Connecticut	Conn. Gen. Stat. Ann. § 54–86g
Delaware	Del. Code Ann. tit. 11, § 5134(b)
Hawaii	Haw. Rev. Stat. Ann. § 621–28 +
Idaho	Idaho Code § 19–3023
Michigan	Mich. Comp. Laws Ann. § 600.2163a(4)
Minnesota	Minn. Stat. Ann. § 631.046
New York	N.Y. Exec. Law § 642-a
Pennsylvania	42 Pa. Cons. Stat. § 5983
Rhode Island	R.I. Gen. Laws § 12–28–9(2)
Washington	Wash. Rev. Code Ann. §§ 7.69A.020, .030
Federal (U.S. Code)	18 U.S.C.A. § 3509(i)

NOTES: This compilation includes all statutes (excluding military and tribal statutes) that allow a person to be present during a criminal proceeding to support the child victim/witness or to represent the interests of a child victim. This table includes all legislation passed through March 2002, as verified through Lexis Nexis.

+ Held unconstitutional as applied

* Statute refers to sexual or inchoate offense to a sexual offense only

2. Child Advocates or Support Persons

Fourteen states and the United States Congress authorize or mandate the appointment of a child advocate or support person to assist child victims and their families. These advocates normally do not play as active a role in criminal proceedings as guardians *ad litem,* but can provide valuable emotional support for child victims and their families throughout the court process. Advocates may be part of a volunteer organization, such as Court Appointed Special Advocates (CASA), or may be employed by the prosecutor's office or other formal victim/witness programs. Support persons usually remain in the courtroom during the child's testimony and are often permitted to sit with the child as the child testifies.

B. Legal Authority

Trial judges have broad discretion regarding general trial procedures, provided the procedure does not create a bias against the defendant or jeopardize due process rights. Most appellate courts have ruled that the presence of support persons for child victims does not create an inherent bias against the defendant. Therefore, the presence of a support person during the child's testimony is within the court's discretion. For example, the Indiana Court of Appeals held that the presence of a silent supportive adult, sitting behind the child witness during her testimony, was not inherently prejudicial and did not violate due process rights. (*Stanger v. State,* 545

N.E.2d 1105 [Ind. Ct. App. 1989]; see also *People v. Patten*, 12 Cal. Rptr. 2d 284 [1992] [finding that the failure of Cal. Penal Code § 868.5 (1997) to require a case-specific showing of necessity for support persons does not violate the defendant's right to a fair trial, and the presence of support persons is not inherently prejudicial even if the person is also a witness]; *State v. Hoyt*, 806 P.2d 204 [Utah Ct. App. 1991] [finding that the presence of a support person did not create an aura of bias against defendant]; *Boatwright v. State*, 385 S.E.2d 298 [Ga. Ct. App. 1989] [upholding trial court's allowing a foster parent to stand behind the child during her testimony]; *State v. Pollard*, 719 S.W.2d 38 [Mo. Ct. App. 1986] [finding defendant's rights not prejudiced by the presence of victim's mother within the railing near counsel's table during victim's testimony]; *Mosby v. State*, 703 S.W.2d 714 [Tex. Ct. App. 1985] [finding that guardian *ad litem's* presence slightly behind the child witness during child's testimony did not prejudice defendant's rights].)

Appellate courts have also permitted child witnesses to sit on a support person's lap or hold a support person's hand to minimize the trauma of testifying. In *State v. Rogers*, the child witness testified on direct and cross-examination while seated on the prosecuting attorney's lap. (692 P.2d 2 [Mont. 1984].) The appellate court held that this did not prejudice the defendant's case, and the defense counsel was sufficiently able to conduct a detailed cross-examination (at 7). The court stressed that the unique seating arrangement helped focus the child's attention on the questioning and provided comfort to her during a difficult and unfamiliar experience (at 8). While the *Rogers* court upheld this procedure, it is far more preferable to use someone other than the prosecutor as a support person. (See *Pressley v. State*, 398 S.E.2d 268 [Ga. 1990] [upholding mother of child victim remaining on witness stand during child's testimony]; *Commonwealth v. Pankraz*, 554 A.2d 974 [Pa. Super. Ct. 1989] [finding that trial court did not abuse discretion by permitting the child witness to sit on grandmother's lap while testifying]; *Baxter v. State*, 522 N.E.2d 362 [Ind. 1988], *cert. denied*, 501 U.S. 1255 [1991] [finding no prejudice when the child testified holding stepmother's hand]; *State v. Dompier*, 764 P.2d 979 [Or. Ct. App. 1988] [upholding trial court's decision to permit the child victim to testify while sitting on aunt's lap]; *State v. Johnson*, 528 N.E.2d 567 [Ohio 1987], *cert. denied*, 498 U.S. 826 [1990] [allowing the 7-year-old victim to testify while sitting on aunt's lap]; *State v. Jones*, 362 S.E.2d 330 [W. Va. 1987] [finding no abuse of discretion where the victim testified from foster mother's knee].)

Prior to allowing the child to sit on someone's lap or hold someone's hand during testimony, the prosecution may need to show that such procedural deviations are necessary. In *State v. Rulona*, Hawaii's Supreme Court reversed a conviction because the 8-year-old witness sat on her counselor's lap during her testimony. (785 P.2d 615 [Haw. 1990].) The court concluded that the child's claim that she was frightened and would feel better if she sat on the counselor's lap was insufficient justification for this procedure. (See also *State v. Suka*, 777 P.2d 240 [Haw. 1989] [reversing conviction where record was silent on the need for a support person to place her hands on the victim's shoulders during testimony].)

Judges must also be careful not to appear overly supportive of the child witness. In *People v. Rogers*, the Colorado Court of Appeals reversed a conviction because the judge escorted the child witness to and from the stand. (800 P.2d 1327 [Colo. 1990].) The court held that a jury instruction professing impartiality was insufficient to overcome the prejudice caused by the judge's actions. As a neutral person, the judge should not have shown such particular attention to the child. The New Jersey Court of Appeals used similar reasoning when reviewing the trial judge's actions in a highly publicized daycare case to reverse the conviction. (*State v. Michaels*, 625 A.2d 489 [N.J. Super. Ct. App. Div. 1993].)

Greater procedural problems arise when the person who is to support the child witness is also a witness. Judges traditionally have discretion to authorize witnesses to remain in the courtroom when essential to the defense or prosecution. In child abuse proceedings, the prosecution can argue that the presence of a parent or other supportive person is essential to ensure accurate testimony from a child victim. In *Commonwealth v. Berry*, the Pennsylvania Superior Court affirmed the trial court's decision that sequestering the victim's mother during her child's testimony was not necessary, where the mother testified about collateral issues and was the most appropriate support person for the child. (513 A.2d 410 [Pa. Super. Ct. 1986]; see also *Government of the Virgin Islands v. Edinborough*, 625 F.2d 472 [3d. Cir. 1980] [concluding that the trial court's failure to sequester the child's mother while her child testified resulted in no prejudice to the defendant where the statements made by the child and her mother at the time the offense was reported did not differ materially from their testimony at trial]; *People v. Wilson*, 430 N.Y.S.2d 715 [N.Y. App. Div. 1980] [declining to vacate indictment when victim's mother, who had already testified, was permitted to remain in the grand jury room while her 6-year-old daughter testified).

Since the purpose of sequestering witnesses is to ensure that their testimony is not influenced by other testimony, the prosecutor may wish to consider calling the child after the support person has testified. However, the Arkansas Court of Appeals overturned a conviction in which a victim's mother remained in the courtroom after testifying, stressing that a witness who has already testified must still be excluded from the courtroom in case there is a retrial. (*Hall v. State*, 692 S.W.2d 769, 774 [Ark. Ct. App. 1985].) This position appears to be the minority opinion.

V. OTHER SPECIAL PROCEDURES

A. Turning the Witness's Chair Slightly Away From the Defendant

Having to face the defendant can be one of the most stressful moments for children in court. Most children, if properly prepared and given the requisite emotional support, are able to appear in court, face the defendant, and give testimony without any special modifications being made. There are, however, situations where forcing a child to see the defendant would cause further trauma and stress to the child witness. In those situations, the courts have allowed the child's witness chair to be turned slightly to allow the child's direct point of view to be the jury rather than the defendant.

The issue that arises in these types of situations is whether the Sixth Amendment requires "eyeball-to-eyeball" confrontation. In the case of *Coy v. Iowa*, 487 U.S. 1012 (1988), the Supreme Court held that "the Confrontation Clause does not, of course, compel the witness to fix his eyes upon the defendant; he may studiously look elsewhere, but the trier of fact will draw its own conclusions" (at 1019). As emphasized in *Maryland v. Craig*, 497 U.S. 835 (1990), the "State's interest in the physical and psychological well-being of child abuse victims may be sufficiently important to outweigh, at least in some cases, a defendant's right to face his or her accusers in court" (at 853).

Whether the Sixth Amendment Confrontation Clause is even triggered may depend upon how far the chair is turned. Basically, face-to-face confrontation consists of the following elements:

1. The defendant must be able to observe and hear the witness sufficiently well to comprehend the witness's answers and evaluate the witness's demeanor. (*State v. Mannion*, 57 P. 542 [Utah 1899].)

2. The witness need not face the defendant directly. (*United States v. Williams*, 37 M.J. 289 [C.M.A. 1993].) At a minimum, however, the defendant should have a full profile of the witness's head. Moreover, the trier of fact must see the witness's face.

3. The witness is not required to look directly at the defendant unless the witness is asked to identify the defendant. (*Coy v. Iowa*, 487 U.S. 1012 [1988].) However, the witness should be able to look directly at the defendant by turning his head less than 90 degrees.

Should one of the foregoing elements be missing, the defendant's Sixth Amendment right is infringed to some degree. When the defendant's right is infringed upon, a case-specific showing of necessity will be required. A lesser showing of necessity is required when the infringement is minor, whereas a major infringement would require a much greater showing.

Arguably, turning the witness chair slightly away from the defendant accommodates all three elements of face-to-face confrontation, eliminating the need for a case-specific showing of necessity. It is clear, however, that a child may not sit with her back to the defendant. It has been routinely held that obscuring a defendant's view of a child by means of a screen or other device is as effective a denial of face-to-face confrontation as turning the chair completely away from the defendant. In *Coy v. Iowa*, the Supreme Court ruled that a defendant's Sixth Amendment right to face-to-face confrontation was violated when a screen was placed between the defendant and the child witness. In *State v. Mannion*, the Utah Supreme Court held that the trial judge's decision to allow a child "to turn her back to the defendant, so that he could not see her while testifying, . . . denied the defendant a constitutional right, and prevented him from having a fair trial." The Massachusetts Supreme Judicial Court also held that "a trial judge may not permit a child witness to testify with his back to the defendant." (*Commonwealth v. Johnson*, 631 N.E.2d 1002 [Mass. 1994].)

Many courts have allowed the courtroom's physical setup to be modified for the comfort of a child witness. In *United States v. Williams*, 37 M.J. 289 (C.M.A. 1993), the defendant's daughter was permitted to testify from a chair placed in the middle of the courtroom. The defendant had a full left-side profile of the child's face. The stated purpose for the modification "was to allow the accused to see the witness against him while allowing C to feel less inhibited than if she were facing her father" (at 289). On appeal, the Court of Military Appeals stated that "while the defendant might not have been able to look into the witness' eyes, we do not think he was deprived of face-to-face confrontation. The witness testified in the presence of the accused, and he could see her face and demeanor at all times. From the angle she was facing, the witness could see the accused without moving her body in the chair" (at 289–90). The court further ruled that since there was no infringement of the defendant's right to confrontation, there was no need for a case-specific finding of necessity.

The Massachusetts' appellate court found it acceptable for a witness to sit at a 45° angle to the defendant, provided the defendant can see the witness's profile and lips. (*Commonwealth v. Conefrey*, 570 N.E.2d 1384 [Mass. 1991].) The Georgia Court of Appeals held that placing the witness's chair at a 90° angle to the defendant is acceptable. (*Ortiz v. State*, 374 S.E.2d 92 [Ga. 1988].) The court reasoned that "although in the present case the angle of the witness' chair did make it possible for the young victims to avoid looking directly into the eyes of the appellant, it was also possible that the victims could see the appellant with the mere turning of their head. There was no physical device in this case that made it impossible for the witness to avoid viewing the appellant. Not only did the appellant have the opportunity to [sic] a thorough a sifting cross-examination of each victim, but the victims' in-court testimony occurred in view of the judge and jury, who were able to observe their demeanor and determine the credibility of their testimony" (at 95).

In *People v. Sharp*, 36 Cal. Rptr. 2d 117 (1994), the issue was not whether the child's chair could be turned, but whether the prosecutor could position herself so the child did not have to look at the defendant while testifying (at 120). The Court of Appeals held that the defendant's right to confrontation was not violated, finding that

> surely, appellant cannot be claiming a constitutional right to stare down or otherwise subtly intimidate a young child who would dare to testify against him. Nor can he claim a right to a particular seating arrangement in the courtroom. A witness who avoids the gaze of the defendant may be exhibiting fear, embarrassment, shyness, nervousness, indifference, mendacity, evasiveness, or a variety of other emotional states or character traits, some or all of which might bear on the witness's credibility. It is, however, the function of the jury to assess such demeanor evidence and 'draw its own conclusions' about the credibility of the witness and her testimony. There was no interference with the jury's ability to perform that function in this case (at 123).

B. Questioning by the Court

Under the Federal Rules of Evidence, the judge may question witnesses. "The court may interrogate witnesses, whether called by itself or by a party . . ." (Fed. R. Evid. 614[b]. The advisory committee note elaborates on the power of the court to question witnesses by stating, "The authority of the judge to question witnesses is also well established . . . The authority is, of course, abused when the judge abandons his proper role and assumes that of advocate, but the manner in which interrogation should be conducted and the proper extent of its exercise are not susceptible of formulation in a rule. The omission in no sense precludes courts of review from continuing to reverse for abuse."

Rule 614(b) has been challenged and discussed in various jurisdictions. The Ninth Circuit interprets this rule as follows: "It is entirely proper for the court to question witnesses in order to clarify questions and develop facts, so long as the questions are nonprejudicial in form and tone, and the court does not become personally involved." (*United States v. Haro-Espinosa*, 619 F.2d 789, 795 [1979].) The Fifth Circuit went farther and stated, "a judge is not a mere moderator, and he has an obligation and duty to question witnesses. . . . [A] trial judge may elicit facts not yet adduced or clarify those previously presented and he may maintain the pace of the trial by interrupting and curtailing counsel's examination as a matter of discretion." (*United States v. Bartlett*, 633 F.2d 1184 [5th Cir. 1981].) Finally, in *State v. Howard*, the Maine Supreme Judicial Court ruled that it is proper for a trial judge to question expert witnesses to "clarify the rather complex and often murky testimony of the expert witnesses. 'So long as the trial judge intervenes for the purpose of clarifying testimony, saving time, or preventing a miscarriage of justice, he must be allowed considerable latitude in his questioning.'" (405 A.2d 206, 211 [Me. 1979].)

The role of the trial court as an active participant in the trial is succinctly stated by two circuit courts. The Seventh Circuit commented that "the trial judge need not sit on the bench like a mummy when his intervention would serve to clarify an issue for the jurors." (*Ross v. Black & Decker, Inc.*, 977 F.2d 1178, 1187 [1992].) The Fourth Circuit made a similar observation when it stated that the judge "is not a bump on a log, nor even a referee at a prize fight. He has not only the right, but he has the duty to participate in the examination of witnesses when necessary to bring out matters that have been insufficiently developed by counsel." (*United States v. Ostendorff*, 371 F.2d 729, 732 [4th Cir. 1967].)

Generally, the allowable scope of judicial questioning will depend upon the proceeding. Bench trials afford a more relaxed atmosphere in the courtroom and allow the judge greater latitude in questioning. However, there may be more of a necessity for court questioning in criminal jury trials, where it may help to clarify the child's testimony. Courts should be careful to avoid an appearance of favoritism. That being said, judges also do not have to be cold and aloof with children. As long as the court's remarks can be categorized as "an incidental, innocent, and a non-prejudicial statement," such statements will be allowable. (*McDuffitt v. State*, 519 N.E.2d 216, 221 [Ind. Ct. App. 1988].)

The trial court must be careful to avoid improper bolstering of the child's testimony. One extreme example of such bolstering can be found in *State v. R.W.*, 491 A.2d 1304 (N.J. 1985), *aff'd as modified*, 514 A.2d 1287 (N.J. 1986). There the judge promised the child—in the jury's presence—that if she gave "real" testimony, the judge would buy her ice cream. After direct examination, the judge gave the child ice cream, restating the conditions for the reward. After cross-examination, the judge invited the child behind the bench and gave her two cookies and a lollipop (at 1306). The appellate court ruled that these actions unequivocally expressed the judge's opinion as to the accuracy of the testimony and therefore improperly bolstered the child's credibility (at 1309).

C. Miscellaneous Special Procedures

A prosecutor's imagination should be used to modify courtroom procedures and setups that were designed with adults in mind. Novelty should not be rejected as long as constitutional constraints, statutes, court rules, and case law are not violated. Many children derive comfort from a favorite toy or blanket. Children should be permitted to bring such comfort items into the stressful courtroom situation. Studies have shown that the presence of these items helps children calm themselves when parents are not immediately on hand. (See Matthews, E., & Saywitz, K. J. [1992]. Child victim witness manual. *California Center for Judicial Education and Research Journal, 1*, 34.) In *State v. Cliff*, the Idaho Court of Appeals approved allowing an 8-year-old child witness to hold a doll to prevent her from twisting her hands and chewing her nails. The court found that it was not prejudicial and did not generate sympathy for the child. (782 P.2d 44 [Idaho 1989].) In *Sperling v. State*, 924 S.W.2d 722 (Tex. Ct. App. 1996), the defendant claimed on appeal that allowing his child to testify before the jury while holding a teddy bear constituted "demonstrative evidence, which engendered sympathy in the minds and hearts of the jurors, validated the child-victim's unimpeached credibility, and deprived him of his constitutional right of confrontation." The Texas Court of Appeals disagreed, writing, " . . . the same accusation could as reasonably be made of the calculated attire of any witness. Rather, under this record, it seems more rational that the trial court, when faced with the general objection made, permitted the child-victim to retain the stuffed animal as one of the discretionary, 'reasonable steps' authorized by the Code of Criminal Procedure in an effort to minimize the psychological, emotional and physical trauma of the child-victim caused by her participation in the prosecution, including her face-to-face confrontation with appellant" (at 726).

Prosecutors can request limits on the length of the child witness's testimony or recesses to permit children to rest and regain composure. The trial judge has discretion to recess the proceedings during a child's testimony and should do so when a child shows signs of fatigue, loss of concentration, or unmanageable stress. (*Commonwealth v. Brusgulis*, 496 N.E.2d 652 [Mass. 1986]; *State v. Kallin*, 877 P.2d 138 [Utah 1994]; but see *People v. Feathers*, 481 N.E.2d 826 [Ill. App. Ct. 1985] [finding a limit of 1 hour and 50 minutes on defense's cross-examination of 14-year-old rape victim significantly and prejudicially denied defendant fair opportunity to confront his accuser].) Recesses during direct examination are not as problematic as cross-examination interruptions, but it is most often during cross-examination that children feel most uncomfortable and in need of a rest. A pre-trial motion that puts defense counsel on notice that the State will request a recess every 20 minutes should solve any appellate issues.

Courtroom configurations can be modified to be more comfortable. In Connecticut, courts can require attorneys to pose questions and objections while seated at a table in front of the child and in a manner that is not intimidating. (Conn. Gen. Stat. § 54–86g[b][4].) A special Michigan statute approves an arrangement in which the defendant is seated as far from the witness stand as reasonable and not directly in front of it, and attorneys must use a podium when questioning a child witness. (Mich. Stat. Ann. § 27A.2163[1].) The Alabama Court of Criminal Appeals ruled that requiring the defendant to sit at a table 20 feet from the witness stand did not infringe on his Sixth Amendment rights. (*Heup v. State*, 549 So. 2d 528 [Ala. Crim. App. 1989].) The court reasoned that the defendant was still physically present and permitted to confront and vigorously cross-examine the child. In *Boatwright v. State*, 385 S.E.2d 298 (Ga. Ct. App. 1989), the child victims were allowed to sit at a small table facing the jury with their backs to the defendants and attorneys. (See Appendix VI.3 for a sample motion to allow victim to be examined while seated in front of the jury box.)

Although legislation may encourage such procedures, they can be implemented without special statutes. Not all accommodations are complicated or controversial. The simple act of placing a stool by the child's seat so her feet will have something to rest on can make a surprising difference in reassuring the child. Prosecutors may have to be tenacious in persuading reluctant officials to be innovative in courtroom arrangements, but a comfortable, truthful, and convincing witness is well worth the effort.

VI. RESOURCE LIST

Armstrong, J. J. (1976). [Comment] The criminal videotape trial: Serious constitutional questions. *Oregon Law Review, 55, 567.*

Bainor, M. H. (1985). The constitutionality of the use of two-way circuit television to take testimony of child victims of sex crimes [Note]. *Fordham Law Review, 53, 995.*

Berliner, L., et al. (1992). Should investigative interviews of children be videotaped? *Journal of Interpersonal Violence, 7(2), 277.*

Brakel, S. J. (1975). Videotape in trial proceedings: A technological obsession. *A.B.A. Journal, 61, 956.*

Bulkley, J. (1986). *Analysis of legal reforms in child sexual abuse cases, in legal advocacy for children and youth: Reforms, trends and contemporary issues* (p. 5). Washington, DC: American Bar Association.

Bulkley, J. (1985). Evidentiary and procedural trends in state legislation and other emergent legal issues in child sexual abuse cases. *Dickinson Law Review, 89, 645.*

Bulkley, J. (1985). Introduction: Background and overview of child sexual abuse: Law reforms in the mid-1980's. *University of Miami Law Review, 40, 5.*

Chaney, A. L. (1985). *Videotaped interviews with child abuse victims, in papers from a national policy conference on legal reforms in child sexual abuse cases* (p. 209). Washintgon, DC: American Bar Association.

Coppel, K. K. (1985). *An analysis of the legal issues involved in the presentation of a child's testimony by two-way closed-circuit television in sexual abuse cases, in papers from a national policy conference on legal reforms in child sexual abuse cases* (p. 241). Washinton, DC: American Bar Association.

Graham, M. H. (1985). Indicia of reliability and face-to-face confrontations: Emerging issues in child sexual abuse prosecutions. *University of Miami Law Review, 40, 19.*

Guy, J. L. (1992). Has Wright made right? The interaction in child sexual abuse cases between the Sixth Amendment Confrontation Clause and hearsay rule exceptions. *University of Louisville Journal of Family Law, 31, 535.*

Haas, D. A. (1984). The uses of videotape in child abuse cases. *Nova Law Review, 8, 373.*

Hoffenberg, E. I. (1984). For the sake of our children: Selected legislative needs of Florida's children. *Nova Law Review, 8, 223.*

Kelly, J. L. (1985). Comment, legislative responses to child sexual abuse cases: The hearsay exception and the videotaped deposition. *Catholic University Law Review, 34, 1021.*

Lloyd, D. W. (1985). *Practical issues in confrontation of a child witness and the defendant in a criminal trial, in papers from a national policy conference on legal reforms in child sexual abuse cases* (p. 275). Washington, DC: American Bar Association.

MacFarlane, K. (1985). Diagnostic evaluations and the use of videotapes in child sexual abuse cases. *University of Miami Law Review, 40, 135.*

MacFarlane, K., Krebs, S. (1986). Videotaping of interviews and court testimony, in sexual abuse of young children (p. 164). In K. MacFarlane et al. (Eds.). *Sexual abuse of young children*. New York: Guilford.

Manhusky, D. (1986). [Comment] Children's testimony in sexual abuse cases: Ohio's proposed legislation. *Akron Law Review, 19*, 441.

Matthews, E., & Saywitz, K. J. (1992). Child victim witness manual. *California Center for Judicial Education and Research Journal*, Vol. 12.

Melton, G. B. (1984). Child witnesses and the First Amendment: A psycholegal dilemma. *Journal of Social Issues, 40*, 109.

Mlyniec, W. J., & Dally, M. M. (1993). See no evil? Can insulation of child sexual abuse victims be accomplished without endangering the defendant's constitutional rights? *Notre Dame Journal of Law Ethics and Public Policy, 7*, 371.

Parker, J. Y. (1982). The rights of child witnesses: Is the court a protector or perpetrator? *New England Law Review, 17*, 643.

Perry, N. W., & Wrightsman, L. S. (1991). *The child witness: Legal issues and dilemmas*. Newbury Park, CA: Sage.

Seitz, V. (1992). Videotaping clinical interviews with child victim witnesses. *Violence Update, 2*(11), 3.

Slicner, N. A., & Hanson, S. R. (1989). Guidelines for videotape interviews in child sexual abuse cases. *American Journal of Forensic Psychology, 7*(1), 61.

Stephenson, C. (1992). Videotaping and how it works well in San Diego. *Journal of Interpersonal Violence, 7*(2), 277.

Stern, P. (1992). Videotaping child interviews: A detriment to an accurate determination of guilt. *Journal of Interpersonal Violence, 7*(2), 277.

Western, P. (1978). Confrontation and compulsory process: A unified theory of evidence for criminal cases. *Harvard Law Review, 91*, 567.

Whitcomb, D., et al. (1992) *When the victim is a child: Issues for judges and prosecutors* (2nd ed.). Washington, DC: National Institute of Justice.

Wise, D. R. (1985). The constitutionality of admitting the videotape testimony at trial of sexually abused children. *Whitter Law Review, 7*, 639.

Wixom, M. B. (1986). Comment, videotaping the testimony of an abused child: Necessary protection for the child or unwarranted compromise of the defendant's constitutional rights? *Utah Law Review*, p. 461.

Case Index

Index